JUVENILE JUSTICE

This book provides a comprehensive and thought-provoking introduction to the juvenile justice system in the United States. It begins by tracing the historical origins of the legal concept of juvenile delinquency and the institutional responses that developed, and analyzes the problem of delinquency, including its patterns, correlates, and causes. With this essential foundation, the greater part of the book examines the full range of efforts to respond to delinquency through both informal and formal mechanisms of juvenile justice. Core coverage includes:

- The history and transformation of juvenile justice,
- The nature and causes of delinquency,
- Policing juveniles,
- Juvenile court processes,
- Juvenile probation and community-based corrections,
- Residential placement and aftercare programs,
- Delinquency prevention,
- Linking systems of care.

This book is designed as a core text for courses on juvenile justice. Each chapter begins with a compelling case study and learning objectives that draw attention to the topics discussed. Each chapter ends with one or two readings that introduce readers to the literature on juvenile justice. In addition, "critical thinking questions" invite analysis of the material covered in the chapter.

A companion website offers an array of resources for students and instructors. For students, this includes chapter overviews, flashcards of key terms, and useful website links. The instructor site is password protected and offers a complete set of PowerPoint slides and an extensive test bank for each chapter—all prepared by the authors.

James Burfeind is Professor of Sociology at the University of Montana.

Dawn Jeglum Bartusch is Associate Professor of Sociology and Criminology at Valparaiso University.

Dusten R. Hollist is Professor of Sociology at the University of Montana.

JUVENILE JUSTICE

An Introduction to Process, Practice, and Research

JAMES BURFEIND,
DAWN JEGLUM BARTUSCH,
DUSTEN R. HOLLIST

Routledge
Taylor & Francis Group
LONDON AND NEW YORK

First published 2019
by Routledge
2 Park Square, Milton Park, Abingdon, Oxon OX14 4RN

and by Routledge
711 Third Avenue, New York, NY 10017

Routledge is an imprint of the Taylor & Francis Group, an informa business

British Library Cataloguing-in-Publication Data
A catalogue record for this book is available from the British Library

Library of Congress Cataloging-in-Publication Data
Names: Burfeind, James W., 1953– author. | Bartusch, Dawn Jeglum, author. | Hollist, Dusten, author.
Title: Juvenile justice : an introduction to process, practice, and research / James Burfeind, Dawn Jeglum Bartusch and Dusten Hollist.
Description: Abingdon, Oxon ; New York, NY : Routledge, 2018. | Includes bibliographical references and index.
Identifiers: LCCN 2018003048| ISBN 9781138843219 (hardback) | ISBN 9781138843226 (pbk.) | ISBN 9781315731087 (ebook)
Subjects: LCSH: Juvenile justice, Administration of—United States. | Juvenile delinquency—United States. | Juvenile corrections—United States.
Classification: LCC HV9104 .B8524 2018 | DDC 364.360973—dc23
LC record available at https://lccn.loc.gov/2018003048

ISBN: 978-1-138-84321-9 (hbk)
ISBN: 978-1-138-84322-6 (pbk)
ISBN: 978-1-315-73108-7 (ebk)

Typeset in Minion Pro
by Florence Production Ltd, Stoodleigh, Devon, UK

Visit the companion website: routledge.com/cw/burfeind

To the men and women, children and youth who comprise the juvenile justice system.

– J.B., D.J.B., D.R.H.

To my wonderful wife, Linda, who puts up with my never-ending work on book projects, and does so with patience, support, and love.

– J.B.

To my family, Mark, Joshua, and Claire, with gratitude for their encouragement and support while I worked on this new project.

– D.J.B.

To Cheri, Mariah and Tristen, for your support and inspiration.

– D.R.H.

CONTENTS IN BRIEF

CONTENTS

FIGURES

TABLES

VISUAL TOUR OF KEY FEATURES

Welcome to *Juvenile Justice: An Introduction to Process, Practice, and Research*! Juvenile justice is a dynamic field of study, filled with much research activity, change, and innovation. We have made every effort to provide readers with up-to-date coverage of juvenile justice process, practice, and research, and to do so in an interesting and thought-provoking manner.

We have also carefully and strategically developed a common set of features for each chapter to aid student learning. These special features are identified by name and brief description below, with visual examples of each resource, indicating to readers what to look for and what can be found in these different features.

TEN KEY FEATURES

(1) Chapter topics and learning objectives

Each chapter begins with a list of the major **topics** and the **learning objectives** that are pursued. The chapter objectives alert students to the juvenile justice processes and practices that they should understand after reading the chapter.

CHAPTER TOPICS

- A separate system of justice for juveniles
- Juvenile justice reform
- Juvenile justice process, practice, and research
- Exploring the literature on juvenile justice: Chapter readings

CHAPTER LEARNING OBJECTIVES

After completing this chapter, students should be able to:

- Convey an initial understanding of the separate and distinctive system of justice that has developed for juveniles in the United States.
- Demonstrate an initial understanding of the series of reforms, beginning in

(2) Case in point

Right at the beginning of each chapter, a **case study** is offered that provides a real life illustration of the content of the chapter.

CASE IN POINT

INTAKE DISCRETION AND THE REHABILITATIVE EMPHASIS OF JUVENILE JUSTICE

Steve Jones is Chief Probation Officer (CPO) of Johnson County Youth Court Services. In this capacity, he screens cases that are referred to the juvenile court, determining whether cases should be dismissed, diverted to a community social service agency, dealt with informally by the juvenile court, or petitioned into youth court for formal court action. The "intake" decision is highly discretionary because few laws define or regulate this process. The primary considerations have to do with what is best for the youth, his or her family, and the community.

One Monday morning in early November, CPO Jones received an offense report of a youth who was taken into custody and placed in detention over the weekend by the local city police department for underage drinking, public drunkenness, and disorderly conduct. He recognized the name immediately: Clay Rogers—a 16-year-old youth who had been on probation with Court Services the previous year for two consecutive six-month terms, each for burglary. The first burglary was not petitioned into youth court, but dealt with through informal probation, which was based on an agreement (technically called a "consent adjustment without petition") between the youth, his parents, and a probation officer. The informal probation included

(3) Application boxes

Application boxes appear throughout the text, containing helpful extra material that will aid student learning. Three types of application boxes are used:

- "**Juvenile justice law**": Examples of statutory and case law that establish and regulate juvenile justice process and practice.

EXPANDING IDEAS: A TYPICAL DAY AT THE NEW YORK HOUSE OF REFUGE

At sunrise, the children are warned, by the ringing of a bell, to rise from their beds. Each child makes his own bed, and steps forth, on a signal, into the Hall. They then proceed, in perfect order, to the Wash Room. Thence they are marched to parade in the yard, and undergo an examination as to their dress and cleanliness; after which, they attend Morning Prayer. The morning school then commences, where they are occupied in summer, until 7 o'clock. A short intermission is allowed, when the bell rings for breakfast; after which, they proceed to their respective workshops, where they labor until 12 o'clock, when they are called from work, and one hour allowed them for washing and eating dinner. At one, they again commence work and continue at it until five in the afternoon, when the labor of the day terminated. Half an hour is allowed for washing and eating their supper, and at half-past five, they are conducted to the school room where they continue at their studies until 8 o'clock. Evening Prayer is performed by the Superintendent; after which, the children are conducted to their dormitories, which they enter, and are locked up for the night, when perfect silence reigns throughout the establishment. The foregoing is the history of a single day, and will answer for every day in the year, except Sundays, with slight variation during stormy weather, and the short days in winter.

- "**Juvenile justice process and practice**": Full description of a particular juvenile justice procedure or program.
- "**Expanding ideas**": Further explanation of a specific key point made in the chapter.

(4) Summary and conclusions

Concisely written summaries draw attention to important points of the chapter and the conclusions that can be drawn.

SUMMARY AND CONCLUSIONS

Contemporary legal definitions of juvenile delinquency distinguish juvenile offenders from adult criminals and provide for a separate system and process of justice. Legal definitions continue to emphasize the dependency of children and adolescents and their need for protection and nurture. In addition, the family unit is affirmed as the key institution of socialization, providing "care, protection, and wholesome mental and physical development of a youth."[2] However, contemporary legal definitions of juvenile delinquency commonly specify at least four different legal classifications of juveniles over which the juvenile court maintains jurisdiction: (1) dependent and neglected children; (2) status offenders, sometimes called "youth in need of intervention" or some variant of that term; (3) delinquent youth who violate the criminal code; and (4) serious delinquent offenders who have committed felony offenses. The authority to make decisions within the juvenile justice system is defined by statutory law. Statutory laws cover each of the major decision points and mandate which officials will be charged with decision making within them.

The term "juvenile justice system" is misleading. There is not a single juvenile justice system; rather, each state has a separate juvenile justice system, and these are "systems" in only a limited sense. The various parts of these systems—police, courts, and corrections—are all operated by different levels and branches of government, sometimes even by private organizations.

(5) Chapter readings

Most chapters include two readings that are carefully chosen to expose students to the scholarly literature on juvenile justice. Some readings are academic journal articles, while others are research briefs and reports from agencies that address the practice of juvenile justice.

READING 2.2

"REPORT BRIEF—REFORMING JUVENILE JUSTICE: A DEVELOPMENTAL APPROACH."

National Research Council. 2012. Committee on Law and Justice, Division of Behavioral and Social Sciences and Education. Washington, DC: The National Academies.

This reading is a "Report Brief" of a much larger document that the National Research Council published in 2013, entitled Reforming Juvenile Justice: A Developmental Approach. The full report resulted from an extensive review of recent research on adolescent development and the implications of that research for juvenile justice reform.

The past decade has seen an explosion of knowledge about adolescent development and the neurobiological underpinnings of adolescent behavior. Much has also been learned about the

(6) Critical-thinking questions

Questions at the end of each chapter invite readers to apply knowledge acquired through reading the chapter and to consider the chapter opening case study in light of the materials presented in the chapter.

CRITICAL-THINKING QUESTIONS

1 How does the case in point about two obnoxious teenagers at the beginning of the chapter demonstrate the importance of police discretion and the factors that influence officer decision making?
2 Explain how the police serve as the "gatekeepers" of the juvenile justice process.
3 Why are "discretion" and "diversion" essential to policing juveniles and the process of juvenile justice?
4 Identify and briefly describe the various roles that police adopt in juvenile law enforcement.
5 How does procedural due process influence the enforcement of laws with juveniles?
6 Research conducted by Lee Ann Slocum and her colleagues shows that juvenile perceptions of mistreatment by the police are more important than perceptions of fair treatment for shaping attitudes toward future delinquency. What are the implications of this finding for policing juveniles?
7 The reading by Richard Dudley discusses the importance of police officers' ability to recognize symptoms of previous trauma. How does previous trauma exposure influence how a juvenile may interact with the police?

(7) Suggested reading

References to primary sources that were discussed in each chapter, or scholarship that is relevant to the chapter topic.

SUGGESTED READING

Feld, Barry. 2013. *Kids, Cops, and Confessions: Inside the Interrogation Room*. New York/London: New York University Press.
Puzzanchera, Charles. 2014. "Juvenile Arrests 2012." *Juvenile Offenders and Victims National Report Series*. Washington, DC: Office of Juvenile Justice and Delinquency Prevention.
Redner-Vera, Erica and Marcus-Antonio Galeste. 2015. "Attitudes and Marginalization: Examining American Indian Perceptions of Law Enforcement among Adolescents." *Journal of Ethnicity in Criminal Justice* 13:283–308.

(8) Useful websites

Links to online resources that complement and expand upon material covered in the chapter, and invite students to further their understanding of particular topics through additional exploration.

USEFUL WEBSITES

For further information relevant to this chapter, go to the following websites.

- **Juvenile Detention Alternatives Initiative (JDAI)**, The Annie E. Casey Foundation, Juvenile Justice: www.aecf.org/work/juvenile-justice/jdai/

(9) Glossary of key terms

Each chapter includes a glossary of key terms, which provides concise definitions of the important terms that have been highlighted in the chapter.

GLOSSARY OF KEY TERMS

Intensive supervision probation (ISP): A development in probation supervision that attempts to provide public safety and offender accountability through intensive monitoring and supervision of the probationer.

Juvenile probation: An informal or formal disposition that is based in the community, involving conditions (court-imposed rules) and supervision by a probation officer.

Probation conditions: Court-imposed rules that are a central part of the disposition of probation. Juveniles placed on probation by the court must obey these conditions in order to live in the community and avoid confinement.

Probation supervision: Monitoring and assistance of probationers by probation officers. The approach to supervision taken by probation officers determines the relative emphasis given to offender rehabilitation or enforcement of probation rules.

Revocation: The legal termination of probation by the court when the youth commits a new offense or violates the conditions of probation.

Visit the companion website at: routledge.com/cw/burfeind.

ABOUT THE AUTHORS

James Burfeind is a Professor of Sociology at the University of Montana. He earned a PhD in Criminology and Urban Sociology from Portland State University in Oregon. Professor Burfeind's teaching and research interests are in criminological theory, juvenile delinquency, juvenile justice, and corrections. With Dawn Jeglum Bartusch, he co-authored the textbook *Juvenile Delinquency: An Integrated Approach* (3rd edition, 2016, Routledge). He has received a number of teaching awards, including "Most Inspirational Teaching," a university-wide award chosen by graduating seniors. He has considerable experience in juvenile probation and parole, and adolescent residential placement.

Dawn Jeglum Bartusch is an Associate Professor of Sociology and Criminology at Valparaiso University in Indiana. She earned a PhD in Sociology from the University of Wisconsin, Madison. Professor Bartusch's teaching and research interests are in juvenile delinquency, criminological theory, crime and inequality, and social stratification. With James Burfeind, she co-authored the textbook *Juvenile Delinquency: An Integrated Approach*. Her research has appeared in *Criminology, Social Forces, Law and Society Review*, and the *Journal of Abnormal Psychology*.

Dusten Hollist is a Professor in the Department of Sociology at the University of Montana. He earned a PhD in Sociology from Washington State University. Professor Hollist's teaching and research interests are in juvenile delinquency, juvenile justice, and sociology of law enforcement. His research has appeared in *Journal of Research in Crime and Delinquency, Journal of Criminal Justice*, and the *Journal of Youth and Adolescence*.

ACKNOWLEDGEMENTS

Many reviewers provided thoughtful comments on our chapters as we prepared this manuscript. The text is much improved as a result of their helpful feedback and suggestions, and we are grateful to these anonymous reviewers.

Several very capable students provided research assistance in the preparation of this manuscript: Ally Guldborg, Tessa DeCunzo, Karyn Kovich, Darby Semenza, Calyn Hitchcock, and Patrick McKay at the University of Montana; and Macy Mullins at Valparaiso University. We are grateful for their careful work and attention to detail.

We thank Elsevier, National Academies Press, SAGE, Wiley, Models for Change, the National Criminal Justice Reference Service, and Laura S. Guy, Gina M. Vincent, Thomas Grisso and Rachael Perrault for their kind permission to reproduce previously published material, including lengthy articles and reports, in this book.

We are especially thankful for the incredible work of the team at Routledge/Taylor & Francis Group. Thomas Sutton is a tremendously gifted and responsive editor. He has been enthusiastic about this book from the beginning, and we are grateful for his commitment to this project. We are also extremely grateful to Hannah Catterall for all of her hard work on this project. We truly marvel at her efficiency and appreciate her assistance in seeking permissions, facilitating the cover design process, and preparing the manuscript for production. We are also grateful for her patience when we were a bit late in submitting chapters. Finally, we thank Ting Baker for her careful copyediting work, Miriam Armstrong for her very capable production work, and the design team that created the cover art for this book. It has been a delight to work with this very talented editorial and production team.

PART I

Introduction to juvenile justice

Chapter 1

THE STUDY OF JUVENILE JUSTICE

CHAPTER TOPICS

- **A separate system of justice for juveniles**
- **Juvenile justice reform**
- **Juvenile justice process, practice, and research**
- **Exploring the literature on juvenile justice: Chapter readings**

CHAPTER LEARNING OBJECTIVES

After completing this chapter, students should be able to:

- Convey an initial understanding of the separate and distinctive system of justice that has developed for juveniles in the United States.
- Demonstrate an initial understanding of the series of reforms, beginning in the 1960s, that redefined the legal concept of juvenile delinquency and significantly transformed juvenile justice philosophy, policy, and practice.
- Understand the book's organization and content.
- Develop skills for effective and efficient reading of scholarly work on juvenile justice.

CHAPTER CONTENTS

CASE IN POINT

INTAKE DISCRETION AND THE REHABILITATIVE EMPHASIS OF JUVENILE JUSTICE

Steve Jones is Chief Probation Officer (CPO) of Johnson County Youth Court Services. In this capacity, he screens cases that are referred to the juvenile court, determining whether cases should be dismissed, diverted to a community social service agency, dealt with informally by the juvenile court, or petitioned into youth court for formal court action. The "intake" decision is highly discretionary because few laws define or regulate this process. The primary considerations have to do with what is best for the youth, his or her family, and the community.

One Monday morning in early November, CPO Jones received an offense report of a youth who was taken into custody and placed in detention over the weekend by the local city police department for underage drinking, public drunkenness, and disorderly conduct. He recognized the name immediately: Clay Rogers—a 16-year-old youth who had been on probation with Court Services the previous year for two consecutive six-month terms, each for burglary. The first burglary was not petitioned into youth court, but dealt with through informal probation, which was based on an agreement (technically called a "consent adjustment without petition") between the youth, his parents, and a probation officer. The informal probation included rules of probation ("conditions") and participation in agreed-upon social services for Clay and his family. The second burglary occurred near the end of the informal probation period. This time, CPO Jones decided that Clay needed to be held accountable, so he recommended that the County Attorney's Office petition the juvenile into youth court for formal court action. At the arraignment hearing, the petition was read and Clay admitted to the charge of burglary. The judge continued the court case for disposition so that a probation officer could conduct an investigation and write a predisposition report. Based on the report's recommendation, the youth court judge determined that Clay was a "delinquent youth" and placed him on six months of formal probation with more restrictive conditions, restitution, and community service.

Now, with the allegations of new offenses specified in the police report, CPO Jones had a discretionary dilemma. Should he suspend a formal referral to the youth court in an effort to pressure Clay to follow his probation expectations more closely—a motivation for compliance? Should he submit a revocation report to the youth court, describing how Clay had violated the condition of probation that required him to follow all local, state, and federal laws? Revocation would result in a disposition that provided a graduated sanction for the new offenses. Or should he recommend that the County Attorney's Office petition Clay into youth court for a new offense, which would result in an entirely new formal adjudication process? Beyond these alternative methods of handling Clay's most recent referral, the third-round intake decision presents CPO Jones with some fundamental questions regarding the appropriate role of juvenile courts and the philosophy of justice that should be pursued, especially when dealing with a repeat offender. Should a juvenile be held fully responsible for his/her actions? Should the juvenile court maintain its rehabilitative focus with a repeat offender? Even more broadly: Should juveniles be dealt with differently from adults by a separate justice system?

Before the establishment of the first juvenile court, legal systems in the United States dealt with young people who violated the criminal law much as they did adult offenders (Feld 2014). Beginning in the 1800s, reformers established institutions designed to deal with juvenile offenders differently than adults. These reformers embraced a view of young people as immature, dependent, and at-risk for problem behaviors due to negative environmental influences (Bishop and Feld 2012). At the end of the 1800s, a separate system of justice was created for juveniles, first in Chicago, and shortly thereafter all across the United States. By 1925, every state but two had established a juvenile justice system (Platt 1977).

The legal concept of "juvenile delinquency" emerged within the context of the legislation that established each state's juvenile justice system. With some variation in wording, youth court acts defined **juvenile delinquency** as actions that violate the law, committed by a person under the legal age of majority. Early youth court acts established the legal age of majority as 16 years old, but over time, 18 years of age became the most common age of majority.

Each state operates its own juvenile justice system but these are "systems" in only a limited sense because the authority to respond "officially" to delinquency is spread broadly across the different levels and branches of government. Juvenile law enforcement, for example, is an executive branch responsibility carried out predominately by local police departments (municipal police departments and county sheriffs' departments). Youth courts, on the other hand, are judicial units that most often operate within state district or county courts, which are part of a state court system. In addition, groups and institutions that are not part of justice systems also respond to the problem behaviors of children and teens through prevention and early intervention efforts. Public and private schools, for instance, usually try to deal with disruptive behaviors in the classroom through teacher and student training programs.

A SEPARATE SYSTEM OF JUSTICE FOR JUVENILES

The juvenile justice systems that developed across the United States in the early 1900s adopted a legal structure, philosophy, and process that separated them from adult criminal justice systems and made them distinct. The Illinois Juvenile Court Act of 1899, which established the first juvenile court in Chicago, provided for an entirely separate system of juvenile justice, complete with law enforcement, judicial, and correctional components. The Act specified the use of a "special courtroom" and separate personnel and records (NCJFCJ 1998; Platt 1977).

The juvenile justice systems that spread across the country were envisioned as child welfare systems, rather than as judicial systems, and their prevailing goal was to protect, nurture, reform, and regulate dependent, neglected, and delinquent children (Feld 1999). These new juvenile justice systems were designed deliberately to remove juveniles from adult criminal justice systems and to create a special rehabilitative approach for delinquent, dependent, and neglected youth. As such, early juvenile justice systems had broad jurisdiction over almost all juvenile matters. Furthermore, juvenile justice proceedings were typically informal and family-like, with personnel exercising extensive discretion in handling juvenile cases. Softer, more rehabilitative, legal terminology was and still is customarily used in the juvenile justice process in order to avoid reference to the harsh, adversarial process of the criminal justice system. For example, police officers "take youth into custody" instead of arresting them, youth are "petitioned" into juvenile court rather than "indicted" into criminal court; juvenile court proceedings are called "hearings" instead of trials, and delinquent youth are given a disposition rather than a sentence.

JUVENILE JUSTICE REFORM

Traditional juvenile justice systems were drawn into question beginning in the 1960s, resulting in a series of reforms that redefined the legal concept of juvenile delinquency and significantly transformed juvenile justice philosophy, policy, and practice. In a wide-ranging critique of juvenile justice in the late 1990s, juvenile justice scholar Barry Feld (1999) examined four areas of change that were evident in the reforms at that time: (1) an increased emphasis on procedural due process with little actual gain in due process rights; (2) a shift in legal philosophy from the rehabilitative ideal to punishment and criminal responsibility, especially for serious, violent juvenile offenders; (3) reforms to divert, deinstitutionalize, and decriminalize status offenders (the "soft end" of the juvenile court), thereby sending them to a "hidden," private sector treatment system of social control, administered by mental health and chemical dependency service providers; and (4) the transfer of serious juvenile offenders (the "hard end" of the juvenile court) to adult criminal court jurisdiction. As a result of these sweeping changes, the structure and process of contemporary juvenile justice systems have come to resemble those of adult criminal justice systems, and the philosophy of juvenile justice has shifted decisively from an emphasis on rehabilitation to punishment and accountability, thereby adopting a "get tough on juvenile crime" approach.

As we will discuss further in later chapters, contemporary juvenile justice reform is driven by research, especially research in two primary areas: adolescent development and evidence-based practice. A growing body of research on adolescent development has questioned the punitive posture of many contemporary juvenile justice systems across the United States, as expressed in get-tough policies and practices. This research shows that adolescents are not developmentally mature, and they are therefore less able to regulate their behavior and make decisions that require future orientation. Because of these findings, a return to rehabilitation in juvenile justice is warranted. Contemporary juvenile justice reform is also being driven by

WHAT'S AHEAD IN *JUVENILE JUSTICE: AN INTRODUCTION TO PROCESS, PRACTICE, AND RESEARCH*?

- **Chapter 1: The study of juvenile justice** provides an overview to the perspective and approach taken in this book.
- **Chapter 2: Origins and transformation of juvenile justice** traces the historical origins and recent transformations of the legal concept of juvenile delinquency and juvenile justice in the United States.
- **Chapter 3: Juvenile justice law, structure, and process** describes contemporary juvenile justice in terms of the statutory laws that form its foundation and the distinctive structures and processes that characterize it.
- **Chapter 4: Data on delinquency and juvenile justice** presents the three major sources of data on delinquency and juvenile justice: "official" records maintained by law enforcement agencies and courts, surveys of individuals who have been victims of crime, and surveys of individuals who self-report involvement in offending.
- **Chapter 5: The nature of delinquency** examines the extent of delinquent offenses and the social correlates of offending (age, gender, race, ethnicity, and social class).
- **Chapter 6: Causes of delinquency** presents an inventory of the key concepts and contexts of delinquency that have been offered in theory and supported through research.
- **Chapter 7: Cops and kids: Policing juveniles** describes the structure and role of juvenile policing, with an emphasis on changes in law enforcement tactics and due process.
- **Chapter 8: Preliminary procedures of juvenile courts: Detention, transfer to criminal court, and intake** surveys three key preliminary procedures: detention, transfer to adult court, and intake screening.
- **Chapter 9: Formal procedures of juvenile courts: Adjudication and disposition** considers the two primary components of formal juvenile court proceedings: adjudication and disposition.
- **Chapter 10: Juvenile probation** examines the most frequently imposed disposition in juvenile courts: juvenile probation—first describing its key features, structure, and use, then exploring conditions of probation, supervision, and revocation.
- **Chapter 11: Community-based corrections and restorative justice** explores community-based responses to delinquency, including diversion of cases before petition or adjudication, community treatment, restorative justice, and teen and problem-solving courts (drug and mental health courts).
- **Chapter 12: Residential placement and aftercare services** surveys the range of residential facilities for out-of-home placement and the aftercare services used to reinterate youth back into communities.
- **Chapter 13: Delinquency prevention** investigates how evidence-based practices have impacted delinquency prevention practices and programs.
- **Chapter 14: Linking systems of care** examines the coordination of care for delinquent youth across the major service delivery systems: child welfare, education, medical, mental health, and substance abuse treatment.

evaluation research that tries to establish whether delinquency prevention and intervention programs effectively reduce the likelihood of offending. The accumulated evidence from evaluation research is then used to develop principles for "best practice" and to establish registries of model programs of proven effectiveness.

JUVENILE JUSTICE PROCESS, PRACTICE, AND RESEARCH

Within the context of expanding knowledge on juvenile delinquency and ongoing juvenile justice reform, this book first describes the historical origins of the legal concept of juvenile delinquency and the early institutional responses that developed. We then provide a thorough analysis of the problem of delinquency, including the patterns of delinquency, the social correlates of offending, and the causes of delinquent behavior. Our analysis of the problem of delinquency draws heavily from delinquency theory and research.

With this essential foundation, the greater part of this book examines the full range of efforts to respond to delinquency through both informal and formal mechanisms of juvenile justice. In a formal sense, the juvenile justice system comprises police, courts, and corrections, but as we will see, much delinquency is dealt with informally, sometimes by agencies not usually considered part of the juvenile justice system. Furthermore, the juvenile justice system is not really a "system" at all, but rather a highly decentralized and fragmented assortment of both public and private agencies. In addition, each element of juvenile justice exercises tremendous discretion and relies on diversion to operate efficiently. As a result, processes of juvenile justice are unique and distinctive, and they differ notably from adult criminal justice.

In a nutshell, this book will thoroughly describe juvenile justice in terms of its structure and process—how the different elements of juvenile justice are organized and how they operate. We have incorporated the latest research on juvenile justice, especially with regard to evidence-based practice in juvenile justice. The application box entitled "What's Ahead in *Juvenile Justice: An Introduction to Process, Practice, and Research*?" provides an outline of the chapters that follow. It is our hope that you gain a full understanding of juvenile justice in the United States!

EXPLORING THE LITERATURE ON JUVENILE JUSTICE: CHAPTER READINGS

One more feature of this book should be highlighted. Each chapter, except this first chapter, includes one or two readings that are used deliberately to expose students to the literature on juvenile justice. This is a lively and engaging field of study, filled with science and practical application. These readings include *peer-reviewed journal articles* that we have shortened to make more manageable, *research briefs* from sponsoring organizations like the Office of Juvenile Justice and Delinquency Prevention (OJJDP), *policy briefs* from agencies with reform initiatives such as the MacArthur Foundation, and *technical reports* that describe the research methods and findings of grant-funded research. Each reading begins with a brief overview and a full reference to identify the source of the reading. The application box entitled "Reading scholarly literature" offers some tips on efficient and effective reading.

READING SCHOLARLY LITERATURE

Four strategic steps to efficient and effective reading that will result in comprehension.

1. ***Actually read and think about the title of the reading.*** While students often skip over or pay little attention to the title of a scholarly publication, writers often spend a great deal of time choosing just the right title so that it accurately and succinctly reflects their discussion. Want to know what the reading is about right from the start? Thoughtfully read the title.
2. ***Page through the reading and pay attention to the headings.*** The headings depict the reading's organization and development, and thereby reveal the author's basic argument.
3. ***Read quickly, but carefully.*** Students too often go through the motions of reading—they read words, sentences, and paragraphs, but they do not concentrate adequately on the key points that are being expressed. *Jot down the key points as you move through the reading.* In essence, this is the author's argument, so it should develop logically. Do not get sidetracked in trying to understand every nuance of the reading; instead, move along and your questions may be answered in later discussion.
4. ***Assess the argument.*** After reading the entire piece, do not simply put it down ("Phew, I'm done!"). Rather, think about the reading in terms of the major points that were made and how clearly and convincingly the arguments were presented. The reading must be assessed in order to gain understanding of the argument.

SUMMARY AND CONCLUSIONS

This introductory chapter provides an overview to the study of juvenile justice that you are about to embark on in this book. The philosophies, processes, and practices of juvenile justice are unique and distinctive from adult criminal justice, and they have undergone continuous change and transformation. Juvenile justice processes and practices will be fully elaborated in the following chapters, as will research findings on juvenile delinquency and evidence-based practice. We trust you will find the study of juvenile justice to be both interesting and challenging!

CRITICAL-THINKING QUESTIONS

1. Should justice systems deal differently with juveniles and adults? Why or why not?
2. Should there be a separate and distinct system of justice for juveniles? If so, how specifically should it differ from the adult criminal justice system?
3. Identify the major areas of reform in contemporary juvenile justice.

SUGGESTED READING

Bishop, Donna M. and Barry C. Feld. 2012. "Trends in Juvenile Justice Policy and Practice." Pp. 899–926 in *The Oxford Handbook of Juvenile Crime and Juvenile Justice*, edited by B. C. Feld and D. M. Bishop. New York: Oxford University Press.

Sickmund, Melissa and Charles Puzzanchera (eds.). 2014. *Juvenile Offenders and Victims: 2014 National Report*. Pittsburgh, PA: National Center for Juvenile Justice.

GLOSSARY OF KEY TERMS

Juvenile delinquency: Actions that violate the law, committed by a person under the legal age of majority.

USEFUL WEBSITES

For further information relevant to this chapter, go to the following websites.

- **National Council of Juvenile and Family Court Judges:** http://www.ncjfcj.org/
- **Office of Juvenile Justice and Delinquency Prevention (OJJDP):** http://www.ojjdp.gov/
- **OJJDP Statistical Briefing Book:** https://www.ojjdp.gov/ojstatbb/

REFERENCES

Bishop, Donna M. and Barry C. Feld. 2012. "Trends in Juvenile Justice Policy and Practice." Pp. 899–926 in *The Oxford Handbook of Juvenile Crime and Juvenile Justice*, edited by B. C. Feld and D. M. Bishop. New York: Oxford University Press.

Feld, Barry C. 1999. *Bad Kids: Race and the Transformation of the Juvenile Court*. New York: Oxford University Press.

Feld, Barry C. 2014. *Juvenile Justice Administration in a Nutshell*. St. Paul, MN: West.

National Council of Juvenile and Family Court Judges (NCJFCJ). 1998. "The Illinois Juvenile Court Act of 1899: Juvenile Courts for Dependent, Neglected and Delinquent Children." *Juvenile and Family Court Journal* 49:1–5.

Platt, Anthony. 1977. *The Child Savers: The Invention of Delinquency*. 2nd ed. Chicago: University of Chicago Press.

Sickmund, Melissa and Charles Puzzanchera (eds.). 2014. *Juvenile Offenders and Victims: 2014 National Report*. Pittsburgh, PA: National Center for Juvenile Justice.

Chapter 2

ORIGINS AND TRANSFORMATION OF JUVENILE JUSTICE

CHAPTER TOPICS

- **The social construction of "juvenile delinquency"**
- **Inventing juvenile justice: Institutional responses to juvenile delinquency**
- **Reforming juvenile justice: Transformation of juvenile justice philosophy, policy, and practice**

CHAPTER LEARNING OBJECTIVES

After completing this chapter, students should be able to:

- Identify the major historical developments that led to the social construction of "juvenile delinquency" as a social and legal concept.
- Describe the roots of the juvenile court in nineteenth-century developments such as poor laws, houses of refuge, placing-out, reform schools, and the child-saving movement.
- Explain the key characteristics of the original juvenile court—its philosophy, jurisdiction, and procedures.
- Describe the transformation of juvenile justice thought and practice.
- Identify and describe the two major areas of research that drive contemporary juvenile justice reform.

CHAPTER CONTENTS

CASE IN POINT

LEGAL PHILOSOPHY OF THE EARLY JUVENILE COURT

A 1909 article in the *Harvard Law Review* by Judge Julian Mack (1909:107), the second judge of the Chicago juvenile court, articulated the distinctive legal philosophy of the early juvenile court.

> Why is it not just and proper to treat these juvenile offenders, as we deal with the neglected children, as a wise and merciful father handles his own child whose errors are not discovered by the authorities? Why is it not the duty of the State, instead of asking merely whether a boy or a girl has committed the specific offense, to find out what he is, physically, mentally, morally, and then if it learns that he is treading the path that leads to criminality, to take him in charge, not so much to punish as to reform, not to degrade but to uplift, not to crush but to develop, not to make him a criminal but a worthy citizen.

This chapter traces the historical origins and recent transformations of juvenile justice in the United States. As perspectives toward juvenile delinquency change, so too do legal responses to it. Focusing on this correspondence, this chapter examines the social construction of "juvenile delinquency" and the origins and character of the early juvenile court. We then consider a series of juvenile justice reforms since the 1960s that have resulted in significant redefinition of juvenile delinquency and redirection of juvenile justice practice. **Figure 2.1** provides a timeline of these major developments in juvenile justice.

THE SOCIAL CONSTRUCTION OF "JUVENILE DELINQUENCY"

Scholars say that juvenile delinquency was "socially constructed" in order to indicate that the concept is a product of sweeping social, political, economic, and religious changes (Feld 1999). Three historical developments are fundamental to the social construction of "juvenile delinquency": (1) the "discovery" of childhood and adolescence, (2) the English common law doctrine of *parens patriae*, and (3) the rise of positivist criminology. As a result, the concept of juvenile delinquency came to signify a separate and distinct status for young people, both socially and legally. Juvenile delinquency is a status determined both by age (younger than the legal age of majority) and behavior (actions that violate the law).

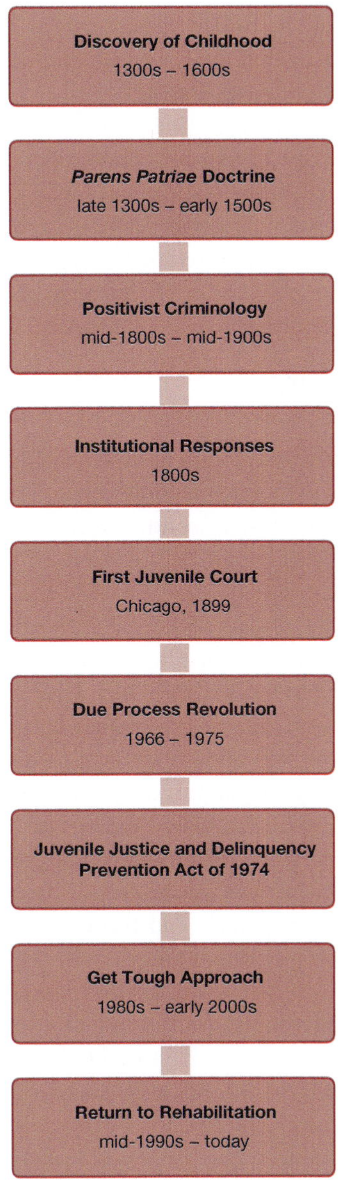

FIGURE 2.1
Timeline of major developments in juvenile justice in the United States.

The discovery of childhood and adolescence

Today, we take for granted that childhood and adolescence are separate stages in life, unique from other stages. However, in his widely cited book, *Centuries of Childhood*, Philippe Aries (1962) argues that the idea of childhood did not emerge until the Renaissance (roughly 1300–1600), and that far greater age distinctions developed during the Enlightenment (mid-1600s to late 1700s) and Industrial Revolution (1760 to mid-1900s). Using a variety of historical records, he argues that attitudes toward children during the Middle Ages were largely "indifferent" and that treatment of children was often harsh and punitive. This changed in the late sixteenth and seventeenth centuries when the special needs of childhood began to be recognized. Aries goes on to point out that, although childhood was established as a separate age category by the seventeenth century, it was not distinguished from adolescence until the late eighteenth century.

Family life and childrearing emerged as matters of great importance in Renaissance society. Numerous treatises and manuals were written in the sixteenth and seventeenth centuries, and many remained popular until the eighteenth century. These manuals instructed parents on how to train their children in the "new morality," involving etiquette, obedience, respect for others, self-control, and modesty. The training tools emphasized in these manuals included supervision and strict discipline. These manuals were clear expressions of a new view of children, childhood, and childrearing: Children began to be viewed as innocent and vulnerable, and it was the responsibility of parents to protect their children from the evils of a corrupt world and to morally train them (Empey and Stafford 1991; Sommerville 1982; deMause 1974; Aries 1962).

At the beginning of the Enlightenment, John Locke (1632–1704) published *Some Thoughts Concerning Education*, a treatise on childrearing that went through twenty-six editions before 1800. He used the term "education" to refer to training by parents in the form of childrearing practices, especially for purposes of supervision, discipline, and moral training. A later Enlightenment philosopher, Jean-Jacques Rousseau (1712–1778), pointed to the "distinctive human plight" confronted by adolescents during the transition from childhood to adulthood, and identified adolescence as a unique stage of development. In his book *Emile* (1762), Rousseau provided the first systematic consideration of the stages of development (Illick 1974; Kaplan 1984; Aries 1962).

The slow discovery of childhood and adolescence was not complete until the Enlightenment, when Rousseau's idea of developmental stages led to a growing awareness of age distinctions across the life course. Ideas about the innocence, vulnerability, and dependence of childhood resulted in an increasing emphasis on the family as the key institution of socialization. Gradually, the view developed that young people require protection, nurturing, supervision, discipline, training, and education in order to grow and mature into healthy and productive adults (Sommerville 1982; Degler 1980).

The *parens patriae* doctrine

The development of the English legal doctrine of *parens patriae* coincided with the discovery of childhood and adolescence. This far-reaching legal doctrine emerged slowly in the late fourteenth and early fifteenth centuries in response to a series of cases heard in English chancery courts (Rendleman 1971; Cogan 1970). The resulting law is referred to as *equity law*. Adopted in the United States as a part of the Anglo-Saxon legal tradition of England, *parens patriae* provided the fundamental legal authority for the idea of juvenile delinquency and the early juvenile court.

The Latin phrase ***parens patriae*** literally means "parent of the country" (Oxford English Dictionary 2015). As a legal doctrine, *parens patriae* vested far-reaching power in the king as supreme ruler and guardian over his land and people. Chancery courts were established to provide just settlements to disputes, but to do so in a way that maintained and extended the king's legal authority and power. These disputes arose mainly with regard to property rights and inheritance. Attached to this authority, however, was a duty that the king had to his subjects in return for the allegiance paid to him. In practice, this duty was concerned primarily with the social welfare of certain dependent groups, especially children, those who were mentally incompetent, and those in need of charity. Under *parens patriae*, the king was established as protector and guardian of these dependent classes (Feld 1999; Cogan 1970).

With regard to children, *parens patriae* was applied most extensively to cases in which the guardianship of young children who were heirs to an estate or who had already inherited an estate from a deceased father was at issue. The primary purpose of *parens patriae* legal authority was to award custody and control of these children and their estates to the government. Gradually the chancery courts extended the doctrine of *parens patriae* to include the general welfare of children; the proper care, custody, and control of children was in the "crown's interests" (Cogan 1970). This included the ability of the courts to assume and exercise parental duties—to act *in loco parentis*—when parents failed to provide for the child's welfare (Feld 1999). As we will see, early juvenile courts in the United States adopted the *parens patriae* doctrine as the foundation of their legal authority—authority to regulate, treat, and control "dependent, neglected and delinquent children" (NCJFCJ 1998).

Positivist criminology

To say that juvenile delinquency is socially constructed means that it is a product of prevailing thoughts and perspectives. The two historical developments we have considered so far correspond closely in time and perspective. A third historical development took root somewhat later but had an equally strong influence on the idea of juvenile delinquency. Positivist criminology is an approach to the study of crime that emerged in the last half of the nineteenth century and came to dominate the field of study for most of the twentieth century.

Positivist criminology is based on **positivism**—the use of scientific methods to study crime and delinquency (Beirne and Messerschmidt 2015). The scientific method involves systematic observation, measurement, description, and analysis so that scientists can look for, uncover, and draw conclusions about patterns of crime and delinquency and the individual characteristics of offenders (Feld 1999; Platt 1977; Allen 1964). The scientific approach advanced by positivism assumes that crime and delinquency are caused by identifiable factors. This cause-and-effect relationship is called determinism. According to positivism, causal factors can be systematically observed and measured, and causal processes can be analyzed and described. A variety of causal factors were advanced by social scientists in the late 1800s and early 1900s, such as "feeblemindedness," "moral intemperance," poverty, unemployment, and lack of education. The prospect of a scientific approach to crime and delinquency quickly became very popular because of the hope it offered to better understand and respond to the problem of delinquency.

Armed with scientific methods to discover the causes of delinquency, positivist criminologists sought to use this understanding to bring about change in juvenile offenders and their social environments. Thus, the scientific methods of positivist criminology had a corresponding emphasis on treatment and rehabilitation, which were thought to be especially appropriate to juvenile delinquency, because children and adolescents, in a developmental sense, are not fully matured, and, if given effective treatment and rehabilitation, they are able to be reformed.

INVENTING JUVENILE JUSTICE: INSTITUTIONAL RESPONSES TO JUVENILE DELINQUENCY

The concept of "juvenile delinquency" is a clear expression of these three historical developments: the discovery of childhood and adolescence, the English equity law doctrine of *parens patriae*, and the growing dominance of positivist thought in criminology. As a legal term, however, "juvenile delinquency" is tied to the creation of the first juvenile court. In this section, we trace the evolution of thought and practice that led to the origins of juvenile justice in the United States.

Poor laws, charities, and pauperism

Three social institutions were emphasized in colonial America: family, church, and community.

> Families were to raise their children to respect law and authority, the church was to oversee not only family discipline but adult behavior, and the members of the community were to supervise one another, to detect and correct first signs of deviancy.
>
> (Rothman 1971:16)

When these institutions functioned well, towns were orderly and stable, and deviance was kept in check.

Civic responsibility in colonial America generated individual and social obligation to the less fortunate in a community, especially the poor. The first colonial **poor laws**, legislated in the late seventeenth century, stipulated a community obligation to support and "relieve" the poor. Sharing similar philosophy and purpose with the *parens patriae* doctrine, colonial communities, and later cities and states, soon developed a system for protecting poor children and, if necessary, separating them from their "undeserving parents" (Rendleman 1971:233; Rothman 1971). This system grew to include laws that regulated the poor, and charitable organizations and relief societies that were designed to fight **pauperism**—the widely held belief that poverty, if left unchecked, will produce children with "a future of crime and degradation" (Fox 1970:1189). These laws provided legal authority for governmental and private agencies to institutionalize poor children separated from their parents. Institutional relief efforts included the almshouse, workhouse, and poor house, which sought to motivate the poor out of poverty by hard work and strict discipline (Fox 1970). However, reformers soon realized that these institutional settings could similarly "pauperize" children by exposing them to adults "addicted to idleness and intemperance" (Rendleman 1971:214).

Houses of refuge and moral reform

In the first quarter of the nineteenth century, the state's parental authority derived from poor laws and institutional efforts to respond to pauperism became increasingly focused on the plight of urban poor children (Mennel 1973). As an expression of this perspective, the New York House of Refuge was established in 1824 by the Society for the Reformation of Juvenile Delinquents. The House of Refuge dealt both with children who were convicted of crimes and those who were vagrant, but in practice almost all of its children were vagrants from pauper families. Reformers were convinced that these children were victims rather than offenders and that they needed to be removed from the corrupting influences of urban poverty. **Houses of refuge** soon followed in Boston (1825) and Philadelphia (1828), and "for a quarter of a century the activities of these three institutions defined institutional treatment of juvenile delinquents" (Mennel 1973:4; Rendleman 1971; Rothman 1971; Fox 1970; Pickett 1969).

Houses of refuge were intended to be a haven where poor children could be isolated from the destructive forces of poverty and where moral reform could take place (Feld 1999; Mennel 1973). Moral reform involved four basic elements: a daily regimen, strict discipline, education, and work (Rothman 1971). Discipline was strictly enforced, based largely on solitary confinement and corporal punishment. As "Expanding ideas: a typical day at the New York House of Refuge" reveals, education and work consumed the daily life of children in houses of refuge. School in the early mornings and late at night, both before and after work, was intended not only to provide academic skills and achievement, but also to promote self-discipline and to instill morality and religion. Children in houses of refuge were also expected to work long and hard, doing physical labor and repetitive tasks. The labor of children was sometimes contracted to manufacturers to provide revenue for houses of refuge. The apprenticeship system was also used, justified as a means for children to develop occupational skills. Apprenticeships accounted for about 90 percent of the children released each year from houses of refuge. The most common apprenticeship placement for boys was with farmers, whereas for girls, maid service was the only socially acceptable form of indenture (Mennel 1973:21–23).

EXPANDING IDEAS: A TYPICAL DAY AT THE NEW YORK HOUSE OF REFUGE

At sunrise, the children are warned, by the ringing of a bell, to rise from their beds. Each child makes his own bed, and steps forth, on a signal, into the Hall. They then proceed, in perfect order, to the Wash Room. Thence they are marched to parade in the yard, and undergo an examination as to their dress and cleanliness; after which, they attend Morning Prayer. The morning school then commences, where they are occupied in summer, until 7 o'clock. A short intermission is allowed, when the bell rings for breakfast; after which, they proceed to their respective workshops, where they labor until 12 o'clock, when they are called from work, and one hour allowed them for washing and eating dinner. At one, they again commence work and continue at it until five in the afternoon, when the labor of the day terminated. Half an hour is allowed for washing and eating their supper, and at half-past five, they are conducted to the school room where they continue at their studies until 8 o'clock. Evening Prayer is performed by the Superintendent; after which, the children are conducted to their dormitories, which they enter, and are locked up for the night, when perfect silence reigns throughout the establishment. The foregoing is the history of a single day, and will answer for every day in the year, except Sundays, with slight variation during stormy weather, and the short days in winter.

Source: Mennel (1973:18–19).

The enthusiasm of house of refuge reformers was contagious and numerous institutions of similar design opened across the United States during the 1840s and 1850s (Rothman 1971). The philosophy and authority for placing children in houses of refuge was derived from the English legal doctrine of *parens patriae*. The doctrine of *parens patriae* was introduced into American law in an 1838 Pennsylvania Supreme Court case called *ex parte Crouse*, in which the commitment of a young girl to a house of refuge was contested. Although this case makes only brief mention of the doctrine, the intent and meaning appears deliberate: Under the philosophy and purpose of *parens patriae*, the government is granted legal authority to assume custody (guardianship) and parental responsibility (Rendleman 1971; Fox 1970). The Pennsylvania Supreme Court held that parental custody and control of children is a natural, but not absolute right, and if parents fail to properly supervise, train, and educate their children, their rights as parents can be taken over by the state.[1]

Placing-out and orphan trains

Even though houses of refuge continued to open during the 1850s, critics began to argue that, rather than being models of care, houses of refuge had become juvenile prisons, unable to nurture and reform children through an institutional approach (Rothman 1971). Beginning in the 1850s, reformers returned to the traditional belief that family homes, not institutions, were the best places for reform. Leading this charge was Charles Loring Brace (1826–1890), who founded the New York Children's Aid Society in 1853. He held that urban poverty bred a "dangerous class," prone to crime and violence. Fueled by this fear, the New York Children's

Aid Society sought to "drain the city" of poor and delinquent children through a practice called **placing-out** (Mennel 1973:37). Placing-out involved taking groups of vagrant children west by railroad, on "orphan trains," for placement with farming families. Brace believed that "the best of all Asylums for the outcast child is the farmer's home . . . the cultivators of the soil are in America our most solid and intelligent class" (Mennel 1973:37).

Placing-out was apparently well received in many communities. Reports indicate that community members were excited and willing to take these youths into their homes, whether because of the prospect of free farm labor or a sense of civic obligation. Placing-out programs were soon implemented by other organizations, but they were not without critics who contended that it is next to impossible to take a poor, vagrant child off the streets and expect him or her to adjust to rural family life (Mennel 1973).

Reform schools

The development of **reform schools**, beginning in the mid-nineteenth century, represents another way in which institutions were used to respond to the problem of dependency and juvenile crime. As the name implies, reform schools emphasized formal schooling. Instead of sandwiching school around a full day of work as houses of refuge did, reform school operated on a traditional school schedule (Mennel 1973).

Many reform schools used a cottage system in which committed youth were divided into "families" of 40 or fewer. Each family had its own cottage, its own matron and/or patron (mother or father), and its own schedule. Cottages were used to make the facility more like a family and less like a prison. Corrective discipline, rather than physical punishment, was used in an effort to generate conformity and instill good citizenship. Cottage reform schools spread across the United States in the latter half of the 1800s, but the degree of emphasis on the family ideal and the roles of school and work varied greatly. Contract labor of children to manufacturers was a part of most reform schools, but after the Civil War, child labor became more exploitative in some schools (Mennel 1973). In addition, changes in the nature of work brought on by the Industrial Revolution meant a significant reduction in apprenticeship opportunities—the means by which most children were released from reform schools. In response to this, some reform schools, especially those in the West, began to emphasize vocational education and to deemphasize a family environment (Schlossman 2005; Mennel 1973).

Commitment to reform schools was based on the legal authority of the state, under *parens patriae*, to take over parental custody and control. But this legal authority was challenged and overruled in the Illinois Supreme Court case *O'Connell v. Turner* (1870).[2] The court's opinion directly questioned the state's *parens patriae* authority, stressing that parents have a right and responsibility to rear and educate their children that cannot be preempted by the government except under "gross misconduct [by the child] or almost total unfitness on the part of the parents" (Fox 1970:1219).

The child-saving movement

By the late nineteenth century, little enthusiasm and hope remained for the programs and institutions that had once been heralded as places of protection and reform for vagrant and delinquent children. The problems of urban poverty and delinquency persisted and, in fact, grew worse. Forces of industrialization, urbanization, and immigration weakened the cohesiveness of communities and the abilities of communities and families to socialize and control children effectively (Feld 1999). Nonetheless, the late nineteenth century was a time of optimism and renewed effort. The **child-saving movement** emerged during this period in an effort to mobilize change in how government dealt with dependent, neglected, and delinquency children. The child-saving movement was comprised almost exclusively of women from middle- and upper-class backgrounds, who formed local groups across the United States (Krisberg and Austin 1993; Sutton 1988; Mennel 1973).

Scholars have long debated the motives behind the child-savers' reform efforts. Traditional explanations of the child-saving movement emphasize the "noble sentiments and tireless energy of middle class philanthropists" (Platt 1977:10). Another point of view holds that child-savers were progressive reformers seeking to alleviate the problems of urban life and to solve social problems by rational, scientific methods. Still others argue that the child-saving movement was an effort by the ruling class to repress newly arriving immigrants and the urban poor and to preserve its own way of life. Putting aside assumptions about their motivation, it is safe to say that child-savers were prominent, influential, philanthropic women, who were "generally well educated, widely traveled, and had access to political and financial resources" (Platt 1977:77, 83). Additionally, child-savers viewed their work as a humanitarian "moral enterprise," seeking to "strengthen and rebuild the moral fabric of society" (Platt 1977:75). Child-saving was largely women's work. Women involved in the child-saving movement proclaimed that the domestic role of women made them better suited than men to work with dependent and delinquent children (Platt 1977; see also Schlossman 2005; Tanenhaus 2004).

Creation of the juvenile court (1899)

The child-savers in the Chicago area were organized as the Chicago Women's Club, and it is this organization that is chiefly responsible for the creation of the first juvenile court—a separate legal system for children. The child-savers, however, realized that "child-welfare reform could only be accomplished with the support of political and professional organizations" (Platt 1977:130–131; see also Tanenhaus 2004; Mennel 1973). Through collaboration between the Chicago Women's Club, the Chicago Bar Association, and the Illinois Conference of Charities, a bill was introduced to the Illinois House of Representatives in February 1899 and shortly thereafter to the Senate. The bill was passed on April 14, the last day of the session. The first reading at the end of the chapter provides the original legislation, entitled "The Illinois Juvenile Court Act of 1899."

The Illinois Juvenile Court Act of 1899 did not represent radical reform; rather, it consolidated existing practices (Feld 1999; Sutton 1988; Hellum 1979; Platt 1977; Mennel 1973). In fact, in the years before the bill was drafted, a number of other states already practiced some of the innovations advanced in the Juvenile Court Act. For example, Massachusetts, in 1874, and New York, in 1892, passed laws that provided for separate trials of minors, apart from adults, and Massachusetts developed a system of juvenile probation in 1846. Nonetheless, the creation of the juvenile court culminated a century-long evolution of thought and practice by which juveniles were differentiated from adults both in terms of development and control (Feld 1999).[3] The new juvenile court established a separate system that is noteworthy in terms of (1) structure and jurisdiction, (2) legal authority under the expansion of *parens patriae*, and (3) legal philosophy and process.

Structure and jurisdiction of the juvenile court

The Illinois Juvenile Court Act of 1899 was the first statutory provision in the United States to provide for an entirely separate system of juvenile justice. As described in Section 3 of the Act, the juvenile court was made up of a designated judge of the circuit court, a "special courtroom," and separate records. The Act specifically refers to this court as the "Juvenile Court." This new court structure was designed to remove children from the adult criminal justice system and to create special programs for delinquent, dependent, and neglected children (Tanenhaus 2004; Feld 1999; Sutton 1988; Platt 1977). The personnel that made up the first juvenile court were distinct from the personnel that made up the adult court. A substantial portion of the personnel were police officers and truant officers; as a result, the juvenile court provided its own policing machinery and removed many distinctions between the enforcement and adjudication of laws (Platt 1977). The full title of the legislation that created the juvenile court indicates that the new court was granted jurisdiction over both juvenile delinquents and dependent and neglected children. As such, the juvenile court was deliberately created to have broad jurisdiction over almost all juvenile matters. The act defined a delinquent child as "any child under the age of sixteen who violates any law of this State or any city or village ordinance." The definition of a dependent and neglected child was much longer and far more sweeping, covering a wide range of conditions from which children must be protected, including homelessness, lack of parental care or guardianship, and parental neglect and abuse.

Legal authority: Parens patriae

A 1905 Pennsylvania Supreme Court case, *Commonwealth v. Fisher*, declared the legal authority of the new juvenile court under *parens patriae*:

> To save a child from becoming a criminal, or from continuing in a career of crime, . . . the legislatures surely may provide for the salvation of such a child, if its parents or guardians be unable or unwilling to do so, by bringing it into one of the courts of the state without any process at all, for the purpose of subjecting it to the state's guardianship and protection.[4]

Sections 7 and 9 of the Illinois Juvenile Court Act prescribe options for "disposition"—court actions or outcomes in dealing with dependent and neglected children, and with delinquent children. A wide variety of "commitment" options are offered in the statute. Commitment refers to the juvenile court's authority to transfer legal custody of the child from the parents to another person or to a public or private agency when the court finds the parents to be inadequate. Regardless of whether cases were dependency and neglect or delinquency, this statute authorized commitment to a probation officer, a "reputable citizen," a training or industrial school, or a private philanthropic association (Ferdinand 1991; Platt 1977; Mennel 1973; Fox 1970). The variety of commitment options specified in the act clearly reflected and authorized the *parens patriae* doctrine in the early juvenile court.

Legal philosophy and process: The "rehabilitative ideal"

In advocating for the juvenile court, the child-savers sought not only a separate legal system for juveniles, but also a legal philosophy and process that distinguished juvenile courts from adult criminal courts. Barry Feld (1999) refers to this distinctive legal philosophy of the original juvenile court as the **rehabilitative ideal** because of its emphasis on assessment and reform, rather than the determination of guilt and punishment as in adult criminal courts (see also Platt 1977; Allen 1959, 1964). The rehabilitative ideal is clearly founded on *parens patriae*, giving juvenile courts authority and obligation to assume parental responsibility. Rehabilitation became the focus of the new juvenile court, and procedures were developed to reflect and facilitate this ideal. The early juvenile court's rehabilitative ideal and *parens patriae* authority resulted in at least three distinctive legal procedures: (1) diminished criminal responsibility of juveniles, (2) a child welfare approach operating on the concept of the "best interests of the child" and (3) informal and family-like procedures.

1 **Diminished criminal responsibility of juveniles:** Drawn from the developmental concepts of childhood and adolescence, the early juvenile court held that children and adolescents younger than 16 years of age lacked the capacity to commit crime. This presumption of incapacity acknowledged that young people could not be held legally responsible for their offenses because they lacked physical and mental maturity (Brummer 2002). Viewed in this way, juveniles were not charged with or convicted of criminal offenses, and rehabilitation, not punishment, was the appropriate outcome of the juvenile court process.
2 **A child welfare approach—the "best interests of the child":** The child-savers envisioned the juvenile court as a welfare system, rather than a judicial system (Feld 1999). As a result, the prevailing goal of the juvenile court was to protect, nurture, reform, and regulate the dependent, neglected, and delinquent child. The role of the juvenile court was not to determine guilt or innocence, but to ascertain the character and needs of an offender by analyzing his or her social background so that the court could make a full determination of what was in the "**best interests of the child.**" The early juvenile court's intense focus on the individual juvenile offender, rather than the offense, coincides with the rise of positivist criminology in the late nineteenth and early twentieth centuries. Using detailed social histories, the juvenile court sought to uncover the causes of a youth's delinquent behavior and thereby provide a "proper diagnosis" or assessment. This assessment was then used to develop a treatment program that was individualized to the child's needs (Feld 1999; Platt 1977; Rothman 1971).[5]
3 **Informal and family-like procedures:** In an effort to bring about the rehabilitative ideal, the original juvenile court discarded the rules of criminal procedure that are part of adult criminal courts. Instead, the juvenile court developed an informal process in which the judge, much like a parent, tried to find out all about the child (Feld 1999; Platt 1977).

The physical setting of the juvenile court was intended to facilitate the rehabilitative ideal. The new juvenile court building that opened in Chicago in 1907 was designed to provide an informal, family-like setting for juvenile court hearings. Hearings were held in "a room fitted up as a parlor rather than a court, around a table instead of a bench" (Platt 1977:143).

Juvenile court reformers also introduced softened legal terminology in order to avoid reference to the harsh, adversarial process of adult criminal courts (Schlossman 2005; Feld 1999). To initiate the juvenile court process, a petition is filed "in the welfare of the child," whereas the formal legal document that initiates the adult criminal process is an indictment or an information. The proceedings of juvenile courts are referred to as "hearings," instead of trials, as in adult courts. Juvenile courts find youths to be "delinquent," rather than guilty of an offense, and juvenile delinquents are given a "disposition," instead of a sentence, as in adult criminal courts.

The juvenile court was clearly an idea ripe for its time. The Illinois Juvenile Court Act of 1899 was a prototype for legislation in a number of other states, including Wisconsin (1901), New York (1901), Ohio (1902), Maryland (1902), and Colorado (1903) (Platt 1977; Mennel 1973). By 1925, all but two states, Maine and Wyoming, had juvenile court laws. The juvenile justice systems that emerged from legislation were composed of newly created juvenile courts together with a collection of private and public institutions and community programs, all embracing the rehabilitative ideal and empowered by *parens patriae* (Ferdinand 1991).

REFORMING JUVENILE JUSTICE: TRANSFORMATION OF JUVENILE JUSTICE PHILOSOPHY, POLICY, AND PRACTICE

Although the new juvenile court system proved wildly popular and spread rapidly, it was not without critics. Some scholars argued that the child-savers' rhetoric of reform was never really achieved in the newly created juvenile justice systems across the United States. They contended that the new juvenile justice systems were even more repressive, punitive, and authoritarian than the earlier child welfare systems that were used in combination with adult criminal courts. In addition, the new juvenile justice systems were given extensive, almost unbridled, authority under the rehabilitative ideal and expanded *parens patriae* (Schlossman 2005; Platt 1977; Feld 1999; Fox 1970). Feminist criminologists have also criticized the early juvenile justice system

JUVENILE JUSTICE PROCESS AND PRACTICE: GENDER DIFFERENCES IN CASE PROCESSING OF THE EARLY JUVENILE JUSTICE SYSTEM

Historical research documents how police and juvenile courts have responded more harshly to female status offenses than to more serious offenses committed by females, or to status and other delinquent offenses committed by males (MacDonald and Chesney-Lind 2001; Odem and Schlossman 1991; Chesney-Lind 1977). Feminist scholar Meda Chesney-Lind attributes this "double standard of juvenile justice" to threats that female status offenses pose to parental authority and female chastity.

> The juvenile justice system is concerned that girls allowed to run wild might be tempted to experiment sexually and thus endanger their marriageability. The court involves itself in the enforcement of adolescent morality and parental authority through the vehicle of status offenses.
>
> (Chesney-Lind 1977:122–123)

Chesney-Lind's critique is supported by evidence of juvenile court practice. Odem and Schlossman (1991) found that almost half of the referrals of girls to the Los Angeles Juvenile Court originated from parents, guardian, or relatives, and that two-thirds of the girls petitioned into court were accused of sexual activity. Another study by Chesney-Lind (1973:56), using data from 1929–1955 found that the juvenile court in Hawaii commonly ordered physical examinations of females in order to determine if the girls were sexually active.

for its double standard of juvenile justices for males and females. For discussion of this issue, see "Juvenile justice process and practice: Gender differences in case processing of the early juvenile justice system."

Despite occasional criticism, juvenile courts across the United States achieved high regard in the decades following their creation. The few reports of problems were viewed as "minor imperfections soon to be corrected by a continually improving system" (Hellum 1979:301). In addition, the confidential records and closed hearings of juvenile courts made them inaccessible and beyond accusation.

Challenges to the traditional juvenile court

Shortly after World War II, criticism of the juvenile court began to mount. In 1946, criminologist Paul Tappan (1946) wrote a widely read and influential article entitled "Treatment without Trial?" Tappan criticized the juvenile court's failure to provide due process of law. **Due process of law** refers to the procedural rights established in the Constitution (especially the Bill of Rights) and extended through appellate court decisions, including procedural rights such as notice of charges, legal counsel, and protection from self-incrimination. Under the guise of the rehabilitative ideal and empowered by *parens patriae*, the procedures of the original juvenile court were informal and family-like, making the rules of criminal procedure inapplicable. Beginning in the 1960s and persisting until the 1980s, legal challenges were mounted against the informalities of the juvenile justice system (Hellum 1979). This movement involved a series of Supreme Court cases that radically altered juvenile justice procedures. The most significant cases will be discussed in the next section.

The 1960s also ushered in empirical challenges to the juvenile justice system. Most actively in the 1970s, evaluation research seriously questioned the effectiveness of individualized treatment and rehabilitation (Feld 1999; Ferdinand 1991; Hellum 1979; Lerman 1975; Lipton, Martinson, and Wilks 1975). Although this research considered both juvenile and adult correctional methods, it directed significant attention at the rehabilitative ideal of the juvenile court. In his book, *Radical Non-Intervention*, Edwin Schur (1973) argued for a drastic reduction in the juvenile justice system's reliance on treatment and rehabilitation. Instead, he advocated a "return to the rule of law," involving the reduction of discretionary powers of the juvenile court, diversion of less serious offenders, and intervention for only the most serious crimes.

In the years following these challenges, the juvenile justice system was altered dramatically. Prevailing views of juvenile delinquency and the proper approach to juvenile justice changed significantly. Four areas of change have been most pronounced: (1) the due process revolution, (2) enactment of the Juvenile Justice and Delinquency Prevention Act of 1974, (3) initiatives for punishment and accountability, and (4) contemporary juvenile justice reform and the return to rehabilitation.

The due process revolution in juvenile justice

With the purpose of protection and reform, the rehabilitative ideal of the juvenile court made due process protections given to criminal defendants unnecessary (Feld 1999; Ferdinand 1991). In the ten-year period from 1966 to 1975, however, the U.S. Supreme Court introduced due process requirements into juvenile justice procedures (Feld 2003). Five U.S. Supreme Court decisions handed down during this period dramatically altered the procedures of traditional juvenile justice systems (Feld 2014; Sickmund and Puzzanchera 2014; Hemmens, Steiner, and Mueller 2013; Siegel and Tracy 2008).

- ***Kent v. United States*** (1966)[6]
  While on probation, 16-year-old Morris Kent was charged with robbery, rape, and breaking into someone's home. Kent confessed to the charges as well as to several similar incidents. Without a formal hearing, the juvenile court judge waived jurisdiction to the criminal court after making a "full investigation," but the judge did not describe the extent of the investigation or the reasons for the waiver. Kent was subsequently found guilty in criminal court on six counts of breaking and entering and robbery, but acquitted by reason of insanity on two rape counts. He was sentenced to 30–90 years in prison.

  The U.S. Supreme Court found the waiver invalid, ruling that Kent was entitled to a hearing that provided "the essentials of due process and fair treatment." This standard includes the right to a formal hearing on the motion of waiver, the right to counsel, defense access to all records involved in the waiver decision, and a written statement of the reasons for waiver.

- ***In re Gault*** (1967)[7]
  Already on probation for a minor property offense, Gerald Gault, age 15, was arrested and placed in detention for allegedly making obscene phone calls to an adult neighbor. His parents were both at work at the time of the arrest and they were not notified that their son had been taken to detention until later that evening. While the neighbor did not appear at the adjudication hearing, and the court never determined whether he in fact made the obscene remarks, Gault was committed to a training school "for the period of his minority"—six years. Had he been an adult, the maximum sentence would have been a $50 fine or not more than two months in jail. Furthermore, no official transcript of the proceeding was made.

  An attorney obtained for Gault by his parents filed a writ of habeas corpus that was eventually appealed to the U.S. Supreme Court. The Court ruled that juveniles are entitled to the constitutional guarantee of due process when court proceedings may result in commitment to a secure facility. The specific due process rights include: (1) fair notice of charges; (2) right to counsel; (3) right to confront and cross-examine witnesses; and (4) privilege against self-incrimination. The Court concluded that the manner in which this case was handled violated the Due Process Clause of the Fourteenth Amendment: "Juvenile court history has again demonstrated that unbridled discretion, however benevolently motivated, is frequently a poor substitute for principle and procedure."

- ***In re Winship*** (1970)[8]
  Samuel Winship, aged 12, was charged with stealing $112 from a woman's purse in a store, a charge that "if done by an adult would constitute the crime or crimes of Larceny." The youth was found delinquent in a New York juvenile court, using the civil law standard of proof, "preponderance of the evidence." Winship was committed to a state training school for an initial period of 18 months with annual extension of no more than six years.

  Upon appeal, the U.S. Supreme Court ruled that "proof beyond a reasonable doubt is among the 'essentials of due process and fair treatment' required during the adjudication stage when a juvenile is charged with an act which would constitute a crime if committed by an adult." The Court acknowledged that juvenile adjudication hearings are designed to be more informal than adult criminal courts, but that confinement dispositions necessitate proof beyond a reasonable doubt.

- ***McKeiver v. Pennsylvania*** (1971)[9]
  In May 1968, Joseph McKeiver, then age 16, was charged with robbery, larceny, and receiving stolen goods, all felonies under state law. He and a large group of youths purportedly chased three youths and took 25 cents from them. At the adjudication hearing, McKeiver was represented by counsel and requested a jury trial; the request was denied. He was subsequently adjudicated a delinquent youth and placed on probation.
  While acknowledging that the informality of juvenile court proceedings is idealistic and far from perfect, the U.S. Supreme Court "asserted that imposing jury trials would not correct those deficiencies but would make the juvenile process unduly formal and adversarial" (Feld 2014:15). Justice Harry A. Blackmun argued that "If the formalities of the criminal adjudicative process are to be superimposed upon the juvenile court system, there is little need for its separate existence. Perhaps that ultimate disillusionment will come one day, but for the moment we are disinclined to give impetus to it".

- ***Breed v. Jones*** (1975)[10]
  At the age of 17, Gary Jones was charged with armed robbery. He appeared in juvenile court and was adjudicated delinquent on the original charge and two other robberies. At the dispositional hearing, the probation officer assigned to the case testified that Jones was not amenable to treatment as a juvenile. The juvenile court subsequently ordered that he be prosecuted as an adult. At the preliminary hearing in criminal court, the defense counsel filed a writ of habeas corpus, arguing that the waiver to criminal court violated the double jeopardy clause of the Fifth Amendment in that he had been prosecuted twice for the same offense, both in juvenile court and now in criminal court. The district court denied the petition, saying that Jones had not been tried twice because juvenile adjudication is not a trial and does not place a youth "in jeopardy."
  The case was eventually appealed to the U.S. Supreme Court, which ruled that adjudication in juvenile court, in which a juvenile is found to have violated a criminal statute, is functionally equivalent to trial in criminal court. Thus, the Court determined that Jones had, in fact, been placed in double jeopardy.

In the years that followed, the U.S. Supreme Court continued to hear cases that impacted juvenile justice proceedings, but the number and scope of these cases lessened. Taken together, these five cases dramatically changed the character and procedures of juvenile justice. The rehabilitative ideal of the traditional juvenile court, with its *parens patriae* authority, was diminished, making juvenile courts more like criminal courts. Nonetheless, the due process revolution acknowledged the need for a separate system and the need for a distinctive approach to juvenile crime.

The Juvenile Justice and Delinquency Prevention Act of 1974

The Juvenile Justice and Delinquency Prevention (JJDP) Act of 1974 embodied a series of reforms to redefine juvenile delinquency and to redirect the legal philosophy, authority, and procedures of juvenile justice systems across the United States. Two federal commissions, established in the 1960s, and a national organization, directly influenced these reform efforts: the President's Commission on Law Enforcement and Administration of Justice, the National Council on Crime and Delinquency, and the National Advisory Commission on Criminal Justice Standards and Goals (Howell 1997; Crank 1995).

Based on thorough examination of crime and delinquency, and the workings of justice systems in the United States, the President's Commission on Law Enforcement and Administration of Justice significantly challenged prevailing approaches to juvenile justice and made four compelling recommendations: (1) handle minor offenders in the community instead of juvenile courts through diversion and development of community-based programs that provide a variety of services to youth and families; (2) narrow the jurisdiction of the juvenile court to youth who violate the criminal law, thereby eliminating jurisdiction over noncriminal conduct; (3) limit the use of detention and incarceration; and (4) for serious offenders, implement a more formal and punitive system of juvenile justice (President's Commission 1967b:22–28). While agreeing with the President's Commission, the National Advisory Commission on Criminal Justice Standards and Goals, went one step further, arguing that "first priority should be given to preventing juvenile delinquency, to minimizing the involvement of young offenders in the juvenile and criminal justice system, and to reintegrating delinquent and young offenders into the community" (National Advisory Commission 1973:23). In addition, the National Council on Crime and Delinquency (NCCD) surveyed state and local correctional agencies and institutions across the United States, finding widespread use of detention facilities for juveniles accused of noncriminal conduct (status offenses, dependency, and neglect), often without court petitions. As a result of the survey, the NCCD recommended that "no child be placed in any detention facility unless he is a delinquent or alleged delinquent and there is substantial probability that he will commit an offense dangerous to himself or the community" (President's Commission 1967a:211).

The findings and recommendations of these three groups formed the basis for the JJDP Act of 1974. This act was the first major federal initiative to address juvenile delinquency in a comprehensive manner (Raley 1995). While primary responsibility for juvenile justice had historically existed at the state and local levels, the JJDP Act established a leadership role for the federal government through the creation of the Office of Juvenile Justice and Delinquency Prevention (OJJDP).

The JJDP Act established juvenile justice goals and policies and committed ongoing financial assistance to aid their implementation at the state and local levels (Shepherd 1999). The most assertive parts of the JJDP Act sought reform in the use of secure detention—both limiting its use and separating juveniles from adult offenders when detention was necessary (Sickmund and Puzzanchera 2014:87; Crank 1995). The JJDP Act also called for a preventive approach to the problem of delinquency, as the name of the act clearly indicates. Federal legislation associated with the JJDP Act authorized a grant funding program for states (block grants) to develop policies, practices, and programs directed at delinquency prevention in local areas. Communities were encouraged to develop alternatives to the juvenile justice system that included community-based, diversionary, and noninstitutional programs aimed at preventing and controlling juvenile delinquency (Sickmund and Puzzanchera 2014; Krisberg et al. 1986).

Getting tough: Initiatives for punishment and accountability

The 1980s saw a dramatic shift in juvenile justice law and practice at both the federal and state levels. Attention focused on the identification and control of serious, violent, and chronic offenders (Krisberg et al. 1986). OJJDP began to sponsor research on chronic, violent offenders and funded state and local programs designed to prevent and control violence and the use of drugs (Wilson and Howell 1993; Krisberg et al. 1986). At the state level, legislatures passed laws to crack down on juvenile crime, reflecting a widespread reconsideration of juvenile justice philosophy, jurisdiction and authority, and a more punitive approach to juvenile delinquency. Four areas of legal change have been most pronounced: (1) transfer provisions in state law, (2) enhanced sentencing authority for juvenile courts, (3) reduction in juvenile court confidentiality, and (4) juvenile offender accountability (Sickmund and Puzzanchera 2014:86; Redding 2008).

Transfer provisions

All states have enacted laws that allow juveniles to be tried in adult criminal courts. Although these statutes vary from state to state, the basic idea is that certain types of offenses and offenders, especially violent ones, are beyond the scope of the juvenile court. Transfer provisions fall into three main categories: judicial waiver, concurrent jurisdiction, and statutory exclusion (Sickmund and Puzzanchera 2014; Kupchik 2006). *Judicial waiver* statutes provide judges authority to waive juvenile court jurisdiction and transfer cases to adult criminal court. *Concurrent jurisdiction* statutes give prosecutors authority to file certain types of cases in either juvenile or criminal court. Some state statutes, for example, allow prosecutors, at their discretion, to file felony offenses directly in adult criminal courts. *Statutory exclusion* statutes eliminate juvenile court jurisdiction for certain types of juvenile offenders and juvenile offenses. For example, a number of state statutes specify that violent felony offenses such as homicide, rape, and robbery, when committed by older adolescents, are automatically sent to adult criminal court.

In addition to these transfer provisions, a number of states (at least 13) have lowered the age of majority to 15, 16, or 17, thereby limiting juvenile court jurisdiction. Youth of the age of majority automatically have their cases heard in adult criminal courts. These statutory law changes are intended to provide procedures whereby serious juvenile offenses and offenders may be dealt with in adult courts, rather than juvenile courts, in an effort to deter youthful offenders and to administer punishment, rather than rehabilitation. The practice and effectiveness of transfer laws will be discussed more fully in Chapter 8.

Sentencing authority

A second area of transformation in the 1980s was the enactment of state laws that give both criminal and juvenile courts expanded sentencing options in juvenile cases. This change resulted in a more punitive approach to juvenile delinquency. Traditionally, juvenile court dispositions were individualized and based on the background characteristics of the offender. State sentencing laws allowed the juvenile court judge to customize the disposition to fit the offender's needs and situation, with rehabilitation as the primary goal. As states shifted the purpose of their juvenile justice systems away from rehabilitation and toward punishment, accountability, and public safety, juvenile case dispositions began to be based more on the offense than the offender.

Beginning in the mid-1970s, a number of states changed their statutes to allow for punishment in juvenile court disposition. For example, New York's Juvenile Justice Reform Act of 1976 provided for secure confinement and mandatory treatment of serious juvenile offenders, followed by strict parole standards and intensive supervision upon release. By 1997, at least 16 states had followed New York's lead by adding or modifying laws to require minimum periods of incarceration for certain violent or serious offenders (Sickmund and Puzzanchera 2014).

In recent years, 14 states have adopted "blended sentencing" laws that authorize juvenile courts to impose criminal sanctions on certain juvenile offenders (depending on age and criminal history) or for certain types of offenses. As a result of this statutory law change, the sanctioning powers of juvenile courts in these states have been expanded such that some juvenile offenders may receive the same penalties faced by adult offenders, even when those juvenile offenders stay under the jurisdiction of the juvenile court (Sickmund and Puzzanchera 2014:105–106).

Confidentiality

A third area of juvenile justice transformation concerns the traditional confidentiality of juvenile justice proceedings and records. Even though the first juvenile court was open to the public, confidentiality became the norm over time. Confidentiality of juvenile court proceedings and records was an operating standard in most states until the latter part of the 1980s. In recent years, most states have provided at least some access to juvenile court hearings, although almost half of the states place limits on such access. In addition, most state legislatures have made significant changes in how information about juvenile offenders is treated by the juvenile justice system. Laws allowing for the release of court records to other justice agencies, social service agencies, schools, victims, and the public have been enacted in most states. These laws also establish the circumstances under which media access is allowed. A number of states also permit or even require the juvenile court to notify school districts about juveniles charged with or convicted of serious or violent crimes (Sickmund and Puzzanchera 2014; Tanenhaus 2004).

Juvenile offender accountability

These initiatives for punishment and accountability have replaced the rehabilitative ideal and *parens patriae* authority of the original juvenile court. Sections of state law that declare the purpose of the juvenile court—"purpose clauses"—now emphasize offender accountability, community safety, and offender competency development (OJJDP 2008; Albert 1998).

This emphasis on juvenile offender accountability was spearheaded by federal legislation called the Balanced Juvenile Justice and Crime Prevention Act of 1996, an act that promoted a more punitive approach to juvenile justice. This act was associated with a large federal grant program, the Juvenile Accountability Block Grants Program (JABG), administered by OJJDP. States requesting funding were required to demonstrate that their laws, policies, and procedures fulfilled a number of federally specified expectations for a more punitive approach to serious delinquency. States used funds from the JABG program to construct and staff juvenile detention and correctional facilities; to hire judges, prosecutors, defense attorneys, and probation officers; and to develop accountability-based sanctioning programs such as drug courts. In addition, the wording of purpose clauses in many state juvenile court acts was changed in order to demonstrate an operating philosophy consistent with the requirements of JABG, thereby making these states eligible for federal funds (Sickmund and Puzzanchera 2014; OJJDP 2008; Danegger et al. 1999; Albert 1998). The wording of the purpose clause of the Wisconsin Juvenile Justice Code reflects this reorientation toward offender accountability and public safety (see "Juvenile justice law: Purpose clause of the Wisconsin juvenile justice code").

JUVENILE JUSTICE LAW: PURPOSE CLAUSE OF THE WISCONSIN JUVENILE JUSTICE CODE

938.01 Title, legislative intent and purposes.

(1) TITLE. This chapter may be cited as "The Juvenile Justice Code", and shall be liberally construed in accordance with the objectives expressed in this section.

(2) LEGISLATIVE INTENT. It is the intent of the legislature to promote a juvenile justice system capable of dealing with the problem of juvenile delinquency, a system which will protect the community, impose accountability for violations of law and equip juvenile offenders with competencies to live responsibly and productively. To effectuate this intent, the legislature declares the following to be equally important purposes of this chapter:

(a) To protect citizens from juvenile crime.

(b) To hold each juvenile offender directly accountable for his or her acts.

(c) To provide an individualized assessment of each alleged and adjudicated delinquent juvenile, in order to prevent further delinquent behavior through the development of competency in the juvenile offender, so that he or she is more capable of living productively and responsibly in the community.

(d) To provide due process through which each juvenile offender and all other interested parties are assured fair hearings, during which constitutional and other legal rights are recognized and enforced.

(e) To divert juveniles from the juvenile justice system through early intervention as warranted, when consistent with the protection of the public.

(f) To respond to a juvenile offender's needs for care and treatment, consistent with the prevention of delinquency, each juvenile's best interest and protection of the public, by allowing the court to utilize the most effective dispositional option.

(g) To ensure that victims and witnesses of acts committed by juveniles that result in proceedings under this chapter are, consistent with this chapter and the Wisconsin constitution, afforded the same rights as victims and witnesses of crimes committed by adults, and are treated with dignity, respect, courtesy, and sensitivity throughout those proceedings.

[Remainder of statute omitted.]

Source: 2015–16 Wisconsin Statutes and Annotations (2017).

Contemporary juvenile justice reform: Return to rehabilitation

Recent reform efforts have been driven by empirical research that seeks to translate research findings into effective juvenile justice practice. Only in the last 25 years have researchers been able to identify clearly both the developmental processes associated with delinquent behavior and the interventions that consistently reduce the likelihood of its occurrence (Greenwood 2008:186; National Research Council 2012, 2013). Research in two principal areas has been applied to juvenile justice reform: adolescent development and evidence-based practice.

A developmental approach to juvenile justice reform

The get-tough approach is based on the assumption that many present-day delinquents commit more adult-like offenses than earlier generations and that contemporary juvenile justice is too lenient to be effective (Grisso and Schwartz 2000; Zimring 1998). In the mid-1990s, this assumption and the get-tough initiatives derived from it were drawn into question. Most influential was the work of the MacArthur Foundation's Research Network on Adolescent Development and Juvenile Justice, a group of national experts on juvenile law and developmental psychology.

Research sponsored by the Network found that adolescents differ from adults in ways that make them potentially less blameworthy than adults for their criminal acts and less competent in the legal system (MacArthur Foundation 2014a, 2014b). More specifically, maturation was found to be associated with increasing cognitive and reasoning skills, including the ability to consider long-term consequences, to control impulses, and to resist peer pressure. Based on these findings, the Network argued that developmental immaturity is a mitigating factor in criminal responsibility, or in their terms, youth are "less guilty by reason of adolescence" (MacArthur Foundation 2014b). Immaturity also makes adolescents less competent to negotiate the legal system. The competence to participate in the legal process and to make reasoned and informed decisions is key to ensuring due process of law, especially when the legal procedures of juvenile courts become increasingly formal and punitive, and state laws expand the options to have juvenile cases tried and sentenced in criminal courts (Grisso and Schwartz 2000). The Network concluded that it is justifiable to consider adolescents to be a "special legal category," and to deal with them through a separate system of justice where they are

> treated as responsible but less blameworthy, and where they . . . receive less punishment and more rehabilitation and treatment than typical adult offenders. The juvenile system does not excuse youths of their crimes; rather, it acknowledges the development stage and its role in the crimes committed, and punishes appropriately.
>
> (MacArthur Foundation 2014b:4)

Spurred by the Network's findings and approach to juvenile justice reform, the National Research Council organized a committee to synthesize recent research on adolescent development and then provide implications for juvenile justice reform (National Research Council 2013). The committee released a lengthy report in 2013, entitled *Reforming Juvenile Justice: A Developmental Approach*. The report cited "important behavioral differences between adults and adolescents with direct bearing on the design and operation of the justice system" (National Research Council 2013:1). Specifically, the Committee concluded that:

- Adolescents are less able to regulate their own behavior in emotionally charged contexts.
- Adolescents are more sensitive to external influences such as peer pressure and immediate rewards.
- Adolescents show less ability to make judgments and decisions that require future orientation.

(National Research Council 2012:2, 2013:91)

The Committee on Juvenile Justice Reform also observed that research consistently shows that most delinquency does not extend beyond the adolescent years and that only a very small proportion of delinquent youth are involved in violent offenses—most are nonserious offenders.

Based on these findings, the Committee concluded that a separate system of justice for juveniles is indeed warranted, but that it needs to be reformed using a developmental approach:

> The overarching goal of the juvenile justice system is to support the positive social development of youths who become involved in the system, and thereby assure the safety of communities. The specific aims of juvenile courts and affiliated agencies are to hold youths accountable for wrongdoing, prevent further offending, and treat youths fairly.
>
> (National Research Council 2012:3)

This chapter's second reading provides the "Report Brief" of the full report, *Reforming Juvenile Justice: A Developmental Approach*.

The implementation of juvenile justice reform using a developmental approach is the focus of an initiative launched by the MacArthur Foundation in 2004 called *Models for Change*. Today, Models for Change (n.d.) promotes and sponsors juvenile justice reform in 35 states, targeting a number of key areas:

- **Juvenile aftercare** that provides support, supervision, and services to delinquent youth after custodial placement.
- **Community-based alternatives** to formal court processing and incarceration.
- Coordinated services to "**dual status youth**"—youth involved in both juvenile justice and child welfare systems.
- **Evidence-based practices**, providing programs and services of proven effectiveness to improve behavior.
- **Juvenile indigent defense** that promotes legal counsel to all youth.
- **Mental health collaboration** that provides mental health services without unnecessary juvenile justice involvement.
- **Racial–ethnic fairness** through "data-driven strategies to reduce racial and ethnic disparities" (Models for Change n.d.).
- **Status offense reform** to divert non-delinquent youth from juvenile justice systems, in an effort to provide effective services and community safety.

Evidence-based practice

Contemporary juvenile justice reform is also being driven by evaluation research that tries to establish whether delinquency prevention and intervention programs effectively reduce the likelihood of offending. Greenwood and Welsh (2012:495) summarize this approach: "**Evidence-based practice** involves the use of scientific principles to assess the available evidence on program effectiveness and to develop principles for best practice in any particular field." While we will discuss this important development in chapter 13 when we take up delinquency prevention, four key points about evidence-based practice are necessary now (Mihalic and Elliott 2015; McKee and Rapp 2014; National Research Council 2013; Greenwood and Welsh 2012; Lipsey and Howell 2012; Vincent, Guy, and Grisso 2012; Lipsey et al. 2010; Drake et al. 2009; Lipsey 2009; Greenwood 2008).

1 Advances in the criteria and methods for assessing program effectiveness through evaluation research provide a growing body of knowledge on program effectiveness—knowledge that has practical usefulness.

2 Several model program guides offer information on the "best practices" in delinquency prevention and intervention.
   - *Blueprints for Healthy Youth Development*, Center for the Study and Prevention of Violence, University of Colorado Boulder
   - *Model Program Guide*, Office of Juvenile Justice and Delinquency Prevention
   - *National Registry of Evidence-Based Programs and Practices*, Substance Abuse and Mental Health Services Administration.

3 Evidence-based intervention practices increasingly use risk–need assessment instruments to identify the needs of youth and to determine the likelihood of reoffending.

4 Evidence-based practice increasingly involves identification and measurement of the benefits and costs of programs, including those that occur during and after participation in the program.

Each wave of reform that we have discussed has brought about substantial change in juvenile justice philosophy, policy, and practice. While these changes may be enduring, they are also cumulative, transforming how our society defines and responds to delinquency.

SUMMARY AND CONCLUSIONS

Juvenile delinquency is a socially constructed concept. This means that it is a product of sweeping social, political, economic, and religious changes. Three historical developments laid the foundation for the idea of juvenile delinquency: (1) the discovery of childhood and adolescence as separate and distinct stages of life; (2) the emergence of *parens patriae* in English equity law, which gave legal authority to the state for protective control of children when parents failed to fulfill childrearing responsibilities; and (3) the rise of positivist criminology, which introduced scientific methods to the study and control of crime and delinquency.

The creation of the juvenile court in Chicago in 1899 clearly reflected these historical developments. Reformers envisioned a child welfare system, rather than a judicial system. As a result, the prevailing goal of the early juvenile court was to protect, nurture, reform, and regulate the dependent, neglected, and delinquent child. Because the court was pursuing the "best interests of the child," little distinction was made between types of offenders. The legal tradition of *parens patriae*, together with the rehabilitative ideal, provided the new juvenile court with a distinctive legal philosophy, structure, and process.

The traditional juvenile court came under attack shortly after World War II. Criticism centered on its disregard of due process and its failure to provide effective rehabilitation through individualized treatment. Beginning in the 1960s, at least four areas of transformation have dramatically changed the legal concept of juvenile delinquency and the character of juvenile justice systems across the United States: (1) the juvenile due process revolution from 1966 to 1975; (2) the Juvenile Justice and Delinquency Prevention Act of 1974; (3) a growing emphasis on punishment and accountability in the 1980s and 1990s; and (4) contemporary juvenile justice reform that is driven by empirical research on adolescent development and evidence-based practice, resulting in a return to rehabilitation.

READING 2.1

"THE ILLINOIS JUVENILE COURT ACT OF 1899: JUVENILE COURTS FOR DEPENDENT, NEGLECTED AND DELINQUENCY CHILDREN."

National Council of Juvenile and Family Court Judges. 1998. ***Juvenile and Family Court Journal*** **49(4):1–5.**

This reading provides the text of the Illinois Juvenile Court Act of 1899. The Act defines juvenile delinquency, establishes juvenile court jurisdiction, gives authority to personnel of the juvenile court, and designates a juvenile justice process.

An Act to regulate the treatment and control of dependent, neglected and delinquency children

. . .

SECTION I. *Be it enacted by the People of the State of Illinois, represented in the General Assembly:*

DEFINITIONS. This act shall apply only to children under the age of 16 years not now or hereafter inmates of a State institution, or any training school for boys or industrial school for girls or some institution incorporated under the laws of this State, except as provided in sections twelve (12) and eighteen (18). For the purposes of this act the words dependent child and neglected child shall mean any child who for any reason is destitute or homeless or abandoned; or dependent upon the public for support; or has not proper parental care or guardianship; or who habitually begs or receives alms; or who is found living in any house of ill fame or with any vicious or disreputable person; or whose home, by reason of neglect, cruelty or depravity on the part of its parents, guardian or other person in whose care it may be, is an unfit place for such a child; and any child under the age of 8 years who is found peddling or selling any article or singing or playing any musical instrument upon the streets or giving any public entertainment. The words delinquent child shall include any child under the age of 16 years who violates any law of this State or any city or village ordinance. The word child or children may mean one or more children, and the word parent or parents may be held to mean one or both parents, when consistent with the intent of this act. The word association shall include any corporation which includes in its purposes the care or disposition of children coming within the meaning of this act.

§2. JURISDICTION. The circuit and county courts of the several counties in this State shall have original jurisdiction in all cases coming within the terms of this act. In all trials under this act any person interested therein may demand a jury of six, or the judge of his own motion may order a jury of the same number, to try the case.

§3. JUVENILE COURT. In counties having over 500,000 population the judges of the circuit court shall, at such times as they shall determine, designate one or more of their number whose duty it shall be to hear all cases coming under this act. A special court room, to be designated as the juvenile court room, shall be provided for the hearing of such cases, and the findings of the court shall be entered in a book or books to be kept for that purpose and known as the "Juvenile Record," and the court may, for convenience, be called the "Juvenile Court."

§4. PETITION TO THE COURT. Any reputable person, being resident in the county, having knowledge of a child in his county who appears to be either neglected, dependent or delinquent, may file with the clerk of a court having jurisdiction in the matter a petition in writing, setting forth the facts, verified by affidavit. It shall be sufficient that the affidavit is upon information and belief.

§5. SUMMONS. Upon the filing of the petition a summons shall issue requiring the person having custody or control of the child, or with whom the child may be, to appear with the child at a place and time stated in the summons, which time shall be not less than 24 hours after service. The parents of the child, if living, and their residence is [if] known, or its legal guardian, if one there be, or if there is neither parent nor guardian, or if his or her residence is not known, then some relative, if there be one and his residence is known, shall be notified of the proceedings, and in any case the judge may appoint some suitable person to act in behalf of the child. If the person summoned as herein provided shall fail, without reasonable cause, to appear and abide the order of the court, or to bring the child, he may be proceeded against as in case of content of court. In case the summons can not be served or the party served fails to obey the same, and in any case when it shall be made to appear to the court that such summons will be ineffectual, a warrant may issue on the order of the court, either against the parent or guardian or the person having custody of the child or with whom the child may be, or against the child itself. On the return of the summons or other process, or as soon thereafter as may be, the court shall proceed to hear and dispose of the case in a summary manner. Pending the final disposition of any case the child may be retained in the possession of the person having the charge of same, or may be kept in some suitable place provided by the city or county authorities.

§6. PROBATION OFFICERS. The court shall have authority to appoint or designate one or more discreet persons of good character to serve as probation officers during the pleasure of the court: said probation officers to receive no compensation from the public treasury. In case a probation officer shall be appointed by any court, it shall be the duty of the clerk of the court, if practicable, to notify the said probation officer in advance when any child is to be brought before the said court: it shall be the duty of the said probation officer to make such investigation as may be required by the court; to be present in court in order to represent the interests of the child when the case is heard; to furnish to the court such information and assistance as the judge may require; and to take such charge of any child before and after trial as may be directed by the court.

§7. DEPENDENT AND NEGLECTED CHILDREN. When any child under the age of sixteen (16) years shall be found to be dependent or neglected within the meaning of this act, the court may make an order committing the child to the care of some suitable State institution, or to the care of some reputable citizen of good moral character, or to the care of some training school or an industrial school, as provided by law, or to the care of some association willing to receive it embracing in its objects the purpose of caring or obtaining homes for dependent or neglected children, which association shall have been accredited as hereinafter provided.

§8. GUARDIANSHIP. In any case where the court shall award a child to the care of any association or individual in accordance with the provisions of this act the child shall, unless otherwise ordered, become a ward and be subject to the guardianship of the association or individual to whose care it is committed. Such association or individual shall have authority to place such child in a family home, with or without indenture, and may be made party to any proceeding for the legal adoption of the child, and may by its or his attorney or agent appear in any court where such proceedings are pending and assent to such adoption. And such assent shall be sufficient to authorize the court to enter the proper order or decree of adoption. Such guardianship shall not include the guardianship of any estate of the child.

§9. DISPOSITION OF DELINQUENT CHILDREN. In the case of a delinquent child the court may continue the hearing from time to time, and may commit the child to the care and guardianship of a probation officer duly appointed by the court, and may allow said child to remain in its own home, subject to the visitation of the probation officer; such child to report to the probation officer as often as may be required and subject to be returned to the court for further proceedings whenever such action may appear to be necessary; or the court may commit the child to the care and guardianship of the probation officer, to be placed in a suitable family home, subject to the friendly supervision of such probation officer; or it may authorize the said probation officer to board out the said child in some suitable family home, in case provision is made by voluntary contribution or otherwise for the payment of the board of such child, until a suitable provision may be made for the child in a home without such payment; or the court may commit the child, if a boy, to a training school for boys, or if a girl, to an industrial school for girls. Or, if the child is found guilty of any criminal offense, and the judge is of the opinion that the best interest requires it, the court may commit the child to any institution within said county incorporated under the laws of this State for the care of delinquent children, or provided by a city for the care of such offenders, or may commit the child, if a boy over the age of ten years, to the State reformatory, or if a girl over the age of ten years, to the State Home for Juvenile Female Offenders. In no case shall a child be committed beyond his or her minority. A child committed to such institution shall be subject to the control of the board of managers thereof, and the said board shall have power to parole such child on such conditions as it may prescribe, and the court shall, on the recommendation of the board, have power to discharge such child from custody whenever in the judgment of the court his or her reformation shall be complete; or the court may commit the child to the care and custody of some association that will receive it embracing in its objects the care of neglected and dependent children and that has been duly accredited as hereinafter provided.

§10. TRANSFER FROM JUSTICES AND POLICE MAGISTRATES. When, in any county where a court is held as provided in section three of this act, a child under the age of 16 years is arrested with or without warrant, such child may, instead of being taken before a justice of the peace or police magistrate, be taken directly before such court; or if the child is taken before a justice of the peace or police magistrate, it shall be the duty of such justice of the peace or police magistrate to transfer the care [case] to such court, and the officer having the child in charge to take such child before that court, and in any such case the court may proceed to hear and dispose of the case in the same manner as if the child had been brought before the court upon petition as herein provided. In any case the court shall require notice to be given and investigation to be made as in other cases under this act, and may adjourn the hearing from time to time for the purpose.

§11. CHILDREN UNDER TWELVE YEARS NOT TO BE COMMITTED TO JAIL. No court or magistrate shall commit a child under twelve (12) years of age to a jail or police station, but if such child is unable to give bail it may be committed to the care of the sheriff, police officer or probation officer, who shall keep such child in some suitable place provided by the city or county outside of the inclosure of any jail or police station. When any child shall be sentenced to confinement in any institution to which adult convicts are sentenced it shall be unlawful to confine such child in the same building with such adult convicts, or to confine such child in the same yard or inclosure with such adult convicts, or to bring such child into any yard or building in which such adult convicts may be present.

§12. AGENTS OF JUVENILE REFORMATORIES. It shall be the duty of the superintendent of the State Reformatory at Pontiac and the board of managers of the State Home for Juvenile. Female Offenders at Geneva, and the board of managers of any other institution to which juvenile delinquents may be committed by the courts, to maintain an agent of such institution, whose duty it shall be to examine the homes of children paroled from such institution for the purpose of ascertaining and reporting to said court whether they are suitable homes; to assist children paroled or discharged from such institution in finding suitable employment, and to maintain a friendly supervision over paroled inmates during the continuance of their parole; such agents shall hold office subject to the pleasure of the board making the appointment, and shall receive such compensation as such board may determine out of any funds appropriated for such institution applicable thereto.

§13. SUPERVISION BY STATE COMMISSIONERS OF PUBLIC CHARITIES. All associations receiving children under this act shall be subject to the same visitation, inspection and supervision of the Board of State Commissioners of Public Charities as the public charitable institutions of this State. The judges of the courts hereinbefore mentioned may require such information and statistics from associations desiring to have children committed to their care under the provisions of this act as said judges deem necessary in order to enable them to exercise a wise discretion in dealing with children. Every such association shall file with the Board of State Commissioners of Public Charities an annual printed or written report which shall include a statement of the number of children cared for during the year, the number received, the number placed in homes, the number died, the number returned to friends; also a financial statement showing the receipts and disbursements of the associations. The statement of receipts shall indicate the amount received from public funds, the amount received from donations and the amount received from other sources, specifying the several sources. The statement of disbursements shall show the amount expended for salaries and other expenses, specifying the same, the amount expended for lands, buildings and investments. The secretary of the board of public charities shall furnish to the judge of each of the county courts a list of associations filing such annual reports, and no child shall be committed to the care of any association which shall not have filed a report for the fiscal year last preceding with the State Board of Commissioners of Public Charities.

§14. INCORPORATION OF ASSOCIATIONS. No association whose objects may embrace the caring for dependent, neglected or delinquent children shall hereafter be incorporated unless the proposed articles of incorporation shall first have been submitted to the examination of the Board of State Commissioners of Public Charities, and the Secretary of State shall not issue a certificate of incorporation unless there shall first be filed in his office the certificate of said Board of State Commissioners of Public Charities that said board has examined the said articles of incorporation and that, in its judgment, the incorporators are reputable and responsible persons, the proposed work is needed, and the incorporation of such association is desirable and for the public good; amendments proposed to the articles of incorporation or association having as an object the care and disposal of dependent, neglected or delinquent children shall be submitted in like manner to the Board of State Commissioners of Public Charities, and the Secretary of State shall not record such amendment or issue his certificate therefor unless there shall first be filed in his office the certificate of said Board of State Commissioners of Public Charities that they have examined the said amendment, that the association in question is, in their judgment, performing in good faith the work undertaken by it, and that the said amendment is, in their judgment, a proper one and for the public good.

§15. SURRENDER OF DEPENDENT CHILDREN: ADOPTION. It shall be lawful for the parents, parent, guardian or other person having the right to dispose of a dependent or neglected child to enter into an agreement with any association or institution incorporated under any public or private law of this State for the purpose of aiding, caring for or placing in homes such children, and being approved as herein provided, for the surrender of such child to such association or institution, to be taken and cared for by such association or institution or put into a family home. Such agreement may contain any and all proper stipulations to that end, and may authorize the association or institution, by its attorney or agent, to appear in any proceeding for the legal adoption of such child, and consent to its adoption, and the order of the court made upon such consent shall be binding upon the child and its parents or guardian or other person the same as if such parents or guardian or other person were personally in court and consenting thereto, whether made party to the proceeding or not.

§16. FOREIGN CORPORATIONS. No association which is incorporated under the laws of any other state than the State of Illinois shall place any child in any family home within the boundaries of the State of Illinois, either with or without indenture, or for adoption, unless the said association shall have furnished the Board of State Commissioners of Public Charities with such guarantee as they may require that no child shall be brought into the State of Illinois by such society or its agents having any contagious or incurable disease, or having any deformity, or being of feeble mind, or of vicious character, and that said association will promptly receive and remove from the State any child brought into the State of Illinois by its agent which shall become a public charge within the period of five (5) years after being brought into this State. Any person who shall receive, to be placed in a home, or shall place in a home, any child in behalf of any association incorporated in any other state than the State of Illinois which shall not have complied with the requirements of this act, shall be imprisoned in the county jail not more than thirty days, or fined not less than $5.00 or more than one hundred (100) dollars, or both in the discretion of the court.

§17. RELIGIOUS PREFERENCES. The court in committing children shall place them as far as practicable in the care and custody of some individual holding the same religious belief as the parents of said child, or with some association which is controlled by persons of like religious faith of the parents of the said child.

§18. COUNTY BOARDS OF VISITORS. The county judge of each county may appoint a board of six reputable inhabitants, who will serve without compensation, to constitute a board of visitation, whose duty it shall be to visit as often as once a year all institutions, societies and associations receiving children under this act. Said visits shall be made by not less than two of the members of the board, who shall go together or make a joint report; the said board of visitors shall report to the court from time to time the condition of children received by or in the charge of such associations and institutions, and shall make an annual report to the Board of State Commissioners of Public Charities in such form as the board may prescribe. The county board may, at their discretion, make appropriations for the payment of the actual and necessary expenses incurred by the visitors in the discharge of their official duties.

§19. POWERS OF JUVENILE COURT. The powers and duties herein provided to be exercised by the county court or the judges thereof may, in counties having over 500,000 population, be exercised by the circuit courts and their judges as hereinbefore provided for.

§20. INDUSTRIAL AND TRAINING SCHOOLS NOT AFFECTED. Nothing in this act shall be construed to repeal any portion of the act to aid industrial school[s] for girls, the act to provide for and aid training schools for boys, the act to establish the Illinois State Reformatory or the act to provide for a State Home for Juvenile Female Offenders. And in all commitments to said institutions the acts in reference to said institutions shall govern the same.

§21. CONSTRUCTION OF THE ACT. This act shall be liberally construed, to the end that its purpose may be carried out, to-wit: That the care, custody and discipline of a child shall approximate as nearly as may be that which should be given by its parents, and in all cases where it can properly be done the child be placed in an improved family home and become a member of the family by legal adoption or otherwise.

Approved April 21, 1899

READING 2.2

"REPORT BRIEF—REFORMING JUVENILE JUSTICE: A DEVELOPMENTAL APPROACH."

National Research Council. 2012. Committee on Law and Justice, Division of Behavioral and Social Sciences and Education. Washington, DC: The National Academies.

This reading is a "Report Brief" of a much larger document that the National Research Council published in 2013, entitled Reforming Juvenile Justice: A Developmental Approach. The full report resulted from an extensive review of recent research on adolescent development and the implications of that research for juvenile justice reform.

The past decade has seen an explosion of knowledge about adolescent development and the neurobiological underpinnings of adolescent behavior. Much has also been learned about the pathways by which adolescents become delinquent, the effectiveness of prevention and treatment programs, and the long-term effects of transferring youths to the adult system and confining them in harsh conditions.

These findings have raised doubts about the wisdom and effectiveness of laws passed in the 1990s that criminalized many juvenile offenses and led more youths to be tried as adults. Some jurisdictions have already taken significant steps to reverse these policies and to overhaul their juvenile justice systems.

A new report from the National Research Council, *Reforming Juvenile Justice: A Developmental Approach*, aims to consolidate the progress that has been made in both science and policymaking and establish a strong platform for a 21st-century juvenile justice system. It takes an in-depth look at evidence on adolescent development and on effective responses to adolescent offending.

Changes are needed if the juvenile justice system is to meet its aims of holding adolescents accountable, preventing reoffending, and treating them fairly, the report concludes. It recommends that state and tribal governments review their laws and policies and align them with emerging evidence on adolescent development and effective interventions.

Emerging science on adolescence

Falling between childhood and adulthood, adolescence is when a person develops an integrated sense of self, which includes separating from parents and developing an individual identity. As part of that process, adolescents often engage in novelty-seeking and risky behavior, such as alcohol and drug use, unsafe sex, and reckless driving.

Research has shown that adolescents differ from adults in at least three important ways that lead to differences in behavior:

- Adolescents are less able to regulate their own behavior in emotionally charged contexts.
- Adolescents are more sensitive to external influences such as peer pressure and immediate rewards.
- Adolescents show less ability to make judgments and decisions that require future orientation.

Evidence suggests that these cognitive tendencies are linked to the biological immaturity of the brain and an imbalance among developing brain systems. The brain system that influences pleasure-seeking and emotional reactivity develops more rapidly than the brain system that supports self-control, leaving adolescents less capable of self-regulation than adults. The likelihood and seriousness of offending are also strongly affected by influences in youths' environment—peers, parents, schools, and communities. In addition, perceived racial discrimination has been linked to antisocial behavior.

Research shows that, for most youths, the period of risky experimentation does not extend beyond adolescence, ceasing as identity settles with maturity. The vast majority of youths who are arrested or referred to juvenile court have not committed serious offenses, and half of them appear in the system only once. Evidence indicates that youths who commit serious offenses such as homicide, aggravated assault, and burglary are a very small proportion of the overall delinquent population, and that their behavior is driven by the same risk factors and developmental processes that influence other juvenile offenders.

The existing juvenile justice system

In 2008, 28 percent of delinquency cases that were adjudicated resulted in youths being placed outside the home, such as in a group home or juvenile correctional facility. Confining youths away from their homes and communities interferes with three social conditions that contribute to adolescents' healthy psychological development:

- the presence of a parent or parent figure who is involved with the adolescent and concerned about his or her successful development;
- association with peers who value and model positive social behavior and academic success; and
- activities that require autonomous decision-making and critical thinking. Schools, extra-curricular activities, and work settings can provide opportunities for adolescents to learn to think for themselves, develop self-reliance and self-efficacy, and improve reasoning skills.

In addition, many youths face collateral consequences of involvement in the justice system, such as the public release of juvenile records that follow them throughout their lives and limit future educational and employment opportunities.

These disadvantages are borne disproportionately by some groups of adolescents. Racial and ethnic minorities are overrepresented at every stage of the juvenile justice system; they are more likely to be arrested, and, for certain offenses, more likely to face harsh punishment. They also remain in the system longer than white youths. Adolescents who move between the child welfare and juvenile justice systems, and those with mental health disorders, are also more likely to be treated harshly.

A developmental approach to juvenile justice

The overarching goal of the juvenile justice system is to support the positive social development of youths who become involved in the system, and thereby assure the safety of communities. The specific aims of juvenile courts and affiliated agencies are to hold youths accountable for wrongdoing, prevent further offending, and treat youths fairly. All three of these aims are compatible with a developmental approach to juvenile justice.

Accountability

Holding adolescents accountable for their offenses aims to ensure that offenders will be answerable for wrongdoing, particularly for conduct that causes harm to identifiable victims. It does not follow, however, that the mechanisms of accountability for juveniles should mimic adult punishments. Condemnation, control, and lengthy confinement ("serving time")—the identifying attributes of criminal punishment—are not ordinarily needed to assure that juveniles are held accountable. Juvenile courts should provide an opportunity for youths to accept responsibility for their actions, make amends to individual victims and the community, and participate in community service or other kinds of programs. Examples of appropriate approaches include restorative justice programs that involve victims and adjudication programs that involve restitution and peers.

Preventing reoffending

Whether a juvenile court can reduce reoffending depends on its ability to intervene with the right adolescent offenders and use the right type of intervention. The first step in enabling courts to do this is by implementing risk and need assessments. Risk assessments gauge whether a youth is at low, medium, or high risk of reoffending based on factors such as prior offending history and school performance. Newer instruments also assess the youth's needs, acknowledging that the risk of reoffending is not a fixed attribute but an estimate that might be lowered by particular interventions, monitoring in the community, or changes in life situation. Using these tools can allow resources to be better targeted, focusing the more intense and costly interventions on those at greater risk of reoffending.

If implemented well, evidence-based interventions—for example, certain types of therapy, such as aggression replacement therapy and cognitive-behavioral therapy—reduce reoffending and produce remarkably large economic returns relative to their costs. In general, community-based interventions show greater reductions in rearrests than programs offered in institutional settings. Once in institutional care, adequate time—arguably up to about six months—is needed to provide sufficiently intense services for adolescents to benefit. There is no convincing evidence, however, that confinement of juvenile offenders beyond the minimum amount needed for this purpose appreciably reduces the likelihood of subsequent offending.

Fairness

Treating youths fairly and with dignity can enhance moral development and legal socialization during adolescence. The juvenile court should assure that youths are represented by properly trained counsel and have an opportunity to participate in the proceedings. However, lawyers in juvenile courts often have too few resources and are overburdened by high caseloads. To improve the quality of representation and enhance youths' perception of justice, states should clarify the obligations of juvenile defense counsel at every stage of the case and should specify caseload limits in accordance with recommended standards.

A critical aspect of achieving a fair juvenile justice system is reducing racial and ethnic disparities. Several interventions and policy initiatives have been undertaken to reduce disparities, but there is little scientific evidence on whether they are effective. Federal, state, and local governments should intensify their efforts to address disparities in a focused and transparent manner.

Role of the Office of Juvenile Justice and Delinquency Prevention (OJJDP)

The juvenile justice field is moving toward a more developmentally appropriate system, with states and local jurisdictions taking the lead as federal dollars have waned. But the need for technical assistance and training is critical. Historically, such assistance has come from the Office of Juvenile Justice and Delinquency Prevention (OJJDP) in the Department of Justice. Congress established this office in 1974, giving it a broad mandate to develop and disseminate knowledge to the juvenile justice field, assist states and local jurisdictions in improving their juvenile justice systems, develop national standards, and coordinate federal activities related to the treatment of juvenile offenders. Unfortunately, OJJDP's capacity to carry out this mandate has dramatically declined over the past decade, in part due to inadequate funding and a severe restriction of its discretion in determining how its resources should be used.

GUIDING PRINCIPLES FOR JUVENILE JUSTICE REFORM IN A DEVELOPMENTAL APPROACH

Accountability

- Use the justice system to communicate the message that society expects youths to take responsibility for their actions and the foreseeable consequences of their actions.
- Encourage youths to accept responsibility for admitted or proven wrongdoing, consistent with protecting their legal rights.
- Facilitate constructive involvement of family members in the proceedings to assist youths to accept responsibility and carry out the obligations set by the court.
- Use restitution and community service as instruments of accountability to victims and the community.
- Use confinement sparingly and only when needed to respond to and prevent serious reoffending.
- Avoid collateral consequences of adjudication such as public release of juvenile records that reduce opportunities for a successful transition to a prosocial adult life.

Preventing reoffending

- Use structured risk and need assessment instruments to identify low-risk youths who can be handled less formally in community-based settings, to match youths with specialized treatment, and to target more intensive and expensive interventions toward high-risk youths.
- Use clearly specified interventions rooted in knowledge about adolescent development and tailored to the particular adolescent's needs and social environment.
- Engage the adolescent's family as much as possible and draw on neighborhood resources to foster positive activities, prosocial development, and law-abiding behavior.
- Eliminate interventions that rigorous evaluation research has shown to be ineffective or harmful.
- Keep accurate data on the type and intensity of interventions provided and the results achieved.

Fairness

- Ensure that youths are represented throughout the process by properly trained counsel unless the right is voluntarily and intelligently waived by the youth.
- Ensure that youths are adjudicated only if they are competent to understand the proceedings and assist counsel.
- Facilitate participation by youths in all proceedings.
- Intensify efforts to reduce racial and ethnic disparities, as well as other patterns of unequal treatment, in the administration of juvenile justice.
- Ensure that youths perceive that they have been treated fairly and with dignity.
- Establish and implement evidence-based measures of fairness based on both legal criteria and perceptions of youths, families, and other participants.

Recommendations

The committee made recommendations for a developmentally informed juvenile justice system and for incorporating new evidence into policy and practice on a continuing basis. Given current realities regarding the role of OJJDP and the role of the federal government in general, the immediate momentum for change will continue to come from the state, local, and tribal jurisdictions.

Among the committee's recommendations:

State and tribal governments should establish bipartisan multistakeholder task forces or commissions under the auspices of the governor or tribal leader, the legislature, or the highest state court to undertake a thorough and transparent assessment of their juvenile justice systems. They should align their laws, policies and practices with evolving knowledge about adolescent development and evidence-based programs. In addition, they should intensify efforts to identify and eliminate policies that tend to disadvantage minorities, to publicly report on the scope of the problem, and to evaluate programs aimed at reducing disparities.

Federal policymakers should restore OJJDP's capacity to carry out its core mission through reauthorization, appropriations, and funding flexibility. OJJDP has been effective in the past in spearheading major reforms that reflect key developmental principles: keeping youths separated from adult offenders, addressing racial disparities, and avoiding unnecessary detention for youths. These protections need to be strengthened by:

- defining status offenses to include offenses such as possession of alcohol or tobacco that apply only to youths under 21.
- removing all exceptions to the detention of youths who commit offenses that would not be punishable by confinement if committed by an adult. For example, a youth should not be confined for an offense such as truancy or running away.
- modifying the definition of an "adult inmate" to give states flexibility to keep youths in juvenile facilities until they reach the age of extended juvenile court jurisdiction.
- expanding the protections to all youths under 18 in pretrial detention, whether they are charged in juvenile or adult courts.

In addition, OJJDP should prioritize its research, training, and technical assistance resources to promote the adoption of developmentally appropriate policies and practices and expand the number of jurisdictions actively engaged in activities to reduce racial disparities.

Federal research agencies, such as the National Science Foundation, Centers for Disease Control and Prevention, and National Institutes of Health, as well as OJJDP, should support research that continues to advance the science of adolescent development, expanding our understanding of the ways developmental processes influence juvenile delinquency and how the juvenile justice system should respond.

The Bureau of Justice Statistics and other government and private statistical agencies should, under OJJDP's leadership, develop a data improvement program on juvenile offending and juvenile justice system processing that provides greater insight into state and local variations.

At the state and local level, data should be collected on the gender, age, race and ethnicity of offenders as well as offense charged or committed; arrest, detention, and disposition practices; and recidivism.

CRITICAL-THINKING QUESTIONS

1. Describe how the statement from Judge Julian Mack that opened this chapter reflects the distinctive legal philosophy of the early juvenile court.
2. What does it mean to say that juvenile delinquency has been socially constructed?
3. How did the due process revolution change the character of the juvenile justice system?
4. In what ways does contemporary juvenile justice emphasize offender accountability?
5. How have recent research findings on adolescent development informed juvenile justice reform efforts?
6. What is evidence-based practice?
7. What are the major objectives of the Illinois Juvenile Court Act of 1899 (first reading, NCJFCJ 1998).
8. According to the second reading, "Reforming Juvenile Justice: A Developmental Approach" (NRC 2012), how do adolescents differ from adults?

SUGGESTED READING

Platt, Anthony. 1977. *The Child-savers: The Invention of Delinquency.* 2nd ed. Chicago, IL: University of Chicago Press.

Tanenhaus, Daniel. 2004. *Juvenile Justice in the Making.* New York: Oxford University Press.

Tanenhaus, Daniel. 2012. "The Elusive Juvenile Court: Its Origins, Practices, and Re-Inventions." Pp. 419–441 in *The Oxford Handbook of Juvenile Crime and Juvenile Justice*, edited by B. C. Feld and D. M. Bishop. Oxford: Oxford University Press.

Tuell, John A., with Jessica Heldman and Kari Harp. 2017. "Developmental Reform in Juvenile Justice: Translating the Science of Adolescent Development to Sustainable Best Practice." Boston, MA: Robert F. Kennedy Children's Action Corps.

USEFUL WEBSITES

For further information relevant to this chapter, go to the following websites.

- **Center for Juvenile Justice Reform**, Georgetown University: http://cjjr.georgetown.edu/
- **Models for Change: Systems Reform in Juvenile Justice**, MacArthur Foundation: http://www.modelsforchange.net/about/index.html
- **Status Offense Reform Center (SORC),** Vera Institute: http://www.statusoffensereform.org
- **The Annie E. Casey Foundation: Juvenile Justice**: http://www.aecf.org/work/#juvenile-justice

GLOSSARY OF KEY TERMS

"Best interests of the child": The overarching interest of the traditional juvenile court to assess the needs of the youth and then to seek physical, emotional, mental, and social well-being for that youth through court intervention.

Child-saving movement: A collection of locally organized groups of women from middle- and upper-class backgrounds who mobilized change in how governments dealt with dependent, neglected, and delinquent children. One particular child-saving group, the Chicago Women's Club, was largely responsible for the creation of the first juvenile court in Chicago.

Due process of law: Procedural rights established in the Constitution (especially the Bill of Rights) and extended through appellate court decisions. They include procedural rights such as notice of charges, legal counsel, and protection from self-incrimination.

Evidence-based practice: The use of evaluation research to assess evidence on program effectiveness and to derive principles for best practice in the field that is being studied (Greenwood and Welsh 2012:495).

Houses of refuge: The first institutional facilities in the United States for poor, vagrant children. Both private and public refuges sought to protect and reform the "predelinquent."

***Parens patriae*:** Literally means "parent of the country." Refers to the legal authority of courts to assume parental responsibilities when the natural parents fail to fulfill their duties.

Pauperism: The view, popularly held throughout the nineteenth century, that children growing up in poverty, surrounded by depravity in their neighborhood and family, are destined to lives of crime and degradation.

Placing-out: A practice begun in the mid-1800s in which philanthropic groups took vagrant children West by railroad to be placed in farm families.

Poor laws: Laws enacted in colonial America that established a civic duty of private citizens to "relieve" the poor. Legal authority was also granted for governmental agencies or private relief societies to separate poor children from their "undeserving" parents.

Positivism: The use of scientific methods to study phenomena. These methods include observation, measurement, description, and analysis.

Reform school: In the mid-1800s a new form of institution began to replace houses of refuge. These institutions emphasized education and operated with traditional school schedules. Many reform schools also used a cottage system in which children were grouped into "families" of 40 or fewer.

Rehabilitative ideal: The traditional legal philosophy of the juvenile court, which emphasizes assessment of the youth and individualized treatment rather than determination of guilt and punishment.

NOTES

1 *Ex parte Crouse*, 4, Wharton (PA) 9 (1838) at 11 (Krisberg and Austin 1993; Pisciotta 1982; Rendleman 1971; Fox 1970).

2 *People ex rel. O'Connell v. Turner*, 55 Ill. (1870) (Rendleman 1971; Fox 1970).

3 Tanenhaus (2004:xxvii) argues that the new juvenile court was not fully formed when it was created; rather it evolved in "structure, rules, and self conception." Nonetheless the early juvenile court was distinctive in terms of the characteristics discussed here.

4 *Commonwealth v. Fisher*, 213 Pennsylvania 48 (1905).

5 Coinciding with the child welfare approach of the juvenile court is the development of child guidance clinics, first implemented in Chicago as the Juvenile Psychopathic Institute under the direction of William Healy (Krisberg 2005; Tanenhaus 2004; Mennel 1973; Hawes 1971).

6 *Kent v. United States*, 383 U.S. 541, 86 S.Ct. 1045 (1966).

7 *In re Gault*, 387 U.S. 1, 87 S.Ct. 1428 (1967).

8 *In re Winship*, 397 U.S. 358, 90 S.Ct. 1068 (1970).

9 *McKeiver v. Pennsylvania*, 403 U.S. 528, 91 S.Ct. 1976 (1971).

10 *Breed v. Jones*, 421 U.S. 519, 95 S.Ct. 1779 (1975).

REFERENCES

Albert, Rodney L. 1998. "Juvenile Accountability Incentive Grants Program." Washington, DC: Office of Juvenile Justice and Delinquency Prevention.

Allen, Francis A. 1959. "Legal Values and the Rehabilitative Ideal." *Journal of Law, Criminology, and Police Science* 50:226–232.

Allen, Francis A. 1964. *The Borderland of Criminal Justice: Essays in Law and Criminology*. Chicago: University of Chicago Press.

Aries, Philippe. 1962. *Centuries of Childhood: A Social History of Family Life*. Translated by Robert Baldick. New York: Random House.

Beirne, Piers and James Messerschmidt. 2015. *Criminology*. 6th ed. New York: Oxford University Press.

Brummer, Chauncey E. 2002. "Extended Juvenile Jurisdiction: The Best of Both Worlds?" *Arkansas Law Review* 54:777–822.

Chesney-Lind, Meda. 1973. "Judicial Enforcement of the Female Sex Role: The Family Court and the Female Delinquent." *Issues in Criminology* 8:51–69.

Chesney-Lind, Meda. 1977. "Judicial Paternalism and the Female Status Offender: Training Women to Know Their Place." *Crime and Delinquency* 23:121–130.

Cogan, Neil Howard. 1970. "Juvenile Law, Before and After the Entrance of '*Parens Patriae*.'" *South Carolina Law Review* 22:147–181.

Crank, Kathleen Kositzky. 1995. "The JJDP Mandates: Rationale and Summary." Washington, DC: Office of Juvenile Justice and Delinquency Prevention. Available online at: www.ncjrs.gov/txtfiles/fs-9522.txt

Danegger, Anna E., Carole E. Cohen, Cheryl D. Hayes, and Gwen A. Holden. 1999. *Juvenile Accountability Incentive Block Grants: Strategic Planning Guide*. Washington, DC: Office of Juvenile Justice and Delinquency Prevention.

Degler, Carl. 1980. *At Odds: Women and the Family in America from the Revolution to the Present*. New York: Oxford University Press.

deMause, Lloyd. 1974. "The Evolution of Childhood." Pp. 1–73 in *The History of Childhood*, edited by L. deMause. New York: Psychohistory Press.

Drake, Elizabeth K., Steve Aos, and Marna G. Miller. 2009. "Evidence-Based Public Policy Options to Reduce Crime and Criminal Justice Costs: Implications for Washington State." *Victims & Offenders* 4:170–196.

Empey, LaMar T. and Mark C. Stafford. 1991. *American Delinquency: Its Meaning and Construction*. 3rd ed. Belmont, CA: Wadsworth.

Feld, Barry C. 1999. *Bad Kids: Race and the Transformation of the Juvenile Court*. New York: Oxford University Press.

Feld, Barry C. 2003. "The Politics of Race and Juvenile Justice: The 'Due Process Revolution' and the Conservative Reaction." *Justice Quarterly* 20:765–800.

Feld, Barry C. 2014. *Juvenile Justice Administration in a Nutshell*. St. Paul, MN: West.

Ferdinand, Theodore N. 1991. "History Overtakes the Juvenile Justice System." *Crime and Delinquency* 37:204–224.

Fox, Sanford J. 1970. "Juvenile Justice Reform: An Historical Perspective." *Stanford Law Review* 22:1187–1239.

Greenwood, Peter W. 2008. "Prevention and Intervention Programs for Juvenile Offenders." *The Future of Children* 18:185–210.

Greenwood, Peter W. and Brandon C. Welsh. 2012. "Promoting Evidence-Based Practice in Delinquency Prevention at the State Level: Principles, Progress, and Policy Directions." *Criminology & Public Policy* 11:493–513.

Grisso, Thomas and Robert G. Schwartz. 2000. "Introduction." Pp. 1–5 in *Youth on Trial: A Developmental Perspective on Juvenile Justice*, edited by T. Grisso and R. G. Schwartz. Chicago: University of Chicago.

Hawes, Joseph. 1971. *Children in Urban Society: Juvenile Delinquency in Nineteenth-Century America*. New York: Oxford University Press.

Hellum, Frank. 1979. "Juvenile Justice: The Second Revolution." *Crime and Delinquency* 25:299–317.

Hemmens, Craig, Benjamin Steiner, and David Mueller. 2013. *Significant Cases in Juvenile Justice*. 2nd ed. New York: Oxford.

Howell, James C. 1997. *Juvenile Justice and Youth Violence*. Thousand Oaks, CA: Sage.

Illick, Joseph E. 1974. "Child-Rearing in Seventeenth-Century England and America." Pp. 303–350 in *The History of Childhood*, edited by L. deMause. New York: Psychohistory Press.

Kaplan, Louise J. 1984. *Adolescence: The Farewell to Childhood*. New York: Simon and Schuster.

Krisberg, Barry. 2005. *Juvenile Justice: Redeeming Our Children*. Newbury Park, CA: Sage.

Krisberg, Barry and James Austin. 1993. *Reinventing Juvenile Justice*. Newbury Park, CA: Sage.

Krisberg, Barry, Ira M. Schwartz, Paul Litsky, and James Austin. 1986. "The Watershed of Juvenile Justice Reform." *Crime and Delinquency* 32:5–38.

Kupchik, Aaron. 2006. *Judging Juveniles: Prosecuting Adolescents in Adult and Juvenile Courts*. New York: New York University Press.

Lerman, Paul. 1975. *Community Treatment and Control*. Chicago: University of Chicago Press.

Lipsey, Mark W. 2009. "The Primary Factors That Characterize Effective Interventions with Juvenile Offenders: A Meta-Analytic Overview." *Victims & Offenders* 4:124–147.

Lipsey, Mark W. and James C. Howell. 2012. "A Broader View of Evidence-Based Programs Reveals More Options for State Juvenile Justice Systems." *Criminology & Public Policy* 11:515–523.

Lipsey, Mark W., James C. Howell, Marion R. Kelly, Gabrielle Chapman, and Darin Carver. 2010. *Improving the Effectiveness of Juvenile Justice Programs: A New Perspective on Evidence-Based Practice*. Washington, DC: Center for Juvenile Justice Reform.

Lipton, Douglas, Robert Martinson, and Judith Wilks. 1975. *The Effectiveness of Correctional Treatment*. New York: Praeger.

MacArthur Foundation Research Network on Adolescent Development and Juvenile Justice. 2014a. "Adolescent Legal Competence in Court" (Issue Brief 1). Retrieved October 7, 2014 (www.adjj.org/downloads/9805issue_brief_1.pdf).

MacArthur Foundation Research Network on Adolescent Development and Juvenile Justice. 2014b. "Less Guilty by Reason of Adolescence" (Issue Brief 3). Retrieved October 7, 2014 (www.adjj.org/downloads/6093issue_brief_3.pdf).

MacDonald, John M. and Meda Chesney-Lind. 2001. "Gender Bias and Juvenile Justice Revisited: A Multiyear Analysis." *Crime and Delinquency* 47:173–195.

Mack, Julian W. 1909. "The Juvenile Court." *Harvard Law Review* 23:104-122.

McKee, Esther Chao and Lisa Rapp. 2014. "The Current Status of Evidence-Based Practice in Juvenile Justice." *Journal of Evidence-Based Social Work* 11:308–314.

Mennel, Robert M. 1973. *Thorns & Thistles: Juvenile Delinquents in the United States 1825–1940*. Hanover, NH: University Press of New England.

Mihalic, Sharon F. and Delbert S. Elliott. 2015. "Evidence-based Programs Registry: Blueprints for Healthy Youth Development." *Evaluation and Program Planning* 48:124–131.

Models for Change. n.d. Webpage. Chicago, IL: John D. and Catherine T. MacArthur Foundation, Juvenile Justice. Retrieved September 25, 2014 (www.modelsforchange.net/index.html).

National Advisory Commission on Criminal Justice Standards and Goals. 1973. Task Force Report on Corrections (Standard 22.3). Washington, DC: GPO.

National Council of Juvenile and Family Court Judges. 1998. "The Illinois Juvenile Court Act of 1899: Juvenile Courts for Dependent, Neglected and Delinquency Children." *Juvenile and Family Court Journal* 49(4):1–5.

National Research Council. 2012. "Report Brief—Reforming Juvenile Justice: A Developmental Approach." Committee on Law and Justice, Division of Behavioral and Social Sciences and Education. Washington, DC: The National Academies.

National Research Council. 2013. *Reforming Juvenile Justice: A Developmental Approach.* Committee on Assessing Juvenile Justice Reform. Richard J. Bonnie, Robert L. Johnson, Betty M. Chemers, and Julie A. Schuck (editors). Committee on Law and Justice, Division of Behavioral and Social Sciences and Education. Washington, DC: The National Academies Press.

Office of Juvenile Justice and Delinquency Prevention. 2008. *Juvenile Accountability Block Grants Program: 2005 Report to Congress.* Washington, DC: Office of Juvenile Justice and Delinquency Prevention.

Odem, Mary E. and Steven Schlossman. 1991. "Guardians of Virtue: The Juvenile Court and Female Delinquency in Early 20th-Century Los Angeles." *Crime and Delinquency* 37:186–201.

Oxford English Dictionary. 2015. "*parens patriae*." Retrieved April 16, 2015 (www.oed.com/).

Pickett, Robert S. 1969. *House of Refuge: Origins of Juvenile Reform in New York State, 1815–1857.* Syracuse, NY: Syracuse University Press.

Pisciotta, Alexander W. 1982. "Saving the Children: The Promise and Practice of *Parens Patriae*, 1838–98." *Crime and Delinquency* 28:410–425.

Platt, Anthony. 1977. *The Child Savers: The Invention of Delinquency.* 2nd ed. Chicago: University of Chicago Press.

President's Commission on Law Enforcement and Administration of Justice. 1967a. *Task Force Report: Corrections.* Washington, DC: GPO.

President's Commission on Law Enforcement and Administration of Justice. 1967b. *Task Force Report: Juvenile Delinquency and Youth Crime.* Washington, DC: GPO.

Raley, Gordon. 1995. "The JJDP Act: A Second Look." *Juvenile Justice Journal* 2:11–18.

Redding, Richard E. 2008. "Juvenile Transfer Laws: An Effective Deterrent to Delinquency?" *Juvenile Justice Bulletin.* Washington, DC: Office of Juvenile Justice and Delinquency Prevention.

Rendleman, Douglas R. 1971. "*Parens Patriae*: From Chancery to the Juvenile Court." *South Carolina Law Review* 23:205–259.

Rothman, David J. 1971. *The Discovery of the Asylum: Social Order and Disorder in the New Republic.* Boston: Little, Brown, and Company.

Schlossman, Steven. 2005. *Transforming Juvenile Justice: Reform Ideals and Institutional Realities, 1825–1920.* DeKalb, IL: Northern Illinois University Press.

Schur, Edwin M. 1973. *Radical Non-Intervention: Rethinking the Delinquency Problem.* Englewood Cliffs, NJ: Prentice Hall.

Shepherd, Robert E., Jr. 1999. "The Juvenile Court at 100 Years: A Look Back." *Juvenile Justice* 6:13–21.

Sickmund, Melissa and Charles Puzzanchera (eds.). 2014. *Juvenile Offenders and Victims: 2014 National Report.* Pittsburgh, PA: National Center for Juvenile Justice.

Siegel, Larry J. and Paul E. Tracy. 2008. *Juvenile Law: A Collection of Leading U.S. Supreme Court Cases.* Upper Saddle River, NJ: Pearson.

Sommerville, John. 1982. *The Rise and Fall of Childhood.* Beverly Hills, CA: Sage.

Sutton, John. 1988. *Stubborn Children: Controlling Delinquency in the United States, 1640–1981*. Berkley, CA: University of California Press.

Tanenhaus, Daniel. 2004. *Juvenile Justice in the Making*. New York: Oxford University Press.

Tappan, Paul. 1946. "Treatment without Trial?" *Social Problems* 24:306–311.

Vincent, Gina M., Laura S. Guy, and Thomas Grisso. 2012. *Risk Assessment in Juvenile Justice: A Guidebook for Implementation*. Models for Change: System Reform in Juvenile Justice. MacArthur Foundation. Retrieved November 19, 2013 (www.modelsforchange.net/publications/346).

Wilson, John J. and James C. Howell. 1993. *Comprehensive Strategy for Serious, Violent, and Chronic Juvenile Offenders: Program Summary*. Washington, DC: Office of Juvenile Justice and Delinquency Prevention.

Zimring, Franklin E. 1998. *American Youth Violence*. New York: Oxford University Press.

Chapter 3

JUVENILE JUSTICE LAW, STRUCTURE, AND PROCESS

CHAPTER TOPICS

- **"Juvenile delinquency" and juvenile justice in statutory law**
- **Structure of juvenile justice systems: Decentralized and fragmented**
- **Juvenile justice process: Discretion, diversion, major decision points, and disproportionate minority contact**

CHAPTER LEARNING OBJECTIVES

After completing this chapter, students should be able to:

- Distinguish the four legal classifications of juvenile delinquency.
- Describe the structure of juvenile justice systems in the United States.
- Provide examples of how discretion and diversion are exercised throughout the juvenile justice process.
- Explain why it is important to examine racial and ethnic disparities across each of the major decision points in the juvenile justice process.

CHAPTER CONTENTS

CASE IN POINT

ARTURO'S STORY—THE HUMAN ELEMENT OF JUVENILE JUSTICE

Arturo's childhood was filled with drugs and abuse, and no parental supervision or discipline. Add in parental criminality, he learned by example. Arturo entered the juvenile justice system at age 12 for burglary, but he was already on course for drug dealing and theft. Here are Arturo's thoughts on the juvenile justice system, as offered in a book entitled *Dispatches from Juvenile Hall: Fixing a Failing System* (Aarons, Smith, and Wagner 2009:18–19).

> But I ended up getting a probation officer, and with his and another counselor's help, they would always talk about opportunities in life, and say that the possibilities weren't just for certain people, that they were for everyone. When I saw good people like that, it opened the door to talk to them—trusting them a little. They seemed like more than just people in the system. They seemed like people who cared about me. But there were other people who were against me. They told me I wasn't going to amount to shit, that I was no different than my dad or my uncle. And I remember what that did to me. It showed me that they were against me. . . . It was just negative reinforcement—I already saw them as part of the system, and when they forced that message on me, it showed me they really were not on my side. . . . That was a lot different than the other people I encountered. The good people in the system that were telling me that I could go to school, that I could graduate, that there were things I could do. They were still part of that system, but I could see that they wanted to help me, and I could open the door to that.

This chapter describes contemporary juvenile justice in terms of the statutory laws that form its foundation and the distinctive structures and processes that characterize it. In a formal sense, the juvenile justice system comprises police, courts, and corrections. However, a substantial amount of juvenile delinquency is dealt with informally, sometimes by agencies not usually considered a part of the "system." In fact, the juvenile justice is really not a "system" at all, but rather a highly decentralized and fragmented array of both public and private agencies. We discuss how each element of juvenile justice exercises tremendous discretion and relies on diversion to operate efficiently. As a part of this discussion, we briefly describe each of the nine major decision points in the juvenile justice process and the increased importance that has been given to examinations of disproportionate minority contact.

"JUVENILE DELINQUENCY" AND JUVENILE JUSTICE IN STATUTORY LAW

In its zeal to save children, the original juvenile court showed little interest in distinguishing the different types of children that came under its jurisdiction (Platt 1977). The juvenile court assumed broad jurisdiction over not only delinquent offenders, but also dependent and neglected children. Although the Juvenile Court Act provided definitions of delinquent and dependent and neglected children, the primary interest of the early court was to act in the "best interests of the child," regardless of the reason the child came before the court. Put simply, the original juvenile court focused on the offender, rather than the offense.

Reformers soon realized, however, that restricting the new juvenile court's definition of delinquency to violations of criminal law would make it function like a criminal court (Feld 1999; Sutton 1988). Within two years of the court's creation, amendments to the Illinois Juvenile Court Act broadened the definition of delinquent to include a youth "who is incorrigible" (Feld 1999). Barry Feld (1999) observes that this undefined term changed the scope of the court's inquiry into a youth's delinquency and introduced a substantial amount of imprecision and subjectivity. This broadened definition of juvenile delinquency now included behavior that was defined by law as illegal only for juveniles. Acts that are illegal only if committed by juveniles are called **status offenses**. Examples include running away, truancy, ungovernability, and liquor law violations.

Traditionally, juvenile courts have had two primary areas of jurisdiction: (1) juvenile delinquency, which includes violations of criminal law and status offenses; and (2) dependency, neglect, and child abuse (Rubin 1985). The working assumption behind both areas of jurisdiction has been the rehabilitative ideal, using *parens patriae* authority: If parents are unable or have failed to provide proper care for their children, then the juvenile court can assume parental responsibility in the best interests of the child.

In the early 1960s, criticism began to mount over the juvenile court's broad jurisdiction and its failure to distinguish different types of offenses and offenders. This criticism was most pronounced with regard to the sweeping legal definitions of status offenders in state laws, whereby almost all youth could fall under the attention of the juvenile court. The popular solution was for state legislatures to enact laws that legally distinguished status offenses and offenders from those that violated the criminal law. The intent here was to have juvenile courts deal differently with criminal law offenders and status offenders.

In 1961, the California legislature created a separate section of the juvenile code to specify three different areas of jurisdiction for the juvenile court: (1) dependent and neglected children (nondelinquents), (2) juveniles who violate the state criminal code (delinquents), and (3) juveniles who are beyond parental control or who engage in conduct harmful to themselves (status offenders) (Gibbons and Krohn 1991). The following year, New York passed legislation that established a family court system with jurisdiction over all areas of family life. In addition, the legislation established a person in need of supervision (PINS) classification to provide a separate designation for status offenders. This legal separation of status and criminal law offenders allowed the juvenile justice system to approach these two groups differently. Following the lead of New York, statutory law in many states soon provided a separate legal category for status offenders. Various acronyms were used: YINS (youth in need of supervision), MINS (minor in need of supervision), CHINS (children in need of supervision), and JINS (juveniles in need of supervision).

JUVENILE JUSTICE LAW: ADJUDICATION CLASSIFICATIONS IN THE MONTANA YOUTH COURT ACT

"**Youth in need of care**" means a youth who has been adjudicated or determined, after a hearing, to be or to have been abused, neglected, or abandoned.

"**Youth in need of intervention**" means a youth who is adjudicated as a youth and who:

(a) commits an offense prohibited by law that if committed by an adult would not constitute a criminal offense, including but not limited to a youth who:
   (i) violates any Montana municipal or state law regarding alcoholic beverages;
   (ii) continues to exhibit behavior, including running away from home or habitual truancy, beyond the control of the youth's parents, foster parents, physical custodian, or guardian despite the attempt of the youth's parents, foster parents, physical custodian, or guardian to exert all reasonable efforts to mediate, resolve, or control the youth's behavior; or

(b) has committed any of the acts of a delinquent youth but whom the youth court, in its discretion, chooses to regard as a youth in need of intervention.

"**Delinquent youth**" means a youth who is adjudicated under formal proceedings under the Montana Youth Court Act as a youth:

(a) who has committed an offense that, if committed by an adult, would constitute a criminal offense; or

(b) who has been placed on probation as a delinquent youth or a youth in need of intervention and who has violated any condition of probation.

"**Serious juvenile offender**" means a youth who has committed an offense that would be considered a felony offense if committed by an adult and that is an offense against a person, an offense against property, or an offense involving dangerous drugs.

Source: Montana Code Annotated 2017. "Child Abuse and Neglect": 41-3-102 (34). "Youth Court Act": 41-5-103 (51), (11), and (38).

This differentiation between status offenders and juvenile criminal law offenders plays an important role in contemporary trends in juvenile justice. The juvenile due process revolution has been applied most extensively to juvenile criminal offenders. Status offenses are normally handled like dependency and neglect cases in terms of both informal procedures and dispositional provisions for social services. Alternatives to the juvenile justice system, in the form of diversion and deinstitutionalization, have been developed most extensively for use with status offenders, while a more punitive approach to juvenile justice has been applied most frequently to serious, violent juvenile offenders.

The state statutes that define juvenile delinquency are similar in form throughout the United States. Contemporary statutes typically use four legal categories, often with varying names but with similar legal conceptualization: "serious delinquent youth," "delinquent youth," "youth in need of intervention," and "dependent and neglected youth." The statutory definitions for these categories under the Montana Youth Court Act illustrate this legal categorization (see "Juvenile justice law: Adjudication classifications in the Montana Youth Court Act").

State statutory law also provides for juvenile justice procedure and authority. Each of the major decision points in the juvenile justice process are authorized in state statutes, and juvenile justice personnel are given authority under statutory law. For example, Montana statutory law gives discretion to the police to determine the arrest (MCA: 4-5-331) and initial detention (MCA: 41-5-322) decisions. The subsequent decisions about whether the case will move forward in the system will be made by probation officers, attorneys, and the juvenile court judge (see "Juvenile justice law: Procedures and authority derived from statutory law").

JUVENILE JUSTICE LAW: PROCEDURES AND AUTHORITY DERIVED FROM STATUTORY LAW

- **taking into custody** (arrest): law enforcement officer and juvenile probation officer (41-5-321, 322, 331)
- **detention**: law enforcement officer and juvenile probation officer (41-5-322—police officers are referred to as "peace officers"), youth court (probable cause hearing 41-5-332, 333, 334)
- **filing in criminal court** (41-5-206); **transfer hearing** (41-5-208)
- **intake**: juvenile probation officer (preliminary inquiry 41-5-1202 through 1205)
- **petition**: county attorney (prosecutor) (41-5-1401, 1402)
- **adjudication**: youth court (41-5-1502)
- **disposition**: *informal disposition* using consent adjustment without petition and consent decree with petition—juvenile probation officer and youth court (41-5-1302, 1304, 1402); *formal disposition*—youth court (41-5-1512 and 1513)
- **corrections**: department of corrections (commitment to department or youth court: 41-5-1522 and 1523), juvenile probation officer (41-5-1703)
- **probation revocation**: youth court and juvenile probation officer (41-5-1431)

Source: "Youth Court Act," *Montana Code Annotated 2017.*

STRUCTURE OF JUVENILE JUSTICE SYSTEMS: DECENTRALIZED AND FRAGMENTED

It may surprise you to learn that there is not a single juvenile justice system in the United States. Rather, each state has a separate juvenile justice system, and they are "systems" in only a limited sense. The various parts of these systems—police, courts, and corrections—are all operated by different levels and branches of government, and sometimes even by private organizations. For example, courts with jurisdiction over juvenile matters are a judicial entity, and they operate at the federal, state, and local levels, but there is not a single, standard structure to juvenile courts. In most states, juvenile courts operate within district courts (courts of original trial jurisdiction). However, some lower courts, such as city and municipal courts have special or limited jurisdiction in juvenile cases. Juvenile traffic violations, for example, are often handled by these lower courts. The federal court system also deals with juvenile matters, usually at the district court level, but the number of juvenile cases dealt with by federal courts is minuscule compared to state juvenile courts. Thus, the juvenile justice system is said to be *decentralized*, operating at every level of government.

The juvenile justice system is also *fragmented* among the different branches of government. Each branch of government—legislative, judicial, and executive—plays an important role in juvenile justice. For example, laws are the foundation of juvenile justice systems. Under the United States Constitution, such laws are the responsibility of legislative bodies at all levels—local, state, and federal. The structure, jurisdiction, and authority of juvenile justice systems are primarily determined by state legislatures. For instance, the law that created the first juvenile court in Chicago was enacted by the Illinois Legislature in 1899. Similarly, contemporary juvenile courts are legally authorized by state youth court acts. State and federal legislatures also pass codes that regulate people's actions (criminal codes) and establish procedures to be followed (procedural codes) when someone breaks the law. Thus, legislatures play a central role in juvenile justice, even though they do not actually operate juvenile justice agencies.

Table 3.1 shows the structural elements of juvenile justice in terms of their level and branch of government. As you can see, the various parts of juvenile justice systems are spread broadly among the different levels and branches of government, making them decentralized and fragmented. Let's look at a few of these components of juvenile justice systems. Beyond statutory law, legislative units also allocate funds for the different components of juvenile justice systems. Courts, including juvenile courts, are a judicial responsibility. Juvenile courts provide both informal and formal procedures to deal with delinquency cases that are referred to them. Appellate courts at both the state and federal levels have tremendous influence on juvenile justice process, establishing due process of law in juvenile matters. The executive branch of government is responsible for law enforcement, the operation of detention centers, prosecution, departments of corrections, and sometimes probation and parole. Probation and parole are perhaps the most structurally varied components of juvenile justice. Juvenile probation is often a judicial function, but in some states is operated by the department of corrections. In addition, parole is sometimes administratively attached to probation, in which case both operate under the same governmental unit—either the courts or the department of correction. In other states, probation is a part of the juvenile court and parole is a part of the department of correction. What can you conclude? The decentralized and fragmented organizational structure of juvenile justice in the United States is extremely complex!

TABLE 3.1 Juvenile justice structure: Decentralized and fragmented

	Legislative	Judicial	Executive
Local	• Ordinances • Funding	• Courts of limited jurisdiction	• Law enforcement • Detention centers • Prosecution • Corrections
State	• Statutory law (criminal codes, youth court acts, procedural codes) • Funding	• Youth courts • Probation • State appellate courts	• Law enforcement • Detention centers • Prosecution • Corrections • Probation
Federal	• Statutory law (criminal codes, procedural codes) • Funding	• Federal appellate courts • Probation	• Law enforcement • Detention centers • Prosecution • Corrections

JUVENILE JUSTICE PROCESS: DISCRETION, DIVERSION, MAJOR DECISION POINTS, AND DISPROPORTIONATE MINORITY CONTACT

The structure and procedures of juvenile justice vary considerably from state to state and from community to community. Nevertheless, a fairly common process can be identified in most juvenile justice jurisdictions. This process is depicted in the figure presented in the first chapter reading from *Juvenile Offenders and Victims: 2014 National Report* (Sickmund and Puzzanchera 2014).

Two features are key to the juvenile justice process in literally every jurisdiction throughout the country: discretion and diversion. Concerns regarding discretion and diversion in contemporary juvenile justice are expressed most concertedly in widespread efforts to reduce disproportionate minority contact at the major decision points in juvenile justice systems.

Discretion and diversion

Well-known legal scholar Roscoe Pound (1960:926) defined **discretion** as "authority conferred by law to act in certain conditions or situations in accordance with an official's or an official agency's considered judgment and conscience." Although discretion is usually discussed with regard to decision making by the police, virtually all decisions in the juvenile justice process carry with them wide-ranging discretion.

A second prevalent feature of the juvenile justice process is diversion. **Diversion** is the tendency of juvenile justice systems to deal with juvenile matters informally, without formal processing and adjudication, by referring cases to special programs and agencies inside or outside the juvenile justice system. Police officers commonly divert some cases to special programs within the department or to a variety of community resources such as family counseling and drug treatment. Probation officers, when screening cases that have been referred to the juvenile court, have legal authority to decide whether cases should be dealt with formally or informally. Informal handling may involve a diversionary referral to a community treatment option.

Prosecutors can choose not to petition a case and instead to provide for informal handling of a case, often involving a referral to community resources.

Discretion and diversion across the juvenile justice process will be discussed more extensively in later chapters. It is important to note here that discretion and diversion are essential to the efficient operation of the juvenile justice process. Although far less common than diversion, juvenile cases can sometimes be transferred from the juvenile system to the adult criminal justice system in one of three ways: (1) through statutory exclusion, in which state law requires that the case be heard in adult court because of the severity of the offense and/or the age of the youth; (2) by decision of the prosecutor, who is given authority in state statutes to file certain types of cases in either juvenile or adult court; and (3) by judicial waiver, which is a decision by a juvenile court judge to transfer the case to adult court.

Major decision points

The juvenile justice process involves nine major decision points: (1) arrest, (2) referral to court, (3) diversion, (4) secure detention, (5) judicial waiver to adult criminal court, (6) case petitioning, (7) delinquency finding/adjudication, (8) probation, and (9) residential placement, including confinement in a secure correctional facility (Sickmund and Puzzanchera 2014:175). For the majority of cases, the initial contact that youth have with the juvenile justice system is with law enforcement. Data reported in *Juvenile Court Statistics 2014* (Hockenberry and Puzzanchera 2017:31) show that a substantial majority of the referrals for delinquency cases (82 percent) were a result of citation and/or arrest by law enforcement. While far less common, the initial contact may also result from non-law enforcement sources, such as referrals from school officials, family members, or service providers.

Once a case is referred to a juvenile court, an intake decision is made. Probation officers and/or county attorneys (prosecutors) determine whether or not a case merits attention by the juvenile court. Often, cases are handled informally through diversion, by referring the youth to community services or informal probation through the juvenile court. For cases that are to be handled formally through the juvenile court, a decision to detain or release the youth is made by a judge at a detention hearing. Two fundamental questions influence the decision to release or detain a youth: (1) Does the youth pose a public safety risk? (2) Does the youth pose a flight risk? Detention is most likely when the answer to either of these questions is yes, or in instances where a parent/adult legal guardian cannot be located, or refuses to take custody of the youth.

Formal youth court action is triggered when the county attorney files a petition with the youth court, which identifies the specific statutory law violation(s). The formal process of hearings in youth court is called "adjudication." A vast majority of all cases result in an admission by the juvenile of the charge(s) filed in the petition. When the youth denies the petition, the case proceeds through an adjudication hearing in which the evidence is presented, first by the prosecutor and then by the defense attorney. Based on the evidence presented in the adjudication hearing, the youth court judge makes a finding (or determination) regarding the charge(s) identified in the petition. The judicial determination that the youth committed the petitioned offense(s) is sometimes referred to as a "finding of delinquency," and the youth is "adjudicated a delinquent youth." A dispositional hearing follows from an admission or an adjudication. The dispositional hearing is separate in time and purpose from the adjudication hearing. Disposition is the youth court equivalent of a sentence in adult court. Dispositions range from dismissal to secure confinement. As the least restrictive dispositional option is normally pursued, probation and other forms of community treatment are far more common than secure confinement. The chapters in Part III: Juvenile justice process, provide a full account of this process.

Disproportionate minority contact

Chapter 2 described the juvenile justice reforms that were initiated by passage of the Juvenile Justice and Delinquency Prevention (JJDP) Act of 1974. The JJDP Act authorized federal grant funding for juvenile justice system reform efforts at the state and local levels (Crank 1995). Foremost was reform in the use of secure detention in four problematic areas: (1) eliminate the use of detention for status offenders who commit offenses such as running away, truancy and disregard of parents (incorrigibility); (2) separate detained juveniles from adult offenders being held in jails; (3) remove juveniles from adult jail facilities; and (4) reduce the disproportionate rate of minority confinement (Sickmund and Puzzanchera 2014:87; Shepherd 1999; Crank 1995).

The 1988 amendment to the JJDP Act required states receiving grant funds through the Act to address disproportionate minority confinement—to "develop and implement plans to reduce the proportion of minority youth detained or confined in secure detention facilities, secure correctional facilities, jails, and lockups if they exceeded the percentage of minority youth in the general population" (OJJDP 2012:1). With a growing recognition that that disparity is not limited to secure confinement and that it may occur at multiple decision points across the juvenile justice process, "DMC" was expanded in the 2002 amendment to the JJDP Act to include not only disproportionate minority *confinement*, but to encompass disproportionate minority *contact* throughout the system. "This change required participating states to address juvenile delinquency prevention efforts and systems improvement efforts designed to reduce the disproportionate number of juvenile members of minority groups who come in contact with the juvenile justice system" (Sickmund and Puzzanchera 2014:175; see also OJJDP 2012; Leiber, Bishop, and Chamlin 2011).

Disproportionate Minority Contact (DMC) can be assessed at each of the major decision points depicted in the figure presented in the first chapter reading from *Juvenile Offenders and Victims: 2014 National Report* (Sickmund and Puzzanchera 2014). DMC is an indicator of minority juvenile over-representation relative to the representation of white juveniles across the decision points. The most common measure used to show DMC is the *relative rate index* (RRI).

> The RRI compares the rates of processing for minority youth to the rates of processing for white youth. The RRI method describes the volume of activity from one contact point to the next and how it differs between white and minority youth.
>
> (DSG 2014:6)

Empirical research on DMC has been conducted at both the national and state level. Several general findings are apparent:

- **Racial disparity**. National and state studies have consistently found minority youth to be over-represented across the points of contact in the juvenile justice process (for reviews of this literature see DSG 2014; Kempf-Leonard 2007; Bishop 2005; Pope and Leiber 2005; Pope, Lovell, and Hsia 2002; see also Leiber et al. 2011). The chapter reading by Nancy Rodriguez (2010) examines how race and ethnicity influence juvenile court decision-making, resulting in harsher treatment of minority youth.

- **Disparity across decision points.** Racial and ethnic disparities are not limited to the secure detention and confinement decision points. In most jurisdictions, evidence shows disproportionate minority representation at nearly all key decision points throughout the juvenile justice system (Sickmund and Puzzanchera 2014; see also Davis and Sorenson 2013; Leiber et al. 2011; DSG 2014). No state, however, showed consistent DMC for a particular minority group throughout all decision points (Davis and Sorenson 2013:118). Furthermore, disparity is greatest at the earliest stages of the juvenile justice process (arrest and intake) and smallest at judicial disposition (Sickmund and Puzzanchera 2014; Leiber et al. 2011; Hartney and Vuong 2009).
- **Early disparity affects later decisions.** As youth proceed through the system, disparate treatment at early stages produces disparity at later stages (Sickmund and Puzzanchera 2014). For example, Rodriguez (2010) found that youth who were detained were more likely to be petitioned into juvenile court, and subsequently more likely to be removed from the home at disposition than youth who were not detained.

Two contrasting explanations have been offered regarding DMC: the *differential offending hypothesis* and the *differential treatment hypothesis*. The differential offending hypothesis contends that minority youth are over-represented at each step of the juvenile justice process because they commit more frequent and more serious offenses, and they have more prior contacts with the juvenile justice system than do white youth. In this explanation, legal factors are the primary influence on decision points in the juvenile justice process. The differential treatment hypothesis asserts that minority youth are dealt with more formally and more harshly than white youth. Differential handling of minority youth by the juvenile justice system is the focal point in this explanation. The bulk of research evidence on these competing explanations of DMC shows persistent racial disparities after accounting for differences pertaining to legal factors. In their meta-analysis of prior state assessment studies, Pope and Leiber (2005) found that race continued to contribute to DMC even after accounting for legal factors in 32 of the 44 studies they reviewed (see also DSG 2014).

As a tool of technical assistance to states, the Office of Juvenile Justice and Delinquency Prevention (OJJDP) has developed a five-stage process to reduce DMC (OJJDP 2012: 3, 4; DSG 2014:3; see also Cabaniss, Frabutt, Kendrick, and Arbuckle 2007).[1]

1. **Identify the extent to which DMC exists.** States calculate disproportionality at nine contact points in the juvenile justice using the relative rate index (RRI). The RRI measures the disparity at each point in terms of volume and methods of handling cases.
2. **Assess the reasons for DMC.** Assess the possible influences on any disparity observed across the contact points. Use relevant data and information to determine the degree to which these influences affect disparity.
3. **Develop an intervention plan to address DMC.** Implement appropriate delinquency prevention and systems improvement. Diversion, alternatives to secure confinement, advocacy, and training on technical assistance on cultural competency are some examples of prevention and intervention activities that have been found to be effective. Some examples of effective system improvement activities include advocating for legislative reforms; making administrative policy, and procedural changes; and implementing structured decision-making tools at various contact points within the juvenile justice system.

4 **Evaluate the effectiveness of interventions.** Develop and conduct systematic, objective evaluation of the prevention and intervention activities. Assess system changes.
5 **Monitor DMC trends.** Consider demographic changes that might affect DMC rates and assess changes in DMC rates. Make adjustments to intervention strategies.

SUMMARY AND CONCLUSIONS

Contemporary legal definitions of juvenile delinquency distinguish juvenile offenders from adult criminals and provide for a separate system and process of justice. Legal definitions continue to emphasize the dependency of children and adolescents and their need for protection and nurture. In addition, the family unit is affirmed as the key institution of socialization, providing "care, protection, and wholesome mental and physical development of a youth."[2] However, contemporary legal definitions of juvenile delinquency commonly specify at least four different legal classifications of juveniles over which the juvenile court maintains jurisdiction: (1) dependent and neglected children; (2) status offenders, sometimes called "youth in need of intervention" or some variant of that term; (3) delinquent youth who violate the criminal code; and (4) serious delinquent offenders who have committed felony offenses. The authority to make decisions within the juvenile justice system is defined by statutory law. Statutory laws cover each of the major decision points and mandate which officials will be charged with decision making within them.

The term "juvenile justice system" is misleading. There is not a single juvenile justice system; rather, each state has a separate juvenile justice system, and these are "systems" in only a limited sense. The various parts of these systems—police, courts, and corrections—are all operated by different levels and branches of government, sometimes even by private organizations. Consequently, juvenile justice is highly decentralized and fragmented. In addition, many juvenile justice cases are diverted from "the system" or dealt with informally with only limited due process of law. As a result, "justice" is highly discretionary in juvenile justice systems across the United States.

Initially, the examination of racial and ethnic disparities in the juvenile justice system was limited to the use of confinement. Since the expansion of this focus to include all nine decision points, research has shown that minority youth tend to be over-represented across multiple points of contact in the juvenile justice process—from arrest to disposition. Issues associated with minority overrepresentation in the juvenile justice system have become a focal concern among policy makers and researchers. Over the last decade, considerable federal and state resources have been devoted to better understanding the factors that lead to racial and ethnic disparities in the juvenile justice system and to use this evidence in policy and programming of DMC reduction strategies.

READING 3.1

JUVENILE OFFENDERS AND VICTIMS: 2014 NATIONAL REPORT.

Melissa Sickmund, and Charles Puzzanchera (eds.). 2014. Pittsburg, PA: National Center for Juvenile Justice. (Pages 93–96)

This excerpt is taken from Chapter 4, "Juvenile Justice System Structure and Process," in the comprehensive national report on juvenile justice. It covers the use of state statutes to define cases under the jurisdiction of the juvenile court and the stages that cases go through as they are processed in the juvenile justice system.

Statutes set age limits for original jurisdiction of the juvenile court

In most states, the juvenile court has original jurisdiction over all youth charged with a law violation who were younger than age 18 at the time of the offense, arrest, or referral to court. Since 1975, five states have changed their age criteria: Alabama raised its upper age from 15 to 16 in 1976 and to 17 in 1977; Wyoming lowered its upper age from 18 to 17 in 1993; New Hampshire and Wisconsin lowered their upper age from 17 to 16 in 1996; and in 2007, Connecticut passed a law that gradually raised its upper age from 15 to 17 by July 1, 2012.

Oldest age for original juvenile court jurisdiction in delinquency matters, 2010:

Age	*State*
15	New York, North Carolina
16	Connecticut, Georgia, Illinois, Louisiana, Massachusetts, Michigan, Missouri, New Hampshire, South Carolina, Texas, Wisconsin
17	Alabama, Alaska, Arizona, Arkansas, California, Colorado, Delaware, District of Columbia, Florida, Hawaii, Idaho, Indiana, Iowa, Kansas, Kentucky, Maine, Maryland, Minnesota, Mississippi, Montana, Nebraska, Nevada, New Jersey, New Mexico, North Dakota, Ohio, Oklahoma, Oregon, Pennsylvania, Rhode Island, South Dakota, Tennessee, Utah, Vermont, Virginia, Washington, West Virginia, Wyoming

Many states have higher upper ages of juvenile court jurisdiction in status offense, abuse, neglect, or dependency matters—typically through age 20. In many states, the juvenile court has original jurisdiction over young adults who committed offenses while juveniles.

States often have statutory exceptions to basic age criteria. For example, many states exclude married or otherwise emancipated juveniles from juvenile court jurisdiction. Other exceptions, related to the youth's age, alleged offense, and/or prior court history, place certain youth under the original jurisdiction of the criminal court. In some states, a combination of the youth's age, offense, and prior record places the youth under the original jurisdiction of both the juvenile and criminal courts. In these states, the prosecutor has the authority to decide which court will initially handle the case.

As of the end of the 2010 legislative session, 16 states have statutes that set the lowest age of juvenile court delinquency jurisdiction. Other states rely on case law or common law. Children younger than a certain age are presumed to be incapable of criminal intent and, therefore, are exempt from prosecution and punishment.

Youngest age for original juvenile court jurisdiction in delinquency matters, 2010:

Age	*State*
6	North Carolina
7	Maryland, Massachusetts, New York
8	Arizona
10	Arkansas, Colorado, Kansas, Louisiana, Minnesota, Mississippi, Pennsylvania, South Dakota, Texas, Vermont, Wisconsin

Juvenile court authority over youth may extend beyond the upper age of original jurisdiction

Through extended jurisdiction mechanisms, legislatures enable the court to provide sanctions and services for a duration of time that is in the best interests of the juvenile and the public, even for older juveniles who have reached the age at which original juvenile court jurisdiction ends. As of the end of the 2011 legislative session, statutes in 33 states extend juvenile court jurisdiction in delinquency cases until the 21st birthday.

Oldest age over which the juvenile court may retain jurisdiction for disposition purposes in delinquency matters, 2011:

Age	*State*
18	Alaska, Iowa, Kentucky, Nebraska, Oklahoma, Rhode Island, Texas
19	Mississippi
20	Alabama, Arizona*, Arkansas, Connecticut, Delaware, District of Columbia, Georgia, Idaho, Illinois, Indiana, Louisiana, Maine, Maryland, Massachusetts, Michigan, Minnesota, Missouri, Nevada**, New Hampshire, New Mexico, New York, North Carolina, North Dakota, Ohio, Pennsylvania, South Carolina, South Dakota, Utah, Virginia, Washington, West Virginia, Wyoming
21	Florida, Vermont
22	Kansas
24	California, Montana, Oregon, Wisconsin
***	Colorado, Hawaii, New Jersey, Tennessee

Note: Extended jurisdiction may be restricted to certain offenses or juveniles.

* Arizona statute extends jurisdiction through age 20, but a 1979 state supreme court decision held that juvenile court jurisdiction terminates at age 18.

** Until the full term of the disposition order for sex offenders.

*** Until the full term of the disposition order.

In some states, the juvenile court may impose adult correctional sanctions on certain adjudicated delinquents that extend the term of confinement well beyond the upper age of juvenile jurisdiction.

Such sentencing options are included in the set of dispositional options known as blended sentencing.

Local processing of juvenile offenders varies

From state to state, case processing of juvenile law violators varies. Even within states, case processing may vary from community to community, reflecting local practice and tradition. Any description of juvenile justice processing in the U.S. must, therefore, be general, outlining a common series of decision points.

Law enforcement agencies divert many juvenile offenders out of the juvenile justice system

At arrest, a decision is made either to send the matter further into the justice system or to divert the case out of the system, often into alternative programs. Generally, law enforcement makes this decision after talking to the victim, the juvenile, and the parents and after reviewing the juvenile's prior contacts with the juvenile justice system. In 2010, 23% of all juvenile arrests were handled within the police department and resulted in release of the youth; in 68 of 100 arrests, the cases were referred to juvenile court. The remaining arrests were referred for criminal prosecution or to other agencies.

Most delinquency cases are referred by law enforcement agencies

Law enforcement accounted for 83% of all delinquency cases referred to juvenile court in 2010. The remaining referrals were made by others, such as parents, victims, school personnel, and probation officers.

Intake departments screen cases referred to juvenile court for formal processing

The court intake function is generally the responsibility of the juvenile probation department and/or the prosecutor's office. Intake decides whether to dismiss the case, to handle the matter informally, or to request formal intervention by the juvenile court.

To make this decision, an intake officer or prosecutor first reviews the facts of the case to determine whether there is sufficient evidence to prove the allegation. If not, the case is dismissed. If there is sufficient evidence, intake then determines whether formal intervention is necessary.

Nearly half of all cases referred to juvenile court intake are handled informally. Many informally processed cases are dismissed. In the other informally processed cases, the juvenile voluntarily agrees to specific conditions for a specific time period. These conditions often are outlined in a written agreement, generally called a "consent decree." Conditions may include such things as victim restitution, school attendance, drug counseling, or a curfew.

In most jurisdictions, a juvenile may be offered an informal disposition only if he or she admits to committing the act. The juvenile's compliance with the informal agreement often is monitored by a probation officer. Thus, this process is sometimes labeled "informal probation."

If the juvenile successfully complies with the informal disposition, the case is dismissed. If, however, the juvenile fails to meet the conditions, the case is referred for formal processing and proceeds as it would have if the initial decision had been to refer the case for an adjudicatory hearing.

If the case is to be handled formally in juvenile court, intake files one of two types of petitions: a delinquency petition requesting an adjudicatory hearing or a petition requesting a waiver hearing to transfer the case to criminal court.

A delinquency petition states the allegations and requests that the juvenile court adjudicate (or judge) the youth a delinquent, making the juvenile a ward of the court. This language differs from that used in the criminal court system, where an offender is convicted and sentenced.

In response to the delinquency petition, an adjudicatory hearing is scheduled. At the adjudicatory hearing (trial), witnesses are called and the facts of the case are presented. In nearly all adjudicatory hearings, the determination that the juvenile was responsible for the offense(s) is made by a judge; however, in some states, the juvenile has the right to a jury trial.

During the processing of a case, a juvenile may be held in a secure detention facility

Juvenile courts may hold delinquents in a secure juvenile detention facility if this is determined to be in the best interest of the community and/or the child.

After arrest, law enforcement may bring the youth to the local juvenile detention facility. A juvenile probation officer or detention worker reviews the case to decide whether the youth should be detained pending a hearing before a judge. In all states, a detention hearing must be held within a time period defined by statute, generally within 24 hours. At the detention hearing, a judge reviews the case and determines whether continued detention is warranted. In 2010, juveniles were detained in 21% of delinquency cases processed by juvenile courts.

Detention may extend beyond the adjudicatory and dispositional hearings. If residential placement is ordered but no placement beds are available, detention may continue until a bed becomes available.

The juvenile court may transfer the case to criminal court

A waiver petition is filed when the prosecutor or intake officer believes that a case under jurisdiction of the juvenile court would be handled more appropriately in criminal court. The court decision in these matters follows a review of the facts of the case and a determination that there is probable cause to believe that the juvenile committed the act. With this established, the court then decides whether juvenile court jurisdiction over the matter should be waived and the case transferred to criminal court.

The judge's decision in such cases generally centers on the issue of the juvenile's amenability to treatment in the juvenile justice system. The prosecution may argue that the juvenile has been adjudicated several times previously and that interventions ordered by the juvenile court have not kept the juvenile from committing subsequent criminal acts. The prosecutor may also argue that the crime is so serious that the juvenile court is unlikely to be able to intervene for the time period necessary to rehabilitate the youth.

If the judge decides that the case should be transferred to criminal court, juvenile court jurisdiction is waived and the case is filed in criminal court. In 2010, juvenile courts waived 1% of all formally processed delinquency cases. If the judge does not approve the waiver request, generally an adjudicatory hearing is scheduled in juvenile court.

Prosecutors may file certain cases directly in criminal court

In more than half of the states, legislatures have decided that in certain cases (generally those involving serious offenses), juveniles should be tried as criminal offenders. The law excludes such cases from juvenile court; prosecutors must file them in criminal court. In a smaller number of states, legislatures have given both the juvenile and adult courts original jurisdiction in certain cases. Thus, prosecutors have discretion to file such cases in either criminal or juvenile court.

What are the stages of delinquency case processing in the juvenile justice system?

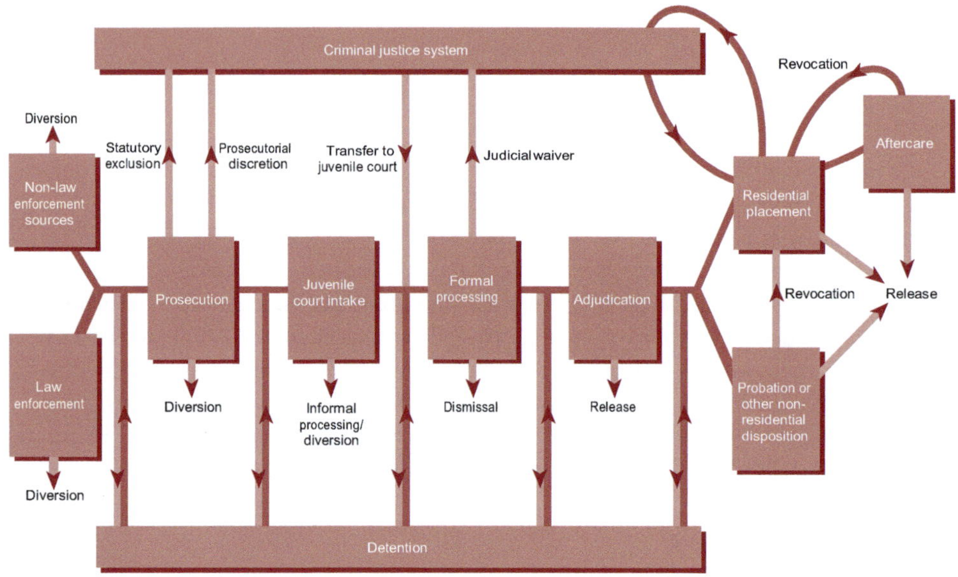

Note: This chart gives a simplified view of caseflow through the juvenile justice system. Procedures may vary among jurisdictions.

After adjudication, probation staff prepare a disposition plan

Once the juvenile is adjudicated delinquent in juvenile court, probation staff develop a disposition plan. To prepare this plan, probation staff assess the youth, available support systems, and programs. The court may also order psychological evaluations, diagnostic tests, or a period of confinement in a diagnostic facility.

At the disposition hearing, probation staff present dispositional recommendations to the judge. The prosecutor and the youth may also present dispositional recommendations. After considering the recommendations, the judge orders a disposition in the case.

Most youth placed on probation also receive other dispositions

Most juvenile dispositions are multifaceted and involve some sort of supervised probation. A probation order often includes additional requirements such as drug counseling, weekend confinement in the local detention center, or restitution to the community or victim. The term of probation may be for a specified period of time or it may be open-ended. Review hearings are held to monitor the juvenile's progress. After conditions of probation have been successfully met, the judge terminates the case. In 2010, formal probation was the most severe disposition ordered in 61% of the cases in which the youth was adjudicated delinquent.

The judge may order residential placement

In 2010, juvenile courts ordered residential placement in 26% of the cases in which the youth was adjudicated delinquent. Residential commitment may be for a specific or indeterminate time period. The facility may be publicly or privately operated and may have a secure, prison-like environment or a more open (even home-like) setting. In many states, when the judge commits a juvenile to the state department of juvenile corrections, the department determines where the juvenile will be placed and when the juvenile will be released. In other states, the judge controls the type and length of stay; in these situations, review hearings are held to assess the progress of the juvenile.

Juvenile aftercare is similar to adult parole

Upon release from an institution, the juvenile is often ordered to a period of aftercare or parole. During this period, the juvenile is under supervision of the court or the juvenile corrections department. If the juvenile does not follow the conditions of aftercare, he or she may be recommitted to the same facility or may be committed to another facility.

Status offense and delinquency case processing differ

A delinquent offense is an act committed by a juvenile for which an adult could be prosecuted in criminal court. There are, however, behaviors that are law violations only for juveniles and/or young adults because of their status. These "status offenses" may include behaviors such as running away from home, truancy, alcohol possession or use, incorrigibility, and curfew violations.

In many ways, the processing of status offense cases parallels that of delinquency cases. Not all states, however, consider all of these behaviors to be law violations. Many states view such behaviors as indicators that the child is in need of supervision. These states handle status offense matters more like dependency cases than delinquency cases, responding to the behaviors by providing social services.

Although many status offenders enter the juvenile justice system through law enforcement, in many states the initial, official contact is a child welfare agency. About 3 in 5 status offense cases referred to juvenile court come from law enforcement.

The federal Juvenile Justice and Delinquency Prevention Act states that jurisdictions shall not hold status offenders in secure juvenile facilities for detention or placement. This policy has been labeled deinstitutionalization of status offenders. There is an exception to the general policy: a status offender may be confined in a secure juvenile facility if he or she has violated a valid court order, such as a probation order requiring the youth to attend school and observe a curfew.

READING 3.2

"THE CUMULATIVE EFFECT OF RACE AND ETHNICITY IN JUVENILE COURT OUTCOMES AND WHY PREADJUDICATION DETENTION MATTERS."

Nancy Rodriguez. 2010. *Journal of Research in Crime and Delinquency* 47:391–413.

Researcher Nancy Rodriguez examines how race and ethnicity influence juvenile court decision-making, resulting in harsher treatment of minority youth.

Introduction

Studies of the juvenile justice system continue to shed light on the complex ways in which race and ethnicity influence court outcomes. Over the past 25 years, prior work has established several key findings regarding racial biases in juvenile court outcomes. These findings can be summarized in the following: (1) race directly and indirectly influences court outcomes (through gender, age, and community context), (2) racial biases are more common in front-end court processes than back-end processes, and (3) racial disparities accumulate as youth are processed further into the system (Engen, Steen, and Bridges 2002; Frazier and Cochran 1986; Leiber and Johnson 2008).

Studies have relied on various theoretical frameworks, including conflict theory, attribution theory, and racial threat, to explain the overrepresentation of minority youth in the justice system. A dominant theme throughout this work is how racial stereotypes influence the differential treatment of racial minorities in court outcomes. While prior work in this area has placed much empirical focus on how race influences certain court outcomes (e.g., detention, disposition), less attention has been given to the cumulative effect of race and ethnicity in juvenile court processes. In fact, few studies have conducted systematic reviews of multiple court outcomes to examine racial and ethnic disparities within the justice system. An important factor in the manifestation of this cumulative effect is preadjudication detention. Studies have found that detention plays a critical role in minority youth overrepresentation as evidenced by the relatively high number of detained minorities and the more severe treatment detained youth receive in subsequent court outcomes.

Consistent with these studies, this research will examine the influence of being white, black, Latino, and Native American on multiple court decision-making outcomes in one southwestern state. By examining the influence of race and ethnicity at the diversion, petition, detention, adjudication, and disposition stages, this study will produce a comprehensive assessment of minority youth overrepresentation in one juvenile justice system. This study will also examine how preadjudication detention affects subsequent court outcomes and capture whether there is a cumulative effect of race and ethnicity in juvenile court outcomes.

Prior research

Cumulative effect of race/ethnicity in court outcomes and the harms of detention

Various studies over the years have documented the overrepresentation of minority youth in the juvenile justice system (Bishop and Frazier 1996; Bridges et al. 1993; Pope and Feyerherm

1990; Secret and Johnson 1997). Work in this area has shown the value associated with examining racial/ethnic biases in multiple stages of processing (Bishop and Frazier 1988, 1996; DeJong and Jackson 1998). Interestingly, studies of multiple outcomes within the juvenile court show inconsistent findings regarding the effect of race. For example, Bishop and Frazier's (1988, 1996) work found that black youth were more likely to be recommended for formal processing, referred to court, found delinquent, and given harsher dispositions than white youth. Similarly, Pope and Feyerherm (1990) found that black youth received more severe court outcomes than white youth and that racial disparity occurred at various stages of juvenile court processing. On the contrary, Leiber and Jamieson (1995) found racial disparities exist at diversion, petition, and initial appearance, yet do not exist in subsequent decisions such as adjudication or disposition. Also, Guevara, Herz, and Spohn (2006) found that although non-white males were more likely than other offenders (non-white females, white males) to be detained prior to adjudication, non-white males were less likely than other offenders to be ordered to an out-of-home placement.

Prior work in this area has not only highlighted the varying effect of race across multiple court outcomes but also how early court outcomes significantly influence later stages of processing (e.g., disposition) and compound racial biases by producing indirect race effects (Bortner and Reed 1985; Engen et al. 2002; Leiber and Fox 2005). This process, referred to by some as "bias amplification" (see Dannefer and Schutt 1982:1129; Liska and Tausig 1979) and cumulative disadvantage (Zatz 1984), has important implications for studies of minority youth overrepresentation. Stated simply, studies that restrict their empirical focus to back-end stages such as disposition are unable to provide insight on whether there is a cumulative race/ethnicity effect in juvenile court processing.

A key component of tests of the cumulative disadvantage of racial and ethnic groups in the justice system is the preadjudication detention decision. Not only are racial and ethnic minorities more likely to be detained (Armstrong and Rodriguez 2005, Bishop and Frazier 1996; Secret and Johnson 1997), but those detained are likely to receive more severe treatment during the adjudication and disposition stages than youth not detained (Bortner 1982; Feld 1989; Leiber and Fox 2005; Wu 1997). Given these findings, national efforts sponsored by the Annie E. Casey Foundation and the W. Haywood Burns Institute have documented the various harms associated with the detention of youth. Unfortunately, how white, black, Latino/a and American Indian youth are affected by the detention decision and the cumulative effect of race and ethnicity associated with the detention outcome remains relatively unknown.

Several studies of juvenile court decision-making processes have proposed a possible "correction" process in back-end stages of processing (Fagan, Slaughter, and Hartstone 1987; Kurtz, Giddings, and Sutphen 1993). According to this explanation, court officials attempt to correct the high rate of minority youth overrepresentation at intake and referral stages by treating minority youth more leniently in later stages of processing. In their study, Dannefer and Schutt (1982) found minorities were more likely than white youth to be referred by police yet black youth were treated more leniently than white youth at the disposition stage. They describe this self correction process as one where court officials make efforts to address the aggressive law enforcement strategies that result in the high referral of (weak) cases involving minorities. In a recent study, Rodriguez (2007) found that arrests by law enforcement showed significant black youth overrepresentation yet preadjudication detention decisions showed white youth treated more severely than black youth. This finding is particularly relevant since the preadjudication detention decision is absent of prosecutorial review where a case might be "corrected" for being "weak." This implies judges as early as during the preadjudication detention phase may be making decisions that counter or "correct" the overrepresentation of minority youth at the arrest and referral stage.

The attributions of race and ethnicity in juvenile courts

One explanation for the overrepresentation of racial and ethnic minorities in the juvenile court system is the "differential treatment" argument (Bishop 2005). At the center of this perspective is the role of stereotypes or attributions that serve to disadvantage racial and ethnic minorities in court processes relative to similarly situated white youth (Bridges and Steen 1998; Feld 1999; Rodriguez 2007; Rodriguez, Smith, and Zatz 2009). According to this theoretical perspective, notions of blameworthiness and risk of reoffending are interrelated with race and class and play an integral part in juvenile court decision-making processes. Often relying on limited information, court officials make individual assessments of youth that highlight situational factors (e.g., family structure, community resources) that are most pronounced among racial/ethnic minorities. These assessments also involve attributions that link minorities to "bad neighborhoods" or "bad families" leading to more severe outcomes for racial minorities (Rodriguez 2007).

The influence of stereotypical perceptions in court processes has been primarily documented in studies that compare white and black youth (Bridges and Steen 1998; Leiber and Johnson 2008). The most extensive review of attributions of race in juvenile court outcomes found that court officials were more likely to assign negative internal attributions (e.g., juvenile's personality, attitude, and cooperativeness) to black youth and negative external attributions (e.g., delinquent peers, poor school performance, family conflict) to white youth (Bridges and Steen 1998). Furthermore, negative internal attributions were associated with perceptions of higher risk of reoffending and more severe disposition outcomes, which support the differential treatment argument. Unfortunately, the extent to which negative attributions serve to disadvantage other racial and ethnic groups is unknown.

Prior work has documented the need to examine how racial and ethnic groups are processed by juvenile court, yet few studies have included Latinos/as and American Indians in such studies. An empirical test of the differential treatment argument clearly warrants the inclusion of various racial and ethnic groups. The life circumstances and situational factors of Latino/a and American Indian youth, coupled with attributions of race and ethnicity, are likely critical elements in decision-making processes. For example, cultural differences may result in attributions that present Latinos/as as gang-involved, violent, and unresponsive to the justice system (Demuth 2002, 2003; Portillos 2006) and American Indians as outsiders (Bachman, Alvarez, and Perkins 1996; Leiber 1994; Zatz, Lujan, and Snyder-Joy 1991). These attributions may ultimately culminate to produce disparate court outcomes.

Studies of racial/ethnic biases in juvenile courts that have included Latinos/as and American Indian youth have produced mixed findings. While some studies show more severe treatment of blacks than Latinos/as (Leonard and Sontheimer 1995), others report Latinos/as are treated more severely than whites and blacks (DeJong and Jackson 1998; Maupin and Bond-Maupin 1999). Researchers have found American Indians receive less severe treatment than blacks (Leiber 1994) and more severe treatment than whites (Dean, Hirschel, and Brame 1996). Rodriguez (2007) found Latinos/as from economically advantaged and disadvantaged communities were more likely to be detained than similarly situated white youth yet no differences were found between American Indian and white youth in detention outcomes. In order to obtain a comprehensive review of racial and ethnic biases in juvenile court outcomes, studies should not only extend beyond the black-white and the white–non-white dichotomies but also review multiple stages of the juvenile justice system as biases may be compounded from one stage to the next (McCord, Spatz-Widom, and Crowell 2002).

Research objectives

Based on prior research on minority youth overrepresentation in the juvenile justice system, the current study examines the following research hypotheses:

Research Hypothesis 1: Diversion, petition, detention, adjudication, and disposition outcomes will vary based on race and ethnicity (e.g., whites, blacks, Latinos/as, and American Indians), producing more severe treatment of minority youth than white youth.

Research Hypothesis 2: Adjudication and disposition outcomes will vary based on detention outcome, producing more severe treatment of detained youth than nondetained youth.

The differential treatment of minority youth has been the focus of an extensive body of work; however, studies have primarily focused on the disparities of black youth relative to white youth (Frazier and Bishop 1996; Sampson and Laub 1993). As previously discussed, blameworthiness, potential for rehabilitation, and risk of reoffending are elements that guide the decision-making process within the justice system. Prior studies have shown that these are often correlated with attributions and stereotypes of race and ethnicity and can lead to biases in court outcomes (Bridges and Steen 1998; Bynum and Paternoster 1984; Mata and Herrerias 2006). Accordingly, it is hypothesized that black, Latino, and American Indian youth will receive more severe treatment than white youth, net the effect of legal criteria. Although most prior studies have focused on stereotypes of black youth and how those stereotypes lead to disparate outcomes, researchers have found language and cultural barriers are instrumental in the creation of ethnic stereotypes of Latinos/as (Demuth 2000, 2003; Portillos 2006). Thus, the more severe treatment Latino/a youth receive relative to their white counterparts may be explained by these stereotypes. Also, perceptions of American Indians as individuals plagued by alcohol and drug abuse problems in Indian country and as "outsiders" would suggest they too experience more severe treatment by the justice system than similarity situated whites.

A review of minority youth overrepresentation in the juvenile justice system must take into account the critical role of preadjudication detention and the possible cumulative effects of race and ethnicity in court outcomes. Consistent with prior studies on the effect of detention in subsequent juvenile court processes (adjudication and disposition; Feld 1989; Leiber and Fox 2005; Secret and Johnson 1997), it is hypothesized that court officials at the adjudication stage will perceive detained youth as more culpable for the alleged delinquent act and adjudicate them at a higher rate than nondetained youth. Also, juvenile court judges at the disposition stage will perceive detained youth as more blameworthy, a significant threat to public safety, and unsuitable for community supervision. As a result, detained youth will be more likely to be ordered to an out-of-home placement than nondetained youth.

In sum, a systematic review of juvenile court outcomes that includes white, black, Latino/a, and American Indian youth will provide the most comprehensive study to date of racial and ethnic disparities in juvenile court outcomes. Also, an examination of race and ethnicity at the diversion, petition, detention, adjudication, and disposition stages is especially relevant as no prior study has included these four racial/ethnic groups in one study to examine possible biases across these particular multiple court outcomes.

Research design and methods

In order to test the hypotheses, data from the Arizona Juvenile On-Line Tracking System (JOLTS) database and the 2000 U.S. census were utilized.

Study site

The setting for this study is Arizona, a state characterized by a vastly growing racial and ethnic minority population. The multiple racial and ethnic groups in the state's population allowed empirical focus on Latinos/as and American Indians, two groups that have received minimal empirical attention in studies of juvenile court outcomes. According to the 2000 U.S. Census, 50 percent of the children (< 18 years old) in Arizona were white, 38.8 percent Latino, 5 percent black, and 1.9 percent American Indian.

Sample and data

A random sample of delinquent and status offenders (N = 23,156) referred to the Arizona juvenile justice system during 2000 was drawn from the JOLTS database to examine juvenile court outcomes. The JOLTS database captures information on youths' court processing from the time the youth is referred to the juvenile court until court disposition. The unit of analysis for this study was the juvenile offender. In instances where a youth was referred to the court multiple times in 2000, the first referral in the year was included in the sample. Each youth was followed through five distinct court outcomes. . . .

Discussion and conclusion

A theme throughout various studies of minority youth overrepresentation is how racial/ethnic stereotypes lead to the differential treatment of minority youth in the juvenile justice system. Consistent with prior studies, findings reveal that attributions of race and ethnicity produce disparities in justice system outcomes. These findings are particularly important as this is the first study to include white, black, Latino/a, and American Indian youth in a study of minority overrepresentation across multiple stages of juvenile court processing. Analyses reveal black, Latino/a, and American Indian youth were treated more severely than white youth. Furthermore, these disparities exist in front-end court processes (i.e., diversion and detention) as well as in back-end processes and outcomes (i.e., out-of-home placement). An important element of these racial and ethnic disparities is how they differ across juvenile court outcomes. For example, black youth received severe (diversion, detention, and out-of-home placement) and lenient (adjudication) treatment at different stages of processing while Latinos/as and American Indians only received more severe treatment across certain court outcomes (diversion and detention).

A central focus of this study was the examination of the cumulative effect of race and ethnicity via detention. As expected, the effect of preadjudication detention was a significant predicator in subsequent court outcomes. Specifically, youth who were detained were more likely to have a petition filed, less likely to have petitions dismissed, and more likely to be removed from the home and ordered to the juvenile state correctional institution. This finding is consistent with prior studies that document how even short-term incarceration of youth can lead to more severe treatment of youth (Bishop and Frazier 1992; Bortner and Reed 1985; Feld 1993). Furthermore, findings reveal detention produces indirect racial/ethnic effects in subsequent stages of processing. An important facet of detention decisions is the role of detention screening instruments. In Arizona, each individual court relies on its own tool to determine detention decisions and therefore it was not included as a control measure in this statewide study. However, efforts to curb the detention of youth must begin with assessing how such instruments directly or indirectly affect minority youth. In the end, these findings highlight the need for multistage studies that incorporate how early court processes, such as detention, affect later court decisions and outcomes. In fact, when race and ethnicity effects are not examined during early stages of processing, analyses of later decision-making processes are likely underestimating the influence of race and ethnicity in court outcomes (Bishop and Frazier 1996; Bortner and Reed 1985).

An important dimension of this study was the inclusion of the control variable structural disadvantage. Findings from this study indicate that structural disadvantage was a significant predictor of detention. While structural disadvantage was not directly associated with petition, adjudication, and the out-of-home placement outcome, youth who lived in structurally disadvantaged areas were treated more severely in those outcomes given the direct effect of disadvantage in the detention outcome. While previous studies have included macro-level measures in studies of juvenile court outcomes (Feld 1991; Frazier and Lee 1992; Rodriguez 2007; Sampson and Laub 1993; Wu, Cernkovich, and Dunn 1997), this is the first study to demonstrate the indirect effect of structural disadvantage in subsequent court outcomes. Findings reported here reveal the importance of examining macro-level factors in studies of juvenile court decision-making processes.

In the end, what insight does this study provide for juvenile justice practice and policy? The current study found racial/ethnic biases exist at initial, front-end processes as well as back-end processes. This is important as efforts aimed at reducing disparities at detention like the Juvenile Detention Alternatives Initiative (JDAI) of the Annie E. Casey Foundation cannot alone reduce disparities that take place across multiple stages of processing (e.g., referral, adjudication, and disposition). In Arizona, only one jurisdiction is currently a JDAI site (Pima County, Arizona). While this collaboration has resulted in a significant drop in the detention population, minority youth overrepresentation continues to be a problem for that juvenile court. Since black, Latino/as and American Indian youth were more likely to be detained than white youth, it is critical to better understand why members of these racial/ethnic groups were detained. Doing so will require better understanding of social and family situational factors of youth. For example, far more insight is needed on whether the reasons black youth are detained are the same for Latinos/as and American Indians. Is the family support system different for racial/ethnic groups and therefore their capacity to work with the juvenile justice system different? Are there cultural barriers (e.g., language and custom) that keep certain parents from becoming involved and engaged in juvenile court activities, and how does this possibly affect the treatment of racial and ethnic youth? Juvenile justice officials must work to identify underlying factors that lead to detention and be sensitive to those factors that keep certain youth in the hands of the juvenile justice system.

Any effort aimed at addressing racial/ethnic biases must consider the context of the juvenile court as well as the community characteristics of the youth who come to the attention of the juvenile court. Attempts at eradicating disparities must first focus on identifying the nature of the disparities at the local level. This will require comprehensive reviews of racial/ethnic disparities across multiple decision points and during an ongoing basis. Second, attention must also be given to community capacity. This includes focusing attention on the resources (or lack of) that are available for juveniles in their respective communities. Like many jurisdictions, localities within Arizona have struggled in obtaining resources for prevention and intervention efforts as well as detention alternatives. The sheer volume of youth who enter the justice system each year, many with dual jurisdictional status (i.e., delinquent and dependent youth), are in need of various resources. The risk factors that lead to antisocial behavior among youth are an important related facet in finding community alternatives for at-risk and delinquent youth. Alternatives to the justice system that are suitable for youth with individual (e.g., illicit drug use), family (e.g., maltreatment), school (e.g., truancy), peer (e.g., gang involvement), and community (e.g., living in impoverished communities) risk factors are difficult to find. In many cases, the child welfare or the mental health systems serve as alternatives when the juvenile justice system lacks the capacity and resources for youth with such needs. At the same time, many nonprofit community agencies have restrictions regarding which type of youth they can serve (e.g., youth with no histories of mental illness and illicit drug use and U.S. citizens). Since public safety often trumps the needs of children, agents of the juvenile justice systems must be active participants at national, state, and local discussions regarding crime prevention and intervention efforts.

While this study represents a comprehensive review of racial and ethnic biases in juvenile court outcomes, several limitations are worth noting. First, the study was unable to include statistical controls for family situational variables. Family living situation (DeJong and Jackson 1998), family dysfunction (Bridges and Steen 1998), and parental incarceration (Rodriguez et al. 2009) have all been shown to play a significant role in juvenile court outcomes. The capacity of youths' family and the perception of a "bad home" may be perceived as risk factors by court officials and lead to more severe treatment. Second, while a measure of urbanization was included in the models, the study did not control for court specific characteristic (e.g., workload) that likely influence case processes in Arizona juvenile courts. Lastly, this study only examined the direct effects of race and ethnicity in court outcomes and controlled for context using multilevel analysis. By examining data at the statewide level, it is possible that the effects of race/ethnicity are not fully specified and underestimate the effect of race/ ethnicity in local jurisdictions. Furthermore, multilevel interactions were not performed and therefore it is unknown whether race/ethnicity and other individual criteria (e.g., gender, age, and offense seriousness) intersect with macro-level factors to produce more severe treatment of youth at specific court outcomes.

[References and notes omitted.]

CRITICAL-THINKING QUESTIONS

1 Using the case of Arturo that opened the chapter, describe the impacts that juvenile justice practitioners have on youth in the system.
2 In what ways are juvenile justice systems decentralized and fragmented among the different levels and branches of government?
3 How is discretion used throughout the juvenile justice process?
4 How is diversion used throughout the juvenile justice process?

5 Why is it important to examine racial and ethnic disparities at each of the juvenile justice process decision points?
6 Based on the reading drawn from *Juvenile Offenders and Victims: 2014 National Report*, identify several decision points in the juvenile justice process in which choices are made between informal and formal processing.
7 According to the Rodriguez (2010) reading, why is preadjudicatory detention a key decision point for understanding racial and ethnic disparities in juvenile justice?

SUGGESTED READING

Feld, Barry C. 2014. *Juvenile Justice Administration: In a Nutshell.* 3rd ed. St. Paul, MN: West.

Sickmund, Melissa and Charles Puzzanchera (eds.). 2014. "Chapter 4: Juvenile Justice System Structure and Process." Pp. 83–114 in *Juvenile Offenders and Victims: 2014 National Report.* Pittsburgh, PA: National Center for Juvenile Justice.

Sickmund, Melissa and Charles Puzzanchera (eds.). 2014. "Identifying Racial/Ethnic Disparity in Justice System Processing." Pp. 175–178 in *Juvenile Offenders and Victims: 2014 National Report*. Pittsburgh, PA: National Center for Juvenile Justice.

USEFUL WEBSITES

For further information relevant to this chapter, go to the following websites.

- **Juvenile Justice Geography, Policy, Practice, & Statistics**: www.jjgps.org
- **National Association of Youth Courts**: www.youthcourt.net
- **National Council of Juvenile and Family Court Judges**: www.ncjfcj.org
- **OJJDP Statistical Briefing Book**: Juvenile Justice System Structure and Process: www.ojjdp.gov/ojstatbb
- **OJJDP DMC Statistical Briefing Book**: www.ojjdp.gov/ojstatbb/dmcdb/

GLOSSARY OF KEY TERMS

Discretion: "Authority conferred by law to act in certain conditions or situations in accordance with an official's or an official agency's considered judgment and conscience" (Pound 1960:926).

Disproportionate Minority Contact: "The disproportionate number of juvenile members of minority groups who come into contact with the juvenile justice system" (OJJDP 2012:1).

Diversion: The tendency to deal with juvenile matters informally, without formal processing and adjudication, by referring cases to agencies outside the juvenile justice system.

Status offense: An act that is illegal for a juvenile, but is not a crime if committed by an adult. Status offenses include acts such as running away, truancy, ungovernability, and liquor law violations.

NOTES

1 See Leiber, Bishop, and Chamlin (2011) and McCarter (2011) for assessment of the effectiveness of OJJDP's DMC mandate.

2 *Montana Code Annotated 2017*, 41-5-102.

REFERENCES

Aarons, John, Lisa Smith, and Linda Wagner. 2009. *Dispatches from Juvenile Hall: Fixing a Failed System*. New York: Penguin Books.

Bishop, Donna M. 2005. "The Role of Race and Ethnicity in Juvenile Justice Processing." Pp. 23–28 in *Our Children, Their Children: Confronting Racial and Ethnic Differences in American Juvenile Justice*, edited by D. F. Hawkins and K. Kempf-Leonard. Chicago: University of Chicago Press.

Cabaniss, Emily R., James M. Frabutt, Mary H. Kendrick, and Margaret B. Arbuckle. 2007. "Reducing Disproportionate Minority Contact in the Juvenile Justice System: Promising Practices." *Aggression and Violent Behavior* 12:393–401.

Crank, Kathleen Kositzky. 1995. "The JJDP Mandates: Rationale and Summary." Washington, DC: Office of Juvenile Justice and Delinquency Prevention. Available online at: www.ncjrs.gov/txtfiles/fs-9522.txt.

Davis, Jaya and Jon R. Sorensen. 2013. "Disproportionate Minority Confinement of Juveniles: A National Examination of Black–White Disparity in Placements, 1997–2006." *Crime and Delinquency* 59:115–139.

Development Services Group, Inc. (DSG). 2014. "Disproportionate Minority Contact." OJJDP Model Programs Guide. Washington, DC: Office of Juvenile Justice and Delinquency Prevention.

Feld, Barry C. 1999. *Bad Kids: Race and the Transformation of the Juvenile Court*. New York: Oxford University Press.

Gibbons, Don C. and Marvin D. Krohn. 1991. *Delinquent Behavior*. 5th ed. Englewood Cliffs, NJ: Prentice Hall.

Hartney, Christopher and Linh Vuong. 2009. *Created Equal: Racial and Ethnic Disparities in the U.S. Criminal Justice System*. Oakland, CA: National Council on Crime and Delinquency. Retrieved March 8, 2015 (http://nccdglobal.org/publications).

Hockenberry, Sarah and Charles Puzzanchera. 2017. *Juvenile Court Statistics 2014*. Pittsburgh. PA: National Center for Juvenile Justice.

Kempf-Leonard, Kimberly. 2007. "Minority Youths and Juvenile Justice Disproportionate Minority Contact after Nearly 20 Years of Reform Efforts." *Youth Violence and Juvenile Justice* 5:71–87.

Leiber, Michael, Donna Bishop, and Mitchell B. Chamlin. 2011. "Juvenile Justice Decision-Making Before and After the Implementation of the Disproportionate Minority Contact (DMC) Mandate." *Justice Quarterly* 28:460–492.

McCarter, Susan A. 2011. "Disproportionate Minority Contact in the American Juvenile Justice System: Where Are We After 20 Years, a Philosophy Shift, and Three Amendments?" *Journal of Forensic Social Work* 1:96–107.

Office of Juvenile Justice and Delinquency Prevention (OJJDP). 2012. "Disproportionate Minority Contact." *OJJDP in Focus*. Washington DC: OJJDP.

Platt, Anthony. 1977. *The Child Savers: The Invention of Delinquency*. 2nd ed. Chicago: University of Chicago Press.

Pope, Carl and Michael Leiber. 2005. "Disproportionate Minority Contact (DMC): The Federal Initiative." Pp. 351–389 in *Our Children, Their Children: Confronting Racial and Ethnic Differences in American Juvenile Justice*, edited by D. Hawkins and K. Kempf-Leonard. Chicago: University of Chicago Press.

Pope, Carl E., Rick Lovell, and Heidi M. Hsia. 2002. "Disproportionate Minority Confinement: A Review of the Research Literature from 1989 through 2001." Washington, DC: Office of Juvenile Justice and Delinquency Prevention.

Pound, Roscoe. 1960. "Discretion, Dispensation, and Mitigation: The Problem of the Individual Special Case." *New York University Law Review* 35:925–937.

Rodriguez, Nancy. 2010. "The Cumulative Effect of Race and Ethnicity in Juvenile Court Outcomes and Why Preadjudication Detention Matters." *Journal of Research in Crime and Delinquency* 47:391–413.

Rubin, H. Ted. 1985. *Juvenile Justice: Policy, Practice, and Law*. 2nd ed. New York: Random House.

Shepherd, Robert E., Jr. 1999. "The Juvenile Court at 100 Years: A Look Back." *Juvenile Justice* 6:13–21.

Sickmund, Melissa and Charles Puzzanchera (eds.). 2014. *Juvenile Offenders and Victims: 2014 National Report.* Pittsburgh, PA: National Center for Juvenile Justice.

Sutton, John. 1988. *Stubborn Children: Controlling Delinquency in the United States, 1640–1981.* Berkley, CA: University of California Press.

PART II

Understanding the problem of delinquency

Chapter 4

DATA ON DELINQUENCY AND JUVENILE JUSTICE

CHAPTER TOPICS

- "Official data"
- Victimization surveys
- Self-report surveys
- Comparing data sources

CHAPTER LEARNING OBJECTIVES

After completing this chapter, students should be able to:

- Identify the strengths and weaknesses of the three major sources of data on delinquency and juvenile justice: Official records, victimization surveys, and self-report surveys.

CHAPTER CONTENTS

CASE IN POINT

NEED FOR MULTIPLE DATA SOURCES

There is an ongoing debate about the relative ability of self-report studies and official statistics to describe juvenile crime and victimization. Self-report studies can capture information on behavior that never comes to the attention of juvenile justice agencies. Compared with official studies, self-report studies find a much higher proportion of the juvenile population involved in delinquent behavior . . .

Although official records may be inadequate measures of the level of juvenile offending, they do monitor justice system activity. Analysis of variations in official statistics across time and jurisdictions provides an understanding of justice system caseloads . . .

Delbert Elliott, founding director of the Center for the Study and Prevention of Violence, has argued that to abandon either self-report or official statistics in favor of the other is "rather shortsighted; to systematically ignore the findings of either is dangerous, particularly when the two measures provide apparently contradictory findings." Elliott stated that a full understanding of the etiology and development of delinquent behavior is enhanced by using and integrating both self-report and official record research.

(Sickmund and Puzzanchera 2014:60)

The scientific study of delinquency is based on the ability to gather accurate and valid data. Social scientists have used various research methods to obtain data on crime and delinquency primarily from three sources: "official" records maintained by law enforcement agencies and courts, surveys of individuals who have been victims of crime, and surveys of individuals who self-report involvement in offending. We discuss each of these, comparing the data gathered from these sources, and considering the strengths and weaknesses of each type of data.

"OFFICIAL DATA"

"Official data" on juvenile delinquency are gathered by governmental agencies within the criminal justice system. These data reveal the extent of delinquency with which these agencies deal and the characteristics of offenses and offenders they encounter. The two primary sources of official data on delinquency are the Uniform Crime Reporting program and *Juvenile Court Statistics.*

Uniform Crime Reporting program

The **Uniform Crime Reporting (UCR) program** was begun by the Federal Bureau of Investigation (FBI) in 1930. The UCR program includes more than 18,000 local, state, and federal law enforcement agencies that voluntarily report data on crimes that come to their attention. The vast majority of law enforcement agencies in the United States report crime data to the FBI as part of the UCR program. In 2015, participating agencies represented 98 percent of the total U.S. population (FBI 2016). As the program title implies, the UCR provides uniformity in crime reporting by requiring law enforcement agencies to use standardized offense definitions. In this way, variation in local statutes does not affect the nature or extent of offenses reported.

Offenses included in the UCR are divided into two categories: Part I (Index) and Part II (non-Index) offenses. Part I offenses include the violent crimes of murder and non-negligent manslaughter, forcible rape, robbery, and aggravated assault, and the property crimes of burglary, larceny-theft, motor vehicle theft, and arson. Part II offenses include all other criminal and delinquent acts. See **Table 4.1** for a list of UCR Part II offenses. Data on both Part I and Part II offenses are gathered and submitted to the UCR program on a monthly basis.

The UCR includes primarily four types of information: offenses known to law enforcement, crimes cleared, persons arrested, and police employee data (e.g., number of law enforcement employees in the U.S.). Offenses known to law enforcement are those reported by victims, witnesses, or other sources, or discovered by police officers. Crimes known to police may be cleared in one of two ways: (1) by arrest of at least one person, who is charged with committing an offense and turned over to the court for prosecution; or (2) by exceptional means when a factor beyond law enforcement control prevents the agency from arresting and formally charging an offender (e.g., death of the offender, or refusal of the victim to cooperate with prosecution after an offender has been identified) (FBI 2017). A law enforcement agency may clear multiple crimes with the arrest of one individual, or it may clear one crime with the arrest of many individuals. In 2016, the nationwide clearance rate was 46 percent for Part I violent crimes and 18 percent for Part I property crimes (FBI 2017). Clearance rates are higher for violent crimes than for property crimes because violent crimes are typically more vigorously investigated than property crimes, and because victims or witnesses of violent crimes often identify the offenders.

For juvenile offenders, a clearance by arrest is recorded when a person under age 18 is cited to appear in juvenile court or before other juvenile authorities, even though a physical arrest

TABLE 4.1 Uniform Crime Reporting program Part II offenses

• Simple assaults • Forgery and counterfeiting • Fraud • Embezzlement • Stolen property offenses (buying, receiving, possessing) • Vandalism • Weapons offenses (carrying, possessing, etc.) • Prostitution and commercialized vice • Sex offenses (except forcible rape, prostitution, and commercialized vice) • Drug abuse violations • Gambling	• Offenses against the family and children (nonviolent acts by a family member, such as nonsupport, neglect, or desertion) • Driving under the influence • Liquor law violations • Drunkenness • Disorderly conduct • Vagrancy • All other offenses ("All violations of state or local laws not specifically identified as Part I or Part II offenses, except traffic violations.") • Suspicion • Curfew and loitering law violations (persons under age 18)

Source: Federal Bureau of Investigation (2017).

may not have occurred (FBI 2016). The UCR reveals that, in 2015, juvenile offenders accounted for 9 percent of clearances for Part I violent crimes and 10 percent of clearances for Part I property crimes (FBI 2016).

The third type of data in the UCR is information about persons arrested, such as age, race, ethnicity, and gender. The UCR provides extensive data on crimes committed by various subgroups based on offender characteristics. For example, the UCR presents data separately on offenses committed by juveniles (those under the age of 18) and adults, and for different racial and ethnic groups. Until 2017, the UCR also presented data separately for males and females. The total number of persons arrested does not equal the total number of persons who have committed crimes, but rather only the number apprehended by law enforcement personnel. In addition, the number of persons arrested does not equal the number of arrests, because an individual offender may be arrested for multiple crimes. For offenders who are arrested for multiple Part I crimes, only the most serious offense is recorded in the UCR. This is another reason that the actual amount of crime committed in the United States is higher than the amount revealed by the UCR.

The Bureau of Justice Statistics (BJS) has developed estimates of the total number of arrests nationally, based on UCR arrest statistics (BJS n.d.). These estimates adjust the UCR arrest numbers to take into consideration the size of the population served by each law enforcement agency that reports data to the FBI. The BJS estimates are higher than the number of arrests shown in UCR data. The *Statistical Briefing Book* presented by the Office of Juvenile Justice and Delinquency Prevention (OJJDP) provides extensive estimated arrest data for juvenile offenders (OJJDP 2017).

Redesign of the UCR program

In the early 1980s, law enforcement agencies called for evaluation and modernization of the UCR program. The result was a new UCR program called the National Incident-Based Reporting System (NIBRS). The NIBRS offers detailed information about criminal incidents, including when and where an incident occurred, the type and value of property stolen, the relationship between victim and offender, and the age, gender, and race of both offender and victim. The major differences between the original UCR program and the NIBRS are the greater detail and larger number of offenses included in the NIBRS and the inclusion in the NIBRS of all Part I offenses occurring in a single incident (compared to the UCR, which records only the most serious offense per incident) (FBI 2011).

Strengths of UCR data

The UCR program provides uniform, nationwide data about crime and delinquency. The FBI ensures that law enforcement agencies across the country use consistent definitions and procedures for reporting crimes as part of the UCR program. This allows researchers to examine the nature and extent of crime for the nation as a whole. Because the UCR program has been in existence for more than 85 years, researchers are also able to use UCR data to explore trends in crime rates over time. Another strength of the UCR program is that it offers information about the demographic characteristics of *arrested* offenders.

Weaknesses of UCR data

The most important weakness of UCR data is the vast number of offenses not included in official statistics. Surveys of crime victims indicate that more than half of the violent and property crime victimizations that occur annually in the United States are not reported to police (Truman and Morgan 2016). The majority of offenses are not known to law enforcement, and therefore are not included in official statistics. In addition, a strong relationship exists between the seriousness of an offense and the likelihood that it will be cleared through an arrest. The less serious the offense, the more likely that it will be excluded from official data. However, serious offenses such as sexual assault are also relatively unlikely to be reported to police, for a variety of reasons. So-called victimless offenses (e.g., drug abuse violations and prostitution) are particularly likely to go unreported and thus be excluded from UCR data.

A second weakness of UCR data concerns the effects of policing practices on official statistics. The criteria that influence arrest decisions may vary among law enforcement agencies and within agencies over time. For example, an agency might decide to "crack down" on prostitution, and conduct operations that result in an increased number of vice arrests. Yet, this increase does not mean that prostitution has increased in that jurisdiction, or that it is necessarily a greater problem there than in other jurisdictions that show fewer arrests for prostitution. Rather, the increase in arrests reflects only changes in policing practices.

A related criticism is that the criteria governing arrest decisions vary for different segments of the population. For example, racial discrimination in the arrest process is well documented and indicates that, for committing the same crimes, blacks are more likely than whites to be arrested (Tapia 2011; Tonry 2010; Beckett et al. 2005; but see also Engel, Smith, and Cullen 2012). Such discrimination distorts official data, particularly about the characteristics of offenders.

As we noted above, according to the "hierarchy rule" in recording crimes, when an individual is arrested for committing multiple Part I crimes, only the most serious offense is recorded in UCR data, and the other offenses in multiple-offenses situations are omitted. While there are exceptions to the hierarchy rule for the offenses of justifiable homicide, motor vehicle theft, and arson, this rule clearly results in the under-estimation of crime using UCR data (FBI 2016).

Finally, police officers sometimes simply make unintentional errors in recording crime data. In addition, although the FBI works hard to achieve uniformity of data across jurisdictions, some variation in crime coding and recording practices is inevitable, given the huge number of agencies participating in the UCR program. Law enforcement agencies may also intentionally manipulate crime data for political purposes and thus provide an inaccurate picture of crime. For example, an agency may under-report offenses in its jurisdiction to try to show that it has curbed crime.

Juvenile Court Statistics

Juvenile court records provide another official source of data about juvenile delinquency. *Juvenile Court Statistics* is compiled from data that state and county agencies provide to the National Juvenile Court Data Archive (Hockenberry and Puzzanchera 2017). The most recent juvenile court statistics from 2014 regarding delinquency cases are based on individual case-level data from 2,256 jurisdictions in 39 states, and court-level aggregate data from 221 jurisdictions in 5 states.[1] Together, these jurisdictions contained 84 percent of the juvenile population in the U.S. in 2014. Juvenile court statistics from 2014 regarding petitioned status offense cases are based on individual case-level and court-level aggregate data from 2,267 jurisdictions containing 77 percent of the juvenile population in the U.S. in 2014. In 2014, *Juvenile Court Statistics* data were based on 730,278 delinquency cases and 72,242 formally handled status offense cases (Hockenberry and Puzzanchera 2017:92). *Juvenile Court Statistics* provides information about offenses charged; age, gender, and race of offenders; referral sources; detention and petitioning decisions; and dispositions ordered. Reporting agencies use their own definitions and coding categories when providing juvenile court data, so the data are not uniform across jurisdictions. However, the National Juvenile Court Data Archive restructures the data into standardized categories (Hockenberry and Puzzanchera 2017).

The "unit of count" in *Juvenile Court Statistics* is the number of "cases disposed." "A 'case' represents a juvenile processed by a juvenile court on a new referral, regardless of the number of law violations contained in the referral" (Hockenberry and Puzzanchera 2017:1). For example, a youth charged in a single referral with three offenses represents one case. "The fact that a case is 'disposed' means that a definite action was taken as a result of the referral—i.e., a plan of treatment was selected or initiated" (Hockenberry and Puzzanchera 2017:1). The treatment plan does not have to be completed for a case to be considered disposed. "For example, a case is considered to be disposed when the court orders probation, not when a term of probation supervision is completed" (Hockenberry and Puzzanchera 2017:1).

Only a portion of juveniles who commit offenses come to the attention of the police, and only a portion of juvenile offenses known to police are processed by juvenile courts. The primary weakness of juvenile court data is that they are available only for juvenile offenders whose cases are handled by juvenile courts. Thus, the offenders included in juvenile court statistics are not representative of all juvenile offenders.

OJJDP databases on youth in custody

OJJDP gathers information on juveniles in residential placement through three mechanisms: Census of Juveniles in Residential Placement, Juvenile Residential Facility Census, and Survey of Youth in Residential Placement.

Census of Juveniles in Residential Placement (CJRP)

The CJRP began in 1997 and is conducted every two years to provide detailed information about juvenile offenders in custody in secure and non-secure facilities. It includes both status and delinquent offenders, and individuals who are detained temporarily by the court as well as those who have been committed to a facility following adjudication for an offense. The Census does not include facilities that are exclusively for abused or neglected youth, or for mental health or drug treatment. The CJRP collects information on juveniles under age 21 held in all juvenile residential facilities on the census reference date, including birth date, race, gender, placement authority, most serious offense charged, court adjudication status, date of admission, and security status. On the census reference date in 2015, residential facilities housed 48,043 juvenile offenders under age 21 (Sickmund et al. 2017).

Juvenile Residential Facility Census (JRFC)

The JRFC also began in the late 1990s and is conducted every two years to gather information about facilities that house juveniles as a result of their contact with the justice system (who have been either charged with or adjudicated for an offense). Like the CJRP, this Facility Census includes secure and non-secure facilities, both detention centers and other facilities to which juveniles are committed following adjudication. In 2010, the JRFC gathered data from 2,519 facilities (Sickmund and Puzzanchera 2014:200). The JRFC gathers data on how facilities operate and the services they provide, including specific questions about facility security, capacity and crowding, facility ownership and operation, and juvenile injuries and deaths while in custody. In select years, additional information is collected regarding specific services, such as education, substance abuse treatment, and mental and physical health services provided to juveniles in placement (Sickmund and Puzzanchera 2014).

Survey of Youth in Residential Placement (SYRP)

The SYRP has been conducted only once, in 2003. It involved the selection of a national sample of youth who were 10–20 years old, and in residential placement in facilities covered by the CJRP and the JRFC because of their involvement with the juvenile justice system (they were charged with or adjudicated for offenses). The SYRP was conducted through anonymous interviews of 7,073 youth in 205 facilities throughout the U.S. It provided information about juveniles' experiences in placement and conditions of their confinement. For example, it asked specific questions about prior experiences of abuse or serious trauma, past offense histories, contact with their families, gang affiliation and gangs within the facilities, contraband within the facilities, treatment by staff, use of isolation within the facilities, and victimization experiences while in placement (including both property and violent crimes) (Sedlak and Bruce 2016; Sickmund and Puzzanchera 2014).

VICTIMIZATION SURVEYS

Crime data are gathered not only from police agencies and courts, but also from those who have been victimized. Begun in 1972, the National Crime Victimization Survey (NCVS) was developed to overcome problems with data from official sources (O'Brien 2000). Criminologists expected NCVS data to give a more accurate picture of crime than UCR data because the NCVS provided a systematic way to gather information about offenses unreported to law enforcement personnel and thus excluded from UCR data.

The NCVS is conducted by the U.S. Census Bureau, which selects the national sample and interviews respondents. In 2015, the sample consisted of 95,760 households, and 163,880 persons age 12 or older living in them (Truman and Morgan 2016). Households selected as part of the NCVS remain in the sample for three years, and individuals are interviewed twice a year. The first interview is conducted in person, and subsequent interviews are conducted either in person or by phone. The NCVS has a high response rate: In 2015, 82 percent of households and 86 percent of eligible individuals selected to participate in the NCVS actually completed the survey (Truman and Morgan 2016).

The NCVS asks respondents about personal crime victimizations (including rape and sexual assault, robbery, aggravated assault, simple assault, and "personal larceny" including purse snatching and pickpocketing) and property crime victimizations (including household burglary, motor vehicle theft, and other theft). During the interview process, one adult answers background questions about the household, such as family income and age and gender of all household members. That same respondent also answers questions about property crime victimizations during the previous six months. Each member of the household age 12 or older is interviewed individually about personal crime victimizations during the previous six months.

The primary objectives of the NCVS were to estimate the number and types of crimes unreported to police and to gather detailed information about the victims and consequences of crime—information not gathered by the UCR. Victimization surveys were designed to provide data about the following:

- **situational factors**, such as where the crime occurred, time of day at which it occurred, how many victims were involved, whether a weapon was used, self-protective actions by the victim, and the results of those actions.
- **victim characteristics**, such as gender, age, race, educational attainment, income, marital status, and relationship to the offender.
- **consequences of the victimization**, such as victim injuries and cost of medical expenses incurred.

Data from the NCVS enable researchers to estimate the likelihood of victimization for various types of crime for the U.S. population as a whole, and for specific demographic subgroups. For example, with data on victim characteristics, researchers can estimate how the likelihood of becoming a robbery victim differs for males and females.

Strengths of victimization surveys

The primary strength of the NCVS, and of victimization surveys in general, is their ability to provide information about crimes that victims do not report to police. According to NCVS data from 2015, victims reported to police only 35 percent of property crimes, 47 percent of violent crimes, and 55 percent of serious violent crimes (Truman and Morgan 2016). By surveying victims directly, the NCVS provides a systematic way to gain information about offenses that would otherwise go unnoticed in crime statistics.

Because the NCVS also gathers information about demographic characteristics of individuals and households that have been victimized, it offers insights into the risks of victimization. Using victimization survey data, researchers can determine how the risks of becoming the victim of various types of crime differ by social characteristics, such as age, gender, race, and social class.

Weaknesses of victimization surveys

The primary weakness of victimization surveys is that they include a more limited range of offenses than UCR data do. Victimization surveys omit homicide, most UCR Part II offenses, "victimless" crimes (e.g., drug use violations), and status offenses (e.g., curfew violations, running away) (O'Brien 1985). The NCVS includes questions about all UCR Part I offenses except homicide and arson, but the only Part II offense it includes is simple assault. Thus, by design, it excludes many crimes. Some types of crime, such as employee theft, income tax violations, and fraud, are difficult to assess from a victim's perspective.

Victimizations are sometimes omitted from NCVS data not by design, but because survey respondents do not report them. Some offenses may go unreported because the adult answering questions about household victimizations is unaware of all victimizations during the previous six months. Other offenses may go unreported because respondents choose not to reveal them. Despite revisions to the survey instrument, designed to encourage respondents to report personal crimes of violence, offenses such as sexual assault may be particularly likely to be under-reported. Such offenses, however, are more likely to be reported in NCVS data than in UCR data because victims are often reluctant to report sexual assaults to the police. Respondents may also under-report offenses because they know or are related to the offender (Turner 1972).

A second limitation of the NCVS is that it underestimates juvenile victimizations (Wells and Rankin 2001).[2] This is true, in part, because the NCVS excludes victims younger than 12 years of age and, in part, because young respondents appear reluctant to provide interviewers with information about crimes committed against them, especially given that those crimes are likely to have been committed by their peers or a family member (Wells and Rankin 2001).

A third weakness of victimization surveys is that they offer limited information about offenders. Obviously, victimization surveys can provide information about offender characteristics, such as gender, race, and estimated age, only for those offenses involving personal contact between offender and victim. In addition, these data on offender characteristics are reliable only to the extent that victims are able to describe *accurately* these characteristics.

Finally, victimization surveys have shortcomings inherent in the survey method. Perhaps the most important limitation is the problem of recall. Respondents may not accurately recall past victimizations and the details related to them. This problem intensifies as the length of time between the victimization event and the survey interview increases. The NCVS tries to minimize this problem by asking respondents only about victimizations that have occurred during the previous six months. Another problem of survey methodology is that respondents may not provide truthful responses to survey questions, or they may provide what they consider to be "socially desirable" responses. Respondents may also simply misunderstand the questions and so give incorrect answers.

SELF-REPORT SURVEYS

Self-report surveys are a third major source of data on delinquency. Their popularity grew in the 1960s and 1970s as researchers began to recognize the problems associated with official statistics and the ability of self-reports to overcome these problems. Rather than asking about victimizations, as in the NCVS, self-report surveys ask individuals directly, through either questionnaires or interviews, about their involvement in committing delinquent acts. Thus, these surveys avoid the filter of the criminal justice system and provide information about offenders, regardless of whether those offenders have been arrested or officially processed.

Self-report surveys provide demographic information about offenders, such as age, race, and gender, as well as information—unavailable through official data or victimization surveys—about personal characteristics of offenders, such as family background and social class. Importantly, self-report surveys enable researchers to explore the attitudes, beliefs, and motivations of offenders.

Self-report surveys can be either cross-sectional or longitudinal. A **cross-sectional survey** is one conducted at a single point in time. A cross-sectional design offers researchers a glimpse of a cross-section, or "slice," of the population at a particular time. Researchers must be extremely cautious when using cross-sectional data to try to address questions of causal order or change. A **longitudinal survey**, which gathers information from the same individuals at more than one point in time, is better suited to answer these questions. Longitudinal surveys are relatively expensive and complex to implement compared with cross-sectional surveys. Yet, longitudinal designs are used by researchers interested in processes of change and in crime and delinquency over the life course.

The Monitoring the Future (MTF) survey, which has been conducted annually since 1975, is an example of a self-report survey. MTF is designed to study beliefs, attitudes, and behavior of adolescents and young adults, and to monitor trends in substance use and delinquency across the United States. The project includes a series of surveys in which the same segments of the population—students in 8th, 10th, and 12th grades; college students; and young adults—are asked the same sets of questions each year. For example, high school seniors are asked annually about their involvement in several types of delinquent offenses. The data gathered show how different classes of high school seniors over the years compare to one another in terms of delinquent acts. The samples of respondents are selected so that they are representative of 8th, 10th, and 12th graders, college students, and young adults in the U.S. These data provide the only annual depiction of self-reported delinquency that is representative of a sizeable segment of youth in the U.S. We examine data from the MTF survey in the next chapter.

Strengths of self-report data

The primary strength of self-report data is that they offer information about the delinquent acts of youth who have not been arrested or officially processed. Thus, they provide a broader and less biased picture of delinquency in the U.S. than official data do. Self-reports also provide data about relatively minor forms of offending and drug and alcohol use. These behaviors are often omitted from official data because more serious offenses are most likely to lead to arrest. Because self-reports capture both minor and serious forms of offending, apart from the filter of criminal justice system processing, they reveal far more delinquency than do official data.

Self-report data also provide researchers with opportunities to consider questions they would be unable to address with either official or victimization data. In addition to questions about involvement in delinquency and drug use, self-report surveys may include questions regarding respondents' beliefs about law violation; perceptions of opportunities for success in school or work; and family interactions, such as parent–child attachment, parental supervision, and disciplinary practices. Answers to these types of questions are needed by researchers interested in testing various theories about the causes of delinquency.

Weaknesses of self-report data

Scholars have raised several concerns about self-report data on delinquency. Among the more serious concerns is the question of whether offenders will candidly report their involvement in delinquency—particularly offenses undetected by police. Some respondents may intentionally under-report their involvement in offending or may simply forget some of their offenses. The problem of recall may be worse for youth who have committed the most offenses (Blumstein et al. 1986). Other respondents may exaggerate their involvement in offending. A recent study suggests that over-reporting of arrests is almost as likely as under-reporting of arrests among adolescent respondents (Krohn et al. 2013). This study also found that respondents who were arrested more frequently were more likely to under-report their arrests.

A second weakness of self-report surveys concerns sampling design and its potential effects on survey responses. In many self-report studies, samples of respondents are drawn from student populations, and surveys are given in schools. Obviously, in these cases, individuals not attending school—including truants, dropouts, and institutionalized youth—are excluded from the samples. Thus, the individuals excluded may be those most likely to be delinquent (Harris and Shaw 2000).

The selection of samples of respondents in school settings also results in samples that are fairly similar in many respects (Kleck 1982). For example, a researcher who draws a sample from a single high school should not expect much variation among respondents in social class, because students who reside in the same neighborhood probably have relatively similar family incomes. The problem with fairly homogeneous samples is that they prevent researchers from exploring the full range of possible responses to some questions. Suppose a researcher is interested in the relationship between social class and delinquency and draws a sample of respondents from a school in a lower-class neighborhood. That researcher will be unable to draw conclusions about the offending of middle- and upper-class individuals because the responses to survey questions about social class will be limited mostly to those indicating lower-class status.

A third criticism of self-report surveys is that *some* fail to capture the full range of delinquent behaviors and focus instead on relatively minor offenses, such as underage drinking, truancy, and petty theft (Morenoff 2005). Serious or violent delinquency is relatively rare, so it is difficult to detect many serious offenses with self-reports, even with fairly large samples. The exclusion of serious offenses limits researchers' abilities to address theoretically significant questions and to compare self-reports of offending to official or victimization data, which better represent serious delinquency.

Finally, self-report surveys have been criticized for reasons of both validity and reliability. **Validity** is the extent to which a measurement instrument measures what it is supposed to measure (Vogt and Johnson 2011). For example, questions about the number of times a respondent has stolen something or damaged someone else's property would be valid measures of delinquency. Questions about lying to parents, however, would not be valid measures of delinquent behavior, because even though lying might be related to delinquency, it is not itself a delinquent act. The validity of measures is compromised when respondents systematically under-report or over-report their delinquent acts. Validity is also threatened when respondents have limited recall or forget past behaviors or when they misunderstand survey questions. For example, if we ask survey respondents to report the number of times they engaged in delinquency in the past two years, the time frame is probably too long for them to be able to provide accurate responses, and so the measure may not be valid.

EXPANDING IDEAS: SOURCES OF DATA ON DELINQUENCY

	Strengths	Weaknesses
"Official data"*	• UCR program provides uniform, nationwide data. • Can be used to explore trends in crime and delinquency rates. • Provide demographic information about individuals brought into juvenile justice systems.	• Exclude offenses and offenders that do not come to the attention of police or enter juvenile justice systems. • Policing practices influence official data, including data on the demographic characteristics of individuals who are arrested. • May be manipulated by law enforcement agencies for political purposes.
Victimization surveys	• Provide information about crimes that victims do not report to police. • Can be used to estimate the risks of victimization based on demographic characteristics.	• Include a more limited range of offenses than UCR data do. • May underestimate victimizations, including juvenile victimizations, if individuals are unwilling to report them or are unaware of all household victimizations. • Offer limited information about offenders.
Self-report surveys	• Avoid the filter of the juvenile justice system and provide information about the delinquent acts of youth who have not been arrested or officially processed. • Provide data about relatively minor forms of offending. • May include a broad range of questions that enable researchers to test various theories about the causes of delinquency.	• Possibility of juveniles inaccurately reporting their involvement in offending. • Sampling designs (e.g., surveys given in schools) may result in the exclusion of individuals most likely to be delinquent and in fairly homogeneous samples. • May fail to capture the full range of delinquent behaviors and focus instead on relatively minor offenses.

* Several sources provide "official data" on delinquency: the Uniform Crime Reporting (UCR) program, in which law enforcement agencies report crime data to the FBI; juvenile court records, which are used to compile *Juvenile Court Statistics*; and the Office of Juvenile Justice and Delinquency Prevention databases on youth in custody.

To assess the validity of self-reports of delinquency, researchers have compared responses from self-report surveys to official police and court records. These researchers have found relatively strong relationships between official records and self-reported delinquency, indicating that those most likely to report involvement in delinquent behavior were also those most likely to have official records of offending (Thornberry and Krohn 2002; Paschall, Ornstein, and Flewelling 2001; Farrington et al. 1996; but see also Kirk 2006). Based on this finding, researchers have concluded that most self-report surveys provide reasonably valid measures of delinquency.

There has been conflicting research, however, about racial differences in the validity of self-reports of delinquency. Early research in the 1980s compared self-reports and official records and suggested that self-reports may be less valid for blacks than for whites because black males tended to under-report their involvement in serious or violent offenses (Huizinga and Elliott 1984, 1986; Hindelang, Hirschi, and Weis 1981; Hindelang 1981). But more recent research since the mid-1990s shows that the validity of self-reports of delinquency is high for both blacks and whites, particularly when data are collected in computerized ways that enhance the privacy of responses (Piquero, MacIntosh, and Hickman 2002; Thornberry and Krohn 2002; Paschall et al. 2001; Maxfield, Weiler, and Widom 2000; Farrington et al. 1996). For example, Krohn and his colleagues (2013) found that, once they took into account an individual's number of prior arrests, race had no effect on under-reporting or over-reporting of arrests.

Reliability is the extent to which repeated measurements of a concept produce the same or similar responses over time. Suppose, for example, an individual takes an IQ test once each year for three years. She scores 132 on the first test, 92 on the second test, and 153 on the third. These three tests are not reliable measures of IQ because of the great variation in scores over time.

Reliability is a concern with self-report surveys for two reasons. First, in longitudinal surveys, repeated measurement itself can affect responses, leading to a decline in the reporting of delinquency at later rounds of data collection and therefore to unreliable estimates of the true amount of delinquency (Lauritsen 1998). Second, reliability is related to sample size. The smaller the sample size, the greater the likelihood of differences in responses due to chance, and the less reliable the measures. Most self-report surveys are conducted with relatively small samples. In addition, serious offenses are relatively rare events, so respondents in a typical self-report survey are unlikely to report involvement in many serious delinquent acts. Thus, small sample sizes, combined with the rarity of serious crime, may decrease the reliability of measures of serious offending in self-report surveys. Although researchers must consider reliability issues when using self-report data, in general, self-report surveys yield "impressive" levels of reliability for delinquency measures (Huizinga and Elliott 1986; Hindelang et al. 1981).

The box insert entitled "Expanding ideas: Sources of data on delinquency" summarizes the strengths and weaknesses of the three primary sources of data on delinquency.

COMPARING DATA SOURCES

What do we see when we compare the pictures of delinquency presented by the three primary data sources?[3]

Comparing UCR and NCVS data

Both UCR and NCVS data are better measures of serious offending than of minor crime and delinquency. The NCVS, by design, includes only relatively serious offenses, and UCR data are available only for offenses known to police, which are likely to be more serious offenses. But because victimization surveys include offenses unknown to police, we should expect them to reveal more offenses than UCR data do. This is, in fact, the case. NCVS estimates suggest that the actual amount of crime is approximately two to four times higher than official statistics suggest, depending on the offense (Wells and Rankin 2001). For example, UCR data for 2015 report 124,047 rapes/sexual assaults, 327,374 robberies, and 1,579,527 burglaries (FBI 2016: Table 1). NCVS data for 2015 show far more offenses: 431,840 rapes/sexual assaults, 578,580 robberies, and 2,904,570 household burglaries (Truman and Morgan 2016:2, 5). Research using NCVS data suggests that, in recent decades, significant increases have occurred in the likelihood of reporting crimes to the police, for both violent and property offenses (Baumer and Lauritsen 2010).

Comparing self-report data to UCR and NCVS data

Self-report data tend to include relatively minor forms of offending, while UCR and NCVS data tend to include more serious forms of offending. Also, self-report surveys are usually given to samples of respondents of a narrow age range, so these data are more limited than UCR or NCVS data (O'Brien 2000). Given these factors, it is somewhat difficult to compare these data sources. The National Youth Survey (NYS), however, contains questions about some serious offenses, such as aggravated assault and drug distribution, which have allowed researchers to compare data from the NYS with UCR and NCVS data.

Given that UCR data represent only crimes known to police, it is not surprising that the NYS reveals much higher rates of offending than do UCR data. Robert O'Brien (2000) examined aggravated assault rates in UCR, NCVS, and NYS data for 1980. The NYS revealed an aggravated assault rate of 1,400 per 10,000 (for 15–21 year-olds), whereas the NCVS and UCR showed rates of 90.3 and 29.9 per 10,000, respectively, for the same year. If the NCVS and UCR data were limited to the same ages represented in the NYS (ages 15–21), the aggravated assault rates in these two sources would be much higher. But these rates still would not come close to the self-report rate (O'Brien 2000). Clearly, compared with self-report data, the UCR and NCVS underestimate some types of offenses.

In a 2003 study, David Farrington and his colleagues compared conclusions about delinquent careers derived from official data (court referrals) with those derived from self-reports. They used longitudinal data from the Seattle Social Development Project, which began in 1985 and included both self-report and court referral data for 808 youths who were ages 11 to 17. The two data sources agreed about some aspects of delinquent careers and disagreed about others. Self-reports and court referrals both showed that the proportion of the sample involved in offending increased during the juvenile years, and that the younger the age at which an individual began offending, the larger the number of offenses committed. When compared to court referral data, however, self-reports showed a higher proportion of the sample involved in offending, a higher frequency of offending among those who committed offenses, offending beginning at younger ages, and less continuity in offending over time (Farrington et al. 2003). In a recent study, Alex Piquero and his colleagues compared official arrest data with self-reports of arrest over a seven-year period. They found moderate agreement between these two data sources. In addition, this level of agreement was fairly stable over time, and was similar across race, ethnicity, and gender (Piquero, Schubert, and Brame 2014).

All three data sources (UCR, NCVS, and self-report surveys) reveal similar patterns in the demographic characteristics of those who commit *serious* crimes. For serious crimes, all three data sources show that, relative to their proportions in the population, males, African Americans, and the young commit substantially more offenses than do females, whites, and older persons (O'Brien 2000).

SUMMARY AND CONCLUSIONS

In this chapter, we examined the three primary sources of data on delinquency and juvenile justice: agencies within the criminal justice system that provide official data, victimization surveys, and self-report surveys of offenders. We discussed the strengths and weaknesses of each data source and tried to convey how each is best suited to address particular types of questions about delinquency and offenders. When evaluating data on delinquency, it is important to keep in mind the strengths and weaknesses of the data source and to consider what that source is designed to tell us about delinquency. Official data tell us about delinquency that is recorded by agencies of the juvenile justice system. Victimization surveys tell us about delinquency that people experience as victims. Self-report surveys tell us about delinquent acts that youth themselves report having committed, even if the offenses are not known to police.

READING 4.1

JUVENILE COURT STATISTICS 2014.

Sarah Hockenberry and Charles Puzzanchera. 2017. Pittsburgh, PA: National Center for Juvenile Justice. (Pages 1–4)

The following excerpt is from the Juvenile Court Statistics 2014 report completed by researchers at the National Center for Juvenile Justice. This selection describes how data for this report are gathered, processed, and analyzed, and what the data represent in terms of cases handled in juvenile courts.

This report describes delinquency and status offense cases handled between 2005 and 2014 by U.S. courts with juvenile jurisdiction. Courts with juvenile jurisdiction may handle a variety of matters, including child maltreatment, traffic violations, child support, and adoptions. This report focuses on cases involving juveniles charged with law violations (delinquency or status offenses). . . .

Coverage

A basic question for this reporting series is what constitutes a referral to juvenile court. The answer depends partly on how each jurisdiction organizes its case-screening function. In many communities, an intake unit within the juvenile court first screens all juvenile matters. The intake unit determines whether the matter should be handled informally (i.e., diverted) or petitioned for formal handling. In data files from communities using this type of system, a delinquency or status offense case is defined as a court referral at the point of initial screening, regardless of whether it is handled formally or informally.

In other communities, the juvenile court is not involved in delinquency or status offense matters until another agency (e.g., the prosecutor's office or a social service agency) has first screened the case. In other words, the intake function is performed outside the court, and some matters are diverted to other agencies without the court ever handling them. Status offense cases, in particular, tend to be diverted from court processing in this manner.

Since its inception, *Juvenile Court Statistics* has adapted to the changing structure of juvenile court processing nationwide. As court processing became more diverse, the *JCS* series broadened its definition of the juvenile court to incorporate other agencies that perform what can generically be considered juvenile court functions. In some communities, data collection has expanded to include departments of youth services, child welfare agencies, and prosecutors' offices. In other communities, this expansion has not been possible. Therefore, while there is extensive data coverage in the *JCS* series of formally handled delinquency cases and adequate data coverage of informally handled delinquency cases and formally handled status offense cases, the data coverage of informally handled status offense cases is limited and is not sufficient to support the generation of national estimates. For this reason, *JCS* reports do not present any information on informally handled status offense cases. . . .

Juvenile court processing

Any attempt to describe juvenile court caseloads at the national level must be based on a generic model of court processing to serve as a common framework. In order to analyze and present data about juvenile court activities in diverse jurisdictions, the Archive strives to fit the processing characteristics of all jurisdictions into the following general model:

Intake. An intake department (either within or outside the court) first screens referred cases. The intake department may decide to dismiss the case for lack of legal sufficiency or to resolve the matter formally or informally. Informal (i.e., nonpetitioned) dispositions may include a voluntary referral to a social service agency, informal probation, or the payment of fines or some form of voluntary restitution. Formally handled cases are petitioned and scheduled in court for an adjudicatory or waiver hearing.

Judicial waiver. The intake department may decide that a case should be removed from juvenile court and handled instead in criminal (adult) court. In such cases, a petition is usually filed in juvenile court asking the juvenile court judge to waive juvenile court jurisdiction over the case. The juvenile court judge decides whether the case merits criminal prosecution.[1] When a waiver request is denied, the matter is usually then scheduled for an adjudicatory hearing in the juvenile court.

Petitioning. If the intake department decides that a case should be handled formally within the juvenile court, a petition is filed and the case is placed on the court calendar (or docket) for an adjudicatory hearing. A small number of petitions are dismissed for various reasons before an adjudicatory hearing is actually held.

Adjudication. At the adjudicatory hearing, a juvenile may be adjudicated (judged) a delinquent or status offender, and the case would then proceed to a disposition hearing. Alternatively, a case can be dismissed or continued in contemplation of dismissal. In these cases, the court often recommends that the juvenile take some actions prior to the final adjudication decision, such as paying restitution or voluntarily attending drug counseling.

Disposition. At the disposition hearing, the juvenile court judge determines the most appropriate sanction, generally after reviewing a predisposition report prepared by a probation department. The range of options available to a court typically includes commitment to an institution; placement in a group home or other residential facility or perhaps in a foster home; probation (either regular or intensive supervision); referral to an outside agency, day treatment, or mental health program; or imposition of a fine, community service, or restitution. Disposition orders often involve multiple sanctions and/or conditions. Review hearings are held to monitor the juvenile's progress. Dispositions may be modified as a result. This report includes only the most severe initial disposition in each case.

Detention. A juvenile may be placed in a detention facility at different points as a case progresses through the juvenile justice system. Detention practices also vary from jurisdiction to jurisdiction. A judicial decision to detain or continue detention may occur before or after adjudication or disposition. This report includes only those detention actions that result in a juvenile being placed in a restrictive facility under court authority while awaiting the outcome of the court process. This report does not include detention decisions made by law enforcement officials prior to court intake or those occurring after the disposition of a case (e.g., temporary holding of a juvenile in a detention facility while awaiting court-ordered placement elsewhere).

Data quality

Juvenile Court Statistics relies on the secondary analysis of data originally compiled by juvenile courts or juvenile justice agencies to meet their own information and reporting needs. Although these incoming data files are not uniform across jurisdictions, they are likely to be more detailed and accurate than data files compiled by local jurisdictions merely complying with a mandated national reporting program.

The heterogeneity of the contributed data files greatly increases the complexity of the Archive's data-processing tasks. Contributing jurisdictions collect and report information using their own definitions and coding categories. Therefore, the detail reported in some data sets is not contained in others. Even when similar data elements are used, they may have inconsistent definitions or overlapping coding categories. The Archive restructures contributed data into standardized coding categories in order to combine information from multiple sources. The standardization process requires an intimate understanding of the development, structure, and content of each data set received. Codebooks and operation manuals are studied, data providers interviewed, and data files analyzed to maximize the understanding of each information system. Every attempt is made to ensure that only compatible information from the various data sets is used in the standardized data files.

While the heterogeneity of the data adds complexity to the development of a national data file, it has proven to be valuable in other ways. The diversity of the data stored in the National Juvenile Court Data Archive enables the data to support a wider range of research efforts than would a uniform, and probably more general, data collection form. For example, the Federal Bureau of Investigation's (FBI's) Uniform Crime Reporting (UCR) Program is limited by necessity to a small number of relatively broad offense codes. The UCR offense code for larceny-theft combines shoplifting with a number of other larcenies. Thus, the data are useless for studies of shoplifting. In comparison, many of the Archive's data sets are sufficiently detailed to enable a researcher to distinguish offenses that are often combined in other reporting series – shoplifting can be distinguished from other larcenies, joyriding from motor vehicle theft, and armed robbery from unarmed robbery. The diversity of these coding structures allows researchers to construct data sets that contain the detail demanded by their research designs.

Validity of the estimates

The national delinquency and status offense estimates presented in this report were generated with data from a large nonprobability sample of juvenile courts. Therefore, statistical confidence in the estimates cannot be mathematically determined. Although statistical confidence would be greater if a probability sampling design were used, the cost of such an effort has long been considered prohibitive. Secondary analysis of available data is the best practical alternative for developing an understanding of the nation's juvenile courts.

National estimates of delinquency cases for 2014 are based on analyses of individual case records from more than 2,200 courts and aggregate court-level data on cases from more than 200 additional courts. Together, these courts had jurisdiction over 84% of the U.S. juvenile population in 2014. National estimates of petitioned status offense cases for 2014 are based on case records from more than 2,100 courts and court-level data from 159 additional courts, covering 78% of the juvenile population. The imputation and weighting procedures that generate national estimates from these samples control for many factors: the size of a community, the age and race composition of its juvenile population, the volume of cases referred to the reporting courts, the age and race of the juveniles involved, the offense characteristics of the cases, the courts' responses to the cases (manner of handling, detention, adjudication, and disposition), and the nature of each court's jurisdictional responsibilities (i.e., upper age of original jurisdiction). . . .

Data access

The data used in this report are stored in the National Juvenile Court Data Archive at the National Center for Juvenile Justice (NCJJ) in Pittsburgh, PA. The Archive contains the most detailed information available on juveniles involved in the juvenile justice system and on the activities of U.S. juvenile courts. Designed to facilitate research on the juvenile justice system, the Archive's data files are available to policymakers, researchers, and students. In addition to national data files, state and local data can be provided to researchers. . . .

Other sources of juvenile court data

With support from OJJDP, NCJJ has developed two web-based data analysis and dissemination applications that provide access to the data used for this report. The first of these applications, *Easy Access to Juvenile Court Statistics 1985–2014,* was developed to facilitate independent analysis of the national delinquency estimates presented in this report while eliminating the need for statistical analysis software. It also enables users to view preformatted tables, beyond those included in this report, describing the demographic characteristics of youth involved in the juvenile justice system and how juvenile courts process these cases. The second application, *Easy Access to State and County Juvenile Court Case Counts*, presents annual counts of the delinquency, status offense, and dependency cases processed in juvenile courts, by state and county. These applications are available from OJJDP's Statistical Briefing Book at ojjdp.gov/ojstatbb.

Endnote

1 Mechanisms of transfer to criminal court vary by state. In some states, a prosecutor has the authority to file juvenile cases directly in criminal court if they meet specified criteria. This report, however, includes only cases that were initially under juvenile court jurisdiction and were transferred as a result of judicial waiver.

READING 4.2

JUVENILE OFFENDERS AND VICTIMS: 2014 NATIONAL REPORT.

Melissa Sickmund and Charles Puzzanchera (eds.). 2014. Pittsburgh, PA: National Center for Juvenile Justice. (Pages 39, 40, 61, 63–65, 116, 117, 150, 186)

The following excerpts are from the comprehensive national report on juvenile offenders and victims published by the National Center for Juvenile Justice. These selections describe various data sources (victimization and self-report surveys, and official data from law enforcement agencies and juvenile courts) used to gather data on juvenile offending. The excerpts also reveal what various sources tell us about the extent of juvenile delinquency and victimization.

Trends in violent victimization of juveniles*

Since 1973, the Bureau of Justice Statistics (BJS) has used the National Crime Victimization Survey (NCVS) to monitor the level of violent crime in the U.S. NCVS gathers information on crimes against persons ages 12 and older from a nationally representative sample of households. NCVS is critical for understanding the volume and nature of crimes against juveniles ages 12–17 as well as trends in these crimes. A major limitation, however, is that crimes against youth younger than age 12 are not captured.

Juveniles are more likely than adults to be victims of violence

NCVS monitors nonfatal violent victimizations (i.e., the crimes of rape, sexual assault, robbery, aggravated assault, and simple assault). A 2012 BJS report summarized NCVS data for the years 1994–2010 to document trends in nonfatal violent victimizations of youth ages 12–17. The report found that youth experienced relatively high levels of violent crimes during the mid-1990s but their rate of victimization had declined substantially through 2010.

On average from 1994 through 2010, youth ages 12–17 were about 2.2 times more likely than adults (i.e., ages 18 and older) to be victims of a serious[1] violent crime. That means, in 2010, in comparable rates of youth ages 12–17, 14 experienced serious violent victimizations, compared with about 7 persons ages 18 and older. Similarly, on average, youth were 2.6 times more likely than adults to be victims of a simple assault.

Between 1994 and 2010, victimization rates for serious violence and simple assault declined for all youth

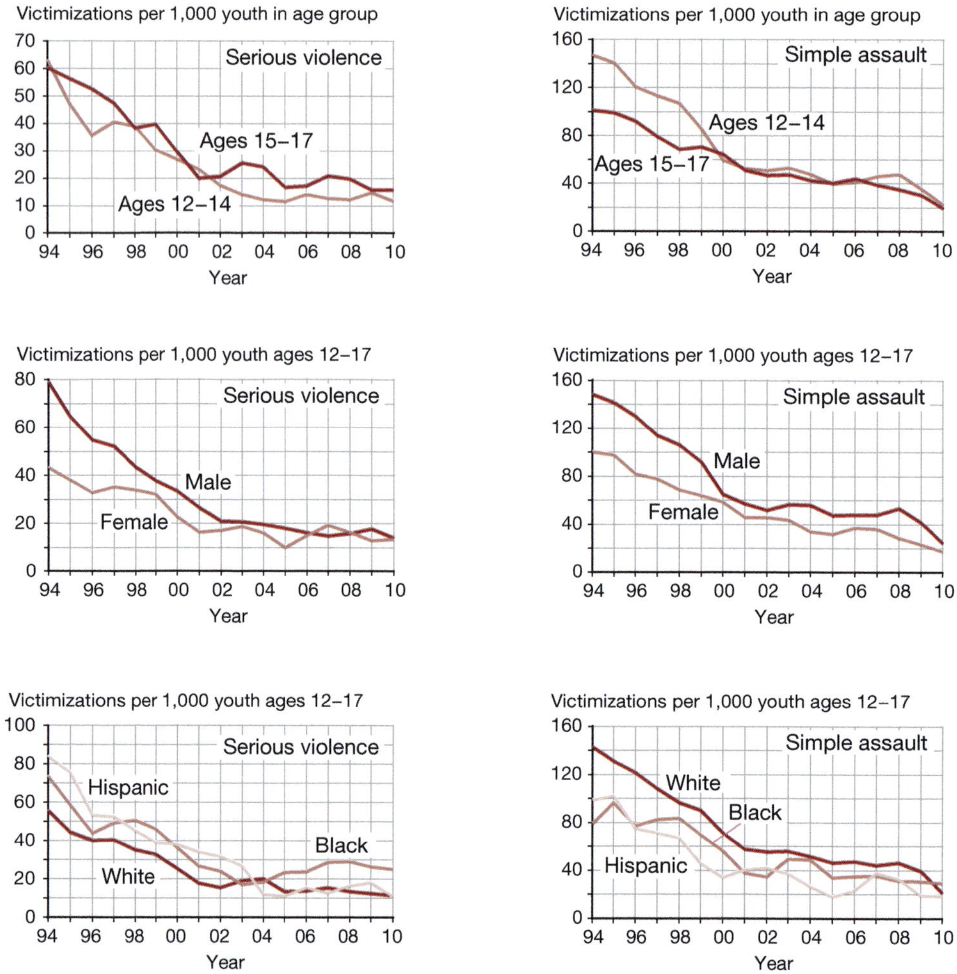

- Most of the decline in both serious violence and simple assault victimization rates took place between 1994 and 2002. During this period, the rate of serious violence against youth ages 12–17 fell 69% and simple assault fell 61%, compared with 27% and 56%, respectively, between 2002 and 2010.
- The relative decline in simple assault victimization rates between 1994 and 2010 was about the same for male (83%) and female (82%) youth, while the decline in the serious violence rate for males (82%) outpaced that of females (69%).
- Among race/ethnicity groups, black non-Hispanic youth had the highest rates of serious violence and simple assault in 2010. Black non-Hispanic youth were more than twice as likely to be victims of serious violence in 2010 as were white non-Hispanic or Hispanic youth and at least 30% more likely to be victims of simple assault.

Source: Authors' adaptation of White and Lauritsen's *Violent Crime Against Youth, 1994–2010.*

In 1994, youth ages 12–17 experienced comparable rates of serious violence committed by strangers and nonstrangers (28.2 vs. 32.4 per 1,000). Between 1994 and 2010, the rate of serious violent crimes committed by strangers declined 84% while the rate for nonstrangers declined 73% so that, by 2010, the rate of serious violence committed by nonstrangers was twice the rate committed by strangers (8.9 vs. 4.5). In 2010, the rate of simple assault committed by nonstrangers was 1.5 times the rate committed by strangers, compared with 2.4 in 1994.

Male and female youth were equally likely to be victims of serious violence in 2010

In 1994, male juveniles were nearly twice as likely to be victims of serious violence as were females (79.4 per 1,000 vs. 43.6 per 1,000, respectively). However, following the relatively larger decline in the serious violence victimization rate among male juveniles (down 82%, compared with 69% for females), the difference in victimization rates for male and female youth was nearly erased by 2010 (14.3 vs. 13.7, respectively). In contrast, 2010 victimization rates for simple assault showed greater gender disparity, as male youth were 36% more likely to be victimized than females (24.8 vs. 18.2).

The rates of serious violence against male and female youth committed by a nonintimate partner were higher than the rates committed by an intimate partner, and female youth were more likely to be victimized by an intimate partner than were males. The same pattern held true for victims of simple assault.

Between 1994 and 2010, rates of serious violence against youth that involved a weapon (e.g., firearm, knife, or club) decreased by 80% (from 40.7 per 1,000 to 8.1). During the same time period, violent crime resulting in serious injuries (broken bones, concussions, or gunshot or stab wounds) declined 63% (from 3.6 to 1.3).

Serious violence committed against youth declined for all locations

In 2010, youth living in urban areas were at greater risk (19.1 per 1,000 youth) of serious violence than youth in suburban (11.7) or rural (12.6) areas. Between 1994 and 2010, the rate of serious violence against juveniles declined 81% in suburban areas, 76% in urban areas, and 72% in rural areas. Youth living in urban areas were also at greater risk (25.2) of simple assault than youth in suburban (22.0) or rural (14.0) areas. The rate of simple assaults decreased at least 80% for each area between 1994 and 2010.

The rate of serious violence at school declined by nearly two-thirds (63%) between 1994 and 2010 and the rate committed in nonschool locations (e.g., parks, playgrounds, or a residence) declined 83%. By 2010, the rate of serious violence at school (6.6) was comparable to the rate at nonschool locations (7.4). Simple assault rates decreased at a similar pace for both school and nonschool locations during the period (81% for school and 85% for nonschool).

In 2010, youth ages 12–17 were at greatest risk of both serious violence and simple assault during the after-school hours of 3 p.m. to 6 p.m. During this time period, youth were 11 times more likely to be victims of either a serious violent act or a simple assault than the period from 9 p.m. to 6 a.m.

Declines in serious violence were similar for white, black, and Hispanic youth

Over the 1994–2010 period, the rate of serious violence declined for all race/ethnicity groups, but the decline was greater for Hispanic youth (87%) than for white non-Hispanic (79%) and black non-Hispanic (66%) youth.

However, in 2010, the rate of serious violence against black youth (25.4) was twice the rate of white (11.7) and Hispanic (11.3) youth. In comparison, black youth in 1994 were 30% more likely to experience serious violence than their white counterparts but 12% less likely than Hispanic youth. The increasing disparity in rates of serious violence against black youth and youth of other racial or ethnic groups is primarily associated with patterns of change that occurred from 2002 to 2010. Specifically, rates of serious violence against white youth and Hispanic youth generally declined throughout the 1994–2010 period, but the rate for black youth declined through 2002 and then increased through 2010. The 2010 simple assault rates for black non-Hispanic youth (29.9) also were higher than those for white non-Hispanic (21.5) and Hispanic (19.0) youth.

Declines in serious violence were similar for juveniles and adults

From 1994 to 2010, rates of serious violence against youth declined across all crime types, a pattern that was replicated among adult victims. During this period, rates of serious violence against youth and adults experienced similar declines (77% and 73%, respectively). Similarly, rates of simple assault victimization decreased (83% for juveniles and 71% for adults).

Serious violent victimization rate (per 1,000 in age group)				
	Juveniles		Adults	
Offense	1994	2010	1994	2010
Serious violence	62.0	14.0	24.1	6.5
Rape/sexual assault	7.0	2.2	3.3	1.0
Robbery	20.1	4.7	6.7	2.1
Aggravated assault	34.8	7.1	14.1	3.3
Simple assault	125.2	21.6	43.3	12.8

Between 1994 and 2010, youth victimization rates for rape/sexual assault declined 68%, robbery declined 77%, and aggravated assault declined 80%. . . .

Prevalence of school-related crime*

The Centers for Disease Control and Prevention's Youth Risk Behavior Survey (YRBS) monitors health risk behaviors that contribute to the leading causes of death, injury, and social problems among youth in the U.S. Every 2 years, YRBS provides data representative of 9th–12th graders in public and private schools nationwide. The 2011 survey included responses from 5,425 students from 43 states and 21 large cities.

More than 3 in 10 high school students were in a physical fight—1 in 25 were injured

According to the 2011 survey, 33% of high school students said they had been in one or more physical fights during the past 12 months. This is consistent with data from the 2003 survey.

Percent of students who were in a physical fight in the past year			
Demographic	Total	Male	Female
Total	32.8%	40.7%	24.4%
9th grade	37.7	46.0	28.8
10th grade	35.3	44.2	25.5
11th grade	29.7	36.3	22.7
12th grade	26.9	34.1	19.4
White	29.4	37.7	20.4
Black	39.1	45.8	32.3
Hispanic	36.8	44.4	28.7

Percent of students who were injured in a physical fight in the past year			
Demographic	Total	Male	Female
Total	3.9%	5.1%	2.6%
9th grade	4.4	5.9	2.7
10th grade	4.1	5.1	3.0
11th grade	3.6	4.8	2.2
12th grade	3.3	4.3	2.1
White	2.8	3.5	1.9
Black	5.7	8.1	3.2
Hispanic	5.5	7.0	3.7

Regardless of grade level or race/ethnicity, males were more likely than females to engage in fighting. Fighting was more common among black and Hispanic students than white students.

Although physical fighting was fairly common among high school students, the proportion of students treated by a doctor or nurse was relatively small (4%). Males were more likely than females to have been injured in a fight. Black and Hispanic students were more likely than white students to suffer fight injuries.

Nationwide, 12% of high school students had been in a physical fight on school property one or more times in the 12 months preceding the survey, down from 16% in 1993. Male students were substantially more likely to fight at school than female students at all grade levels and across racial/ethnic groups. Black and Hispanic students were more likely to fight at school. Fighting at school decreased as grade level increased.

Percent of students who were in a physical fight in school in the past year			
Demographic	Total	Male	Female
Total	12.0%	16.0%	7.8%
9th grade	16.2	21.7	0.4
10th grade	12.8	17.0	8.0
11th grade	9.2	12.3	6.0
12th grade	8.8	11.4	6.1
White	9.9	13.8	5.6
Black	16.4	19.6	13.1
Hispanic	14.4	19.4	9.0

Fewer than 3 in 10 high school students had property stolen or vandalized at school

High school students were less likely to experience property crime than fights at school. Nationally, 26% said they had property such as a car, clothing, or books stolen or deliberately damaged on school property one or more times during the past 12 months. A greater proportion of male than female students experienced such property crimes at school, regardless of grade level or race/ethnicity.

Percent of students who had property stolen or deliberately damaged at school in the past year			
Demographic	**Total**	**Male**	**Female**
Total	26.1%	28.8%	23.4%
9th grade	26.6	27.7	25.5
10th grade	30.6	33.4	27.4
11th grade	23.5	26.7	20.1
12th grade	23.3	26.9	19.5
White	24.0	26.8	21.0
Black	27.3	28.7	25.9
Hispanic	30.7	33.3	27.8

Fear of school-related crime kept 6 in 100 high schoolers home at least once in the past month

Nationwide in 2011, 6% of high school students missed at least 1 day of school in the past 30 days because they felt unsafe at school or when traveling to or from school, up from 4% in 1993. Hispanic and black students were more likely than white students to have missed school because they felt unsafe. Sophomores were more likely than other high school students to miss school because of safety concerns.

Percent of students who felt too unsafe to go to school in the past 30 days			
Demographic	**Total**	**Male**	**Female**
Total	5.9%	5.8%	6.0%
9th grade	5.8	5.4	6.3
10th grade	6.8	6.4	7.1
11th grade	5.2	5.3	5.1
12th grade	5.5	5.9	5.1
White	4.4	4.0	4.7
Black	6.7	8.0	5.3
Hispanic	9.1	8.5	9.6

The proportion of high school students who said they avoided school because of safety concerns ranged from 3% to 9% across state surveys. . . .

Prevalence of drug use among students*

Each year, the Monitoring the Future (MTF) Study asks a nationally representative sample of nearly 50,000 secondary school students in approximately 400 public and private schools to describe their drug use patterns through self-administered questionnaires. Surveying seniors since 1975, the study expanded in 1991 to include 8th and 10th graders. By design, MTF excludes dropouts and institutionalized, homeless, and runaway youth.

Half of seniors in 2010 said they had used illicit drugs

In 2010, nearly half (48%) of all seniors said they had at least tried illicit drugs. The figure was 37% for 10th graders and 21% for 8th graders. Marijuana is by far the most commonly used illicit drug. In 2010, 44% of high school seniors said they had tried marijuana. About half of those in each grade who said they had used marijuana said they had not used any other illicit drug.

Put another way, about half of the 8th, 10th, and 12th graders who have ever used an illicit drug have used something in addition to, or other than, marijuana. About 1 in 4 seniors (25%) (or half of seniors who used any illicit drugs) used an illicit drug other than marijuana. Almost half of high school seniors had used marijuana at least once, 35% used it in the past year, and 21% used it in the previous month. MTF also asked students if they had used marijuana on 20 or more occasions in the previous 30 days. In 2010, 6% of high school seniors said they had used marijuana that frequently.

In 2010, 13% of high school seniors reported using a narcotic such as Vicodin, Percocet, or OxyContin at least once, making narcotics other than heroin the second most prevalent illicit drug after marijuana. Almost 4% of seniors reported using narcotics in the past month. Amphetamines were the next most prevalent drugs after narcotics other than heroin: 11% of seniors reported using amphetamines at least once. Specifically, 2% had used methamphetamine at least once and 2% had used ice (crystal methamphetamine). About 3% of high school seniors reported using amphetamines in the past month.

In 2010, 6% of seniors said they had used cocaine at least once in their life. More than half of this group (3% of all seniors) said they used it in the previous year, and less than one-quarter of users (1% of seniors) had used it in the preceding 30 days. About 2% of seniors reported previous use of crack cocaine: 1% in the previous year, and less than 1% in the previous month. Heroin was the least commonly used illicit drug, with less than 2% of seniors reporting they had used it at least once. More than half of seniors who reported heroin use said they used it only without a needle.

Alcohol and tobacco use is widespread at all grade levels

In 2010, 7 in 10 high school seniors said they had tried alcohol at least once; 2 in 5 said they used it in the previous month. Even among 10th graders, the use of alcohol was common: more than half had tried alcohol, and almost one-third used it in the month prior to the survey.

Perhaps of greater concern are the juveniles who indicated heavy drinking (defined as five or more drinks in a row) in the preceding 2 weeks. Twenty-three percent (23%) of seniors, 16% of 10th graders, and 7% of 8th graders reported recent heavy drinking.

More high school seniors use marijuana on a daily basis than drink alcohol daily

	Proportion of seniors in 2010 who used			
Substance	**in lifetime**	**in last year**	**in last month**	**daily***
Alcohol	71.0%	65.2%	41.2%	2.7%
Been drunk	54.1	44.0	26.8	1.6
Cigarettes	42.2	–	19.2	10.7
Marijuana/hashish	43.8	34.8	21.4	6.1
Amphetamines	11.1	7.4	3.3	0.3
Narcotics, not heroin	13.0	8.7	3.6	0.2
Inhalants	9.0	3.6	1.4	0.1
Tranquilizers	8.5	5.6	2.5	0.1
Sedatives	7.5	4.8	2.2	0.1
MDMA (ecstasy)	7.3	4.5	1.4	0.1
Cocaine, not crack	5.5	2.9	1.3	0.2
Methamphetamine	2.3	1.0	0.5	0.1
LSD	4.0	2.6	0.8	0.1
Crystal methamphetamine	1.8	0.9	0.6	0.1
Crack cocaine	2.4	1.4	0.7	0.2
Steroids	2.0	1.5	1.1	0.4
PCP	1.8	1.0	0.8	0.2
Heroin	1.6	0.9	0.4	0.1

- More than 1 in 4 seniors said they were drunk at least once in the past month.

* Used on 20 or more occasions in the last 30 days or had 1 or more cigarettes per day in the last 30 days.

– Not included in survey.

Source: Authors' adaptation of Johnston et al.'s *Monitoring the Future National Survey on Drug Use, 1975–2010. Volume I: Secondary School Students.*

Tobacco use was less prevalent than alcohol use, but it was the most likely substance to be used on a daily basis. In 2010, 42% of 12th graders, 30% of 10th graders, and 18% of 8th graders had tried cigarettes, and 19% of seniors, 12% of 10th graders, and 6% of 8th graders smoked in the preceding month. In addition, 11% of seniors, 7% of 10th graders, and 3% of 8th graders reported currently smoking cigarettes on a daily basis. Overall, based on various measures, tobacco use is down compared with use levels in the early to mid-1990s.

Higher proportions of males than females were involved in drug and alcohol use, especially heavy use

In 2010, males were more likely than females to drink alcohol at all and to drink heavily. Among seniors, 44% of males and 38% of females reported alcohol use in the past 30 days, and 28% of males and 18% of females said they had five or more drinks in a row in the previous 2 weeks. Males were twice as likely as females to report daily alcohol use (4% vs. 2%).

Drug use was more common among males than females and among whites than blacks

	Proportion of seniors who used in previous year				
Substance	Male	Female	White	Black	Hispanic
Alcohol*	44.2%	37.9%	45.4%	31.4%	40.1%
Been drunk*	31.2	21.8	31.6	14.7	20.5
Cigarettes*	21.9	15.7	22.9	10.1	15.0
Marijuana/hashish	38.3	30.7	34.8	30.8	31.6
Narcotics, not heroin	9.9	7.4	11.1	4.0	5.1
Amphetamines	8.3	6.4	8.6	2.8	4.4
Tranquilizers	5.9	5.2	7.3	2.2	3.9
Sedatives	4.8	4.6	5.8	2.7	3.8
Cocaine, not crack	4.0	1.9	3.4	0.9	3.5
Inhalants	4.7	2.5	3.8	2.0	3.6
MDMA (ecstasy)	5.3	3.6	4.5	2.6	4.6
Steroids	2.5	0.3	1.5	1.7	1.3
LSD	3.6	1.4	2.7	0.8	0.9
Crack cocaine	1.9	0.9	1.2	0.7	1.8
Heroin	1.1	0.5	0.8	0.6	0.6

* Alcohol and cigarette proportions are for use in the last 30 days.

Note: Male and female proportions are for 2010. Race/ethnicity proportions include data for 2009 and 2010 to increase subgroup sample size and provide more stable estimates.

Source: Authors' adaptation of Johnston et al.'s *Monitoring the Future National Survey on Drug Use, 1975–2010. Volume I: Secondary School Students.*

Males were also more likely than females to have used marijuana in the previous year (38% vs. 31%), in the previous month (25% vs. 17%), and daily during the previous month (9% vs. 3%). The proportions of male and female high school seniors reporting overall use of illicit drugs other than marijuana in the previous year were more similar (19% and 15%), but there are variations across drugs. Annual prevalence rates for 12th-grade males, compared with 12th-grade females, are 3 to 6 times greater for salvia, heroin with a needle, Provigil, methamphetamine, Rohypnol, GHB, and steroids, and more than twice as high for hallucinogens, LSD, hallucinogens other than LSD, cocaine, crack, cocaine powder, heroin, heroin without a needle, Ritalin, and ketamine. Male use rates for inhalants, OxyContin, and crystal methamphetamine (ice) are 1.5 to 2 times the rates among females. Furthermore, males account for an even greater proportion of frequent or heavy users of many of these drugs.

Blacks had lower tobacco, alcohol, and drug use rates than whites or Hispanics

In 2010, 10% of black seniors said they had smoked cigarettes in the past 30 days, compared with 23% of whites and 15% of Hispanics. About one-third (31%) of black seniors reported alcohol use in the past 30 days, compared with 45% of white seniors and 40% of Hispanic seniors. Whites were more than twice as likely as blacks to have been drunk in the past month (32% vs. 15%). The figure for Hispanics was 21%.

For nearly all drugs, black seniors report lifetime, annual, 30-day, and daily prevalence rates that are lower than those for their white and Hispanic counterparts. The proportion of seniors who reported using amphetamines in the past year was lower among blacks (3%) than whites (9%) and Hispanics (4%). White and Hispanic seniors were 3 times more likely than blacks to have used cocaine in the previous year.

Fewer than 1 in 10 high school students used alcohol or marijuana at school

According to the Centers for Disease Control and Prevention's 2010 Youth Risk Behavior Survey, 5% of high school students said they had at least one drink of alcohol on school property in the past month. During the same time period, 6% said they had used marijuana on school property.

Overall, males are more likely than females to drink alcohol or use marijuana at school. This was true for most grades and racial/ethnic groups. Females showed more variations across grade levels than males, with a greater proportion of ninth graders drinking alcohol at school than 12th graders. Hispanic students were more likely than white or black students to drink alcohol or use marijuana at school.

Nationally, 26% of high school students said they were offered, sold, or given an illegal drug on school property at least once during the past 12 months. The proportion was higher for

Percent who used on school property in the past 30 days			
Demographic	**Total**	**Male**	**Female**
ALCOHOL			
Total	5.1%	5.4%	4.7%
9th grade	5.4	5.6	5.2
10th grade	4.4	4.2	4.5
11th grade	5.2	5.4	4.9
12th grade	5.1	6.4	3.8
White	4.0	4.2	3.8
Black	5.1	6.5	3.8
Hispanic	7.3	7.9	6.6
MARIJUANA			
Total	5.9%	7.5%	4.1%
9th grade	5.4	7.0	3.7
10th grade	6.2	8.0	4.2
11th grade	6.2	7.5	4.7
12th grade	5.4	7.2	3.5
White	4.5	5.6	3.4
Black	6.7	9.3	4.1
Hispanic	7.7	9.6	5.7

Percent who were offered, sold, or given an illegal drug on school property in the past 12 months			
Demographic	**Total**	**Male**	**Female**
Total	25.6%	29.2%	21.7%
9th grade	23.7	25.9	21.3
10th grade	27.8	30.8	24.6
11th grade	27.0	32.5	21.3
12th grade	23.8	28.1	19.3
White	22.7	26.3	18.8
Black	22.8	28.7	17.0
Hispanic	33.2	35.8	30.5

males than for females, especially among black students and among 11th grade students. Hispanic students were more likely than white or black students to report being offered, sold, or given illegal drugs at school. Among females, seniors were less likely than 9th, 10th, and 11th graders to say they were offered, sold, or given an illegal drug on school property. . . .

High school seniors were more than twice as likely to use alcohol than use marijuana before age 13						
	Percent who had used before age 13					
	ALCOHOL			**MARIJUANA**		
Demographic	**Total**	**Male**	**Female**	**Total**	**Male**	**Female**
Total	20.5%	23.3%	17.4%	8.1%	10.4%	5.7%
9th grade	26.6	28.9	24.1	9.7	12.7	6.6
10th grade	21.1	24.3	17.6	7.5	10.1	4.8
11th grade	17.6	20.9	14.2	7.6	9.6	5.6
12th grade	15.1	17.9	12.2	7.0	8.7	5.3
White	18.1	21.1	14.8	6.5	8.5	4.4
Black	21.8	24.1	19.4	10.5	14.2	6.9
Hispanic	25.2	27.2	23.0	9.4	11.6	7.1

- About 1 in 5 high school students said they had drunk alcohol (more than just a few sips) before they turned 13; fewer than 1 in 10 high school students reported trying marijuana before age 13.
- Females were less likely than males to have used alcohol or marijuana before age 13, and whites were less likely than blacks and Hispanics.

Source: Authors' adaptation of the Centers for Disease Control and Prevention's *Youth Risk Behavior Surveillance—United States*, 2011.

UCR program data on juvenile crime*

Since the 1930s, police agencies have reported to the UCR Program

Each year, thousands of police agencies voluntarily report the following data to the Federal Bureau of Investigation's (FBI's) Uniform Crime Reporting (UCR) Program:

- Number of Index crimes reported to law enforcement.
- Number of arrests and the most serious charge involved in each arrest.
- Age, sex, and race of arrestees.
- Proportion of reported Index crimes cleared by arrest, and the proportion of these Index crimes cleared by the arrest of persons younger than 18.
- Police dispositions of juvenile arrests.
- Detailed victim, assailant, and circumstance information in murder cases.

What can the UCR arrest data tell us about crime and young people?

The UCR arrest data provide a sample-based portrait of the volume and characteristics of arrests in the United States. Detailed national estimates are developed by the Bureau of Justice Statistics (BJS) based on these sample data. The estimates include detailed juvenile age groups as well as details by sex, race, and specific offense. The data can be used to analyze the number and rates of juvenile arrests within offense categories and demographic subgroups and to track changes over various periods. They can also be used to compare the relative number of juvenile and adult arrests by offense categories and demographics and to monitor the proportion of crimes cleared by arrests of juveniles.

What do arrest statistics count?

To interpret the material in this chapter properly, the reader needs a clear understanding of what these statistics count. Arrest statistics report the number of arrests that law enforcement agencies made in a given year—not the number of individuals arrested nor the number of crimes committed. The number of arrests is not the same as the number of people arrested because an unknown number of individuals are arrested more than once during the year. Nor do arrest statistics represent the number of crimes that arrested individuals commit, because a series of crimes that one person commits may culminate in a single arrest, and a single crime may result in the arrest of more than one person. This latter situation, where many arrests result from one crime, is relatively common in juvenile law-violating behavior because juveniles are more likely than adults to commit crimes in groups. For this reason, one should not use arrest statistics to indicate the relative proportions of crime that juveniles and adults commit. Arrest statistics are most appropriately a measure of entry into the justice system.

Arrest statistics also have limitations in measuring the volume of arrests for a particular offense. Under the UCR Program, the FBI requires law enforcement agencies to classify an arrest by the most serious offense charged in that arrest. For example, the arrest of a youth charged with aggravated assault and possession of a weapon would be reported to the FBI as an arrest for aggravated assault. Therefore, when arrest statistics show that law enforcement agencies made an estimated 31,400 arrests of young people for weapons law violations in 2010, it means that a weapons law violation was the most serious charge in these 31,400 arrests. An unknown number of additional arrests in 2010 included a weapons charge as a lesser offense.

What do clearance statistics count?

Clearance statistics measure the proportion of reported crimes that were cleared (or "closed") by either arrest or other, exceptional means (such as the death of the offender or unwillingness of the victim to cooperate). A single arrest may result in many clearances. For example, 1 arrest could clear 10 burglaries if the person was charged with committing all 10 crimes. Or multiple arrests may result in a single clearance if a group of offenders committed the crime.

For those interested in juvenile justice issues, the FBI also reports the proportion of clearances that involved only offenders younger than age 18. This statistic is a better indicator of the proportion of crime that this age group commits than is the proportion of arrests, although there are some concerns that even the clearance statistic overestimates the proportion of crimes that juveniles commit. Research has shown that juvenile offenders are more easily apprehended than adult offenders; thus, the juvenile proportion of clearances probably overestimates juveniles' responsibility for crime.

To add to the difficulty in interpreting clearance statistics, the FBI's reporting guidelines require that clearances involving both juvenile and adult offenders be classified as clearances for crimes that adults commit. Because the juvenile clearance proportions include only those clearances in which no adults were involved, they underestimate juvenile involvement in crime. Although these data do not present a definitive picture of juvenile involvement in crime, they are the closest measure generally available of the proportion of crime known to law enforcement that is attributed to persons younger than age 18. . . .

The juvenile proportion of arrests exceeded the juvenile proportion of crimes cleared by arrest in each offense category

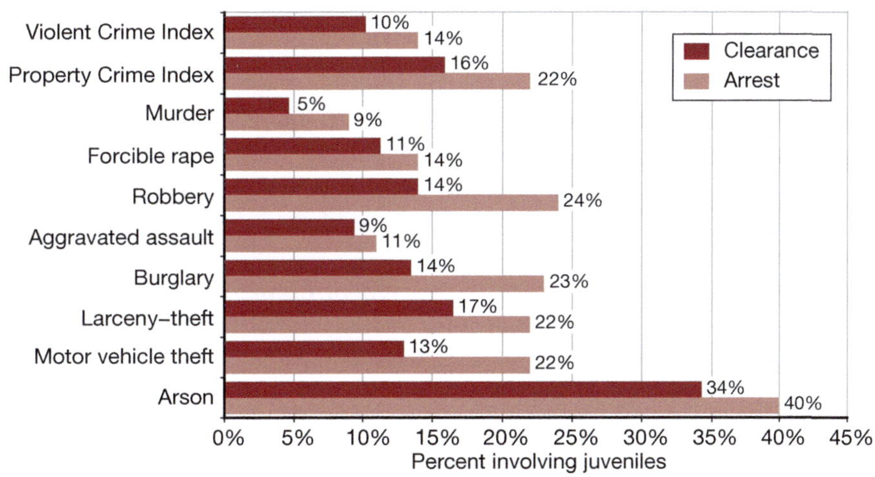

Source: Authors' analysis of the FBI's *Crime in the United States 2010*.

Data from juvenile courts*

The *Juvenile Court Statistics* series is the primary source of information on the activities of the nation's juvenile courts. The first *Juvenile Court Statistics* report, published in 1929 by the Children's Bureau of the U.S. Department of Labor, described cases handled in 1927 by

42 courts. In 1974, the Office of Juvenile Justice and Delinquency Prevention (OJJDP) took on the project. Since 1975, the National Center for Juvenile Justice (NCJJ) has been responsible for this OJJDP data collection effort through the National Juvenile Court Data Archive project. The project not only produces the *Juvenile Court Statistics* reports but also conducts research and archives data for use by other researchers.

Throughout its history, the *Juvenile Court Statistics* series has depended on the voluntary support of courts with juvenile jurisdiction. Courts contribute data originally compiled to meet their own information needs. The data NCJJ receives are not uniform but reflect the natural variation that exists across court information systems. To develop national estimates, NCJJ restructures compatible data into a common format. In 2010, juvenile courts with jurisdiction over virtually 100% of the U.S. juvenile population contributed at least some data to the national reporting program. Because not all contributed data can support the national reporting requirements, the national estimates for 2010 were based on data from more than 2,300 jurisdictions containing nearly 83% of the nation's juvenile population (i.e., youth age 10 through the upper age of original juvenile court jurisdiction in each state).

Juvenile Court Statistics documents the number of cases courts handled

Just as the FBI's Uniform Crime Reporting Program counts arrests made by law enforcement (i.e., a workload measure, not a crime measure), the *Juvenile Court Statistics* series counts delinquency and status offense cases handled by courts with juvenile jurisdiction during the year. Each case represents the initial disposition of a new referral to juvenile court for one or more offenses. A youth may be involved in more than one case in a year. Therefore, the *Juvenile Court Statistics* series does not provide a count of individual juveniles brought before juvenile courts.

Cases involving multiple charges are categorized by their most serious offense

In a single case where a juvenile is charged with robbery, simple assault, and a weapons law violation, the case is counted as a robbery case (similar to the FBI Uniform Crime Reporting Program's hierarchy rule). Thus, the *Juvenile Court Statistics* series does not provide a count of the number of crimes committed by juveniles. In addition, given that only the most serious offense is used to classify the case, counts of—and trends for—less serious offenses must be interpreted cautiously.

Similarly, cases are categorized by their most severe or restrictive disposition. For example, a case in which the judge orders the youth to a training school and to pay restitution to the victim would be characterized as a case in which the juvenile was placed in a residential facility.

Juvenile Court Statistics describes delinquency and status offense caseloads

The *Juvenile Court Statistics* series describes delinquency and status offense cases handled by juvenile courts. The reports provide demographic profiles of the youth referred and the reasons for the referrals (offenses). The series documents the juvenile courts' differential use of petition, detention, adjudication, and disposition alternatives by case type. The series also can identify trends in the volume and characteristics of court activity. However, care should be exercised when interpreting gender, age, or racial differences in the analysis of juvenile delinquency or status offense cases because reported statistics do not control for the seriousness of the behavior leading to each charge or the extent of a youth's court history.

The *Juvenile Court Statistics* series does not provide national estimates of the number of youth referred to court, their prior court histories, or their future recidivism. Nor does it provide data on criminal court processing of juvenile cases. Criminal court cases involving youth younger than age 18 who are defined as adults in their state are not included. The series was designed to produce national estimates of juvenile court activity, not to describe the law-violating careers of juveniles. . . .

OJJDP data on juveniles in residential placement*

Since its inception, the Office of Juvenile Justice and Delinquency Prevention (OJJDP) has collected information on the juveniles held in juvenile detention and correctional facilities. Until 1995, these data were gathered through the biennial Census of Public and Private Juvenile Detention, Correctional, and Shelter Facilities, better known as the Children in Custody (CIC) Census. In the late 1990s, OJJDP initiated two new data collection programs to gather comprehensive and detailed information about juvenile offenders in residential placement and the facilities that house them:

- Census of Juveniles in Residential Placement (CJRP)
- Juvenile Residential Facility Census (JRFC)

CJRP and JRFC are generally administered in alternating years and collect information from all secure and nonsecure residential placement facilities that house juvenile offenders, defined as persons younger than 21 who are held in a residential setting as a result of some contact with the justice system (they are charged with or adjudicated for an offense). This encompasses both status offenders and delinquent offenders, including those who are either temporarily detained by the court or committed after adjudication for an offense. These censuses do not include federal facilities or those exclusively for drug or mental health treatment or for abused/neglected youth. They also do not capture data from adult prisons or jails. Therefore, CJRP and JRFC do not include all juveniles sentenced to incarceration by criminal courts.

CJRP typically takes place on the fourth Wednesday in October of the census year. However, the census that would have occurred October 28, 2009, was postponed until the fourth Wednesday in February 2010. CJRP asks all juvenile residential facilities in the U.S. to describe each offender under age 21 assigned a bed in the facility on the census date. Facilities report individual-level information on gender, date of birth, race, placement authority, most serious offense charged, court adjudication status, admission date, and security status.

JRFC also uses the fourth Wednesday in October as its census date and, in addition to information gathered on the census date, it includes some past-month and past-year variables. JRFC collects information on how facilities operate and the services they provide. It includes detailed questions on facility security, capacity and crowding, injuries and deaths in placement, and facility ownership and operation. Supplementary information is also collected in various years on specific services, such as mental and physical health, substance abuse, and education.

The Survey of Youth in Residential Placement (SYRP) is the third component of OJJDP's multitiered effort to collect information on the juvenile custody population. SYRP collects a broad range of self-report information (on youth's placement experience, past offense histories, education, and other important life events) from interviews with individual youth in placement.

One-day count and admission data give different views of residential populations

CJRP provides a 1-day population count of juveniles in residential placement facilities. Such counts give a picture of the standing population in facilities. One-day counts are substantially different from annual admission or release data, which provide a measure of facility population flow.

Juveniles may be committed to a facility as part of a court-ordered disposition, or they may be detained prior to adjudication or after adjudication while awaiting disposition or placement elsewhere. In addition, a small proportion of juveniles are admitted voluntarily in lieu of adjudication as part of a diversion agreement. Because detention stays tend to be short compared with commitment placement, detained juveniles represent a much larger share of population flow data than of 1-day count data.

State variations in upper age of juvenile court jurisdiction influence placement rates

Although state placement rate statistics control for upper age of original juvenile court jurisdiction, comparisons among states with different upper ages are problematic. Youth ages 16 and 17 constitute 26% of the youth population ages 10–17, but they account for more than 50% of arrests of youth under age 18, more than 40% of delinquency court cases, and more than 50% of juveniles in residential placement. If all other factors were equal, one would expect higher juvenile placement rates in states where older youth are under the juvenile court jurisdiction.

Differing age limits of extended jurisdiction also influence placement rates. Some states may keep a juvenile in placement for several years beyond the upper age of original jurisdiction; others cannot. Laws that control the transfer of juveniles to criminal court also have an impact on juvenile placement rates. If all other factors were equal, states with broad transfer provisions would be expected to have lower juvenile placement rates than other states.

Demographic variations among jurisdictions should also be considered. The urbanicity and economy of an area are thought to be related to crime and placement rates. Available bedspace also influences placement rates, particularly in rural areas.

Endnotes

1 Serious violence refers to rape, sexual assault, robbery, and aggravated assault.

* Authors' note: This heading does not appear in the original source.

CRITICAL-THINKING QUESTIONS

1 Consider again the "Case in point" on the need for multiple data sources that opened this chapter. Why do different data sources sometimes provide contradictory findings about the amount of delinquency in the U.S.?

2 Identify the strengths and weaknesses of the three major sources of data on delinquency: official data, victimization survey data, and self-report survey data. What is each source designed to tell us?
3 Imagine that you want to answer this research question: Are there gender differences in involvement in minor forms of delinquency such as vandalism and shoplifting? Which of the three major data sources discussed in this chapter would be best for addressing this research question and why?
4 Develop your own research question related to juvenile delinquency that you would like to explore. Which data source would you use to address your research question and why is it the best source for your particular question?
5 Based on your reading of the excerpt from *Juvenile Court Statistics 2014*, describe two factors that might impact the quality of data presented in *Juvenile Court Statistics* publications.
6 The excerpts from *Juvenile Offenders and Victims: 2014 National Report* describe UCR data and what they can tell us about juvenile offending. What are the primary problems with relying on UCR data to examine delinquency in the United States?

SUGGESTED READING

Hindelang, Michael J., Travis Hirschi, and Joseph G. Weis. 1981. *Measuring Delinquency*. Beverly Hills, CA: Sage.

Mosher, Clayton J., Terance D. Miethe, and Timothy C. Hart. 2011. *The Mismeasure of Crime*. 2nd ed. Thousand Oaks, CA: Sage.

USEFUL WEBSITES

For further information relevant to this chapter, go to the following websites.

- **Uniform Crime Reporting Program, Federal Bureau of Investigation**: https://ucr.fbi.gov/
- ***Statistical Briefing Book***: www.ojjdp.gov/ojstatbb/
- ***Juvenile Court Statistics*, National Center for Juvenile Justice**: www.ncjj.org/Publication/Juvenile-Court-Statistics-2014.aspx
- **National Crime Victimization Survey, Office of Justice Programs, Bureau of Justice Statistics:** www.bjs.gov/index.cfm?ty=dcdetail&iid=245

GLOSSARY OF KEY TERMS

Cross-sectional survey: A self-report survey conducted at a single point in time. A cross-sectional research design provides a glimpse of a cross section of the population at a particular time.

Longitudinal survey: A self-report survey that gathers information from the same individuals at more than one point in time. A longitudinal research design is better suited than a cross-sectional design to address questions of causal order and change.

Reliability: The extent to which repeated measurements of a variable produce the same or similar responses over time.

Uniform Crime Reporting program: Provides "official data" on crime and delinquency, voluntarily reported by over 18,000 law enforcement agencies across the United States, and compiled by the FBI. These data reveal the extent of crime and delinquency with which the reporting agencies deal, and the characteristics of offenses and offenders they encounter.

Validity: The degree to which a measurement instrument measures what it is supposed to measure.

NOTES

1 Individual case-level data include detailed information about "the characteristics of each delinquency and status offense case handled by courts, generally including the age, gender, and race of the youth referred; the date and source of referral; the offenses charged; detention and petitioning decisions; and the date and type of disposition" (Hockenberry and Puzzanchera 2017:91). Court-level aggregate data "typically provide counts of the delinquency and status offense cases handled by courts in a defined time period (calendar or fiscal year)" (Hockenberry and Puzzanchera 2017:91). These aggregate data are sometimes abstracted from courts' annual reports.

2 Wells and Rankin (2001) compared NCVS data and self-report victimization data from the National Youth Survey and the Monitoring the Future study, both national samples of young people. Both self-report surveys indicated much higher juvenile victimization rates than did the NCVS.

3 The FBI (2009) cautions users of UCR data against comparing UCR and NCVS data, stating that these two data sources rely on different methodologies, include different crimes, and examine crime from different perspectives. The UCR and NCVS are intended only to complement each other. However, the FBI also notes that these two data sources use similar offense definitions and measure a similar subset of serious offenses, including forcible rape, robbery, aggravated assault, burglary, theft, and motor vehicle theft. Thus, any attempt to compare UCR and NCVS data must examine only offenses that are similarly measured in both data sources, recognizing the effects of methodological differences in the two sources.

REFERENCES

Baumer, Eric P. and Janet L. Lauritsen. 2010. "Reporting Crime to the Police, 1973–2005: A Multivariate Analysis of Long-Term Trends in the National Crime Survey (NCS) and National Crime Victimization Survey (NCVS)." *Criminology* 48:131–185.

Beckett, Katherine, Kris Nyrop, Lori Pfingst, and Melissa Bowen. 2005. "Drug Use, Drug Possession Arrests, and the Question of Race: Lessons from Seattle." *Social Problems* 52:419–441.

Blumstein, Alfred, Jacqueline Cohen, Jeffrey A. Roth, and Christy A. Visher. 1986. *Criminal Careers and "Career Criminals."* Vol. I. Washington, DC: National Academy Press.

Bureau of Justice Statistics. n.d. *Arrest Data Analysis Tool.* Retrieved September 6, 2017 (www.bjs.gov/index.cfm?ty=datool&surl=/arrests/index.cfm#).

Engel, Robin S., Michael R. Smith, and Francies T. Cullen. 2012. "Race, Place, and Drug Enforcement: Reconsidering the Impact of Citizen Complaints and Crime Rates on Drug Arrests." *Criminology and Public Policy* 11:603–635.

Farrington, David P., Darrick Jolliffe, David J. Hawkins, Richard F. Catalano, Karl G. Hill, and Rick Kosterman. 2003. "Comparing Delinquency Careers in Court Records and Self-Reports." *Criminology* 41:933–958.

Farrington, David P., Rolf Loeber, Magda Stouthamer-Loeber, Welmoet B. Van Kammen, and Laura Schmidt. 1996. "Self-Reported Delinquency and a Combined Delinquency Seriousness Scale Based on Boys, Mothers, and Teachers: Concurrent and Predictive Validity for African-Americans and Caucasians." *Criminology* 34:493–517.

Federal Bureau of Investigation. 2009. *Uniform Crime Reporting (UCR) Summary Reporting: Frequently Asked Questions (FAQs).* Washington, DC: U.S. Department of Justice.

Federal Bureau of Investigation. 2011. *Effects of NIBRS on Crime Statistics.* Washington, DC: U.S. Department of Justice.

Federal Bureau of Investigation. 2016. *Crime in the United States, 2015: Uniform Crime Reports.* Washington, DC: U.S. Department of Justice. Retrieved September 6, 2017 (https://ucr.fbi.gov/crime-in-the-u.s/2015/crime-in-the-u.s.-2015).

Federal Bureau of Investigation. 2017. *Crime in the United States, 2016: Uniform Crime Reports.* Washington, DC: U.S. Department of Justice. Retrieved October 12, 2017 (https://ucr.fbi.gov/crime-in-the-u.s/2016/crime-in-the-u.s.-2016).

Harris, Anthony R. and James W. Shaw. 2000. "Looking for Patterns: Race, Class, and Crime." Pp. 129–161 in *Criminology*, edited by J. F. Sheley. Belmont, CA: Wadsworth.

Hindelang, Michael J. 1981. "Variations in Sex-Race-Age-Specific Incidence Rates of Offending." *American Sociological Review* 46:461–474.

Hindelang, Michael J., Travis Hirschi, and Joseph G. Weis. 1981. *Measuring Delinquency.* Beverly Hills: Sage.

Hockenberry, Sarah and Charles Puzzanchera. 2017. *Juvenile Court Statistics 2014.* Pittsburgh, PA: National Center for Juvenile Justice.

Huizinga, David A. and Delbert S. Elliott. 1984. *Self-Reported Measures of Delinquency and Crime: Methodological Issues and Comparative Findings.* Boulder, CO: Behavioral Research Institute.

Huizinga, David A. and Delbert S. Elliott. 1986. "Reassessing the Reliability and Validity of Self-Report Delinquency Measures." *Journal of Quantitative Criminology* 2:293–327.

Kirk, David S. 2006. "Examining the Divergence across Self-Report and Official Data Sources on Inferences about the Adolescent Life-Course of Crime." *Journal of Quantitative Criminology* 22:107–129.

Kleck, Gary. 1982. "On the Use of Self-Report Data to Determine the Class Distribution of Criminal and Delinquent Behavior." *American Sociological Review* 47:427–433.

Krohn, Marvin D., Alan J. Lizotte, Matthew D. Phillips, Terence P. Thornberry, and Kristin A. Bell. 2013. "Explaining Systematic Bias in Self-Reported Measures: Factors that Affect the Under- and Over-Reporting of Self-Reported Arrests." *Justice Quarterly* 30:501–528.

Lauritsen, Janet L. 1998. "The Age–Crime Debate: Assessing the Limits of Longitudinal Self-Report Data." *Social Forces* 77:127–155.

Maxfield, M. G., B. L. Weiler, and C. S. Widom. 2000. "Comparing Self-Reports and Official Records of Arrest." *Journal of Quantitative Criminology* 16:87–110.

Morenoff, Jeffrey D. 2005. "Racial and Ethnic Disparities in Crime and Delinquency in the United States." Pp. 139–173 in *Ethnicity and Causal Mechanisms*, edited by M. Rutter and M. Tienda. Cambridge, UK: Cambridge University Press.

O'Brien, Robert M. 1985. *Crime and Victimization Data.* Beverly Hills, CA: Sage.

O'Brien, Robert M. 2000. "Crime Facts: Victim and Offender Data." Pp. 59–83 in *Criminology: A Contemporary Handbook*, 3rd ed., edited by J. F. Sheley. Belmont, CA: Wadsworth.

OJJDP Statistical Briefing Book. Released March 27, 2017. National Center for Juvenile Justice. Retrieved September 6, 2017 (www.ojjdp.gov/ojstatbb/crime/faqs.asp).

Paschall, Mallie J., Miriam L. Ornstein, and Robert L. Flewelling. 2001. "African American Male Adolescents' Involvement in the Criminal Justice System: The Criterion Validity of Self-Report Measures in a Prospective Study." *Journal of Research in Crime and Delinquency* 38:174–187.

Piquero, Alex R., Randall MacIntosh, and Matthew Hickman. 2002. "The Validity of a Self-Reported Delinquency Scale: Comparisons across Gender, Age, Race, and Place of Residence." *Sociological Methods and Research* 30:492–529.

Piquero, Alex R., Carol A. Schubert, and Robert Brame. 2014. "Comparing Official and Self-Report Records of Offending across Gender and Race/Ethnicity in a Longitudinal Study of Serious Youthful Offenders." *Journal of Research in Crime and Delinquency* 51:526–556.

Sedlak, Andrea J. and Carol Bruce. 2016. *Survey of Youth in Residential Placement: Youth's Characteristics and Backgrounds.* SYRP Report. Rockville, MD: Westat.

Sickmund, Melissa and Charles Puzzanchera (eds.). 2014. *Juvenile Offenders and Victims: 2014 National Report*. Pittsburgh, PA: National Center for Juvenile Justice.

Sickmund, Melissa, T. J. Sladky, Wei Kang, and Charles Puzzanchera. 2017. "Easy Access to the Census of Juveniles in Residential Placement." Retrieved September 6, 2017 (www.ojjdp.gov/ojstatbb/ezacjrp/).

Tapia, Mike. 2011. "Gang Membership and Race as Risk Factors for Juvenile Arrest." *Journal of Research in Crime and Delinquency* 48:364–395.

Thornberry, Terence P. and Marvin D. Krohn. 2002. "Comparison of Self-Report and Official Data for Measuring Crime." In *Measurement Problems in Criminal Justice Research: Workshop Summary*, edited by J. V. Pepper and C. V. Petrie. Washington, DC: National Academies Press.

Tonry, Michael. 2010. "The Social, Psychological, and Political Causes of Racial Disparities in the American Criminal Justice System." *Crime and Justice* 39:273–312.

Truman, Jennifer L. and Rachel E. Morgan. 2016. "Criminal Victimization, 2015." *Bureau of Justice Statistics Bulletin*. Washington, DC: U.S. Department of Justice.

Turner, A. G. 1972. *The San Jose Methods Test of Known Crime Victims*. National Criminal Justice Information and Statistics Service, Law Enforcement Assistance Administration. Washington, DC: GPO.

Vogt, W. Paul and R. Burke Johnson. 2011. *Dictionary of Statistics and Methodology: A Nontechnical Guide for the Social Sciences*. 4th ed. Thousand Oaks, CA: Sage.

Wells, Edward L. and Joseph H. Rankin. 2001. "Juvenile Victimization: Convergent Validation of Alternative Measurements." Pp. 267–287 in *Voices from the Field: Readings in Criminal Justice Research*, edited by C. Pope, R. Lovell, and S. Brandl. Belmont, CA: Wadsworth.

Chapter 5

THE NATURE OF DELINQUENCY

CHAPTER TOPICS

- **Prevalence and incidence of delinquent offenses**
- **Relative frequency of different types of offenses**
- **Trends in delinquent offenses**
- **Social correlates of offending**

CHAPTER LEARNING OBJECTIVES

After completing this chapter, students should be able to:

- Describe the extent to which juveniles are involved in crime.
- Identify the types of delinquent offenses that occur most frequently.
- Give an accurate account of the trends in juvenile crime.
- Describe how involvement in delinquency is related to age, gender, race, ethnicity, and social class.
- Demonstrate interpretive skills developed through exposure to delinquency data presented in tables and figures.

CHAPTER CONTENTS

CASE IN POINT

THE OFFENSE SECTION OF A PREDISPOSITION REPORT

The predisposition report is written by a probation officer to provide background information on a youth who has been formally adjudicated a "delinquent youth" so that disposition can be individualized and rehabilitative (discussed in Chapter 9, "Formal procedures of juvenile courts: Adjudication and disposition"). The first section of the report deals with the youth's current offense and offense history, assessing the severity and patterning of offending. Are the offenses depicted in this case typical of those committed by most youth? This chapter addresses that question by describing the nature of delinquency.

PREDISPOSITION REPORT

Youth Court Services
5th Judicial District
Laurel, Ohio

To the Honorable Mary M. Malloy of the Youth Court, 5th Judicial District

Kent Clausen, age 16, is pending for disposition after he admitted to a petition of five counts of residential burglary. Based on the admission, the Court determined him to be a **Delinquent Youth**.

Current Offense

Together with another youth who is pending adjudication, Kent burglarized five houses over the course of a two-week period, April 3, 2016 – April 16, 2016. The two youths targeted specific items that they intended to steal when the neighbors were not at home. All homes were in Kent's neighborhood. The youth entered each home through an unlocked door and took items into their possession with the intent of selling them for money. Items stolen included laptop computers from three houses and Apple TV devices from two other houses. The youth offered the stolen items for sale on Craigslist where Detective Baker from the Lancaster Police Department discovered the stolen items. Detective Baker met with the youth separately, at which time they each admitted involvement and gave statements.

Offense History

Date	Offense	Disposition
08/28/2017	Burglary (IC 35-43-2-1): current offense	Pending
02/12/2017	Theft (IC 35-43-4-2): took laptop computer from school; arrested by School Resource Officer	Adjudicated a delinquent youth; formal probation, community service
10/10/2015	Theft (IC 35-43-4-2): electronic cables taken from retail store; apprehended by store security	Consent decree without petition; six months informal probation
04/15/2015	Criminal mischief (IC 35-43-1-2): broke two windows of neighbor's property	Not petitioned; paid restitution
09/21/2014	Residential entry (IC 35-43-2-1.5): unauthorized entry into two residences	Dismissed; warned and released

[The Predisposition Report includes additional sections dealing with the social background of the youth and an evaluative summary and recommendation for disposition.]

This chapter explores the nature of delinquency by examining the extent of delinquent offenses and the social correlates of offending. Are most juveniles involved in delinquent offenses? If so, how frequently are they involved? What types of delinquent offenses occur most often? Is delinquency increasing, decreasing, or staying the same? We will address these questions by briefly summarizing the research in three key areas of study with regard to the extent of delinquent offenses: prevalence and incidence, relative frequency, and trends. Taken together, these considerations provide a basic understanding of the extent of juvenile delinquency. A working understanding of both the nature of delinquency (Chapter 5) and the causes of delinquency (Chapter 6) is foundational to subsequent discussion of juvenile justice processes and practices. We must understand the nature of delinquency before we attempt to respond to it through prevention and control efforts.

PREVALENCE AND INCIDENCE OF DELINQUENT OFFENSES

One of the most basic considerations regarding delinquency is the extent to which youth engage in delinquent behavior. This consideration begins with the prevalence and incidence of delinquency among adolescents. **Prevalence** refers to the proportion of youth involved in delinquent acts, and is usually stated as a percentage. **Incidence**, a measure of the frequency of offending, is the average number of delinquent offenses committed by adolescents in general or by delinquent youth.

Self-report data

Self-report studies consistently indicate that the number of youth who commit crimes is far greater than official statistics lead us to believe. The National Longitudinal Survey of Youth (NLSY) is a nationwide survey that interviews nearly 9,000 youth annually, asking them about many aspects of their lives, including delinquent behaviors. The NLSY reveals that a sizable portion of youth report involvement in minor delinquent acts, but relatively few report involvement in serious forms of lawbreaking (Snyder and Sickmund 2006). Similarly, the National Youth Survey, which began in 1976 and gathered data from more than 1,700 youth for a decade, revealed that almost two-thirds of the youth reported involvement in less serious offenses like minor theft, minor assault, and property damage, but only about one-sixth reported involvement in serious forms of assault including aggravated assault, sexual assault, and gang fights (Huizinga and Elliott 1987).

To gauge the amount of crime committed by youth, it is also useful to consider the frequency or incidence of their involvement. **Table 5.1** reports both prevalence and incidence findings from the Monitoring the Future survey (MTF), described in the previous chapter (Bachman, Johnston, and O'Malley 2014). Table 5.1 shows that a significant portion of high school seniors report involvement in delinquent offenses (prevalence). Although most self-reported offenses are minor, a surprising percentage of high school seniors reported involvement in fairly serious offenses. Only 6 percent, however, said they were arrested or taken to the police station. The incidence of self-reported delinquency indicates that delinquency tends to be infrequent and sporadic—seldom do youth continue in a repetitive pattern of delinquency (Sickmund and Puzzanchera 2014; Huizinga et al. 2000). For example, while 14 percent of the youth reported that they had participated in a group fight, only 3 percent had been involved three or more times. MTF data from 2016 also show that drug use is common among high school seniors, as indicated by use in the last 12 months: 56 percent report alcohol use, 37 percent report having been drunk, 36 percent report marijuana use, 14 percent report illicit drug use other than marijuana, and 12 percent report prescription drug misuse (Johnston et al. 2017).

Official data

When juvenile offenders come to the attention of the police and are arrested, they are counted in the Uniform Crime Reporting (UCR) program. In order to limit discussion of the extent of offending to *juvenile* offenders, one must examine arrest data because until an arrest is made, the age of the offender is not known. Thus, UCR data report *arrest* prevalence, rather than *offense* prevalence. The proportion of youth actually involved in delinquency is not represented by arrest data because many offenses are not reported to police or do not result in arrest. UCR

TABLE 5.1 Prevalence and incidence of self-reported delinquency by high school seniors in the Monitoring the Future survey, 2012

In the last 12 months, how often have you . . .	Not at all (%)	Once (%)	Twice (%)	3–4 times (%)	≥ 5 times (%)
Damaged school property on purpose?	92.4	3.9	1.5	1.2	1.1
Gone into some house or building when you weren't supposed to be there?	78.9	10.3	5.6	2.7	2.4
Taken a car that didn't belong to someone in your family without permission of the owner?	96.1	1.9	0.9	0.5	0.5
Taken something from a store without paying for it?	77.9	9.2	4.8	4.0	4.2
Taken something not belonging to you worth under $50?	77.9	11.0	2.0	2.9	3.2
Taken something not belonging to you worth over $50?	92.7	3.7	1.6	0.7	1.4
Gotten into a serious fight in school or at work?	88.9	7.0	1.9	1.3	1.0
Hurt someone badly enough to need bandages or a doctor?	89.7	6.4	2.0	0.8	1.1
Taken part in a fight where a group of your friends were against another group?	85.7	7.1	4.2	1.6	1.4
Been arrested and taken to a police station?	94.4	3.9	1.0	0.5	0.3

Source: Bachman et al. (2014:27–28, 115–117).

data show the percentage of arrests that are attributable to juveniles, and thus, they provide insight into the delinquency problem encountered by police and the rest of the juvenile justice system. We present these data in Table 5.2, later in this chapter.

RELATIVE FREQUENCY OF DIFFERENT TYPES OF OFFENSES

The prevalence and incidence of juvenile delinquency provide a general understanding of the extent to which young people are involved in crime. It is also useful to consider the types of crime that juveniles are most involved in. Relative to each other, what types of juvenile offenses are most common? This is referred to as the **relative frequency** of juvenile offenses.

Self-report data

Self-report surveys reveal that a sizable portion of youth report involvement in a wide variety of minor misconduct, but relatively few youth are involved in serious forms of lawbreaking. According to self-report data, the most common forms of adolescent misconduct are using alcohol and marijuana, lying about age, skipping school, committing minor theft, damaging others' property, entering a house or building without permission, engaging in disorderly conduct, making threats of physical harm, and fighting (Bachman et al. 2014; Sickmund and Puzzanchera 2014). Self-report data show that youth are also involved in serious crime, but minor delinquency significantly outpaces serious delinquency (see Table 5.1).

Official data

Official data from both the UCR and *Juvenile Court Statistics* confirm the relative frequency of delinquent offenses that is revealed in self-report data. UCR data show that juveniles make up a larger share of those arrested for Part I property offenses than for Part I violent offenses (see Table 5.2). UCR data, however, are problematic for understanding the relative proportions of crime that juveniles commit because they represent arrests, rather than offenses (Puzzanchera 2014). A single offense may result in the arrest of multiple people. This situation is relatively common with regard to delinquency because juveniles are more likely than adults to commit crimes in groups. Even though the percentage of arrests involving juveniles overestimates the amount of crime committed by juveniles, UCR data are useful for understanding the types of offenses that bring juveniles into the system.

Juvenile Court Statistics show that, in 2014, the largest portion of delinquency cases handled in juvenile courts were property offenses (34 percent), followed by person offenses (27 percent), public order offenses (26 percent), and drug law violations (13 percent) (Hockenberry and Puzzanchera 2017:6).

TRENDS IN DELINQUENT OFFENSES

If we were to ask the general public how juvenile delinquency has changed in recent years, most would probably respond that juvenile offenses are growing in number and juveniles are becoming increasingly violent. Is this true? To answer this question, we examine trends in delinquent offenses.

It is important to understand that different sources of data provide different pictures of trends in delinquency. MTF, which provides a self-reported indication of high school seniors' involvement in delinquency, tends to concentrate on less serious forms of offending. Less serious offenses have low rates of reporting to law enforcement, making them more difficult to track with official sources of data, such as the UCR. For this reason, self-report surveys are good indicators of trends in less serious juvenile crime. Reporting crime to police is less problematic for violent crime, making arrest data more valid and reliable as a measure of violent crime trends. We must keep in mind what the data are measuring in order to draw accurate conclusions about trends.

Self-report data

Figure 5.1, which presents data from MTF's survey of high school seniors, shows the 25-year trends in annual prevalence from 1988 through 2012. Represented are the percentages of high school seniors reporting that they had gotten into a serious fight, taken something worth under $50, taken something worth over $50, entered a house or building without permission, and been arrested and taken to a police station in the past year. These offenses were chosen because they are among the most common juvenile offenses. Although the data show fluctuations from year to year, the general trend for these four offenses has been one of decline since 1997, except for unauthorized entry, which stayed fairly consistent until 2008 and then declined.

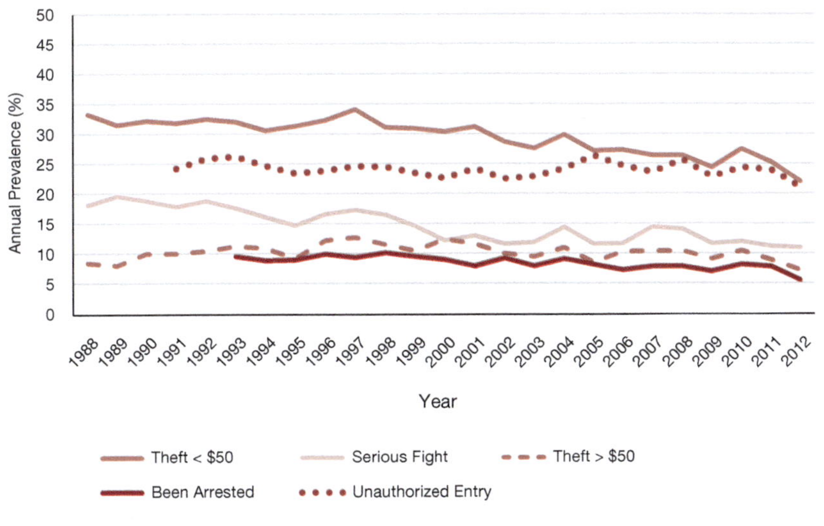

FIGURE 5.1 *Prevalence trends in self-reported delinquency among high school seniors: Serious fight, theft, unauthorized entry, and arrest, 1988–2012 (arrest since 1993; unauthorized entry since 1991).*

Note: Data for this graph were drawn from published documents reporting questionnaire responses for 1988–1995, and from the MTF website noted in the references for 1996–2012.

Source: Bachman et al. (2014:115–117).

Official data

UCR data can be used to assess trends in the volume of juvenile arrests. The Violent Crime Index is made up of murder and non-negligent manslaughter, forcible rape, robbery, and aggravated assault. The Property Crime Index includes burglary, larceny-theft, motor vehicle theft, and arson. To analyze trends, it is most accurate to express these Indexes in terms of arrest rate—the number of juvenile arrests for Index crimes per 100,000 juveniles, ages 10 through 17 (Puzzanchera 2014).

The first reading in this chapter by Charles Puzzanchera (2014) presents a wealth of information about juvenile arrests, including trends in arrests for Violent and Property Crime Index offenses. The figures in this reading show significant declines in juvenile arrests for serious violent and property crimes since the mid-1990s.

SOCIAL CORRELATES OF OFFENDING

Who are the offenders? What do age, gender, race, ethnicity, and social class have to do with the likelihood of offending? The social characteristics that tend to distinguish offenders from non-offenders are often called the **social correlates** of delinquency. By social correlates, we mean social characteristics that are statistically associated with each other. Here we are interested in the social characteristics of individuals that are related to involvement in delinquency.

Age

There are few factors that criminologists agree are undeniably related to involvement in crime. Age is one of those rare factors. The **age effect** refers to the fact that, although juveniles constitute a small portion of the U.S. population, they commit a disproportionate share of crime. Involvement in crime tends to increase with age during the teenage years, peak in mid-adolescence to early adulthood (the "crime-prone years"), and then decline rapidly with age. Relatively few people who are involved in crime during adolescence and young adulthood continue offending into later adulthood. When we graph the relationship between age and crime, we generally see a bell-shaped curve called the **age–crime curve**. This relationship between age and crime holds up across all three data sources: official data, self-reports of offending (Elliott et al. 1983), and victimization surveys (Hindelang 1981).

Figure 5.2 shows the age-crime curve for 2016, when the arrest rate increased steadily from about age 10, peaked at ages 19–20, and then declined. The age–crime relationship varies somewhat depending on the type of offense. Compared to arrests for serious violent offenses, arrests for serious property offenses peak at a slightly earlier age and decline more rapidly.

In 2016, 22.8 percent of the U.S. population was under age 18. To understand the extent of juvenile delinquency, however, it is important to consider ages 13 through 17—the age range in which juveniles are most involved in delinquency. In 2016, this group comprised 6.5 percent of the U.S. population (U.S. Census Bureau 2017). **Table 5.2** shows the number and proportion of offenders arrested who are juveniles (under the age of 18) and adults (ages 18 and over), for each type of offense. In 2016, juveniles accounted for 8.0 percent of all arrests, 12.6 percent of arrests for UCR Part I offenses, and 7.1 percent of arrests for UCR Part II offenses (less serious).[1]

Arrest rates, which take into account the size of a population group, are another measure of the extent of juvenile crime. The arrest rates presented in Table 5.2 are stated in terms of the

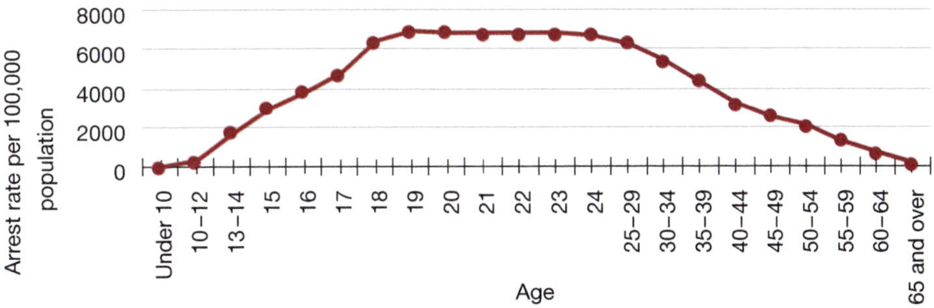

FIGURE 5.2 *The "age–crime curve."*

This figure shows the bell-shaped curve one typically sees when graphing the relationship between age and crime. This curve illustrates the consistent finding that crime tends to increase with age during the teenage years, peak in mid-adolescence to early adulthood, and then decline rapidly with age.

Note: This graph is based on arrests for all Part I and Part II offenses. Arrest figures based on 13,055 reporting agencies, with 2016 estimated U.S. population of 257,118,573.

Sources: Federal Bureau of Investigation (2017: Table 20); U.S. Census Bureau (2017).

number of arrests per 100,000 juveniles, ages 13–17 (column 5) and the number of arrests per 100,000 adults, ages 18–39 (column 6). We limited the calculations to these particular age groups because they are the ages when juveniles and adults are most likely to commit offenses. In 2016, the juvenile arrest rate was 3,039.9 for all UCR crimes, compared to the adult arrest rate of 5,847.6. The juvenile arrest rate exceeded the adult arrest rate for several offenses: forcible rape, robbery, motor vehicle theft, and arson.

The conclusion based on data in Table 5.2 is clear: When one considers that juveniles, ages 13–17, made up 6.5 percent of the U.S. population in 2016 (U.S. Census Bureau 2017), juveniles accounted for a disproportionate number of arrests, given their share of the population.

Gender

Evidence from self-report and official data shows that crime and delinquency are committed primarily by males. But the strength of the relationship between gender and crime varies depending on data source (self-report surveys vs. official data) and type of offense. Compared to self-report data, UCR data show a wider gender gap in offending. Multiple data sources show that the gender gap in offending is particularly large for serious violent offenses.

In a widely cited study, Rachelle Canter (1982) used National Youth Survey (NYS) data to examine gender differences in self-reported delinquency. She found gender differences in overall delinquency, with boys reporting roughly twice as many delinquent acts as girls. These gender differences are due to a higher number of male offenders and a higher frequency of offending among males. Although Canter found consistent gender differences in involvement in delinquency, these differences were much smaller than those indicated by UCR data.[2]

Canter (1982) also found that males and females generally report involvement in the same types of offenses. The exception to this similarity is for serious offenses, particularly violent

TABLE 5.2 Juvenile and adult arrests and arrest rates, by type of crime, 2016

	Number of arrests		Percentage of arrests		Arrest rate per 100,000 in age group	
Type of crime	Juveniles 0–17	Adults 18 & over	Juveniles 0–17	Adults 18 & over	Juveniles 13–17	Adults 18–39
All crimes	681,701	7,799,901	8.0	92.0	3,039.9	5,847.6
Part I crimes	188,685	1,303,419	12.6	87.4	846.4	1,001.1
Violent crimes	41,335	369,382	10.1	89.9	184.9	280.7
Homicide	682	8,745	7.2	92.8	3.2	7.3
Forcible rape	2,952	15,850	15.7	84.3	12.4	11.5
Robbery	15,339	61,164	20.1	79.9	71.6	54.1
Aggravated assault	22,362	283,623	7.3	92.7	97.6	207.9
Property crimes	147,350	934,037	13.6	86.4	661.5	720.3
Burglary	25,513	139,863	15.4	84.6	113.7	114.4
Larceny–theft	107,287	732,330	12.8	87.2	482.0	554.0
Motor vehicle theft	12,520	56,047	18.3	81.7	58.5	47.9
Arson	2,030	5,797	25.9	74.1	7.3	4.1
Part II crimes	493,016	6,496,482	7.1	92.9	2,193.5	4,846.5

Note: Arrest figures based on 13,055 reporting agencies, with 2016 estimated U.S. population of 257,118,573. Population figures from U.S. Census data for 2016: juvenile population ages 13–17 = 20,870,650; adult population ages 18–39 = 96,294,959; total population = 323,127,513. See Table 4.1 in Chapter 4 for a list of all Part II crimes.

Sources: Federal Bureau of Investigation (2017: Table 20); U.S. Census Bureau (2017).

crimes. Males are substantially more likely than females to report involvement in serious offenses. This finding is consistent with other self-report research and with UCR data (Steffensmeier et al. 2005; Smith and Visher 1980; Steffensmeier and Steffensmeier 1980).

Consistent with self-report data, UCR data show that males are disproportionately likely to be arrested. Males and females constitute roughly equal shares of the U.S. population, yet 70.7 percent of juveniles arrested in 2015 were male (FBI 2016). **Table 5.3** presents juvenile arrest percentages by gender for various offenses. Males made up the largest percentage of juveniles arrested for all crimes except prostitution, and were particularly overrepresented among those

TABLE 5.3 Juvenile arrests, by gender and type of crime, 2015

Type of crime	Total number	Male (%)	Female (%)
All crimes	709,333	70.7	29.3
Part I crimes	201,211	69.1	30.9
Violent crimes	39,519	81.6	18.4
Homicide	605	93.6	6.4
Forcible rape	2,745	96.1	3.9
Robbery	14,176	89.4	10.6
Aggravated assault	21,993	74.4	25.6
Property crimes	161,692	66.1	33.9
Burglary	27,473	86.6	13.4
Larceny-theft	120,967	59.6	40.4
Motor vehicle theft	11,169	82.1	17.9
Arson	2,083	84.1	15.9
Part II crimes	508,122	71.3	28.7
Other assaults	100,980	63.3	36.7
Vandalism	32,145	83.2	16.8
Weapons offenses	14,779	89.2	10.8
Forgery and counterfeiting	791	73.8	26.2
Fraud	3,474	66.6	33.4
Prostitution	442	24.4	75.6
Sex offenses (except forcible rape, prostitution)	6,699	87.3	12.7
Drug abuse violations	76,172	78.8	21.2
Curfew violations	33,908	71.8	282

Note: Arrest figures based on 12,706 reporting agencies, with 2015 estimated U.S. population of 246,947,242.

Source: Federal Bureau of Investigation (2016: Table 39).

arrested for violent offenses. In 2015, males accounted for 82 percent of arrests for Part I violent crimes and 66 percent of arrests for Part I property crimes. The gender differences in arrests were largest for murder, rape, robbery, burglary, weapons offenses, and sex offenses other than rape and prostitution. For these crimes, more than 86 percent of juveniles arrested were male. Although crime in general is a male phenomenon, this is especially true for violent crime.

Victimization survey data are consistent with official data in terms of the picture of gender and crime that they present (Hindelang 1979). This similarity across data sources demonstrates that the relationship between gender and crime is a consequence of females being less involved in crime, rather than of biases in the criminal justice system that might lead to fewer female arrests.

The second reading in this chapter examines trends in violence by teenage girls and presents findings from research conducted by the Girls Study Group convened by the Office of Juvenile Justice and Delinquency Prevention (Zahn et al. 2008).

Race and ethnicity

The relationship between race and involvement in delinquency is not entirely straightforward. To understand this relationship, one must consider the data source and the biases that exist in different data sources.[3]

Self-report data

Because self-report surveys ask individuals directly about their involvement in delinquency, they avoid potential biases in official and victimization data. Recent data from the MTF survey show some racial differences in the *prevalence* of delinquency (Bachman, Johnston, and O'Malley 2011, 2014; Eaton et al. 2010; Johnston, Bachman, and O'Malley 2010, 2013). The MTF survey asked respondents about 15 delinquent offenses, some of them serious (see **Table 5.4**). Data from 2009–2012 show racial differences in self-reported offenses against persons (violent offending) and in some property offenses. Compared to white respondents, blacks were substantially more likely to report involvement in all offenses against persons. Black respondents were also twice as likely as whites to report having been arrested or taken to a police station.

Earlier research, using NYS data, also shows some racial differences in the *incidence* of offending, but only for serious property crimes, for which blacks reported more than twice as many offenses as whites (Elliott and Ageton 1980). For serious violent offenses and less serious types of delinquency, there were no significant racial differences in frequency of offenses. The racial differences that exist in frequency of offending occur primarily among high-frequency offenders (Elliott and Ageton 1980; Wolfgang, Figlio, and Sellin 1972).[4]

Official data

The UCR includes data on individual characteristics only for people who have been arrested. However, offenses committed by members of some racial or ethnic groups may be more likely to result in arrest (Brame et al. 2014; Tapia 2010). Because many factors come into play in the arrest process, those who are arrested are not representative of all offenders. In other words, we cannot look at those who have been arrested and accurately assume that others who have offended but avoided arrest are similar in terms of race, age, gender, or other social characteristics. This is an important point to keep in mind when using official data to explore the relationship between delinquency and social characteristics.

TABLE 5.4 Racial differences in self-reported offending, by offense type: Monitoring the Future, 2009–2012 (four-year average of percent reporting involvement)

Delinquent activity (During the last 12 months, have you . . .)	White (%)	Black (%)
Offenses against persons		
Used a weapon to get something from a person	2.1	6.5
Hit an instructor or supervisor	1.9	6.1
Hurt someone badly enough to need bandages or a doctor	10.4	15.5
Gotten into a serious fight in school or at work	9.6	15.6
Taken part in a group fight	14.5	20.5
Property offenses		
Set fire to someone's property on purpose	1.9	4.5
Taken part of a car without permission of the owner	2.4	6.7
Taken a car not belonging to your family without permission	3.1	7.0
Damaged property at work on purpose	3.4	4.8
Taken something not belonging to you worth over $50	7.0	12.3
Damaged school property on purpose	8.6	11.2
Gone into some house or building when you weren't supposed to be there	22.9	22.0
Taken something from a store without paying for it	21.2	30.5
Taken something not belonging to you worth under $50	24.2	24.0
Contact with police		
Been arrested or taken to a police station	5.6	11.2

Sources: Bachman et al. (2011, 2014); Johnston et al. (2010, 2013).

UCR data show that African Americans are overrepresented among those who are arrested. In 2016, African Americans constituted 15.1 percent of the juvenile population and whites constituted 72.5 percent (U.S. Census Bureau 2017). Yet, 34.7 percent of juveniles arrested in 2016 were black and 62.1 percent were white (see **Table 5.5**, which compares across race and ethnicity the percentages of juveniles arrested for various offenses) (FBI 2017). (The first four columns of Table 5.5 present data for various races, and the last two columns present data based on ethnicity.) Racial differences in arrest rates become more glaring when we look at serious violent offenses, particularly homicide and robbery. The numbers are less striking for property crimes, but here, too, black juveniles are overrepresented in arrests. Victimization survey data show racial differences in serious, violent juvenile offending similar to those revealed in UCR data (Hawkins et al. 2000; Sampson and Lauritsen 1997).

UCR data indicate that juveniles of Hispanic origin are not similarly overrepresented in arrests. In 2016, persons of Hispanic origin constituted 24.9 percent of the juvenile population

TABLE 5.5 Juvenile arrests, by race, ethnicity, and type of crime, 2016

	White		Black		American Indian or Alaska Native		Asian		Hispanic or Latino		Not Hispanic or Latino	
Type of crime	Number	%	Number	%	Number	%	Number	%	Number	%	Number	%
All crimes	419,393	62.1	234,092	34.7	11,509	1.7	7,424	1.1	113,244	22.8	382,989	77.2
Part I crimes	103,772	55.5	77,086	41.3	2,819	1.5	2,515	1.3	30,070	23.0	100,860	77.0
Violent crimes	18,675	45.5	21,375	52.0	476	1.2	404	1.0	7,620	24.4	23,625	75.6
Homicide	244	35.9	413	60.8	9	1.3	11	1.6	103	24.8	313	75.2
Forcible rape	1,877	64.7	956	33.0	23	0.8	31	1.1	455	21.3	1,682	78.7
Robbery	4,468	29.2	10,520	68.8	94	0.6	139	0.9	2,462	21.9	8,792	78.1
Aggravated assault	12,068	54.4	9,486	42.7	350	1.6	223	1.0	4,600	26.4	12,838	73.6
Property crimes	85,097	58.4	55,711	38.2	2,343	1.6	2,111	1.4	22,450	22.5	77,235	77.5
Burglary	14,036	55.3	10,606	41.8	531	1.4	302	1.2	4,874	27.8	12,686	72.2
Larceny–theft	63,842	60.2	38,364	36.2	1,754	1.7	1,672	1.6	15,155	20.8	57,537	79.2
Motor vehicle theft	5,810	46.9	6,255	50.5	190	1.5	106	0.9	2,123	26.6	5,856	73.4
Arson	1,409	71.1	486	24.5	48	2.4	31	1.6	298	20.5	1,156	79.5
Part II crimes	315,621	64.7	157,006	32.2	8,690	1.8	4,909	1.0	83,174	22.8	282,129	77.2

Note: Arrest figures based on 13,049 reporting agencies, with 2016 estimated U.S. population of 257,112,535.

Source: Federal Bureau of Investigation (2017: Table 21B).

(U.S. Census Bureau 2017). This percentage is relatively consistent with the percentage of juveniles arrested who are Hispanic or Latino: 22.8 percent (see Table 5.5).

In summary, African Americans and whites are equally likely to report involvement in some types of delinquency, especially property offenses. African Americans, however, appear to be disproportionately represented among the population of offenders who commit serious violent offenses. In terms of frequency, there are no racial differences in the frequency of *minor* forms of delinquency. However, racial differences exist in the frequency of *serious* property offenses, with blacks more likely than whites to be high-frequency offenders.

Social class

Self-reports of offending provide the only way to examine the relationship between social class and delinquency because official data and victimization surveys do not include information about the social class of offenders. Some early self-report studies supported the assumption that delinquency is a lower-class phenomenon (e.g., Wolfgang et al. 1972), while other studies found no relationship between social class and offending (Johnson 1980; Krohn et al. 1980; Williams and Gold 1972). These early studies were criticized for several reasons, including their inclusion of "trivial" offenses that the majority of adolescents, regardless of social class, might be expected to commit (Kleck 1982). So what do studies that examine more than trivial offenses tell us about social class and delinquency?

Using NYS data, Elliott and Ageton (1980) examined the full range of delinquent behaviors, from minor to serious offenses (see also Elliott, Huizinga, and Ageton 1985; Elliott and Huizinga 1983). The striking class difference in this study was for serious violent crimes. For these offenses, lower-class youth reported almost four times as many offenses as did middle-class youth and one and a half times as many offenses as working-class youth (Elliott and Ageton 1980:160). The class differences in serious violent crime were primarily at the high end of the frequency continuum, where lower-class youth were disproportionately represented.

Elliott and Huizinga (1983) extended this study to include data gathered annually over a five-year period. They examined both prevalence and incidence of offending for persons from different social classes. They found no class differences in prevalence when they measured delinquency using a general scale of offenses. But they did find class differences in prevalence for serious offenses (felony assault, felony theft, and robbery), for males only. Middle-class males were less likely to engage in serious offenses than lower- or working-class males. They also found that class differences in delinquency appear greater with incidence than with prevalence measures, and greater for serious violent crimes than for other types of offenses (Elliott and Huizinga 1983).

Other self-report studies have demonstrated how the measurement of social class and delinquency impacts research results. For example, Margaret Farnworth and her colleagues (1994) found that, when social class was measured in terms of the education and occupation of wage earners in the household (the kinds of variables used most often in prior research), no strong or consistent relationship existed between class and delinquency. But when class was measured in terms of "underclass" status (households below the poverty level, households receiving welfare, unemployment of the principal wage earner), a relationship existed between class and serious street crime. The lower one's social class, the greater the likelihood of involvement in serious street crime. Similarly, the measurement of delinquency also affected research results. Farnworth and her colleagues concluded that, when social class and delinquency are measured in ways most consistent with theories of delinquency, the expected negative relationship exists between class and involvement in serious offending (Farnworth et al. 1994).

The conclusion we can draw from self-report data is that, when we focus on *minor* forms of offending, there is little or no relationship between social class and delinquency. Youth of all social classes are equally likely to engage in minor offenses. But when we focus on *serious* forms of offending, particularly violent offenses, a negative relationship exists between social class and delinquency. Lower-class youth are more likely than those in higher social classes to engage in serious violent offending, and to commit offenses with greater frequency.

SUMMARY AND CONCLUSIONS

This chapter addressed the nature and extent of delinquency by exploring the proportion of juveniles involved in delinquent offenses, the frequency of their involvement, the relative frequency of different types of offenses, and trends in delinquency. It also examined age, gender, race, ethnicity, and social class as social correlates of offending.

To understand the extent of delinquency we examined prevalence and incidence. Self-report data lead to the clear conclusion that a substantial portion of adolescents report involvement in delinquency, but relatively few indicate that their involvement is frequent or repetitive. Furthermore, among those youth who commit delinquent acts, only a small portion come to the attention of the police, relatively few are arrested, and even fewer are processed by juvenile courts. This is why arrest data and juvenile court data fail to provide an adequate depiction of the prevalence and incidence of delinquent offenses.

Virtually all sources of data indicate that minor forms of delinquency are far more common than serious, violent offenses. Property offenses (especially property damage, vandalism, and theft) and alcohol and marijuana use are among the most common types of offenses. Among violent offenses, less serious forms are most common, particularly fighting and simple assault. Truancy is the most common status offense.

Despite data limitations, we can draw certain conclusions about delinquency trends. Because much crime goes unreported, self-report data provide the most accurate indication of trends in offenses. Across different offense types, self-report delinquency data generally show a fairly stable pattern since the late 1980s, with a slight decline beginning in 1997. Self-report drug use in the last 30 days similarly shows a decline since 1997, with the exception of marijuana use, which has shown a gradual increase since 2007. Even though juvenile arrests for property offenses fluctuated in the first half of the 1990s, a notable drop followed in the second half of the decade—one that persists into the new century. Juvenile arrests for violent offenses increased in the late 1980s and into the early 1990s, but have steadily declined since then. In general, with the exception of an increase in violent juvenile crime in the late 1980s and early 1990s, the trend for most types of juvenile crime has been one of decline since the latter part of the 1990s.

Our exploration of the social correlates of offending revealed that age and gender are strongly and consistently related to involvement in crime, which is primarily a pursuit of young males. Multiple data sources all point to the same fact: The period of adolescence and young adulthood is the peak time of offending for most individuals. The peak age of offending for violent crimes, however, is somewhat older than for most property offenses.

The gender gap in crime also varies by type of offense and is particularly wide for violent offenses, which are committed overwhelmingly by males. All three data sources—official data, victimization surveys, and self-report surveys—show that males are disproportionately involved in delinquency. The gender gap in crime revealed in self-report data, however, is generally smaller than the gap suggested by official data.

The relationships between race and social class and involvement in delinquency are less clear-cut than those observed for age and gender. The bulk of evidence suggests that African Americans are disproportionately represented among the population of offenders who commit serious offenses. For decades, some social scientists argued that official data on offenders are suspect because of biases inherent in the criminal justice system. Yet victimization data tend to confirm the conclusions drawn from official data. Both official and victimization data are weighted more heavily toward serious offenses. However, self-report data, which best capture minor offenses, show that blacks and whites are equally likely to engage in some types of delinquency (prevalence), but blacks are more likely than whites to report involvement in violent offending.

Self-reports of offending reveal no social class differences in involvement in *minor* offenses, which youth of all social classes are equally likely to commit. But there are significant class differences in *serious* forms of offending, particularly violent offenses. Lower-class youth are more likely than working- and middle-class youth to engage in serious delinquency and to commit a higher frequency of offenses.

READING 5.1

"JUVENILE ARRESTS 2012."

Puzzanchera, Charles. 2014. *Juvenile Offenders and Victims: National Report Series Bulletin*. Washington, DC: Office of Juvenile Justice and Delinquency Prevention.

This bulletin provides an overview of juvenile delinquency in the United States by analyzing arrest data from the Uniform Crime Reporting Program. As you consider these data, it is important to keep in mind that many juvenile offenses do not result in an arrest.

What do arrest statistics count?

Findings in this bulletin are drawn from data that local law enforcement agencies across the country report to the Federal Bureau of Investigation's (FBI's) Uniform Crime Reporting (UCR) Program. To properly interpret the material presented, the reader needs a clear understanding of what arrest statistics count. Arrest statistics report the number of arrests that law enforcement agencies made in a given year—not the number of individuals arrested nor the number of crimes committed. The number of arrests is not the same as the number of people arrested because an unknown number of individuals are arrested more than once during the year. Nor do arrest statistics represent the number of crimes that arrested individuals commit because a series of crimes that one person commits may culminate in a single arrest, and a single crime may result in the arrest of more than one person. This latter situation, where many arrests result from one crime, is relatively common in juvenile law-violating behavior because juveniles are more likely than adults to commit crimes in groups. For this reason, one should not use arrest statistics to indicate the relative proportions of crime that juveniles and adults commit. Arrest statistics are most appropriately a measure of entry into the justice system.

The number of arrests of juveniles in 2012 was 37% fewer than the number of arrests in 2003							
Most serious offense	2012 estimated number of juvenile arrests	Percent of total juvenile arrests			Percent change		
		Female	Younger than 15	White	2003–2012	2008–2012	2011–2012
Total	1,319,700	29%	28%	65%	–37%	–34%	–10%
Violent Crime Index	61,070	19	28	46	–33	–36	–10
Murder and nonnegligent manslaughter	720	9	11	46	–43	–42	–14
Forcible rape	2,500	2	37	64	–39	–24	–10
Robbery	21,500	10	20	29	–15	–39	–10
Aggravated assault	36,300	26	33	55	–40	–35	–11
Property Crime Index	295,400	35	29	61	–36	–32	–12
Burglary	53,800	12	28	59	–36	–36	–13
Larceny-theft	224,200	42	29	61	–30	–30	–12
Motor vehicle theft	13,100	16	21	57	–71	–47	–7
Arson	4,400	15	59	72	–46	–33	–11
Nonindex							
Other (simple) assaults	173,100	37	39	59	–28	–25	–9
Forgery and counterfeiting	1,400	30	14	67	–69	–44	–9
Fraud	4,700	32	18	56	–36	–35	–10
Embezzlement	400	39	7	63	–61	–65	6
Stolen property (buying, receiving, possessing)	12,900	16	23	52	–47	–38	–3
Vandalism	59,900	16	39	75	–43	–44	–12
Weapons (carrying, possessing, etc.)	24,700	10	34	60	–37	–38	–13
Prostitution and commercialized vice	800	76	7	40	–44	–46	–19

Sex offense (except forcible rape and prostitution)	12,400	10	50	71	–32	–14	–1
Drug abuse violations	140,000	17	17	74	–29	–22	–6
Gambling	1,000	6	10	10	–44	–41	–2
Offenses against the family and children	3,300	38	32	68	–51	–42	–6
Driving under the influence	9,400	26	2	92	–55	–41	–7
Liquor laws	77,800	40	10	88	–42	–40	–12
Drunkenness	9,900	28	12	87	–43	–36	–14
Disorderly conduct	120,100	35	38	55	–38	–36	–14
Vagrancy	1,400	22	26	62	–30	–64	–22
All other offenses (except traffic)	239,600	27	24	68	–37	–33	–10
Suspicion (not included in totals)	300	27	34	73	–79	25	141
Curfew and loitering	70,200	29	28	57	–49	–47	–9

- All four offenses that make up the Violent Crime Index decreased considerably between 2008 and 2012: murder (–42%), rape (–24%), robbery (–39%), and aggravated assault (–35%).
- In 2012, there were an estimated 224,200 juvenile arrests for larceny-theft. More than 4 of every 10 (42%) of these arrests involved females, 29% involved youth younger than age 15, and 61% involved white youth.
- Youth younger than age 15 accounted for more than half (59%) of all juvenile arrests for arson in 2012 and nearly 40% of juvenile arrests for simple assault, vandalism, and disorderly conduct.
- Females accounted for 9% of juvenile arrests for murder but one-fourth (26%) of juvenile arrests for aggravated assault and 37% of juvenile arrests for simple assault.

Note: Detail may not add to totals because of rounding.

Data source: Analysis of Snyder, H., and Mulako-Wantota, J., Bureau of Justice Statistics, *Arrest Data Analysis Tool* [online, retrieved 10/14/14].

Arrest statistics also have limitations in measuring the volume of arrests for a particular offense. Under the UCR Program, the FBI requires law enforcement agencies to classify an arrest by the most serious offense charged in that arrest. For example, the arrest of a youth charged with aggravated assault and possession of a weapon would be reported to the FBI as an arrest for aggravated assault. Therefore, when arrest statistics show that law enforcement agencies made an estimated 24,700 arrests of young people for weapons law violations in 2012, it means that a weapons law violation was the most serious charge in these 24,700 arrests. An unknown number of additional arrests in 2012 included a weapons charge as a lesser offense.

How do arrest statistics differ from clearance statistics?

Clearance statistics measure the proportion of reported crimes that were cleared (or "closed") by either arrest or other, exceptional means (such as the death of the offender or unwillingness of the victim to cooperate). A single arrest may result in many clearances. For example, 1 arrest could clear 10 burglaries if the person was charged with committing all 10 crimes, or multiple arrests may result in a single clearance if a group of offenders committed the crime. The FBI's reporting guidelines require that clearances involving both juvenile and adult offenders be classified as clearances for crimes that adults commit. Because the juvenile clearance proportions include only those clearances in which no adults were involved, they underestimate juvenile involvement in crime. Although these data do not present a definitive picture of juvenile involvement in crime, they are the closest measure generally available of the proportion of crime known to law enforcement that is attributed to persons younger than age 18.

Juvenile arrests for violent crimes fell 36% in the past 5 years

The FBI assesses trends in violent crimes by monitoring four offenses that law enforcement agencies nationwide consistently report. These four crimes—murder and nonnegligent manslaughter, forcible rape, robbery, and aggravated assault—form the Violent Crime Index.

Following 10 years of declines between 1994 and 2004, juvenile arrests for Violent Crime Index offenses increased from 2004 to 2006 and then declined each year through 2012. As a result, the number of juvenile violent crime arrests in 2012 was less than any of the previous 33 years and 24% less than the previous low point in 1984.

In fact, juvenile arrests for all violent crimes reached historically low levels in 2012. Following a 39% decline since 2008, the number of juvenile robbery arrests in 2012 was at its lowest level since 1980. Similarly, the number of juvenile arrests for forcible rape fell 40% in the past 10 years to reach its lowest level of the 1980–2012 period. After falling to a relatively low level in 2004, juvenile arrests for murder increased through 2007 and then declined 46% by 2012 to reach the lowest level in three decades. The number of juvenile arrests for aggravated assault was cut in half between 1994 and 2012, also reaching its lowest level since at least 1980.

Between 2003 and 2012, the number of arrests in all offense categories declined for juveniles and the relative decline for juveniles exceeded that of adults.

Juvenile property crime arrests declined for the fourth straight year

As with violent crime, the FBI assesses trends in the volume of property crimes by monitoring four offenses that law enforcement agencies nationwide consistently report. These four

	Percent change in arrests 2003–2012	
Most serious offense	**Juvenile**	**Adult**
Violent Crime Index	–33%	–9%
Murder	–43	–13
Forcible rape	–39	–30
Robbery	–15	0
Aggravated assault	–40	–9
Property Crime Index	–36	18
Burglary	–36	11
Larceny-theft	–30	29
Motor vehicle theft	–71	–49
Simple assault	–28	2
Weapons law violations	–37	–3
Drug abuse violations	–29	–5

Data source: Analysis of Snyder, H., and Mulako-Wantota, J., Bureau of Justice Statistics, *Arrest Data Analysis Tool* [online, retrieved 10/14/14].

crimes, which form the Property Crime Index, are burglary, larceny-theft, motor vehicle theft, and arson.

For the period 1980–1994, during which juvenile violent crime arrests increased substantially, juvenile property crime arrests remained relatively constant. After this long period of relative stability, juvenile property crime arrests began to fall. Between 1994 and 2006, the number of juvenile Property Crime Index arrests was cut in half, reaching its lowest level since at least 1980. This decline was interrupted briefly as the number of juvenile Property Crime Index arrests increased in 2007 and 2008. By 2012, the number of juvenile Property Crime Index arrests fell 32%, reaching its lowest level since at least 1980. Between 2008 and 2012, juvenile arrests declined for individual property offenses: burglary (36%), larceny-theft (30%), motor vehicle theft (47%), and arson (33%). As a result, juvenile arrests for all Property Crime Index offenses in 2012 were at their lowest levels since at least 1980.

Females accounted for 29% of juvenile arrests in 2012

Law enforcement agencies made 383,600 arrests of females younger than age 18 in 2012. From 2003 through 2012, arrests of juvenile females decreased less than male arrests in several offense categories (e.g., aggravated and simple assault, larceny-theft, vandalism, liquor law violations, and disorderly conduct).

Gender differences also occurred in the assault arrest trends for adults. Between 2003 and 2012, adult male arrests for aggravated assault fell 12% while female arrests increased 1%. Similarly, adult male arrests for simple assault fell 3% between 2003 and 2012 while adult female arrests rose 20%. Therefore, the female proportion of arrests grew for both types of assault. It is likely that the disproportionate growth in female assault arrests over this period was related to factors that affected both juveniles and adults.

	Percent change in juvenile arrests 2003–2012	
Most serious offense	Female	Male
Violent Crime Index	–31%	–34%
Robbery	–2	–16
Aggravated assault	–35	–42
Simple assault	–19	–32
Property Crime Index	–29	–39
Burglary	–36	–36
Larceny-theft	–26	–33
Motor vehicle theft	–73	–70
Vandalism	–35	–45
Weapons	–45	–36
Drug abuse violations	–26	–30
Liquor law violations	–34	–46
Driving under influence	–43	–58
Disorderly conduct	–29	–42

Data source: Analysis of Snyder, H., and Mulako-Wantota, J., Bureau of Justice Statistics, *Arrest Data Analysis Tool* [online, retrieved 10/14/14].

Gender differences in arrest trends also increased the proportion of arrests involving females in other offense categories for both juveniles and adults. Between 2003 and 2012, the number of larceny-theft arrests of juvenile females fell 26% while juvenile male arrests declined 33%, and adult female arrests grew more than adult male arrests (55% and 14%, respectively). For Property Crime Index offenses, juvenile arrests declined more for males than for females between 2003 and 2012, and adult arrests increased less for males (5%) than for females (48%).

Juvenile arrests disproportionately involved minorities

The racial composition of the U.S. juvenile population ages 10–17 in 2012 was 76% white, 17% black, 5% Asian/Pacific Islander, and

Most serious offense	Black proportion of juvenile arrests in 2012
Murder	52%
Forcible rape	33
Robbery	69
Aggravated assault	43
Simple assault	39
Burglary	39
Larceny-theft	35
Motor vehicle theft	40
Weapons	37
Drug abuse violations	23
Vandalism	23
Liquor laws	7

Data source: Analysis of Snyder, H., and Mulako-Wantota, J., Bureau of Justice Statistics, *Arrest Data Analysis Tool* [online, retrieved 10/14/14].

2% American Indian. Most juveniles of Hispanic ethnicity were included in the white racial category. More than half (52%) of all juvenile arrests for violent crimes in 2012 involved black youth, 46% involved white youth, 1% involved Asian youth, and 1% involved American Indian youth. For property crime arrests, the proportions were 61% white youth, 36% black youth, 2% Asian youth, and 1% American Indian youth. Black youth were overrepresented in juvenile arrests.

Violent crime arrest rates reached a new historic low in 2012

The juvenile Violent Crime Index arrest rate (i.e., the number of arrests per 100,000 juveniles in the population) was essentially constant through the late 1980s and then increased sharply through 1994. This rapid growth led to speculation about changes in the nature of juvenile offenders—concerns that spurred state legislators to pass laws that facilitated an increase in the flow of youth into the adult justice system. Since the 1994 peak, however, the juvenile violent crime arrest rate generally declined each year since the mid-1990s. Following the past 4 consecutive years of decline, the rate in 2012 was 63% below the 1994 peak, resting at its lowest level since at least 1980.

In 2012, juveniles were involved in about 1 in 14 arrests for murder and about 1 in 5 arrests for robbery, burglary, and motor vehicle theft

Most serious offense	Juvenile arrests as a percentage of total arrests				
	All	Male	Female	White	Black
Total	10%	10%	11%	10%	12%
Violent Crime Index	12	12	11	9	16
Murder and nonnegligent manslaughter	7	7	5	6	7
Forcible rape	14	14	22	14	14
Robbery	21	21	16	14	26
Aggravated assault	9	9	11	8	12
Property Crime Index	18	19	17	16	22
Burglary	19	20	14	17	24
Larceny-theft	17	18	17	16	21
Motor vehicle theft	19	20	16	17	25
Arson	38	39	32	38	41
Nonindex					
Other (simple) assaults	14	13	19	13	18
Vandalism	26	28	21	27	24
Weapons (carrying, possessing, etc.)	17	16	19	17	15
Drug abuse violations	9	9	8	10	7

Data source: Analysis of Snyder, H., and Mulako-Wantota, J., Bureau of Justice Statistics, *Arrest Data Analysis Tool* [online, retrieved 10/14/14].

The juvenile Violent Crime Index arrest rate fell 35% between 2008 and 2012

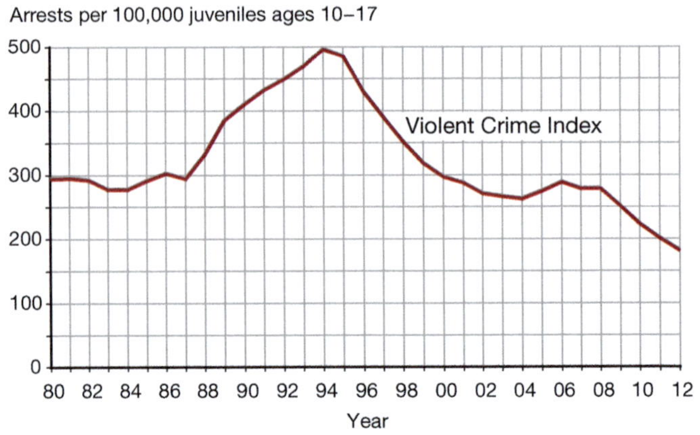

Violent Crime Index arrest rate trends by gender and race

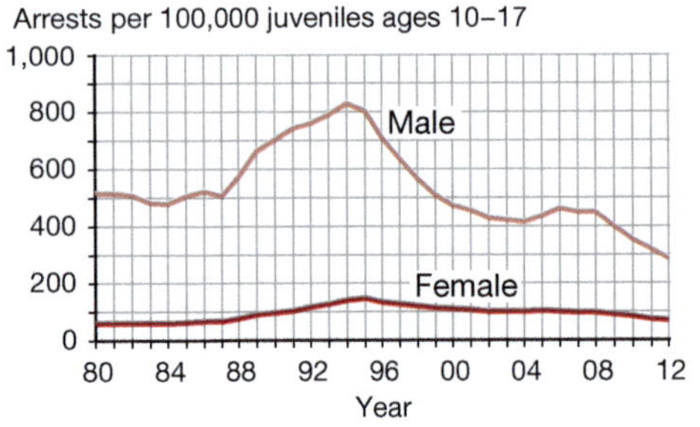

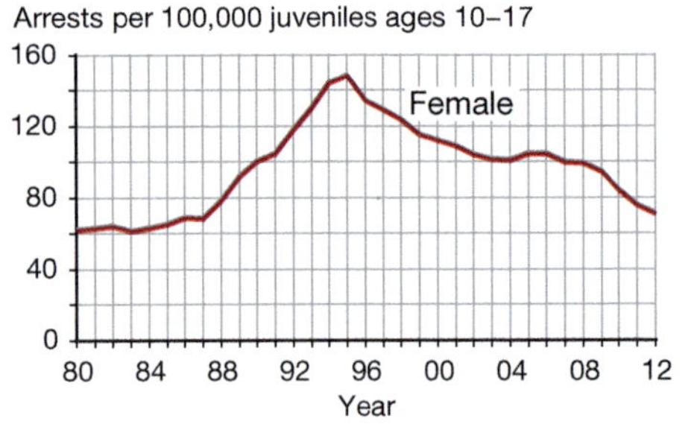

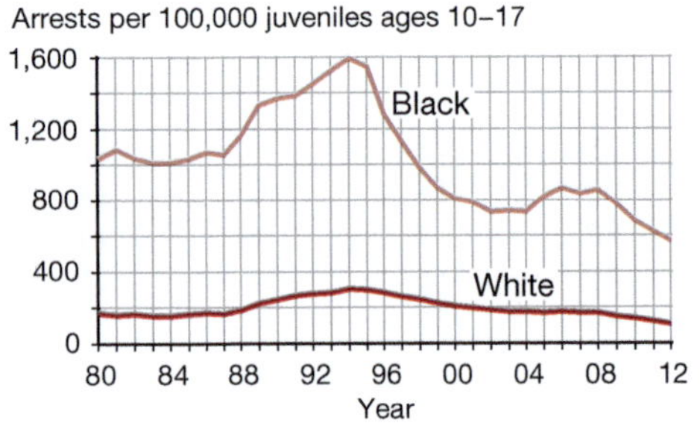

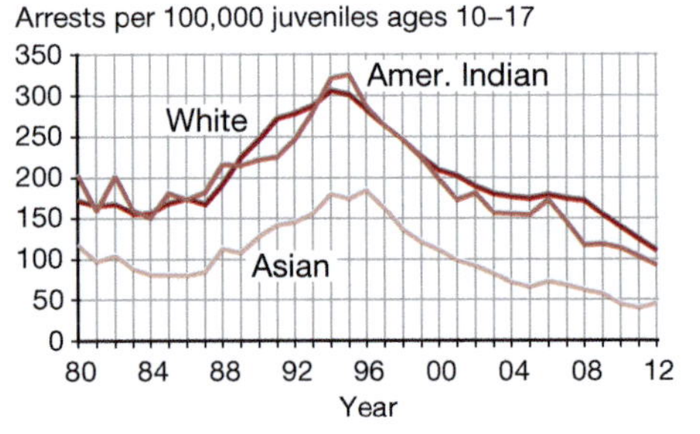

- The Violent Crime Index arrest rate declined considerably for all racial subgroups in the last 10 years. The relative decline between 2003 and 2012 was greatest for Asian youth (44%), followed by American Indian (41%), white (39%), and black (23%) youth.

Data source: Analysis of arrest data from the Bureau of Justice Statistics and population data from the U.S. Census Bureau.

Declines in violent crime arrest rates were evident across gender and racial groups

Male juvenile violent crime arrest rates exceed the rates for females. For example, during the 1980s, the male violent crime arrest rate was nearly 8 times greater than the female rate. However, by 2012, the male rate was only 4 times greater. This convergence of male and female arrest rates is due to the large relative increase in the female rate. Between 1980 and 1994, the male rate increased 60% while the female rate more than doubled. By 2012, the male rate was 65% below its 1994 peak and at its lowest level in at least three decades. Although the female rate also declined since the mid-1990s (down 52%), the rate in 2012 was 16% above its 1983 low point.

With few exceptions, violent crime arrest rates have declined for all racial groups for nearly two decades. In fact, violent crime arrest rates for each racial group declined 64% or more since the mid-1990s. As a result of these declines, the rates in 2012 for white, black, and American Indian youth were at their lowest level since at least 1980, and rates for Asian youth were near their lowest level.

Property crime arrest rates fell in each of the past 4 years

After years of relative stability between 1980 and the mid-1990s, the juvenile Property Crime Index arrest rate began a decline that continued annually until reaching a then-historic low in 2006, down 54% from its 1988 peak. This nearly two-decade decline was interrupted by a slight increase over the next 2 years, followed by a 31% decline between 2008 and 2012. As a result, juveniles were less likely to be arrested for property crimes in 2012 than at any point in the past 33 years.

Male property crime arrest rates declined more than female rates

The male property crime arrest rate has generally declined each year since the late 1980s. In the 10 years since 2003, the male rate fell 37%, reaching its lowest level in at least three decades. In comparison, the decline in the female rate began nearly 10 years after that for males, and the relative decline was less for females (down 27% since 2003). Unlike the pattern for males, the female rate varied considerably in the past 10 years. However, after 3 consecutive years of decline, in 2012 the female rate reached its lowest point since at least 1980.

Property crime arrest rates declined for all racial groups

Similar to the pattern for violent crime, property crime arrest rates have declined for all racial groups for nearly two decades. As a result, in 2012 the rates for youth in each racial group except for Asian were at their lowest level since at least 1980, and rates for Asian youth were near their lowest level. The decline over the past 10 years was greatest for American Indian youth (47%), followed by Asian (43%), white (40%), and black (17%) youth.

Since 2008, juvenile Property Crime Index arrest rates fell 20% or more for all demographic groups

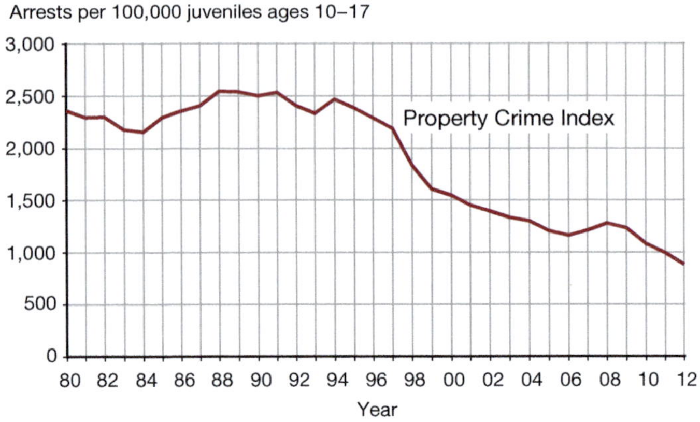

Property Crime Index arrest rate trends by gender and race

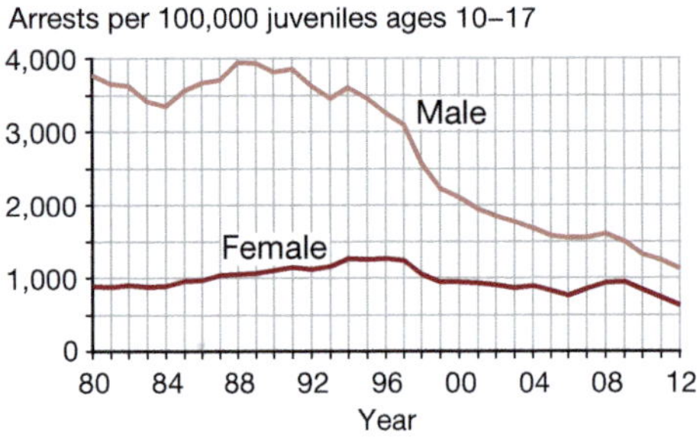

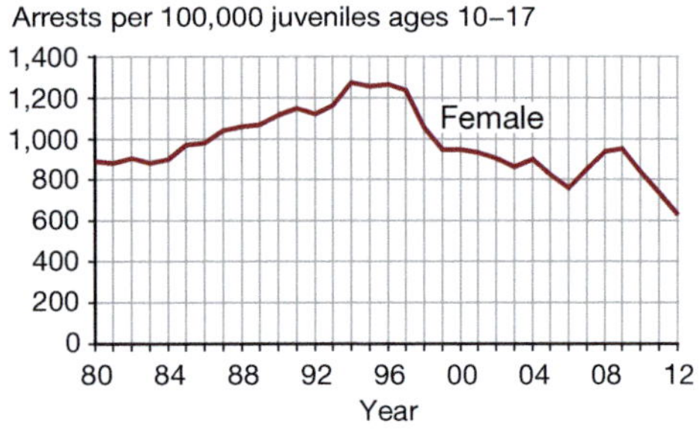

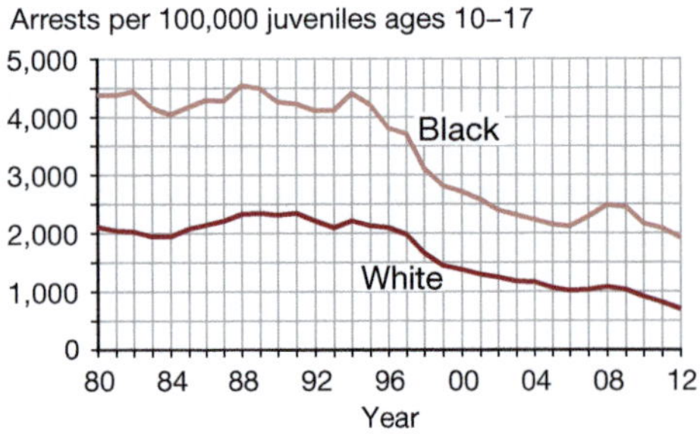

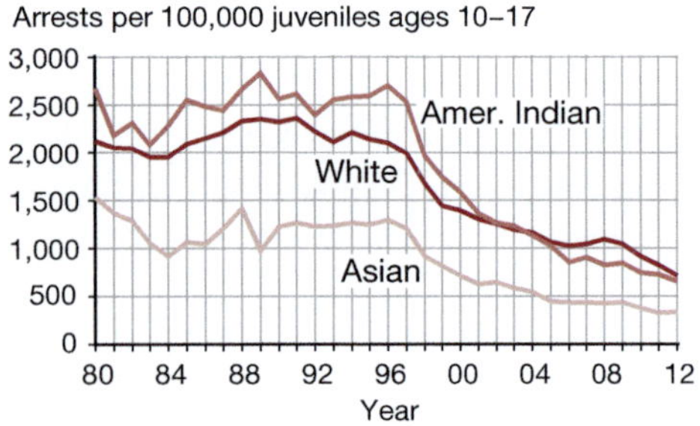

- Larceny-theft accounted for 76% of all juvenile Property Crime Index arrests in 2012. As such, the trends in Property Crime Index arrest rates largely reflect the trends in larceny-theft.

Data source: Analysis of arrest data from the Bureau of Justice Statistics and population data from the U.S. Census Bureau.

Murder

- After reaching a peak in 1993, the juvenile arrest rate for murder declined substantially through 2000 (down 72%), falling below 4.0 (per 100,000 juveniles) for the first time in at least two decades. The juvenile murder arrest rate was less than 3.0 in the past 2 years.
- Compared with the previous 20 years, the juvenile murder arrest rate between 2000 and 2012 was historically low and relatively stable. In fact, the number of juvenile arrests for murder in 1993 (the peak year for juvenile murder arrests) exceeded the combined total number of such arrests in the past 4 years.

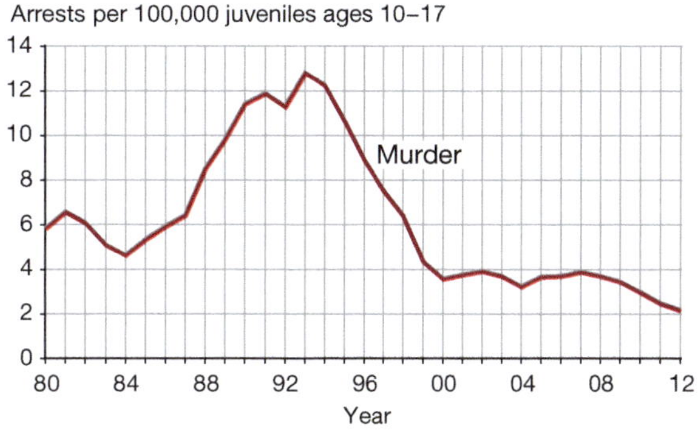

Forcible rape

- With few exceptions, the juvenile arrest rate for forcible rape dropped annually from its 1991 peak, falling 66% through 2012. The 2,500 estimated juvenile arrests for forcible rape in 2012 were the fewest such arrests in at least three decades.
- Juveniles accounted for 14% of all forcible rape arrests reported in 2012. Nearly two-thirds (63%) of these juvenile arrests involved youth ages 15–17. Similarly, white youth accounted for 64% of juvenile arrests for forcible rape in 2012. Males accounted for the overwhelming majority (98%) of juvenile arrests for forcible rape.

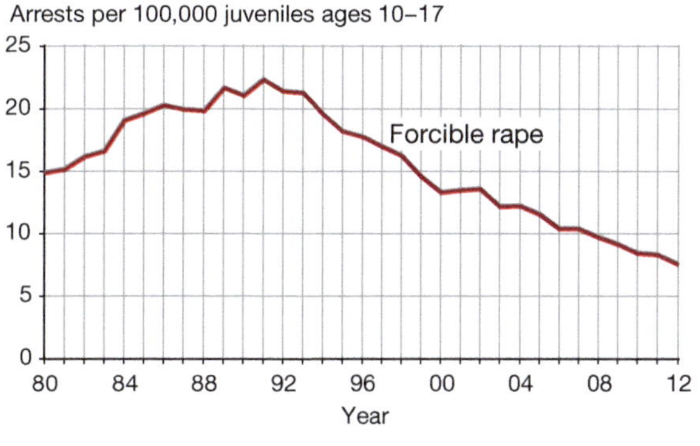

Data source: Analysis of arrest data from the Bureau of Justice Statistics and population data from the U.S. Census Bureau.

Robbery

- Similar to other violent crimes, the juvenile robbery arrest rate declined steadily from the mid-1990s into the early 2000s. However, unlike the other violent crimes, the robbery rate increased between 2004 and 2008. The rate has declined each of the past 4 years (down 38%), resting in 2012 at its lowest point of the 33-year period.
- Juvenile robbery arrest rates declined for all gender and racial subgroups since 2008: 38% for males, 32% for females, 41% for whites, 35% for blacks, 24% for Asians, and 8% for American Indians. Rates in 2012 were at historic lows for males and white youth.

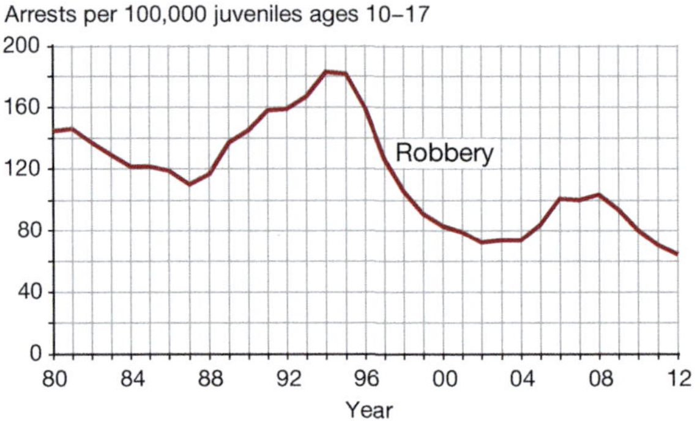

Aggravated assault

- After doubling between 1980 and 1994, the juvenile arrest rate for aggravated assault fell substantially and consistently through 2012, down 62% from its 1994 peak. As a result of this decline, the rate in 2012 reached its lowest point since at least 1980 and was 15% below the previous low point in 1983.
- Aggravated assault rates declined for males and females and all racial groups since the mid-1990s. In fact, in 2012 the rates were at their lowest level of the 1980–2012 period for males and for white, black, and American Indian youth.

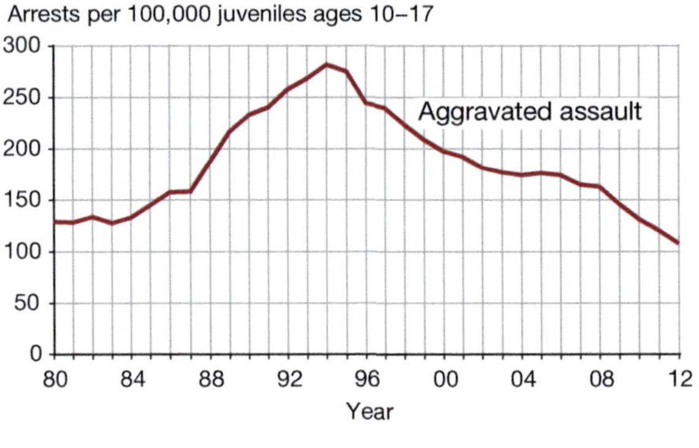

Data source: Analysis of arrest data from the Bureau of Justice Statistics and population data from the U.S. Census Bureau.

Burglary

- Unlike the pattern for other property crimes, a steady decline marked the trend in the juvenile arrest rate for burglary during the 1980–2012 period. The rate in 2012 reached its lowest level of the 33-year period, which was 78% below the level in 1980.
- This large decline in juvenile burglary arrests was not reflected in the adult statistics. For example, between 2000 and 2012, the number of juvenile burglary arrests fell 44%, while adult burglary arrests increased 12%. As a result of this decline, only one-fifth (19%) of all burglary arrests in 2012 were juvenile arrests, compared with one-third in 2000.

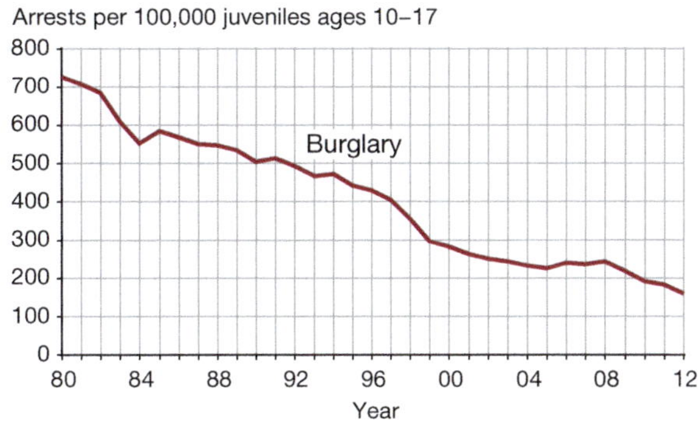

Larceny-theft

- With few exceptions, the juvenile larceny-theft arrest rate declined annually over the past two decades, falling 60% since the mid-1990s. Following 4 years of decline (down 29% since 2008), in 2012 the juvenile arrest rate for larceny-theft was at its lowest level in more than three decades and 16% below the previous low point in 2006.
- In 2012, three-fourths (76%) of all juvenile arrests for Property Crime Index offenses were for larceny-theft. As such, juvenile Property Crime Index arrest trends largely reflect the pattern of larceny-theft arrests (which is dominated by shoplifting—the most common larceny-theft offense).

Data source: Analysis of arrest data from the Bureau of Justice Statistics and population data from the U.S. Census Bureau.

Motor vehicle theft

- After reaching a peak in 1989, the juvenile arrest rate for motor vehicle theft declined annually for more than 20 years. By 2012, the rate was 89% below the 1989 peak.
- This large decline in motor vehicle arrests was greater for juveniles than adults. For both groups, motor vehicle arrests reached a peak in 1989; since that time, the number of juvenile arrests for motor vehicle theft declined 86%, while adult arrests decreased 59%.
- In 2012, most (79%) juvenile arrests for motor vehicle theft involved youth ages 15–17.

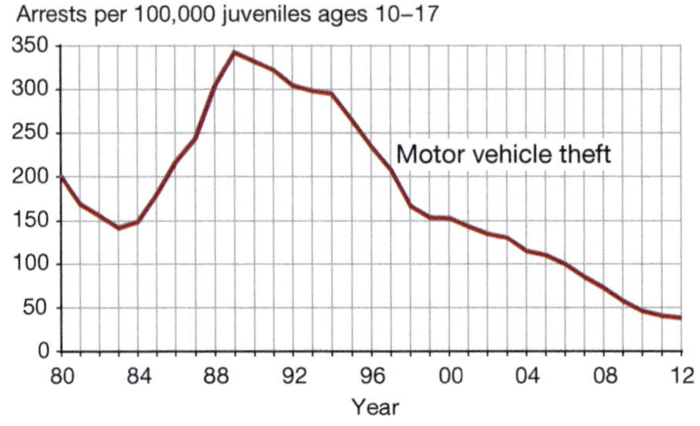

Arson

- The pattern of stability, growth, and decline in the juvenile arrest rate for arson was similar in magnitude and character to the trend in juvenile violent crime arrest rates. After years of stability, the juvenile arrest rate for arson increased more than 50% between 1987 and 1994 before falling 63% between 1994 and 2012.
- Arson is the criminal act with the largest proportion of juvenile arrestees—38% in 2012—and most juvenile arrests (59%) involved youth younger than 15. In comparison, the juvenile proportion for larceny-theft was 17%, and 29% of those involved youth younger than 15.

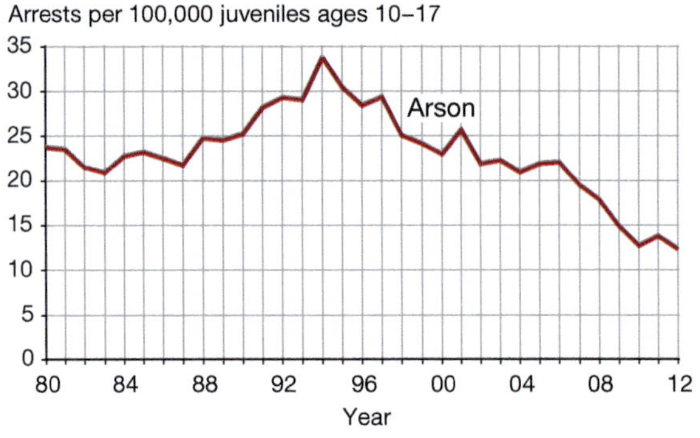

Data source: Analysis of arrest data from the Bureau of Justice Statistics and population data from the U.S. Census Bureau.

Among states with at least minimally adequate reporting (above 74%), those with high juvenile violent crime arrest rates in 2012 were Delaware, Florida, Maryland, Pennsylvania, and Tennessee

	2012 Reporting population coverage	Arrests of juveniles under age 18 per 100,000 juveniles ages 10–17, 2012					2012 Reporting population coverage	Arrests of juveniles under age 18 per 100,000 juveniles ages 10–17, 2012			
		Violent Crime Index	Property Crime Index	Drug abuse	Weapon			Violent Crime Index	Property Crime Index	Drug abuse	Weapon
U.S. total	84%	187	914	417	72	Missouri	93%	187	1,259	468	61
Alabama	2	57	698	286	11	Montana	94	113	1,535	406	15
Alaska	64	246	1,485	622	50	Nebraska	91	115	1,711	719	57
Arizona	91	152	1,109	653	34	Nevada	100	243	941	405	40
Arkansas	85	143	1,001	328	44	New Hampshire	88	54	650	543	0
California	98	225	669	253	123	New Jersey	97	199	523	526	80
Colorado	91	111	1,108	611	65	New Mexico	85	202	1,278	644	78
Connecticut	94	162	599	211	45	New York	55	218	1,024	485	56
Delaware	100	389	1,245	546	73	North Carolina	90	162	969	319	138
District of Columbia	0	NA	NA	NA	NA	North Dakota	98	89	1,343	501	37
Florida	100	263	1,264	480	56	Ohio	62	100	703	252	43
Georgia	89	169	927	302	61	Oklahoma	94	130	958	354	49
Hawaii	11	248	826	880	67	Oregon	93	133	1,215	699	45
Idaho	99	87	1,198	549	70	Pennsylvania	96	303	770	387	90
Illinois	22	751	1,395	1,337	291	Rhode Island	99	128	735	407	130
Indiana	64	160	981	387	45	South Carolina	87	146	911	516	87
Iowa	88	183	1,347	403	49	South Dakota	90	87	1,495	1,043	60
Kansas	72	112	809	369	23	Tennessee	91	281	949	431	85
Kentucky	96	91	562	166	20	Texas	97	121	785	471	29

Continued

	2012 Reporting population coverage	Arrests of juveniles under age 18 per 100,000 juveniles ages 10–17, 2012					2012 Reporting population coverage	Arrests of juveniles under age 18 per 100,000 juveniles ages 10–17, 2012			
		Violent Crime Index	Property Crime Index	Drug abuse	Weapon			Violent Crime Index	Property Crime Index	Drug abuse	Weapon
Louisiana	50	445	1,385	477	90	Utah	98	76	1,328	492	85
Maine	100	54	1,133	412	26	Vermont	89	70	391	239	17
Maryland	91	295	1,100	617	102	Virginia	100	74	620	337	41
Massachusetts	92	177	305	84	28	Washington	75	163	1,039	399	60
Michigan	93	135	658	274	53	West Virginia	73	57	323	138	10
Minnesota	87	114	1,267	525	47	Wisconsin	94	234	1,793	648	143
Mississippi	51	63	1,004	377	64	Wyoming	90	51	1,264	1,122	66

NA = Arrest counts were not available for the District of Columbia or Hawaii in the FBI's *Crime in the United States 2012*.

Notes: Arrest rates for jurisdictions with less than complete reporting may not be representative of the entire state. Although juvenile arrest rates may largely reflect juvenile behavior, many other factors can affect the magnitude of these rates. Arrest rates are calculated by dividing the number of youth arrests made in the year by the number of youth living in the jurisdiction. Therefore, jurisdictions that arrest a relatively large number of nonresident juveniles would have a higher arrest rate than jurisdictions where resident youth behave similarly. Jurisdictions (especially small ones) that are vacation destinations or that are centers for economic activity in a region may have arrest rates that reflect the behavior of nonresident youth more than that of resident youth. Other factors that influence arrest rates in a given area include the attitudes of citizens toward crime, the policies of local law enforcement agencies, and the policies of other components of the justice system. In many areas, not all law enforcement agencies report their arrest data to the FBI. Rates for such areas are necessarily based on partial information and may not be accurate. Comparisons of juvenile arrest rates across jurisdictions can be informative. Because of factors noted, however, comparisons should be made with caution.

Data source: Analysis of arrest data from *Crime in the United States 2012* (Washington, DC: Federal Bureau of Investigation, 2013) tables 5 and 69, and population data from the National Center for Health Statistics' *Vintage 2013 Postcensal Estimates of the Resident Population of the United States (April 1, 2010, July 1, 2010–July 1, 2013), by Year, County, Single-Year of Age (0, 1, 2, . . . , 85 Years and Over), Bridged Race, Hispanic Origin, and Sex* [machine-readable data files available online at www.cdc.gov/nchs/nvss/bridged_race.htm, as of 6/26/14].

[Notes omitted.]

READING 5.2

"VIOLENCE BY TEENAGE GIRLS: TRENDS AND CONTEXT."

Margaret A. Zahn, Susan Brumbaugh, Darrell Steffensmeier, Barry C. Feld, Merry Morash, Meda Chesney-Lind, Jody Miller, Allison Ann Payne, Denise C. Gottfredson, and Candace Kruttschnitt, Girls Study Group. 2008. *Understanding and Responding to Girls' Delinquency*. Washington, DC: Office of Juvenile Justice and Delinquency Prevention. (Pages 1–10, 15, 16)

The following excerpts are from a bulletin that presents the results of research conducted by the Girls Study Group, convened by the Office of Juvenile Justice and Delinquency Prevention to inform the understanding of and responses to girls' delinquency. This research uses data from three different sources to try to determine whether girls' violence has actually increased in recent years, or whether changes in the policing of girls' behavior have given a false impression of increases in girls' violence.

In June 2005, *Newsweek* ran a story titled "Bad Girls Go Wild," which described "the significant rise in violent behavior among girls" as a "burgeoning national crisis" (Scelfo, 2005)—a depiction that echoes other recent media accounts. This Bulletin assesses the accuracy of these assertions using the best available data. Drawing on information from official arrest sources, nationally based self-report and victimization surveys, and studies reported in the social science literature, the Bulletin examines the involvement of girls in violent activity (including whether such activity has increased relative to the increase for boys) and the contexts in which girls engage in violent behavior.

One of the most consistent and robust findings in criminology is that, for nearly every offense, females engage in much less crime and juvenile delinquency than males. In recent years, however, the extent and character of this gender difference in offending are increasingly being called into question by statistics and media reports suggesting the increasing involvement of girls in the juvenile and criminal justice systems. During the past two-and-a-half decades, official statistics suggest that female delinquency has undergone substantial changes compared with male delinquency. Between 1980 and 2005, arrests of girls increased nationwide, while arrests of boys decreased (Federal Bureau of Investigation, 2006). These arrest trends, along with high-profile cases of female delinquency, have become the main support for media headlines.

However, because arrest counts are a product of both delinquent behavior and official responses to it, researchers and policymakers face a dilemma about how to interpret the arrest statistics. Do the increases in arrests indicate real changes in girls' behaviors, or are the increases a product of recent changes in public sentiment and enforcement policies that have elevated the visibility and reporting of girls' delinquency and violence? This Bulletin attempts to answer this question.

Trends in girls' violence

This Bulletin relies on three data sources—official arrest data, self-report data, and victimization data—to examine trends in girls' violence from 1980 through 2005. Each source has strengths and weaknesses and provides a somewhat different picture of crime.

Data sources

Official sources of data on delinquency include information collected and disseminated by local agencies such as police, as well as State and national organizations that disseminate information collected at the local level. The primary source of official data on delinquency comes from the Federal Bureau of Investigation's (FBI's) Uniform Crime Report (UCR), published annually. Each UCR reflects thousands of local police reports on crimes known to police and on arrests, from which the FBI compiles statistics on the type of crime (roughly 30 broad categories), the location of the arrest (urban, suburban, or rural), and the demographic characteristics of the offender (e.g., age, gender).

VIOLENCE DEFINED

Many different sources of data examine violence and girls' involvement in it. However, these sources often rely on different definitions and measures of violence. Official criminal justice system data sources (e.g., Uniform Crime Reports) use legal definitions focusing on homicide, rape, robbery, aggravated assault (which usually involves assault with a weapon or assault producing injury), and simple assault (a behavior defined differently in various jurisdictions). Self-report studies and those involving interviews with adolescents focus on a variety of behaviors including, for example, fighting and weapon-carrying. Some studies include relational aggression in their definitions of violent behavior. In general, this Bulletin defines violence as behaviors that inflict or threaten to inflict bodily injury on other persons.

Self-report surveys on juvenile crime and its correlates are another major source of information. In addition to the detailed information on respondent characteristics, the main benefit of self-report data is the information obtained on crimes that were committed by youth but not known to the police. Most self-report delinquency surveys are cross-sectional (i.e., cover only one point in time) and localized (i.e., limited to a particular community or region). Among the surveys that provide longitudinal or trend data on youth delinquency for the Nation as a whole, the authors use Monitoring the Future (MTF).[1] MTF is an ongoing study of the behaviors, attitudes, and values of American secondary school students. Each year, a total of approximately 50,000 8th, 10th, and 12th grade students are surveyed (12th graders since 1975, and 8th and 10th graders since 1991).

Victimization surveys provide a third important source of information on delinquent behavior. These types of data provide a different perspective. Whereas information on self-reported delinquent activity is collected from the offender, the source of information for victimization surveys is the victim of criminal activity. The Census Bureau has conducted the National Crime Victimization Survey (NCVS) for the Bureau of Justice Statistics annually since 1973. Each year, NCVS interviews individuals age 12 and older in a nationally representative sample of approximately 50,000 households. Victims of various types of crimes (including violent and property crimes) report detailed characteristics of criminal events, including time and location, level of physical and property damage, and—in the case of violent crime—the perceived characteristics (e.g., age, gender, race) of the offender(s).

LIMITATIONS

All three data sources have limitations. The official or arrest data capture only detected offenses—those that are known to the police or that result in an arrest. Reporting police agencies also vary widely in their reporting coverage. Some jurisdictions have 100-percent reporting, while other jurisdictions are underrepresented. Moreover, because offense categories are very broad, conclusions may be misleading.* For example, the increase in girls' arrests for "serious crimes" (i.e., UCR Index Crimes, as discussed and defined later in this Bulletin) is largely attributable to the inclusion of larceny-theft in that category. Furthermore, arrest data may be affected by changes in enforcement policy that may affect one gender more than the other. Given the gender difference in the character and context of delinquency (i.e., that girls generally engage in less serious forms of crime), changes in laws and enforcement toward targeting less serious forms of lawbreaking may disproportionately impact the risk of arrest for females.

Limitations of self-report and victimization data are that they typically cover only a few forms of lawbreaking and have sampling deficiencies (e.g., MTF is administered in schools and so would underreport crimes committed by youth who have dropped out of school or are frequently truant, and NCVS only interviews victims who are age 12 and older). These data are, however, particularly useful for thinking about whether girls' delinquency trends reflect changes in underlying behavior or changes in enforcement and arrest policies—at least when data sources overlap for the forms of law-violating behavior being measured. For example, longitudinal arrest data on assault can be compared with information on assaults collected in self-report and victimization surveys over time. Confidence in recent assertions regarding levels of violence among girls is enhanced if all of these sources agree on the nature of the trends, whereas confidence is diminished if the sources disagree.

*Reporting agencies classify each arrest by the most serious offense charged in that arrest. If a juvenile is arrested for an aggravated assault and a simple assault, only the aggravated assault is counted in the report—the accompanying simple assault would not be represented in the data. This means that UCR data may be underrepresenting certain offenses when they are committed at the same time as more serious offenses.

Trends in arrests for violent offenses: UCR data

In 2005, out of 14 million arrests, 2.1 million involved juveniles (Snyder, forthcoming).[2] Juveniles comprised about 15 percent of arrests for all offenses, about 16 percent of arrests for Violent Crime Index[3] offenses, and about 26 percent of arrests for Property Crime Index[4] offenses. Girls comprised nearly one-third (29 percent) of all juvenile arrests, about one-third (34 percent) of arrests for Property Crime Index offenses, and less than one-fifth (18 percent) of arrests for Violent Crime Index offenses. Although serious and violent crimes capture media and public attention, the vast majority of juvenile arrests are for less serious offenses—nonindex and status offenses[5] accounted for three-quarters (76 percent) of all juvenile arrests.

Only 4 percent of juvenile arrests in 2005 were for Violent Crime Index offenses; aggravated assaults accounted for two-thirds (64 percent) of Violent Crime Index juvenile arrests (3 percent of all juvenile arrests). Girls comprised about one-quarter (24 percent) of all juvenile arrests for aggravated assault. By contrast, simple assaults accounted for 12 percent of all juvenile arrests; other than larceny-theft and "all other offenses," simple assault was the offense for which police made the largest number of juvenile arrests (247,900). Significantly, girls accounted for one-third (33 percent) of juvenile arrests for simple assault, the largest female proportion of arrests for any type of violent crime.

Although girls comprise a smaller overall portion of juvenile arrests than boys, the two groups' arrest patterns have diverged somewhat over the past decade. As the percentage changes in table 1 indicate, juvenile arrests generally decreased between 1996 and 2005, but the decrease was greater for boys than for girls; the exception to the general trend was arrests for simple assault, which increased for girls while decreasing for boys.[6]

Arrests for aggravated assault comprise the single largest component of the Violent Crime Index, and arrests for simple assault are the largest component of nonindex violent arrests. As shown in table 1, boys' arrests for aggravated assault decreased nearly one-quarter (–23 percent) between 1996 and 2005, while girls' arrests decreased far less (–5 percent). In contrast, girls' arrests for simple assault increased nearly one-quarter (24 percent), while boys' arrests decreased slightly (–4 percent). For Violent Crime Index offenses, arrests of males decreased more substantially (–28 percent) than did arrests of females (–10 percent). Between 1996 and 2005, the overall total of juvenile arrests dropped about 22 percent, primarily because arrests of males decreased 29 percent, whereas arrests of females decreased 14 percent.

Steffensmeier and colleagues (2005) assess statistically whether the gender difference in arrest trends over the past two decades has been narrowing, widening, or has remained essentially stable. Based on UCR arrest data from 1980 through 2003, their analysis found that the gender difference in arrest rates is essentially stable for homicide, rape, and robbery but has narrowed considerably for aggravated assault and simple assault (Steffensmeier et al., 2005).

The gender difference for the Violent Crime Index has also narrowed significantly, but this narrowing is largely attributable to the rise in female juvenile arrest rates for aggravated assault during the 1990s (see figure 1). If arrests for aggravated assault are omitted from the Index, the trend is essentially stable.

To better show what a narrowing or widening gender difference in violence means, figure 1 plots juvenile female and male arrest rate trends for aggravated assault, simple assault, and the Violent Crime Index (sum of arrests for homicide, robbery, rape, and aggravated assault), along with the female percentage of arrests, according to the UCR.

Over the past two decades, clear changes have occurred in girls' arrests and between boys' and girls' patterns of arrests in aggravated and simple assault. As figure 1 indicates, boys' and

TABLE 1 Percent change in male and female juvenile arrests for violent crimes, 1996–2005

Type	Girls	Boys
Aggravated assault	–5.4%	–23.4%
Simple assault	24.0	–4.1
Violent Crime Index	–10.2	–27.9
All crimes	–14.3	–28.7

Source: Crime in the United States, 2005—Table 33 (FBI, 2006).

FIGURE 1 Trends in juvenile female and male arrest rates[a] (per 100,000) and juvenile female percentage of arrests[b] for violent offending: Uniform Crime Reports, 1980–2003

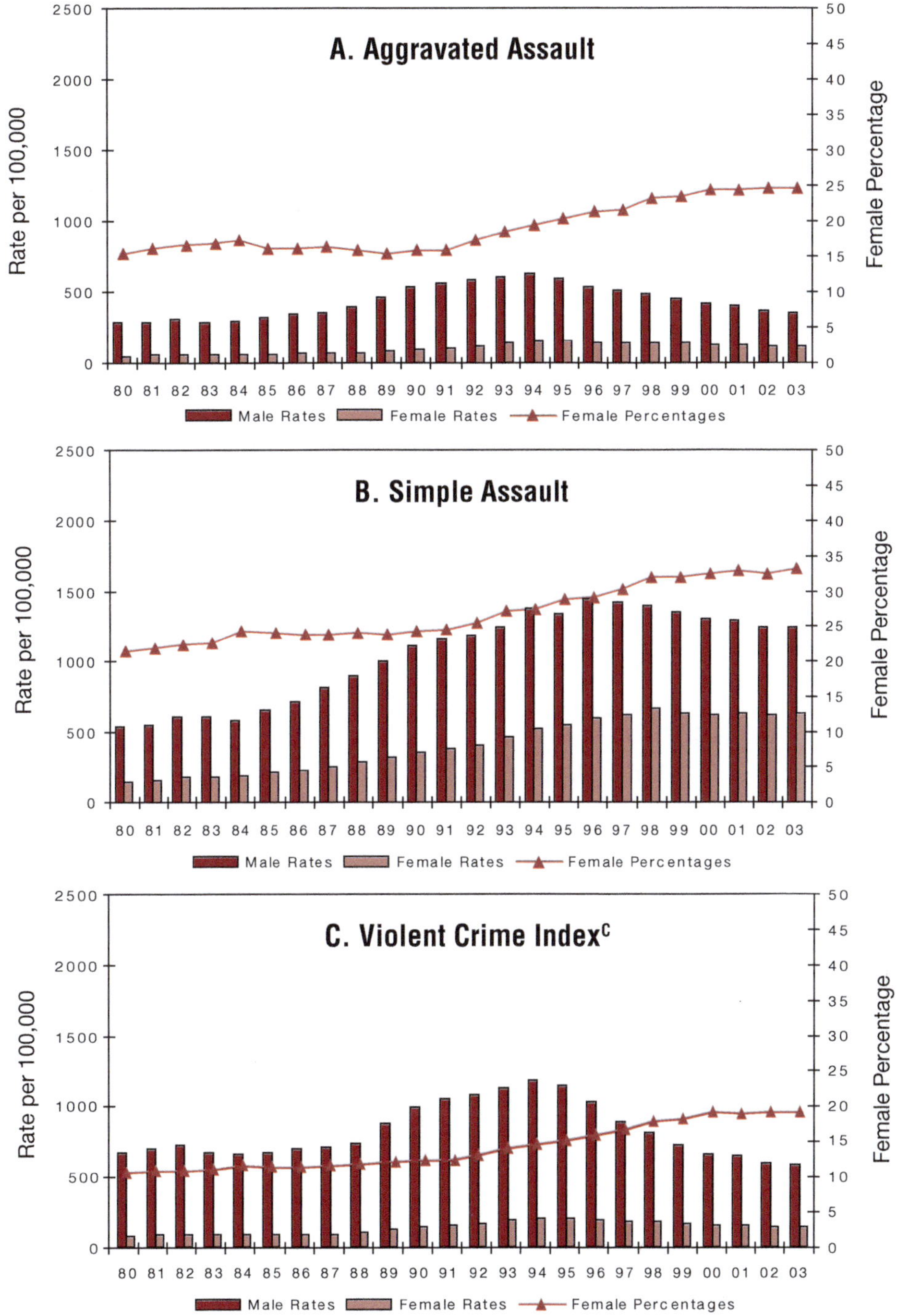

[a] Rates are adjusted for the gender composition of the population and for changes in UCR coverage over time. The population base includes ages 12–17.

[b] Female Percentage = Female Rate / (Female Rate + Male Rate) x 100%

[c] The Violent Crime Index includes homicide, aggravated assault, rape, and robbery

Source: Steffensmeier et al., 2005. Permission was given by the American Society of Criminology to reprint this figure, which was originally published in *Criminology* (Vol. 43, No. 2).

girls' arrests for aggravated assault diverged conspicuously—the female arrest rate in 2003 (88.3 girls per 100,000) was nearly double the arrest rate in 1980 (45 girls per 100,000). Although males' arrest rate for aggravated assault was five times higher than that of females, males' proportional increase from 1980 to 2003 (12.5 percent, from 239.4 to 269.5 boys per 100,000) was much more modest than that of girls.

The juvenile arrest rate for simple assaults is more than three times greater than the rate for aggravated assaults. Again, changes in the arrest rates of females for simple assault over the past two decades have greatly outpaced those of males. The arrest rate of girls for simple assault in 2003 was more than triple (3.5 times) the rate in 1980 (478.3 versus 129.7 per 100,000). Although male arrests for simple assaults started from a higher base rate, that rate barely doubled over the same period (934.4 versus 462.7 per 100,000). Arrest rates for both groups peaked in the mid-1990s, and then male rates exhibited a much sharper dropoff than female rates. Moreover, while the male juvenile arrest rate for Violent Crime Index offenses was lower in 2003 than in 1980, the rate for girls was much higher—the girls' arrest rate for Violent Crime Index offenses rose from 70.4 to 103.1 per 100,000 between 1980 and 2003, a 46-percent increase. Thus, the juvenile "crime drop" of the past decade reflects primarily changes in arrest rates for boys.

In general, the gender difference in arrests has narrowed considerably for aggravated assault and simple assault and has also narrowed for the Violent Crime Index—the female percentage of juvenile arrests held steady during the 1980s, followed by a fairly steep rise in the female share of juvenile arrests during the 1990s. The Index trend essentially matches the pattern for aggravated assault, primarily because the large arrest volumes for aggravated assault (two-thirds of all Violent Index offenses) swamped the effects of arrest trends in the other Index violent crimes during the 1990s.

Figure 1 helps clarify whether the movement in arrest rates is similar for both genders and whether substantial gender differences in juvenile arrests for violent offenses still exist. Data indicate that trends in arrest rates are roughly similar for both genders across all violent crime categories, but with some divergence since the mid-1990s. For example, arrest rates rose for both boys and girls over much of the past two decades, particularly during 1986–94. Then rates leveled off or declined in the late 1990s for boys, while rates for girls merely stabilized or continued to inch upward. Therefore, the narrowing difference in trends (particularly for both types of assault) is at least partly a function of the recent downward movement in boys arrest rates for violence.

Figure 2 compares the simple/aggravated assault arrest rate ratios (arrest rate for simple assault divided by the arrest rate for aggravated assault) over two decades for boys and girls. These ratios and changes in the ratios indicate the relative seriousness of offenses for which police have arrested juveniles. In 1980, the ratio for girls was 2.9, which means that police arrested girls for simple assault about three times as often as they arrested girls for aggravated assault. They arrested boys for simple assault about twice (1.9 times) as often as they arrested boys for aggravated assault. By 2003, police arrested girls more than five times (5.4) as often for simple assault as for aggravated assault. By contrast, the ratio of boys' arrests for simple to aggravated assault was just over threefold (3.5). These ratios show that (1) arrests for simple assault are more common than for aggravated assault (i.e., the ratios for both boys and girls are greater than 1.0) and (2) simple assaults comprise a larger percentage of arrests for girls than for boys (i.e., the simple/aggravated assault ratios are consistently higher for girls than for boys), particularly in recent years.

FIGURE 2 Ratio of simple/aggravated assault rates for juvenile males and females, 1980–2003

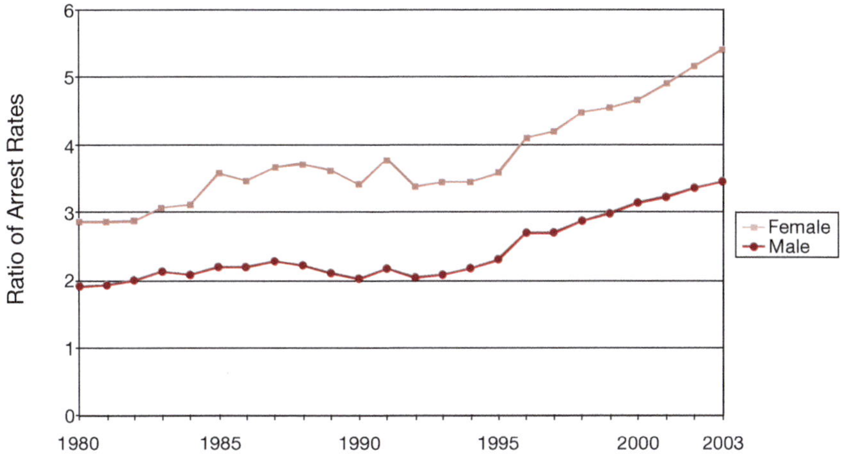

Source: National Center for Juvenile Justice (February 28, 2005), available at www.ojjdp.ncjrs.org/ojstatbb/crime/excel/jar_20050228.xls.

These differences in ratios are partly explained by gender differences in the underlying trends for aggravated and simple assaults. The large decline in boys' arrests for aggravated assaults over the past decade raised their ratio of simple to aggravated assault. By contrast, the larger increase in the girls' ratio of simple to aggravated assault is attributable to their large increase in arrests for simple assault over the same period.

The statistics on juvenile arrests for assault point to certain conclusions about the seriousness of girls' violence, especially relative to the seriousness of boys' violence. Although juvenile arrests for assault—regardless of gender—are far more likely to involve simple assault than aggravated assault, the fact that the ratio of simple to aggravated assault arrests is much higher for girls than boys suggests that most girls' violence is of a less serious nature than boys' violence. Moreover, one of the reasons that boys are more likely than girls to be charged with aggravated assault is that boys use weapons more frequently and physically inflict more injury on their victims—both indicators of the relative seriousness of boys' versus girls' violence. Finally, although girls' rate of arrest for simple assault has increased over the decades, their arrest rate for aggravated assault has not.

Despite dramatic changes in the number and rate of arrests and in simple/aggravated assault ratios, the question remains whether these trends signify a real change in girls' underlying violent behavior or reflect other factors.

Researchers have examined the changing nature of assaults over the past decades by comparing ratios of aggravated assaults to homicides (e.g., Zimring, 1998) or ratios of assaults to robberies (e.g., Zimring and Hawkins, 1997; Snyder and Sickmund, 2000). Because arrests for assault increased without corresponding increases in arrests for homicide or robbery, these analysts attribute the increases in assault arrests to changes in law enforcement policies, such as responses to domestic violence, rather than to actual increases in assaults. Several factors relevant to interpreting statistics on girls' arrests for assault must be considered:

- Law enforcement policies that lower the threshold for reporting an assault or for classifying an assault as aggravated may create the appearance of a "crime wave" when the underlying behavior remains relatively stable.
- Heightened sensitivity to domestic violence has led many States and localities to implement "mandatory arrest" policies in response to domestic disturbances. Behaviors once considered "ungovernable" (a status offense) may, in a domestic situation, result instead in an arrest for simple assault—possibly in response to the Juvenile Justice and Delinquency Prevention Act of 2002, which requires States to decriminalize and deinstitutionalize status offenses (Schneider, 1984; Mahoney and Fenster, 1982; Chesney-Lind and Sheldon, 2004; Girls Inc., 1996).
- Family dynamics may also contribute to gender differences in juvenile arrests for assault. Parents have different expectations about their sons' and daughters' obedience to parental authority (Chesney-Lind, 1988), and these expectations may affect how the justice system responds to a girl's behavior when she "acts out" within the home (Krause and McShane, 1994). Research indicates that girls fight with family members or siblings more frequently than boys, who more often fight with friends or strangers (Bloom et al., 2002). Some research suggests that girls are three times as likely as boys to assault a family member (Franke, Huynh-Hohnbaum, and Chung, 2002).
- Policies of mandatory arrest for domestic violence, initially adopted to protect victims from further attacks, also provide parents with another method for attempting to control their "unruly" daughters. Regardless of who initiates a violent domestic incident, law enforcement first responders may consider it more practical and efficient to identify the youth as the offender, especially when the parent is the caretaker for other children in the home (Gaarder, Rodriguez, and Zatz, 2004).
- It is possible that school officials' adoption of zero-tolerance policies toward youth violence may increase the number of youth referred to police for schoolyard tussles that schools previously handled internally.

One way of assessing the "policy change hypothesis" is to compare girls' arrest trends for violent offenses to trends reflected in self-report and victimization data, using MTF and NCVS. Unlike the UCR, these data are not limited to cases that come to the attention of the police or result in arrests. If higher female arrest rates for violent crime are a byproduct of policy changes, then one would expect to find disagreement between official and unofficial data sources, with arrest data showing noticeably larger gains in female violence than found in self-report or victimization data. In contrast, if higher female rates reflect true changes in the aggressive tendencies of girls, then data sources should generally be in agreement.

Trends in self-reported assaults: Monitoring the Future data

As with the UCR arrest data, Steffensmeier and colleagues (2005) used MTF data from 1980 through 2003 to explore female-versus-male trends with tests to determine any statistical differences. Focusing on self-reported assaults, the researchers calculated prevalence (one or more incidents) and high frequency (five or more incidents) estimates for an assault index comprising three assault items[7] for 12th graders (ages 17–18). Data indicate marked stability in the separate trends for both boys and girls for the assault index over the 1980–2003 period, regardless of whether prevalence or high-frequency measures are used.

WHAT DO WE LEARN FROM SELF-REPORT DATA?

In contrast to official arrest statistics, self-report data from the Monitoring the Future surveys show that levels of assault for juvenile females and males have been fairly constant over the past two decades and that female involvement in violence has not increased relative to male violence.

FIGURE 3 Trends in female and male self-reported assault* and female percentage of violent offending: Monitoring the Future, 1980–2003 (17- and 18-year-olds)

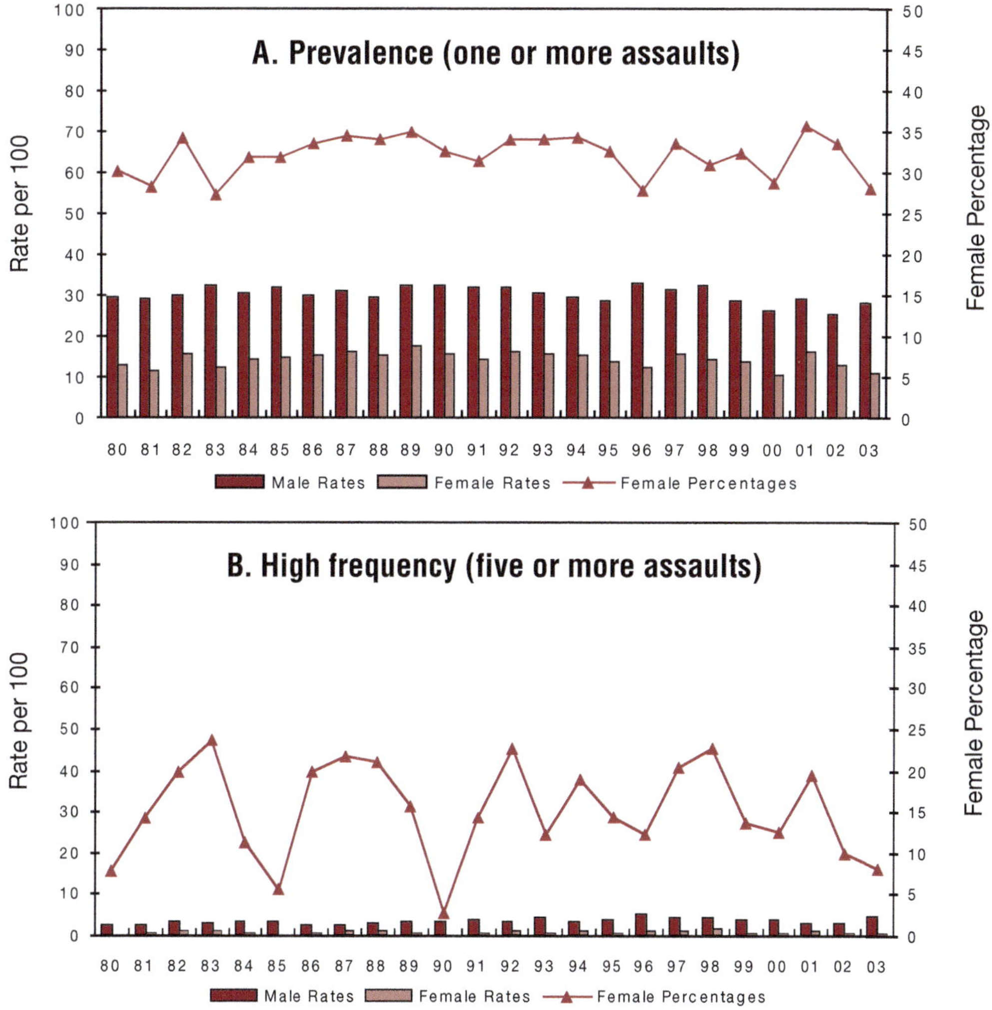

* Items in the assault index include (1) hit instructor/supervisor, (2) fight at school/work, and (3) hurt somebody badly in a fight.

Source: Steffensmeier et al., 2005. Permission was given by the American Society of Criminology to reprint this figure, which was originally published in *Criminology* (Vol. 43, No. 2).

These statistical patterns are illustrated in figure 3, where the trends over the past two decades show overall stability (i.e., random fluctuations rather than any consistent upward or downward trend). Assault rates among both girls and boys are relatively unchanged over this period, although female assault levels are consistently lower than male levels for both prevalence and high-frequency measures. Also, the gender difference in high-frequency violent assaults is quite large: Girls account for an average of about 15 percent of high-frequency assaults, compared with about 35 percent for less frequent or minor involvement in violence.

Trends in victims' reports of assaults: National Crime Victimization Survey data

Steffensmeier and colleagues (2005) also analyzed NCVS data to explore trends in assault and violence as reported by victims. Again, their analysis relies on statistical tests and illustrative plots of female-versus-male trends during 1980–2003. The results indicate that the rates of violence among adolescent females relative to rates among adolescent males have changed very little during this period (i.e., year-to-year changes in female-versus-male rates are not statistically significant). This is true for violent offenses in general and assault in particular. The trends for both aggravated assault and simple assault are stable, a pattern contrary to UCR arrest trends, which show a narrowing gender gap. The gender difference in NCVS trends is also stable for the Violent Crime Index, also contrary to the UCR trends.

Figure 4 illustrates these findings by showing NCVS rates of violence for juvenile males and females (per 100,000), along with the relevant female percentages. Based on NCVS reports, girls' violence levels are much lower than boys' levels. Girls' rates typically rise when boys' rates rise and decline when boys' rates decline (i.e., male and female rates move in tandem), yielding a stable gender gap in overall violence. Similar to UCR data, girls' and boys' assault rates rose during the late 1980s through the early 1990s and then tapered off, but the rise is smaller and the decline is greater in the NCVS series than in the UCR series.

The NCVS data show both girls' and boys' rates of assault dropping considerably in recent years, whereas the UCR data show that assault arrest rates declined only for boys. This telling difference between the two data sources supports the conclusion that policy shifts and changes in enforcement may have had a greater impact on arrest rates than have actual changes in the behavior of girls.

The gender difference in violence is fairly comparable between NCVS and UCR figures in earlier years, but the two sources diverge in more recent years, as would be expected based on the policy change hypothesis. For example, the female percentage for the assault index (defined the same in the NCVS as in the UCR as aggravated assaults, simple assaults, and other offenses against persons) in the early 1980s was about 18–20 percent in both the NCVS and the UCR—essentially no difference; by the late 1990s, however, the percentage holds steady at about 20 percent in the NCVS but jumps to about 30 percent in the UCR. Sizable declines

WHAT DO WE LEARN FROM VICTIMIZATION DATA?

In contrast to official arrest statistics, victimization data from the National Crime Victimization Survey show very little change in the gender gap for assault crimes and the Violent Crime Index over the past two decades and since the 1994 peak in violent crimes.

FIGURE 4 Trends in juvenile female and male violence rates[a] (per 100,000) and female percentage of violent offending: National Crime Victimization Survey, 1980–2003

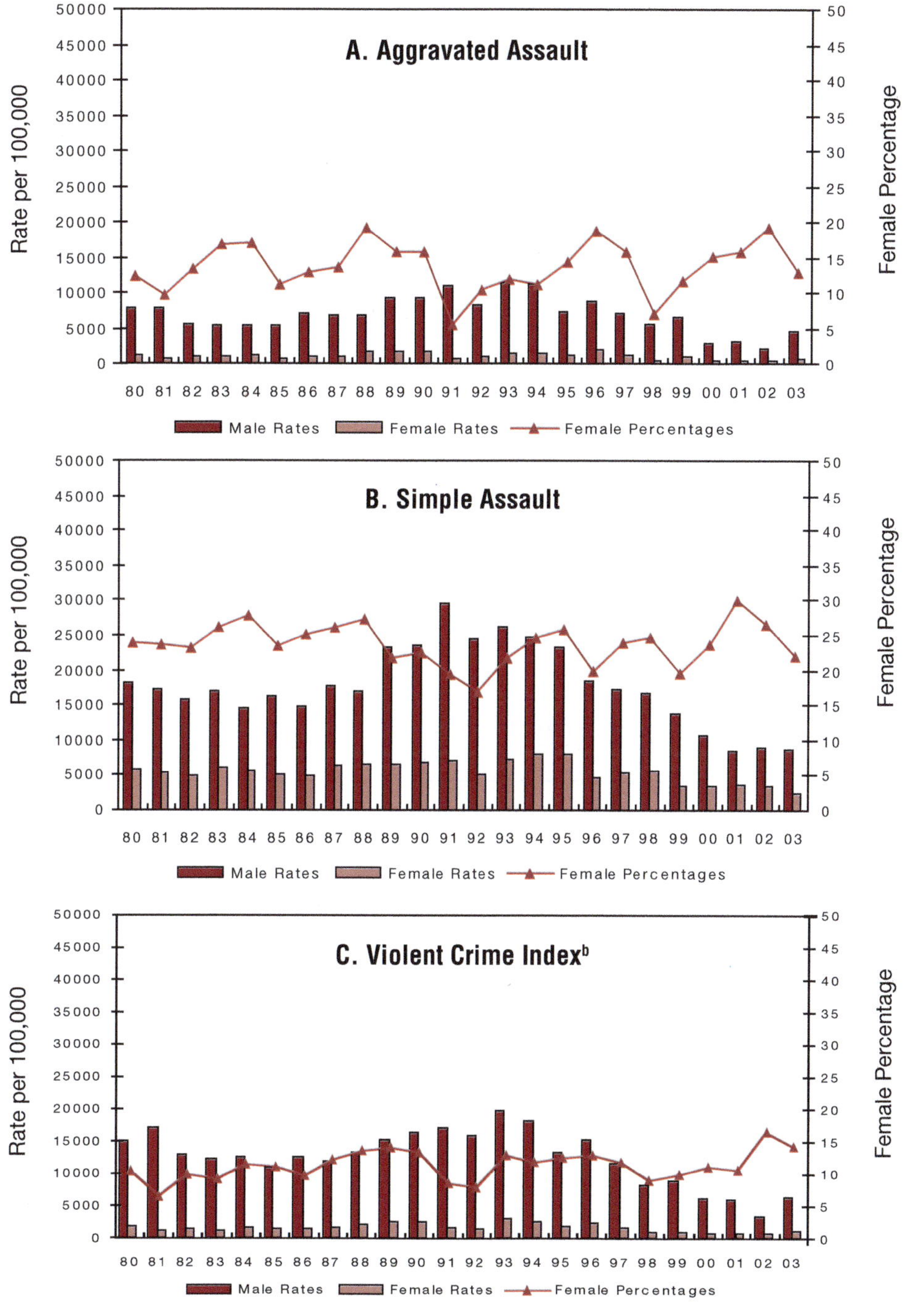

[a] Data are adjusted to take into account effects of the survey redesign in 1992. The multiplier is offense and sex specific and is calculated based only on juvenile data. The formula is: Multiplier = (n92 + n93 + n94)/(n90 + n91 + n92).

[b] The Violent Crime Index includes aggravated assault, rape, and robbery.

Source: Steffensmeier et al., 2005. Permission was given by the American Society of Criminology to reprint this figure, which was originally published in *Criminology* (Vol. 43, No. 2).

FIGURE 5 Summary of trends in juvenile gender gap for assault in arrest data compared with victimization and self-report sources: Uniform Crime Reports, National Crime Victimization Survey, and Monitoring the Future,1980–2003

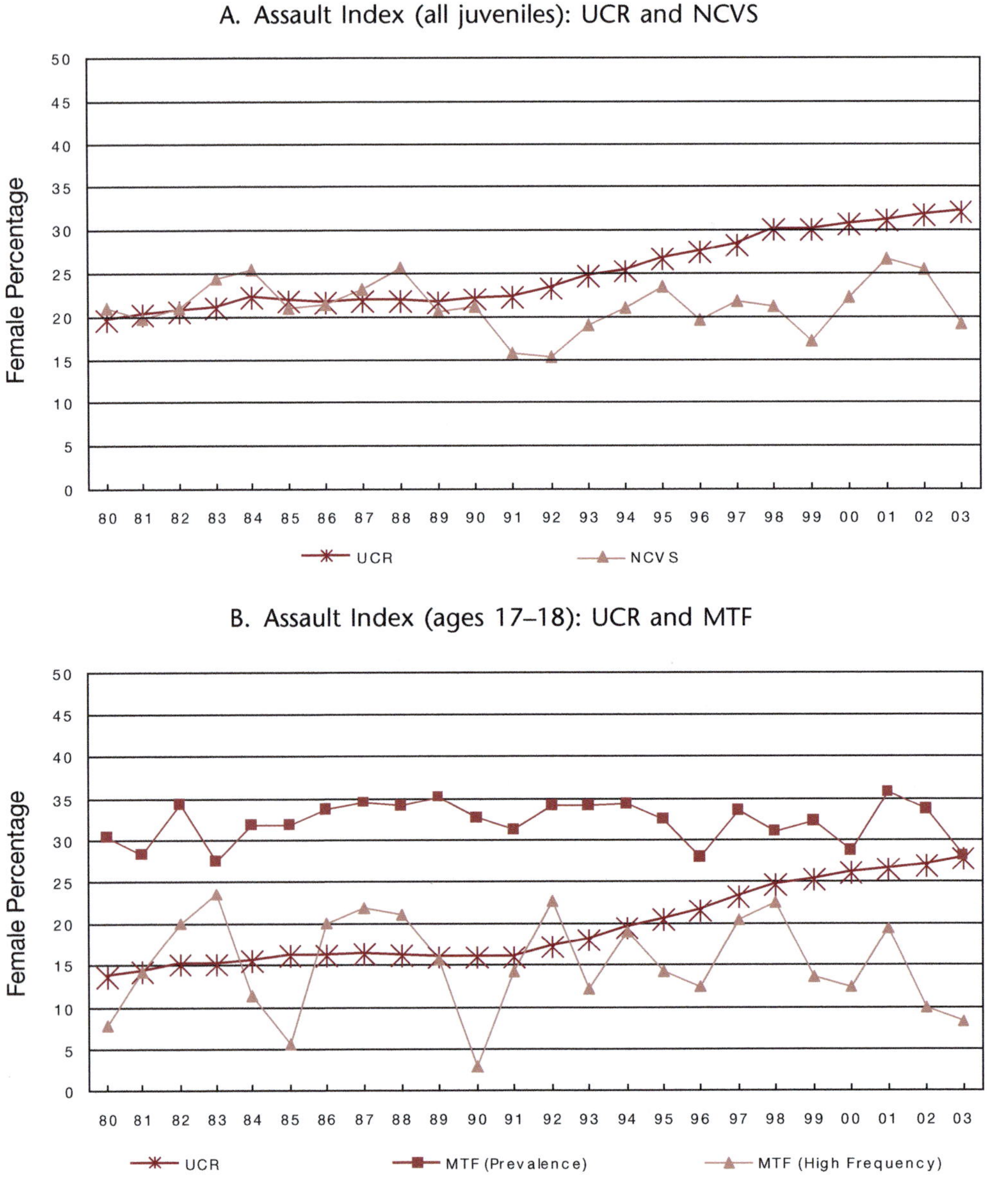

Source: Steffensmeier et al., 2005. Permission was given by the American Society of Criminology to reprint this figure, which was originally published in *Criminology* (Vol. 43, No. 2).

in NCVS assault rates in recent years have considerably outpaced the much smaller declines in UCR assault arrest rates, particularly among adolescent girls.

Several conclusions can be drawn from the NCVS data:

- First, gender differences in juvenile violent offending, including assault, have not changed meaningfully or systematically in the NCVS data since 1980. The NCVS assault finding stands in sharp contrast to UCR arrest statistics, where the gender difference has narrowed significantly for both simple and aggravated assault.
- Second, the NCVS series reveals sharp declines in assault crimes among both girls and boys since about the mid-1990s, but girls' declines are not seen in the UCR arrest data. This discrepancy in the two data sources may be caused in part by changes in policies and practices.
- Third, these possible changes in policy are particularly salient for girls, whose arrest figures have continued to rise or barely level off compared with victim reports that show sizable declines in girls' assaults since at least the mid-1990s.

Summary

Figure 5 highlights the differences in trends between official arrest data (UCR) and victimization (NCVS) and self-report (MTF) sources. These graphs clearly show the upward trend in the female percent of arrests for assaults based on UCR arrest data, while the trends based on victimization data and self-reports have been fairly stable over time.

Conclusions

What we know about girls and violence

Trends

Available evidence based on arrest, victimization, and self-report data suggests that although girls are currently arrested more for simple assaults than previously, the actual incidence of their being seriously violent has not changed much over the last two decades. This suggests that increases in arrests may be attributable more to changes in enforcement policies than to changes in girls' behavior. Juvenile female involvement in violence has not increased relative to juvenile male violence. There is no burgeoning national crisis of increasing serious violence among adolescent girls.

Endnotes

1 The MTF study is funded by the National Institute on Drug Abuse. Findings are available online at www.monitoringthefuture.org.

2 Note that UCR data count the number of arrests, not the number of individuals arrested. An unknown number of individuals are arrested more than once during a year.

3 The Violent Crime Index includes homicide, forcible rape, robbery, and aggravated assaults.

4 The Property Crime Index includes burglary, larceny-theft, motor vehicle theft, and arson.

5 Nonindex offenses are simple assault, weapons offenses, drug and liquor law violations, driving under the influence, disorderly conduct, vandalism, and other categories not included in the FBI's Crime Indexes. Status offenses are acts that are offenses only when committed by juveniles (e.g., running away).

6 Aggravated assault is defined as "an unlawful attack by one person upon another for the purpose of inflicting severe or aggravated bodily injury. This type of assault usually is accompanied by the use of a weapon or by means likely to produce death or great bodily harm" (FBI, 2004, p. 23). Simple assault is defined as including "all assaults which do not involve the use of a firearm, knife, cutting instrument, or other dangerous weapon and in which the victim did not sustain serious or aggravated injuries. Agencies must classify as simple assault such offenses as assault and battery, injury caused by culpable negligence, intimidation, coercion, and all attempts to commit these offenses" (FBI, 2004, p. 26).

7 The 12th graders were asked how often during the past 12 months they had: (1) "hit an instructor or supervisor," (2) "gotten into a serious fight at school or at work," and (3) "hurt someone badly enough to need bandages or a doctor."

[References omitted.]

CRITICAL-THINKING QUESTIONS

1. Are Kent Clausen's offenses, depicted in the predisposition report at the beginning of this chapter, typical of those committed by most youth?
2. With regard to delinquency, what do the terms *prevalence* and *incidence* mean? How might distinguishing between prevalence and incidence impact delinquency prevention efforts?
3. What types of delinquent offenses are most common? Why do you think these forms of delinquent behavior occur more frequently than others?
4. Why do official statistics and self-report data paint somewhat different pictures of the social correlates of offending?
5. Given what you have learned about the disproportionate involvement in serious violent crime of young people, males, African Americans, and those who are economically disadvantaged, describe the kinds of programs you believe would be most successful in preventing violent delinquency.
6. Based on the trend data presented in the chapter reading *Juvenile Arrests 2012*, has there been a juvenile crime wave in recent years? How might the perception of a juvenile crime wave impact juvenile justice policy?
7. Summarize recent trends in teenage girls' violent behavior, which are described in the reading by Margaret Zahn and her colleagues. Are girls becoming more violent, or are the trends attributable simply to changes in police responses to violent behavior?

SUGGESTED READING

Morenoff, Jeffrey D. 2005. "Racial and Ethnic Disparities in Crime and Delinquency in the United States." Pp. 139–173 in *Ethnicity and Causal Mechanisms*, edited by M. Rutter and M. Tienda. Cambridge, UK: Cambridge University Press.

Sickmund, Melissa and Charles Puzzanchera (eds.). 2014. *Juvenile Offenders and Victims: 2014 National Report*. Pittsburgh, PA: National Center for Juvenile Justice.

Steffensmeier, Darrell, Emilie Anderson Allan, Miles D. Harer, and Cathy Streifel. 1989. "Age and the Distribution of Crime." *American Journal of Sociology* 94:803–831.

USEFUL WEBSITES

For further information relevant to this chapter, go to the following websites.

- **Crime in the United States,** Uniform Crime Reports publications, Federal Bureau of Investigation: https://ucr.fbi.gov/ucr-publications
- **Statistical Briefing Book,** Office of Juvenile Justice and Delinquency Prevention: www.ojjdp.gov/ojstatbb/default.asp
- **Monitoring the Future,** Institute for Social Research, University of Michigan: http://monitoringthefuture.org/
- **Criminal Victimization publications,** Bureau of Justice Statistics: www.bjs.gov/index.cfm?ty=pbse&sid=6
- **Girls Study Group research,** Office of Juvenile Justice and Delinquency Prevention: www.ojjdp.gov/programs/girlsatrisk.html

GLOSSARY OF KEY TERMS

Age–crime curve: The bell-shaped curve observed when one graphs the relationship between age and crime. The age–crime curve typically shows an increase in delinquent involvement during the teenage years, a peak in mid-adolescence to early adulthood, and then a rapid decline.

Age effect: The disproportionate involvement of young people in crime.

Incidence: The average number of delinquent offenses committed by adolescents in general or by delinquent youth.

Prevalence: The proportion of youth involved in delinquent acts.

Relative frequency: In comparison to each other, the types of delinquent offenses that occur most often.

Social correlates: Social characteristics (such as age, gender, race, and social class) that are statistically related to involvement in delinquency and that tend to distinguish offenders from non-offenders.

NOTES

1 Statistics on the proportion of arrests attributable to juveniles can be somewhat misleading if a small number of juveniles is responsible for a large percentage of arrests. It may be, for example, that one juvenile is arrested six times for burglary. The percentages in Table 5.2 correctly state the proportions of juvenile and adult arrests, but they mask the reality that a relatively small number of repeat offenders account for a disproportionate share of crimes and arrests. However, it is also true that more than one offender may be arrested for a single crime.

2 But see also Hindelang, Hirschi, and Weis (1981), who argue that gender differences in delinquency are similar across data sources (self-report and official data), at least for more serious offenses.

3 In our discussion of race and delinquency, we try to be as inclusive as possible. But limited data on delinquency exist for races other than African American and Caucasian. Similarly, data examining delinquency and ethnicity are rather limited. Official data include only five race categories (the four listed in Table 5.5, as well as Hawaiian or other Pacific islander) and only two ethnicity categories (Hispanic and non-Hispanic).

4 But see also the study by Piquero and Brame (2008) in which the authors used a sample of *serious* offenders to explore the race-delinquency relationship. They used both official and self-report data on offending and

did not find the kinds of racial differences in offending that are typically found with samples that include broad cross-sections of the population.

REFERENCES

Bachman, Jerald G., Lloyd D. Johnston, and Patrick M. O'Malley. 2011. *Monitoring the Future: Questionnaire Responses from the Nation's High School Seniors, 2010*. Ann Arbor, MI: Institute for Social Research, The University of Michigan. Retrieved December 8, 2014 (www.monitoringthefuture.org/pubs.html#refvols).

Bachman, Jerald G., Lloyd D. Johnston, and Patrick M. O'Malley. 2014. *Monitoring the Future: Questionnaire Responses from the Nation's High School Seniors, 2012*. Ann Arbor, MI: Institute for Social Research, The University of Michigan. Retrieved December 30, 2014 (www.monitoringthefuture.org/pubs.html#refvols).

Brame, Robert, Shawn D. Bushway, Ray Paternoster, and Michael G. Turner. 2014. "Demographic Patterns of Cumulative Arrest Prevalence by Ages 18 and 23." *Crime and Delinquency* 60:471–486.

Canter, Rachelle J. 1982. "Sex Differences in Self-Reported Delinquency." *Criminology* 20:373–393.

Eaton, Danice K., Laura Kann, Steve Kinchen, Shari Shanklin, James Ross, Joseph Hawkins, William A. Harris, Richard Lowry, Tim McManus, David Chyen, Connie Lim, Lisa Whittle, Nancy D. Brener, and Howell Wechsler. 2010. "Youth Risk Behavior Surveillance—United States, 2009." *CDC Surveillance Summaries, Morbidity and Mortality Weekly Report* 59, No. SS-5. Washington, DC: USGPO. Cited in *Sourcebook of Criminal Justice Statistics Online*, Table 3.56.2009. Retrieved December 8, 2014 (www.albany.edu/sourcebook/index.html).

Elliott, Delbert S. and Suzanne S. Ageton. 1980. "Reconciling Race and Class Differences in Self-Reported and Official Estimates of Delinquency." *American Sociological Review* 45:95–110.

Elliott, Delbert S., Suzanne S. Ageton, David Huizinga, B.A. Knowles, and Rachelle J. Canter. 1983. *The Prevalence and Incidence of Delinquent Behavior: 1976–1980. National Estimates of Delinquent Behavior by Sex, Race, Social Class and Other Selected Variables*. Boulder, CO: Behavioral Research Institute.

Elliott, Delbert S. and David Huizinga. 1983. "Social Class and Delinquent Behavior in a National Youth Panel." *Criminology* 21:149–177.

Elliott, Delbert S., David Huizinga, and Suzanne S. Ageton. 1985. *Explaining Delinquency and Drug Use*. Beverly Hills, CA: Sage.

Farnworth, Margaret, Terence P. Thornberry, Marvin D. Krohn, and Alan J. Lizotte. 1994. "Measurement in the Study of Class and Delinquency: Integrating Theory and Research." *Journal of Research in Crime and Delinquency* 31:32–61.

Federal Bureau of Investigation. 2016. *Crime in the United States, 2015: Uniform Crime Reports*. Washington, DC: U.S. Department of Justice. Retrieved October 25, 2017 (https://ucr.fbi.gov/crime-in-the-u.s/2015/crime-in-the-u.s.-2015).

Federal Bureau of Investigation. 2017. *Crime in the United States, 2016: Uniform Crime Reports*. Washington, DC: U.S. Department of Justice. Retrieved October 25, 2017 (https://ucr.fbi.gov/crime-in-the-u.s/2016/crime-in-the-u.s.-2016).

Hawkins, Darnell F., John H. Laub, Janet L. Lauritsen, and Lynn Cothern. 2000. *Race, Ethnicity, and Serious and Violent Juvenile Offending*. Washington, DC: Office of Juvenile Justice and Delinquency Prevention.

Hindelang, Michael J. 1979. "Sex Differences in Criminal Activity." *Social Problems* 27:143–156.

Hindelang, Michael J. 1981. "Variations in Sex-Race-Age-Specific Incidence Rates of Offending." *American Sociological Review* 46:461–474.

Hindelang, Michael J., Travis Hirschi, and Joseph G. Weis. 1981. *Measuring Delinquency*. Beverly Hills: Sage.

Hockenberry, Sarah and Charles Puzzanchera. 2017. *Juvenile Court Statistics 2014*. Pittsburgh, PA: National Center for Juvenile Justice.

Huizinga, David A. and Delbert S. Elliott. 1987. "Juvenile Offenders: Prevalence, Offender Incidence, and Arrest Rates by Race." *Crime and Delinquency* 33:206–223.

Huizinga, David A., Rolf Loeber, Terence P. Thornberry, and Lynn Cothern. 2000. "Co-Occurrence of Delinquency and Other Problem Behaviors." *Juvenile Justice Bulletin.* Washington, DC: Office of Juvenile Justice and Delinquency Prevention.

Johnson, Richard E. 1980. "Social Class and Delinquent Behavior: A New Test." *Criminology* 18:86–93.

Johnston, Lloyd D., Jerald G. Bachman, and Patrick M. O'Malley. 2010. *Monitoring the Future: Questionnaire Responses from the Nation's High School Seniors, 2009.* Ann Arbor, MI: Institute for Social Research, The University of Michigan. Retrieved December 8, 2014 (www.monitoringthefuture.org/pubs.html#refvols).

Johnston, Lloyd D., Jerald G. Bachman, and Patrick M. O'Malley. 2013. *Monitoring the Future: Questionnaire Responses from the Nation's High School Seniors, 2011.* Ann Arbor, MI: Institute for Social Research, The University of Michigan. Retrieved December 8, 2014 (www.monitoringthefuture.org/pubs.html#refvols).

Johnston, Lloyd D., Patrick M. O'Malley, Richard A. Miech, Jerald G. Bachman, and John E. Schulenberg. 2017. *Monitoring the Future National Survey Results on Drug Use, 1975-2016: Overview, Key Findings on Adolescent Drug Use.* Ann Arbor: Institute for Social Research. The University of Michigan.

Kleck, Gary. 1982. "On the Use of Self-Report Data to Determine the Class Distribution of Criminal and Delinquent Behavior." *American Sociological Review* 47:427–433.

Krohn, Marvin D., Ronald L. Akers, Marcia J. Radosevich, and Lonn Lanza-Kaduce. 1980. "Social Status and Deviance." *Criminology* 18:303–318.

OJJDP Statistical Briefing Book. 2014. National Center for Juvenile Justice. Retrieved May 27, 2014 (www.ojjdp.gov/ojstatbb/crime/excel/JAR_2012.xls).

Piquero, Alex R. and Robert W. Brame. 2008. "Assessing the Race-Crime and Ethnicity-Crime Relationship in a Sample of Serious Adolescent Delinquents." *Crime and Delinquency* 54:390–422.

Puzzanchera, Charles. 2014. "Juvenile Arrests 2012." *Juvenile Offenders and Victims National Report Series.* Washington, DC: Office of Juvenile Justice and Delinquency Prevention.

Sampson, Robert J. and Janet Lauritsen. 1997. "Racial and Ethnic Disparities in Crime and Criminal Justice in the United States." Pp. 311–374 in *Crime and Justice: An Annual Review of Research.* Vol. 22, edited by M. Tonry. Chicago: University of Chicago Press.

Sickmund, Melissa and Charles Puzzanchera (eds.). 2014. *Juvenile Offenders and Victims: 2014 National Report.* Pittsburgh, PA: National Center for Juvenile Justice.

Smith, Douglas A. and Christy A. Visher. 1980. "Sex and Involvement in Deviance/Crime: A Quantitative Review of Empirical Literature." *American Sociological Review* 45:691–701.

Snyder, Howard N. and Melissa Sickmund. 2006. *Juvenile Offenders and Victims: 2006 National Report.* Washington, DC: Office of Juvenile Justice and Delinquency Prevention.

Steffensmeier, Darrell, Jennifer Schwartz, Hua Zhong, and Jeff Ackerman. 2005. "An Assessment of Recent Trends in Girls' Violence Using Diverse Longitudinal Sources: Is the Gender Gap Closing?" *Criminology* 43:355–405.

Steffensmeier, Darrell and Renee Hoffman Steffensmeier. 1980. "Trends in Female Delinquency: An Examination of Arrest, Juvenile Court, Self-Report, and Field Data." *Criminology* 18:62–85.

Tapia, Michael. 2010. "Untangling Race and Class Effects on Juvenile Arrests." *Journal of Criminal Justice* 38:255–265.

U.S. Census Bureau. 2017. *Annual Estimates of the Resident Population, 2016.* Retrieved October 28, 2017 (www.census.gov/data/tables/2016/demo/popest/nation-detail.html).

Williams, Jay R. and Martin Gold. 1972. "From Delinquent Behavior to Official Delinquency." *Social Problems* 20:209–229.

Wolfgang, Marvin E., Robert M. Figlio, and Thorsten Sellin. 1972. *Delinquency in a Birth Cohort.* Chicago: University of Chicago Press.

Zahn, Margaret A., Susan Brumbaugh, Darrell Steffensmeier, Barry C. Feld, Merry Morash, Meda Chesney-Lind, Jody Miller, Allison Ann Payne, Denise C. Gottfredson, and Candace Kruttschnitt, Girls Study Group. 2008. "Violence by Teenage Girls: Trends and Context." *Understanding and Responding to Girls' Delinquency.* Washington, DC: Office of Juvenile Justice and Delinquency Prevention.

Chapter 6

CAUSES OF DELINQUENCY

CHAPTER TOPICS

- Understanding and responding to delinquency: The role of theory and research
- Key contexts, theories, and concepts
- The developmental perspective: Spanning multiple contexts

CHAPTER LEARNING OBJECTIVES

After completing this chapter, students should be able to:

- Describe the basic components of theory.
- Identify the key contexts that are considered to be important in explaining the causes of delinquency and understand how these contexts fit within theory.
- Summarize the major theories of delinquency.
- Describe the key concepts that various theories of delinquency emphasize.

CHAPTER CONTENTS

CASE IN POINT

THE CAUSES AND CONTEXTS OF DELINQUENCY FOR SAM

Sam, the second son born to his hard-working parents, grew up in a low-income part of Baltimore. From the beginning, his parents struggled with his difficult temperament. Though they tried hard to be good parents, they lacked the skills to deal effectively with Sam's forceful personality. His impulsive and oppositional behavior made it impossible for Sam's parents to bond with him in the same way that they bonded with his older brother. Sam and his parents never had what anyone would consider a particularly close relationship.

Because Sam's parents were not able to discipline him effectively for his problem behaviors in childhood, he began school by engaging in behaviors that were difficult for teachers to control as well. Sam was diagnosed relatively early in his school career with learning disabilities, and he struggled greatly in school. He did not perform well academically, and this was a source of great frustration for Sam. He certainly was not optimistic about his future, given that his grades in school would prohibit college attendance. So Sam just gave up on school. He started skipping classes and hanging out in a local park during the day with other teenagers who had also given up on school.

Sam and his peers engaged in minor acts of vandalism in the park. Because they had little hope for their futures and little to lose by engaging in delinquency, their involvement in offending eventually escalated to more serious offenses, such as theft, burglary, and drug use. The neighborhood in which they lived, characterized by low socioeconomic status and a constantly changing population of residents who cared little about the neighborhood, provided plenty of opportunities for these types of offenses.

Theoretical explanations of delinquency are at the foundation of any attempt to respond to delinquent behavior. In this chapter, we briefly describe the major theories of delinquency and the particular contexts they emphasize (e.g., peer groups, family, and schools). We also identify the key concepts that are central to each theory. The major theories are presented here only in abbreviated form, so we encourage you to consult a juvenile delinquency textbook (e.g., Burfeind and Bartusch 2016) for a more complete discussion of delinquency theory. Before turning to specific theories, we first discuss the basic components of theory.

UNDERSTANDING AND RESPONDING TO DELINQUENCY: THE ROLE OF THEORY AND RESEARCH

Delinquency theory and research are useful to the degree that they can help us understand and respond to delinquency. A **theory** is an explanation that makes a systematic and logical argument about what is important and why.

Like other scientific theories, theories of delinquency are composed of two basic parts: concepts and propositions. **Concepts** isolate and categorize features of the world that are thought to be causally important. Different theories of delinquency incorporate and emphasize different concepts, including personality traits, routine activities of adolescents, attachments to others, associations with delinquent friends, and social disorganization of neighborhoods. **Propositions** are theoretical statements that tell how concepts are related. In research, hypotheses are the testable counterpart of propositions, and variables are the measurable counterpart of concepts.

A *theory of delinquency* is a set of logically related propositions that explain why and how selected concepts are related to delinquent behavior. Theories of delinquency offer logically developed arguments that identify certain factors as being causally important and then describe how these factors are interrelated in producing delinquent behavior. Different theories may offer competing propositions.

Research is also essential to the task of understanding and responding to delinquency. It is used to empirically identify the key factors that predict delinquent behavior and to test theories that have been developed to explain delinquency.

So what do theory and research reveal that might be useful in trying to understand and respond to delinquency? To answer this question, we offer a brief inventory of key concepts that have been identified in delinquency theory and supported by research. We place these concepts within particular contexts and briefly describe the theories most closely associated with these contexts.

KEY CONTEXTS, THEORIES, AND CONCEPTS

Delinquency theory and research are usually embedded in particular contexts that are held to be of special importance. Biosocial criminology, for example, considers *individual traits* and the environmental context in which they are expressed. Theories that emphasize the *situational context* of delinquency focus on the activities, social dynamics, and immediate settings that surround offending decisions. Social control theories focus on the central importance of *family relations*, and social learning theories give attention to the importance of *peer group influences*. The larger social context of *schools*, *neighborhoods*, and *communities* is the focus for social structure theories of delinquency. When we think about the practical application of delinquency theory, it is useful to be mindful of the different contexts that various theories emphasize. Key theories are in bold and theoretical concepts are italicized in the discussion that follows. "Expanding ideas: Key criminological theories" summarizes the contexts, specific theories, and theorists and researchers discussed below.

EXPANDING IDEAS: KEY CRIMINOLOGICAL THEORIES

Context	Specific theories and emphases	Theorists and researchers
Individual traits	Biosocial criminology	Raine Fishbein
	Personality	Miller and Lynam
Situational contexts	Routine activities theory	Cohen and Felson Osgood
	Rational choice theory	Cornish and Clarke
Family relations • Social control theories	Social bond theory	Hirschi
	Life-course theory	Sampson and Laub
	General theory of crime (or self-control theory)	Gottfredson and Hirschi
Peer group influences • Social learning theories	Differential association theory	Sutherland
	Social learning theory	Akers
Neighborhood and community influences • Social structure theories	Social disorganization theory	Shaw and McKay
	Collective efficacy theory	Sampson, Raudenbush and Earls
	Anomie theory	Merton
	Strain theory	Merton
	General strain theory	Agnew
School experiences	Fit primarily into social bond theory and general strain theory	
Spanning multiple contexts	Developmental perspective	Moffitt Sampson and Laub

Individual traits

Several theoretical perspectives consider individual traits and the environmental contexts that shape them. Contemporary **biosocial criminology** contends that delinquency and other forms of antisocial behavior result from a combination of biological, psychological, and social causes (Brennan and Raine 1997). This approach is interdisciplinary and based on the fundamental concept of *nature–nurture interaction*. Nature–nurture interaction refers to the process by which biological, psychological, and environmental factors influence each other, as together they affect the likelihood of delinquency.

Biosocial criminology includes three major areas of study. First, *neurological deficits* associated with the prefrontal cortex have been studied extensively in relation to antisocial behavior. Such deficits may reduce executive functioning, resulting in poor self-regulation of impulses, emotions, and behaviors (Peskin et al. 2013; Walsh and Bolen 2012; Wright et al. 2009). Another neurological deficit is autonomic system underarousal, which results in risk-taking, sensation-seeking, and impulsive actions. The autonomic nervous system controls involuntary bodily functions such as blood pressure, heart rate, intestinal activity, and hormone levels. Several theories have been offered to explain the relationship between autonomic system underarousal and antisocial and criminal behavior. One theory argues that individuals with low levels of autonomic arousal are relatively fearless in reaction to stress and thus, underaroused individuals experience little restraint against antisocial acts and little fear of punishment (Raine 2002; Rowe 2002).

Second, *biochemical factors* influence behavior by affecting the central and peripheral nervous systems. Two key aspects of biochemistry have been connected most extensively with antisocial behavior: neurotransmitters and the hormone testosterone (Walsh 2002; Fishbein 2001). Neurotransmitters are the chemical compounds that carry signals between neurons in the intricate communication system of the brain. These include dopamine, serotonin, and norepinephrine. The concentration and metabolism of neurotransmitters play a critical role in how various parts of the brain evoke and regulate behavior, especially as a part of the fight-or-flight response. Testosterone levels have been implicated in displays of dominance and control. However, social variables such as level of social integration appear to intervene in the relationship between testosterone and behavior (Mazur 2009; Booth and Osgood 1993).

Third, the study of *behavioral genetics* seeks to establish the contributions of heredity and environment to individual traits such as impulsivity, risk-taking, self-control, aggressiveness, and negative emotionality (Burt and Simons 2014; Walsh 2002; Fishbein 2001). Whether these traits are given full expression in the form of delinquent and criminal behavior depends on environmental conditions. Genetic factors refer to traits and characteristics that are handed down from parent to child, based on the influence of genes. The measure of this genetic influence is called heritability (Beaver et al. 2014; Burt and Simons 2014).

Researchers have used two designs—adoption studies and twin studies—to try to disentangle genetic and environmental influences on behavior. These studies suggest that there is a heritable component to individual traits that underlie delinquent and criminal behavior—traits such as impulsivity, negativity, aggressiveness, and low intelligence. These studies, however, do not identify the genetic mechanism that may contribute to these traits (Guo, Roettger, and Cai 2008; Baker, Bezdjian, and Raine 2006; Fishbein 2001). Studies in molecular genetics attempt to measure more directly genetic influences on behavior and individual traits.

Personality and biosocial criminology

Biosocial criminology does not contend that biological factors have direct effects on delinquency. Rather, biological factors, in combination with environmental conditions, produce personality traits and behavioral tendencies that are conducive to delinquent behavior. *Personality* refers to reasonably stable patterns of perceiving, thinking, feeling, and responding to the environment (Kleinmuntz 1982). "Traits are the basic building blocks of personality," providing foundation to thought, emotion, character, and behavior (Miller and Lynam 2001:767). Contemporary theory and research contend that personality can be characterized along a number of key dimensions, sometimes called "superfactors," that organize the array of personality traits into a limited number of categories according to the interrelatedness of personality traits (John, Naumann, and Soto 2008). Research shows that antisocial individuals are low on the superfactors of *agreeableness* and *conscientiousness*.

Research on individual traits and delinquency

Biosocial criminology and personality research have produced the following key findings.

- Impaired executive functioning is implicated in the poor self-regulation of impulses, emotions, and behaviors, including delinquency (Peskin et al. 2013; Wright et al. 2009; Raine et al. 2005; Raine 2002; Fishbein 2001).
- In the past decade, there has been a great deal of research on the physical development of the adolescent brain and its relationship with antisocial behavior, particularly the age-linked patterning of delinquent offending (National Research Council 2013). Research shows that adolescents are less capable of self-regulation than adults in part because "the brain system that influences pleasure-seeking and emotional reactivity develops more rapidly than the brain system that supports self-control" (National Research Council 2013:97).
- The physiological condition of autonomic system underarousal is related to antisocial, criminal, and violent behavior in both children and adults (Armstrong et al. 2009; Raine 2002).
- Research on neurotransmitters has produced mixed results. The overproduction of dopamine has been associated with psychotic behavior and with aggression and violence. However, research findings have been inconsistent, and researchers have not uncovered a direct effect of dopamine levels on aggression (Baker et al. 2006; Fishbein 2001). Abnormally low levels of serotonin have been connected with impulsive and aggressive behavior in both juveniles and adults. Although research specifically relates low serotonin activity with impulsivity, the expression of that impulsivity depends on a variety of predisposing and environmental factors (Baker et al. 2006; Fishbein 2001; Moffitt et al. 1998). Although several studies seem to establish a link between antisocial behavior, including violence, and levels of norepinephrine, others do not. Actual behavioral outcomes depend on individual predispositions, circumstances, and social settings (Walsh and Beaver 2009; Fishbein 2001).
- Genetic influences on antisocial behavior have been studied most extensively in terms of how genes influence neurotransmitter levels and, to a lesser degree, how genes influence brain circuitry, especially circuitry of the prefrontal cortex and amygdala. Structural differences in specific genes have been tied to individual traits such as temperament and intelligence and to behavioral tendencies such as aggressiveness, novelty-seeking, and risk-taking (Beaver 2009; DeLisi 2009; Guo et al. 2008; Guo, Roettger, and Shih 2007; Rutter 2006). The expression of genes, however, is dependent on environmental conditions, and

the influence of environmental conditions is dependent on genetic predispositions (Schwartz and Beaver 2011; DeLisi 2009).

- Personality research has established clearly that antisocial individuals are socially indifferent, self-centered, and hostile (low agreeableness) and that they lack self-control (low conscientiousness). Thus, delinquent youth tend to be "hostile, self-centered, spiteful, jealous and indifferent to others" and "they tend to lack ambition, motivation and perseverance, have difficulty controlling their impulses and hold nontraditional and unconventional values and beliefs" (Miller and Lynam 2001:780; Caspi et al. 1994).

Situational contexts

The notion that a youth was "in the wrong place at the wrong time" suggests that the delinquent event has some relevance to how and why delinquency occurs. The term *event* conveys an episodic quality to delinquent acts—they occur at particular times, in particular places, and involve particular people (Sacco and Kennedy 2002). Several theoretical perspectives focus on the situational context of offending decisions and delinquent acts.

Situational characteristics of delinquent events can be described in terms of their objective and subjective content. The *objective content of situations* may motivate and provide opportunity for delinquency by "imposing negative experiences such as frustration, threats, humiliation, and boredom; by offering positive attractions such as money, property, image-building, thrills, and sexual satisfaction; or by providing models to be imitated" (Birkbeck and LaFree 1993:129–130). Experiencing adverse situations such as abuse or homelessness, and the situational strains of daily adolescent life (e.g., the badgering of peer pressure) may also provoke delinquent acts. The *subjective content of situations* encompasses the "individual's perception and interpretation of the immediate setting" (Birkbeck and LaFree 1993:129). Subjective content of situations also includes how delinquent acts are experienced by youths and what these experiences mean to them (Katz 1988).

Routine activities: Opportunities for delinquency

Routine activities theory holds that the likelihood of participating in delinquent acts depends on the degree to which the daily routines of everyday life provide situational opportunity for crime (Osgood et al. 1996; Cohen and Felson 1979). According to routine activities theory, three basic elements of the situation are necessary for crime or delinquency to occur: *motivated offenders* must come in contact with *suitable targets* in the *absence of capable guardians* (Cohen and Felson 1979). Wayne Osgood and his colleagues (1996) examined how the *routine activities* of adolescents in particular are related to delinquent behavior. Involvement in delinquency is more likely to the extent that the routine activities of adolescents lack structure and controls and involve peers. Youths' daily lives tend to expose them to situations that provide opportunity and reward for deviance because their routine activities involve both time with peers (who may increase the situational potential for deviance) and unstructured, unsupervised leisure activities that are beyond the direct control of authority figures. Osgood and his colleagues (1996) called this "situational motivation."

Choosing delinquency: Rational choice theory

Rational choice theory, developed in the 1980s by Derek Cornish and Ronald Clark (1986), focuses on decisions to engage in delinquency. While the word "rational" implies that delinquent acts are deliberate and motivated by self-interest, rational choice theory contends that a series of offending decisions are made over time, involving a variety of individual, social, and legal factors that are sometimes specific to particular types of crime. Furthermore, perceptions of risk and reward appear to change over time and vary according to the situation. The study of rational choice in delinquent offending considers a broad range of influences relating to material gain, legal consequences, normative controls associated with relationship ties, moral beliefs, and guilt and shame. Rational choice is not simply a matter of getting caught and punished. Offending decisions are also subject to individual criminal propensity and morality.

Research on the situational context of delinquency

Research on situational influences on offending has revealed these key findings.

- Research has explored the adverse situations encountered by homeless youth. Life on the "mean streets" provides temptations and opportunities for involvement in delinquency. Without resources of money or employment, many homeless youth resort to street crimes, such as theft, robbery, drug selling, and prostitution, to obtain food and shelter. The adverse situations of homelessness have strong direct effects on street crime (Hagan and McCarthy 1997; McCarthy and Hagan 1992).
- Testing their theory regarding the routine activities of adolescents, Osgood and his colleagues found that unstructured socializing activities (riding around in a car for fun, getting together with friends informally, going to parties, and spending evenings out for fun and recreation) accounted for the largest share of the variation in deviant involvement (Osgood et al. 1996). They concluded that it is not merely spending time outside the home that leads to deviance. Rather, it is the unstructured and unsupervised nature of these activities that is associated with involvement in deviant behavior (see also Bernasco et al. 2013; Miller 2013; Thomas and McGloin 2013).
- Research on the role of rational choice in delinquent behavior found that the deterrent effect of formal sanctions (perceived certainty and severity of punishment) was relatively unimportant to delinquency and that other considerations were far more influential in youths' offending decisions. These considerations included moral beliefs, opportunities to engage in delinquency (shaped by parental supervision and peer involvement), and affective ties (specifically, attachment to parents) (Paternoster 1989). Social costs including loss of respect and friendship, shame, and embarrassment also play a significant role in offending decisions (Wenzel 2004; Piquero and Tibbetts 1996).
- The perceptions of risk and reward that impact offending decisions change over time and vary according to the situation (Matthews and Agnew 2008; Paternoster 1987, 1989; Piliavin et al. 1986). For example, an active social life, in which peers support and encourage delinquent involvement, provides opportunity to engage in delinquent acts and encouragement to do so. One group of researchers concluded that assessments of risk and reward are "to some extent situationally-induced, transitory, and unstable" (Piliavin et al. 1986:116).
- Past experience also influences perceptions of risk and reward, but research findings are inconsistent. Some research shows that past involvement in offending and experience with formal sanctions actually reduce perceptions of risk and thereby increase the possibility of future crime and delinquency (Paternoster 1987; Piliavin et al. 1986). Other research shows that perceived risk of arrest, which is shaped by prior experiences with crime and arrest, decreases involvement in offending (Matsueda, Kraeger, and Huizinga 2006).

Family relations

Social control theories emphasize the important role that social relationships, especially within the family, play in controlling behavior. Social controls that originate from family relationships are an example of *informal social controls*. These are characteristics of social relationships that encourage people to conform, such as parental supervision, emotional attachment, and sensitivity to others' feelings and expectations. The most notable social control theories are Travis Hirschi's social bond theory, Robert Sampson and John Laub's life-course theory, and Michael Gottfredson and Travis Hirschi's general theory of crime.

Hirschi's social bond theory

Hirschi's **social bond theory** emphasizes indirect controls, which are based on affectional identification with others, especially parents, such that individuals conform in order to maintain relationship bonds and avoid disappointing others. The thesis of social bond theory, which attempts to explain why people conform to the expectations of society, is that individuals are free to engage in delinquent acts when their bond to society is weak or broken (Hirschi 1969). Hirschi's theory argues that four elements of the *social bond* provide a reason to conform: Attachment, commitment to conventional lines of action, involvement in conventional activities, and belief in the moral validity of law.

Attachment is generally regarded as the primary element of the social bond. Although Hirschi considered attachments to parents, school, and peers, he presented parent–child attachment as most important in inhibiting delinquent behavior. Attachment results in conformity because of the vested interest a youth has in maintaining relationships that he or she values (Hirschi 1969). *Commitment*, the "rational component" of the social bond, concerns individuals' investments of time and energy in conventional activities such as school and work. Whatever possible gains might come from delinquency must be weighed against the risk of losing the positions, reputations, and possessions individuals have acquired through conventional behavior. The more that is acquired, the more invested the individual is in conforming. *Involvement* in conventional activities controls delinquency by consuming a youth's time and energy, though the type of activity is important in determining the commitment that arises from such involvement and the degree of opportunity for delinquent acts. Hirschi (1969) found that the more time youth spent on education-related activities (e.g., doing homework), the less their involvement in delinquency. Finally, social bond theory considers the strength of *belief* in the moral validity of law and the legal system. As Hirschi notes, "the less a person believes he should obey the rules, the more likely he is to violate them" (Hirschi 1969:26).

Sampson and Laub's life-course theory

While Hirschi's social bond theory focuses on social bonds in adolescence, Sampson and Laub's (1993) **life-course theory** examines social bonds over the life course, considering their origins and how changes in these bonds influence informal social control and behavior (see also Sampson and Laub 2005; Laub and Sampson 1993, 2003). Family processes of attachment, supervision, and discipline are key to the development of social bonds in childhood, and they explain conformity or involvement in delinquency in adolescence. These processes are influenced by the family's structural background and by early childhood difficulties, such as difficult temperament and disruptive and antisocial behavior.

Sampson and Laub also considered social bonds in adulthood, which they refer to as *social capital*—a term that more explicitly links relationship bonds to institutional roles within the family, school, work, and community. The informal social controls of social capital involve not only affective attachment, but also social obligations and restraints that are attached to particular roles, such as marriage and work. Significant changes in the life-course pathway or "trajectory," called *turning points* (e.g., getting married, enlisting in the military, or beginning college), affect social capital and thereby influence informal social control. For example, when an individual begins college, she has a significant investment to lose by engaging in crime, and may leave behind peers with whom she had previously engaged in delinquency. Thus, the obligations of school and the new relationships she forms in college may explain why she stops offending. Sampson and Laub refer to the causal process that supports the termination of offending as *desistance*. Because of the potential for change in life-course trajectories, Sampson and Laub's theory can explain both change and continuity in offending over the life course.

Gottfredson and Hirschi's general theory of crime

Gottfredson and Hirschi's (1990) general theory of crime is often referred to as **self-control theory**. This theory shifts from an emphasis on the informal controls of relationship bonds to focus instead on controls within the individual. As a result of effective childrearing practices of monitoring and discipline, some children develop skills to respond effectively to situations that require delayed gratification, planning, sensitivity to others, independence, cognitive and verbal skills, and a willingness to accept restraints on their activities. In contrast, individuals with *low self-control* are "impulsive, insensitive, physical (as opposed to mental), risk taking, short-sighted, and nonverbal" (Gottfredson and Hirschi 1990:90). They are unable to resist temptations not only of crime, but also of analogous acts such as reckless driving, smoking, and alcohol and drug use. As a result, low self-control fosters problems in interpersonal relations, social activities, and involvement in social institutions, such as family, school, and work. Individuals with low self-control have difficulty making and keeping friends, are less able to succeed in school and the workplace, and tend to enter marriages that are destined to fail.

Research on the family and delinquency

Research documents that characteristics of family life, including the quality of the parent–child relationship, family management techniques (especially monitoring, supervision, and discipline), family disruption, family size, and parental criminality, influence informal social controls and subsequently delinquent behavior.

- Parent–child attachment plays an important role in explaining delinquency. Delinquent behavior is associated with low levels of parental acceptance, sense of belonging, identification with parents, parental caring and trust, positive communication, and parental support (Canter 1995; Rankin and Wells 1990).
- In contrast to attachment, parent–child relationships characterized by hostility, conflict, and rejection have been found to result in limited parental control and increases in delinquency (Fagan et al. 2011; Sampson and Laub 1993).
- Direct parental controls (monitoring children's behavior and consistently providing rewards to encourage and reinforce conformity and restrictions and punishments to constrain behavior) are related to low levels of delinquency, even when other causal factors are taken into consideration (Fagan et al. 2011; Wasserman et al. 2003; Wright and Cullen 2001).

This research reveals that the direct controls of parents have at least as great an effect on delinquency as do indirect relational controls.

- Sampson and Laub found that social capital in the form of social bonds in marriage (marital attachment) and work (job stability) significantly reduced deviant behavior during adulthood, even among those with a history of delinquent behavior in childhood and adolescence. Both continuity and change in behavior were strongly predicted by prior social bonds and the development of adult social bonds (Sampson, Laub, and Wimer 2006; Sampson and Laub 1993; see also Jang 2013; Eitle, Taylor, and Eitle 2010; Christie-Mizell and Peralta 2009).
- Low self-control has consistently been found to be related to self-reported delinquency and adult crime (Holt, Bossler, and May 2012; Pratt and Cullen 2000; LaGrange and Silverman 1999; Arneklev et al. 1993; Grasmick et al. 1993). Low self-control is related not only to the likelihood of involvement in crime, but also to the frequency of involvement, persistence in crime, and desistance from crime (DeLisi and Vaughan 2008; Piquero, Moffitt, and Wright 2007; Doherty 2006).
- Family disruption (due to divorce, separation, or the desertion or death of one or both parents) is related to delinquency largely because of the effect of such disruption on relationship bonds and parental monitoring and supervision (Demuth and Brown 2004; Wasserman et al. 2003; Rebellon 2002; Thornberry et al. 1999; Van Voorhis et al. 1998; Sampson and Laub 1993).
- The research is very clear on one problematic aspect of family life: Child maltreatment (physical abuse, sexual abuse, and neglect) is a risk factor for delinquency. Maltreated children and adolescents are more likely to be involved in delinquent behavior, especially serious and violent delinquency (Colman et al. 2009; Rebellon and Van Gundy 2005; Thornberry, Huizinga, and Loeber 2004; Wasserman et al. 2003; Ireland, Smith, and Thornberry 2002; Smith and Thornberry 1995; Zingraff et al. 1993; Widom 1989). Physical abuse is related to delinquency beyond its impact on self-control and social bonds. Researchers suggest that the negative emotions resulting from physical abuse may increase the probability of delinquency as a coping mechanism.

Peer group influences

Peer groups are a crucial context for understanding delinquency. The causal processes connecting peer group influences and delinquent behavior have been examined mostly through the lens of **social learning theories**, including Edwin Sutherland's differential association theory and Ronald Akers' social learning theory. These theories point to peer groups as the social context in which delinquent behavior is learned and reinforced.

Sutherland's differential association theory

A revised version of **differential association theory**, published in 1947, remains the best-known formal statement of the learning processes that occur in delinquent peer groups (Sutherland, Cressey, and Luckenbill 1992). Differential association theory is stated in the form of nine propositions. Though these propositions are phrased in terms of criminal behavior, Sutherland intended for his theory to explain a broad range of crimes, including delinquency.

Differential association theory is a theory of *social learning*; it holds that criminal behavior is learned through social interaction in groups. According to Sutherland, the vehicle for learning is verbal communication, and learning occurs within intimate personal groups. Through such interaction, individuals learn both techniques for committing delinquent acts and attitudes and motivations toward offending. The theory goes on to state that association with different groups—*differential association*—varies in "frequency, duration, priority, and intensity." In other words, the influence of relationships within groups is greatest when interaction occurs frequently (frequency), for long periods (duration), and early in life (priority), and when those relationship ties are strong (intensity). At the heart of the theory are *definitions of the law.* A person defines the law as favorable or unfavorable—either as rules to obey or as rules to violate—and such definitions are learned through social interaction. The direction of these definitions involves motives and drives that either support obedience to the law or encourage violation of it. The central proposition of differential association theory states that "a person becomes delinquent because of an excess of definitions favorable to violation of law over definitions unfavorable to violation of law" (Sutherland et al. 1992:88–90). Sutherland assigned special importance to delinquent peer groups as a context in which adolescents learn "definitions favorable to the violation of the law." In fact, he contended that adolescent peer groups are much more important than the family in teaching delinquent behavior.

A criticism of differential association theory is that it says little about *how* the learning of crime and delinquency occurs, other than noting that the "process of learning criminal behavior . . . involves all the mechanisms that are involved in any other learning" (Sutherland et al. 1992:88–90). Social learning theory was developed to overcome this shortcoming.

Akers' social learning theory

Ronald Akers' (1985) **social learning theory** elaborates on the processes of learning by emphasizing four particular aspects: differential association, definitions, differential reinforcement, and imitation. The idea of *differential association* builds on Sutherland's use of the term to include not only the group context in which delinquent attitudes and behaviors are learned, but also the group's ability to model and reinforce these attitudes and behaviors. Also drawing on Sutherland's original theory, social learning theory points to the importance of delinquent *definitions.* Attitudes and beliefs that encourage delinquent acts are acquired in groups through imitation and reinforcement. Akers asserts that delinquent definitions are "basically positive or neutralizing. Positive definitions are beliefs or attitudes that make the behavior morally desirable or wholly permissible. Neutralizing definitions favor the commission of crime by justifying or excusing it" (Akers and Sellers 2013:83, emphasis omitted). The third aspect of learning is *differential reinforcement.* This term refers to learning processes that involve rewards and punishments. Rewards and punishments may be actual or anticipated, social or nonsocial (Akers and Sellers 2013). The fourth aspect of learning is *imitation*, in which the behavior modeled by others is copied. Sometimes, people behave in particular ways after observing other people's behavior. Imitation may result in new kinds of behavior or serve to maintain current behaviors. In some cases, it can result in the discontinuation of behavior. Akers (1985), for example, argues that imitation is key to learning how to use drugs. Seeing how other people actually take drugs and then observing the effect that they experience provides an important first step into drug use.

Research on peers and delinquency

Research examining the relationship between peers and delinquency has produced the following key findings.

- The number of delinquent friends a youth has and the extent of their delinquency are closely related to the level of a youth's own delinquency (Megens and Weerman 2012; Miller 2010; Elliott and Menard 1996).
- Learning delinquent attitudes and behaviors occurs through communication, modeling, imitation, and reinforcement among peers. These social learning processes are an important component of peer influence (Akers 1985).
- Peer group associations have the greatest influence on behavior when they occur often, for longer periods, and when relationship ties are strong and intimate (Kreager, Rulison, and Moody 2011; Haynie and Osgood 2005; Giordano, Cernkovich, and Pugh 1986).
- The groups in which youth commit delinquency tend to be small and transitory. Adolescents typically commit offenses in groups of only two or three youth, and these companions change frequently, being drawn from a larger network of friends (Warr 1996).
- A key question in the literature on peers and delinquency is which comes first? Does association with delinquent peers come before delinquency (as learning theories suggest), or do youth engage in delinquency and then associate with delinquent peers? Studies show that both views are partially correct. Some youth, particularly younger adolescents and those who engage in serious delinquency, make delinquent friends before getting involved in delinquency (Elliott and Menard 1996), while other youth engage in delinquent acts and then seek out delinquent friends (Inciardi, Horowitz, and Pottieger 1993).
- Research on drug use also supports both views of the causal ordering of peers and delinquency. Youth who use drugs tend to choose friends who also use drugs, and once friendships are established, peer group interactions promote attitudes and behaviors that encourage continued drug use (Krohn et al. 1996).
- Gender differences exist in peer group influence. Males are substantially more likely than females to be exposed to delinquent friends; they spend more time with friends than females do, and are roughly twice as likely to have friends who have broken the law. Males are also more strongly affected by delinquent friends than females are (Chapple, Vaske, and Worthen 2014; Augustyn and McGloin 2013; Mears, Ploeger, and Warr 1998).
- Street gangs provide a key context in which serious delinquency is learned from and reinforced by peers. Gang members commit more frequent and more serious crime (particularly violent crime), compared with delinquent youth who are not gang members (Melde and Esbensen 2013, 2014; Gordon et al. 2004, 2014; Thornberry et al. 1993, 2003). The link between gang involvement and delinquency suggests that membership and social interaction within gangs have strong influence on the behaviors and attitudes of gang members. Group processes related to group cohesion, status within the group, and threats of violence are central to understanding how gangs influence the behavior of members (Hughes 2013; Papachristos 2013; Decker and Van Winkle 1996; Short and Strodtbeck 1965). In addition, group characteristics such as gang culture and organizational structure provide the social context for group processes (Decker, Katz, and Webb 2008; Coughlin and Venkatesh 2003; Padilla 1992; Jankowski 1991; Moore 1991).

Neighborhood and community influences

Social structure theories consider the social and societal characteristics that integrate and regulate people's daily lives. Sociologists refer to these organizational features of the social environment as *social structures*. Social structure theories examine societal characteristics such as cultural traditions; institutionalized social relations within the context of families, schools, and employment; and ecological dimensions, such as population mobility and the residential concentration of ethnic groups and social classes. When these societal characteristics disrupt social organization, social control breaks down, and crime and delinquency flourish.

Social disorganization theory

In the early to mid-1900s, Clifford Shaw and Henry McKay studied delinquency in Chicago (Shaw et al. 1929; Shaw and McKay 1931, [1942] 1969). The primary purpose of their research was to investigate how delinquent behavior was geographically distributed across the city and to discover the community characteristics that were associated with high rates of delinquency. Based on this research, Shaw and McKay developed **social disorganization theory**, which emphasizes three structural characteristics of urban environments that disrupt social organization: *low economic status, ethnic heterogeneity* (or diversity), and *residential mobility* (the movement of residents into or out of a community). Urban areas characterized by these structures typically lack effective social control mechanisms and, as a result, experience high rates of crime and delinquency. These delinquency areas often have strong criminal traditions, or subcultures, in which involvement in illegal activity is a way of life, passed on from adults to youth and youth to youth. Delinquency areas also lack legitimate economic opportunities, resulting in personal frustration or strain that can motivate involvement in delinquency.

Collective efficacy

Robert Sampson and his colleagues have recently revitalized social disorganization theory by advancing their theory of **collective efficacy** (Sampson, Raudenbush, and Earls 1997). They argue that structural characteristics related to the social composition of neighborhoods are strongly related to rates of violence. These structural characteristics include a community's levels of poverty and family disruption, race and age composition, concentration of immigrants, and residential stability (the rates at which people are moving into or out of a neighborhood). The influence of these structural features of neighborhoods, however, depends on the degree to which local residents are interdependent, cohesive, and willing to exercise informal social control. Together these elements of cohesion among community residents and their willingness to exert informal control make up *collective efficacy*.

Anomie theory

Delinquency theories that focus on the lack of regulation in society are referred to as **anomie theories**. The origins of anomie and strain theories can be traced to the work of Robert Merton (1938). He argued that the *cultural goal* of economic success permeates all of American society, but that the *institutional means* or norms to achieve success are neither stressed to the same degree nor equally available to all people. Merton used the term *anomie* to describe the societal condition of normlessness that results when societal goals are stressed to a much greater degree than are the institutionalized means for achieving those goals. According to Merton, it is this inconsistent emphasis on cultural goals and institutional means that explains why some societies have high rates of crime and deviance. In a society characterized by anomie, where norms are no longer binding, people are free to pursue economic success by whatever means necessary, including crime.

Strain theories

Building on anomie theory, Merton's **strain theory** explains how groups and individuals adapt to the condition of anomie in society. Merton (1938) argued that individuals experience *strain* when the acceptable means for achieving economic success are unclear or unavailable, and that they must adapt to such strain. Although blocked opportunities for success might seem to be the primary source of strain, strain theory centers on an individual's response to anomie in terms of acceptance or rejection of cultural goals and the institutional means to reach those goals. In its most basic form, strain theory argues that "delinquency results when individuals cannot get what they want through legitimate channels" (Agnew 1995:113). Although strain is experienced at the individual level, it results from structural factors, especially social class placement and the resulting level of opportunity (Farnworth and Leiber 1989).

Merton proposed five *modes of adaptation* to the societal condition of anomie: conformity, ritualism, innovation, retreatism, and rebellion. Conformity, which represents an acceptance of cultural goals and the institutional means to obtain those goals, is the most common adaptation. Ritualism involves rigid compliance with rules, without a clear commitment to the goals. Innovation involves the use of illegitimate means to achieve cultural goals. With the accepted means to success underemphasized or unavailable, some individuals turn to illegitimate means. Retreatism, the least common adaptation, involves individuals dropping out of society when the goals and means to achieve them are unattainable. Rebellion depicts individuals who not only reject cultural goals and means, but replace them with new ones. Deviant behavior occurs as part of the adaptations of innovation, retreatism, and rebellion.

Robert Agnew's (1985, 1992, 2006) **general strain theory** identifies additional sources of strain beyond the structural feature of anomie. In particular, Agnew emphasizes the social psychological aspect of strain, focusing on strains of adolescent life that result from negative social relationships and efforts to avoid unpleasant or painful situations. According to Agnew, three types of *strain* are most common: (1) losing something of value; (2) being treated by others in an aversive or negative manner; and (3) being unable to achieve goals. These strains may increase the likelihood of delinquency because they may breed negative emotions (e.g., anger, frustration, jealousy, depression, and fear); they may produce personality traits such as negative emotionality and low constraint; they may reduce levels of social control; and they may foster the social learning of crime (Agnew 2006). General strain theory does not fit neatly in this section on neighborhood and community influences. We include it here, however, because Agnew presented this theory as flowing out of Merton's strain theory, which builds on anomie theory. General strain theory actually spans multiple contexts, including family relations and peer group influences.

Research on neighborhood and community influences

The social structure theories described above have been tested extensively. Research on neighborhood and community influences on delinquency has produced the following results.

- Shaw and his colleagues (1929) found that variation in delinquency and crime rates across the city of Chicago reflected differences in community characteristics. Delinquency and crime rates were highest in areas characterized by declining population and physical deterioration.

- Testing social disorganization theory with survey data gathered in Great Britain, Sampson and Groves (1989:799) found that "communities characterized by sparse friendship networks, unsupervised teenage peer groups, and low organizational participation had disproportionately high rates of crime and delinquency." In addition, variation in these dimensions of community social disorganization mediated much of the effects of community structural characteristics on crime and delinquency, as predicted by social disorganization theory.
- Testing their theory of collective efficacy, Sampson and his colleagues (1997) found that the social composition of neighborhoods—measured using the structural characteristics of concentrated disadvantage, concentration of immigrants, and residential stability—was related strongly to neighborhood rates of violence. This relationship was heavily dependent, however, on the collective efficacy of neighborhoods. Communities that were characterized by collective disadvantage and residential instability, but where residents still maintained cohesive social relationships and engaged readily in informal social control, had low rates of crime and delinquency. Sampson and his associates concluded that the effects of concentrated disadvantage and residential instability on rates of violence are mediated by collective efficacy. Several recent studies have provided additional support for the theory of collective efficacy (MacDonald et al. 2013; Kirk and Matsuda 2011; Mazerolle, Wickes, and McBroom 2010), while other research has provided mixed or no support for the theory (Sutherland, Brunton-Smith, and Jackson 2013; Wickes 2010).
- Research testing the basic premise of strain theory has provided only limited empirical support (Agnew 2000; Jensen 1995; Burton et al. 1994; Hirschi 1969). For example, research has provided only limited support for the proposition that strain results when goals for success go unfulfilled because of blocked opportunities (Agnew 2000; Burton et al. 1994). Margaret Farnworth and Michael Leiber (1989) contend that the lack of empirical support for strain theory has more to do with the way in which strain has been measured than with the theory's lack of legitimacy.
- General strain theory has received strong empirical support. For example, research found that adolescents who scored high on a composite measure of strain were far more likely to engage in delinquent acts than those who scored lower. Thus, the experience of strain pressured or motivated youth to engage in delinquency (Agnew and White 1992). Another study examined the degree to which delinquent acts are a coping response to strain and found that the experience of strain was associated with feelings of anger, resentment, anxiety, and depression. Brezina (1996) concluded that involvement in delinquency enables adolescents to minimize the negative emotional consequences of strained social relationships (see also Moon et al. 2009; Hay and Evans 2006). More recent studies also provide support for general strain theory and demonstrate its value in explaining both juvenile and adult offending and its applicability to offending in the United States and other countries (Sigfusdottir, Kristjansson, and Agnew 2012; Piquero and Sealock 2004, 2010; Rebellon et al. 2009; Froggio and Agnew 2007; Ostrowsky and Messner 2005).

School experiences

School provides an important context for understanding involvement in delinquency. School experiences are linked to delinquent behavior through several mechanisms, including school performance, attachment to school, commitment to education, and school characteristics. These mechanisms fit primarily into two bodies of theory discussed above: social bond theory and general strain theory.

School performance

As a measure of *intelligence,* IQ scores are most accurately viewed as a measure of academic preparedness and aptitude, rather than innate intellect. As such, low IQ places youth at risk for poor *school performance* and frustration, leading indirectly to delinquency (Hirschi and Hindelang 1977). A variety of factors other than school performance also impact the relationship between intelligence and delinquency. For example, low IQ also contributes to delinquency indirectly by inhibiting the development of self-control and increasing the likelihood of experiencing pressure from deviant peers (Loeber et al. 2012; Beaver et al. 2008; Beaver, Wright, and DeLisi 2008; McGloin, Pratt, and Maahs 2004). The relationship between intelligence and delinquency also varies by gender, race, and social class; for various types of offenders; and according to temperament (Hampton, Drabick, and Steinberg 2014; Block 1995; Lynam and Moffitt 1995; Lynam, Moffitt, and Stouthamer-Loeber 1993).

Attachment to school

Many have argued, from the perspective of social bond theory, that students who are strongly attached to school—who, for example, like school, "feel a part of their school," and care what teachers think of them—are less likely than others to engage in delinquency (Gottfredson, Wilson, and Najaka 2002; Johnson, Crosnoe, and Elder 2001; Hirschi 1969). Numerous studies support this hypothesis regarding *attachment to school.* Research also suggests that school capital and high-quality school environments "serve as substitutes for poor parental attachment and a lack of parental involvement in children's schooling," and thus diminish involvement in delinquency in part "by compensating for high-risk family environments" (Hoffman and Dufur 2008:29).

The link between poor relationships with teachers and involvement in delinquent behavior can also be explained in terms of general strain theory, which argues that being treated by others in a negative way is conducive to delinquency. Delinquents are more likely than non-delinquents to report that they dislike their teachers and have negative relationships with them (Agnew 1985).

Commitment to education

Criminologists have also argued, from a social bond perspective, that weak *commitment to education* (i.e., weak valuing of educational goals) and low educational aspirations are related to school misconduct and delinquency (Gottfredson et al. 2002; Hirschi 1969). General strain theory also predicts that, compared with non-delinquents, delinquents have more limited educational and occupational aspirations and expectations (Agnew and Brezina 2015; Carroll et al. 2013). Commitment to education is likely related to academic performance as well as to school misconduct and delinquency. Students who perform well academically are likely to be more committed to education and have higher aspirations and expectations for success than those who perform poorly (Siennick and Staff 2008; Wasserman et al. 1996).

Truancy and dropping out of school are manifestations of weak social bonds to school, especially lack of commitment to academic achievement. Research has shown that truancy is a precursor to more serious delinquency (both violent and nonviolent offenses) and is also related to substance abuse and marital and job problems later in life (Baker et al. 2001). Dropping out of school also indicates weak bonds to school, and some research has shown that dropping out is related to delinquency and crime, including violence (Henry, Knight, and Thornberry 2012; Staff and Kreager 2008; Jarjoura 1993; see also Sweeten, Bushway, and Paternoster 2009).

School characteristics

Various school characteristics are sources of strain and have been linked through empirical research to delinquency. School characteristics that contribute to *lower* rates of in-school delinquency include schools that provide opportunities for student success and praise student accomplishments; schools with good discipline, where rules for behavior are clear and consistently enforced in a fair manner; schools with high expectations and pleasant working conditions for students, strong community involvement, and good cooperation between administration and teachers; and small schools with good resources (Agnew and Brezina 2015).

From a strain theory perspective, the relationship between these school characteristics and delinquency might be explained in this way: Schools with these characteristics are less likely to create strain for students because they are perceived as pleasant and fair, students are likely to achieve their success goals, and students are likely to have positive relationships with teachers and others in the school (Agnew and Brezina 2015).

Research on school experiences and delinquency

Research on school experiences and delinquency provides the following key findings.

- Poor academic performance predicts delinquent behavior. Specifically, research has found that children who perform poorly academically commit more frequent, serious, and violent offenses and persist longer in their offending than children with higher academic achievement (Maguin and Loeber 1996). A more recent study, however, suggests that the relationship between poor academic performance and delinquency is spurious and due to the effects of self-control on both academic performance and delinquent behavior (Felson and Staff 2006). On the flip side, strong academic performance by incarcerated delinquents appears to serve as a turning point, contributing to a return to school following incarceration and a decrease in the likelihood of re-arrest (Blomberg, Bales, and Piquero 2012; see also Hoffman, Erickson, and Spence 2013).
- Students who are strongly attached to school are less likely than others to engage in delinquency (Hirschfield and Gasper 2011; Stewart 2003; Jang 1999). Some researchers found, though, that the relationship between attachment to school and delinquency is reciprocal—attachment influences delinquency and delinquency influences attachment (Siennick and Staff 2008).
- Weak school commitment is strongly related to school misconduct and various forms of delinquency, including violence (Siennick and Staff 2008; Stewart 2003). Compared with at-risk and not at-risk adolescents, delinquent adolescents report fewer educational and occupational goals, set fewer challenging goals, and have a lower commitment to their goals (Carroll et al. 2013). Research shows that educational expectations combined with effort in school explain delinquents' lower educational attainment (Siennick and Staff 2008). Research also suggests that commitment to education has a greater protective effect in preventing delinquency for boys than for girls (Payne 2009).
- Research generally has not supported the hypothesis that involvement in school-related activities will inhibit delinquency (Guest and McRee 2009; Stewart 2003; Hoffman and Xu 2002). In particular, research has challenged the assumption that participation in high school sports would have a deterrent effect on delinquency. Research shows that being a highly involved athlete tends to be associated with higher levels of delinquency (Kelley and

Sokol-Katz 2011), and that sports participation increases involvement in particular types of delinquency, such as drunk driving (Hartmann and Massoglia 2007).

- School failure, measured in part as dropping out of school, operates as a significant adolescent turning point, amplifying later delinquency (Bersani and Chapple 2007). Being suspended or expelled greatly increases a child's risk of dropping out of school and of being drawn into the juvenile justice system (Monahan et al. 2014; Fabelo et al. 2011). Suspension or expulsion increases the likelihood of arrest, particularly for youth who do not have a history of behavior problems (Monahan et al. 2014).

THE DEVELOPMENTAL PERSPECTIVE: SPANNING MULTIPLE CONTEXTS

The **developmental perspective**, which emerged in the early 1990s, invites us to think about how involvement in crime and delinquency might span multiple contexts. This perspective helps to explain the patterning of offending that we tend to see over the life course by focusing on five key elements: age of onset of problem behaviors, continuity and change in problem behaviors, progression of seriousness, generality of deviance, and desistance from offending.

The developmental perspective suggests different patterns of offending based, in part, on *age of onset of problem behaviors*. Most offenders begin involvement in delinquency during adolescence and relatively quickly age out of crime in late adolescence or early adulthood. Other offenders, however, display problem behaviors early in the life course and are more likely to develop stable patterns of offending into adulthood (DeLisi et al. 2013; Tzoumakis et al. 2013; LeBlanc and Loeber 1998). Research has shown that, compared with late-onset offenders, early-onset offenders show more stability in offending over time, a higher rate of offending, and more serious offenses (DeLisi 2006; Nagin, Farrington, and Moffitt 1995; Loeber and LeBlanc 1990). The developmental perspective also considers different patterns of offending based on level of *continuity or change in problem behaviors* over time. For most offenders, problem behaviors are not stable over time. Involvement in delinquency is brief and represents a change in behavior patterns. However, for a relatively small number of offenders with "extreme" behavior problems, antisocial behavior is stable over time, from childhood through adulthood (Piquero and Moffitt 2014; Piquero et al. 2010; Thornberry 2005; Sampson and Laub 1993).

A third pattern that developmental theories consider is *progression of seriousness* in offending. Research reveals a progression from minor to serious offenses. Most individuals who engage in delinquency do not progress to the most serious offenses. Among those who do become serious delinquents, though, criminal careers tend to start with minor offenses and escalate to more serious ones (MacDonald et al. 2014; Loeber et al. 2008; Kelley et al. 1997). Fourth, the developmental perspective considers the *generality of deviance* or co-occurrence of problem behaviors. Studies suggest that delinquency is often a component of a larger group of problem behaviors—including drug and alcohol use, mental health problems, behavior problems and underachievement in school, and risky sexual behavior—that tend to occur together (Hirschfield et al. 2006; Huizinga et al. 2000; Farrington 1998). Finally, the developmental perspective examines the process of *desistance from offending*. Research indicates that attachment to law-abiding others (especially a spouse), stable employment, the aging process, and changes in personal identity all influence desistance from crime and delinquency (Steinberg, Cauffman, and Monahan 2015; Bersani and Doherty 2013; Sampson, Laub, and Wimer 2006; Laub and Sampson 2001, 2003; Giordano, Cernkovich, and Rudolph 2002; Maruna 2001; Uggen 2000).

These five elements of the developmental perspective suggest ways in which the patterning of delinquency spans multiple contexts. For example, individual traits or the context of the family may be more important in explaining delinquent behavior for those who begin offending earlier in the life course and for whom antisocial behavior is more stable over the life course. The context of peer groups, on the other hand, may be more important in explaining patterns of offending characterized by change, a later onset of offending, and desistance in earlier adulthood. Specific developmental models are based on these propositions. For example, Terrie Moffitt's (1993, 1997) influential developmental model argues that there are primarily two patterns of offending: adolescence-limited and life-course-persistent offending.

Adolescence-limited offenders are those who participate in antisocial behavior for a relatively brief period of time during adolescence. For this relatively large group of offenders, involvement in antisocial behavior is temporary and situational. Moffitt (1993) argues that adolescence-limited offenders begin offending because of the "maturity gap" between biological and sexual maturity in early adolescence and social maturity in late adolescence or early adulthood, which leaves adolescents searching for a means of achieving status. According to Moffitt, adolescents view antisocial behavior as a way of achieving mature status. Peer groups provide reinforcement for these efforts to achieve status and are important for explaining delinquency among adolescence-limited offenders.

Life-course-persistent offenders are those characterized by continuity of antisocial behavior from early childhood through adulthood. For this small group of offenders, antisocial behavior is stable across time and circumstance. Moffitt (1993) attributes the early onset of antisocial behavior for life-course-persistent offenders to a combination of (1) structures and processes within the child's nervous system that influence psychological characteristics such as temperament and cognitive abilities and (2) a negative child-rearing environment. Thus, individual traits and family relations are important for explaining the offending pattern for this group.

Numerous tests of Moffitt's developmental approach offer support for her hypotheses about these two types of offenders (Moffitt 2006; Piquero and Brezina 2001; Bartusch et al. 1997). The reading included in this chapter considers not only developmental pathways to offending, but also presents key research findings and policy implications from the Program of Research on the Causes and Correlates of Delinquency regarding multiple contexts that impact involvement in delinquency.

SUMMARY AND CONCLUSIONS

Theories of delinquency, made up of concepts and propositions, identify certain factors as being causally important and then describe how these factors are interrelated in producing delinquent behavior. In this chapter, we discussed six contexts of delinquency—individual traits, situational contexts, family relations, peer groups, neighborhoods and communities, and schools—and briefly described the major theories that have focused on each of those contexts to explain delinquency. These theories include biosocial criminology (focusing on individual traits), routine activities and rational choice theories (focusing on situational contexts), social control theories (focusing on family relations), social learning theories (focusing on peer group influences), social disorganization and anomie theories (focusing on neighborhood and community influences), and social control and strain theories (focusing on school experiences). In our discussion of theories, we identified the key concepts that are central to each theory.

Theories must be "put to the test" through research. We highlighted findings of research that has tested the various theories we presented in this chapter. Delinquency theory and research are useful to the degree that they help us understand and respond to delinquency.

Finally, we described the developmental perspective, which spans multiple contexts of delinquency. This perspective helps to explain the patterning of offending that we tend to see over the life course by focusing on five key elements: age of onset of problem behaviors, continuity and change in problem behaviors, progression of seriousness, generality of deviance, and desistance from offending. These five elements suggest ways in which the patterning of delinquency spans multiple contexts, including individual traits, family relations, and peer group influences.

READING 6.1

"THE CAUSES AND CORRELATES STUDIES: FINDINGS AND POLICY IMPLICATIONS."

Terence P. Thornberry, David Huizinga, and Rolf Loeber. 2004. *Juvenile Justice* 9:3–19.

This reading presents research findings from the Program of Research on the Causes and Correlates of Delinquency, which consists of three longitudinal studies: the Denver Youth Survey, the Pittsburgh Youth Study, and the Rochester Youth Development Study. This summary of findings focuses specifically on childhood aggression, developmental pathways to delinquency, and the overlap of problem behaviors, as well as two key risk factors for delinquency: child maltreatment and gang membership. This reading also considers the policy implications of these research findings.

Delinquent behavior has long been a serious and costly problem in American society. Although the U.S. delinquency rate has declined since the mid-1990s, it is still among the highest in the industrialized countries. To reduce delinquent behavior and improve societal well-being, it is essential to develop effective intervention programs. In turn, effective programs depend on a firm, scientific understanding of the origins of delinquency. The Office of Juvenile Justice and Delinquency Prevention's (OJJDP's) Program of Research on the Causes and Correlates of Delinquency constitutes the largest, most comprehensive investigation of the causes and correlates of delinquency ever undertaken.

For the past 17 years, the program, which consists of three longitudinal studies (the Denver Youth Survey, the Pittsburgh Youth Study, and the Rochester Youth Development Study) has contributed substantially to an understanding of delinquent behavior. This article summarizes a few of the many empirical findings generated by these studies and policy implications arising therefrom.[1]

The studies

Each study uses a longitudinal design in which a sample of children and/or adolescents was selected and then followed over time to chart the course of their development. The studies oversampled youth at high risk for serious delinquency; however, because the studies used statistical weighting, the samples represent the broader population of urban adolescents.

Denver Youth Survey

The Denver Youth Survey is based on a probability sample of households in high-risk neighborhoods of Denver, CO, selected on the basis of their population, housing characteristics, and high official crime rates. The survey respondents include 1,527 children who were ages 7, 9, 11, 13, or 15 in 1987 and who lived in one of the more than 20,000 randomly selected households. The sample of children includes 806 boys and 721 girls. These respondents, along with a parent or primary caretaker, were interviewed annually from 1988 until 1992 and from 1995 until 1999. The younger two age groups were reinterviewed in 2003. The sample is composed of African Americans (33 percent), Latinos (45 percent), whites (10 percent), and youth of other ethnic groups (12 percent). To date, Denver researchers have studied subjects ranging in age from 7 through 27.

Pittsburgh Youth Study

The Pittsburgh Youth Study is based on a sample of 1,517 boys from Pittsburgh, PA, selected in 1987–88. To identify high-risk subjects, an initial screening assessment of problem behaviors was conducted in the first, fourth, and seventh grades of the Pittsburgh public school system. Boys who scored above the upper 30th percentile for their grade were identified as high risk, and approximately 250 of them were randomly selected for followup, along with 250 boys from the remaining 70 percent. The subjects, parents or primary caretakers, and teachers were interviewed at 6-month intervals for the first 5 years of the study, although the fourth grade sample was discontinued after seven assessments. Since the sixth year of the study, followups of the first and seventh grade samples have been conducted annually. In the followup period, researchers are studying data regarding the sampled youth from when they were age 7 to their current age of 25.

Rochester Youth Development Study

The Rochester Youth Development Study is based on a sample of 729 boys and 271 girls who were in the seventh and eighth grades (ages 13–14) in the public schools of Rochester, NY, in 1988. The sample is composed of African American (68 percent), Hispanic (17 percent), and white (15 percent) youth. Each student, along with a parent or primary caretaker, was interviewed at 6-month intervals for the first 4 1/2 years of the study. From ages 20–22, the subjects and their caretakers were interviewed annually, and the subjects are currently being reinterviewed at ages 28 and 30.

The studies collectively

These studies provide data on delinquent behavior from 1987 to the present, and have included more than 4,000 subjects ranging in age from as young as 7 to as old as 30. The samples have a strong representation of serious, violent, and chronic offenders. To date, more than 100,000 personal interviews have been conducted, and volumes of additional data from schools, police, courts, social services, and other agencies have been collected.

The Causes and Correlates studies have addressed scores of different topics related to juvenile delinquency and juvenile justice. In the following pages, the authors summarize just a few of these many investigations. Some of the topics are specific to one of the projects; other topics are investigated with data from two or all three projects.

Patterns of delinquency

The Causes and Correlates studies have provided descriptive data that trace the onset and development of delinquency. Three key topics are childhood aggression, developmental pathways to delinquency, and the overlap of problem behaviors.

Childhood aggression

The vast majority of the youth in the Denver and Pittsburgh studies reported involvement in some form of physical aggression before age 13 (85 percent of the boys and 77 percent of the girls in Denver and 88 percent of the boys in Pittsburgh) (Espiritu et al., 2001). Well over half (roughly 60 percent of both genders in Denver and 80 percent of the Pittsburgh boys) reported such aggression before age 9. In addition, approximately half of the Denver children (57 percent of the boys, 40 percent of the girls) and 32 percent of the Pittsburgh boys reported more serious aggression in which the victim was hurt (bruised or worse), and 47 percent of the boys and 28 percent of the girls in Denver and 14 percent of the Pittsburgh boys reported assaults that resulted in more serious injuries to the victim (e.g., cuts, bleeding wounds, or injuries requiring medical treatment).

As these findings indicate, aggression during childhood is quite common, although exactly how widespread depends on how aggression is defined. Involvement in aggression, however, is not necessarily extensive or long lasting. A substantial amount of delinquency, including aggression, is limited to childhood. For example, only about half (49 percent) of the Denver children involved in minor violence in which the victim was hurt or injured continued this behavior for more than 2 years. In fact, much aggressive behavior, and an even larger proportion of other delinquency, appears to be limited to childhood. However, a large proportion—about half—of aggressive children continue to be aggressive for several years into at least early adolescence. Exactly what distinguishes children who cease to be aggressive and those who continue remains to be determined.

Developmental pathways

Childhood aggression that continues and escalates as individuals age raises two key questions: does the movement to serious delinquency progress in an orderly fashion, and is there a single dominant pathway or are there multiple pathways?

The onset of minor aggression (e.g., arguing, bullying) tends to occur first, followed by the onset of physical fighting (including gang fighting), and then by the onset of other violence such as robbery or rape (Loeber and Hay, 1997). These results suggest that development toward serious forms of delinquency tends to be orderly.

Initial research comparing single and multiple pathways found that a model of three distinct pathways (see figure 1) provided the best fit to the data:

- The Authority Conflict Pathway, which starts with stubborn behavior before age 12 and progresses to defiance and then to authority avoidance (e.g., truancy).
- The Covert Pathway, which starts with minor covert acts before age 15 and progresses to property damage and then to moderate and then to serious delinquency.
- The Overt Pathway starts with minor aggression and progresses to physical fighting and then to more severe violence (no minimum age is associated with this pathway).

These results were replicated for African American and white boys in Pittsburgh across three age samples (Loeber et al., 1993, 1998). They have also been replicated in a sample of African American and Hispanic adolescents in Chicago and in a nationally representative U.S. sample of adolescents (Tolan, Gorman-Smith, and Loeber, 2000). Replications also have been successfully undertaken in the Denver Youth Survey and the Rochester Youth Development Study (Loeber et al., 1999).

As they became older, some boys progressed on two or three pathways, indicating an increasing variety of problem behaviors over time (Kelley et al., 1997; Loeber et al., 1993; Loeber, Keenan, and Zhang, 1997). Researchers found some evidence that development along more than one pathway was orderly. For example, aggressive boys committing overt acts were particularly at risk of also committing covert acts, but not vice versa. Further, conflict with authority figures was either a precursor or a concomitant of boys' escalation in overt or covert acts (Loeber et al., 1993). Also, an early age of onset of problem behavior or delinquency was associated with escalation to more serious behaviors in all the pathways (Tolan, Gorman-Smith, and Loeber, 2000). The pathway model accounted for the majority of the most seriously delinquent boys, that is, those who self-reported high rates of offending (Loeber et al., 1993; Loeber, Keenan,

FIGURE 1 Developmental pathways to serious and violent offending

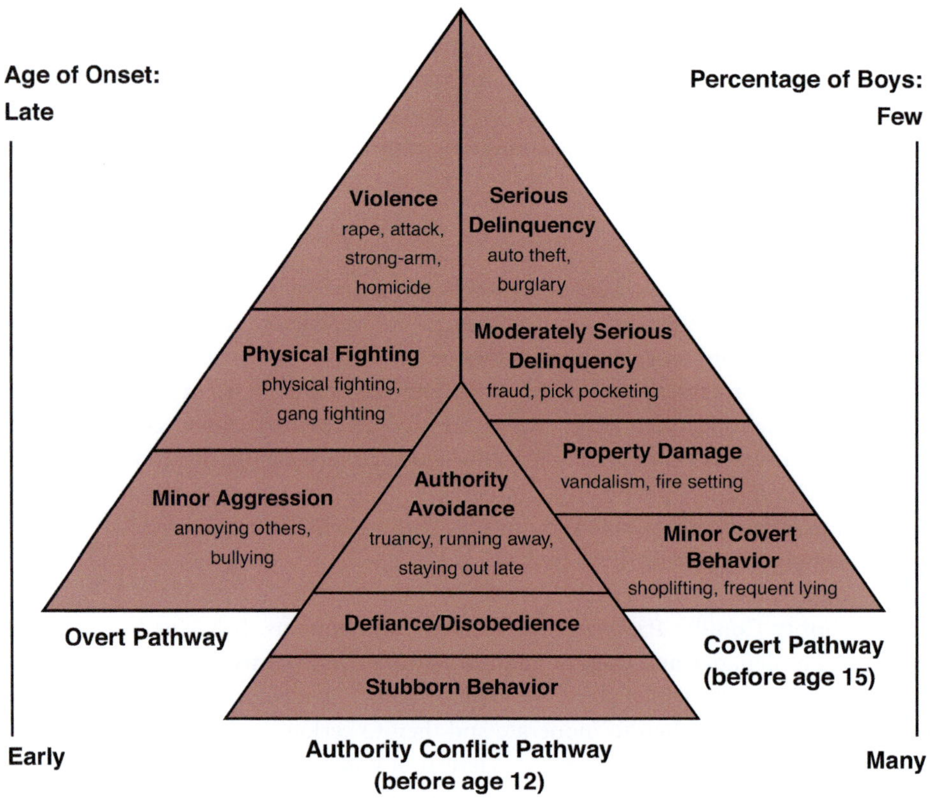

and Zhang, 1997) or those who were court-reported delinquents (Loeber, Keenan, and Zhang, 1997).

The pathway model shows that the warning signs of early onset of disruptive behavior cannot necessarily be dismissed with a "this-will-soon-pass" attitude (Kelley et al., 1997). However, it is not yet possible to distinguish accurately between boys whose problem behaviors will worsen over time and those who will improve. The pathway model is a way to help identify youth at risk and optimize early interventions before problem behavior becomes entrenched and escalates.

The overlap of problem behaviors

The pathways analyses found that many delinquent youth, especially the more serious offenders, engaged in multiple forms of delinquency. Many youth who commit serious offenses also experience difficulties in other areas of life. With the exception of drug use, however, little is known about the overlap of these problem behaviors in general populations. Do most youth who commit serious delinquent acts have school and mental health problems? Are most youth who have school or mental health problems also seriously delinquent?

The Causes and Correlates studies examined these questions in all three sites (Huizinga and Jakob-Chien, 1998; Huizinga, Loeber, and Thornberry, 1993; Huizinga et al., 2000). Recognizing that involvement in delinquency or in other problem behaviors can be transitory or intermittent, the studies examined the level of overlap of more persistent drug use, school problems, and mental health problems[2] that lasted for at least 2 of the 3 years examined (Huizinga et al., 2000).

There was some consistency of findings for males across sites. Although a sizeable proportion of persistent and serious offenders do have other behavioral problems, more than half do not. Thus, it would be incorrect to characterize persistent and serious delinquents generally as having drug, school, or mental health problems. On the other hand, drug, school, and mental health problems are strong risk factors for involvement in persistent and serious delinquency, and more than half (55–73 percent) of the male respondents in all three sites with two or more persistent problems were also persistent and serious delinquents.

For females, the findings were different and varied by site. As with the males, fewer than half of the persistent and serious female delinquents had drug, school, or mental health problems. In contrast to males, however, these problems alone or in combination were not strong risk factors for serious delinquency. This result stems, in part, from the fact that a substantially smaller proportion of girls (5 percent) than boys (20–30 percent) was involved in persistent and serious delinquency, while their rates (within sites) of other problem behaviors were roughly similar to those of males.

It is important to note that these findings are for general population samples. Additional analyses of the Denver data found substantial differences between population findings and findings among youth who had been arrested and became involved in the juvenile justice system (Huizinga and Elliott, 2003). Among males who were persistent and serious offenders, 69 percent of those who had been arrested had one or more problems, whereas only 37 percent of those who had not been arrested had such problems. Although there were too few persistent serious offenders among females to permit control of delinquent involvement, 81 percent of the females who were arrested had one or more problems compared with only 1–2 percent among females who were not arrested.

Thus there appears to be a concentration of offenders entering the juvenile justice system who have drug use, school, or mental health-related problems. Accordingly, the capability to identify the particular configuration of problems facing individual offenders and provide interventions to address these problems is critical to the effectiveness of the juvenile justice system.

Two key risk factors for delinquency

The Causes and Correlates studies have investigated a host of risk factors involving child behavior, family functioning, peer behavior, school performance, and neighborhood characteristics that precede and potentially lead to delinquency. Findings on just two topics—child maltreatment and gangs—are summarized here.

Child maltreatment

Prior research indicates that child maltreatment (e.g., physical abuse, sexual abuse, neglect) that occurs at some point prior to age 18 is a risk factor for delinquency (Widom, 1989; Zingraff et al., 1993). This relationship was also observed in the Pittsburgh and Rochester studies (Smith and Thornberry, 1995; Stouthamer-Loeber et al., 2001, 2002). In the Rochester study, for example, Smith and Thornberry (1995) found that subjects maltreated before age 12, who may or may not also have been maltreated between ages 12 and 18, were significantly more likely to be arrested and to self-report more delinquency, especially serious and violent delinquency, than subjects who had not been maltreated prior to age 12 (see also Widom, 1989; Zingraff et al., 1993).

While prior studies have made important contributions to the literature, they do not explicitly take adolescent maltreatment into account. This results in two problems. First, the victims of childhood maltreatment referred to above actually contain two groups: those victimized in childhood only and those victimized in childhood and adolescence. Second, the comparison group, youth who were never maltreated, is likely to include some youth who were actually maltreated in adolescence (i.e., after age 12), but not in childhood. Because of these issues, it is hard to know if the previous conclusion—that childhood maltreatment is a risk factor for delinquency—is accurate. Relying on its longitudinal design, the Rochester project was able to reexamine the link between maltreatment and delinquency, taking into account when the maltreatment occurred (Ireland, Smith, and Thornberry, 2002; Thornberry, Ireland, and Smith, 2001).

Of the subjects in the Rochester study, 78 percent were never maltreated and 22 percent were. Of the latter, 11 percent were maltreated in childhood only (before age 12 but not after), 8 percent were maltreated in adolescence only, and 3 percent were persistently maltreated (i.e., they had at least one substantiated case in childhood and at least one in adolescence).

The relationship to delinquency is intriguing. Figure 2 presents self-reported and official arrest data on the prevalence of delinquency for four groups of youth: those who were never maltreated, those who were maltreated in childhood only, those who were maltreated in adolescence only, and those who were persistently maltreated. For self-reported general delinquency that occurs from ages 16 to 18,[3] the subjects who were maltreated during childhood only were not at significantly greater risk for delinquency (53.8 percent) than those who were never maltreated (49.6 percent). Subjects maltreated during adolescence, however, were at

FIGURE 2 Maltreatment and delinquency

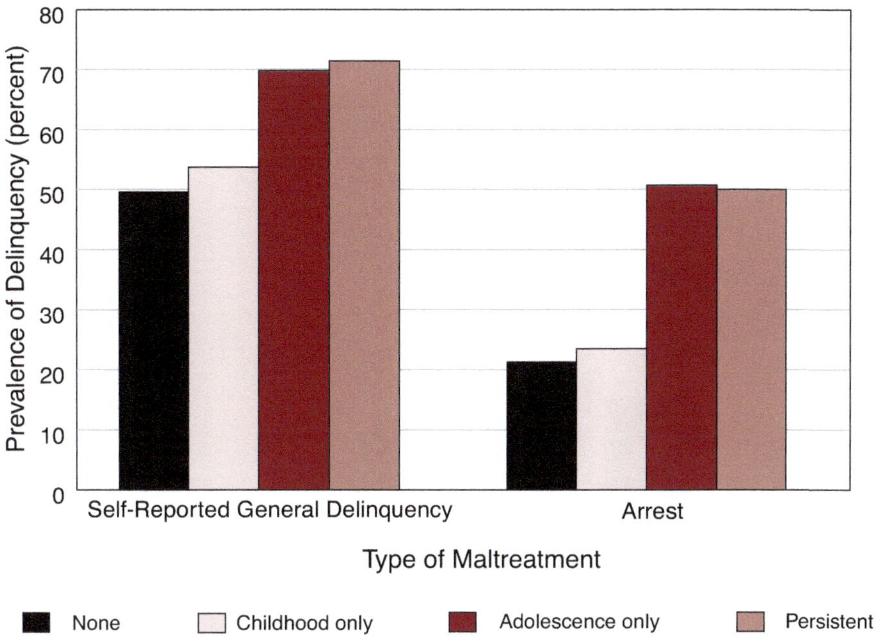

significantly greater risk. The delinquency level for the adolescence-only group (69.8 percent) was significantly higher than that for those who were never maltreated, and the delinquency level for those persistently maltreated—in both childhood and adolescence—was the highest (71.4 percent). The same pattern of results applies to other self-reported measures of delinquency: drug use, violent crime, and street crime (Ireland, Smith, and Thornberry, 2002). For official arrest records, 21.3 percent of youth who were never maltreated had arrest records and 23.5 percent of youth who were maltreated in childhood only had arrest records. In contrast, 50.7 percent of youth maltreated in adolescence had arrest records and 50.0 percent of youth maltreated in both developmental stages had been arrested. The latter rates are significantly higher than the rate for those never maltreated.

Gangs

The Rochester project also investigated how gang membership influences adolescent development. The results have recently been published in *Gangs and Delinquency in Developmental Perspective* (Thornberry et al., 2003). Key findings are summarized here, as are findings from the Denver Youth Survey.

Approximately 30 percent of the Rochester subjects joined a gang at some point during the 4-year period covering ages 14–18. The membership rate was virtually identical for boys (32 percent) and girls (29 percent). Gang membership turned out to be a rather fleeting experience for most of these youth. Half of the male gang members reported being in a gang for 1 year or less, and only 7 percent reported being a gang member for all 4 years. Two-thirds

(66 percent) of the females were in a gang for 1 year or less and none reported being a member for all 4 years.

Although fleeting, gang membership had a tremendous impact on the lives of these youth. Gang members—both male and female—accounted for the lion's share of all delinquency. Although gang members were only 30 percent of the studied population, they were involved in

FIGURE 3 Self-reported general delinquency for males active in a gang for 1 out of 4 years studied

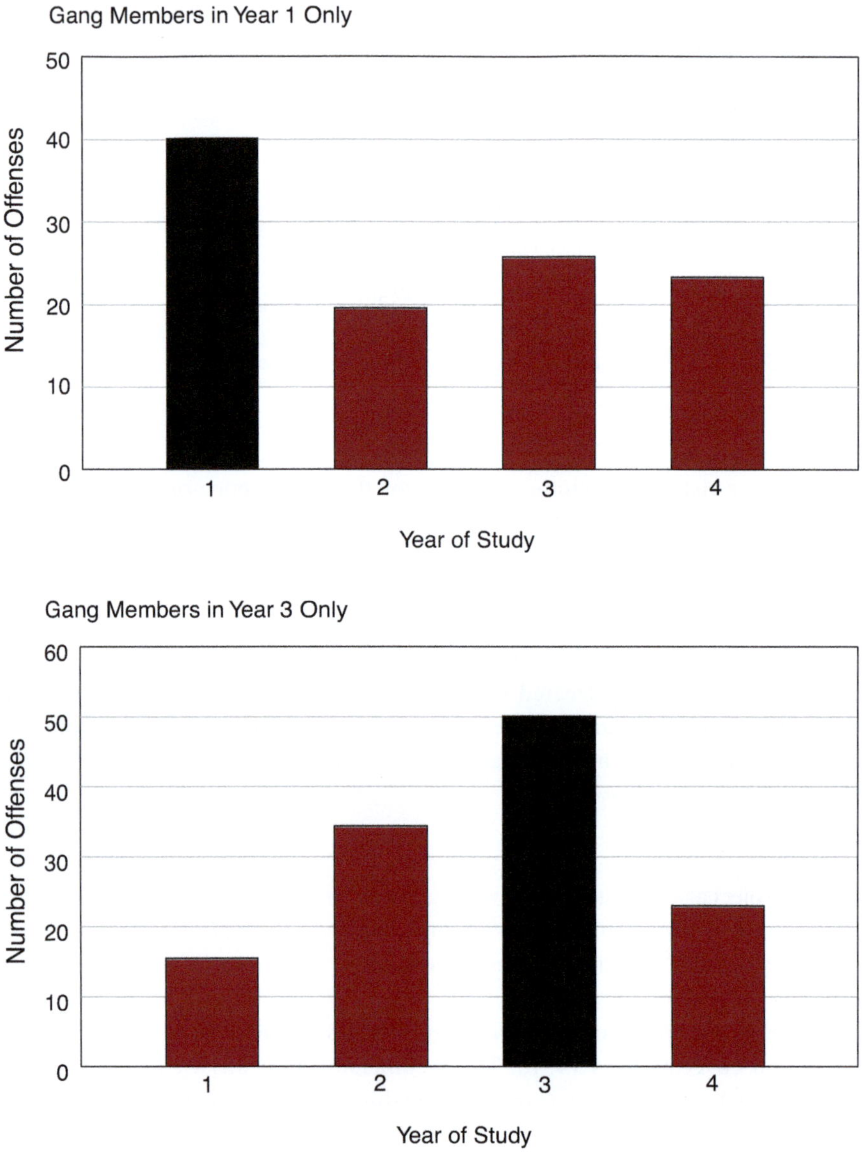

63 percent of all delinquent acts (excluding gang fights), 82 percent of serious delinquencies, 70 percent of drug sales, and 54 percent of all arrests.

Two explanations for the strong association between gang membership and delinquency are frequently raised. One focuses on the individual: gangs attract antisocial adolescents who will likely get into trouble whether or not they are in a gang. The second focuses on the group: individual gang members are not fundamentally different from nonmembers, but when they are in the gang, the gang facilitates their involvement in delinquency.

If the second explanation is correct, gang members should have higher rates of delinquency only during the period of membership, not before or after that period. That is precisely what the Rochester data showed, as illustrated in figure 3. This pattern is found across the 4-year period studied and is observed for various offenses, particularly violence, drug sales, and illegal gun ownership and use.

The impact of being in a street gang is not limited to its short-term effect on delinquent behavior. It also contributes to disorderly transitions from adolescence to adulthood. As compared with individuals who were never members of a gang, male gang members were significantly more likely to drop out of school, get a girl pregnant, become a teenage father, cohabit with a woman without being married, and have unstable employment. Female gang members were significantly more likely to become pregnant, become a teenage mother, and to have unstable employment.

The relationship between gang membership and delinquency has also been investigated in the Denver Youth Survey and in other studies, including a companion project in Bremen, Germany (Esbensen and Huizinga, 1993; Esbensen, Huizinga, and Weiher, 1993; Hill et al., 1996; Huizinga, 1997, 1998; Huizinga and Schumann, 2001). Many of Rochester's findings about gang membership were replicated in Denver's high-risk sample.

For example, a fair proportion of both genders in Denver—18 percent of the males and 9 percent of the females—have been gang members. Denver findings also reveal that gang members accounted for a very disproportionate amount of crime, as do findings in the other studies (Hill et al., 1996; Huizinga and Schumann, 2001). Denver male and female gang members accounted for approximately 80 percent of all serious and violent crime (excluding gang fights) committed by the sample. Further, over a 5-year period, these individuals committed the vast majority of crimes while they were gang members (e.g., 85 percent of their serious violent offenses, 86 percent of their serious property offenses, and 80 percent of their drug sale offenses). The social processes of being an active gang member clearly facilitate or enhance involvement in delinquent behavior.

The studies have also investigated the developmental processes leading to gang membership. In the Denver sample, although gang members and nonmembers were similar in many respects, there were substantial differences between gang members and other serious delinquents in the years preceding gang membership. In the years before they became gang members, individuals were more likely to be involved in higher levels of minor and serious delinquency and drug use, were more involved with delinquent peers, and were less involved with conventional peers. They also displayed weaker beliefs about the wrongfulness of delinquent behavior and a greater willingness to make excuses for involvement in delinquent behavior. The Rochester project found these variables, measured in early adolescence, to be significant risk factors for joining a gang as well (Thornberry et al., 2003). Poor school performance and brittle parent-child relationships also increased the risk of gang membership.

Because of the very high contribution of gang members to the volume of crime, developing effective gang prevention and intervention programs is important and urgent. Police data on gang crimes are helpful in identifying sites particularly affected by gang activity and in providing information for the evaluation of gang intervention activities. Among police departments that collect gang-related data, however, some define gang crimes as any crime committed by a gang member, others require that several gang members be involved in the offense, and yet others collect both kinds of information. The Denver study found that although gang members committed more group crimes than other delinquent youth, both before and after joining a gang, they also committed more offenses while alone than other youth. For example, more than one-third of their serious assaults were committed while alone (Huizinga, 1996). Thus, the measurement difference appears to be significant.

Given the large contribution of gang members to the total volume and location of crime, it would seem helpful for police departments to collect and separate both kinds of data to provide information about the nature of the local gang problem and to help plan local intervention activities. . . .

Responding to delinquency

There are various ways to respond to juvenile crime, including interventions through the juvenile justice system and the provision of general social services or specialized prevention and treatment programs. The Causes and Correlates studies have investigated these different strategies, and the longitudinal results suggest alternative strategies.

Arrest

The Denver study conducted several examinations of the impact of arrest using various analytical strategies (Esbensen, Thornberry, and Huizinga, 1991; Huizinga and Esbensen, 1992; Huizinga, Esbensen, and Weiher, 1996; Huizinga et al., 2003). The findings from these studies are quite consistent. In general, arrest has little impact on subsequent delinquent behavior, and when it does have an impact, it is most likely an increase in future delinquent behavior. These findings are in agreement with several other studies of the impact of arrest (Klein, 1986; Sherman et al., 1997). In addition, those who are arrested and incarcerated as juveniles are substantially more likely to be incarcerated as adults (Huizinga, 2000).

There are different possible explanations for these findings. For example, those arrested may be more serious offenders who are on a different life trajectory than delinquents who are not arrested. However, arrest and sanctioning do not appear to have had the desired effect on the future offending of many delinquent youth. It should be noted that arrest and sanctions need not demonstrate an ameliorative effect to justify their use because the need to protect public safety, perceived needs for retribution, and the influence of these actions on general deterrence within the population cannot be disregarded. Nevertheless, the findings do suggest that arrest and subsequent sanctions generally have not been a particularly viable strategy for the prevention of future delinquency and that other alternatives are needed. The findings also suggest that the use of the least restrictive sanctions, within the limits of public safety, and enhanced reentry assistance, monitoring, and support may reduce future delinquency.

Given these general observations, it also must be observed that progress has been made and continues to be made. There are some intervention programs within the juvenile justice system that have been shown to reduce future delinquency; other promising programs are currently being evaluated (Aos et al., 2001; Howell, 2003; Huizinga and Mihalic, 2003; Lipsey and Wilson, 1998; Mihalic et al., 2001; U.S. Department of Health and Human Services, 2001).

Utilization of services

Several service-providing agencies can potentially help both youth involved in delinquency and their families. These agencies include the juvenile justice system and external agencies such as schools and social services. Are they utilized? The Pittsburgh Youth Study investigated this question by examining the extent to which the parents of delinquent boys received help for dealing with their problems (Stouthamer-Loeber, Loeber, and Thomas, 1992; Stouthamer-Loeber et al., 1995). The study considered help received from anyone (including lay people) and from professionals (especially mental health professionals). In general, seeking help for behavior problems was twice as common for the oldest boys as compared with the youngest (21 percent versus 11 percent, respectively). In 25 percent of the cases, however, seeking help resulted in only one contact with a help provider, and it is doubtful that positive results were achieved in one session.

The percentage of parents who sought any help—help for behavior problems or help from mental health professionals—increased with the seriousness of the delinquency. However, less than half of the parents of seriously delinquent boys received any help, and only one-quarter of the parents of these boys received help from a mental health professional (Stouthamer-Loeber, Loeber, and Thomas, 1992).

Help in schools. Division of the Pittsburgh sample into four groups (nondelinquents, persistent nonserious offenders, persistent property offenders, and persistent violent offenders) showed that all three persistent offender groups were placed in special education classes for learning problems at the same rate as non-delinquents (less than 10 percent). However, more of the persistently delinquent boys, as compared with the non-delinquent boys, were placed in classes for behavior problems; this was particularly true for the violent boys (22.3 percent versus 2.8 percent of the nondelinquents). Nevertheless, three-quarters (77.7 percent) of the persistent violent offenders were never placed in a class for behavior problems, and two-thirds were never placed in any special class.

It is commonly believed that certain groups of boys receive a disproportionate share of resources from various agencies. When researchers examined persistent property and persistent violent offenders, they found that just under half did not receive any help inside or outside of school (about 48 percent), and only 15.4 percent of the persistent property offenders and persistent violent offenders received help from mental health professionals in addition to help in school.

Steps in developmental pathways. Stouthamer-Loeber and colleagues (1995) compared movement along the developmental pathways described above with seeking help for services. In general, the higher the advancement in multiple pathways, the higher the chances that help was sought. An early onset of disruptive behaviors, however, did not increase the frequency at which help was sought.

Court contact. Comparison of court-involved boys with those who had not had court contact showed that the former group received more intensive help. It may be possible that court intervention brought the necessity for help to the parents' attention. Only 17 percent of the boys' parents sought help before the year in which their boys were referred to the juvenile court.

In summary, the development of disruptive and delinquent behaviors was largely left unchecked by parents and helping agencies. These findings have important implications for policymakers and planners of preventive interventions. Merely having programs available may not be adequate; outreach to the most seriously delinquent youth and their families may also be essential.

Implications for prevention

Although the projects of the Program of Research on the Causes and Correlates of Delinquency were not designed to evaluate preventive interventions, program findings have important implications for the design of appropriate interventions. Knowledge of developmental pathways is relevant for interventions, in that pathways reflect current problem behaviors in the context of the history of problem behaviors. Knowledge of pathways also helps identify future problem behaviors that need to be prevented.

The studies examined how long disruptive behaviors had been apparent in boys who eventually were referred to the juvenile court for an index offense[4] (Office of Juvenile Justice and Delinquency Prevention, 1998). The average age at which individuals took their first step in any of the pathways was approximately 7; moderately serious problem behavior began at about age 9.5 and serious delinquency at about age 12. The average age at which youth first came into contact with the juvenile court was 14.5. Thus, approximately 7½ years elapsed between the earliest emergence of disruptive behavior and the first contact with the juvenile court. It should be noted that delinquent boys who were not referred to the juvenile court also tended to have long histories of problem behaviors.

Research findings from all three Causes and Correlates projects show that youth who start their delinquency careers before age 13 are at higher risk of becoming serious and violent offenders than those who start their delinquency careers later (Huizinga, Esbensen, and Weiher, 1994; Krohn et al., 2001; Loeber and Farrington, 1998, 2001). These results imply that preventive interventions to reduce offending should be available at least from the beginning of elementary school-age onward. However, it is important to be mindful of the results of the studies' investigation of childhood offending. Many of the aggressive children did not progress to serious involvement in serious juvenile crime. This suggests that great care is needed in the design of intervention programs for aggressive children. Not all programs are benign, and some may lead to or exacerbate later problems (Dishion, McCord, and Poulin, 1999).

Further research is needed to identify those individuals whose childhood aggression leads to violent behavior later in life. Intervention programs for aggressive children must be developed, and the outcomes for the children served by these programs must be carefully evaluated. The pathways model may be particularly helpful in designing these interventions. Overall, it seems that the judicious use of early interventions known to have long-term effectiveness is warranted.

In addition, although it is "never too early" to try to prevent offending, it is also "never too late" to intervene and attempt to reduce the risk of recidivism for serious offending (Loeber and Farrington, 1998). There is a complex relationship between when individuals begin to commit offenses and how long they persist. A full range of developmentally appropriate and scientifically validated programs is needed.

The Causes and Correlates results regarding the impact of maltreatment are consistent with the importance of developmentally appropriate interventions. It does not appear that childhood-only maltreatment, as long as it does not continue into adolescence, is a risk factor for delinquency. Sources of resiliency, including, perhaps, effective services, must come into play to help children overcome this adversity. Understanding these resiliency processes is an important goal for future research, as these processes have important implications for the design of programs.

Maltreatment that occurs during adolescence, however, appears to be a substantial risk factor for later delinquency. This suggests the need for enhanced services for adolescent victims and, in particular, for services that reduce the chances of delinquent behavior. As Garbarino (1989) has pointed out, however, few treatment programs for adolescent victims exist, and it is often quite difficult to enroll adolescent victims and their families in the available programs. Much greater attention needs to be devoted to the topic of adolescent maltreatment and how it functions as a risk factor for delinquency.

A general strategy for reducing youth crime also needs to be mindful of the sizeable impact that gang membership has on serious and violent delinquency. Working directly with gangs, however, has not yet proved successful and can even be counterproductive. It may be more productive for juvenile justice practitioners to use gang membership as a marker variable and send gang members, on an individual basis, to programs for serious delinquency that are proven effective (see Thornberry et al., 2003). Several excellent summaries identify and describe these programs (see Howell, 2003; Huizinga and Mihalic, 2003; Loeber and Farrington, 1998 (Part II); Mihalic et al., 2001; U.S. Department of Health and Human Services, 2001). Regardless of whether an indirect approach is used or whether gang members are sent individually to proven effective programs, intervening with gang members is an important component in reducing a community's level of youth crime and violence.

Notes

1 Longer, more detailed summaries of these studies can be found in *Taking Stock of Delinquency: An Overview of Findings from Contemporary Longitudinal Studies* (Thornberry and Krohn, 2003).

2 Drug use included use of marijuana, inhalants, and hard drugs. School problems included poor grades and dropping out of school. Mental health problems were indicated by scores in the top 10 percent of either an emotional problem or nondelinquent behavioral problem measure.

3 The authors focused on these ages to preserve proper temporal order, but the pattern of results presented here applies more generally.

4 The index crimes of the Federal Bureau of Investigation include homicide, rape, robbery, aggravated assault, burglary, larceny, auto theft, and arson.

[References omitted.]

CRITICAL-THINKING QUESTIONS

1 Referring back to the case at the beginning of the chapter, what concepts and contexts are important in explaining Sam's delinquent offending?
2 Select one of the major theories of delinquency discussed in this chapter. Imagine that you are developing a delinquency prevention program based on that theory. What would be the key elements of that program and how are they linked to specific elements of the theory?
3 Which context of offending do you think is most important in explaining delinquency? Why did you pick this particular context?
4 Based on the reading "The Causes and Correlates Studies," describe the developmental pathways to delinquency and the policy implications of those pathways.

SUGGESTED READING

Fagan, Abigail A., M. Lee Van Horn, Susan Antaramian, and J. David Hawkins. 2011. "How Do Families Matter? Age and Gender Differences in Family Influences on Delinquency and Drug Use." *Youth Violence and Juvenile Justice* 9:150–170.

Kreager, Derek A., Kelly Rulison, and James Moody. 2011. "Delinquency and the Structure of Adolescent Peer Groups." *Criminology* 49:95–127.

Miller, Joel. 2013. "Individual Offending, Routine Activities, and Activity Settings: Revisiting the Routine Activity Theory of General Deviance." *Journal of Research in Crime and Delinquency* 50:390–416.

Moffitt, Terrie E. 2006. "A Review of Research on the Taxonomy of Life-Course Persistent Versus Adolescence-Limited Antisocial Behavior." Pp. 277–311 in *Taking Stock: The Status of Criminological Theory (Advances in Criminological Theory.* Vol. 15, edited by F. Cullen, J. Wright, and K. Blevins. New Brunswick, NJ: Transaction.

Moon, Byongook, Merry Morash, Cynthia Perez McCluskey, and Hye-Won Hwang. 2009. "A Comprehensive Test of General Strain Theory: Key Strains, Situational- and Trait-Based Negative Emotions, Conditioning Factors, and Delinquency." *Journal of Research in Crime and Delinquency* 46:182–212.

USEFUL WEBSITES

For further information relevant to this chapter, go to the following websites.

- **Program of Research on the Causes and Correlates of Delinquency**, Office of Juvenile Justice and Delinquency Prevention: www.ojjdp.gov/Programs/ProgSummary.asp?pi=19.
- **MacArthur Foundation Research Network on Adolescent Development and Juvenile Justice**: www.adjj.org/content/index.php.
- **Office of Juvenile Justice and Delinquency Prevention**: www.ojjdp.gov.

GLOSSARY OF KEY TERMS

Anomie theories: Argue that crime and delinquency rates are high when the cultural goal of economic success is emphasized more strongly than the institutionalized means of achieving that goal. Merton (1938) used the term anomie to describe the societal condition of normlessness that results when societal goals are stressed to a much greater degree than are the institutionalized means for achieving those goals.

Biosocial criminology: An interdisciplinary approach that views delinquency and other forms of antisocial behavior as resulting from a combination of biological, psychological, and social causes.

Collective efficacy: A combination of cohesion among community residents and their willingness to exert informal social control. The theory of collective efficacy argues that the influence of neighborhood structural characteristics on rates of crime and violence depends on the degree to which local residents are interdependent, cohesive, and willing to exercise informal control.

Concepts: Isolate and categorize features of the world that are thought to be causally important. Different theories of delinquency incorporate and emphasize different concepts.

Developmental perspective: Argues that the development of problem behaviors tends to occur in an orderly, progressive way that is highly age-determined. Examines the patterning of offending in terms of five elements: age of onset of problem behaviors, continuity and change in problem behaviors, progression of seriousness, generality of deviance, and desistance from offending.

Differential association theory: Argues that criminal behavior is learned through social interaction in groups. Through such interaction, individuals learn both techniques for committing delinquent acts and definitions favorable to offending.

General strain theory: Emphasizes the social psychological aspect of strain and focuses on three types of strains of adolescent life: (1) losing something of value; (2) being treated by others in an aversive or negative manner; and (3) being unable to achieve goals.

Life-course theory: Examines social bonds over the life course, considering their origins and how changes in these bonds influence informal social control and behavior.

Propositions: Theoretical statements that tell how concepts are related.

Rational choice theory: Focuses on perceptions of risk and reward related to delinquency and argues that a series of offending decisions are made over time, involving a variety of individual, social, and legal factors that are sometimes specific to particular types of crime.

Routine activities theory: Argues that the likelihood of participating in delinquency depends on the degree to which the daily routines of everyday life provide situational opportunity for crime.

Self-control theory: Contends that individuals with low self-control are impulsive, insensitive risk takers who are less able than others to resist the temptations of crime and analogous acts such as reckless driving, smoking, and alcohol and drug use.

Social bond theory: Contends that individuals conform in order to maintain relationship bonds and avoid disappointing others and are free to engage in delinquent acts when their bond to society is weak or broken. Social bond theory argues that four elements of the social bond provide a reason to conform: attachment, commitment to conventional lines of action, involvement in conventional activities, and belief in the moral validity of law.

Social control theories: Emphasize informal social controls that social relationships, especially within the family, provide to control behavior.

Social disorganization theory: Emphasizes three structural characteristics of urban environments that disrupt social organization: low economic status, ethnic heterogeneity, and residential mobility. Areas characterized by these structures typically lack effective social control mechanisms, have strong criminal traditions, and as a result, experience high rates of crime and delinquency.

Social learning theories: Argue that delinquency is learned through social interaction, particularly in peer groups.

Social learning theory: Elaborates on the processes of learning specified in earlier learning theories by emphasizing four particular aspects: differential association, definitions, differential reinforcement, and imitation.

Social structure theories: Consider the social and societal characteristics that integrate and regulate people's daily lives. When societal characteristics disrupt social organization, social control breaks down, and crime and delinquency flourish.

Strain theory: Explains how groups and individuals adapt to the condition of anomie in society. Strain theory centers on an individual's response to anomie in terms of acceptance or rejection of cultural goals and the institutional means to reach those goals.

Theory: An explanation that makes a systematic and logical argument about what is important and why. A theory of delinquency is a set of logically related propositions that explain why and how selected concepts are related to delinquent behavior.

REFERENCES

Agnew, Robert. 1985. "A Revised Strain Theory of Delinquency." *Social Forces* 64:151–167.

Agnew, Robert. 1992. "Foundation for a General Strain Theory of Crime and Deviance." *Criminology* 30:47–87.

Agnew, Robert. 1995. "The Contribution of Social-Psychological Strain Theory to the Explanation of Crime and Delinquency." Pp. 113–137 in *The Legacy of Anomie Theory*, edited by F. Adler and W. S. Laufer. New Brunswick, NJ: Transaction.

Agnew, Robert. 2000. "Sources of Criminality: Strain and Subcultural Theories." Pp. 349–371 in *Criminology*, 3rd ed., edited by J. F. Sheley. Belmont, CA: Wadsworth.

Agnew, Robert. 2006. *Pressured into Crime: An Overview of General Strain Theory*. Los Angeles, CA: Roxbury.

Agnew, Robert and Timothy Brezina. 2015. *Juvenile Delinquency: Causes and Control*. 5th ed. New York: Oxford University Press.

Agnew, Robert and Helene Raskin White. 1992. "An Empirical Test of General Strain Theory." *Criminology* 30:475–499.

Akers, Ronald L. 1985. *Deviant Behavior: A Social Learning Approach*. 3rd ed. Belmont, CA: Wadsworth.

Akers, Ronald L. and Christine S. Sellers. 2013. *Criminological Theories: Introduction, Evaluation, and Application*. 6th ed. New York: Oxford University Press.

Armstrong, Todd A., Shawn Keller, Travis W. Franklin, and Scott N. MacMillan. 2009. "Low Resting Heart Rate and Antisocial Behavior: A Brief Review of Evidence and Preliminary Results from a New Test." *Criminal Justice and Behavior* 36:1125–1140.

Arneklev, Bruce J., Harold G. Grasmick, Charles R. Tittle, and Robert J. Bursik, Jr. 1993. "Low Self-Control and Imprudent Behavior." *Journal of Quantitative Criminology* 9:225–247.

Augustyn, Megan Bears and Jean Marie McGloin. 2013. "The Risk of Informal Socializing with Peers: Considering Gender Differences across Predatory Delinquency and Substance Use." *Justice Quarterly* 30:117–143.

Baker, Laura A., Serena Bezdjian, and Adrian Raine. 2006. "Behavioral Genetics: The Science of Antisocial Behavior." *Law and Contemporary Problems* 69:7–46.

Baker, Myriam L., Jane Nady Sigmon, and M. Elaine Nugent. 2001. "Truancy Reduction: Keeping Students in School." Washington, DC: Office of Juvenile Justice and Delinquency Prevention.

Bartusch, Dawn R. Jeglum, Donald R. Lynam, Terrie E. Moffitt, and Phil Silva. 1997. "Is Age Important? Testing a General Versus a Developmental Theory of Antisocial Behavior." *Criminology* 35:13–48.

Beaver, Kevin M. 2009. "Molecular Genetics and Crime." Pp. 50–72 in *Biosocial Criminology: New Directions in Theory and Research*, edited by A. Walsh and K. M. Beaver. New York: Routledge.

Beaver, Kevin M., Matt DeLisi, Michael G. Vaughn, John Paul Wright, and Brian B. Boutwell. 2008. "The Relationship between Self-Control and Language: Evidence of a Shared Etiological Pathway." *Criminology* 46:939–970.

Beaver, Kevin M., Michael G. Vaughn, Matt DeLisi, John Paul Wright, Richard Weibe, H. Harrington Cleveland, and Anthony Walsh. 2014. "The Heritability of Common Risk and Protective Factors to Crime and Delinquency." Pp. 99–114 in *Criminological Theory: A Life-Course Perspective*, 2nd ed., edited by M. DeLisi and K. M. Beaver. Burlington, MA: Jones and Bartlett Learning.

Beaver, Kevin M., John Paul Wright, and Matt DeLisi. 2008. "Delinquent Peer Group Formation: Evidence of a Gene x Environment Correlation." *The Journal of Genetic Psychology* 169:227–244.

Bernasco, Wim, Stijn Ruiter, Gerben J. N. Bruinsma, Lievan J. R. Pauwels, and Frank M. Weerman. 2013. "Situational Causes of Offending: A Fixed-Effects Analysis of Space–Time Budget Data." *Criminology* 51:895–926.

Bersani, Bianca E. and Constance L. Chapple. 2007. "School Failure as an Adolescent Turning Point." *Sociological Focus* 40:370–391.

Bersani, Bianca E. and Elaine Eggleston Doherty. 2013. "When the Ties That Bind Unwind: Examining the Enduring and Situational Processes of Change Behind the Marriage Effect." *Criminology* 51:399–433.

Birkbeck, Christopher and Gary LaFree. 1993. "The Situational Analysis of Crime and Deviance." *Annual Review of Sociology* 19:113–137.

Block, Jack. 1995. "On the Relation between IQ, Impulsivity and Delinquency: Remarks on the Lynam, Moffitt and Stouthhamer-Loeber (1993) Interpretation." *Journal of Abnormal Psychology* 104:395–398.

Blomberg, Thomas G., William D. Bales, and Alex R. Piquero. 2012. "Is Educational Achievement a Turning Point for Incarcerated Delinquents across Race and Sex?" *Journal of Youth and Adolescence* 41:202–216.

Booth, Alan and D. Wayne Osgood. 1993. "The Influence of Testosterone on Deviance in Adulthood: Assessing and Explaining the Relationship." *Criminology* 31:93–117.

Brennan, Patricia A. and Adrian Raine. 1997. "Biosocial Bases of Antisocial Behavior: Psychophysiological, Neurological and Cognitive Factors." *Clinical Psychology Review* 17:589–604.

Brezina, Timothy. 1996. "Adapting to Strain: An Examination of Delinquent Coping Responses." *Criminology* 34:39–60.

Burfeind, James and Dawn Jeglum Bartusch. 2016. *Juvenile Delinquency: An Integrated Approach*. London and New York: Routledge.

Burt, Callie and Ronald L. Simons. 2014. "Pulling Back the Curtain on Heritability Studies: Biosocial Criminology in the Postgenomic Era." *Criminology* 52:223–262.

Burton, Velmer S., Jr., Francis T. Cullen, T. David Evans, and R. Gregory Dunaway. 1994. "Reconsidering Strain Theory: Operationalization, Rival Theories, and Adult Criminality." *Journal of Quantitative Criminology* 10:213–239.

Canter, Rachelle J. 1995. "Family Correlates of Male and Female Delinquency." *Criminology* 20:149–167.

Carroll, Annemaree, Kellie Gordon, Michele Haynes, and Stephen Houghton. 2013. "Goal Setting and Self-Efficacy among Delinquent, At-Risk and Not At-Risk Adolescents." *Journal of Youth and Adolescence* 42:431–443.

Caspi, Avashalom, Terrie E. Moffitt, Phil A. Silva, Magda Stouthamer-Loeber, Robert F. Krueger, and Pamela S. Schmutte. 1994. "Are Some People Crime-Prone? Replications of the Personality–Crime Relationship across Countries, Genders, Races and Methods." *Criminology* 32:163–195.

Chapple, Constance, Jamie Vaske, and Meredith G. F. Worthen. 2014. "Gender Differences in Associations with Deviant Peer Groups: Examining Individual, Interactional, and Compositional Factors." *Deviant Behavior* 35:394–411.

Christie-Mizell, C. André and Robert L. Peralta. 2009. "The Gender Gap in Alcohol Consumption during Late Adolescence and Young Adulthood: Gendered Attitudes and Adult Roles." *Journal of Health and Social Behavior* 50:410–426.

Cohen, Lawrence E. and Marcus Felson. 1979. "Social Change and Crime Rate Trends: A Routine Activity Approach." *American Sociological Review* 44:588–608.

Colman, Rebecca A., Do Han Kim, Susan Mitchell-Herzfeld, and Therese Shady. 2009. "Delinquent Girls Grown Up: Young Adult Offending Patterns and Their Relation to Early Legal, Individual, and Family Risk." *Journal of Youth and Adolescence* 38:355–366.

Cornish, Derek and Ronald Clarke. 1986. "Introduction." Pp. 1–16 in *The Reasoning Criminal: Rational Choice Perspectives on Offending*, edited by D. B. Cornish and R. V. Clarke. New York: Springer-Verlag.

Coughlin, Brenda C. and Sudhir Alladi Venkatesh. 2003. "The Urban Street Gang after 1970." *Annual Review of Sociology* 29:41–64.

Decker, Scott H., Charles M. Katz, and Vincent J. Webb. 2008. "Understanding the Black Box of Gang Organization: Implications for Involvement in Violent Crime, Drug Sales, and Violent Victimization." *Crime and Delinquency* 54:153–172.

Decker, Scott H. and Barrik Van Winkle. 1996. *Life in the Gang: Family, Friends, and Violence*. New York: Cambridge University Press.

DeLisi, Matt. 2006. "Zeroing in on Early Arrest Onset: Results from a Population of Extreme Career Criminals." *Journal of Criminal Justice* 34:17–26.

DeLisi, Matt. 2009. "Neuroscience and the Holy Grail: Genetics and Career Criminality." Pp. 209–224 in *Biosocial Criminology: New Directions in Theory and Research*, edited by A. Walsh and K. M. Beaver. New York: Routledge.

DeLisi, Matt, Tricia K. Neppl, Brenda J. Lohman, Michael G. Vaughn, and Jeffrey J. Shook. 2013. "Early Starters: Which Type of Criminal Onset Matters Most for Delinquent Careers?" *Journal of Criminal Justice* 41:12–17.

DeLisi, Matt and Michael G. Vaughn. 2008. "The Gottfredson-Hirschi Critique Revisited: Reconciling Self-Control Theory, Criminal Careers, and Career Criminals." *International Journal of Offender Therapy and Comparative Criminology* 52:520–537.

Demuth, Stephen and Susan L. Brown. 2004. "Family Structure, Family Processes, and Adolescent Delinquency: The Significance of Parental Absence versus Parental Gender." *Journal of Research in Crime and Delinquency* 41:52–81.

Doherty, Elaine Eggleston. 2006. "Self-Control, Social Bonds, and Desistance: A Test of Life-Course Interdependence." *Criminology* 44:807–833.

Eitle, David, John Taylor, and Tamela McNulty Eitle. 2010. "Heavy Episodic Alcohol Use in Emerging Adulthood: The Role of Early Risk Factors and Young Adult Social Roles." *Journal of Drug Issues* 40:295–320.

Elliott, Delbert S. and Scott Menard. 1996. "Delinquent Friends and Delinquent Behavior: Temporal and Developmental Patterns." Pp. 28–67 in *Delinquency and Crime*, edited by J. D. Hawkins. New York: Cambridge University Press.

Fabelo, Tony, Michael D. Thompson, Martha Plotkin, Dottie Carmichael, Miner P. Marchbanks, III, and Eric A. Booth. 2011. *Breaking Schools' Rules: A Statewide Study of How School Discipline Relates to Students' Success and Juvenile Justice Involvement*. New York: Council of State Governments Justice Center.

Fagan, Abigail A., M. Lee Van Horn, Susan Antaramian, and J. David Hawkins. 2011. "How Do Families Matter? Age and Gender Differences in Family Influences on Delinquency and Drug Use." *Youth Violence and Juvenile Justice* 9:150–170.

Farnworth, Margaret and Michael J. Leiber. 1989. "Strain Theory Revisited: Economic Goals, Educational Means, and Delinquency." *American Sociological Review* 54:263–274.

Farrington, David P. 1998. "Predictors, Causes, and Correlates of Male Youth Violence." Pp. 421–475 in *Youth Violence*, edited by M. Tonry and M. Harrison Moore. Chicago: University of Chicago Press.

Felson, Richard B. and Jeremy Staff. 2006. "Explaining the Academic Performance–Delinquency Relationship." *Criminology* 44:299–320.

Fishbein, Diana. 2001. *Biobehavioral Perspectives in Criminology*. Belmont, CA: Wadsworth.

Froggio, Giacinto and Robert Agnew. 2007. "The Relationship between Crime and 'Objective' Versus 'Subjective' Strains." *Journal of Criminal Justice* 35:81–87.

Giordano, Peggy C., Stephen A. Cernkovich, and M. D. Pugh. 1986. "Friendship and Delinquency." *American Journal of Sociology* 5:1170–1202.

Giordano, Peggy C., Stephen A. Cernkovich, and Jennifer L. Rudolph. 2002. "Gender, Crime, and Desistance: Toward a Theory of Cognitive Transformation." *American Journal of Sociology* 107:990–1064.

Gordon, Rachel A., Benjamin B. Lahey, Eriko Kawai, Rolf Loeber, Magda Stouthamer-Loeber, and David P. Farrington. 2004. "Antisocial Behavior and Youth Gang Membership: Selection and Socialization." *Criminology* 42:55–89.

Gordon, Rachel A., Hillary L. Rowe, Dustin Pardini, Rolf Loeber, Helene Raskin White, and David P. Farrington. 2014. "Serious Delinquency and Gang Participation: Combining and Specializing in Drug Selling, Theft, and Violence." *Journal of Research on Adolescence* 24:235–251.

Gottfredson, Denise C., David B. Wilson, and Stacy S. Najaka. 2002. "The Schools." Pp. 149–189 in *Crime: Public Policies for Crime Control*, 2nd ed., edited by J. Q. Wilson and J. Petersilia. Oakland, CA: Institute for Contemporary Studies Press.

Gottfredson, Michael R. and Travis Hirschi. 1990. *A General Theory of Crime*. Stanford, CA: Stanford University Press.

Grasmick, Harold G., Charles R. Tittle, Robert J. Bursik, Jr., and Bruce J. Arneklev. 1993. "Testing the Core Empirical Implications of Gottfredson and Hirschi's General Theory of Crime." *Journal of Research in Crime and Delinquency* 30:5–29.

Guest, Andrew M. and Nick McRee. 2009. "A School-Level Analysis of Adolescent Extracurricular Activity, Delinquency, and Depression: The Importance of Situational Context." *Journal of Youth and Adolescence* 38:51–62.

Guo, Guang, Michael E. Roettger, and Tianji Cai. 2008. "The Integration of Genetic Propensities into Social-Control Models of Delinquency and Violence among Male Youths." *American Sociological Review* 73:543–568.

Guo, Guang, Michael E. Roettger, and Jean C. Shih. 2007. "Contributions of the *DAT1* and *DRD2* Genes to Serious and Violent Delinquency among Adolescents and Young Adults." *Human Genetics* 121:125–136.

Hagan, John and Bill McCarthy. 1997. *Mean Streets: Youth Crime and Homelessness*. Cambridge: Cambridge University Press.

Hampton, Ashley S., Deborah A. G. Drabick, and Laurence Steinberg. 2014. "Does IQ Moderate the Relation between Psychopathy and Juvenile Offending?" *Law and Human Behavior* 38:23–33.

Hartmann, Douglas and Michael Massoglia. 2007. "Reassessing the Relationship between High School Sports Participation and Deviance: Evidence of Enduring, Bifurcated Effects." *Sociological Quarterly* 48:485–505.

Hay, Carter and Michelle M. Evans. 2006. "Violent Victimization and Involvement in Delinquency: Examining Predictions from General Strain Theory." *Journal of Criminal Justice* 34:261–274.

Haynie, Dana L. and D. Wayne Osgood. 2005. "Reconsidering Peers and Delinquency: How Do Peers Matter?" *Social Forces* 84:1109–1130.

Henry, Kimberly L., Kelly E. Knight, and Terence P. Thornberry. 2012. "School Disengagement as a Predictor of Dropout, Delinquency, and Problem Substance Use during Adolescence and Early Adulthood." *Journal of Youth and Adolescence* 41:156–166.

Hirschfield, Paul and Joseph Gasper. 2011. "The Relationship between School Engagement and Delinquency in Late Childhood and Early Adolescence." *Journal of Youth and Adolescence* 40:3–22.

Hirschfield, Paul, Tina Maschi, Helene Raskin White, and Rolf Loeber. 2006. "Mental Health and Juvenile Arrests: Criminality, Criminalization, or Compassion?" *Criminology* 44:593–630.

Hirschi, Travis. 1969. *Causes of Delinquency*. Berkeley, CA: University of California Press.

Hirschi, Travis and Michael J. Hindelang. 1977. "Intelligence and Delinquency: A Revisionist Review." *American Sociological Review* 42:571–587.

Hoffman, John P. and Mikaela J. Dufur. 2008. "Family and School Capital Effects on Delinquency: Substitutes or Complements?" *Sociological Perspectives* 51:29–62.

Hoffman, John P., Lance D. Erickson, and Karen R. Spence. 2013. "Modeling the Association between Academic Achievement and Delinquency: An Application of Interactional Theory." *Criminology* 51:629–660.

Hoffman, John P. and Jiangmin Xu. 2002. "School Activities, Community Service, and Delinquency." *Crime and Delinquency* 48:568–591.

Holt, Thomas J., Adam M. Bossler, and David C. May. 2012. "Low Self-Control, Deviant Peer Associations, and Juvenile Cyberdeviance." *American Journal of Criminal Justice* 37:378–395.

Hughes, Lorine A. 2013. "Group Cohesiveness, Gang Member Prestige, and Delinquency and Violence in Chicago, 1959–1962." *Criminology* 51:795–832.

Huizinga, David A., Rolf Loeber, Terence P. Thornberry, and Lynn Cothern. 2000. "Co-Occurrence of Delinquency and Other Problem Behaviors." *Juvenile Justice Bulletin.* Washington, DC: Office of Juvenile Justice and Delinquency Prevention.

Inciardi, James A., Ruth Horowitz, and Anne E. Pottieger. 1993. *Street Kids, Street Drugs, and Street Crime: An Examination of Drug Use and Serious Delinquency in Miami.* Belmont, CA: Wadsworth.

Ireland, Timothy O., Carolyn A. Smith, and Terence P. Thornberry. 2002. "Developmental Issues in the Impact of Child Maltreatment on Later Delinquency and Drug Use." *Criminology* 40:359–399.

Jang, Sung Joon. 1999. "Age-Varying Effects of Family, School, and Peers on Delinquency: A Multilevel Modeling Test of Interactional Theory." *Criminology* 37:643–685.

Jang, Sung Joon. 2013. "Desistance and Protection from Binge Drinking between Adolescence and Emerging Adulthood: A Study of Turning Points and Insulators." *Sociological Focus* 46:1–24.

Jankowski, Martin Sanchez. 1991. *Islands in the Street: Gangs in American Urban Society.* Berkeley, CA: University of California Press.

Jarjoura, G. Roger. 1993. "Does Dropping Out of School Enhance Delinquent Involvement? Results from a Large-Scale National Probability Sample." *Criminology* 31:149–172.

Jensen, Gary F. 1995. "Salvaging Structure through Strain: A Theoretical and Empirical Critique." Pp. 139–158 in *The Legacy of Anomie Theory,* edited by F. Adler and W. S. Laufer. New Brunswick, NJ: Transaction.

John, Oliver P., Laura P. Naumann, and Christopher J. Soto. 2008. "Paradigm Shift to the Integrative Big Five Taxonomy: History, Measurement, and Conceptual Issues." Pp. 114–158 in *Handbook of Personality: Theory and Research,* 3rd ed., edited by O. P. John, R. W. Robins and L. A. Pervin. New York: Guilford.

Johnson, Monica Kirkpatrick, Robert Crosnoe, and Glen H. Elder, Jr. 2001. "Students' Attachment and Academic Engagement: The Role of Race and Ethnicity." *Sociology of Education* 74:318–340.

Katz, Jack. 1988. *Seductions of Crime: Moral and Sensual Attractions in Doing Evil.* New York: Basic Books.

Kelley, Barbara Tatem, Rolf Loeber, Kate Keenan, and Mary DeLamatre. 1997. "Developmental Pathways in Boys' Disruptive and Delinquent Behavior." *Juvenile Justice Bulletin.* Washington, DC: Office of Juvenile Justice and Delinquency Prevention.

Kelley, Margaret S. and Jan Sokol-Katz. 2011. "Examining Participation in School Sports and Patterns of Delinquency Using the National Longitudinal Study of Adolescent Health." *Sociological Focus* 44:81–101.

Kirk, David S. and Mauri Matsuda. 2011. "Legal Cynicism, Collective Efficacy, and the Ecology of Arrest." *Criminology* 49:443–472.

Kleinmuntz, Benjamin. 1982. *Personality and Psychological Assessment.* New York: St. Martin's.

Kreager, Derek A., Kelly Rulison, and James Moody. 2011. "Delinquency and the Structure of Adolescent Peer Groups." *Criminology* 49:95–127.

Krohn, Marvin D., Alan J. Lizotte, Terence P. Thornberry, Carolyn Smith, and David McDowall. 1996. "Reciprocal Causal Relationships among Drug Use, Peers, and Beliefs: A Five-Wave Panel Model." *Journal of Drug Issues* 26:405–428.

LaGrange, Teresa C. and Robert A. Silverman. 1999. "Low Self-Control and Opportunity: Testing the General Theory of Crime as an Explanation for Gender Differences in Delinquency." *Criminology* 37:41–72.

Laub, John H. and Robert J. Sampson. 1993. "Turning Points in the Life Course: Why Change Matters to the Study of Crime." *Criminology* 31:301–325.

Laub, John H. and Robert J. Sampson. 2001. "Understanding Desistance from Crime." Pp. 1–69 in *Crime and Justice: A Review of Research*. Vol. 28, edited by M. Tonry. Chicago: University of Chicago Press.

Laub, John H. and Robert J. Sampson. 2003. *Shared Beginnings, Divergent Lives: Delinquent Boys to Age 70*. Cambridge, MA: Harvard University Press.

LeBlanc, Marc and Rolf Loeber. 1998. "Developmental Criminology Updated." In *Crime and Justice: An Annual Review of Research*. Vol. 23, edited by M. Tonry. Chicago: University of Chicago Press.

Loeber, Rolf and Marc LeBlanc. 1990. "Toward a Developmental Criminology." Pp. 375–437 in *Crime and Justice: An Annual Review of Research*. Vol. 12, edited by M. Tonry and N. Morris. Chicago: University of Chicago Press.

Loeber, Rolf, David P. Farrington, Magda Stouthamer-Loeber, and Helene Raskin White. 2008. *Violence and Serious Theft: Development and Prediction from Childhood to Adulthood*. New York: Routledge.

Loeber, Rolf, Barbara Menting, Donald R. Lynam, Terri E. Moffitt, Magda Stouthamer-Loeber, Rebecca Stallings, and Dustin Pardini. 2012. "Findings from the Pittsburgh Youth Study: Cognitive Impulsivity and Intelligence as Predictors of the Age–Crime Curve." *Journal of the American Academy of Child and Adolescent Psychiatry* 51:1136–1149.

Lynam, Donald and Terrie Moffitt. 1995. "Delinquency and Impulsivity and IQ: A Reply to Block (1995)." *Journal of Abnormal Psychology* 104:399–401.

Lynam, Donald, Terrie Moffitt, and Magda Stouthamer-Loeber. 1993. "Explaining the Relationship between IQ and Delinquency: Class, Race, Test Motivation, School Failure, or Self-Control?" *Journal of Abnormal Psychology* 102:187–196.

MacDonald, John, Amelia Haviland, Rajeev Ramchand, Andrew R. Morral, and Alex R. Piquero. 2014. "Linking Specialization and Seriousness in Criminal Careers." *Advances in Life Course Research* 20:43–55.

MacDonald, John, Robert J. Stokes, Ben Grunwald, and Ricky Bluthenthal. 2013. "The Privatization of Public Safety in Urban Neighborhoods: Do Business Improvement Districts Reduce Violent Crime among Adolescents?" *Law and Society Review* 47:621–652.

Maguin, Eugene and Rolf Loeber. 1996. "Academic Performance and Delinquency." Pp. 145–264 in *Crime and Justice: A Review of Research*. Vol. 20, edited by M. Tonry. Chicago: University of Chicago Press.

Maruna, Shadd. 2001. *Making Good: How Ex-Offenders Reform and Reclaim Their Lives*. Washington, DC: American Psychological Association Books.

Matsueda, Ross L., Derek A. Kreager, and David Huizinga. 2006. "Deterring Delinquents: A Rational Choice Model of Theft and Violence." *American Sociological Review* 71:95–122.

Matthews, Shelley Keith and Robert Agnew. 2008. "Extending Deterrence Theory: Do Delinquent Peers Condition the Relationship Between Perceptions of Getting Caught and Offending?" *Journal of Research in Crime and Delinquency* 45:91–118.

Mazerolle, Lorraine, Rebecca Wickes, and James McBroom. 2010. "Community Variations in Violence: The Role of Social Ties and Collective Efficacy in Comparative Context." *Journal of Research in Crime and Delinquency* 47:3–30.

Mazur, Allan. 2009. "Testosterone and Violence among Young Men." Pp. 190–204 in *Biosocial Criminology: New Directions in Theory and Research*, edited by A. Walsh and K. M. Beaver. New York: Routledge.

McCarthy, Bill and John Hagan. 1992. "Mean Streets: The Theoretical Significance of Situational Delinquency among Homeless Youths." *American Journal of Sociology* 98:597–627.

McGloin, Jean Marie, Travis Pratt, and Jeff Maahs. 2004. "Rethinking the IQ–Delinquency Relationship: A Longitudinal Analysis of Multiple Theoretical Models." *Justice Quarterly* 21:603–635.

Mears, Daniel, Matthew Ploeger, and Mark Warr. 1998. "Explaining the Gender Gap in Delinquency: Peer Influence and Moral Evaluations of Behavior." *Criminology* 35:251–266.

Megens, Kim C. I. M. and Frank M. Weerman. 2012. "The Social Transmission of Delinquency: Effects of Peer Attitudes and Behavior Revisited." *Journal of Research in Crime and Delinquency* 49:420–443.

Melde, Chris and Finn-Aage Esbensen. 2013. "Gangs and Violence: Disentangling the Impact of Gang Membership on the Level and Nature of Offending." *Journal of Quantitative Criminology* 29:143–166.

Melde, Chris and Finn-Aage Esbensen. 2014. "The Relative Impact of Gang Status Transitions: Identifying the Mechanisms of Change in Delinquency." *Journal of Research in Crime and Delinquency* 51:349–376.

Merton, Robert K. 1938. "Social Structure and Anomie." *American Sociological Review* 3:672–682.

Miller, Holly Ventura. 2010. "If Your Friends Jumped Off of a Bridge, Would You Do It Too? Delinquent Peers and Susceptibility to Peer Influence." *Justice Quarterly* 27:473–491.

Miller, Joel. 2013. "Individual Offending, Routine Activities, and Activity Settings: Revisiting the Routine Activity Theory of General Deviance." *Journal of Research in Crime and Delinquency* 50:390–416.

Miller, Joshua D. and Donald Lynam. 2001. "Structural Models of Personality and Their Relation to Antisocial Behavior: A Meta-Analytic Review." *Criminology* 39:765–798.

Moffitt, Terrie E. 1993. "Adolescence-Limited and Life-Course-Persistent Antisocial Behavior: A Developmental Taxonomy." *Psychological Review* 100:674–701.

Moffitt, Terrie E. 1997. "Adolescence-Limited and Life-Course-Persistent Offending: A Complementary Pair of Developmental Theories." Pp. 11–54 in *Developmental Theories*, edited by T. P. Thornberry. New Brunswick, NJ: Transaction.

Moffitt, Terrie E. 2006. "A Review of Research on the Taxonomy of Life-Course Persistent Versus Adolescence-Limited Antisocial Behavior." Pp. 277–311 in *Taking Stock: The Status of Criminological Theory (Advances in Criminological Theory)*. Vol. 15, edited by F. Cullen, J. Wright, and K. Blevins. New Brunswick, NJ: Transaction.

Moffitt, Terrie E., Gary L. Brammer, Avshalom Caspi, Paul Fawcett, Michael Raleigh, Arthur Yuwiler, and Phil Silva. 1998. "Whole Blood Serotonin Relates to Violence in an Epidemiological Study." *Biological Psychiatry* 43:446–457.

Monahan, Kathryn C., Susan Vanderhei, Jordan Bechtold, and Elizabeth Caufmann. 2014. "From the School Yard to the Squad Car: School Discipline, Truancy, and Arrest." *Journal of Youth and Adolescence* 43:1110–1122.

Moon, Byongook, Merry Morash, Cynthia Perez McCluskey, and Hye-Won Hwang. 2009. "A Comprehensive Test of General Strain Theory: Key Strains, Situational- and Trait-Based Negative Emotions, Conditioning Factors, and Delinquency." *Journal of Research in Crime and Delinquency* 46:182–212.

Moore, Joan W. 1991. *Going Down to the Barrio: Homeboys and Homegirls in Change*. Philadelphia: Temple University Press.

Nagin, Daniel S., David P. Farrington, and Terrie E. Moffitt. 1995. "Life-Course Trajectories of Different Types of Offenders." *Criminology* 33:111–139.

National Research Council. 2013. *Reforming Juvenile Justice: A Developmental Approach*. Committee on Assessing Juvenile Justice Reform. Richard J. Bonnie, Robert L. Johnson, Betty M. Chemers, and Julie A. Schuck (editors). Committee on Law and Justice, Division of Behavioral and Social Sciences and Education. Washington, DC: The National Academies Press.

Osgood, D. Wayne, Janet K. Wilson, Patrick M. O'Malley, Jerald G. Bachman, and Lloyd D. Johnston. 1996. "Routine Activities and Individual Deviant Behavior." *American Sociological Review* 61:635–655.

Ostrowsky, Michael K. and Steven F. Messner. 2005. "Explaining Crime for a Young Adult Population: An Application of General Strain Theory." *Journal of Criminal Justice* 33:463–476.

Padilla, Felix M. 1992. *The Gang as an American Enterprise*. New Brunswick, NJ: Rutgers University Press.

Papachristos, Andrew V. 2013. "The Importance of Cohesion for Gang Research, Policy, and Practice." *Criminology and Public Policy* 12:49–58.

Paternoster, Raymond. 1987. "The Deterrent Effect of Perceived Certainty and Severity of Punishment: A Review of Evidence and Issues." *Justice Quarterly* 42:173–217.

Paternoster, Raymond. 1989. "Decisions to Participate and Desist from Four Types of Common Delinquency: Deterrence and the Rational Choice Perspective." *Law and Society Review* 23:7–40.

Payne, Allison Ann. 2009. "Girls, Boys, and Schools: Gender Differences in the Relationships between School-Related Factors and Student Deviance." *Criminology* 47:1167–1200.

Peskin, Melissa, Yu Gao, Andrea L. Glenn, Anna Rudo-Hutt, Yaling Yang, and Adrian Raine. 2013. "Biology and Crime." Pp. 22–39 in *The Oxford Handbook of Criminological Theory*, edited by F. T. Cullen and P. Wilcox. New York: Oxford.

Piliavin, Irving, Rosemary Gartner, Craig Thornton, and Ross L. Matsueda. 1986. "Crime, Deterrence and Rational Choice." *American Sociological Review* 51:101–119.

Piquero, Alex R. and Timothy Brezina. 2001. "Testing Moffitt's Account of Adolescence-Limited Delinquency." *Criminology* 39:353–370.

Piquero, Alex R., David P. Farrington, Daniel S. Nagin, and Terrie E. Moffitt. 2010. "Trajectories of Offending and Their Relation to Life Failure in Late Middle Age: Findings from the Cambridge Study in Delinquent Development." *Journal of Research in Crime and Delinquency* 47:151–173.

Piquero, Alex R., Terrie E. Moffitt, and Bradley E. Wright. 2007. "Self-Control and Criminal Career Dimensions." *Journal of Contemporary Criminal Justice* 23:72–89.

Piquero, Alex R. and Stephen Tibbetts. 1996. "Specifying the Direct and Indirect Effect of Low Self-Control and Situational Factors in Offenders' Decision-Making: Toward a More Complete Model of Rational Offending." *Justice Quarterly* 13:481–510.

Piquero, Nicole Leeper and Terrie E. Moffitt. 2014. "Can Childhood Factors Predict Workplace Deviance?" *Justice Quarterly* 31:664–692.

Piquero, Nicole Leeper and Miriam D. Sealock. 2004. "Gender and General Strain Theory: A Preliminary Test of Broidy and Agnew's Gender/GST Hypotheses." *Justice Quarterly* 21:125–158.

Piquero, Nicole Leeper and Miriam D. Sealock. 2010. "Race, Crime, and General Strain Theory." *Youth Violence and Juvenile Justice* 8:170–186.

Pratt, Travis C. and Francis T. Cullen. 2000. "The Empirical Status of Gottfredson and Hirschi's General Theory of Crime: A Meta-Analysis." *Criminology* 39:931–964.

Raine, Adrian. 2002. "Annotation: The Role of Prefrontal Deficits, Low Autonomic Arousal and Early Health Factors in the Development of Antisocial and Aggressive Behavior in Children." *Journal of Child Psychology and Psychiatry* 43:417–434.

Raine, Adrian, Terrie E. Moffitt, Avshalom Caspi, Rolf Loeber, Magda Stouthamer-Loeber, and Don Lynam. 2005. "Neurocognitive Impairments in Boys on the Life-Course Persistent Antisocial Path." *Journal of Abnormal Psychology* 114:38–49.

Rankin, Joseph H. and L. Edward Wells. 1990. "The Effect of Parental Attachments and Direct Controls on Delinquency." *Journal of Research in Crime and Delinquency* 27:140–165.

Rebellon, Cesar J. 2002. "Reconsidering the Broken Homes/Delinquency Relationship and Exploring Its Mediating Mechanism(s)." *Criminology* 40:103–136.

Rebellon, Cesar J., Nicole Leeper Piquero, Alex R. Piquero, and Sherod Thaxton. 2009. "Do Frustrated Economic Expectations and Objective Economic Inequity Promote Crime?: A Randomized Experiment Testing Agnew's General Strain Theory." *European Journal of Criminology* 6:47–71.

Rebellon, Cesar J. and Karen Van Gundy. 2005. "Can Control Theory Explain the Link between Parental Physical Abuse and Delinquency: A Longitudinal Analysis." *Journal of Research in Crime and Delinquency* 42:247–274.

Rowe, David C. 2002. *Biology and Crime*. Los Angeles: Roxbury.

Rutter, Michael. 2006. *Genes and Behavior: Nature-Nurture Interplay Explained*. Malden, MA: Blackwell.

Sacco, Vincent F. and Leslie W. Kennedy. 2002. *The Criminal Event: Perspectives in Space and Time*. Belmont, CA: Wadsworth.

Sampson, Robert J. and W. Byron Groves. 1989. "Community Structure and Crime: Testing Social Disorganization Theory." *American Journal of Sociology* 94:774–802.

Sampson, Robert J. and John H. Laub. 1993. *Crime in the Making: Pathways and Turning Points through Life*. Cambridge, MA: Harvard University Press.

Sampson, Robert J. and John H. Laub. 2005. "The Life-Course View of the Development of Crime." *The Annals of the American Academy of Political and Social Science* 602:12–45.

Sampson, Robert J., John H. Laub, and Christopher Wimer. 2006. "Does Marriage Reduce Crime? A Counterfactual Approach to Within-Individual Causal Effects." *Criminology* 44:465–508.

Sampson, Robert J., Steven W. Raudenbush, and Felton Earls. 1997. "Neighborhoods and Violent Crime: A Multilevel Study of Collective Efficacy." *Science* 277:918–924.

Schwartz, Joseph A. and Kevin M. Beaver. 2011. "Evidence of a Gene × Environment Interaction between Perceived Prejudice and MAOA Genotype in the Prediction of Criminal Arrests." *Journal of Criminal Justice* 39:378–384.

Shaw, Clifford R. and Henry D. McKay. 1931. *Social Factors in Juvenile Delinquency: A Study of the Community, the Family, and the Gang in Relation to Delinquent Behavior*. Report of the National Commission on Law Observance and Enforcement, Causes of Crime. Vol. II. Washington, DC: GPO.

Shaw, Clifford R. and Henry D. McKay. [1942] 1969. *Juvenile Delinquency and Urban Areas: A Study of Rates of Delinquency in Relation to Differential Characteristics of Local Communities in American Cities*. Rev. ed. Chicago: University of Chicago Press.

Shaw, Clifford R., Frederick M. Zorbaugh, Henry D. McKay, and Leonard S. Cottrell. 1929. *Delinquency Areas: A Study of the Geographic Distribution of School Truants, Juvenile Delinquents, and Adult Offenders in Chicago*. Chicago: University of Chicago Press.

Short, James F., Jr. and Fred L. Strodtbeck. 1965. *Group Process and Gang Delinquency*. Chicago: University of Chicago Press.

Siennick, Sonja E. and Jeremy Staff. 2008. "Explaining the Educational Deficits of Delinquent Youths." *Criminology* 46:609–635.

Sigfusdottir, Inga Dora, Alfgeir Logi Kristjansson, and Robert Agnew. 2012. "A Comparative Analysis of General Strain Theory." *Journal of Criminal Justice* 40:117–127.

Smith, Carolyn A. and Terence P. Thornberry. 1995. "The Relationship between Childhood Maltreatment and Adolescent Involvement in Delinquency." *Criminology* 33:451–481.

Staff, Jeremy and Derek A. Kreager. 2008. "Too Cool for School? Violence, Peer Status and High School Dropout." *Social Forces* 87:445–471.

Steinberg, Laurence, Elizabeth Cauffman, and Kathryn C. Monahan. 2015. "Psychosocial Maturity and Desistance from Crime in a Sample of Serious Juvenile Offenders." *Juvenile Justice Bulletin*. Washington, DC: Office of Juvenile Justice and Delinquency Prevention.

Stewart, Eric A. 2003. "School Social Bonds, School Climate and School Misbehavior: A Multilevel Analysis." *Justice Quarterly* 20:575–604.

Sutherland, Alex, Ian Brunton-Smith, and Jonathan Jackson. 2013. "Collective Efficacy, Deprivation and Violence in London." *British Journal of Criminology* 53:1050–1074.

Sutherland, Edwin H., Donald R. Cressey, and David F. Luckenbill. 1992. *Principles of Criminology*. 11th ed. Dix Hills, NY: General Hall.

Sweeten, Gary, Shawn D. Bushway, and Raymond Paternoster. 2009. "Does Dropping Out of School Mean Dropping into Delinquency?" *Criminology* 47:47–91.

Thomas, Kyle J. and Jean Marie McGloin. 2013. "A Dual-Systems Approach for Understanding Differential Susceptibility to Processes of Peer Influence." *Criminology* 51:435–474.

Thornberry, Terence P. 2005. "Explaining Multiple Patterns of Offending Across the Life Course and Across Generations." *Annals of the Academy of Political and Social Science* 602:156–195.

Thornberry, Terence P., David Huizinga, and Rolf Loeber. 2004. "The Causes and Correlates Studies: Findings and Policy Implications." *Juvenile Justice* 9:3–19.

Thornberry, Terence P., Marvin D. Krohn, Alan J. Lizotte, and Deborah Chard-Wierschem. 1993. "The Role of Juvenile Gangs in Facilitating Delinquent Behavior." *Journal of Research in Crime and Delinquency* 30:55–87.

Thornberry, Terence P., Marvin D. Krohn, Alan J. Lizotte, Carolyn A. Smith, and Kimberly Tobin. 2003. *Gangs and Delinquency in Developmental Perspective*. New York: Cambridge University Press.

Thornberry, Terence P., Carolyn A. Smith, Craig Rivera, David Huizinga, and Magda Stouthamer-Loeber. 1999. "Family Disruption and Delinquency." *Juvenile Justice Bulletin*. Washington, DC: Office of Juvenile Justice and Delinquency Prevention.

Tzoumakis, Stacy, Patrick Lussier, Marc LeBlanc, and Garth Davies. 2013. "Onset, Offending Trajectories, and Crime Specialization in Violence." *Youth Violence and Juvenile Justice* 11:143–164.

Uggen, Christopher. 2000. "Work as a Turning Point in the Life Course of Criminals: A Duration Model of Age, Employment, and Recidivism." *American Sociological Review* 65:529–546.

Van Voorhis, Patricia, Francis T. Cullen, Richard A. Mathers, and Connie Chenoweth Garner. 1998. "The Impact of Family Structure and Quality on Delinquency: A Comparative Assessment of Structural and Functional Factors." *Criminology* 26:235–261.

Walsh, Anthony. 2002. *Biosocial Criminology: Introduction and Integration*. Cincinnati, OH: Anderson.

Walsh, Anthony and Kevin M. Beaver (eds.). 2009. *Biosocial Criminology: New Directions in Theory and Research*. New York: Routledge.

Walsh, Anthony and Jonathan D. Bolen. 2012. *The Neurobiology of Criminal Behavior: Gene-Brain-Culture Interaction*. Burlington, VT: Ashgate Publishing Company.

Warr, Mark. 1996. "Organization and Instigation in Delinquent Groups." *Criminology* 34:11–37.

Wasserman, Gail A., Kate Keenan, Richard E. Tremblay, John D. Cole, Todd I. Herrenkohl, Rolf Loeber, and David Petechuk. 2003. "Risk and Protective Factors of Child Delinquency." Washington, DC: Office of Juvenile Justice and Delinquency Prevention.

Wasserman, Gail A., Laurie S. Miller, E. Pinner, and B. S. Jaramillo. 1996. "Parenting Predictors of Early Conduct Problems in Urban, High-Risk Boys." *Journal of the American Academy of Child and Adolescent Psychiatry* 35:1227–1236.

Wenzel, Michael. 2004. "The Social Side of Sanctions: Personal and Social Norms as Moderators of Deterrence." *Law and Human Behavior* 28:547–567.

Wickes, Rebecca L. 2010. "Generating Action and Responding to Local Issues: Collective Efficacy in Context." *The Australian and New Zealand Journal of Criminology* 43:423–443.

Widom, Cathy S. 1989. "The Cycle of Violence." *Science* 244:160–166.

Wright, John Paul, Danielle Boisvert, Kim Dietrich, and M. Douglas Ris. 2009. "The Ghost in the Machine and Criminal Behavior: Criminology for the 21st Century." Pp. 73–89 in *Biosocial Criminology: New Directions in Theory and Research*, edited by A. Walsh and K. M. Beaver. New York: Routledge.

Wright, John Paul and Francis T. Cullen. 2001. "Parental Efficacy and Delinquent Behavior: Do Control and Support Matter?" *Criminology* 39:677–705.

Zingraff, Matthew T., Jeffrey Leiter, Kristen A. Myers, and Matthew C. Johnsen. 1993. "Child Maltreatment and Youthful Problem Behavior." *Criminology* 31:173–202.

PART III

Juvenile justice process

Chapter 7

COPS AND KIDS: POLICING JUVENILES

CHAPTER TOPICS

- **Cops and kids: The police role**
- **Discretion and diversion in juvenile law enforcement**
- **Due process in juvenile law enforcement**

CHAPTER LEARNING OBJECTIVES

After completing this chapter, students should be able to:

- Explain the role conflict that officers experience when interacting with juveniles.
- Discuss the four different roles that have been prominent in the history of police encounters with juveniles.
- Provide examples of why police discretion and diversion of juveniles through informal actions are essential to the juvenile justice process.
- Define due process of law and describe how it affects juvenile law enforcement.

CHAPTER CONTENTS

CASE IN POINT

TWO OBNOXIOUS TEENAGERS

Dispatch notified the young city police officer of a citizen complaint about two intoxicated teenagers. They were rambling around the downtown area and being generally obnoxious. The officer had recently completed field training with an experienced training officer who stressed the importance of a quick and significant response to citizen complaints—it made for positive rapport with the public—the taxpayers who provided funding for the police department.

The officer responded to the call and promptly found the offending youth. It was a busy Friday evening and the streets were full of families enjoying the shops and restaurants. Loud, intoxicated teenagers were clearly unwanted, but an aggressive police intervention would be inappropriate. The officer stopped the youth and asked them a few questions. The responses confirmed that the youth were drunk and being disruptive. He took them into custody by placing them in the back of the squad car. His decisive action was made more complicated when the officer learned that one of the youth was the son of his boss, the Chief of Police. In addition, both youth were on probation for a string of misdemeanor offenses, including shoplifting and possession of marijuana—offenses they had committed together. While the Chief of Police's son had been placed on informal probation (discussed in Chapter 8), his partner in crime, a youth from a single-parent, lower-class family, was placed on formal probation.

What options does the officer have in handling this case? What factors might enter into the officer's decision? The latitude in decision-making that police have is called discretion. A variety of legal and extralegal factors influence police discretion. Police discretion, however, is not unbridled. Law enforcement decisions and actions are regulated by procedural due process extended in constitutional, statutory, and administrative law.

The young officer somewhat reluctantly decided to take the youth to the police station and contact their parents. The Chief of Police was extremely embarrassed and responded right away, yet he also seemed a bit perturbed with the arresting officer, at least that's what the officer thought. The mother of the other youth was working late at her second job as a bartender; she could not leave work and her son spent the night in detention.

This chapter describes the role of the police in the juvenile justice system. Contact with the police is typically the initial entry point in to the juvenile justice system. We begin with a discussion of changes in the police role over time and how these changes have impacted the way in which police interact with juveniles and view their work with them. Next, we move to the role of police discretion and diversion of juvenile away from formal processing. The police are often referred to as the "gatekeepers" to the justice system and are given broad decision-making authority to use professional judgment to decide between formal and informal courses of action. The chapter concludes with an examination of the impact of due process decisions by the U.S. Supreme Court on juvenile law enforcement, especially search and seizure, arrest, and custodial interrogation of juveniles.

Juveniles constitute a unique population that poses a special set of challenges for the police (Slocum, Wiley, and Esbensen 2016; Brown, Novak, and Frank 2009). First, police have frequent contact with juveniles. In 2012, police made over 1.3 million arrests of juveniles nationwide, but this number represents only a fraction of all police–juvenile encounters, many of which never result in arrest (Puzzanchera 2014). Nonetheless, juveniles account for a significant portion of the crime problem. Second, law enforcement with juveniles includes a broad array of offenses, ranging from status offenses to violent crime. Third, police commonly view juvenile delinquency as minor crime, and "taking a youth into custody" is often not considered a "real arrest." Fourth, police are often expected to take an approach with juveniles that involves prevention, protection, and rehabilitation; while at the same time enforcing the law. There is often role conflict that emerges when the time and effort associated with crime prevention efforts for juveniles compete with another charge of the police, the apprehension of criminals. Fifth, juveniles must be processed through a justice system that is different from the adult system in philosophy, jurisdiction, structure, and process. This is unfamiliar terrain for many officers. Moreover, some police have little support for a system that they view as pandering—one that does not hold youth accountable for their actions. Because of this, some police officers have little interest in working with juveniles. The feeling is apparently mutual, because much research indicates that most high school students are lukewarm in their attitudes toward police (Walker and Katz 2005).

Most police departments of at least moderate size have specialized juvenile units to deal with juveniles and delinquency. According to Criminologist Larry Gaines (2003), juvenile units within police departments are common, most notably because many patrol officers are not familiar with the complexity involved in juvenile cases. The rules that have been implemented in juvenile courts are distinct from the adult criminal procedures. The coordination and collaboration among a variety of systems (e.g. juvenile court, schools, child protective services) requires specific knowledge and is a primary reason juvenile units are housed alongside criminal investigation and detective units within departments.

COPS AND KIDS: THE POLICE ROLE[1]

Police role refers to the expectations associated with the position of police officer. It must be noted, however, that there is much controversy over the proper police role toward juveniles. Some citizens place emphasis on the importance of the police to arrest law violators, others favor an approach, in particular for juveniles, that is based on alternatives to formal law enforcement (e.g. prevention, counseling, diversion). Police officers sometimes struggle with conflict stemming from apparently inconsistent expectations of their work by the public. This conflict places at odds the duty to protect citizens by apprehending criminals, with the mandate to provide services to the public. Such role conflict can make police work difficult to manage for officers and the departments where they work. This inconsistency in role expectations seems especially pertinent to the policing of juveniles. In addition, unclear and undefined departmental policies regarding juveniles create further confusion for police officers.

Parens patriae policing: The original protective role

Historically, police have been viewed as an extension of the juvenile court. Police officers comprised a substantial portion of the staff of the first juvenile court in Chicago, removing many distinctions between the enforcement and adjudication of laws (Wolcott 2005; Platt 1977). Although these officers were assigned to assist probation officers in supervision, their authority was derived from the court's *parens patriae* doctrine, and their role was consistent with the rehabilitative ideal that came to dominate juvenile justice. As an extension of the juvenile court, police were expected to deal with juveniles in an informal, parent-like fashion, acting in the "best interests of the child" (Feld 1999). Recall from Chapter 2 that the early juvenile justice system was deliberately established to operate as a child-welfare system, not as a judicial system. This **protective role** was adopted extensively by the police, giving them broad discretion in dealing with juveniles. In fact, the legal distinction between "taking into custody" and adult arrest was created to signify the protective approach that police traditionally have taken with juveniles. Under authority of statutory law, **taking into custody** involves gaining control of a youth, much like in an arrest, but for protective purposes; this is sometimes referred to as *protective custody*. If the police officer believes that the youth is in need of protection or has violated the law, the police officer may take control of the youth and remove him or her from their surroundings. This can be accomplished by physical control or by voluntary submission of the youth. The youth may be placed in the back of the squad car, told to sit in a chair in the waiting area of the police station, or placed in a holding cell. Taking into custody may or may not involve placement in a detention facility.

The degree to which individual police officers and police departments adopted this protective role is a matter of debate (Wolcott 2005). Nonetheless, the protective origins of the police role established broad discretion for dealing with juveniles. This discretion was exercised in a wide range of police activities related to juveniles. These range from prevention education and truancy reduction in school to investigation of criminal activity and arrest. Sociologists refer to this broad range of activities and expectations associated with a given position as *role diversity*, and such role diversity aptly characterizes juvenile policing.

Professional policing: The crime-fighting role

Beginning in the early 1920s, during the historical period of policing known as the Reform Era, a movement emerged that significantly influenced juvenile policing, both in terms of its structure and role. Referred to as *professional policing*, this movement produced at least two important innovations. First, bureaucratic structure and authority were implemented in local police departments across the United States. Police organization and management became more hierarchical, involving a chain and unit of command. Bureaucratic policing also resulted in specialization, in which different units performed special tasks simultaneously. Besides the creation of patrol, detective, and vice divisions, juvenile units were put in place in most medium and large police departments. Second, the protective role of policing juveniles was to a great degree replaced with the **crime-fighting role**. Enforcement of laws and crime control became the primary interest of local police. The relationship between the police and public was redefined, with the police being portrayed as the "thin blue line" that protected the lives and property of a passive and dependent public. Although the protective role of the police was not out of line with the notion of the "thin blue line," youth who formerly were viewed as dependent and at risk, requiring police protection, now began to be viewed as juvenile suspects who were most likely to violate the law.

In the mid-1960s, the due process revolution in juvenile justice introduced a variety of procedural requirements in law enforcement that can be viewed as either a limitation on crime fighting or an enhancement of professional policing. Some police officers believed that due process requirements limited their abilities to gain evidence and statements, making arrest less likely; other officers, especially supervising officers, believed that procedural requirements actually enhanced professional policing by requiring officers to know the law and to enforce it in a standardized and objective manner. Regardless of the point of view, the introduction of due process into juvenile policing substantially reduced the protective role of police, while emphasizing the importance and quality of arrest.

Community-oriented policing: The collaborative role

Beginning in the 1960s, research, public sentiment, and changing views among the police themselves began to raise questions about professional policing. In response, community-oriented policing (COP) was born, representing a significant change in the philosophy, structure, and authority of law enforcement, especially in terms of policing juveniles (Goldstein 1990). Community-oriented policing is made up of four basic elements: (1) community crime prevention, (2) reorientation of patrol activities to emphasize service and public order, (3) increased accountability to the public, and (4) decentralization of command through the creation of neighborhood police centers. Under community-oriented policing, it is assumed that the police cannot fight crime effectively without the public's cooperation and involvement. As a result, the crime-fighting role began to be viewed as inadequate to prevent and control crime. In contrast, the **collaborative role** emphasizes that police are to engage the public in order to cooperatively prevent crime, maintain public order, and solve community problems.

To varying degrees, most police departments have incorporated the idea of community-oriented policing, which has affected how they deal with juveniles and juvenile crime (Hickman and Reaves 2001). The community-oriented policing role includes police efforts to foster relationships with neighborhood youth in order to prevent crime and maintain order. This role has been implemented most extensively through school resource officer (SRO) programs. Officers are assigned to schools (usually junior high and high schools) and provide a number of services to the school, including crime-related education in the classroom, crime prevention by walking the halls and outside the school building, and investigation of crimes on or near campus. The underlying strategy is to develop relationships with students and school personnel in an effort to prevent crime and to respond to crime committed by students. The school resource officer is primarily a collaborator between police, the schools, families, and the community. Thus, SRO programs provide crime prevention, order maintenance, and problem-solving collaboration between police and students, families, and school staff (Na and Gottfredson 2013).

Getting tough: The law-enforcer role

Beginning in the early 1980s, the "get tough" approach to crime introduced a **law-enforcer role** for police, even as community-oriented policing was emerging in law enforcement. Greater attention has been given to public safety and holding juvenile offenders accountable for law violations. As a result, contemporary juvenile policing is increasingly characterized by the law-enforcer role, emphasizing vigorous enforcement of laws, both criminal laws and status offense laws. Reflecting this, the legal distinction between taking into custody and arrest in statutory law has been reduced in some states, authorizing police to arrest juveniles just as adults.

Perhaps the clearest example of the contemporary law-enforcer role in juvenile policing lies in the increasing tendency of police to deal formally with juveniles taken into custody through a "referral to juvenile court" or "referral to adult criminal court." Consequently, police are also far less likely to deal informally with juveniles taken into custody through what is known as "warn and release." **Figure 7.1** shows that in the early 1970s almost half of all juveniles taken into custody were handled informally within police departments and then released. In recent years, however, this has been true for only about one-fifth of all juveniles that the police have taken into custody. In contrast, almost two-thirds of all juveniles taken into custody are now referred to juvenile court, and a small but increasing portion are referred to adult criminal court. These trends in handling juveniles taken into custody are a clear indication of a shift in law enforcement efforts toward greater accountability and public safety.

Is the law-enforcer role beginning to wane? The Models for Change initiative, sponsored by the McArthur Foundation, advocates a developmental model of juvenile justice reform. Reform efforts are portrayed as "system reforms," seeking to generate change across juvenile justice systems—from police to courts to corrections. These efforts are based on a growing body of knowledge on adolescent development and, corresponding to that, appropriate juvenile justice strategies and techniques. How might the developmental model of juvenile justice reform impact the police role with juveniles? "Juvenile justice process and practice: ten strategies to improve law enforcement interactions with youth" describes tactics offered by the International Association of Chiefs of Police for police interaction with youth.

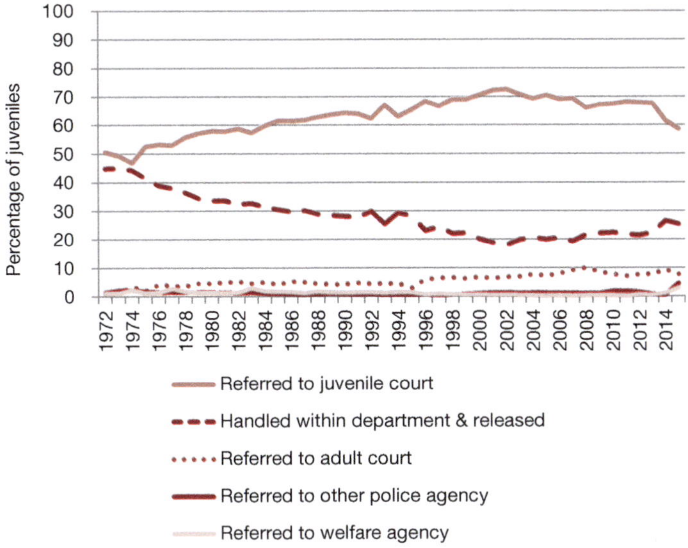

FIGURE 7.1 *Method of handling juveniles taken into custody, 1972–2015. Over this period, local police have shown an increasing tendency to deal formally with juveniles taken into custody through "referral to juvenile court" or "referral to adult criminal court," and a decreasing tendency to deal informally with juveniles taken into custody by handling them within the department and then releasing them—a practice commonly referred to as "warn and release."*
Sources: Federal Bureau of Investigation (2012–2016); University at Albany, Hindelang Criminal Justice Research Center (2013).

JUVENILE JUSTICE PROCESS AND PRACTICE: TEN STRATEGIES TO IMPROVE LAW ENFORCEMENT INTERACTIONS WITH YOUTH

The "developmental approach to juvenile justice reform" seeks to foster positive youth development in all phases of juvenile justice, including law enforcement (National Research Council 2013). The International Association of Chiefs of Police (IACP) has recently offered a brief guide called "The Effects of Adolescent Development on Policing." The guide seeks to facilitate positive law enforcement interaction with youth by promoting police officer understanding of "why teenagers think and act the way they do" (IACP 2015). Here are ten strategies that are offered.

1 Approach youth with a calm demeanor, conveying that you are there to help them. Aggression may cause the youth to shut down and make the situation worse. Refrain from pushing back (arguing). If necessary, de-escalate using a calm, focused, and non-confrontational verbal approach. Use a nonjudgmental tone. Youth are particularly attune to both verbal and non-verbal judgment from adults.
2 Establish rapport. Developing rapport is fundamental to successful youth interactions. They are not likely to open up if they feel unsupported or uncomfortable. Give them your undivided attention. Convey that you want to listen and can be trusted. Listen openly and non-judgmentally.

3 Be patient. Don't act hurried, like you don't have time to talk with the youth. Give the youth a chance to ask questions and be honest with your responses. Convey that you want to hear what they have to say. Give them a chance to explain what happened. Build in extra time to assess their emotions and to work around blocked thinking due to emotion.
4 Model the respect you expect in return. Avoid criticism and lecture. Refer to them by name as much as possible. Avoid correcting them or making statements that may communicate disrespect. You may lessen their aggression and defiance by demonstrating respect and support for their autonomy, views, and choices.
5 Use age-appropriate language. Adolescents do not have adult capacity to organize thoughts. They may not fully understand what you tell them and may need time to process information. Keep it simple. Use open-ended questions and be prepared to help them sort out information. Don't expect a long attention span.
6 Repeat or paraphrase their statements. Affirm their emotions. Seek clarity and understanding through the use of these three methods. Repeating what they say gives you a chance to confirm you heard what they said. Paraphrasing shows them you are listening. Affirming their emotions (e.g. You're frustrated with your parents) shows them genuine interest.
7 Take caution with nonverbal communication. Avoid challenging gestures. Approach youth in a natural manner, not actively seeking or avoiding eye contact. Don't demand eye contact. Convey your warmth over your authority. Get on their level (e.g. sit if they are sitting), lean in when listening, and hold your arms and body in a relaxed manner.
8 Model and praise calm confidence. Adolescents seek validation and praise while acting indifferent towards it. They act confident, even when feeling self-doubt. They tend to be most calm and cooperative when provided with adult modeling and sincere praise for their ability to make good decisions.
9 Empower them through choices. Adolescents need to feel they have choice and control over their thoughts and actions. They are sensitive to external influence and likely to feel coerced, even when there is no explicit effort to coerce them. Yet, they rely on others to validate their decisions. Provide them a range of options and explain their choices in simple terms. Give them a chance to ask questions.
10 Serve as a positive adult role model. Positive relationships with adults are a vital component of healthy youth development. Develop programs in your agency that focus on positive youth development, such as mentoring, job skills.

Source: Reprinted from International Association of Chiefs of Police (IACP) (2015). Copyright held by IACP. Further reproduction without express permission from IACP is strictly prohibited.

DISCRETION AND DIVERSION IN JUVENILE LAW ENFORCEMENT

Regardless of changes in the police role toward juveniles, it is local police (municipal and county) that have the most frequent contact with juveniles. State and federal law enforcement officers have comparatively few encounters with juveniles. Local patrol officers are typically the first point of contact with juveniles in everyday activities and with juveniles suspected of crime involvement. State statutory laws provide authority to police officers to stop and talk to individuals and to investigate suspicious situations and crime incidents. These laws also give police officers arrest authority and authority to take a youth into custody. The application of this statutory law enforcement authority gives police officers broad, wide-ranging discretion.

As we saw in Figure 7.1, the evidence shows a decreasing tendency by the police to deal informally with juveniles that are taken into custody. Instead, referral to juvenile court has become far more common. However, it should be noted that these data represent only those juveniles who were "taken into custody." Those contacts that were dealt with by the police in a more informal manner are not reported. We are left to speculate about the proportion of police contacts that do not result in a youth being taken into custody. We get a sense of how police respond to juveniles they come into contact with in an old but classic study by David Bordua (1967). Bordua found that in a one-year period during 1964, the Detroit police had 106,000 encounters with juveniles. Only 9 percent (9,445) of these were classified as "official contacts" by the police, resulting in formal enforcement action. Bordua concluded that a majority of police–juvenile contacts are dealt with informally and never result in official action, such as issuing a ticket or citation, taking the youth into custody, or referring the youth to juvenile court (see also Piliavin and Briar 1964). Assuming that these findings are still relevant to contemporary policing, a substantial portion of all police encounters with juveniles are dealt with informally, rather than through formal referral to the juvenile court.

Informal handling of juveniles by the police involves a number of diversionary approaches intended to keep youth out of the juvenile justice system (Krisberg and Austin 1978). These include: (1) warn and release at the scene—a "street adjustment"; (2) take the youth into custody, but release the youth to the parents at the police station—a "station house adjustment"; (3) refer the case to a juvenile officer or juvenile unit within the department for further investigation or for involvement in an intervention program operated by the police department; (4) refer the youth to community-based services, such as a youth services bureau, school, or church; (5) refer the case to a child protective service agency for services, family intervention, or dependency and neglect investigation.

Whether taking a youth into custody involves the use of secure detention is also a discretionary decision. Police usually begin the initial detention decision. In most states, the decision for detention requires the officer to inform or request authorization from the probation department and provide a written report that specifies why the officer believes the youth must be held in detention. After initial authorization, statutory law typically requires that a detention hearing be held within a set time period, often within 24 hours (Sickmund and Puzzanchera 2014). The detention decision is based on a consideration of whether the youth poses a risk to him- or herself, or a public safety risk to others; and whether detention is needed to ensure the youth's appearance at upcoming court hearings.

Police discretion involves much broader authority than just decisions regarding whether to take a youth into custody or make an arrest and whether to detain the youth. Patrol officers make decisions regarding where, when, and how intensely to patrol; whether to engage in high-speed pursuit; whether to stop, question, or frisk a suspect; and how much force to use in the process of taking someone in to custody. Detectives and juvenile officers make decisions related to criminal investigation, including how vigorously to investigate the case; whom to talk to; and whether to conduct surveillance, seek a warrant, or involve other police investigative agencies. Additionally, police administrators have discretion in the style of law enforcement that they encourage among their officers, the type of crimes they emphasize for enforcement, and the degree to which they emphasize supervision and accountability of officers.

Factors influencing the use of discretion

Prior research shows that police officers consciously or unconsciously consider a number of factors when deciding how to handle juveniles suspected of crime (see Brown et al. 2009; Lundman, Sykes, and Clark 1978; Black and Reiss 1970; Piliavin and Briar 1964). Several key factors influence police discretion. These can be broken into two types, legal and extralegal factors. Among the legal factors, formal outcomes are more likely among juveniles who have committed more serious offenses. As the seriousness of the offense increases, the amount of discretion for informal outcomes that an officer can use decreases. Juveniles with prior police contacts are also more likely to be dealt with formally. This is particularly true for juveniles whose prior contacts with the police resulted in arrest. Furthermore, the demeanor of the juvenile influences the likelihood of informal outcomes. Juveniles who are oppositional and exhibit a lack of respect in their interactions with police are more likely to be dealt with formally. Police–citizen interactions involve an expectation of reciprocity. If an officer treats a juvenile offender with respect, the officer will be more likely to consider alternatives to formal action if he or she receives respect in return from the juvenile.

In addition to legal factors, extralegal factors influence discretionary decision-making in police officers' interactions with juveniles. The source of the complaint against a juvenile impacts the level of authority that officers use. Most complaints against juveniles originate from the public. The degree to which a citizen advocates for the arrest of a juvenile in a particular instance influences the likelihood of formal action by police. The structure and organization of the police department also influences the course of action officers will take. In some departments, officers are expected to operate "by the book" and strictly adhere to written guidelines and policies in their interactions with juveniles. In addition, the availability of alternatives to formal processing of juveniles and public opinion about alternatives influences discretionary decision-making. Officers will be less likely to search for alternatives in communities where residents advocate for formal processing and in places where there are few alternatives to formal processing. Social characteristics of juveniles such as race, gender, and social class are also extralegal factors considered by police officers in making discretionary decisions. However, these characteristics cannot be studied in isolation from other factors, including legal factors, that influence discretion (see Ousey and Lee 2008; Bishop and Frazier 1988; Sampson 1986). "Expanding ideas: Gender and police discretion" explores the ways in which gender impacts police decision-making.

EXPANDING IDEAS: GENDER AND POLICE DISCRETION

Comparisons of arrest data from the Uniform Crime Reporting (UCR) program and self-report and victimization data raise important concerns about the ways in which gender influences police decision making.

Research comparing UCR and self-report data has shown that females are more likely than males to be arrested for some status offenses, such as running away and incorrigibility, even though males are more likely to report engaging in status offenses (Gavazzi, Yarcheck, and Chesney-Lind 2006; Hindelang, Hirschi, and Weis 1981; Teilmann and Landry 1981; Chesney-Lind 1977). Rachelle Canter (1982) attributed this discrepancy between self-report and UCR data to harsher responses by law enforcement officials when females commit such acts than when males do. Feminist criminologists such as Meda Chesney-Lind have examined the paternalistic attitudes of police and juvenile court judges, who historically have been less concerned with girls' serious delinquent offenses than with their sexual behavior (or even the potential for it, suggested by status offenses such as running away or incorrigibility, which indicate that girls are beyond parental control) (Chesney-Lind and Shelden 2014; Chesney-Lind and Pasko 2013; MacDonald and Chesney-Lind 2001; Chesney-Lind 1999).

For more serious forms of delinquency, though, gender bias might operate in the opposite direction. Girls may be less likely than boys to be arrested for serious offenses because police officers, subscribing to traditional notions of appropriate gender-role behavior, treat female delinquents more leniently than males. Also, female involvement in serious delinquency may be less "visible" to police because it contradicts gender stereotypes that portray serious delinquent behavior as a male phenomenon. Research from the 1980s and 1990s pro-vided support for both of these hypotheses (Horowitz and Pottieger 1991; Morash 1984).

More recent research, however, suggests that juvenile justice systems are currently *less* tolerant of serious offending than they once were, including serious offending by females. Darrell Steffensmeier and his colleagues (Steffensmeier et al. 2005, 2006; Schwartz et al. 2009) examined trends in girls' violence from 1980 to 2003 using UCR data, victimization data from the National Crime Victimization Survey (NCVS), and self-report data from two separate national surveys. Media accounts of sensational incidents of girls' violence have created the widespread belief that girls' violence is increasing. UCR data clearly indicate an increase in girls' violence. From 1980 to 2000, the female proportion of juvenile arrests increased from 21 to 33 percent for simple assault, from 15 to 24 percent for aggravated assault, and from 10 to 19 percent for the Violent Crime Index, which includes homicide, forcible rape, robbery, and aggravated assault (Steffensmeier et al. 2005). However, when Steffensmeier and his colleagues looked at victimization and self-report data, they did not find similar increases in girls' violence. They concluded that several recent shifts in juvenile justice policy have increased the likelihood of girls' arrests for violence, fueling an inaccurate perception of increases in girls' violent behavior. These policy shifts include:

> first, stretching definitions of violence to include more minor incidents that girls in relative terms are more likely to commit; second, increased policing of violence between intimates and in private settings (for example, home, school) where girls' violence is more widespread; and, third, less tolerant family and societal attitudes toward juvenile females.
>
> (Steffensmeier et al. 2005:355; see also Zahn et al. 2008; Chesney-Lind and Paramore 2001)

Other researchers, however, have found that UCR and NCVS data show a similar narrowing of the gender gap in violent crimes and have challenged the conclusions reached by Steffensmeier and his colleagues (Lauritsen, Heimer, and Lynch 2009; Heimer, Lauritsen, and Lynch 2009).

DUE PROCESS IN JUVENILE LAW ENFORCEMENT

Though police discretion in juvenile matters is broad and extensive, it is not unbridled. During the 1960s and 1970s, the due process revolution in juvenile justice addressed several key law enforcement methods. Drawn into question was whether constitutionally protected due process rights apply to juveniles in a system and process that is intentionally protective and rehabilitative in nature. Also of concern was whether the due process revolution, as advanced by state and federal appellate courts, is binding on local law enforcement practices with juveniles. Three methods of law enforcement have been addressed most extensively by state and federal appellate court decisions: (1) search and seizure, (2) arrest, and (3) custodial interrogation.

Search and seizure

The Fourth Amendment to the U.S. Constitution protects citizens from unauthorized **search and seizure**. Law enforcement may be authorized to conduct searches and to seize evidence through warrants that are issued by courts. Warrants are based on probable cause—the reasoned conclusion, drawn from knowledge and facts, that a particular person committed a particular crime.[2] The outcome of police violations of "unreasonable search and seizure," as specified in the Fourth Amendment, is a case law doctrine called the *exclusionary rule*, which requires that illegally obtained evidence be ruled inadmissible in court. With several significant exceptions, the Fourth Amendment prohibits search and seizure without a valid search warrant.

In *State v. Lowry* (1967), the Supreme Court considered whether Fourth Amendment protections against unreasonable search and seizure apply to juveniles. The Court first acknowledged that the juvenile justice system is distinct in purpose, in that it attempts to protect and reform youth who are dependent and at risk. While recognizing the distinctiveness of the juvenile court, the Court ruled decisively that juveniles have the right of protection from unreasonable search and seizure.

A juvenile's right against unreasonable search and seizure is conditioned in the school context, however, when school safety takes priority. In the 1985 landmark decision *New Jersey v. T.L.O.*, the Supreme Court ruled that school officials can search students and their possessions if the students are suspected of violating school rules.[3] In this case, a 14-year-old high school freshman was observed smoking in a school lavatory by a teacher. When the assistant vice-principal confronted her, she denied that she had been smoking and claimed that she did not smoke at all. The assistant vice-principal opened her purse and found a pack of cigarettes and a package of cigarette rolling papers, commonly used to smoke marijuana. Upon a more thorough search of the purse, he found some marijuana, a pipe, a list of students who owed the young woman money, and two letters implicating her in marijuana dealing. Based on the need for schools to provide a safe and secure learning environment, this case grants school officials search and seizure authority beyond that of the police. In addition, evidence seized by school officials can be turned over to the police for use in their own criminal investigation (Hemmens, Steiner, and Mueller 2004).

Arrest

Most states do not have specific statutory provisions distinguishing the arrest of juveniles from the arrest of adults. Even when states maintain the legal distinction between "taking into custody"

JUVENILE JUSTICE LAW: STATUTORY AUTHORIZATION FOR TAKING A YOUTH INTO CUSTODY

41-5-331. Rights of youth taken into custody—questioning—waiver of rights. (1) When a youth is taken into custody for questioning upon a matter that could result in a petition alleging that the youth is either a delinquent youth or a youth in need of intervention, the following requirements must be met:

(a) The youth must be advised of the youth's right against self-incrimination and the youth's right to counsel.

(b) The investigating officer, probation officer, or person assigned to give notice shall immediately notify the parents, guardian, or legal custodian of the youth that the youth has been taken into custody, the reasons for taking the youth into custody, and where the youth is being held. If the parents, guardian, or legal custodian cannot be found through diligent efforts, a close relative or friend chosen by the youth must be notified . . .

Source: *Montana Code Annotated 2017*.

and arrest, the protective purpose of taking a youth into custody has diminished in recent years. In practice, taking into custody has come to mean almost the same as arrest; the due process rights applied to a youth taken into custody are very similar to those applied to juveniles who are arrested (see "Juvenile justice law: Statutory authorization for taking a youth into custody").

As we have seen, the police have very broad arrest authority because of the protective origins of juvenile policing and because of the extended range of juvenile offenses, particularly status offenses. Authority for arrest is granted in state statutory law (see "Juvenile justice law: Statutory authorization for arrest"). **Arrest** involves the deprivation of an individual's freedom by a person of authority on the grounds that there is probable cause to believe that the individual has committed a criminal offense. Arrest is purposive: to protect the public and to initiate a legal response to the suspected crime. The legality of arrest lies in the Fourth Amendment's "right against unreasonable . . . seizures." The seizure that is specified refers to both property and people; therefore, the requirement of a warrant applies to arrest as well as to searches. However, just as there are exceptions to the constitutional requirement for search warrants, there are also exceptions to the requirement that arrests be accomplished through the use of warrants.

Use of force is the primary legal issue arising from arrest. Under Common Law tradition, most state statutes authorize that "all necessary and reasonable force may be used in making an arrest, but the person arrested may not be subjected to any greater restraint than is necessary to hold or detain that person" (see "Juvenile justice law: Statutory authorization for arrest").[4] The defining Supreme Court case regarding use of deadly force involved a juvenile—a 15-year-old youth from Tennessee named Edward Garner. *Tennessee v. Garner* (1985) is a tragic case dealing with an officer's hard-pressed, spur-of-the-moment interpretation of "all necessary and reasonable force."[5] During a response to a burglary call, a Memphis police officer shot and killed a suspect attempting to flee. The officer ordered the suspect to stop, but he continued to flee over a fence. The suspect was later determined to be Edward Garner. The Supreme Court ruled

JUVENILE JUSTICE LAW: STATUTORY AUTHORIZATION FOR ARREST

46-6-104. Method of arrest. (1) An arrest is made by an actual restraint of the person to be arrested or by the person's submission to the custody of the person making the arrest.

(2) All necessary and reasonable force may be used in making an arrest, but the person arrested may not be subject to any greater restraint than is necessary to hold or detain that person.

(3) All necessary and reasonable force may be used to effect an entry into any building or property or part thereof to make an authorized arrest.

Source: Montana Code Annotated 2017.

that use of deadly force against an apparently unarmed and non-dangerous fleeing felon is an illegal seizure under the Fourth Amendment (Ferdico 1993).

Custodial interrogation

Custodial interrogation involves police questioning of suspects while they are under arrest or when their freedom is restricted in a significant way. There is no other juvenile justice topic that has been decided on more by the Supreme Court (Feld 2013). Two Constitutional Amendments are drawn into question with the practice of custodial interrogation: the Fifth Amendment's right against self-incrimination and the Sixth Amendment's right to counsel. These two fundamental rights were linked together for the first time in *Miranda v. Arizona* (1966), in which the Supreme Court ruled that in order to ensure the right against self-incrimination, it is necessary for the accused to have counsel.[6] The Miranda warning requires police to notify persons arrested that they have a right to remain silent and that any statements they make can and will be used against them; and that they have a right to counsel, and that if they cannot afford counsel, it will be provided at public expense. It should be noted, however, that Ernesto Miranda was 23 years old when he was charged with kidnapping and rape. Do these same rights apply to juveniles?

One year after the *Miranda* decision, the Supreme Court extended due process rights to juvenile court proceedings in the case *In re Gault* (1967).[7] However, the Court intentionally declined to address whether the right to counsel and the right against self-incrimination are guaranteed in pre-adjudication stages of juvenile justice, including police procedures with juveniles. Two earlier Supreme Court cases ruled that statements made by juveniles when under custodial interrogation must be considered in terms of the "totality of circumstances"—a variety of considerations including the absence of parents and lawyers, the age of the suspect, the length of questioning, and the approach used by officers.[8] In one of these cases, *Haley v. Ohio* (1948), five hours of apparently coercive interrogation, without parents or attorney present, led the Supreme Court to conclude that children, to include juveniles, have a constitution right of protection against self-incrimination.[9]

After *Miranda,* the totality-of-circumstances standard was enhanced by the requirement that juveniles be given the Miranda warning by the police when questioning may extract incriminating statements. The critical question that follows is whether a juvenile is able to knowingly, intelligently, and voluntarily waive the rights stated in the Miranda warning. In most circumstances, a juvenile can waive Miranda rights only in the presence of parents or lawyers. In *California v. Prysock* (1981), the U.S. Supreme Court addressed the adequacy of the Miranda warning when it was paraphrased by a police officer to allow the youth to better understand the expressed rights.[10] The Court ruled that even though the Miranda warning was not given verbatim, its meaning was plain and easily understandable for a juvenile. Thus, an officer's attempt to make Miranda understandable for youth is permissible law enforcement practice.

SUMMARY AND CONCLUSIONS

Police encounters with juveniles are the most common entry point into juvenile justice systems. As gatekeepers, police make the initial decision about whether a youth is warned and released or diverted to some community resource, or referred to the juvenile court for possible formal processing. Juveniles and the juvenile justice system pose specific challenges for police officers. Many officers report conflicting expectations that contrast the long-held view that interactions with juveniles should focus on the offender and not the offense, against a responsibility to ensure public safety through enforcement of the law.

Over the past 35 years, formal juvenile court referrals by the police have become increasingly common compared to informal police processing. Recently, over two-thirds of all juveniles taken into custody by the police have been referred to juvenile courts. This is in stark contrast to the informal counsel and release process that had been most common in juvenile policing. Police have extensive discretion in dealing with juvenile matters. This authority is broad and extensive, but it is not unbridled. Departmental policy, state statutes, and even public sentiment influence decision making in police interactions with juveniles. Furthermore, the due process revolution in juvenile justice during the 1960s and 1970s, addressed several key law enforcement practices related to juveniles. The case decisions that make up the due process revolution established procedural law that attempts to extend basic rights and freedoms advanced in state and federal constitutions, especially with regard to search and seizure, custodial interrogation, and arrest.

More recently, juvenile policing has been characterized by contrasting emphases on vigorous enforcement of the law—the law-enforcer role, to enhance public safety, and, at the same time, community-oriented policing—the collaborative role, to promote positive police–citizen relationships. What does the future hold for the police role with juveniles? Will a more rehabilitative approach, reminiscent of the protective role of juvenile policing, become prominent again because of significant juvenile justice reform efforts resulting from recent research on adolescent development?

READING 7.1

"THE IMPORTANCE OF BEING SATISFIED: A LONGITUDINAL EXPLORATION OF POLICE CONTACT, PROCEDURAL INJUSTICE, AND SUBSEQUENT DELINQUENCY."

Lee Ann Slocum, Stephanie Ann Wiley, and Finn-Aage Esbensen. 2016. *Criminal Justice and Behavior* 43:7–26.

Lee Ann Slocum and her colleagues explore the ways in which juvenile satisfaction with treatment by the police during previous stops or arrests influence future involvement in delinquency.

Police–citizen interactions have received a great deal of scrutiny in recent years. Although much of this attention surrounds highly publicized police–citizen encounters that are racially charged and involve excessive police force (e.g., Rodney King, Michael Brown, Eric Garner), the typical police stop or arrest is mundane and does not make national news. But, even these mundane encounters can have negative consequences. As a result, practitioners and researchers alike have sought to understand how the police can effectively do their job, yet minimize the potential harms associated with police-initiated encounters.

One negative consequence of being stopped or arrested is that it can amplify the behavior that it is designed to curb—delinquency (Liberman, Kirk, & Kideuk, 2014; Lopes et al., 2012; Morris & Piquero, 2013; Wiley & Esbensen, 2013). Studies have replicated this finding in different samples using a variety of methods, but we know less about the processes through which this amplification occurs. The procedural justice literature provides one explanation. According to this perspective, people who perceive that the police perform their duties in an unfair and unjust manner are less likely to comply with the law because they do not view the law as legitimate (Tyler, 1990/2006). Perceptions of procedural justice also affect law-violating behavior by shaping people's social identity and their norms regarding the use of violence (Bradford, 2012; Jackson, Huq, Bradford, & Tyler, 2013). Although a number of factors—including community norms, the media, and experiences of friends and family members—influence people's perceptions of the police, chief among these is personal experience (Antrobus, Bradford, Murphy, & Sargeant, 2015; Brunson, 2007; Callanan & Rosenberger, 2011; Weitzer & Tuch, 2005). Thus, changing how people view their personal encounters with the police, including stops and arrests, has the potential to mitigate the negative consequences of these interactions for subsequent offending.

This study examines this idea by exploring how youth's personal experiences with the police and their perceptions of these interactions influence their subsequent delinquent behavior. Using longitudinal survey data, we consider multiple ways in which being stopped or arrested and procedural justice act in concert to affect later delinquency. More specifically, we test whether police contact sets in motion a process whereby youth develop negative orientations toward the police, become alienated from their community, and endorse norms that promote the use of violent self-help, the culmination of which is more delinquency. . . . The procedural justice framework indicates that it is not merely police contact but citizen perceptions of the interaction that matter, so unlike most work on deviance amplification, we examine whether the effects of contact depend on youth's satisfaction with their police encounters. Specifically, we assess whether only youth who are dissatisfied with their encounters engage in higher levels of subsequent delinquency than their counterparts with no contact, or whether being stopped or arrested leads to deviance amplification even among those who rate their interactions as satisfactory. Our focus is on adolescents because their orientations toward the law are still developing, making them more susceptible to the consequences of police contact (Leiber, Nalla, & Farnworth, 1998; Taylor, Turner, Esbensen, & Winfree, 2001). In addition, being stopped or arrested is not an uncommon experience for youth. One estimate suggests that between 16% and 27% of American youth report being arrested before the age of 18 (Brame, Turner, Paternoster, & Bushway, 2012), mostly for non-serious offenses (Office of Juvenile Justice and Delinquency Prevention, 2014).

Although research has generally supported the main propositions of the procedural justice framework, our data allow us to extend prior work in several ways. Namely, because the data are longitudinal, not cross-sectional like most research on this issue, we can assess how the link between police contact and subsequent delinquency unfolds over time and can control for factors related to the initial police encounter and youth's evaluations of these interactions, procedural justice, and subsequent delinquency. This is important because, as Skogan (2012) noted, "People doubtless bring 'priors' to bear when they encounter the police, and when they later interpret what happened" (p. 276). In addition, we look at a broad range of pathways that link contact, procedural justice, and subsequent delinquency—including social identity and norms regarding the personal use of violence—while controlling for alternate mechanisms like peer delinquency and academic achievement. Finally, we are able to focus on law-violating behavior as our outcome rather than willingness to break the law. Although intentions and behaviors are certainly related, their relationship is imperfect, and they may have different antecedents (Ajzen, 1991).

Police-initiated contact can have serious consequences, particularly for youth. Yet the police cannot be expected to turn a blind eye to law-violating behavior. The challenge, therefore, is to identify methods for minimizing or counteracting any potentially harmful effects of these encounters. A necessary first step to achieving this goal is to understand the conditions under which police contact is harmful and why.

Theoretical background

The idea that perceptions of the legal system shape compliance with the law is not new. Crime surveys and reports from the early 1900s indicate that individuals are more inclined to participate in illegal behaviors if they feel they have been unfairly accused or convicted (e.g., Bettman, 1931; Chafee, Pollak, & Stern, 1931). More recent work, such as Tyler's (1990/2006) procedural justice framework, also emphasizes how evaluations of the justness and fairness of the law are formed and the impact of these perceptions on future attitudes and behavior. This framework views compliance with the law as rooted in normative rather than instrumental concerns (e.g., sanction avoidance). Simply put, people obey the law when they view the police and other legal authorities as legitimate. Legitimacy and law-abiding behavior are determined, in large part, by assessments of police, particularly whether they perform their duties in a fair and just (i.e., procedurally just) manner.

Police contact and procedural justice

A number of factors contribute to how people perceive the police, but chief among these is personal experience (Bradford, Jackson, & Stanko, 2009). Studies indicate that youth perceive police-initiated contacts as unwanted, at best (e.g., Carr, Napolitano, & Keating, 2007), and thus, any police-initiated contact may translate into negative perceptions of the police. In fact,

Bradford, Jackson, and Hough (2013) called the association between police contact and negative attitudes toward the police "one of the most reliably replicated findings in criminology" (p. 9).

Work on procedural justice, however, emphasizes that contact generates negative perceptions of the police and amplifies delinquency only when youth perceive that law enforcement treated them unfairly. Favorable interactions, however, should breed positive global assessments of law enforcement. Yet, research points to a different reality: Most studies find that the effect of police-initiated contact is asymmetrical such that satisfactory interactions with the police have weak or null effects on perceptions of the police while unsatisfactory interactions are more salient (e.g., Bradford et al., 2009; Skogan, 2006).

There is evidence that personal contact with the police is related to cooperation or willingness to obey the law and this relationship is partially or fully mediated by procedural justice and legitimacy (Mazerolle, Antrobus, Bennett, & Tyler, 2013; Sunshine & Tyler, 2003).

Fewer studies explicitly examine the association between police contact, procedural justice, and law-violating behavior. Paternoster, Brame, Bachman, and Sherman (1997) provided one of the first assessments of these relationships. They found that arrestees for spousal assault who perceive the police followed fair and just procedures have levels of violence similar to those given warnings, while recidivism rates are higher for arrestees who perceive the police used unfair and unjust procedures. These findings provide some evidence that satisfaction with police encounters can buffer the negative effects of contact, at least for adults. A few studies have focused on youth. For example, Fagan and Tyler (2005) found that encounter-based evaluations of procedural justice are related to some aspects of legitimacy, which, in turn, are correlated with past-year self-reported delinquency. However, the researchers' use of cross-sectional data does not allow for proper causal ordering and confounds the factors that influence perceptions of police encounters, such as prior attitudes toward the police and delinquency, with the consequences of contact. Fagan and Piquero (2007) reached similar conclusions using panel data, but as is the case with Paternoster et al.'s (1997) study, their sample was taken exclusively from individuals with police contact and does not allow for a comparison of those with and without police-initiated encounters.

In Tyler's (1990/2006) early work, legitimacy provides the key link between experiences with the police, procedural justice, and willingness to obey the law. Others argue that there are additional mechanisms through which contact and procedural justice affect subsequent delinquency. For example, perceptions of procedural injustice may directly lead to defiance of the law independent of legitimacy by generating negative reactions such as anger (Agnew, 2001; Paternoster et al., 1997; Sherman, 1993), a pathway supported by research (e.g., Barkworth & Murphy, 2015). As discussed below, social identity and attitudes toward the personal use of violence may be important also. Therefore, although legitimacy is one link between procedural justice and offending, it is not the only one.

Social identity

The group-value model (Lind & Tyler, 1988; Tyler & Lind, 1992) suggests that information about an individual's standing within the group is conveyed by authority figures during encounters with citizens, primarily through the quality of the interaction. These interactions, as well as global assessments of how fairly authority figures treat members of the individual's social group, influence whether a person views him or herself as a respected community member or as an outsider. Because police officers act as representatives of the mainstream, their actions influence the extent to which youth feel connected to the dominant social group and adopt prosocial values and norms (Bradford, 2012; Bradford, Murphy,& Jackson, 2014). When youth perceive that the police are procedurally just, it signals they are respected and worthwhile members of the community. This identification inhibits law violating behavior because youth feel they are obligated to follow societal norms. In contrast, when youth believe the police are unfair or unjust, it alienates them from the prosocial mainstream, delegitimizes the police, and reduces their willingness to comply with the law (Bradford, 2012; Fagan & Tyler, 2005). Because formal intervention signifies that individuals are not part of the "in" group (see McAra & McVie, 2012), any unwanted police contact may be enough to trigger this shift in social identity; however, marginalization is most likely when youth perceive they have been treated poorly.

The limited research on these relationships supports the idea that perceptions of procedural justice affect social identity. For example, Bradford's (2012) study of minority males in London found a significant relationship between global assessments of procedural justice and identification with the local community and larger entities (London or Britain). In turn, social identity predicted willingness to cooperate with the police, but only for those who did not view themselves as citizens of the United Kingdom. Furthermore, a study that surveyed people involved in vehicle stops found that it was social identity, not legitimacy, that mediated the effect of encounter-based assessments of procedural justice on intentions to commit future traffic offenses (Bradford, Hohl, Jackson, & MacQueen, 2015). Finally, longitudinal research has linked neighborhood identification with willingness to cooperate with the police (Tyler & Fagan, 2008) and found that citizens who believe the police are more just and fair have stronger social identities (Bradford et al., 2014).

Support for the personal use of violence

Attitudes toward violence provide a final link between police contact, procedural justice, and subsequent delinquency. This mechanism is rooted in the idea that when people grant legitimacy to authorities such as the police, they implicitly acknowledge that the right to use violence belongs to the state (Jackson et al., 2013). When the justness of the criminal justice system is questioned, private violence may be tolerated because people feel they cannot turn to the police for help and must take responsibility for their own safety (Gau & Brunson, 2015). Under these circumstances, retaliation becomes an acceptable response to interpersonal conflict, and violence is viewed as a way to prevent future victimization (see Anderson, 1999; Black, 1983 for different perspectives). Therefore, police contact viewed as unsatisfactory should promote delinquent behavior via procedural injustice and the adoption of norms that support the personal use of violence to resolve disputes.

Jackson and colleagues (2013) found support for this hypothesis using data from a cross sectional survey of young, minority males. Compared with those who did not experience police contact in the past 12 months, individuals who were stopped and/or arrested by the police and received no procedural justice were more likely to support the personal use of violence. This relationship was explained by overall trust in procedural justice by the police and, in turn, perceptions of police legitimacy. Similar results have been found in studies of vigilantism (Tankebe, 2009). One of the few qualitative examinations of procedural justice and self-help describes how young men in high-crime neighborhoods engage in self-protective behaviors because of their alienation from and distrust of the police (Gau & Brunson, 2015). To our knowledge, research has not looked at these relationships as they relate to delinquency.

In sum, the full procedural justice framework outlined here includes three primary components that link police contact to subsequent delinquency: an evaluative component (procedural justice), an affective component (social identity), and a normative component (support for the personal use of violence).

Current study

The procedural justice framework suggests that perceptions of the police, social identity, and norms regarding the use of violence are intimately intertwined and affect one's willingness to violate the law. There is empirical support for the main propositions of this framework, but research is needed to examine simultaneously and over time the multiple mechanisms that link police contact and youth's perceptions of these encounters to future delinquency. This research contributes to the literature by exploring whether police contact is associated with increased delinquency via its effects on procedural injustice, social identity, and norms regarding the personal use of violence. We argue that the negative ramifications of police contact on subsequent delinquency will emerge for youth who are dissatisfied with their treatment, but not youth who are satisfied. Youth who voice ambivalent feelings toward their contact will fall somewhere between the two.

We also expect contact will have a direct effect on delinquency. As described above, procedural injustice may directly lead to defiance of the law and this may be true for both generalized evaluations of procedural justice as well as those rooted in specific interactions with the police. Also, there are likely other mechanisms implicated in the delinquency amplification process that are not captured by our model, including legitimacy.

Method

Data

To test these hypotheses, we use data from the second National Evaluation of the Gang Resistance Education and Training (G.R.E.A.T.) program (2006–2013). The program is aimed at preventing youth violence and gang membership (see Esbensen, Osgood, Peterson, Taylor, & Carson, 2013). At the start of the evaluation, participants were in 6th or 7th grade in 31 middle schools across seven U.S. cities. A total of 3,820 youth (77.9%) returned active parental consent, and attempts were made to survey these youth 6 times over the course of 5 years (see Esbensen, Melde, Taylor, & Peterson, 2008). Because questions regarding police contact were not added until Wave 3, we use data from Waves 2 through 5 for this study. For ease of reference, we refer to these waves as Time 1 through Time 4 (T1-T4).

As is the case with longitudinal and school-based surveys, attrition and missing data are concerns. The majority (68%) of youth was surveyed at all 4 time points; however, 15% were missing one survey, 8% were missing two, 7% were missing three, and 2% were missing all four waves of data. To help retain youth who were not surveyed at all 4 time points, we utilized full information maximum likelihood (FIML) estimation, which uses all cases that are not missing data on the exogenous variables (see "Analytic Procedure" section). After excluding cases missing on exogenous variables, our final sample size was 2,919. Our final sample was racially and ethnically diverse (28.4% White, 16.9% Black, 40.4% Latino, and 14.3% Other or multiple races/ethnicities) and was evenly divided between males and females. . . .

Discussion

It is important for scholars to explore the processes that link experiences with the police to detrimental outcomes not only to address issues of fairness, equal treatment, and respect but also for a much more pragmatic reason: Police encounters have the potential to amplify the delinquent behaviors they are intended to combat. We rely on recent extensions of the procedural justice framework that include evaluative, affective, and normative components to provide a more nuanced exploration of the links between personal experiences with the police, procedural justice, and subsequent law-violating behavior.

We proposed four hypotheses related to police contact, procedural justice, and the amplification of deviance. Our findings support some of the direct relationships predicted in our first hypothesis, but there is no evidence that the relationship between contact and subsequent delinquency is mediated by procedural injustice alone. Specifically, our results indicate that relative to those with no contact, youth with police-initiated encounters perceived as unsatisfactory or neutral view the police as more procedurally unjust. Views of procedural injustice do not differ between youth with no police contact and those with satisfactory encounters. These findings provide support for Skogan's (2006) argument that negatively perceived police contact is more salient than satisfactory encounters for shaping attitudes toward the police. They also suggest that even though satisfactory encounters may not improve youth's overall assessments of the police, they can mitigate the negative consequences of contact for youth, at least with regard to their orientation toward law enforcement.

Although our results are consistent with the well-replicated finding that interactions with the police influence procedural justice, our work does not support a direct link between procedural justice and subsequent delinquency. There could be several explanations for this finding. First, most research has examined willingness to obey the law and not actual behavior. Procedural justice may be more important for explaining attitudes and intentions whereas other factors, such as peers and instrumental concerns, are more important for behavior. This may be particularly true during adolescence, when delinquency is normative and youth strive for acceptance from their social groups. Second, Tyler (1990/2006) noted that among individuals who have negative perceptions of the performance of legal authorities, other factors such as peer disapproval shape compliance. Negative attitudes toward the law and its actors tend to reach their peak during mid-adolescence (see Fagan & Tyler, 2005); thus, procedural justice and legitimacy may be less important for youth, who place increased emphasis on peer groups. Finally, our measure of procedural justice primarily captures the quality of treatment. A more robust measure that includes quality of decision making might lead to different results.

This is not to say that procedural justice is irrelevant for delinquency amplification. Consistent with our third hypothesis, we find that procedural injustice mediates the effects of police contact on delinquency via its relationship with support for the personal use of violence. Consistent with the procedural justice framework, this amplification only occurs when youth are not satisfied with their contact. This implies that positively perceived interactions with the police can limit to some small extent the negative consequences of being stopped or arrested for youth. Although the relationship between procedural justice and compliance with the law traditionally has been attributed to legitimacy, norms supporting the personal use of violence offer an alternative link, but the magnitude of these effects is substantively small. We cannot assess whether these relationships are independent of legitimacy. Future research should explore the simultaneous effects of procedural justice, support for personal violence, and legitimacy on delinquency. More work is also needed to understand why contact—even satisfactory contact—is associated with more delinquency via violence norms, controlling for procedural justice.

We find no evidence that identification with the community mediates the effect of police contact on subsequent delinquency, although adolescents with negative or neutral encounters as well as those who view the police as more unjust are more isolated from the community.

It may be that the state or nation-state is the relevant identification group and not the local community. This may be especially true if youth view the police as enforcing laws that are made by those outside their community and that do not necessarily reflect the community's best interests or values. More generally, there is a need to explicitly address the question of "Who do the police represent?" and explore whether changes in other types of social identity are relevant for explaining the link between police contact and subsequent delinquency. It is also possible that social identity may be more relevant for other outcomes, such as willingness to cooperate with the police.

Controlling for these three paths as well as other potential deviance amplification mechanisms, we find that police contact retains a direct effect on subsequent delinquency, regardless of how it is perceived. Considering that we control for other potential links in the deviance amplification process such as negative peers, poor school performance, and a proxy for identity change, these significant direct effects highlight that deviance amplification is not fully understood. One potential missing link between negative contact and delinquency is emotions. Sherman (1993) argues that when sanctions are viewed as unjust or unfair, they increase delinquency by generating defiant pride and unacknowledged shame (see also Agnew, 2001). We cannot rule out that some of the observed direct effect may be a result of measurement error, or that despite our rigorous controls and attention to causal ordering, we have not adequately accounted for the tendency for youth with a high propensity for delinquency to be stopped or arrested by the police.

An important possibility that we have not explored here is that the effects of police contact may depend on the characteristics of the youth or the context in which the interactions occur. There are well-established differences between racial and ethnic groups as well as males and females in the extent of their police contacts and their perceptions of these encounters (Brunson & Miller, 2006; Langton & Durose, 2013). People from different backgrounds also bring a unique set of experiences and personal histories that may differentially affect the consequences of police contact. In addition, it is possible that the effects of contact are conditioned by neighborhood or school context (Hagan, Shedd, & Payne, 2005; Skogan, 1978). For example, youth living in heavily policed neighborhoods may have very different experiences and expectations than their counterparts residing in other types of communities and these effects may be further contingent on race. Future research also should extend analyses to other types of contact (e.g., interactions with school resource officers) and vicarious and accumulated experiences because these encounters are likely to shape procedural justice and related outcomes (Brunson, 2007; Fagan & Tyler, 2005; Smith, 2007).

Conclusion

Sherman (1998) argues that making "the style and substance of police practices more 'legitimate' in the eyes of the public, particularly high-risk juveniles, may be one of the most effective long-term police strategies for crime prevention" (p. 8). Our findings generally support this idea: To the extent that law enforcement behavior influences youth's satisfaction with their encounters, the police can alter their actions to minimize the overall harm associated with contact. But, the relationships among perceptions of encounters with the police, procedural justice, and delinquent behavior are imperfect and complex. It is important to recall that although research has found that the actions and demeanor of the police are the primary factors driving citizens' satisfaction with these interactions (Skogan, 2005), the attitudes and experiences adolescents bring to these interactions as well as the experiences of other community members, family, and friends influence how they are interpreted (Brandl, Frank, Worden, & Bynum, 1994; Brick, Taylor, & Esbensen, 2009). As a result, it may not be enough to change how police interact with youth; we also need to address the priors that people bring to their encounters.

All youth deserve to be treated in a fair and just manner, and it is important for police departments to conduct training programs to teach officers about the principles and benefits of procedural justice (Skogan, Van Craen, & Hennessy, 2014). If police treat youth in a manner that increases the likelihood they will leave the encounter feeling satisfied, it can dampen to some extent the negative ramifications of being stopped and arrested, including subsequent delinquency. However, some negative consequences of contact—including its effects on violent norms—emerge regardless of youth's perceptions of their experiences. There may be a limit to what fair and just police actions can contribute to crime control. Other actors are required to do their part to mitigate the damage of police contact—this onus cannot fall entirely on the police.

[References and notes omitted.]

READING 7.2

CHILDHOOD TRAUMA AND ITS EFFECTS: IMPLICATIONS FOR POLICE.

Richard G. Dudley, Jr. 2015. *New Perspectives in Policing.* Washington, DC: U.S. Department of Justice, National Institute of Justice.

Psychiatrist Richard Dudley examines the importance of police recognizing the symptoms and impacts of childhood trauma and offers recommendations for dealing with trauma in police interactions with juveniles.

Repeated exposure to traumatic events during childhood can have dramatic and long-lasting effects. During the past 20 years, there has been an enormous increase in our understanding of how being repeatedly traumatized by violence affects the growth and development of pre-adolescent children, especially when such traumatized children lack a nurturing and protective parental figure that might mitigate the impact of the trauma. In this paper, I summarize the current understanding of the effects of ongoing trauma on young children, how these effects impair adolescent and young adult functioning, and the possible implications of this for policing.

To demonstrate this, I describe the case of a 17-year-old African American male who was charged with attempted murder. I was asked to perform a psychiatric evaluation because (1) everyone who knew him was shocked about what happened because, before the crime, he had never been in trouble and he had always appeared to be functioning well; and (2) he appeared to be extremely unemotional about what happened, which his attorney viewed as either a lack of remorse or a failure to appreciate how much trouble he was in.

Although this young man had always lived in an extremely violent and drug-infested neighborhood, he was neither a drug dealer nor a gang member. Instead, he had shown such promise that his single mother had gotten him a scholarship to a private school. He was performing well in school despite the problems in his neighborhood and his home, including his mother's involvement in a series of relationships in which she had been physically abused. When I asked him about the multiple homemade tattoos on his body, he told me that each represented a family member or friend who had been killed. He cried as he described the first in this series of deaths, including the death of his best friend, which occurred when they were 8 years old and walking home from school. He also noted that the most recent death, that of his brother, occurred about a year ago. As he spoke of these deaths, that first one, which occurred about 9 years ago, seemed just as fresh to him as the recent death of his brother. In addition, I was struck by the fact that this young man had never been given any parental support that might have helped him begin to cope with these losses. When he was only 8 years old, instead of helping her young son cope with his trauma, his mother yelled at him for being on a street that she had told him not to go on.

During his psychiatric evaluation, it became clear that the young man's initial unemotional presentation was a psychological defense against his enormous fear that he would be killed. He had been carrying a gun since his brother was killed; the shooting incident for which he was charged was the first time he had used the gun. Furthermore, the fear for his life, coupled with his almost taking another's life, made the incident yet another traumatic experience for him.

It also became clear that his history of trauma influenced his interaction with the police at the time of his arrest. The police had shown no sensitivity to him when he was 8 years old, found holding and crying over his dead friend's body. Instead, they simply pulled him away from his friend, pushed him into the background, and never attempted to assess his physical or emotional status or make sure that someone else did so. During his early adolescent years, he had seen police officers mistreat others, which made it harder for him to trust or feel comfortable with police officers. His interaction with the police was further complicated by their initial presumption that he, like the victim, was a gang member and that the attempted murder was gang-related, which influenced not only perceptions of him but also how they treated him, even though he presented no physical threat to them. As a result, the police were physically aggressive with him. Being roughed up made him fearful of the police, and his attempts to manage that high level of anxiety and fear with an unemotional and cold presentation caused the police to be suspicious that he would suddenly act out, which in turn caused them to be even more confrontational and physical with him.

Police officers may also suffer from trauma-related difficulties that impair their ability to do their work. These may be long-standing difficulties stemming from their own childhood that were never identified or adequately addressed, or they may stem from traumatic experiences that occurred while working as a police officer. However, a fuller discussion of that is beyond the scope of this paper.

Stress, trauma and parental protection

Understanding the stress response in children requires consideration of both the persistence and the severity of the stressor—which can range from those experienced by all children to the most severe traumatic events—and the availability of parental nurture, support and protection.

All children have stressful experiences, such as the anxiety associated with the first day of school, being frustrated by a friend's behavior, or being frightened by a big dog. Stresses such as these can be positive experiences when a nurturing adult helps the child learn healthy ways to manage anxiety, frustration and fear (Briere and Lanktree, 2008; Gunnar and Quevedo, 2008; Tarullo and Gunnar, 2006). Some children are also exposed to far more stressful experiences, such as the death of a parent or other close family member, their own childhood illness, or exposure to an isolated incident of violence. Here, too, a nurturing, protective adult can help the child overcome the distress associated with the event and thereby help the child not only tolerate the stressor but also grow from the event (Goslin et al., 2013; Maschi, 2006).

Some children are exposed to events that are exceptionally stressful. The impact of such traumatic events is more severe when they occur repeatedly (Breslau et al., 1999). Various types of violence can traumatize children, including sexual abuse and nonsexual physical abuse (Beitchman et al., 1992; Saywitz et al., 2000). Trauma can also result if a child witnesses acts of violence, including domestic violence and street violence (Berton and Stabb, 1996; Fitzpatrick and Boldizar, 1993). Additionally, psychological abuse that threatens violence, especially when the child has seen the perpetrator become violent, can traumatize children (Levendosky et al., 2002).

Although parental support can attenuate the effects of repeated exposure to extremely traumatic events, this support tends not to be available to these children, who need it the most (Green et al., 1991; Terr, 1991). In the vast majority of these cases, the parents of these children are either abusive (i.e., perpetrators of the abuse) or neglectful (i.e., they have failed to protect the child from exposure to the violence) or both, instead of nurturing and protecting the child. This repeated violent traumatization in the absence of parental nurture and protection is toxic to developing children. The group of children who suffer from this harmful combination are the focus of this paper. The resulting psychiatric impairments and associated dysfunction they exhibit as children and adolescents significantly increase their risk of coming into contact with police officers and present a significant challenge to police officers when such contact occurs.

Parents who fail to adequately nurture and protect their children usually have problems of their own (Green et al., 1991), including their own history of abuse or neglect; serious mental health problems, including intellectual deficits and substance abuse; and situational difficulties that have so overwhelmed them that they cannot parent, such as poverty or their own victimization by a partner (Gewirtz and Edleson, 2007; Lieberman, Van Horn and Ippen, 2005). Therefore, in addition to having to cope with repeated trauma without parental nurture and support, often these children also have to cope with a range of other problems related to the difficulties that their parents might be having. For example, in addition to not adequately protecting his or her child, a parent might be so depressed, drug addicted or cognitively impaired that he or she fails to meet the child's most basic needs.

For example, I was involved in a case where a woman had become involved with a man who seemed to be a "good man" until he moved in with her, when he began to psychologically control and severely physically abuse her and her 6-year-old son. Due to her own history and associated psychiatric difficulties, she was so overwhelmed by the psychological domination and physical abuse that she could not protect herself or extricate herself from the situation. She was also repeatedly abused in front of her son, thereby repeatedly exposing him to violence. She was so overwhelmed by her predicament that she could not protect her son from the abuse that he was enduring. As a result, her son felt constantly at risk of harm, constantly feared that his mother would be harmed or killed, felt there was no place where he would be safe, and saw no reason why things would or even might soon be better. Not surprisingly, the boy developed multiple trauma-related symptoms, such as extreme hypervigilance and overreactivity, that were never identified and treated (these symptoms are described in more detail later). Therefore, as he got older, he repeatedly overreacted violently to perceived threats of harm in all sorts of interactions, including his interactions with police officers. . . .

Implications for policing

In the course of their duties, police officers often encounter individuals who have suffered repeated exposure to traumatic events during their childhood. Understanding the effects of such childhood trauma, and the behaviors that these individuals are likely to exhibit as a result, has practical implications for police operations in three areas: first, where police deal with violence and children are victims or witnesses; second, where police encounter individuals already affected by childhood trauma who exhibit behaviors often attributed to aggressiveness and callousness; and, third, when a suspect in police custody or under interrogation manifests behaviors symptomatic of a history of trauma, case officers need to recognize those symptoms and make appropriate referrals, as they would for any other mental disorder.

Police challenges in encounters with traumatized individuals

Because of their tendency to violent and erratic behavior, these sizable numbers of individuals who experience trauma-related difficulties are at an increased risk of coming into contact with police officers. The likelihood of police contact is even greater if these traumatized individuals live in violent neighborhoods. This is for two reasons. First, violent neighborhoods tend to have a large police presence, meaning that all residents of these neighborhoods come into contact with police more frequently (Hangartner, 1994). Second, if an individual already suffers from trauma-related difficulties, a new traumatic experience will exacerbate those difficulties. This combination of past trauma and subsequent exposure to violence increases the likelihood that an individual will have violent reactions of the type that would bring them into contact with police officers and complicate that contact (Donley et al., 2012).

Without training focused on issues related to childhood trauma, it is unlikely that police officers will recognize that individuals may be acting out due to difficulties stemming from past traumatic experiences. Although anxiety, fear and impaired regulation of the brain's stress response drive the behavior of traumatized individuals, their visible symptoms are more obvious. Attention to these visible symptoms at the expense of their underlying causes results in police misperceiving these children, adolescents and young adults. Traumatized individuals tend to be hypervigilant and hypersensitive to perceived threats, and they tend to overreact to such threats, often violently. This extreme reaction becomes the focus of police attention. For example, a traumatized person may mask anxiety with an extreme bravado, which police view as arrogance or a lack of caring instead of the psychological defense mechanism that it is (Arroyo, 2001). Also, the brain's impaired regulation of the stress response makes it difficult, if not impossible, for traumatized individuals to calm themselves down, even when it would be in their best interest to do so, which makes them seem more aggressive (Van der Kolk et al., 2009). In addition, associated difficulties such as substance abuse can also become a focus of police attention, with no thought about whether underlying psychiatric difficulties might have contributed to such substance abuse.

Factors other than the absence of police training on childhood trauma contribute to a misunderstanding of individuals with a history of such trauma, especially when the individual is a young man of color. Many believe that children and adolescents who have been exposed to violence—a sizable portion of whom are African American children—have become immune to violence (Gottlieb, 2004). In my experience, this notion is readily expanded into a belief that such children and adolescents have become hardened to violence and its effects and that they virtually embrace violence instead of being frightened by it. However, for most children repeatedly exposed to violence, this is not the case (Thomas et al., 2012; Cooley-Strickland et al., 2011). Furthermore, recent studies have begun to confirm the common anecdotal observation that African American boys are viewed as older, less childlike and less innocent than white same-age peers (Goff et al., 2014). Because they are viewed as more like adults, African American boys are seen as more responsible for their behavior and, as a result, they are at risk of being treated more harshly than their white counterparts by police and other components of the criminal justice system (Goff et al., 2014). Therefore, any training on childhood trauma and its effects must address how race frames one's understanding of behavior and how, for many, such race-based beliefs overshadow other well-established factors in their perception of the behavior of young men of color. In other words, if a goal of this training is to influence the thinking and alter the behavior of police officers toward traumatized young men of color, the training must first undo the false belief that such young men may have never been that traumatized and instead became immune to violence.

An increased awareness of the high prevalence of severe childhood trauma and an increased appreciation of its effects on both the developing child and later adolescent and adult functioning might impact the thinking and behavior of police officers in several ways as they go about the work of policing.

Considerations for dealing with traumatized individuals

First, with regard to prevention, or at least early intervention, in the development of trauma-related disorders, police officers can learn more about traumatized children when regularly called to investigate alleged cases of domestic violence (Butzer, Bronfman and Stipak, 1996). An increased appreciation for the impact of exposure to domestic violence on developing children might lead police to develop better mechanisms for reporting domestic violence to their local child protective services and to better advocate for the development of mental health services to address the needs of children so exposed. Furthermore, because a significant subset of children living in homes where there is domestic violence are victims of child abuse and neglect, those children will also need services to address these issues.

Police officers already recognize that one of their roles is to enhance a sense of safety in the communities they serve (Plant and Scott, 2009). However, recognizing that this effort also helps decrease the prevalence of childhood trauma-related difficulties—and guard against the exacerbation of symptoms in those who already suffer from such difficulties—might help police understand how important this aspect of their work is, and how central it is to decreasing crime. Ideally, this would also prompt police to explore whether certain police practices that seem to undercut this goal might be altered without impeding police work.

One police chief, with whom I spoke in connection with writing this article and who wished to be unnamed, noticed that many violent crime scenes were left undisturbed far longer than was required for officers to do their work. In his view, having to constantly see these crime scenes—with blood and police tape or evidence markers and medical refuse—made citizens more fearful and caused them to be all the more traumatized by the crimes that had occurred. The police chief instituted an effort to clean up crime scenes as quickly as possible, which significantly reduced citizens' exposure to reminders of neighborhood violence. Recognizing that this decreased exposure was particularly critical to the well-being of children, this chief also began a practice where his department notified local schools when there were violent crimes in the neighborhood. Such notifications allowed school personnel to keep an eye out for students with any trauma-related difficulties.

In addition, the list of possible causes of any behavior that the police are called upon to investigate and address could be broadened to include the cluster of psychiatric and neuropsychiatric difficulties that result from childhood trauma. This might change how police officers view and treat alleged perpetrators.

Armed with such knowledge, possibly from internal databases and made available at dispatch or, in smaller departments, common knowledge about an individual, police officers would come to understand that, when managing individuals with a childhood trauma history, certain interventions may escalate rather than control difficulties. For example, interventions involving displays of aggression such as yelling, rough physical contact and intense eye contact ("the stare"), though meant to curb aggressive behavior, may provoke aggression. This understanding reinforces the notion that police need not behave in an overly aggressive manner, except when officers deem it necessary to ensure the safety of themselves or those around them. It may also prompt police organizations to develop new interventions that might help manage individuals whom the police already know to suffer from trauma-related difficulties.

Recommendations for dealing with traumatized individuals

With regard to developing trauma-specific interventions, much can be learned from many police organizations' efforts to develop alternative interventions to manage individuals who suffer from a range of psychiatric and neuropsychiatric issues. For example, many police organizations have developed units of officers who understand and appreciate the impact of paranoid delusions. They also learned (a) how to respond to individuals suffering from such delusions in a way that helps calm them instead of making them more paranoid, and (b) what to do if attempts to calm individuals suffering from delusions fail. Although the fears of traumatized individuals are not delusional, neither are they rational—their fears are greater than the situation merits. Furthermore, as with persons suffering from paranoid delusions, the fears of persons suffering from trauma-related difficulties can be exacerbated by the behavior of those they come in contact with. Therefore, it is reasonable for police organizations to develop a protocol for trauma-specific interventions, with goals and objectives similar to those developed to manage other mentally ill individuals.

Moving beyond on-street dealings with traumatized individuals, once a suspect is taken into custody and is being questioned and a full investigation is under way, understanding childhood trauma and its effects might inform next steps. At this point, trained officers can recognize, better than they can during on-street encounters, that they are dealing with a person with a trauma history, and they can use the knowledge, understanding and associated skills that they have developed to deal with such a person. This knowledge and these skills may help officers obtain the cooperation of a suspect instead of making the suspect so much more fearful that he or she shuts down and refuses to cooperate or even speak. This knowledge may also help officers better understand the suspect's responses to questioning and determine the best approach to further questioning. In addition, this new awareness may help officers understand more accurately what happened during the course of the alleged crime.

When individuals suffering from the psychiatric and neuropsychiatric effects of childhood trauma are victimized again as adolescents or young adults, or when someone close to them is victimized, this can significantly exacerbate their symptoms. Unfortunately, this problem is far too common in poor communities of color, and there are virtually no victim services, mental health treatment or social services programs specifically designed for young men of color who are revictimized (Bell and Jenkins, 1991; Edwards and Foley, 1997; Snowden, 2001). Because leaving their difficulties unaddressed causes them additional pain, suffering and dysfunction and further increases their risk of coming into contact with the police, an awareness of these issues might help police become important advocates for the development of treatment and service programs for these victims.

As police and police organizations increase their understanding of childhood trauma and its effects, they will be more invested in and better able to develop and institute police practices that take this serious mental health problem into consideration. In addition, if this training is integrated with training on how race frames our understanding of human behavior, then the relationships that the police have with communities of color could be significantly enhanced.

Summary and conclusion

For children, repeated exposure to violent trauma, particularly in the absence of parental nurture, support and protection that might mitigate the impact of such trauma, can have devastating effects on their psychiatric and neuropsychiatric development. These include the development of mutually exacerbating disorders: neurological difficulties, trauma-specific psychological difficulties, developmental difficulties and other associated functional difficulties.

These psychiatric and neuropsychiatric difficulties become evident when traumatized children are still children, long before they understand what is happening to them or can assume responsibility for addressing what is happening to them. Early therapeutic intervention can help enormously. However, when such early therapeutic intervention does not occur, many of these difficulties become irreversible. Individuals continue to suffer from these difficulties during their adolescent and adult years, and they are vulnerable to exacerbation of their symptoms by subsequent traumatic events as well as events that remind them of or symbolize the childhood traumas that they endured.

Although children from any neighborhood can be exposed to the type of trauma described here, children from poor communities of color are particularly at risk for such exposure. Because these communities are often the focus of police attention, it is important that police be aware of the high prevalence of severe childhood trauma in such communities, appreciate its effects on the developing child, and understand its impact on adolescent and adult functioning. With this knowledge, police officers will have a greater capacity to help decrease the prevalence of this major public mental health problem and will be able to better manage those they come in contact with who suffer from trauma-related psychiatric and neuropsychiatric difficulties.

[References omitted.]

CRITICAL-THINKING QUESTIONS

1 How does the case in point about two obnoxious teenagers at the beginning of the chapter demonstrate the importance of police discretion and the factors that influence officer decision making?
2 Explain how the police serve as the "gatekeepers" of the juvenile justice process.
3 Why are "discretion" and "diversion" essential to policing juveniles and the process of juvenile justice?
4 Identify and briefly describe the various roles that police adopt in juvenile law enforcement.
5 How does procedural due process influence the enforcement of laws with juveniles?
6 Research conducted by Lee Ann Slocum and her colleagues shows that juvenile perceptions of mistreatment by the police are more important than perceptions of fair treatment for shaping attitudes toward future delinquency. What are the implications of this finding for policing juveniles?
7 The reading by Richard Dudley discusses the importance of police officers' ability to recognize symptoms of previous trauma. How does previous trauma exposure influence how a juvenile may interact with the police?

SUGGESTED READING

Feld, Barry. 2013. *Kids, Cops, and Confessions: Inside the Interrogation Room*. New York/London: New York University Press.

Puzzanchera, Charles. 2014. "Juvenile Arrests 2012." *Juvenile Offenders and Victims National Report Series*. Washington, DC: Office of Juvenile Justice and Delinquency Prevention.

Redner-Vera, Erica and Marcus-Antonio Galeste. 2015. "Attitudes and Marginalization: Examining American Indian Perceptions of Law Enforcement among Adolescents." *Journal of Ethnicity in Criminal Justice* 13:283–308.

USEFUL WEBSITES

For further information relevant to this chapter, go to the following websites.

- **Community Oriented Policing Services (COPS)**, Supporting Safe Schools: cops.usdoj.gov/supportingsafeschools
- **Office of Juvenile Justice and Delinquency Prevention**, Topics: Law Enforcement: www.ojjdp.gov/search/topiclist.asp
- **Models for Change (Systems Reform in Juvenile Justice)**: http://www.modelsforchange.net/about
- **International Association of Chiefs of Police**: www.theiacp.org

GLOSSARY OF KEY TERMS

Arrest: The deprivation of an individual's freedom by a person of authority on the grounds that there is probable cause to believe that the individual has committed a criminal offense.

Collaborative role: The police and community working together to prevent crime, maintain public order, and solve community problems.

Crime-fighting role: The police role associated with professional policing that emphasizes enforcement of laws and crime control. The primary strategies for crime fighting involve motorized preventive patrol, rapid response, and reactive investigation.

Custodial interrogation: Police questioning of suspects when custody involves arrest or significant deprivation of freedom and the questioning is possibly incriminating.

Law-enforcer role: Associated with the "get tough" approach to crime and delinquency, the law-enforcer role emphasizes public safety and offender accountability and involves vigorous enforcement of laws through arrest and referral to the juvenile court.

Protective role: The original role of police in dealing with juveniles in which police were expected to practice "kindly discipline" in place of parents—to function *in loco parentis*. As an extension of the juvenile court, police were to deal with juveniles in an informal, parent-like fashion, acting in the "best interests of the child."

Search and seizure: The Fourth Amendment protects against unreasonable search and seizure by the police. A search requires a search warrant, which is issued by the courts and is based on probable cause.

Taking into custody: The statutory authority given to police officers to take control of a juvenile, either physically or by the youth's voluntary submission, in an effort to separate that youth from his or her surroundings. Taking into custody is used when the juvenile has broken the law or is in need of protection.

NOTES

1 "Cops and Kids" is the title of a book by David B. Wolcott (2005): *Cops and Kids: Policing Juvenile Delinquency in Urban America, 1890–1940*. Columbus, OH: Ohio State University Press.

2 *Brinegar v. U.S.*, 338 U.S. 160 (1948).

3 *New Jersey v. T. L. O.*, 469 U.S. 325 (1985).

4 *Montana Code Annotated 2014*. 46-6-14. Method of arrest.

5 *Tennessee v. Garner*, 471 U.S. 1 (1985).

6 *Miranda v. Arizona*, 384 U.S. 436 (1966).

7 *In re Gault*, 387 U.S. 1 (1967).

8 *Haley v. Ohio*, 332 U.S. 596 (1948) and *Gallegos v. Colorado*, 370 U.S. 49 (1962).

9 *Haley v. Ohio*, 332 U.S. 596 (1948).

10 *California v. Prysock*, 453 U.S. 355 (1981).

REFERENCES

Bishop, Donna and Charles Frazier. 1988. "The Influence of Race in Juvenile Justice Processing." *Journal of Research in Crime and Delinquency* 25:242–261.

Black, Donald J. and Albert J. Reiss, Jr. 1970. "Police Control of Juveniles." *American Sociological Review* 35: 63–77.

Bordua, David J. 1967. "Recent Trends: Deviant Behavior and Social Control." *Annals of the American Academy of Political and Social Science* 369:149–163.

Brown, Robert A., Kenneth J. Novak, and James Frank. 2009. "Identifying Variation in Police Officer Behavior between Juveniles and Adults." *Journal of Criminal Justice* 37:200–208.

Canter, Rachelle J. 1982. "Sex Differences in Self-Reported Delinquency." *Criminology* 20:373–393.

Chesney-Lind, Meda. 1977. "Judicial Paternalism and the Female Status Offender: Training Women to Know Their Place." *Crime and Delinquency* 23:121–130.

Chesney-Lind, Meda. 1999. "Challenging Girls' Invisibility in Juvenile Court." *The Annals of the American Academy of Political and Social Science* 564:185–202.

Chesney-Lind, Meda and Vickie V. Paramore. 2001. "Are Girls Getting More Violent? Exploring Juvenile Robbery Trends." *Journal of Contemporary Criminal Justice* 17:142–166.

Chesney-Lind, Meda and Lisa Pasko. 2013. *The Female Offender: Girls, Women, and Crime*. 3rd ed. Thousand Oaks, CA: Sage.

Chesney-Lind, Meda and Randall G. Shelden. 2014. *Girls, Delinquency, and Juvenile Justice*. 4th ed. Hoboken, NJ: Wiley-Blackwell.

Federal Bureau of Investigation (FBI). 2012–2016. *Crime in the United States, 2011–2015: Uniform Crime Reports*. Washington, DC: U.S. Department of Justice.

Feld, Barry C. 1999. *Bad Kids: Race and the Transformation of the Juvenile Court*. New York: Oxford University Press.

Feld, Barry C. 2013. "Real Interrogation: What Actually Happens When Cops Question Kids." *Law & Society Review* 47:1–36.

Ferdico, John N. 1993. *Criminal Procedure for the Criminal Justice Professional*. 5th ed. St. Paul, MN: West.

Gaines, Larry K. 2003. "Police Responses to Delinquency." Pp. 286–290 in *Encyclopedia of Juvenile Justice*, edited by M. D. McShane and F. P. Williams. Thousand Oaks, CA: Sage.

Gavazzi, Stephen M., Courtney M. Yarcheck, and Meda Chesney-Lind. 2006. "Global Risk Indicators and the Role of Gender in a Juvenile Detention Sample." *Criminal Justice and Behavior* 33:597–612.

Goldstein, Herman. 1990. *Problem-Oriented Policing*. New York: McGraw-Hill.

Heimer, Karen, Janet L. Lauritsen, and James P. Lynch. 2009. "The National Crime Victimization Survey and Gender Gap in Offending: Redux." *Criminology* 47:427–438.

Hemmens, Craig, Benjamin Steiner, and David Mueller. 2004. *Significant Cases in Juvenile Justice*. Los Angeles: Roxbury.

Hickman, Matthew J. and Brian A. Reaves. 2001. "Community Policing in Local Police Departments, 1997 and 1999." *Special Report*. Washington, DC: Bureau of Justice Statistics.

Hindelang, Michael J., Travis Hirschi, and Joseph G. Weis. 1981. *Measuring Delinquency*. Beverly Hills: Sage.

Horowitz, Ruth and Anne E. Pottieger. 1991. "Gender Bias in Juvenile Justice Handling of Seriously Crime-Involved Youths." *Journal of Research in Crime and Delinquency* 28:75–100.

International Association of Chiefs of Police. 2015.*The Effects of Adolescent Development on Policing*. Office of Justice Programs, U.S. Department of Justice. Retrieved March 31, 2016 (http://theiacp.org/Portals/0/documents/pdfs/IACPBriefEffectsofAdolescentDevelopmentPolicing.pdf).

Krisberg, Barry and James Austin (eds.). 1978. *The Children of Ishmael: Critical Perspective on Juvenile Justice*. Palo Alto, CA: Mayfield.

Lauritsen, Janet L., Karen Heimer, and James P. Lynch. 2009. "Trends in the Gender Gap in Violent Offending: New Evidence from the National Crime Victimization Survey." *Criminology* 47:361–399.

Lundman, Richard J., Richard E. Sykes, and John P. Clark. 1978. "Police Control of Juveniles: A Replication." *Journal of Research in Crime and Delinquency* 15:74–91.

MacDonald, John M. and Meda Chesney-Lind. 2001. "Gender Bias and Juvenile Justice Revisited: A Multiyear Analysis." *Crime and Delinquency* 47:173–195.

Morash, Merry. 1984. "Establishment of a Juvenile Record: The Influence of Individual and Peer Group Characteristics." *Criminology* 22:97–112.

Na, Chongmin and Denise C. Gottfredson. 2013. "Police Officers in Schools: Effects on School Crime and the Processing of Offending Behaviors." *Justice Quarterly* 30:619–650.

National Research Council. 2013. *Reforming Juvenile Justice: A Developmental Approach*. Washington, DC: The National Academies Press.

Ousey, Graham C. and Matthew R. Lee. 2008. "Racial Disparity in Formal Social Control: An Investigation of Alternative Explanations of Arrest Rate Inequality." *Journal of Research in Crime and Delinquency* 45:322–355.

Piliavin, Irving and Scott Briar. 1964. "Police Encounters with Juveniles." *American Journal of Sociology* 70:206–214.

Platt, Anthony. 1977. *The Child Savers: The Invention of Delinquency*. 2nd ed. Chicago: University of Chicago Press.

Puzzanchera, Charles. 2014. "Juvenile Arrests 2011." *Juvenile Offenders and Victims National Report Series*. Washington, DC: Office of Juvenile Justice and Delinquency Prevention.

Sampson, Robert J. 1986. "Effects of Socioeconomic Context of Official Reaction to Juvenile Delinquency." *American Sociological Review* 51:876–885.

Schwartz, Jennifer, Darrell Steffensmeier, Hua Zhong, and Jeff Ackerman. 2009. "Trends in the Gender Gap in Violence: Reevaluating NCVS and Other Evidence." *Criminology* 47:401–425.

Sickmund, Melissa and Charles Puzzanchera (eds.). 2014. *Juvenile Offenders and Victims: 2014 National Report*. Pittsburgh, PA: National Center for Juvenile Justice.

Slocum, Lee Ann, Stephanie Ann Wiley, and Finn-Aage Esbensen. 2016. "The Importance of Being Satisfied: A Longitudinal Exploration of Police Contact, Procedural Injustice, and Subsequent Delinquency." *Criminal Justice and Behavior* 43:7–26.

Steffensmeier, Darrell, Jennifer Schwartz, Hua Zhong, and Jeff Ackerman. 2005. "An Assessment of Recent Trends in Girls' Violence Using Diverse Longitudinal Sources: Is the Gender Gap Closing?" *Criminology* 43:355–405.

Steffensmeier, Darrell, Hua Zhong, Jeff Ackerman, Jennifer Schwartz, and Suzanne Agha. 2006. "Gender Gap Trends for Violent Crimes, 1980–2003." *Feminist Criminology* 1:72–98.

Teilmann, Katherine S. and Pierre H. Landry, Jr. 1981. "Gender Bias in Juvenile Justice." *Journal of Research in Crime and Delinquency* 18:47–80.

University at Albany, Hindelang Criminal Justice Research Center. 2013. *Sourcebook of Criminal Justice Statistics*. Table 4.26.2011. Retrieved November 28, 2017 (www.albany.edu/sourcebook/pdf/t4262011.pdf).

Walker, Samuel and Charles M. Katz. 2005. *Police in America: An Introduction*. 5th ed. Boston: McGraw-Hill.

Wolcott, David B. 2005. *Cops and Kids: Policing Juvenile Delinquency in Urban America, 1890–1940*. Columbus, OH: Ohio State University Press.

Zahn, Margaret A., Susan Brumbaugh, Darrell Steffensmeier, Barry C. Feld, Merry Morash, Meda Chesney-Lind, Jody Miller, Allison Ann Payne, Denise C. Gottfredson, and Candace Kruttschnitt, Girls Study Group. 2008. "Violence by Teenage Girls: Trends and Context." *Understanding and Responding to Girls' Delinquency*. Washington, DC: Office of Juvenile Justice and Delinquency Prevention.

Chapter 8

PRELIMINARY PROCEDURES OF JUVENILE COURTS: DETENTION, TRANSFER TO CRIMINAL COURT, AND INTAKE

CHAPTER TOPICS

- **Juvenile detention**
- **Transfer to criminal court**
- **Intake**

CHAPTER LEARNING OBJECTIVES

After completing this chapter, students should be able to:

- Characterize the use of detention in terms of extent, trends, and demographic characteristics of the youth who are detained.
- Describe the reform efforts of the Juvenile Detention Alternatives Initiative (JDAI).
- Identify the three main mechanisms for transferring juvenile offenders to adult criminal courts.
- Describe the extent to which transfer to criminal courts is used and trends in the use of transfer.
- Explain how juvenile cases that are transferred to criminal courts are handled, compared to cases that remain in juvenile courts and cases of adult offenders.
- Identify legal and extralegal factors that influence the decision to transfer a juvenile to criminal court.
- Characterize the delinquency caseloads of juvenile courts in terms of age, gender, and race.
- Describe the intake process, including the key determinations, common procedures, and major options.
- Identify legal and extralegal factors that influence the intake decision.

CHAPTER CONTENTS

CASE IN POINT

INTAKE SCREENING OF A STATUS OFFENDER

At their wits' end, Billy's mother and step-father came into the Court Services office late Friday afternoon. Billy never showed up at school that day and he did not come home after school. They quickly added that he had not been listening to them or obeying them. "What should we do?" The receptionist ushered the upset parents into the office of the probation officer (PO) who was scheduled to be on-call that weekend. The PO gathered more information, learning that Billy had been skipping school, staying out late, and associating with kids who were "in trouble." The parents also said that Billy was easily agitated at home—he argued and fought with his younger brother and sister for little or no reason. The PO instructed the parents to report Billy as a runaway to the local police and to call the police and the PO when Billy returned home. The PO also had the parents sign a "complaint" that alleged Billy was a "youth in need of intervention." The state statute defined such a status offender as a youth who "exhibit[s] behavior, including running away from home or habitual truancy, beyond the control of the youth's parents . . . despite the attempt of the youth's parents . . . to exert all reasonable efforts to mediate, resolve, or control the youth's behavior" (Montana Code Annotated 41-5-103-5).

Late that evening, Billy came home offering no explanation of where he had been or what he had been doing. As instructed, the parents called the police and an officer responded, issuing Billy a ticket for runaway. They also called the PO, who came to the home and engaged in crisis counseling with the parents and youth. Threatening detention, the PO was able to solicit Billy's cooperation, and together with the parents, they developed a short-term intervention plan, with the understanding that Billy would stay home over the weekend.

Based on the complaint filed by the parents, the PO scheduled an "intake conference" at the Court Services office for the following Monday. At the conference, the PO read the complaint aloud and explained the different processes that cases can follow in the juvenile court. The PO offered the option to deal with the complaint informally, without Billy having to go before a juvenile court judge. This option involved a "consent adjustment without petition," which is a mutually agreed upon intervention plan to deal with the problem behavior(s) that prompted the referral to juvenile court. The consent adjustment is based on an admission of the allegations by the youth and results in an "informal disposition," which must be approved by the juvenile court judge. Through the consent adjustment, Billy was placed on informal probation and the parents agreed to participate in a program promoting effective parenting. The informal probation involved rules that were specified in the consent adjustment and supervision by the PO.

Preliminary procedures of juvenile courts involve three main determinations: detention, transfer to adult court, and intake screening of referred cases. Just as police encounters with juveniles involve much discretion and diversion, so too do the preliminary procedures of juvenile courts. It is often said that juvenile courts would collapse from the sheer number of cases referred by the police if such discretion and diversion did not exist. Consequently, juvenile courts rely heavily on discretion and diversion, as many cases are diverted or handled informally. Despite these actions, juvenile courts across the United States handled an estimated 1.06 million delinquency cases and 109,000 petitioned status offense cases in 2013 (Hockenberry and Puzzanchera 2015:6, 66).

This chapter examines these three key preliminary procedures: detention, transfer to adult court, and intake screening. Juvenile detention has been an on-going focal point of juvenile justice reform during the past half century. As discussed in Chapter 2, another prevalent area of juvenile justice reform addresses the original jurisdiction of juvenile courts and their rehabilitative focus. Virtually all states have changed their statutory laws to authorize and facilitate transfer of juvenile cases to adult courts, especially for serious and repetitive offenders that may be outside the scope of the rehabilitative emphasis of juvenile courts. Intake involves screening cases that are referred to juvenile courts in order to determine the most appropriate way to handle each case—formally, informally, or by dismissal. Juvenile court intake is a discretionary decision which is usually the responsibility of the juvenile probation department. Cases are sometimes dismissed, but they often involve diversion to a community-based program, or are handled informally by the juvenile court through a mutual agreement with the youth, family, and probation department. Less common is formal processing of juvenile cases through petitioning and adjudication—the topic of the next chapter.

JUVENILE DETENTION

One of the most crucial decisions involved in the preliminary procedures of juvenile courts is whether to detain a youth pending court action. **Detention** is the short-term, secure confinement of a youth under court authority, pending court action, disposition, or placement. Less often, detention may also be used as a disposition or sentence of secure confinement for youth who have been adjudicated delinquent in juvenile court or convicted in adult court. In most states, the initial decision to detain a youth is made by a police officer, followed by a probation officer's authorization. Police officers are usually required to provide a written report that describes why the youth must be held in detention.

Continued detention requires court authorization through a judicial hearing within a statutorily specified period of time, often 24 hours. In cases involving detention, the detention hearing is the first official court action. These hearings are sometimes called "probable cause" hearings because, according to statutory law, the hearing must establish probable cause that the youth is a delinquent youth or status offender. The juvenile court judge must also decide whether the youth meets certain detention criteria that are specified in state statutory law; common criteria include: commission of a criminal offense, escape from a correctional facility, and/or violation of a court order of probation or parole. The court may also deem that secure confinement is necessary to protect the youth, other persons or property, or to ensure appearance at a pending court hearing. The detention hearing follows procedural rules, also set forth in statutory law. These due process rights usually include the right to be represented by counsel, the presence of a parent or guardian at the hearing, and the right against self-incrimination. Some, but not all states provide for the right to bail (Feld 2014).

The application of due process rights to preventive detention of juveniles was taken up in the U.S. Supreme Court case *Schall v. Martin* (1984).[1] In this case, Martin was arrested for first-degree robbery, second-degree assault, and criminal possession of a weapon. At issue was whether the statutory provisions for preventive detention provided adequate due process of law under the Fourteenth Amendment of the Constitution. The statutory provisions in question here were part of the New York Family Court Act, which allowed for preventive detention of juveniles charged with delinquent acts, pending completion of juvenile court adjudication. The Supreme Court ruled that the use of preventive detention was constitutional because the Family Court Act provided specific procedures that must be followed for a juvenile to be detained (Feld 2014; Hemmens, Steiner, and Mueller 2004).

The primary purpose of detention is to protect the community, ensure a youth's appearance at subsequent court hearings, secure the youth's own safety, or facilitate evaluation of the youth (Puzzanchera and Sickmund 2008). **Table 8.1** shows the status of youth held in detention centers in 2015, using the *Census of Juveniles in Residential Placement* (Sickmund et al. 2017). These data provide a one-day count of all youth in residential placement, including detention centers. Almost one-half (48 percent) of the youth in detention centers were being held before adjudication, almost 30 percent were awaiting disposition or placement, and 22 percent were in detention as a result of a juvenile court commitment or a criminal court conviction, with a sentence of detention.

Research reveals a number of factors that influence the likelihood of detention. Legal factors such as the number of prior offenses, age at first offense, and the number of prior adjudications have been shown to be important considerations when examining detention placements. Many studies also show that extralegal factors such as age, gender, race, family structure, community context, and mental health issues influence detention outcomes (Hockenberry and Puzzanchera 2017; Fix et al. 2016; Rodriguez 2007, 2010). The role that race plays in detention decisions is of central importance to the contemporary concern with *disproportionate minority contact.* Research evidence consistently reveals that minority youth are overrepresented in detention centers, and that these racial and ethnic differences persist even when legal and extralegal factors have been accounted for (Leiber 2013; Leiber and Boggess 2012; Davis and Sorensen 2012; Thomas, Moak, and Walker 2012; Rodriguez 2010).

TABLE 8.1 Status of youth held in detention centers, 2015

Adjudication status	Hearing status	Number	Percent
Preadjudication	Diversion	162	0.9%
Preadjudication	Awaiting transfer hearing	165	0.9
Preadjudication	Awaiting criminal court hearing	1,052	5.8
Preadjudication	Awaiting juvenile court adjudication	7,242	40.1
Post adjudication	Awaiting disposition	2,535	14.0
Post adjudication	Awaiting placement	2,816	15.6
Post adjudication	Committed, placed in detention	3,910	21.6
Post adjudication	Convicted in criminal court, placed in detention	62	0.3
Other/unknown		135	0.7
Total		18,079	100

Adapted from: Sickmund et al. (2017).

Detention: Extent, trends, and demographics

Most delinquency cases handled by juvenile courts do not involve detention. In 2014, 212,900 delinquency cases involved detention between referral and disposition. This number represents 22 percent of the delinquency cases processed by juvenile courts in 2014. The number of delinquency cases involving detention peaked in 2002 and then declined by 46 percent through 2014, reaching its lowest level since 1985. The decline in the number of delinquency cases involving detention occurred for all categories of delinquency cases: property, person, public order, and drug offenses. The detention reforms discussed below, especially the development of detention risk assessment instruments and the expansion of alternatives to secure preadjudication detention, have contributed to the reduced use of detention. Despite this decline, the proportion of delinquency cases that are detained has remained relatively constant since 1985—around 20 percent. The proportion of delinquency cases involving detention, however, shows variation across different offense categories: 33 percent of all person offenses involve detention, 29 percent of all public order offenses, 28 percent of all property offenses, and 9 percent of all drug offenses (Hockenberry and Puzzanchera 2017:34; Sickmund et al. 2017).

Males were more likely than females to be detained for all types of delinquency, and youth age 16 or older were more likely to be detained than youth age 15 or younger. With regard to race, black youth represented 36 percent of the overall delinquency caseload in 2014, but 42 percent of the detention caseload. This disparity was greatest for drug offense cases, where black youth accounted for 22 percent of cases involving drug offense violations, but 33 percent of drug offense cases resulting in detention (Hockenberry and Puzzanchera 2017:33–34). These data indicate that, although disproportionate minority contact at the point of detention has been clearly identified and documented for over 40 years, the problem persisted in cases processed in 2014.

Compared to delinquency cases, a much lower percentage of petitioned status offenses involved detention: 7 percent of petitioned status offense cases versus 22 percent of delinquency cases. The percentage of petitioned status offense cases that involve detention varies by type of offense, with 17 percent of the runaway cases, 9 percent of the ungovernability and liquor law cases, 7 percent of the curfew cases, and 5 percent of the truancy cases involving detention. Between 2005 and 2014, the number of petitioned status offenses that involved detention decreased by 50 percent (8,400 to 4,200 cases). When looking at the types of cases that make up the detained status offense cases, the largest portion involve truancy (33 percent), followed by liquor law violations (19 percent), runaway (14 percent), miscellaneous status offenses (13 percent), ungovernability (11 percent), and curfew violations (9 percent) (Hockenberry and Puzzanchera 2017:81).

Conditions of confinement

The secure confinement of juveniles in detention centers occurs almost always in public facilities (92 percent) that are operated by local sheriff's departments. Half (49 percent) of the detention centers hold 20 or fewer residents; whereas almost one-fifth (19 percent) are larger than 50 residents. Most detention facilities are physically secure, with controlled entry and fences or walls with razor wire. Operational security features in detention centers commonly include locking residents in their sleeping rooms to confine them, secure day rooms, and locked internal doors to secure specific areas. While almost all detention centers screen for suicide risk (98 percent) and educational needs (89 percent), only about one-third (38 percent) screen for mental health problems. About 9 out of 10 detention centers provide middle school and high school educational services. Onsite treatment services are usually limited in detention centers with short-term mental health services being the most common (Hockenberry, Wachter, and Sladky 2016; OJJDP 2016; Sedlak and McPherson 2010).

Research on the consequences of detention shows that detaining youth may not improve community safety, may negatively impact youth's ability to avoid future involvement with the juvenile justice system, and may expose youth to a larger community of rule violating peers. Detention also negatively impacts youths' current employment and future job prospects, disrupts educational continuity, and separates youth from their families (Feld 2014). Furthermore, as many as 70 percent of detained youth are arrested or returned to secure detention within one year of release (Holman and Ziedenberg 2006).

Detention reform

The Juvenile Justice and Delinquency Prevention (JJDP) Act of 1974 sought to provide federal assistance to states in dealing with juvenile delinquency. Of particular concern were problematic detention practices across the United States. In particular, the Act sought to: (1) remove status offenders from detention or secure confinement, (2) promote sight and sound separation of juveniles from adults while in detention, (3) remove juveniles from adult jail facilities, and (4) reduce the number of minorities in secure facilities—"disproportionate minority confinement." The Office of Juvenile Justice and Delinquency Prevention (OJJDP) provided technical assistance, consultation, and grant money to deal with these problematic detention practices (Sickmund and Puzzanchera 2014; Hsia, Bridges, and McHale 2004).

Evaluation research indicates that federal initiatives through OJJDP significantly changed state and local juvenile detention practices in each of the areas addressed in the JJDP Act:

(1) the number of status offenders held in secure detention or secure corrections was reduced substantially; (2) new and remodeled state and local detention facilities provided greater levels of sight and sound separation of juveniles from adults while in detention; (3) the number of juveniles held in adult jails declined considerably; and (4) the number of minorities held in secure detention facilities was reduced (Hsia et al. 2004; Pope, Lovell, and Hsia 2002). Despite notable progress, the problem of disproportionate minority confinement, indicating the existence of disparities and biases in juvenile justice processing, demands continued attention (Sickmund and Puzzanchera 2014; Pope et al. 2002).

At the forefront of detention reform is The Annie E. Casey Foundation's Juvenile Detention Alternatives Initiative (JDAI) that began in 1992. Through eight core strategies for detention reform, JDAI promotes changes to policies, practices, and programs in an effort to reduce reliance on secure detention and to reduce racial disparities and bias in the use of secure detention

JUVENILE JUSTICE POLICY AND PRACTICE: EIGHT CORE STRATEGIES OF THE JUVENILE DETENTION ALTERNATIVES INITIATIVE (JDAI)

1 **Collaboration:** A formal structure for collaboration across agencies and among key stakeholders in planning and policymaking will support shared understanding, well delineated roles and responsibilities, and mutual accountability. Without strong interconnectedness, mutual ownership and ongoing joint decision-making, initiatives such as JDAI may lose steam or end up, unintentionally or actively, subverted.

2 **Use of accurate, comprehensive data:** Use of data is required, both to diagnose a system's problems and proclivities, as well as to assess the impact of various reforms. Subjectivity, perceptions, anecdotes, and perceived limitations may rule a system and preclude agreement on key aspects of policy and practice unless hard facts are collected and analyzed by trusted sources.

3 **Use of objective admissions criteria and instruments:** Objective criteria and instruments must be developed to support decision-making at all points where choices to place youth in secure custody are made, rather than relying on subjective decisions.

4 **New or enhanced alternatives to detention:** Alternatives to detention must be put in place—ideally in, or very close to, the home community of affected youth and families. This way, opportunities for community-based placement, monitoring, reporting, and services provided to arrested youth and their families are significantly increased. Such alternatives to secure detention must be carefully targeted to serve youth who would otherwise be locked up.

5 **Case processing reforms:** Changes made to expedite case processing can greatly reduce lengths of stay for juveniles in custody, expand the availability of non-secure program slots, and ensure that interventions with youth are timely and appropriate.

6 **Careful management of "special" detention cases:** Youth in custody as a result of probation violations, writs, and warrants, or while awaiting placement, must have their cases reexamined to reduce placements of such youth in secure facilities.

7 **Deliberate commitment to reducing racial disparities:** It is critical to identify, understand, and eliminate any bias that may lead youth of color to receive more

severe sanctions as compared with white youth in similar circumstances. Inclusive, sustained leadership grounded in the use of data can catalyze changes in law enforcement, detention, judicial, and probation practices to guard against any unintended or institutional racial/ethnic disparities.

8 **Improving conditions of confinement:** To fully understand and address conditions of confinement, it is essential to employ routine monitoring and inspection of detention facilities by knowledgeable and reliable individuals. Such monitors should apply rigorous protocols and standards. Absent consistent scrutiny, conditions in secure facilities are not likely to improve and may deteriorate, even while the detention population declines.

Source: Coalition for Juvenile Justice (2008:6–7). See also Mendel (2014:8–9).

JUVENILE JUSTICE POLICY AND PRACTICE: MONTANA DETENTION RISK ASSESSMENT INSTRUMENT

The Montana Detention Risk Assessment Instrument (MDRAI) is intended to provide information about the safety and failure to appear risks for juveniles who have been issued a citation for a detainable offense. The MDRAI was developed for administration at the initial point of contact with law enforcement. It can be administered in the field by police officers or at intake by detention center staff or juvenile probation officers. In 2013, the MDRAI was automated so it can be completed entirely online. The scores are generated automatically when the current offense information is entered into the online system, which ensures systematic calculation of scores. There is a place for comments by the person administering the MDRAI and a set of justification boxes that must be selected whenever the actual decision to release, place in a detention alternative, or detain is different from the indicated decision based on the score that is generated. The MDRAI score is based on seven predictive factors:

1 Most serious offense alleged in the current referral.
2 Number of prior admissions of guilt for various types of offenses (felony, misdemeanor, and status offenses, and probation or parole violations).
3 Number of referrals pending adjudication.
4 History of failure to appear, runaways from home, or escape from secure custody or non-secure placement such as a group home or treatment facility.
5 Warrant history.
6 Aggravating factors, such as history of drug or alcohol problems, first offense before age 13, or multiple offenses alleged in the current referral.
7 Mitigating factors, such as no arrests in the past 12 months, stability in school or employment, or this offense being the juvenile's first law violation.

Adapted from: McKay et al. (2014).

(see "Juvenile justice policy and practice: Eight core strategies of the Juvenile Detention Alternatives Initiative"). The Annie E. Casey Foundation provides funds to nearly 300 local JDAI sites in 39 states and the District of Columbia (Annie Casey Foundation 2014). The JDAI emphasizes effective detention decisions by: (1) developing and using objective risk assessment instruments; (2) using screening teams for detention decisions; and (3) increasing community-based alternatives for detention, including shelter care, home detention (house arrest), electronic monitoring, and day reporting centers.

Detention risk assessment instruments have become an important element of evidence-based practice in detention reform efforts. These assessment tools use objective criteria to aide detention admission decisions. The application box entitled "Juvenile justice policy and practice: Montana Detention Risk Assessment Instrument" provides a description of a detention risk assessment that uses seven predictive factors as criteria for determining risk. Detention risk assessment instruments are evidence-based practice when they are validated through evaluation research, which shows that a particular instrument accurately predicts risk of reoffending prior to court appearance and failure to appear in court (Steinhart 2006).

TRANSFER TO CRIMINAL COURT

All states have enacted laws that allow juveniles to be transferred to adult criminal courts. Although these statutes vary from state to state, the basic idea is that certain types of offenses and offenders, especially violent ones, are beyond the scope of the juvenile court (Fagan and Zimring 2000). The transfer of juveniles to adult courts began in earnest in the mid-1980s as part of the "get-tough" response to serious juvenile offenders that de-emphasized rehabilitation and focused instead on accountability, punishment, and public safety.

Transfer provisions fall into three main categories: judicial waiver, concurrent jurisdiction, and statutory exclusion (Sickmund and Puzzanchera 2014; Griffin et al. 2011; Redding 2010). These statutory mechanisms allow juvenile court judges, prosecutors, and the state legislature to designate the types of offenders and offenses that are beyond the jurisdiction of the juvenile court.

Judicial waiver provides statutory authority for juvenile court judges to waive the court's original jurisdiction and transfer cases to adult criminal court. The decision to waive cases to adult court is typically at the discretion of the judge, although some states require waiver in certain types of cases (Griffin et al. 2011). In making waiver decisions, judges consider factors such as offense severity, public safety, juveniles' offense histories, juveniles' maturity levels, and the likelihood of rehabilitation in the juvenile justice system. Judicial waiver requires a transfer hearing, which provides some procedural due process protections, including effective assistance of counsel (Feld 2014). States may use terms other than judicial waiver, including certification, remand, or bind over for criminal prosecution.

Concurrent jurisdiction gives statutory authority to prosecutors to file certain types of offenses in either juvenile or adult court. Some state statutes, for example, allow prosecutors, at their discretion, to file felony offenses committed by 16 or 17 year-olds directly in adult criminal courts. About a dozen states have concurrent jurisdiction provisions (Feld 2014). Concurrent jurisdiction is sometimes referred to as direct file.

Under **statutory exclusion**, state statutes exclude certain juvenile offenders and offenses from juvenile court jurisdiction. These cases originate in criminal rather than juvenile court. State statutes providing for statutory exclusion usually set age and offense limits for excluded offenses. For example, a number of state statutes specify that violent felony offenses such as homicide, rape, and robbery, when committed by 16 or 17 year-olds, are automatically sent to adult criminal court. More than half of the states use statutory exclusion to remove certain offenses, typically serious crimes committed by older juveniles, from juvenile court jurisdiction (Feld 2014).

Although judicial waiver is the oldest transfer provision, almost all states have expanded their statutory provisions for transferring juvenile cases to adult court. In addition, nine states currently have an upper age boundary for juvenile court jurisdiction of 15 or 16, thereby limiting juvenile court authority and automatically sending 17-year-olds to adult court (Zang 2016). An estimated 137,000 adolescents are sent directly to adult court each year, based on lower ages of juvenile court jurisdiction (Sickmund and Puzzanchera 2014). These statutory law changes are intended to provide procedures whereby serious cases of juvenile crime may be dealt with in adult courts, rather than juvenile courts, in an effort to deter youthful offenders and to administer punishment, rather than rehabilitation. Although judicial waiver relies on individualized consideration of various factors in determining whether or not to transfer particular cases, newer forms of transfer, such as statutory exclusion and adjustment of age boundaries for juvenile court jurisdiction, emphasize the offense rather than individualized consideration of the offender (Steiner, Hemmens, and Bell 2006).

Transfer to criminal court: Extent, trends, and demographics

The most recent data available show that 45 states have judicial waiver provisions, 15 states have concurrent jurisdiction provisions, and 29 states have statutory exclusion provisions (Griffin et al. 2011). Though almost all states have expanded their statutory provisions for transferring juvenile cases to adult courts, the number of juvenile cases transferred annually is relatively small. The total number of juveniles transferred is unknown because data are collected nationally only on transfers that occur by judicial waiver. But it is estimated that approximately 100,000 juvenile offenders are transferred annually to adult criminal courts (Redding 2016). This number is in addition to the estimated 137,000 juveniles sent to adult courts based on the upper age boundaries for juvenile court jurisdiction. The OJJDP estimates that nationwide approximately 4,000 juvenile offenders were transferred by judicial waiver in 2013; this represents approximately 1 in 250 referred delinquency cases (Furdella and Puzzanchera 2015). In 2013, juvenile courts transferred by judicial waiver less than 1 percent of all petitioned delinquency cases (Hockenberry and Puzzanchera 2015). Clearly, most juvenile cases transferred to adult courts today are transferred by mechanisms other than judicial waiver (Griffin et al. 2011).

The number of juveniles transferred annually has decreased significantly from the estimated 200,000 per year during the 1990s (Woolard et al. 2005). When focusing only on cases that are judicially waived to adult court, the number of juvenile cases transferred peaked in 1994 with 13,600 cases. This is more than double the number of cases judicially waived in 1985. This increase was followed by a decline to 5,400 cases judicially waived in 2011 and the estimated 4,000 cases judicially waived in 2013 (Furdella and Puzzanchera 2015; Hockenberry and Puzzanchera 2014). This declining trend in juvenile transfers mimics the trend in juvenile crime.

Juvenile court data show that from 1985 to 1992, the largest number of judicially waived cases involved property offenses. Since 1992, the largest number of judicially waived cases have involved person offenses. **Figure 8.1** shows that, in 2013, approximately 2,000 person offenses, 1,200 property offenses, 500 drug offenses, and fewer than 500 public order offenses were judicially waived to adult criminal courts (Hockenberry and Puzzanchera 2015:38).

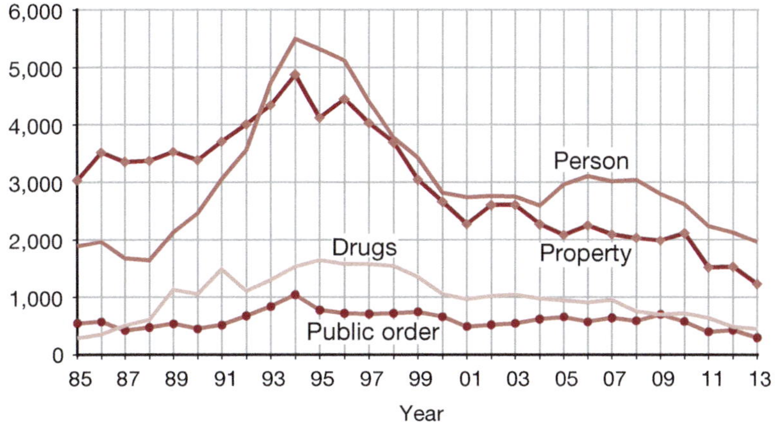

FIGURE 8.1 *Cases judicially waived to criminal court, 1985–2013.*

Source: Hockenberry and Puzzanchera (2015:38). Used with permission of the National Center for Juvenile Justice.

In recent years, as juvenile justice policy has begun to shift away from solely punitive responses, several states have revised their juvenile codes to decrease the number of juveniles tried and sentenced in adult courts and to provide more effective and evidence-based responses to juvenile offending (Redding 2015, 2016). Between 2011 and 2015, at least 14 states limited their criteria for transferring juvenile offenders or placed greater emphasis on the developmental maturity of juveniles as a rationale for diminishing transfers (MacArthur Foundation 2015). Several states have created more options for juvenile courts to use, in order to reduce transfers to adult courts. In addition, some states have reversed the trend to lower the maximum age of juvenile court jurisdiction that began in the 1990s and have raised the age boundary once again to 17. This prevents the automatic transfer of 16 and 17-year-old offenders to adult courts.

In exploring the demographic characteristics of transferred juveniles, we focus on those sent to adult courts through judicial waiver, as this is the only form of transfer for which demographic data are available. Judicial waiver is more common for older juveniles than for younger juveniles, for males than for females, and for black and American Indian youth than for white and Asian youth. In 2013, 1.2 percent of all petitioned delinquency cases involving juveniles age 16 or older were waived to adult court, while only 0.1 percent of cases involving juveniles age 15 or younger were waived. In 2013, 0.8 percent of petitioned delinquency cases involving males were waived, compared to 0.2 percent of cases involving females. Finally, in 2013, 0.8 percent of petitioned delinquency cases involving black juveniles and 0.8 percent of cases involving American Indian juveniles were waived to adult court, compared to 0.6 percent of cases involving white juveniles and 0.3 percent of cases involving Asian youth (Hockenberry and Puzzanchera 2015:40).

Research on disproportionate minority contact has examined racial disparities in the likelihood of cases being transferred to adult criminal courts and has found evidence of minority over-representation. African-American youth comprise approximately 30 percent of youth arrested in the U.S., but 62 percent of youth prosecuted in adult courts (Jones 2016). Recent research finds that race, ethnicity, and gender had substantial effects on transfer decisions, even after legally relevant factors, such as severity of the offense and the number or prior petitions in juvenile court, were taken into consideration. Black and Hispanic youth were approximately three times more likely than white youth to be transferred to adult court, and males were almost seven times more likely than females to be transferred (Brown and Sorensen 2013; see also Jones 2016; Cheesman, Waters, and Hurst 2010).

Handling of transferred cases in criminal court

Before the "get-tough" initiatives of the 1990s, most juveniles transferred to criminal court were transferred for property offenses, and waived offenders tended to be treated leniently, compared to adult offenders. This changed in the 1990s, when transfer policies began to target violent juvenile offenders. Juveniles transferred to criminal court and convicted of violent crimes are more likely to be incarcerated, compared to juveniles who were not transferred, and they receive longer sentences (Kupchik 2006; Kupchik, Fagan, and Liberman 2003).

Juveniles convicted in adult criminal courts are also sometimes sentenced more harshly than young adults convicted of similar crimes (Feld and Bishop 2014; Jordan 2014; Kurlychek and Johnson 2004, 2010). For example, youth convicted of murder are more likely than adults convicted of murder to receive life-without-parole sentences (Feld 2008). Kurlychek and Johnson (2010) found that juveniles were sentenced more harshly than adults particularly for drug offenses, for which juveniles received sentences that were more than six times more severe than those imposed on comparable adult offenders. Research shows that judges are not only more likely to incarcerate transferred juveniles, compared to young adult offenders, but also more likely to deny bail for transferred juveniles than for adults (Steiner 2009). Summarizing these research findings, Feld and Bishop (2014:830) write, "In short, judges treat youthfulness as an aggravating factor and attach a penalty to juvenile status, quite apart from the offense, prior record, and other legally relevant variables."

Kupchik (2006) argues that judges and other courtroom actors in adult courts often advocate a more rehabilitative approach to juvenile offenders, but they have been constrained by the sentencing options available in criminal courts. Many states have now created mechanisms to give criminal court judges the flexibility to review cases and make individualized decisions regarding juvenile offenders. In 24 states, criminal court judges are able to "reverse waive" or "transfer back" to juvenile court cases filed in criminal court as a result of mandatory judicial waiver, statutory exclusion or prosecutors' direct file decisions. **Reverse waiver** provisions allow juveniles whose cases are being handled in adult courts to petition to have their cases heard instead in juvenile courts, for either adjudication or disposition. In 17 states, **criminal blended sentencing** provisions give criminal court judges the option to sentence juveniles convicted in adult court as delinquents in the juvenile justice system (Sickmund and Puzzanchera 2014). These provisions often require that convicted juveniles receive a suspended criminal court sentence, in addition to the juvenile court disposition (Griffin et al. 2011). More than half of the jurisdictions that have mandatory judicial waiver, statutory exclusion or concurrent jurisdiction provisions use reverse waivers and/or criminal blended sentencing to provide more individualized responses to juvenile offenders (Feld 2014).

Criminal blended sentencing is distinct from **juvenile blended sentencing**, which exists in 14 states. In its most common form, juvenile blended sentencing allows youth to be tried in juvenile court and given a juvenile disposition, but also a suspended criminal sentence (Griffin et al. 2011). Juveniles sentenced in this way remain in the juvenile correctional system on a conditional basis. If they successfully complete the juvenile disposition and do not commit any

EXPANDING IDEAS: TYPES OF BLENDED SENTENCES

Type	Description
Juvenile – exclusive blend	A juvenile court judge imposes *either* a juvenile (delinquency) or an adult (criminal) sanction and makes that sanction effective immediately.
Juvenile – inclusive blend	A juvenile court judge imposes *both* juvenile and adult sanctions, typically suspending the adult sanction and imposing it only in the event of a subsequent violation.
Juvenile – contiguous	A juvenile court judge imposes a sanction that begins in the juvenile system but lasts beyond the maximum age of extended juvenile court jurisdiction. When extended juvenile court jurisdiction ends, the juvenile court judge determines whether the offender is moved to the adult correctional system to serve the remainder of the sentence.
Criminal – exclusive blend	A criminal court judge imposes *either* a juvenile or an adult sanction and makes that sanction effective immediately.
Criminal – inclusive blend	A criminal court judge imposes *both* juvenile and adult sanctions, typically suspending the adult sanction and imposing it only in the event of a subsequent violation.

Source: Cheesman (2011:114).

new offenses, the adult criminal sentence is not imposed. But if they do not cooperate or fail to complete the juvenile disposition, the criminal sanction is imposed. "Blended sentencing laws meld the authority of juvenile with criminal courts, provide longer sentences than juvenile courts otherwise could impose, or increase the rehabilitative options available to criminal courts" (Feld 2014:253). "Expanding ideas: Types of blended sentences" explains each of the specific types of blended sentences.

In 34 states, "once an adult, always an adult" laws require that once a child has been prosecuted in adult criminal courts, he or she must be prosecuted in adult courts for all subsequent juvenile offenses, typically regardless of the severity of those offenses (Griffin et al. 2011). Most states with this type of legislation require that the original prosecution in adult court must have resulted in a conviction.

Deterrent effects of transfer to criminal court?

Transfer provisions were created with the expectation that transferring serious juvenile offenders to the adult criminal court would deter juvenile crime. Although the research is not entirely conclusive, findings typically indicate that transferring juvenile offenders does not prevent serious juvenile crime. In fact, most studies show that youth who are transferred to and convicted in adult criminal courts re-offend at higher rates than youth who remain in the juvenile justice system (Johnson, Lanza-Kaduce, and Woolard 2011; Redding 2010; McGowan et al. 2007; Kupchik 2006; Lanza-Kaduce et al. 2005; Myers 2005; Fagan, Kupchik, and Liberman 2003; Sickmund 2003).

The lack of a deterrent effect of transfer to criminal court appears to apply to both specific and general deterrence, although the research on general deterrence is somewhat inconsistent (Redding 2010; McGowan et al. 2007). Research on *specific* deterrence considers whether transferring juvenile offenders to criminal court decreases the likelihood that they will re-offend, while research on *general* deterrence considers whether transferring juvenile offenders prevents offending in the general juvenile population.

In 2007, the Task Force on Community Preventive Services published a systematic review of research that compared recidivism rates of violent offending for youth transferred to criminal courts and youth who remained in juvenile courts (McGowan et al. 2007). The studies examined in this review were conducted using different methodologies, in different jurisdictions, at different times, and focusing on different transfer mechanisms. Yet, they reached a similar conclusion that transfer to criminal courts increases recidivism, particularly for violent crime (see also Redding 2010). Research by Jeffrey Fagan and his colleagues indicates that transfer to criminal courts increases recidivism not only for violent crime, but also for felony property crime and weapons offenses (Fagan et al. 2003).

A recent meta-analysis by Steven Zane and his colleagues suggests the need for a more nuanced examination of transfer provisions and specific deterrence (Zane, Welsh, and Mears 2016). Their sophisticated review of prior research found no significant overall effect of juvenile transfer on recidivism. They argue that the effects of transfer may depend on type of transfer, characteristics of transferred youth, and the punishments and interventions used in both juvenile and adult courts (Zane et al. 2016; see also Kurlychek 2016; Loughran et al. 2010; Steiner et al. 2006; Steiner and Wright 2006). The end-of-chapter reading by Redding (2010) considers whether juvenile transfer laws are an effective deterrent to delinquency.

Other effects of transfer to criminal court

Compared to fairly extensive research on deterrence and recidivism, relatively little research explores other effects of transferring juveniles to criminal court, though these effects are substantial. Being convicted of a serious offense in criminal court often results in a sentence of incarceration, and transferred juveniles typically serve those sentences in adult prisons or jails. This environment has several negative consequences for juvenile offenders, including physical and sexual victimization, the disruption of identity formation and of skill and competency development, and interruption in the accumulation of "human and social capital" during adolescence (Mulvey and Schubert 2012). Human and social capital refers to individuals' skills and relationships that can open up new opportunities or enable people to deal with hardships they face. In adolescence, the development of human and social capital has to do primarily with skills and networking that allow entry into the workforce and the development of supportive social networks independent of parents.

Physical and sexual violence is a harsh reality of prison life, and age is one of the most consistent predictors of victimization in prison (MacKenzie 1987). Adolescents placed in adult facilities are at greater risk than incarcerated adults of violent victimization (Beck and Harrison 2008; Lane et al. 2002). In addition, juveniles incarcerated in adult facilities are unable to accomplish normal developmental tasks associated with adolescence such as identity formation because they lack supportive adults and healthy relationships with peers (Scott and Steinberg 2008; Lane et al. 2002). Prison life also diminishes opportunities to take greater control of decision-making and to acquire various skills and competencies—processes that are part of normal adolescent development (Mulvey and Schubert 2012). In addition, prison life removes adolescents from the contexts of family, school, and neighborhoods, where they typically develop human and social capital. The loss of opportunities to develop skills, competencies, and human and social capital has serious consequences for incarcerated adolescents when they eventually return to the community and try to accomplish tasks such as finding employment and establishing positive relationships. Thus, although an adolescent and an adult might receive the same sentence (e.g., five years in prison), adolescents may experience more significant consequences of this sentence, given its negative impacts on the developmental process.

A developmental view of transfer to criminal court

In light of empirical evidence regarding adolescent development, some researchers have questioned the appropriateness of transferring juveniles to adult courts. Compared to adults, adolescents are less capable of considering fully the consequences of their actions and less knowledgeable about legal processes. They also have different educational and programming needs than adult offenders do. Yet, research suggests that, in making decisions about juvenile transfers, courts tend to focus more on public safety, potential deterrence, and retribution than on juveniles' developmental maturity and competence to enter the adult criminal justice system (Sellers and Arrigo 2009).

Based on the findings of developmental research, some scholars and policy advocates have argued that the process of transferring juvenile offenders to adult courts must be individualized and involve judges' careful consideration of juveniles' competence. They argue that transfer should not be mandated by law (as in statutory exclusion) or at the discretion of the prosecutor (as in concurrent jurisdiction) (MacArthur Foundation 2015; Feld and Bishop 2014; Sellers and Arrigo 2009). The MacArthur Foundation has also called for transfer of juveniles to be reserved for youth age 16 and over.

INTAKE

The juvenile court process is initiated by a **referral** to the juvenile court. Referrals are written documents that request court consideration of a particular juvenile matter. Referrals take various forms: Police make referrals through incident reports, citations, and tickets; and parents, schools, and victims sign complaints. Over 80 percent of all delinquency referrals nationwide come from the police, almost always from local law enforcement (Hockenberry and Puzzanchera 2017:33). The remaining referrals come from probation officers, parents, schools, and victims. Compared to referrals of delinquency cases, police refer a smaller percentage of the petitioned status offense cases dealt with by juvenile courts. For example, in 2014, 53 percent of the runaway cases, 42 percent of the juvenile courts' truancy cases, and 28 percent of the ungovernability cases were referred by the police (Hockenberry and Puzzanchera 2017:80). Status offense cases are more commonly referred by other entities such as schools, social welfare agencies, and relatives.

Delinquency cases in juvenile courts: Extent, trends, and demographics

Table 8.2 shows that in 2014 an estimated 974,900 delinquency cases were handled by juvenile courts across the United States. This represents a 52 percent decline in juvenile court caseloads from the peak year in 1997. Property offenses constituted the largest percentage of delinquency cases in 2014 at 34 percent, person offenses and public order offenses comprised 27 percent and 26 percent of the juvenile court caseload, and drug violations comprised 13 percent. When differences in the size of the juvenile population are taken into consideration by calculating an annual case rate per 1,000 juveniles, the resulting case rates declined by 41 percent from 2005 through 2014. This 10-year analysis showed declines in case rates for all categories of offenses—45 percent for property offenses, 40 percent for public order offenses, 39 percent for person offenses, and 28 percent for drug law violations (Hockenberry and Puzzanchera 2017:6–8).

Although 72 percent of all delinquency cases handled by juvenile courts in 2014 involved males, caseloads have grown at a faster rate for females than for males. During the period of greatest growth in juvenile court caseloads, 1985–1997, the female caseload grew by 99 percent, compared to a 53 percent increase for males (Hockenberry and Puzzanchera 2015:12). Also noteworthy is that less than half (43 percent) of all delinquency cases in juvenile courts involved white youth, while about one-third (36 percent) involved black youth and almost one-fifth (18 percent) involved Hispanic youth. However, a disproportionate number of delinquency cases involved black and Hispanic youth, given their proportion of the juvenile population (15 percent and 23 percent, respectively). American Indian (2 percent) and Asian (1 percent) youth constituted a very small portion of the delinquency cases in juvenile courts. In the ten-year period from 2005–2014, the racial makeup of delinquency cases in juvenile courts showed a decrease for white youth, but an increase for black and Hispanic youth (Hockenberry and

TABLE 8.2 Juvenile court delinquency caseload, 2014

Most serious offense	Number of cases	Percent change, ten years 2005–2014	Percent of total delinquency cases
Total	974,900	–42	100
Person offenses	262,800	–40	27
Property offenses	333,500	–46	34
Drug law violations	128,900	–30	13
Public order offenses	249,700	–44	26

Person offenses: homicide, rape, robbery, aggravated assault, simple assault, other violent sex offenses, other person offenses.
Property offenses: burglary, larceny-theft, motor vehicle theft, arson, vandalism, trespassing, stolen property, other property offenses.
Drug law violations: a broad offense category, including unlawful sale, purchase, cultivation, transportation, or use of controlled or prohibited drug.
Public order offenses: obstruction of justice, disorderly conduct, weapons offenses, liquor law violation, nonviolent sex offenses, other public order offenses.

Source: Hockenberry and Puzzanchera (2017:6, 7, 100–102).

Puzzanchera 2017:21). Delinquency case rates increase progressively with the referral age of the youth: 13-year-olds have a case rate of 20.9 per 1,000 juveniles, while17-year-olds have a case rate of 67.9 per 1,000 juveniles (Hockenberry and Puzzanchera 2017:10).

Intake screening of cases referred to juvenile courts

Cases referred to the juvenile court are screened to determine the most appropriate way to handle each case—formally, informally, or by dismissal. Juvenile court **intake** is a discretionary decision, normally the responsibility of the juvenile probation department and, less typically, the prosecutor's office. Some probation departments have intake officers who specialize in the intake decision and process.

Intake **screening** typically involves three key legal determinations. The first is a consideration of probable cause: Are there legally admissible facts and information to warrant formal processing of the case in juvenile court? Second, do the facts of the case allow the juvenile court to have jurisdiction? This is especially important because contemporary juvenile courts do not always have original jurisdiction in juvenile matters. Recall that two recent trends limit the original jurisdiction of some juvenile courts: statutory exclusion of certain offenses and offenders, and concurrent jurisdiction, which allows prosecutors discretion in filing certain types of cases in either juvenile or criminal court. Third, is formal processing by the juvenile court in the best interests of the child? Although this determination was the overarching concern of the traditional juvenile court, the contemporary emphasis on offender accountability and public safety has introduced another question: Is formal processing by the juvenile court in the best interests of the community?

Four screening options are most common at intake: (1) case dismissal; (2) diversion for non-judicial handling, usually through community-based services; (3) informal processing by the probation department; and (4) formal processing by the juvenile court, called *adjudication.*

In some jurisdictions, intake screening is based on a **preliminary inquiry** (or preliminary investigation), conducted by a probation officer under authority of statutory law. The application box entitled "Juvenile justice law: Statutorily prescribed content of the preliminary inquiry" provides an example from the *Indiana Code 2015* of this statutory law. A preliminary inquiry collects pertinent information about the alleged offense and the youth, and it sometimes involves a "youth assessment" when it includes evaluation of chemical dependency, educational achievement, and mental health and family service needs. Thus, the preliminary inquiry provides information relevant for determining probable cause, juvenile court jurisdiction, and the "best interests" of the youth and community (Griffin and Torbet 2002).

The intake screening decision commonly calls for an **intake conference**—an informal meeting of the youth, parents, and probation/intake officer (Feld 2014; see also Griffin and Torbet 2002). The youth and his or her parents are summoned to the meeting by an official letter or citation and the meeting typically occurs in the office of the probation officer or a probation department conference room. Due process rights have not been extended to the intake conference because the procedures are preliminary to formal adjudication and they are intended to lead to informal resolution of the alleged offense (Feld 2014). The intake process is explained to the youth and parents, and the allegations are discussed. The youth is usually given an opportunity to admit the allegations, with the understanding that they can be resolved informally, without formal petitioning into the juvenile court. These informal resolutions usually involve a **consent adjustment without petition**—a voluntary agreement between the youth and his or her parents

JUVENILE JUSTICE LAW: STATUTORILY PRESCRIBED CONTENT OF THE PRELIMINARY INQUIRY

IC 31-37-8-2

Contents of preliminary inquiry

Sec. 2. A preliminary inquiry is an informal investigation into the facts and circumstances reported to the court. Whenever practicable, the preliminary inquiry should include the following information:

(1) The child's background.

(2) The child's current status.

(3) The child's school performance.

(4) If the child has been detained:

(A) efforts made to prevent removal of the child from the child's home, including the identification of any emergency situation that prevented reasonable efforts to avoid removal;

(B) whether it is in the best interests of the child to be removed from the home environment; and

(C) whether remaining in the home would be contrary to the health and welfare of the child.

(5) The results of a dual status screening tool to determine whether the child is a dual status child, as described in IC 31-41-1-2.

Source: Indiana Code 2015. 31-37-8-2.

that is approved by a juvenile court judge. The written agreement is legally authorized in state statutory law and it normally includes a wide variety of options for **informal disposition** that are aimed at rehabilitation, such as referral to another agency for services (e.g., chemical dependency treatment, family therapy, academic tutoring, restorative justice), community service, restitution, and informal probation through the probation department. When informal probation is a part of the consent adjustment, the agreement includes rules or conditions that the youth is expected to follow, under supervision by a probation officer. Informal dispositions are diversionary in scope and purpose, seeking to keep the youth from the formal processes of adjudication in juvenile court. "Juvenile justice law: Statutory authority for informal disposition at intake" provides the abridged statutory sections from the Montana Youth Court Act that authorizes informal disposition. In many juvenile courts, these options for informal disposition represent the most common mechanism by which referred cases are handled.

Figure 8.2 shows that in 2014, 44 percent of all delinquency cases in juvenile courts were *not* petitioned. Of these delinquency cases, 17 percent (or 40 percent of the "not petitioned" cases) were dismissed at intake, "generally for lack of legal sufficiency" (Furdella and Puzzanchera 2015:3). Twenty-seven percent of all delinquency cases (or 61 percent of the "not petitioned" cases) were handled informally at intake using some informal disposition, most often informal probation (Hockenberry and Puzzanchera 2017).

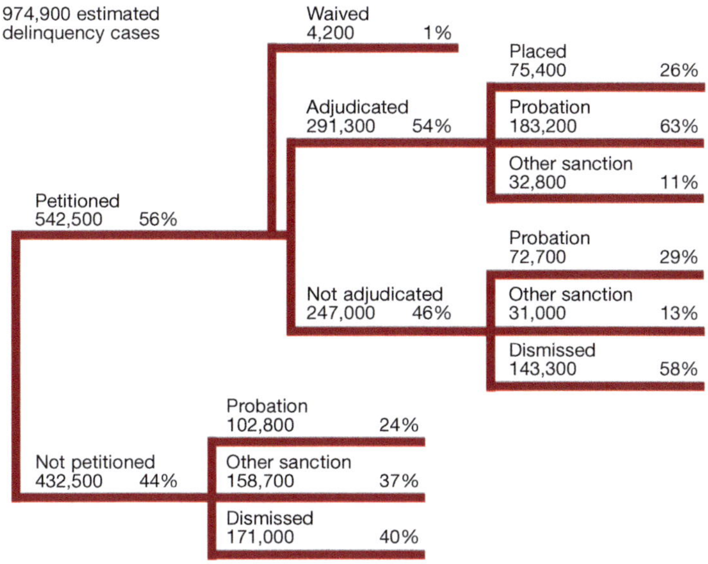

FIGURE 8.2 *Juvenile court processing of delinquency cases, 2014. While a majority of cases (56%) referred to juvenile courts are petitioned, a sizeable proportion (44%) are not petitioned and are either dismissed or provided some form of informal disposition. Of the cases that are petitioned, over half (55%) result in adjudication.*

Source: Hockenberry and Puzzanchera (2017:54). Used with permission of the National Center for Juvenile Justice.

JUVENILE JUSTICE LAW: STATUTORY AUTHORITY FOR INFORMAL DISPOSITION AT INTAKE

41-5-1301. Informal disposition. After a preliminary inquiry . . . the juvenile probation officer or assessment officer upon determining that further action is required and that referral to the county attorney is not required may:

(1) provide counseling, refer the youth and the youth's family to another agency providing appropriate services, or take any other action or make any informal adjustment that does not involve probation or detention; or

(2) provide for treatment or adjustment involving probation or other disposition . . .

41-5-1304. Disposition permitted under consent adjustment. (1) The following dispositions may be imposed by consent adjustment:

(a) probation;

(b) placement of the youth in substitute care in a youth care facility . . .;

(c) placement of the youth with a private agency responsible for the care and rehabilitation of the youth . . .;

(d) restitution, . . ., upon approval of the youth court judge;

(e) placement of the youth under home arrest . . .;

(f) confiscation of the youth's driver's license, if the youth has one, by the juvenile probation officer for a specified period of time, not to exceed 90 days. . . .

(g) a requirement that the youth receive counseling services;

(h) placement in a youth assessment center for up to 10 days;

(i) placement of the youth in detention for up to 3 days on a space-available basis at the county's expense, which is not reimbursable under part 19 of this chapter;

(j) a requirement that the youth perform community service;

(k) a requirement that the youth participate in victim-offender mediation;

(l) an agreement that the youth pay a contribution covering all or a part of the costs for the adjudication, disposition, attorney fees for the costs of prosecuting or defending the youth, costs of detention, supervision, care, custody, and treatment of the youth, including the costs of counseling;

(m) an agreement that the youth pay a contribution covering all or a part of the costs of a victim's counseling or restitution for damages that result from the offense for which the youth is disposed;

(n) any other condition ordered by the court to accomplish the goals of the consent adjustment, including but not limited to mediation or youth assessment . . .

Source: Montana Code Annotated 2015. 41-3-1301 and 1304.

Petition: Extent, trends, and demographics

If intake screening determines that a case should be dealt with formally by the juvenile court, a **petition** is written by the prosecutor's office to initiate the formal juvenile justice process. The petition is a legal document that specifies the facts of the case, the charges, and basic identifying information on the youth and his or her parents. Figure 8.1 shows that 56 percent of all delinquency cases handled by juvenile courts in 2014 were petitioned. Compared to cases that are not petitioned into juvenile court, formally processed cases tend to involve violent offenses, older juveniles (age 16 and over), and juveniles with longer court histories. In addition, males are more likely than females, and blacks are more likely than youth of other races, to have their cases petitioned (Hockenberry and Puzzanchera 2017:38–39).

Recent research shows that the intake decision is a product of a complex mix of both legal and extralegal factors, including: (1) characteristics of the youth, such as age, race, gender, and social class; (2) prior record of the youth and seriousness of the alleged offense; (3) family structure and social class; (4) gender of the intake decision-maker (probation officer); and (5) the decentralized structure and inter-agency interaction of juvenile justice systems. With some inconsistency in findings, females are more likely to have their cases informally processed at intake, as compared to males. Furthermore, the joint effects of gender, race, and class has been found to influence intake decisions in complex ways (Leiber, Peck, and Beaudry-Cyr 2016; Leiber and Peck 2015; Leiber 2013; Bishop, Leiber, and Johnson 2010; Rodriguez 2010; Leiber, Brubaker, and Fox 2009; Tracy, Kempf-Leonard, and Abramoske-James 2009; Leiber and Mack 2003). Intake outcomes for white youth, for example, are affected by both gender and family social class (Leiber and Mack 2003). The end-of-chapter reading by Leiber et al. (2016) provides a thorough review of this literature and extends it by considering how the gender of intake probation officers influences how race and gender affect intake screening (see also Leiber and Brubaker 2010).

Petitioned status offense cases

Juvenile Court Statistics provides information about status offenses only for cases that are handled formally through petition into juvenile courts. Therefore, we have no indication of how many or what types of status offense cases are referred to juvenile courts or what portion are petitioned. Instead, *Juvenile Court Statistics* reports on the case processing of five major categories of petitioned status offenses: running away, truancy, curfew violations, ungovernability, and underage liquor law violations (e.g., minor in possession of alcohol and underage drinking). In 2014, 100,100 status offense cases were petitioned into juvenile courts nationwide. Of these cases, 53 percent involved truancy, 14 percent liquor law violations, 9 percent ungovernability, 8 percent curfew, and 8 percent runaway; the remaining 9 percent were categorized as miscellaneous (Hockenberry and Puzzanchera 2017:68). "Between 1995 and 2002, the formally handled status offense caseload increased considerably (61 percent) and then declined 50 percent through 2014" (Hockenberry and Puzzanchera 2017:68). Although males accounted for 58 percent of all petitioned status offense cases in juvenile courts, females (42 percent) made up a substantially larger portion, compared to the delinquency caseload (Hockenberry and Puzzanchera 2017:73). Almost two-thirds of petitioned status offense cases involve juveniles younger than age 16 at the time of referral (Stahl 2008:1). Between 2005 and 2014, the number of petitioned status offense cases declined for all racial and ethnic groups. Data from 2014 show that truancy cases made up the highest percentage of petitioned status offense caseloads for all races (Hockenberry and Puzzanchera 2017:76).

SUMMARY AND CONCLUSIONS

Juvenile courts rely heavily on discretion and diversion during preliminary procedures. Many cases are diverted or handled informally. This chapter has examined the three main preliminary procedures of juvenile courts: detention, juvenile case transfer to adult court, and intake screening.

Detention is the short-term, secure confinement of a youth under court authority, pending court action, disposition, or placement. Less often, detention may also be used as a disposition or sentence of secure confinement for youth who have been adjudicated delinquent in juvenile court or convicted in adult court. The primary purpose of detention is "to protect the community, to ensure a juvenile's appearance at subsequent court hearings, to secure the juvenile's own safety, or for the purpose of evaluating the juvenile" (Puzzanchera and Sickmund 2008:29). The initial decision to detain a youth is made by a police officer, but the need for continued detention is reviewed by the juvenile court, usually within 24 hours. Most delinquency cases handled by juvenile courts do not involve detention. Detention is used in about 1 out of 5 delinquency cases and 1 out of 15 petitioned status offense cases. Males, older juveniles, and black youth are disproportionately detained. Although disproportionate minority contact at the point of detention has been clearly identified and documented for over 40 years, the problem persists.

Detention reform efforts, notably the Juvenile Detention Alternatives Initiative (JDAI), seek to expand community alternatives to detention, to develop objective admission criteria and risk assessment, and to promote unbiased practices in the use of detention.

All states have enacted laws that allow juveniles to be transferred to adult criminal courts. Several transfer provisions are used, including judicial waiver, concurrent jurisdiction, and statutory exclusion. Relatively few juvenile cases are transferred annually, and this number has decreased significantly since the 1990s. It is currently estimated that approximately 100,000 juvenile offenders are transferred annually to criminal courts, and an additional 137,000 juveniles are sent to adult courts based on upper age boundaries for juvenile court jurisdiction. Research examining racial disparities in the likelihood of cases being transferred finds evidence of minority over-representation. Gender also has a substantial effect on transfer decisions; males are more likely than females to be transferred to adult courts.

Research reveals that juveniles transferred to criminal courts tend to be sentenced more harshly than juveniles who are not transferred and sometimes more harshly than young adults convicted of similar crimes. To give criminal court judges greater flexibility in cases involving juveniles, many states have created mechanisms such as reverse waiver provisions and criminal blended sentencing. Although transfer provisions were created with the expectation that transferring serious juvenile offenders to criminal courts would deter juvenile crime, research suggests that transfer actually leads to higher rates of re-offending among transferred youth, compared to youth who remain in the juvenile justice system.

Juvenile court intake is a screening decision that is usually the responsibility of the juvenile probation department. Intake screening determines the most appropriate way to handle cases that are referred to juvenile courts—formally, informally, or dismissal. While 56 percent of delinquency cases handled by juvenile courts are dealt with formally through petition, 44 percent are not petitioned, and are either dismissed or dealt with through some form of informal disposition. Informal disposition is aimed at rehabilitation and includes a wide variety of options such as referral to another agency for services (e.g., chemical dependency treatment, family therapy, academic tutoring, restorative justice), community service, restitution, and informal probation through the probation department. These informal dispositions usually involve a consent adjustment without petition, a voluntary agreement between the youth and his or her parents that is approved by a juvenile court judge. Informal dispositions are diversionary in scope and purpose, seeking to keep the youth from the formal processes of adjudication in juvenile court. If intake screening determines that the case should be dealt with formally by the juvenile court, a petition is written by the prosecutor's office to initiate the formal juvenile justice process. In 2013, 55 percent of all delinquency cases handled by juvenile courts were petitioned. Formal processing is more likely for violent offenses, African-Americans, males, older juveniles (age 16 and over), and juveniles with longer court histories.

READING 8.1

"WHEN DOES RACE AND GENDER MATTER? THE INTERRELATIONSHIPS BETWEEN THE GENDER OF PROBATION OFFICERS AND JUVENILE COURT DETENTION AND INTAKE OUTCOMES."

Michael J. Leiber, Jennifer H. Peck, and Maude Beaudry-Cyr. 2016. *Justice Quarterly* 33:614–641.

Researchers Leiber, Peck, and Beaudry-Cyr examine how race and gender of the youth, together with gender of the probation officer, influence two key decisions in the early stages of the juvenile court process: detention and intake screening.

. . . Using over 20 years of data from one juvenile court in Iowa, the first objective of the present study is to examine how race and gender, individually and in combination, influence case outcomes. The second objective focuses on how differences in detention and intake outcomes may vary for certain race/gender (e.g. black male, black female, white male, white female) combinations depending on the gender of the court officer. The results have the potential to provide a better understanding of the complexities of juvenile justice decision-making and ensure the equitable treatment of all youth, regardless of the gender of the court officer.

Background

The current study focuses on the individual and combined effects of race and gender on decision-making, with a more detailed inquiry on how the gender of the court officer may condition race and gender relationships. In the following section, prior research and theoretical explanations surrounding the impact of the relationship between race and gender on case outcomes are highlighted, especially how race/gender stereotypes influence the perceptions of decision-makers. Theory and results from past studies relating to the influence of court officer gender on juvenile justice processing are then discussed.

Race and court outcomes

It can be argued that the relationship between race and juvenile justice decision-making is complex in nature. Controlling for both legal (e.g. crime severity, prior record) and extralegal (e.g. age, family status) factors, research has shown that minority youth are often the recipients of disadvantaged outcomes when compared to similarly situated whites (Bishop and Leiber 2012). While certain legal factors are known to consistently predict case outcomes (Tracy 2005), prior research has also shown that race indirectly influences social control to the disadvantage of black youth through other factors (i.e. detention) (Frazier and Cochran 1986; Leiber and Fox 2005).

Theoretical explanations for the overrepresentation of minority youth across court outcomes have been attributed to the role that racial stereotypes play in the decisions of court officers. Micro-level interpretations of the symbolic threat hypothesis, for example, have argued that certain characteristics of youth evoke negative stereotypes and emotions from juvenile court officers (Tittle and Curran 1988), particularly among black youth. Tittle and Curran (1988) argue that decision-makers harbor feelings of fear, resentment, and jealousy towards minority youth who they view as aggressive, sexual, and not taking responsibility for their delinquent behavior. These perceptions subsequently result in increases in social control of black youth compared to whites (Freiburger and Jordan 2011), yet the stereotypical perceptions of court officers are not based on the youth's specific behavior or offense. In other words, the threat is more symbolic than real, still the threatening feelings that decision-makers encompass result in racial differences in social control.

In addition, racial stereotypes and the role of attributions are shown to influence juvenile justice decision-making. Bridges and Steen (1998) found that probation officers' perceptions of black and white youth influenced case outcomes to the disadvantage of blacks. Specifically, court officers were more likely to assign negative internal attributes (individual characteristics) to black youth, and negative external attributes (environmental characteristics) to white youth. Both types of attributions contributed to recidivism risk and sentence recommendations, yet decision-makers viewed blacks as more dangerous, culpable, and less amenable to treatment compared to whites referred to the juvenile court.[1]

Gender and court outcomes

Similar to the research surrounding race and juvenile justice decision-making, the effect of gender on court outcomes has also generated conflicting results. Some studies have found that females are the recipients of more lenient outcomes compared to males (Price and Sokoloff 2004), while additional research has shown that females are treated harsher throughout court proceedings (Tracy, Kempf-Leonard, Abramoske-James 2009). Furthermore, other studies have found both severe and lenient treatment of females depending on the stage examined (Leiber et al. 2009; MacDonald and Chesney-Lind 2001), or that gender did not significantly predict social control net of legal and extralegal factors (Kempf-Leonard and Sontheimer 1995).

Theoretical explanations for both the lenient and harsh treatment of female youth compared to males across court outcomes have focused on the perceptions of court actors and the role of gender bias and stereotypes in influencing decision-making. According to the traditional sexrole approach and paternalism position (see Chesney-Lind 1973), juvenile justice decision-makers may treat females more harshly than males in order to reinforce proper female behavior and punish females who do not adhere to feminine attitudes and demeanor (Gaarder, Rodriguez, Zatz 2004). If decision-makers perceive that female youth violated gender roles, or are in need of protection and guidance, harsher treatment may be imposed as a means of helping and protecting the girls from adverse home and community environments (Guevara et al. 2006). For example, Gaarder and colleagues examined the court actors' perceptions of female youth referred to the juvenile court and found that decision-makers often based court outcomes on stereotypes of "proper girl behavior" and conduct assessments, rather than realities (Gaarder et al. 2004:575).

Contrary to the paternalism explanation, support for the chivalry perspective is found when females receive lenient court outcomes compared to males (Belknap 2001). The chivalry perspective posits that female youth are viewed as less dangerous, less threatening, and have a lower likelihood of recidivism compared to males, which translates to male youth receiving more severe court outcomes compared to their female counterparts (Guevara et al. 2006). Decision-makers may view females as weaker, innocent, and less culpable for their offenses (Price and Sokoloff 2004). Regardless of the theoretical reasoning for severe and/or lenient outcomes of females, the overarching theme is that decision-makers utilize gender stereotypes as influencing factors when making assessments and judgments about youth.

Race, gender, and court outcomes

As shown above, the juvenile justice literature has separately explored the individual relationships between race and gender as they pertain to court outcomes. Only a limited number of studies have focused on the interrelationships of race and gender on the processing of youth (Guevara et al. 2006; Leiber and Mack 2003). Leiber, Brubaker, and Fox (2009), for example, found that race and gender, individually and in combination, influenced the social control of youth. Severe and lenient treatment, however, appeared for different race/gender combinations across varying decision-making stages. Specifically, disparities across court outcomes were not evident for white females, while black females received lenient outcomes at intake and petition. Black males were treated harshly at detention, yet also received both lenient and severe outcomes at intake and judicial disposition. Although unexpected, these results are consistent with prior research that examined the intersections of race and gender with decision-making (Leiber and Mack 2003; Peck, Leiber, Brubaker 2014).

One theoretical approach that has focused on explaining the differential treatment of particular race and gender combinations with social control is the intersectionality perspective (Daly and Stevens 1995). This broad theoretical framework focuses on the intersections of race, gender, and class. In particular, the perspective argues that the experiences of women vary based on different characteristics and social structures built on oppression and privilege (Burgess-Proctor 2006; Gaarder et al. 2004; Leiber et al. 2009). When this approach is applied to juvenile court outcomes to explain the presence of race and gender bias, the perspective argues that all females' experiences and treatment within the juvenile court are not the same, but instead, vary by race and class. Furthermore, the contact that black youth experience within the juvenile justice system is not the same, but varies by gender, sexuality, and class (Chesney-Lind 2006; Peck et al. 2014). Aspects of both race and gender influence the perceptions of decision-makers, and based on different life circumstances (and potential stereotypes) of youth, these dimensions will influence court outcomes to the disadvantage of certain race/gender combinations.

Gender of the decision-maker and court outcomes

One neglected area of research surrounding the complexities of court decision-making is the role that the gender of the decision-maker plays in the court outcomes of offenders. Within the adult criminal justice system, some prior research has indicated that female judges sentence more harshly than males (Spohn 2008; Steffensmeier and Hebert 1999), yet the conditions whereby female judges make these decisions differ across offender and offense characteristics. Steffensmeier and Hebert (1999) found that women judges were to some degree, harsher than males in terms of the likelihood and length of incarceration, yet this finding was extended primarily to property offenders. Decision-makers, irrespective of gender, sentenced white females similarly, but women judges imposed harsher sentences on black males, black females, and white males compared to male judges. This effect was amplified even more when a black male had a prior record.

In a more recent investigation, taking into consideration various modes of conviction (e.g. non-negotiated plea, negotiated plea, trial) within the adult criminal justice system and the actual level of discretion judges can exercise in sentencing outcomes, the gender of judges was shown to differentially impact court decisions based on the level of discretion exercised at sentencing. Specifically, Johnson (2014) found that while the gender of judges did not impact sentencing outcomes for neither negotiated nor non-negotiated pleas, being a female judge was shown to decrease the odds of conviction and incarceration at trial, as more discretion could be exercised at this mode of conviction. Additional judge-level factors shown to decrease the likelihood of conviction at trial included being older and a minority, while judicial tenure on the bench appeared to increase the rates of conviction and incarceration at trial.

When strictly focusing on juvenile justice decision-making, less than a handful of studies have investigated whether decision-maker gender influences how youth are processed throughout different court outcomes (Davis, Severy, Kraus, Whitaker 1993; Leiber and Brubaker 2010). Leiber and Brubaker (2010) examined whether male and female intake probation officers rely on similar legal (e.g. crime severity, offense type) or extralegal (e.g. race, age) considerations when determining the intake outcomes of male youth. Results indicated that overall, female officers were more lenient than male officers; however, race and additional characteristics conditioned this relationship. In particular, black males who lived in a single-parent household were more likely to receive an intake referral, and this effect was larger for female decision-makers compared to males. White males who lived in single-parent households were not predictive of intake outcomes for female officers, but they received leniency at intake from male officers. Crime severity, prior referrals, number of charges, and court authority status were legal factors that predicted severe treatment for all boys, regardless of race and gender of the court officer.

In light of these findings, the feminist and organizational literature suggests two sides of a theoretical framework to disentangle when decision-maker gender may or may not matter throughout decision-making (Epstein 1988; Giele 1988). First, according to the maximalist approach, males and females are fundamentally different across their cognitive, emotional, and behavioral beliefs. Due to innate biological and psychological differences between males and females, the process of development across gender results in more independence and autonomy for males as adults, and more relational connections for females (Chodorow 1978; Gilligan 1982). Females develop through primary identification with their mother, and identify themselves as nurturing, responsive, and protective (Gilligan 1982). Males develop throughout the life course as more independent, and identify themselves as objective and nonintervening. These developmental differences, in turn, translate to differences in decision-making across gender, based on the assumptions of the maximalist approach (Lehman 1993). Second, the minimalist approach, which is the alternative side to the integrated feminist and organizational framework, argues that gender differences existing between males and females are caused by contextual factors (Epstein 1988). Education, opportunities, rules, and procedures are argued to nullify any potential gender differences that may exist due to inherent biological or psychological factors (Cook 1981).

In regards to decision-making, the maximalist approach would argue that differences across court outcomes would be evident based on the gender of the court actor (Steffensmeier and Hebert 1999). On the one hand, female court actors may subject youth to lenient outcomes compared to males, due to feelings of empathy and compassion towards the youth. On the other hand, female decision-makers may impose more severe court outcomes because they consider themselves moralistic and feel that youth should be punished for their behavior. It may also be that female officers encompass various stereotypes, perceptions, and fears of being a victim of crime. These stereotypes can result in differences across court outcomes depending on various offender and offense characteristics. The minimalist approach would assume that male and female court actors would rely on similar case and offender characteristics when making decisions (Steffensmeier and Hebert 1999). Instead of differences across court outcomes based on the gender of the decision-maker, it may be that there are no differences in the way that male and female court officers make decisions. Both legal and extralegal factors are viewed with the same weight and in a similar manner, and as a result, regardless of the decision-making gender, youth of different race and gender combinations would receive similar outcomes whether the court actor was male or female.

Implications for the current research

Prior research has investigated the extent to which race and gender, individually and in combination, influence juvenile court outcomes. A limited amount of research has also attempted to explain if the gender of decision-makers affects the social control of youth, net both legal and extralegal considerations. However, the examinations have been limited to only male youth referred to the juvenile court and one decision-making stage (Leiber and Brubaker 2010). When only one court outcome is examined, potential race and/or gender effects may be evident in additional stages that were not taken into consideration or may be underestimated.

Up until this point in time, research has failed to examine how the juvenile court outcomes of different race and gender combinations (black male, black female, white male, white female) are influenced by the gender of the decision-maker. It may be that above and beyond potential race effects, differences across gender of the youth also emerge. As shown in prior research, female court officers responded differently to a black male compared to a white female (Steffensmeier and Hebert 1999). Disaggregating different race/ gender comparisons within juvenile justice decision-making and the increased level of discretion on behalf of court actors may result in more or less race/ gender effects (Harris 2007).

Noting these voids and limitations throughout the literature, the present study examines two general research questions. First, does race and gender individually and in combination affect detention and intake decision-making? Second, does the gender of the intake probation officer influence the juvenile court outcomes of male and female youth of different racial backgrounds? The research questions can be answered through five hypotheses.

The first hypothesis states:

> H(1): Black youth will be more likely than Whites to receive disadvantaged court outcomes at the stages of detention and intake.

Justification for the first hypothesis rests with the breadth of prior research that suggests that net of legal and extralegal considerations, minorities are often the recipients of severe juvenile court outcomes compared to similarly situated whites (Bishop and Leiber 2012). Detention and intake are two of the stages where discretion is most prevalent amongst juvenile justice decision-makers (Bishop and Leiber 2012). This situation provides the opportunity for court officers' perceptions and attributions to influence the treatment of youth. It is anticipated that black youth will be stereotyped by decision-makers as dangerous, delinquent, in need of supervision, and at an increased risk for recidivism. These stereotypes will result in a higher likelihood of detention and being referred for further court proceedings at intake for blacks compared to whites (Bridges and Steen 1998; Freiburger and Jordan 2011; Steffensmeier and Hebert 1999).

The second hypothesis that guides the study is:

> H(2): Females will be less likely than males to receive disadvantaged court outcomes at the stages of detention and intake.

Although prior research has been mixed, we side with the chivalry position which argues that decision-makers perceive female youth compared to males as less dangerous, threatening, and culpable for their actions. It is anticipated that court officers will view female youth through stereotypical typescripts as being weak or innocent. Therefore, more lenient court outcomes (i.e. lower likelihood of being detained, greater likelihood of being released or diverted from the system at intake) is predicted to occur for female youth compared to males based on gender-specific stereotypes.

The third hypothesis states:

> H(3): The gender of the court officer will be predictive of detention and intake outcomes.

Paralleling the predictions put forth by Leiber and Brubaker (2010) and Steffensmeier and Hebert (1999), we side with the maximalist theoretical approach and anticipate that the gender of the decision-maker will influence the court outcomes of youth. The cognitive and emotional uniqueness of males and females translates to different approaches to solving issues and problems, since there is a divergent imagery between male and female decision-making (Lehman 1993). One side of the argument contends that female court actors may be more lenient in their decision-making. For example, according to Goldman (1999), a growth in female court actors in the judicial system brings an increase in sensitivity to decision-making. The other side of the argument contends that since females are more likely to be the victims of rape, sexual harassment, and domestic violence, these experiences as actual or potential victims will translate to harsher court outcomes (Spohn 2008). While some prior research contends that female decision-makers are more nurturing and caring which translates to lenient case outcomes compared to males (Chodorow 1978; Gilligan 1982), other research has found that females are less tolerant of rule violation, and as a result, impose more severe sanctions (Spohn 1990; Steffensmeier and Hebert 1999).

It is also predicted that race and gender stereotypes will jointly predict the treatment of youth of different race and gender combinations. Prior research has shown that depending on the stage examined, black males, black females, white males, and white females have received harsh and lenient outcomes (Guevara et al. 2006; Leiber and Mack 2003; Leiber et al. 2009). Therefore, racial stereotypes in decision-making will be conditioned by gender perceptions, and gender stereotypes will be influenced by the race of male and female youth. Thus, the fourth hypothesis states:

> H(4): Race and gender in combination will influence court outcomes at the stages of detention and intake.

Differences in court outcomes based on decision-maker gender are also predicted to emerge in the current study and inform the fifth hypothesis. The final hypothesis framing the study is:

> H(5): Any observed race and/or gender relationships with court outcomes will be conditioned by the gender of the intake probation officer.

As with the third hypothesis, justification for the fifth hypothesis aligns with the maximalist approach that inherent psychological and biological differences in males and females will translate to what decision-makers consider important and influential when determining case outcomes (Chodorow 1978; Gilligan 1982). For example, female decision-makers may take into consideration stereotypical race and gender attributions underlying a fear of crime to subject youth to social control in a different manner compared to male decision-makers (Steffensmeier and Hebert 1999; Leiber and Brubaker 2010). In other words, the "lived experiences" of females will translate to different detention and intake decisions (Leiber and Brubaker 2010:56). These effects will be further enhanced depending on the race and gender of youth referred to the juvenile court.

The present study

This research examines juvenile justice decision-making in a single county in Iowa. In the study jurisdiction, juveniles are defined by law as persons under the age of 18. The county in which the study was undertaken has the largest black presence (11–13% of the population) in the state. In the largest city within this county, black youth comprise nearly 20% of the youth population (US Census Bureau 2000). Case files involving youth referred to court for a delinquent offense were examined for the years 1980 through 2000 and 2003 through 2004. . . .

Variables

Central to the research questions and hypotheses are race, gender, and gender of the intake decision-maker. These variables and those commonly used in the assessment of the predictors of juvenile court decision-making were included in the analyses (e.g. Freiburger and Jordan 2011; Guevara et al. 2006). . . .

Race distinguished between whites (56%) and blacks (44%). There were insufficient numbers of youth of other races or identified ethnicities to support an analysis that included other racial or ethnic categories. The *gender* distribution of the sample was 73% male and 27% female. The *race/gender* subgroup distributions show that white males comprised 42% of the sample; followed by black males at 30%, and both white females and black females at 14%. The *gender of the probation officer* was differentiated by male intake officer (40%) and female intake officer (60%).

Indicators of extralegal considerations include age, family status, and school status. The average age of offenders in the sample was approximately 15 years. *Family status* was coded to differentiate between youth from two-parent families and from single-parent homes. Fifty-six percent of the youth resided in single-parent households. The variable *school status* was measured by youth who were attending school regularly without any behavioral problems noted in the school record versus those who were attending school but with problems (e.g. detention, suspension, dropped out). Nineteen percent of the youth had evidence of problems at school.

Several legal measures were also used to capture the severity of the delinquent referral. *Court authority* attempts to reflect whether a youth was under supervision at the time of the current referral, and is differentiated by no vs. yes. Thirty percent of the youth were under court authority. *Prior referrals* represent the number of prior court referrals, and youth on average had 2.06 prior contacts with the juvenile court. On average, youth also had 1.39 current charges. *Crime severity* distinguished between misdemeanors (83%) and felonies (17%). Type of delinquency was also included because of the theoretical importance of offense type in juvenile justice decision-making (e.g. Freiburger and Jordan 2011). Dummy variables were created to differentiate between *property offenses*, *person crimes*, and *drug offenses*. Offenses against public order comprised the reference category. Most cases involved property crimes (53%). Only 16% of the sample was charged with a crime against persons, and 26% were charged with a drug offense. The offense distribution for the sample, for the most part, parallels with national aggregate juvenile arrest data (Puzzanchera and Kang 2013). An ordinal variable designated as year was created to take into account possible differences in court outcomes over time. Year was differentiated by "1980 through 1989," "1990 through 2000," and "2003 through 2004."

Detention was treated as both a dependent variable and an independent variable. As a dependent variable, 8% of the sample was held in detention. As an independent variable, detention was included as an additional predictor of intake to assess for indirect effects of detention status on the intake outcome. Probation officers make the decision to refer youth to detention and are the decision-maker at intake. *Intake* was defined as release/diversion vs. court referral. Most youth received a release or diversion (64%) rather than the more severe outcome of referral to court (36%). . . .

Discussion

Framed within theory, prior research, and five research hypotheses that emphasized perceptions involving racial and gender stereotyping, we examined how race and gender, individually and in combination, influenced juvenile justice detention and intake decision-making. It was expected that black youth would receive more disadvantaged court outcomes than similarly situated whites, and that females would be less likely to be detained and be referred for further court proceedings at intake than males. Further, we anticipated that possible race/gender relationships with justice outcomes would differ by the gender of the court officer. Mixed support was found for the expected effects.

Consistent with expectations, black youth and females were found to receive different detention and intake outcomes than whites and males. Black youth were more likely to be detained and receive an intake referral net of legal and extralegal factors. The findings that black youth are at a disadvantage relative to whites at detention and intake are consistent with most prior research (Shook and Goodkind 2009). Also consistent with prior research is the finding that detention is a strong determinant of intake decision-making (Holman and Ziedenberg 2006). This relationship is especially acute for blacks. Race was found to have an indirect effect on intake decision-making through detention. This was concluded based on the finding that black youth were more likely to be detained, and detention was a significant and positive predictor of receiving an intake referral. This finding further contributes to the disproportionate representation of blacks in the juvenile justice system (Frazier and Cochran 1986; Leiber 2013). Once relevant legal and extralegal factors were taken into account, females were less likely than males to be detained and receive a recommendation for further court intervention. This finding is consistent with some prior research (Guevara et al. 2006; Leiber et al. 2009).

Although speculative, we interpret the discovered race and gender relationships involving severe and lenient detention and intake outcomes as evidence that court actors not only rely on legal and extralegal criteria but also on potential racial and gender stereotypes. It may be that court officers perceive black youth as aggressive, dangerous, and in need of intervention (Bridges and Steen 1998; Freiburger and Jordan 2011; Tittle and Curran 1988). The findings that black youth received disadvantaged court outcomes could possibly be attributed by negative race perceptions on behalf of court officers. However, given the inclusion of specific measures and statistical analyses in the present study, it cannot be entirely concluded that the reason for significant race effects is due to the presence of stereotypical beliefs.

Concomitantly, the findings involving gender have been explained in prior research by beliefs that court officers treat females with greater leniency because they have been socialized to protect females, or they have stereotypical beliefs or perceptions that females do not engage in criminal behavior. This finding also parallels prior research that female youth are considered less dangerous, weaker, and less culpable for their offense than her male counterparts (Guevara et al. 2006; Leiber and Mack 2003; Price and Sokoloff 2004). Once again, while the present study cannot be entirely certain that the presence of gender effects translates to the use of gender stereotypes in court decision-making, the results parallel prior research that has made this specific conclusion.

Anticipated racial and gender stereotyping also guided the focus on the expected possible race/gender relationships with justice outcomes and that the gender of the court officer may condition these relationships. Modest support was discovered for these expectations. Prior research has shown that gender effects on intake outcomes may intersect with race (e.g. Leiber et al. 2009; Rodriguez, Smith, Zatz 2009). In the current study, comparisons involving specific race/gender subgroup combinations showed that black males were more likely than other youth to be detained and be referred on at intake. The finding that race and gender interacted to impact detention and intake decision-making is consistent with a micro-level interpretation of the symbolic threat hypothesis where black males are perceived as the "most dangerous" and in need of social control. A similar argument has been posited by the focal concerns perspective (e.g. Steffensmeier, Ulmer, Kramer 1998) and subsequent research (e.g. Spohn and Holleran 2000). Still, it could be that court officers are simply doing their job, in that the court is acting in accordance with the concept of parens patriae by responding in a protective and benevolent way to meet the needs of black youth (e.g. Bridges, Conley, Engen, Price-Spratlen 1995). Although this may be a valid interpretation and further research may be needed to improve our understanding of the findings, there is no denying that race and the relationship with gender at detention and intake raises questions concerning fairness and the equitable treatment of youth.

The reported individual and joint relationships involving race and gender with decision-making were anticipated to be tempered by the gender of the decision-maker. This expectation was based on the maximalist theoretical approach and the results from Leiber and Brubaker (2010) and Steffensmeier and Hebert (1999). Men and women are believed to differ in problem-solving and coping with issues due to different cognitive, emotional, and life experiences. Some argue that female decision-makers are more nurturing and caring which translates to lenient case outcomes compared to males (Chodorow 1978; Gilligan 1982), while others posit that females are less tolerant of rule violation and as a result, sanction more severely (Spohn 1990; Steffensmeier and Hebert, 1999). Further, since females are more likely to be the victims of rape, sexual harassment, and domestic violence, these experiences as actual or potential victims will translate to harsher court outcomes for black offenders (Leiber and Brubaker 2010; Steffensmeier and Hebert 1999).

Rather than imposing more severe sanctions, female probation officers were less likely than male officers to detain youth and to recommend further court proceedings at intake. This finding is consistent with the maximalist perspective and expectations. These findings appear to lend support to those that suggest that women espouse an ethic of care more so than men (Chodorow 1978; Gilligan 1982), based on the limited past research that has examined the effects of the gender of the court officer on juvenile court outcomes (Leiber and Brubaker 2010). Although speculative, female officers may be more sympathetic toward offenders, want to give youth another chance, and consequently, attempt to avoid detention and recommendations at intake that involve further court intervention.

Although the gender of the decision-maker had a direct effect on detention and intake outcomes, for the most part, being a male or a female officer did not condition the treatment of blacks compared to whites, females to males, and/or most combinations of race/gender. There are a few exceptions to this conclusion. Two of the exceptions involved male officers who were found to be more likely to impose severe intake outcomes for males (white or black) relative to black females. Further, compared to male officers, female officers responded to white males with leniency relative to black females at intake. Leniency at intake by female officers was also evident for white females relative to black females. Despite these exceptions, the overall results failed to show that female officers respond to black offenders and in particular, black male offenders, severely. In fact, few differences were found to exist between male and female officers involving the race and/or the gender of the youth. Thus, overall support is provided for the minimalist perspective rather than the maximalist perspective.

The failure to find gender of the decision-maker relationships with the race and gender of the offender and case outcomes raises potential questions that female officers may be more biased under certain circumstances than male officers (e.g. Leiber and Brubaker 2010; Steffensmeier and Hebert 1999). Challenges also emerge concerning the claim that women are less racist than men (e.g. Sabin, Nosek, Greenwald, Rivara 2009). The similarity between male and female officers when it comes to the race and gender of the youth suggests that the bias found (i.e. blacks more harsh, black males more harsh, females more lenient), whether pervasive in the larger culture or inherent to the juvenile justice system, impacts case outcomes irrespective of gender differences in the treatment of youth in general.

The results indicate that additional research that delves into when and how race and/or gender of the youth matter in juvenile justice proceedings is needed. The use of qualitative methods in the form of observations and interviews may prove to be fruitful in further understanding the dynamics involved. Interviews and observations have the potential to examine, in more detail, attitudes about race, gender, and the goals of the juvenile justice system based on the beliefs of court officers (see Bishop and Frazier 1996). Additional research is also needed that not only includes the gender of the decision-maker, but also the race of the court officer. Recall that all but two of the officers in the present study were white. While minimal support for significant race-of-judge sentencing differences exists at the adult level (Spohn 1990; Steffensmeier and Britt 2001; c.f. Welch, Combs, Gruhl 1988), there remains a void of research addressing the effects of the race of court actors on juvenile court outcomes.

Furthermore, the probation officers formed a group that was highly homogeneous, in that most were white, worked in a relatively small jurisdiction, had similar educational attainment, as well as lengthy tenured careers with low rates of turnover. More research that includes both a more diversified sample of decision-makers and replication across urban and rural jurisdictions is, therefore, needed to assess the generalizability of the reported findings. While the focus of this study was on two stages at the front end of the juvenile justice system, future research should also consider the inclusion of additional stages (i.e. adjudication and judicial disposition), as different juvenile court actors in combination with sociodemographic, legal, and extralegal variables, have the potential to differentially influence decision-making outcomes across stages (Bishop, Leiber, Johnson 2010). In light of this being the first study to assess the individual and joint effects of race and gender on the decision-making process of both male and female court officers, findings should be interpreted with a certain level of caution until further replications are conducted.

Despite the need for more research in this area, the results once again demonstrate the continuing influence of race and gender on the social control of youth within the juvenile justice system. While the gender of the court officer appears to affect the treatment of youth in general, male and female officers tend to respond more alike than differently to females and black offenders, especially black male offenders. This non-tempering effect results in lenient outcomes at detention and intake for females, and disadvantaged outcomes involving greater social control for blacks and, in particular, black males.

Note

1 For more comprehensive reviews of the literature on race and juvenile court outcomes, see Bishop and Leiber (2012); for gender, see Tracy and colleagues (2009); for race and gender, see Zatz (2000) and Guevara et al. (2006).

[References omitted.]

READING 8.2

"JUVENILE TRANSFER LAWS: AN EFFECTIVE DETERRENT TO DELINQUENCY?"

Redding, Richard E. 2010. *Juvenile Justice Bulletin.* Washington, DC: Office of Juvenile Justice and Delinquency Prevention.

"The nationwide policy shift toward transferring juvenile offenders to the criminal court is based largely on the assumption that more punitive, adult criminal sanctions will act as a deterrent to juvenile crime" (Redding 2010:2). The OJJDP bulletin presented here examines this fundamental assumption of deterrence.

Beginning in the 1980s, many States passed legal reforms designed to get tough on juvenile crime. One important reform was the revision of transfer (also called waiver or certification) laws (Griffin, 2003) to expand the types of offenses and offenders eligible for transfer from the juvenile court for trial and sentencing in the adult criminal court.[1] These reforms lowered the minimum age for transfer, increased the number of transfer-eligible offenses, or expanded prosecutorial discretion and reduced judicial discretion in transfer decisionmaking (Fagan and Zimring, 2000; Redding, 2003, 2005). In 1979, for example, 14 States had automatic transfer statutes requiring that certain juvenile offenders be tried as adults; by 1995, 21 States had such laws, and by 2003, 31 States (Steiner and Hemmens, 2003). In addition, the age at which juvenile court jurisdiction ends was lowered to 15 or 16 years in 13 States (see Snyder and Sickmund, 2006), although very recently, some States have reduced the scope of transfer laws (Bishop, 2004), and one State has raised the age at which juvenile court jurisdiction ends from 16 to 18.

In the wake of these legislative changes, the number of youth convicted of felonies in criminal courts and incarcerated in adult correctional facilities has increased (Redding, 2003), reaching a peak in the mid-1990s and then declining somewhat (Snyder and Sickmund, 2006) due, in part, to the decrease in juvenile crime. An estimated 4,100 youth were committed to State adult prisons in 1999, representing 1 percent of new prison commitments (Snyder and Sickmund, 2006). Sixty-one percent of these youth were incarcerated for person offenses, 23 percent for property offenses, 9 percent for drug offenses, and 5 percent for public order offenses (e.g., weapons possession) (Snyder and Sickmund, 2006). Transferred juveniles, particularly those convicted of violent offenses, typically receive longer sentences than those sentenced in the juvenile court for similar crimes (Bishop, 2000; Kupchik, Fagan, and Liberman, 2003; Myers, 2005; Virginia Department of Criminal Justice Services, 1996). But, they may be released on bail for a considerable period of time while they await trial in the criminal court (Myers, 2005), and many youth incarcerated in adult facilities serve no longer than the maximum time they would have served in a juvenile facility (Bishop, 2000; Fritsch, Caeti, and Hemmens, 1996; Myers, 2001). Seventy-eight percent were released from prison before their 21st birthday, and 95 percent were released before their 25th birthday, with an average of 2 years, 8 months of time served on their sentences (Snyder and Sickmund, 2006).

General and specific deterrence

The nationwide policy shift toward transferring juvenile offenders to the criminal court is based largely on the assumption that more punitive, adult criminal sanctions will act as a deterrent to juvenile crime. In terms of specific deterrence—in other words, whether trying and sentencing juvenile offenders as adults decreases the likelihood that they will reoffend—six large-scale studies have found higher recidivism rates among juveniles convicted for violent offenses in criminal court when compared with similar offenders tried in juvenile court. With respect to general deterrence—whether transfer laws deter any would-be juvenile offenders—the picture is less clear. The studies on this issue have produced somewhat conflicting findings; however, the bulk of the empirical evidence suggests that transfer laws have little or no general deterrent effect.

This Bulletin reviews all of the extant research on the general and specific deterrent effects of transferring juveniles to adult criminal court (Redding, 2005), focusing in particular on recent large-scale studies on specific deterrence funded by the Office of Juvenile Justice and Delinquency Prevention (Fagan, Kupchik, and Liberman, 2003; Lane et al., 2002; Lanza-Kaduce et al., 2005). It also identifies gaps in the field's knowledge base, notes challenges for further research, and discusses whether effective deterrence may be achieved through transfer.

General deterrence: Do transfer laws prevent juvenile crime?

Two studies conducted in the 1980s found that transfer laws did not lower juvenile crime rates. Jensen and Metsger's (1994) time-series analysis for the years 1976 to 1986 found a 13-percent increase in arrest rates for violent crime committed by 14- to 18-year-olds in Idaho after the State implemented its transfer law in 1981. In comparison, between 1982 and 1986, the arrest rates for similarly aged juveniles decreased in the neighboring States of Montana and Wyoming (which retained transfer procedures similar to those Idaho had before 1981). In a similar time-series analysis comparing juvenile arrest rates between 1974 and 1984 in New York and Philadelphia, Singer and McDowall (1988) found that a 1978 New York State law that automatically sent violent juvenile offenders to criminal court (by lowering the ages for criminal court jurisdiction to 13 for murder and 14 for assault, arson, burglary, kidnapping, and rape) had no deterrent effect on violent juvenile crime. The law was applied widely and publicized extensively in the media.[2] Although limited, evidence available at the time suggested that juvenile offenders in New York were aware of the law (Singer and McDowall, 1988).

On the other hand, the results of a multistate analysis for the years 1978 to 1993 suggest that adult sanctions, under certain conditions, may have moderate deterrent effects on juvenile crime (Levitt, 1998). Controlling for demographic and economic variables, the researchers compared the juvenile arrest rates for violent crime across States as a function of each State's minimum age for criminal court jurisdiction to the relative punitiveness of its juvenile and criminal justice systems. Punitiveness is defined as the ratio of the number of incarcerated offenders to the number of total offenders in each State system for different age groups. Researchers found relative decreases in youth crime as youth reached the age of criminal responsibility, but only in those States in which juvenile and criminal justice systems differed significantly in severity of punishment. This suggests that significantly more punitive punishments meted out by criminal courts may deter youth from offending once they reach the age of criminal responsibility.

Two multistate studies reached a different conclusion. Examining data on all felony arrests in the State of Florida between 1989 and 2002, including each offender's age and arrest history, Lee and McCrary (2005) evaluated the effect of turning age 18 on criminal offending. This study found that young people did not lower their offending rates upon turning age 18, suggesting that the prospect of adult sanctions was not a deterrent.

Steiner and Wright (2006) examined the effects of prosecutorial transfer laws in the 14 States that had such laws as of 2003.[3] These States enacted their laws at different times (between 1975 and 2000), thereby providing data over different historical time periods. Using time-series analyses, researchers compared monthly juvenile arrest rates for violent index crime (homicide, rape, robbery, and aggravated assault) for each month in the 5 years before and the 5 years after each State enacted its prosecutorial transfer law. In addition, 2 States were selected as controls for each of the 14 target States. The control States resembled the target States in size, location, and juvenile arrest rates, but implemented no transfer law during or near the relevant time period. The study found that transfer laws had no general deterrent effect. Only in Michigan did juvenile crime decrease after the State enacted its prosecutorial transfer law; in the other 13 States, juvenile crime either remained constant or increased after the enactment of the law (see also Risler, Sweatman, and Nackerud, 1998).

A few researchers have interviewed juvenile offenders about the effects of transfer. Before the widespread expansion of transfer laws, Glassner and colleagues (1983) reported the results of interviews with a small number of juvenile offenders in New York, who said they had decided to stop offending once they reached the age at which they knew they could be tried as adults.

Researchers in another small-scale study (Redding and Fuller, 2004) interviewed 37 juvenile offenders who had been charged with murder or armed robbery and automatically tried as adults in Georgia. The study examined their knowledge and perceptions of transfer laws and criminal sanctions. Georgia had undertaken a public awareness campaign to inform juveniles about the State's new automatic transfer law. Nevertheless, juvenile offenders reported being unaware of the law; only 8 of the 37 youth knew that juveniles who committed serious crimes could be tried as adults. Even among those who knew about the law, none expected that it would be enforced against them for the serious crime they had committed. Many thought they would only get light sentences (e.g., a sanction of probation, boot camp, or a several-month stay in a juvenile detention facility) from the juvenile court. These results are consistent with those from a Canadian study (Peterson-Badali, Ruck, and Koegl, 2001) finding that only 22 of the 53 juvenile offenders interviewed thought that they would receive a serious punishment if caught.

Seventy-five percent of the transferred juveniles interviewed by Redding and Fuller (2004) felt that their experiences in the adult criminal justice system had taught them the serious consequences of committing crimes. As one juvenile explained, "[Being tried as an adult] showed me it's not a game anymore. Before, I thought that since I'm a juvenile I could do just about anything and just get 6 months if I got caught" (Redding and Fuller, 2004:39). Seventy-five percent of the juvenile offenders said that if they had known they could be tried and sentenced as adults, they may not have committed the crime (Redding and Fuller, 2004).

In sum, the limited empirical research on the general deterrent effect of juvenile transfer is somewhat inconsistent and does not permit strong conclusions. The bulk of the evidence suggests that transfer laws, at least as currently implemented and publicized, have little or no general deterrent effect in preventing serious juvenile crime. Substantial further research is needed to examine whether transfer laws have—or, under the appropriate conditions, could have—a general deterrent effect. In particular, it is important to examine the following questions:

- Are juveniles aware of transfer laws?
- Do they believe the laws will be enforced against them?
- Does this awareness and belief deter criminal behavior?

In conjunction with such research, there is a need to implement and evaluate well targeted public awareness campaigns on the State and local levels designed to apprise juveniles of the legal consequences of committing serious crimes (Redding and Fuller, 2004). Public awareness campaigns have proved effective in reducing adult crime in some contexts (e.g., Elder et al., 2004; Johnson and Bowers, 2003).

Potential deterrence

It is possible that transfer laws resulting in significant adult sentences might have general deterrent effects if would-be juvenile offenders were made aware of such laws and if the laws were widely implemented. With respect to adult offenders, studies "plainly suggest that when potential offenders are made aware of substantial risks of being punished, many of them are induced to desist" (Von Hirsch et al., 1999:47). However, research with adults suggests that the severity of punishment appears to have little or no effect on crime rates (Pratt and Cullen, 2005; Robinson and Darley, 2004), perhaps because potential offenders typically have much more information about the likelihood of being arrested than they do about likely sentences (Von Hirsch et al., 1999). Studies show that the general public knows little about potential sentences and tends to underestimate their severity (Robinson and Darley, 2004; Von Hirsch et al., 1999). In addition, offenders tend to discount punishment as an uncertain future event, whereas the short-term rewards of crime are more powerful pull factors (Wilson and Herrnstein, 1985). "[F]uture contingent costs may be discounted less, if their magnitude is sufficiently great *and* their likelihood of being incurred increases. Severe sentencing policies thus might possibly have an impact if coupled with much higher probabilities of conviction" (Von Hirsch et al., 1999:48).

Although studies of juvenile offenders are few in number, they suggest that arrests and sanctions have deterrent effects. For example, Mocan and Rees (2005) examined self-reported delinquency data (for drug selling, assault, robbery, burglary, and theft) for 14,942 adolescents from the 1995 National Longitudinal Study of Adolescent Health. They compared county-level arrests (of adults and juveniles) for violent crime reported in 1993 with county-level juvenile crime rates in 1995, thus providing a measure of the deterrent effects of arrest rates on subsequent juvenile crime rates. They found that the arrest rate had a general deterrent effect on the crimes of drug dealing and assault; for each additional arrest, there was a 3.6-percent decrease in the likelihood that juveniles would sell drugs and a 6.6-percent decrease in the likelihood that they would commit an assault. According to Mocan and Rees (2005:344), "this pattern of results runs counter to claims that at-risk young Americans are so present-oriented that they do not respond to incentives and sanctions."

Similarly, Smith and Gartin (1989) found that being arrested reduced recidivism among youthful male offenders, particularly first-time offenders. A 2003 study of serious juvenile offenders incarcerated in a maximum security facility found a negative relationship between their sentence severity and self-reported intent to reoffend and a positive correlation between their self-reported intent and the number of offenses they actually committed after their release. Researchers found evidence that these offenders made "some explicit calculations about the advantages and disadvantages of committing future crimes" (Corrado et al., 2003:197).

Criminal sanctions will only have deterrent effects if potential offenders: (1) believe there is a significant likelihood of getting caught, (2) believe there is a significant likelihood of receiving a substantial sentence, and (3) consider the risk of the penalty when deciding whether to offend (see Von Hirsch et al., 1999). It is useful to consider, however, each of the necessary preconditions for successful deterrence in the context of juvenile offending. A law can act as a deterrent only if the targeted population is aware that the law exists and believes that it will be enforced.

Redding and Fuller (2004) found that few violent juvenile offenders knew that they could be tried as adults, none thought it would happen to them, and few thought they would face serious punishment. Moreover, few reported thinking about the possibility of getting caught when they committed the offense. Indeed, it seems that offenders generally underestimate the risk of arrest (Robinson and Darley, 2004). Juveniles' psychosocial immaturity, including their tendency to focus on the short-term benefits of their choices (Beckman, 2004; Scott, Reppucci, and Woolard, 1995; Steinberg and Cauffman, 1996), may reduce the likelihood that they will perceive the substantial risk of being arrested or punished as an adult (Schneider and Ervin, 1990).

Specific deterrence

To date, six published studies have been conducted to examine the specific deterrence effects of transfer. These large-scale studies indicate that youth tried in adult criminal court generally have greater recidivism rates after release than those tried in juvenile court. It is unclear, however, whether transfer affects recidivism for nonviolent property or drug offenders.

Fagan (1996) examined the recidivism rates of 800 randomly selected 15- and 16-year-old juvenile offenders charged with robbery or burglary during 1981–82. Controlling for eight variables (race, gender, age at first offense, prior offenses, offense severity, case length, sentence length, and court), as well as for time residing in the community, researchers compared offenders charged in New Jersey's juvenile courts with offenders charged in New York's criminal courts under that State's automatic transfer law (under which 16 is the age of full criminal responsibility). Both areas shared similar demographic, socioeconomic, and crime indicator characteristics. Thus, the study provides a comparison of recidivism rates as a function of whether cases were processed in the juvenile or criminal court, without the sample selection problems inherent in studies comparing cases within a single jurisdiction where prosecutors or judges decide which cases to transfer.

A higher percentage of youth who were tried for robbery in criminal court were rearrested (91 percent) than those tried for robbery in juvenile court (73 percent). Of youth who were rearrested, those tried in the criminal court also were rearrested sooner and more often. However, there were no differences in recidivism rates (in terms of the percent rearrested, rearrest rate, and time to rearrest) for burglary offenders tried in the criminal court versus those tried in juvenile court. The findings on robbery offenders suggest that criminal court processing alone, irrespective of whether youth are incarcerated in juvenile or adult facilities, produces a higher recidivism rate. This finding is emphasized by the parallel finding that even those youth sentenced to probation in criminal court had a substantially higher recidivism rate than those incarcerated in the juvenile justice system (see also Mason and Chang, 2001).

Juveniles with the highest recidivism rates were those who were incarcerated after being tried in the criminal court. The study indicated that, overall, youth adjudicated in juvenile court had a 29-percent lower risk of rearrest than those tried in criminal court. Drug offenses were the one exception. Criminal court adjudication substantially reduced the risk of rearrest in those cases.

Bishop and colleagues (1996) compared the 1-year recidivism rate of 2,738 juvenile offenders transferred to criminal court in Florida in 1987 with a matched sample of 2,738 juvenile offenders who had not been transferred. Florida relies almost exclusively on prosecutorial transfer. These transfer decisions are largely offense-driven and made soon after arrest, before the prosecutor has much information about the youth's background. Therefore, it is less likely that the youth retained in the juvenile justice system had lower recidivism rates due to variables other than those controlled for in the analysis, such as the youth's mental health status or amenability to treatment (Bishop and Frazier, 2000). The study controlled for seven variables (race, gender, age, number of referrals to juvenile court, most serious prior offense, number of charges, and most serious charge). Researchers found that the rearrest rates were higher (0.54 versus 0.32 offenses per person, per year of time living in the community) among transferred youth. Also, the average time to reoffending was shorter (135 versus 227 days) for the transferred youth across seven offense types (including violent felonies, property offenses, and minor misdemeanors).

Following the same Florida offenders 7 years after the initial study by Bishop et al. (1996), Winner et al. (1997) compared transferred versus nontransferred offenders matched for gender, age, race, and offending history. They found that the rearrest rates were higher and the time to reoffending shorter (adjusting for time residing in the community following release from incarceration) among those who had been transferred to criminal court. The exception was transferred property felons who had lower recidivism rates than similar offenders who remained under juvenile court jurisdiction.

Myers (2001, 2003) examined the 18-month recidivism rates of 494 juvenile offenders charged with robbery or aggravated assault in Pennsylvania in 1994, using a statistical model to control for the possibility that the transferred juveniles were the more serious offenders in the first place (and therefore more likely to recidivate) or those less amenable to treatment in the juvenile system. The study controlled for age at referral, race, geographical location, school and family status, various indices of prior offending history, use of a weapon, and various case-processing variables. Youth who were judicially transferred to criminal court were twice as likely to be rearrested, and were rearrested more quickly (and often for more serious offenses) upon their return to the community, than youth who were retained in the juvenile justice system during the same period.

Finally, two recent large-scale studies funded by OJJDP are particularly informative:

Recent OJJDP-funded studies

Lanza-Kaduce and colleagues (2005) conducted a second Florida study that included 950 young adult offenders.[4] Half of the offenders had been prosecutorially transferred to the criminal court in 1995 or 1996 for offenses they had committed as juveniles; the other half had remained in the juvenile system. This resulted in a sample of 475 matched pairs of transferred and retained cases.

The cases were drawn from six urban and rural judicial circuits in Florida that differed considerably in their rates of transfer. The cases were matched within each judicial circuit (thus controlling for geographical effects in case processing and decisionmaking) along seven relevant demographic, criminal history, and offense variables: age, gender, race, number of previous juvenile referrals, most serious prior offense, offense, and number of charges. In addition, a subset of this group, consisting of 315 best matched pairs, were further matched according to an offense seriousness index created by examining local records to obtain data about 12 other case characteristics: prior juvenile referrals, multiple charges at arrest, multiple incidents involved in the case, charge consolidation, legal problems during case processing, gang involvement, codefendants or accomplices, property loss or damage, victim injury, use of weapons, felony charges, and the presence of mitigating and aggravating factors. The measure of recidivism was the number of offenses committed after youth turned age 18, and data analyses were conducted on the 475 matched pairs, as well as on the subset of 315 best matched pairs.

Transferred juveniles more likely to offend

The Lanza-Kaduce study expands on the earlier Florida studies (i.e., Bishop et al., 1996; Winner et al., 1997). It includes reoffense types and a detailed matching on relevant case and offense characteristics (see Frazier et al., 1999). Its recidivism data draws on information from two different State databases. To reduce a potential lack of comparability in recidivism measures between transfers and juvenile court retainees due to differences in decisionmaking and recordkeeping between the two systems, it examines offending after age 18. "The focus on adult recidivism . . . captures the persistence of a criminal career into adulthood—a pivotal policy concern" (Lanza-Kaduce et al., 2005:64). Moreover, the data "include cases transferred in 1995 and 1996, after the 'get tough' idea was fully entrenched in the American culture and after prosecutorial transfer had been used in Florida for a long time" (Lanza-Kaduce et al., 2005:65).

Like the earlier Florida studies, this study found that transferred offenders, particularly violent offenders, were significantly more likely to reoffend.

- Overall, 49 percent of the transferred offenders reoffended, compared with 35 percent of the retained offenders.
- For violent offenses, 24 percent of the transferred offenders reoffended, compared with 16 percent of the retained offenders.
- For drug offenses, 11 percent of the transferred offenders reoffended, compared with 9 percent of the retained offenders.
- For property offenses, 14 percent of the transferred offenders reoffended, compared with 10 percent of the retained offenders.

The results were virtually identical for the subset of 315 best matched pairs. In addition, researchers conducted paired-comparison analyses in which each matched pair was the unit of analysis. This analysis classified each pair according to whether both offenders reoffended (21 percent of cases), only the transferred offender reoffended (29 percent of cases), only the retained offender reoffended (15 percent of cases), or neither reoffended (36 percent of cases).[5] Again, the results were virtually identical for the subgroup of best-matched pairs. However, the study failed to replicate the 1997 Florida study finding of lower recidivism rates among transferred property offenders (Winner et al., 1997).

In addition to the recidivism study, the Florida research group conducted detailed interviews with 144 serious male offenders between the ages of 17 and 20, half of whom had been transferred and the other half of whom were retained in the juvenile system (Bishop and Frazier, 2000; Lane et al., 2002). Eighty-three percent had more than one prior arrest, 60 percent began offending before the age of 14, and 47 percent had committed a violent offense as their most serious current offense. Interviews were conducted in four "deep-end" juvenile correctional institutions (i.e., 9–36 month placements in highly secure juvenile correctional facilities designed for high and medium-risk offenders) and eight adult prisons in Florida (mostly youthful offender facilities designed to house young adults up to age 24), with youth at different stages in serving their sentence. Of the 71 youth who had been transferred to the adult system, 63 also had prior experience in the juvenile system. Fifty-eight percent of the youth rated the deep-end juvenile placements as beneficial, 33 percent rated the adult prison as beneficial, 20 percent rated the less restrictive juvenile dispositions (for example, probation, placement in low restrictive residential programs) as beneficial, and 12 percent rated adult probation as beneficial.

The youth rated the deep-end juvenile programs the most beneficial largely because these programs provided intensive, long-term job skills training and treatment. In addition, the lengthier period of incarceration gave them more time to consider their futures and the consequences of reoffending, suggesting that the longer sanctions had an impact (Lane et al., 2002). But "[o]ften when adult sanctions were perceived as being beneficial, the benefit was not attributed to anything gained from the disposition. Rather, many youth indicated that they expected to remain crime-free because their experiences in the adult system had been so horrible. Youth who believed the adult sanctions would keep them from committing crimes primarily pointed to three reasons: pain and denigration, time spent in prison, and fear of future consequences, especially tougher sentences. Paradoxically, most of those who said the adult experience was negative also mentioned pain, denigration, and/or anger, but they gave these as reasons why the adult dispositions had made matters worse. Others attributed a negative impact to adult sanctions because they 'learned more crime while there'" (Lane et al., 2002:444). While a substantial minority of the youth said that prison had taught them a lesson—declaring that they would not reoffend because they did not want to endure the pain of imprisonment again—61 percent said that prison had either no impact or a negative impact on their behaviors (Lane et al., 2002:448). Overall, the "findings call into question the practice of [incarcerating juveniles in adult prison and] 'skipping' the deep-end juvenile programs when sentencing youth for serious crimes" (p. 452).

In another OJJDP-sponsored study, Fagan and colleagues (2003) extended and largely replicated previous research (Fagan, 1996). This time, they examined the time at-risk (i.e., residing in the community) recidivism rates for 2,382 15- and 16-year-old juveniles charged in 1992 or 1993 with robbery, burglary, or assault. The 2003 study used a larger sample drawn from more counties in each State as well as more detailed measures of important variables, such as offenders' prior juvenile record. The study compared those charged in selected counties in northern New Jersey, where such cases originate in the juvenile court, with those charged in matched counties in New York, where such cases originate in the criminal court. The New York and New Jersey counties are contiguous, and part of a large metropolitan area that shares common demographic, economic, and social characteristics as well as similar criminogenic influences and crime rate characteristics. Thus, the study design allows for comparison of recidivism rates as a function of whether cases are processed in juvenile court or criminal court, without the sample selection problems inherent in designs that compare cases retained in the juvenile court with those transferred in a single jurisdiction wherein decisionmakers decide which cases to transfer. All cases were followed for a 7-year period until 2000, by which time almost all of the offenders had served their sentences and had spent at least 2 years living in the community. The study statistically controlled for a variety of relevant demographics (age, gender, ethnicity), case and offense characteristics (for example, most serious charge, weapon use, whether detained, case length), criminal history variables (age at first arrest, number of prior arrests, previous incarcerations), and sentence length. It used statistical techniques that analyzed recidivism in different ways (first rearrest, severity of rearrest charges, time until rearrest, likelihood of subsequent incarceration).

Greater likelihood of rearrest

The study found a 100-percent greater likelihood of rearrest for a violent offense and a 47-percent greater likelihood of rearrest for a property offense, among the New York juveniles whose cases were processed in the criminal court than for the New Jersey juveniles. They also had a greater number of rearrests for such offenses and a 26-percent greater chance of being reincarcerated. The pattern of findings was even stronger for first-time offenders. For drug offense rearrests, however, the results were reversed, with the juveniles tried in juvenile court having a 31-percent greater likelihood of rearrest for drug offenses. Finally, the study found that the differences in recidivism were unrelated to periods of incarceration in adult versus juvenile facilities. Thus, incarceration in adult prisons "does not seem to be responsible for the criminogenic effect of adult court processing" (Fagan et al., 2003:66).

These findings fully replicate those of the earlier Fagan (1996) study, except with respect to property offenses. The 1996 study found no difference in recidivism rates for burglary, whereas the 2003 study found that criminal court processing increased the recidivism rates for property offenses.

Transfer found to increase recidivism

In sum, to date, six large-scale studies have been conducted on the specific deterrent effects of transfer. These studies used large sample sizes (between 494 and 5,476 participants), different methodologies (natural experiment across two jurisdictions, matched groups within the same jurisdictions, or statistical controls), multiple measures of recidivism, and were conducted in five jurisdictions (Florida, New Jersey, New York, Minnesota, Pennsylvania) having different types of transfer laws (automatic, prosecutorial, or judicial). The strong consistency in results across the studies is all the more compelling given that they used different samples and methodologies, thereby providing a degree of convergent validity for the findings. All of the studies found higher recidivism rates among offenders who had been transferred to criminal court, compared with those who were retained in the juvenile system. This held true even for offenders who only received a sentence of probation from the criminal court. Thus, the extant research provides sound evidence that transferring juvenile offenders to the criminal court does not engender community protection by reducing recidivism. On the contrary, transfer substantially increases recidivism. A recent review of the extant research on transfer conducted by the Centers for Disease Central arrived at the same conclusion (McGowan et al., 2007). Only two apparent exceptions challenge this pattern of findings. For nonviolent property offenders, the effects of transfer remain unclear, with one study finding that transfer had no effect on recidivism (Fagan, 1996) and another finding that transfer decreased recidivism (Winner et al., 1997), but with two studies (conducted in the same jurisdiction as the first two studies) finding that it increased recidivism (Fagan et al., 2003; Lanza-Kaduce et al., 2005). In addition, with respect to drug offenders, two studies (Fagan, 1996; Fagan et al., 2003) found decreased recidivism rates among those tried in the criminal court.

Why do juveniles tried as adults have higher recidivism rates?

Experts (see Bazemore and Umbreit, 1995; Myers, 2003; Thomas and Bishop, 1984; Winner et al., 1997) have identified several possible explanations for the higher recidivism rates of violent juvenile offenders tried in criminal court as compared to those adjudicated in juvenile court:

- The stigmatization and other negative effects of labeling juveniles as convicted felons.
- The sense of resentment and injustice juveniles feel about being tried and punished as adults.
- The learning of criminal mores and behavior while incarcerated with adult offenders.
- The decreased focus on rehabilitation and family support in the adult system.

A felony conviction also results in the loss of a number of civil rights and privileges (see Redding, 2003), further reducing the opportunities for employment and community reintegration.

Findings from several studies (Fagan, 1996; Fagan, Kupchik and Liberman, 2003) show that criminal court processing alone, even without the imposition of any criminal sentence, increases recidivism. Juveniles' sense of injustice at criminal court processing may cause them to react defiantly by reoffending, and it may further harden an emergent criminal self-concept (see Sherman, 1993; Thomas and Bishop, 1984; Winner et al., 1997). "The concept of fairness appears to be an important variable in an individual's perception of sentence severity and its subsequent relationship to future recidivism" (Corrado et al., 2003:183). Furthermore, it appears that many adolescents with conduct disorders already have a sense of having been dealt an unfair hand by authority figures (Chamberlain, 1998). Bishop and Frazier (2000) interviewed 95 serious and chronic juvenile offenders in Florida, roughly half of whom were transferred to the criminal court and were incarcerated in adult correctional facilities, and half of whom had been adjudicated in the juvenile court and were incarcerated in maximum-security juvenile facilities. According to the authors, many of the juveniles felt a strong sense of injustice about being tried as adults:

> Many experience the court process not so much as a condemnation of their behavior as a condemnation of them. Unlike the juvenile court, the criminal court failed to communicate that young offenders retain some fundamental worth. What the youths generally heard was that they were being punished not only because their behavior was bad but also because

> they were personifications of their behavior. Far from viewing the criminal court and its officers as legitimate, the juvenile offenders we interviewed saw them more often as duplicitous and manipulative, malevolent in intent, and indifferent to their needs. It was common for them to experience a sense of injustice and, then, to condemn the condemners. (Bishop and Frazier, 2000:263).

These findings are consistent with those of Redding and Fuller (2004), who found that juveniles tried as adults clearly felt that transfer laws were unfair. Many felt that their juvenile status and immaturity dictated that they should be tried as juveniles, despite the serious crimes they had committed. They also did not understand why the legal system was trying them as adults, and they saw themselves as being treated differently from other similarly situated juveniles. Both perceptions contributed to their sense of unfairness, perhaps leading to greater cynicism about the legal system as a result of being incarcerated (see Piquero et al., 2005).

Some studies indicate that prison incarceration "does not seem to be responsible for the criminogenic effect of adult court processing" (Fagan, Kupchik, and Liberman, 2003:66). One reason for the increased recidivism of these offenders, however, might be the reduced opportunities for meaningful rehabilitation in adult prison. Forst, Fagan, and Vivona's 1989 study, for example, found that youth in juvenile facilities gave higher marks than youth in adult facilities to the available treatment and case management services. Youth in juvenile detention described these services as helpful in providing counseling, enabling them to obtain needed services, encouraging participation in programs, teaching the consequences of rule breaking, and deepening their understanding of their problems. Similarly, in a recent study comparing the experiences of youths in adult versus juvenile correctional facilities in a large Northeastern State, all of whom had been tried in adult criminal court, Kupchik (2007) found that youths in juvenile facilities reported far more positive, mentoring-style staff-inmate interactions than did the youths in adult facilities. However, youths in adult facilities reported having greater access to counseling and educational services, perhaps because of the larger size of the adult facilities.

Bishop and Frazier's recent Florida study (2000) vividly portrays the differences between juvenile and adult correctional facilities. They found that the juvenile correctional institutions were treatment oriented and adhered to therapeutic models of rehabilitation (Bishop and Frazier, 2000:255). "Compared to the criminal justice system, the juvenile system seems to be more reintegrative in practice and effect" (Bishop and Frazier, 2000:265). Youths in juvenile facilities had positive feelings about the staff, who they felt cared about them and taught them appropriate behaviors. Most of the juveniles incarcerated in juvenile facilities felt confident that they would not reoffend, often crediting the staff with helping them make this positive change. Conversely, only a third of the juveniles in adult prisons said that they would not reoffend.

Juveniles in adult prison reported that much of their time was spent learning criminal behavior from the inmates and proving how tough they were. They also were much more fearful of being victimized than they had been when incarcerated in juvenile facilities, and more than 30 percent had been assaulted or had witnessed assaults by prison staff. Indeed, Beyer (1997) paints a bleak picture of life in adult prison for juveniles, who are at greater risk for suicide, as well as for physical and sexual abuse from older inmates. As compared with those in juvenile facilities, juveniles incarcerated in adult prison are eight times more likely to commit suicide, five times more likely to be sexually assaulted, and almost twice as likely to be attacked with a weapon by inmates or beaten by staff (Beyer, 1997). Because juveniles in adult prisons are exposed to a criminal culture in which inmates commit crimes against each other, these institutions may socialize delinquent juveniles into true career criminals. In an older study about life in prison (Eisikovits and Baizerman, 1983), violent juvenile offenders reported that their daily survival required finding ways to fit into the inmate culture, dealing with difficult and authoritarian relationships with adult inmates, and adjusting to the institution by accepting violence as a part of daily life and, thus, becoming even more violent.

Finally, Redding and Fuller (2004) found that juveniles whose jail or prison experiences were worse than they had expected, and those who reported witnessing or experiencing violence while incarcerated, were less likely to say that their incarceration would deter them from committing crimes in the future. This finding raises the possibility that incarceration in adult facilities may have brutalizing effects on juveniles, which may partly account for their increased recidivism. (The term "brutalization effect" describes the finding that homicide rates in a State often increase after an execution (Bowers, 1998), perhaps because executions model and communicate that violence is an acceptable and psychologically cathartic alternative.) Likewise, juveniles' brutal experiences in adult prison may teach the wrong lessons about the acceptability and psychological benefits of criminal conduct, particularly violent crime, while also contributing to their sense of being treated unfairly, both of which may increase recidivism. Further research is needed on this issue.

Implications for policymakers and practitioners

The research findings on juvenile transfer have the potential to impact both policy and practice. In a recent study, Hensl and Redding (2005) found that juvenile court judges who were knowledgeable about the ineffectiveness of transfer in reducing recidivism were somewhat less likely to transfer juvenile offenders to the criminal court. This finding suggests that educating judges, prosecutors, court personnel, and legislators about the research on transfer may reduce the number of cases transferred to criminal court or the number of transferred cases that result in criminal sanctions. The Miami-Dade County Public Defender's Office developed the Juvenile Sentencing Advocacy Project, which produced a 350-percent increase in the number of transferred cases receiving a juvenile rather than an adult sanction from criminal court judges (Mason, 2000). In Florida, which has had some of the most aggressive transfer policies in the Nation, the number of juveniles prosecuted in the criminal court decreased by two thirds between 1996 and 2003 (whereas the total number of juvenile court cases decreased by only 9 percent), apparently due, in part, to research disseminated showing the counter-deterrent effects of transfer (Bishop, 2004). Moreover, in the last several years, some States have reduced the scope of transfer laws to make fewer juvenile offenders eligible for prosecutorial or judicial transfer (Bishop, 2004; Griffin, 2003).

Yet in Florida, for example, the data show that the transferred cases were generally no more serious, and sometimes were less serious, than the cases retained in the juvenile justice system (Lanza-Kaduce, Frazier, and Bishop, 1999). Forty-three percent of the 1,100 juveniles incarcerated in adult prisons for offenses committed when they were 15 years old or younger had not previously been committed to a juvenile justice program (Annino, 2000). Thus, the juvenile justice system never had an opportunity to rehabilitate these youth before they were transferred to the adult system, despite the fact that serious juvenile offenders in Florida report that intensive juvenile placements are relatively more beneficial than either adult prison or mild juvenile sanctions (Lane et al., 2002).

But Florida is not unique in transferring first-time offenders to the criminal court. Transfer laws, particularly automatic transfer laws, often target first-time offenders, even though they do not pose the greatest recidivism risk or threat to community safety. The frequency of offending, instead of the seriousness of the first offense, best predicts overall recidivism and the risk for committing a subsequent violent offense (see Bishop, 2004; Piquero, 2000; Redding, 1997). To best achieve reductions in recidivism, the overall number of juvenile offenders transferred to the criminal justice system should be minimized. Moreover, those who are transferred should be the chronic repeat offenders—rather than first-time offenders—particularly in cases where the first-time offense is a violent offense.

Conclusion

Most practitioners would agree, consistent with the extant research, that it is important that the juvenile courts' response to juvenile offenders be calibrated to have sufficient effectiveness as a deterrent while not being overly punitive. The practice of transferring juveniles for trial and sentencing in adult criminal court has, however, produced the unintended effect of increasing recidivism, particularly in violent offenders, and thereby of promoting life-course criminality (Scott, 2000). But, if it was indeed true that transfer laws had a deterrent effect on juvenile crime, then some of these offenders would not have offended in the first place. Although the limited extant research falls far short of providing definitive conclusions, the bulk of the empirical evidence suggests that transfer laws, as currently implemented, probably have little general deterrent effect on would-be juvenile offenders.

Notes

1 Seventeen States currently have "blended sentencing" laws (see Redding and Howell, 2000) that permit the criminal court, after its adjudication of the youthful offender, to impose juvenile sentences in certain cases. Fifteen States permit the juvenile court to impose limited criminal sanctions (Snyder and Sickmund, 2006).

2 In addition, brochures were sent to public schools announcing the law and the legal risks juvenile offenders faced, and juvenile court judges warned youth about the risks of committing violent offenses (S. Singer, 2004, personal communication).

3 These States included Arizona, Arkansas, California, Colorado, Florida, Georgia, Louisiana, Michigan, Montana, Nebraska, Oklahoma, Vermont, Virginia, and Wyoming.

4 This is the most recent in a series of studies conducted by the Florida research group. These studies, which have been funded by the Florida Department of Justice and OJJDP, are part of an ongoing research program, beginning in the mid-1980s, studying the effects of transfer in Florida. For an overview of the Florida research program, see Frazier et al., 1999.

5 The total does not equal 100 because of rounding.

[References omitted.]

CRITICAL-THINKING QUESTIONS

1. Referring back to the status offense case of Billy that opened the chapter, what are some reasons why the case was dealt with informally at intake screening?
2. What are the purposes of preadjudication juvenile detention?
3. What are some of the issues and agencies driving detention reform?
4. Describe the three primary mechanisms for transferring juvenile offenders to criminal courts. Based on the research presented in this chapter, would you advocate for the use of one mechanism over the others? Why or why not?
5. Based on the research presented in this chapter, do you believe serious juvenile offenders should be transferred to adult criminal courts? Why or why not?
6. Describe the intake process, including the key determinations, common procedures, and major options.
7. Describe the range of "informal dispositions" used in cases that are processed informally by juvenile courts.
8. Drawing from the first reading by Leiber and his colleagues (2016), summarize how race and gender, individually and in combination, influence detention and intake decisions.
9. Based on the reading by Richard Redding about juvenile transfer laws, how would you answer this question: Do transfer laws prevent juvenile crime? Be sure to consider both specific and general deterrence.

SUGGESTED READING

Bishop, Donna M., Michael Leiber, and Joseph Johnson. 2010. "Contexts of Decision Making in the Juvenile Justice System: An Organizational Approach to Understanding Minority Overrepresentation." *Youth Violence and Juvenile Justice* 8:213–233.

Griffin, Patrick, Sean Addie, Benjamin Adams, and Kathy Firestine. 2011. "Trying Juveniles as Adults: An Analysis of State Transfer Laws and Reporting." *Juvenile Offenders and Victims: National Report Series*. Washington, DC: Office of Juvenile Justice and Delinquency Prevention.

Leiber, Michael. J. 2013. "Race, Pre-and Postdetention, and Juvenile Justice Decision Making." *Crime and Delinquency* 59:396–418.

Mendel, Richard A. 2014. "Juvenile Detention Alternatives Initiative Progress Report." Baltimore, MD: The Annie E. Casey Foundation. Retrieved March 7, 2017 (www.aecf.org/resources/2014-juvenile-detention-alternatives-initiative-progress-report/).

Rodriguez, Nancy. 2010. "The Cumulative Effect of Race and Ethnicity in Juvenile Court Outcomes and Why Pre-Adjudication Detention Matters." *Journal of Research in Crime and Delinquency* 47:391–413.

Zane, Steven N., Brandon C. Welsh, and Daniel P. Mears. 2016. "Juvenile Transfer and the Specific Deterrence Hypothesis: Systematic Review and Meta-Analysis." *Criminology and Public Policy* 15:901–925.

USEFUL WEBSITES

For further information relevant to this chapter, go to the following websites.

- **Juvenile Detention Alternatives Initiative (JDAI)**, The Annie E. Casey Foundation, Juvenile Justice: www.aecf.org/work/juvenile-justice/jdai/

- **Juvenile Justice Geography, Policy, Practice and Statistics (JJGPS)**, jurisdictional age boundaries and transfer to criminal court: www.jjgps.org/jurisdictional-boundaries
- **Juvenile Transfer to Criminal Court Provisions by State**, 2009, National Center for Juvenile Justice (NCJJ): www.ncjj.org/pdf/JuvenileTransferStateSummaries2009.pdf
- **Structured Decision Making Model** in Juvenile Justice, National Council of Crime and Delinquency (NCCD): www.nccdglobal.org/assessment/structured-decision-making-sdm-model/the-sdm-model-in-juvenile-justice

GLOSSARY OF KEY TERMS

Concurrent jurisdiction: A transfer provision that gives statutory authority to prosecutors to file certain types of offenses in either juvenile or adult court.

Consent adjustment without petition: A voluntary agreement between the youth and his or her parents that is approved by a juvenile court judge. The written agreement is legally authorized in state statutory law and normally includes a wide variety of options for informal disposition, aimed at rehabilitation.

Criminal blended sentencing: A provision that gives criminal court judges the option to sentence juveniles convicted in adult court as delinquents in the juvenile justice system. This provision often requires that convicted juveniles receive a suspended criminal court sentence, in addition to the juvenile court disposition.

Detention: Detention is the short-term, secure confinement of a youth under court authority, pending court action, disposition, or placement.

Informal disposition: Resolution of cases that were referred to juvenile court, but were not petitioned for formal adjudication. A variety of informal dispositional options are available to juvenile courts, including referral to another agency for services (e.g., chemical dependency treatment, family therapy, academic tutoring, restorative justice), community service, restitution, and informal probation through the probation department.

Intake: The initial screening of cases referred to juvenile courts in order to determine the most appropriate way to handle each case—formally, informally, or by dismissal. Juvenile court intake is a discretionary decision, usually the responsibility of the juvenile probation department.

Intake conference: An informal meeting of the youth, parents, and probation/intake officer, usually in the probation department office, used to develop an agreement (consent adjustment without petition) that provides informal disposition of the referral, without formal petitioning into the juvenile court.

Judicial waiver: A transfer provision that gives statutory authority to juvenile court judges to waive the court's original jurisdiction and transfer cases to adult criminal court.

Juvenile blended sentencing: A provision that typically allows youth to be tried in juvenile court and given a juvenile disposition, but also a suspended criminal sentence, which can be imposed if an individual does not cooperate, fails to complete the juvenile disposition, or commits a new offense.

Petition: A legal document filed in juvenile court by the prosecutor's office that specifies the facts of the case, the charge(s), and the basic identifying information of the youth and his or her parents.

Preliminary inquiry: A youth assessment conducted by probation officers, used to inform the intake screening decision. The assessment collects pertinent information about the alleged offense and the youth, including a chemical dependency evaluation, educational assessment, and determination of mental health and family service needs.

Referral: A written document, usually from the police, parents, or schools, that requests or results in juvenile court consideration of a particular matter involving a juvenile.

Reverse waiver: A provision that allows juveniles whose cases are being handled in adult courts to petition to have their cases heard instead in juvenile courts, for either trial or disposition.

Screening: The review of cases referred to the juvenile court, usually by the probation department. Intake screening results in a determination of how the case will be handled—formally, informally, or by dismissal.

Statutory exclusion: A transfer provision in which state statutes exclude certain juvenile offenders and offenses from juvenile court jurisdiction, and these cases originate in criminal rather than juvenile court. State statutes providing for statutory exclusion usually set age and offense limits for excluded offenses.

NOTE

1 *Schall v. Martin* 104 U.S. 2403 (1984).

REFERENCES

Annie E. Casey Foundation. 2014. "Juvenile Detention Alternatives Initiative (JDAI) 2013 Annual Results Report: Inter-Site Conference Summary." Retrieved February 26, 2015 (www.aecf.org/resources/juvenile-detention-alternatives-initiative-2013-annual-results-report/).

Beck, Allen and Paige M. Harrison. 2008. "Sexual Victimization in State and Federal Prisons Reported by Inmates." Washington, DC: U.S. Department of Justice, Bureau of Justice Statistics.

Bishop, Donna M., Michael Leiber, and Joseph Johnson. 2010. "Contexts of Decision Making in the Juvenile Justice System: An Organizational Approach to Understanding Minority Overrepresentation." *Youth Violence and Juvenile Justice* 8:213–233.

Brown, Joe M. and Jon R. Sorensen. 2013. "Race, Ethnicity, Gender, and Waiver to Adult Court." *Journal of Ethnicity in Criminal Justice* 11:181–195.

Cheesman, Fred. 2011. "A Decade of NCSC Research on Blended Sentencing of Juvenile Offenders." Pp. 112–117 in *Future Trends in State Courts 2011*, edited by Carol R. Flango, Amy M. McDowell, Charles F. Campbell, and Neal B. Kauder. Williamsburg, VA: National Center for State Courts.

Cheesman, Fred L., II, Nicole L. Waters, and Hunter Hurst IV. 2010. "Who Gets a Second Chance? An Investigation of Ohio's Blended Juvenile Sentence." *Journal of Health and Human Services Administration* 33:406–450.

Coalition for Juvenile Justice. 2008. "State-Level Detention Reform: A Practice Guide for State Advisory Groups." Juvenile Detention Alternatives Initiative, The Annie E. Casey Foundation. Retrieved March 7, 2017 (www.jdaihelpdesk.org/JDAI%20Practice%20Guides/Practice%20Guide%203-%20State-Level%20Detention%20Reform.pdf).

Davis, Jaya and Sorensen, Jon. R. 2012. "Disproportionate Juvenile Minority Confinement: A State-Level Assessment of Racial Threat." *Youth Violence and Juvenile Justice* 11:296–312.

Fagan, Jeffrey, Aaron Kupchik, and Akiva Liberman. 2003. "Be Careful What You Wish for: The Comparative Impacts of Juvenile versus Criminal Court Sanctions on Recidivism among Adolescent Felony Offenders." Columbia Law School Working Paper No. 03-62.

Fagan, Jeffrey and Franklin E. Zimring. 2000. *The Changing Borders of Juvenile Justice: Transfer of Adolescents to the Criminal Court.* Chicago: University of Chicago.

Feld, Barry C. 2008. "A Slower Form of Death: Implications of *Roper v. Simmons* for Juveniles Sentenced to Life without Parole." *Notre Dame Journal of Law, Ethics, and Public Policy* 22:9–65.

Feld, Barry C. 2014. *Juvenile Justice Administration in a Nutshell.* St. Paul: West.

Feld, Barry C. and Donna M. Bishop. 2014. "Transfer of Juveniles to Criminal Court." Pp. 801–842 in *The Oxford Handbook of Juvenile Crime and Juvenile Justice,* edited by B. C. Feld and D. M. Bishop. New York: Oxford University Press.

Fix, Rebecca L., Spencer T. Fix, Christine M. Wienke Totura, and Barry R. Burkhart. 2016. "Disproportionate Minority Contact among Juveniles Adjudicated for Sexual, Violent, and General Offending: The Importance of Home, School, and Community Contexts." *Crime & Delinquency* 63:189–209.

Furdella, Julie and Charles Puzzanchera. 2015. "Delinquency Cases in Juvenile Court, 2013." *Juvenile Offenders and Victims: National Report Series, Fact Sheet.* Pittsburgh, PA: National Center for Juvenile Justice.

Griffin, Patrick, Sean Addie, Benjamin Adams, and Kathy Firestine. 2011. "Trying Juveniles as Adults: An Analysis of State Transfer Laws and Reporting." *Juvenile Offenders and Victims: National Report Series.* Washington, DC: Office of Juvenile Justice and Delinquency Prevention.

Griffin, Patrick and Patricia Torbet (editors). 2002. "Desktop Guide to Good Probation Practice." Pittsburgh, PA: National Center for Juvenile Justice. Retrieved March 20, 2016 (www.ncjj.org/pdf/DesktopGuide2002_full.pdf).

Hemmens, Craig, Benjamin Steiner, and David Mueller. 2004. *Significant Cases in Juvenile Justice.* Los Angeles: Roxbury.

Hockenberry, Sarah and Charles Puzzanchera. 2014. "Delinquency Cases Waived to Criminal Court, 2011." *Juvenile Offenders and Victims: National Report Series.* Washington, DC: Office of Juvenile Justice and Delinquency Prevention.

Hockenberry, Sarah and Charles Puzzanchera. 2015. *Juvenile Court Statistics 2013.* Pittsburgh, PA: National Center for Juvenile Justice.

Hockenberry, Sarah and Charles Puzzanchera. 2017. *Juvenile Court Statistics 2014.* Pittsburgh, PA: National Center for Juvenile Justice.

Hockenberry, Sarah, Andrew Wachter, and Anthony Sladky. 2016. "Juvenile Residential Facility Census, 2014." *National Report Series Bulletin.* Washington, DC: Office of Juvenile Justice and Delinquency Prevention.

Holman, Barry and Jason Ziedenberg. 2006. *The Dangers of Detention: The Impact of Incarcerating Youth in Detention and Other Secure Facilities.* Washington, DC: Justice Policy Institute.

Hsia, Heidi M., George S. Bridges, and Rosalie McHale. 2004. *Disproportionate Minority Confinement 2002 Update.* Washington, DC: Office of Juvenile Justice and Delinquency Prevention.

Johnson, Kristin, Lonn Lanza-Kaduce, and Jennifer Woolard. 2011. "Disregarding Graduated Treatment: Why Transfer Aggravates Recidivism." *Crime and Delinquency* 57:756–777.

Jones, Chenelle A. 2016. "Is Disproportionate Minority Contact Improving? An Exploratory Analysis of the Arrest, Confinement, and Transfer Stages in Rural and Urban Settings." *Journal of Ethnicity in Criminal Justice* 14:40–57.

Jordan, Kareem L. 2014. "Juvenile Status and Criminal Sentencing: Does It Matter in the Adult System?" *Youth Violence and Juvenile Justice* 12:315–331.

Kupchik, Aaron. 2006. *Judging Juveniles: Prosecuting Adolescents in Adult and Juvenile Courts.* New York: New York University Press.

Kupchik, Aaron, Jeffrey Fagan, and Akiva Liberman. 2003. "Punishment, Proportionality, and Jurisdictional Transfer of Adolescent Offenders: A Test of the Leniency Gap Hypothesis." *Stanford Law and Policy Review* 14:57–83.

Kurlychek, Megan C. 2016. "Effectiveness of Juvenile Transfer to Adult Court: Implications from Current Research and Directions for Future Study." *Criminology and Public Policy* 15:897–900.

Kurlychek, Megan and Brian D. Johnson. 2004. "The Juvenile Penalty: A Comparison of Juvenile and Young Adult Sentencing Outcomes in Criminal Court." *Criminology* 42:485–517.

Kurlychek, Megan and Brian D. Johnson. 2010. "Juvenility and Punishment: Sentencing Juveniles in Adult Criminal Court." *Criminology* 48:725–757.

Lane, Jodi, Lonn Lanza-Kaduce, Charles E. Frazier, and Donna M. Bishop. 2002. "Adult versus Juvenile Sanctions: Voices of Incarcerated Youths." *Crime and Delinquency* 48:431–455.

Lanza-Kaduce, Lonn, Jodi Lane, Donna M. Bishop, and Charles E. Frazier. 2005. "Juvenile Offenders and Adult Felony Recidivism: The Impact of Transfer." *Journal of Crime and Justice* 28:59–77.

Leiber, Michael J. 2013. "Race, Pre- and Post-Detention, and Juvenile Justice Decision Making." *Crime and Delinquency* 59:396–418.

Leiber, Michael. J. and Lyndsay N. Boggess, 2012. "Race, Probation Violations, and Structured Secure Detention Decision Making in Three Jurisdictions." *Youth Violence and Juvenile Justice* 10:333–353.

Leiber, Michael J. and Sarah Jane Brubaker. 2010. "Does the Gender of the Intake Probation Officer Contextualize the Treatment of Black Youth?" *Justice Research and Policy* 12:51–76.

Leiber, Michael J., Sarah Jane Brubaker, and Kristan C. Fox. 2009. "A Closer Look at the Individual and Joint Effects of Gender and Race on Juvenile Justice Decision Making." *Feminist Criminology* 4:333–358.

Leiber, Michael J. and Kristin Y. Mack. 2003. "The Individual and Joint Effects of Race, Gender, and Family Status on Juvenile Justice Decision-Making." *Journal of Research in Crime and Delinquency* 40:34–70.

Leiber, Michael J. and Jennifer H. Peck. 2015. "Race, Gender, Crime Severity, and Decision Making in the Juvenile Justice System." *Crime and Delinquency* 61:771–797.

Leiber, Michael J., Jennifer H. Peck, and Maude Beaudry-Cyr. 2016. "When Does Race and Gender Matter? The Interrelationships between the Gender of Probation Officers and Juvenile Court Detention and Intake Outcomes." *Justice Quarterly* 33:614–641.

Loughran, Thomas A., Edward P. Mulvey, Carol A. Schubert, Laurie A. Chassin, Laurence Steinberg, Alex R. Piquero, Jeffrey Fagan, Sonia Cota-Robles, Elizabeth Cauffman, and Sandy Losoya. 2010. "Differential Effects of Adult Court Transfer on Juvenile Offender Recidivism." *Law and Human Behavior* 34:476–488.

MacKenzie, Doris. 1987. "Age and Adjustment to Prison." *Criminal Justice and Behavior* 14:427–447.

Mendel, Richard A. 2014. "Juvenile Detention Alternatives Initiative Progress Report." Baltimore, MD: The Annie E. Casey Foundation. Retrieved March 7, 2017 (www.aecf.org/resources/2014-juvenile-detention-alternatives-initiative-progress-report/).

MacArthur Foundation. 2015. *Juvenile Justice in a Developmental Framework: A 2015 Status Report.* John D. and Catherine T. MacArthur Foundation.

McGowan, Angela, Robert Hahn, Akiva Liberman, Alex Crosby, Mindy Fullilove, Robert Johnson, Eve Moscicki, LeShawndra Price, Susan Snyder, Farris Tuma, Jessica Lowy, Peter Briss, Stella Cory, and Glenda Stone, Task Force on Community Preventive Services. 2007. "Effects on Violence of Laws and Policies Facilitating the Transfer of Juveniles from the Juvenile Justice System to the Adult Justice System: A Systematic Review." *American Journal of Preventive Medicine* 32:S7–S28.

McKay, Patrick, Dusten Hollist, Jacob Coolidge, Wesley Delano, Ian Greenwood, Michael King, Tyson McLean, James Burfeind, Chuck Harris, Daniel Doyle. 2014 "The Montana Pre-Adjudicatory Detention Risk Assessment Instrument." Retrieved March 8, 2017 (http://mbcc.mt.gov/Portals/130/Data/Reports/2014 RAI_DRAI_Coma.pdf).

Mulvey, Edward P. and Carol A. Schubert. 2012. "Youth in Prison and Beyond." Pp. 843–867 in *The Oxford Handbook of Juvenile Crime and Juvenile Justice*, edited by B. C. Feld and D. M. Bishop. New York: Oxford University Press.

Myers, David. L. 2005. *Boys among Men: Trying and Sentencing Juveniles as Adults.* Westport, CT: Praeger.

Office of Juvenile Justice and Delinquency Prevention (OJJDP). 2016. *Statistical Briefing Book.* Washington, DC: Office of Juvenile Justice and Delinquency Prevention. Retrieved July 3, 2017 (www.ojjdp.gov/ojstatbb/corrections/qa08502.asp?qaDate=2014).

Pope, Carl E., Rick Lovell, and Heidi M. Hsia. 2002. "Disproportionate Minority Confinement: A Review of the Research Literature from 1989 through 2001." Washington, DC: Office of Juvenile Justice and Delinquency Prevention.

Puzzanchera, Charles and Melissa Sickmund. 2008. *Juvenile Court Statistics 2005*. Pittsburgh, PA: National Center for Juvenile Justice.

Redding, Richard E. 2010. "Juvenile Transfer Laws: An Effective Deterrent to Delinquency?" *Juvenile Justice Bulletin*. Washington, DC: Office of Juvenile Justice and Delinquency Prevention.

Redding, Richard E. 2015. "Lost in Translation No More: Marketing Evidence-Based Policies for Reducing Juvenile Crime." Pp. 139–155 in *A New Juvenile Justice: Total Reform for a Broken System*, edited by Nancy E. Dowd. New York: NYU Press.

Redding, Richard E. 2016. "One Size Does Not Fit All: The Deterrent Effect of Transferring Juveniles to Criminal Court." *Criminology and Public Policy* 15:939–948.

Rodriguez, Nancy. 2007. "Juvenile Court Context and Detention Decisions: Reconsidering the Role of Race, Ethnicity, and Community Characteristics in Juvenile Court Processes." *Justice Quarterly* 24:629–656.

Rodriguez, Nancy. 2010. "The Cumulative Effect of Race and Ethnicity in Juvenile Court Outcomes and Why Preadjudication Detention Matters." *Journal of Research in Crime and Delinquency* 47:391–413.

Scott, Elizabeth and Laurence Steinberg. 2008. *Rethinking Juvenile Justice*. Cambridge, MA: Harvard University Press.

Sedlak, Andrea J. and Karla S. McPherson. 2010. "Conditions of Confinement: Findings from the Survey of Youth in Residential Placement." Washington, DC: Office of Juvenile Justice and Delinquency Prevention.

Sellers, Brian G. and Bruce A. Arrigo. 2009. "Adolescent Transfer, Developmental Maturity, and Adjudicative Competence: An Ethical and Justice Policy Inquiry." *The Journal of Criminal Law and Criminology* 99:435–487.

Sickmund, Melissa. 2003. "Juveniles in Court." *Juvenile Offenders and Victims: National Report Series*. Washington, DC: Office of Juvenile Justice and Delinquency Prevention.

Sickmund, Melissa, T.J. Sladky, Wei Kang, and Charles Puzzanchera. 2017. "Easy Access to the Census of Juveniles in Residential Placement." Retrieved September 26, 2017 (www.ojjdp.gov/ojstatbb/ezacjrp/).

Sickmund, Melissa and Charles Puzzanchera (editors). 2014. *Juvenile Offenders and Victims: 2014 National Report*. Pittsburgh, PA: National Center for Juvenile Justice.

Stahl, Anne L. 2008. "Petitioned Status Offense Cases in Juvenile Courts, 2004." *OJJDP Fact Sheet*. Washington, DC: Office of Juvenile Justice and Delinquency Prevention.

Steiner, Benjamin. 2009. "The Effects of Juvenile Transfer to Criminal Court on Incarceration Decisions." *Justice Quarterly* 26:77–106.

Steiner, Benjamin, Craig Hemmens, and Valerie Bell. 2006. "Legislative Waiver Reconsidered: General Deterrent Effects of Statutory Exclusion Laws Enacted Post-1979." *Justice Quarterly* 23:34–59.

Steiner, Benjamin and Emily Wright. 2006. "Assessing the Relative Effects of State Direct File Waiver Laws on Violent Juvenile Crime: Deterrence or Irrelevance?" *Journal of Criminal Law and Criminology* 96:1451–1477.

Steinhart, David. 2006. "Juvenile Detention Risk Assessment: A Guide to Juvenile Detention Reform." Baltimore, MD: The Annie E. Casey Foundation, Juvenile Detention Alternatives.

Thomas, Shaun A., Stacy C. Moak, and Jeffrey T. Walker. 2012. "The Contingent Effect of Race in Juvenile Court Detention Decisions: The Role of Racial and Symbolic Threat." *Race and Justice* 3:239–265.

Tracy, Paul E., Kimberly Kempf-Leonard, and Stephanie Abramoske-James. 2009. "Gender Differences in Delinquency and Juvenile Justice Processing Evidence from National Data." *Crime and Delinquency* 55:171–215.

Woolard, Jennifer L., Candice Odgers, Lonn Lanza-Kaduce, and Hayley Daglis. 2005. "Juveniles within Correctional Settings: Legal Pathways and Developmental Considerations." *International Journal of Forensic Mental Health* 4:1–18.

Zane, Steven N., Brandon C. Welsh, and Daniel P. Mears. 2016. "Juvenile Transfer and the Specific Deterrence Hypothesis: Systematic Review and Meta-Analysis." *Criminology and Public Policy* 15:901–925.

Zang, Angel. 2016. *U.S. Age Boundaries of Delinquency*. JJGPS StateScan. Pittsburgh, PA: National Center for Juvenile Justice.

Chapter 9

FORMAL PROCEDURES OF JUVENILE COURTS: ADJUDICATION AND DISPOSITION

CHAPTER TOPICS

- **Petition**
- **Adjudication hearings**
- **Disposition**

CHAPTER LEARNING OBJECTIVES

After completing this chapter, students should be able to:

- Describe the purpose and content of juvenile court petitions.
- Distinguish the series of hearings that make up the adjudication process.
- Depict due process rights during adjudication.
- Differentiate adjudication and disposition in terms of purpose and process.
- Inventory the range of dispositional options that are typically authorized under state statutory law.
- Provide examples of contemporary changes in the philosophy and practice of juvenile disposition.

CHAPTER CONTENTS

CASE IN POINT

A DISPOSITIONAL ORDER IN JUVENILE COURT

While the names and places of this dispositional order are made-up, its structure and content are similar to the dispositional orders used in many juvenile courts. In this case, Kent Clausen, age 16, appeared for disposition before the Youth Court of Morris County on a petition of five counts of residential burglary, which he admitted to at arraignment. The dispositional order includes an adjudication as a "delinquent youth" and a suspended execution of "commitment" to the state department of corrections, resulting in probation.

MARY M. MALLOY
District Court Judge
Fifth Judicial District
Morris County Courthouse
Lancaster, Indiana

FIFTH JUDICIAL DISTRICT COURT, MORRIS COUNTY

IN THE MATTER OF: Cause No. DJ 96 - 58

KENT CLAUSEN ***ORDER TO ADJUDICATE A DELINQUENT YOUTH***

A Youth Under the Age of 18.

On the 1st day of October 2016, Kent Clausen, a youth of this County, 16 years of age, was brought before the Court pursuant to a Petition of Felony Burglary. The youth appeared with his parents, Kirk and Karen Clausen, and his attorney, Michael Langley. The Court fully advised the youth and his parents of all legal rights accorded by the laws of the State of Indiana. Also present were Deputy County Attorney Jamie Kline, and Juvenile Probation Officer Charles Stevens.

Upon being questioned by the Court concerning the allegations in the petition, the youth admitted the offense. Based on the admission, the Court hereby makes a **Finding of Delinquency**, in addition to a finding that the youth had violated his informal probation, as stipulated in a consent adjustment without petition [an informal agreement between the youth, parents, and probation officer, and approved by judge] for a previous offense of trespass. After reviewing the predispositional report, and having established that every reasonable effort was made to deal with the youth's delinquent behavior informally, in the least restrictive manner, the Court enters the following Order:

IT IS HEREBY ORDERED that Kent Clausen is **adjudicated a Delinquent Youth.**

IT IS HEREBY ORDERED that Kent Clausen is **committed to the Indiana State Department of Correction** for placement in the Logansport Juvenile Correctional Facility Treatment Unit. The commitment order is hereby suspended on the following conditions.

1. The youth will obey all local, state, and federal laws.
2. The youth will be placed on formal probation for an indefinite period of time, as determined by this Court. The Court will review progress on probation every six months.
3. The youth will attend school regularly and will follow all rules of the school; and he will maintain passing grades.
4. The youth will make no change in address, school, or employment without first consulting his probation officer.
5. The youth will obey parents and let them know where he is going and with whom.
6. The youth will report promptly to his probation officer as directed.
7. The youth will not leave the State of Indiana without consulting his probation officer.
8. The youth shall avoid undesirable places and bad companions.
9. The youth will not be in possession or consume any alcohol or illicit drugs.
10. The youth will participate in cognitive behavior therapy until the youth successfully completes treatment, as determined by the counselor. The parents will arrange and pay for this course of treatment.
11. The youth will submit to random drug testing and UA's upon request of his probation officer.
12. The youth will submit to a search of his person or living area at the request of his probation officer.
13. The youth is liable for payment of restitution in the amount to be determined by the Court, to be paid in full by the time the youth turns 18 years of age. The Court will retain jurisdiction over the youth should he fail to pay restitution.

If the youth fails to abide by these conditions, the order of commitment to the Department will be executed after a revocation hearing before the Court.

DONE IN OPEN COURT this 1st day of October, 2016.
DATED this 2nd day of October, 2016.

Mary M. Malloy
Mary M. Malloy
DISTRICT COURT JUDGE

Until fairly recently, formal proceedings in juvenile courts were confidential and closed to the public (Sickmund and Puzzanchera 2014). As a result, they were not widely known or understood. The two primary components of formal juvenile court proceedings are adjudication and disposition. Adjudication is initiated by a legal document called a petition. **Adjudication** involves a series of court hearings that make judicial findings or determinations regarding the "facts of the case." The ultimate purpose of adjudication is twofold: (1) to determine whether the youth is responsible for the offense(s) charged in the petition, and (2) to determine whether the youth should be legally declared a "delinquent youth," a "serious juvenile offender," or a "status offender" by the juvenile court.

While disposition is similar to sentencing in adult court, it is distinctive in purpose and process. **Formal disposition** is the juvenile court's response to a youth's admission of a petition or the court's finding that a youth violated statutory law. Recall from Chapter 8 that disposition may also be informal, providing resolution of cases that are not petitioned into juvenile court for adjudication. Formal disposition follows from adjudication, and it seeks to provide an individualized, rehabilitative, and least restrictive resolution to cases that are officially processed by the juvenile court. The court order of formal disposition may require involvement in rehabilitation programs, community service, restitution, formal probation, out-of-home placement, or confinement.

Figure 9.1 depicts the juvenile court processes of intake, adjudication, and disposition. Juvenile court intake was covered in Chapter 8 and the present chapter discusses adjudication and disposition, beginning with the legal document that charges a youth in juvenile court: the petition.

PETITION

If intake screening determines that the case should be dealt with formally by the juvenile court, a **petition** is filed by the prosecutor's office or the probation department to initiate the formal juvenile court process of adjudication. The petition specifies the jurisdiction of the juvenile court, the charges in statutory and ordinary language, the facts of the offense including time and place of occurrence, and basic identifying information for the youth and his or her parents.

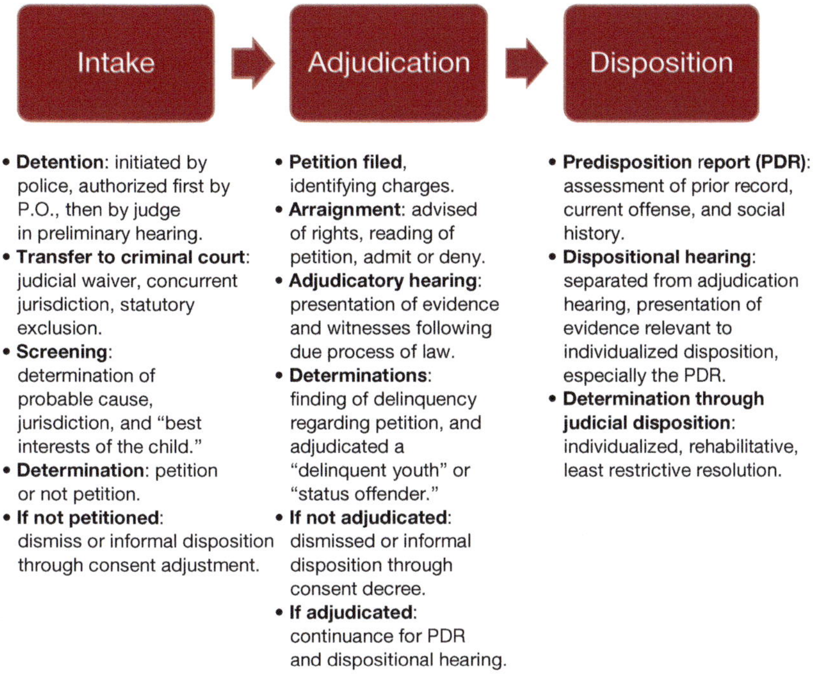

FIGURE 9.1 *The juvenile court processes of intake, adjudication, and disposition.*

Petition: Extent, trends, and demographics

Figure 9.2 shows that 56 percent of all delinquency cases handled by juvenile courts in 2014 were petitioned. The number of petitioned delinquency cases peaked in 1997 and then fell by almost half in 2014. Compared to cases that are not petitioned into juvenile court, delinquency cases that are formally processed through a petition tend to involve older juveniles (over age 15) with longer court histories, who are charged with more serious offenses. In addition, males are more likely than females, and blacks are more likely than youth of other races to have their cases petitioned (Hockenberry and Puzzanchera 2017; Sickmund and Puzzanchera 2014).

Petitioned status offense cases

Juvenile Court Statistics provides information about status offenses for cases that are handled formally in juvenile courts through petition. Therefore, we have no indication of how many or what types of status offense cases are referred to juvenile courts or what portion of these cases are petitioned. Instead, *Juvenile Court Statistics* reports on the case processing of five major categories of petitioned status offenses: running away, truancy, curfew violations, ungovernability, and underage liquor law violations (e.g., minor in possession of alcohol and underage drinking) (Hockenberry and Puzzanchera 2017). In 2014, an estimated 100,100 status offense cases were petitioned into juvenile courts nationwide. Of these cases, 53 percent involved truancy, 14 percent liquor law violations, 9 percent ungovernability, 8 percent curfew, and 8 percent runaway; the remaining 9 percent were categorized as miscellaneous. "Between 1995 and 2002, the formally

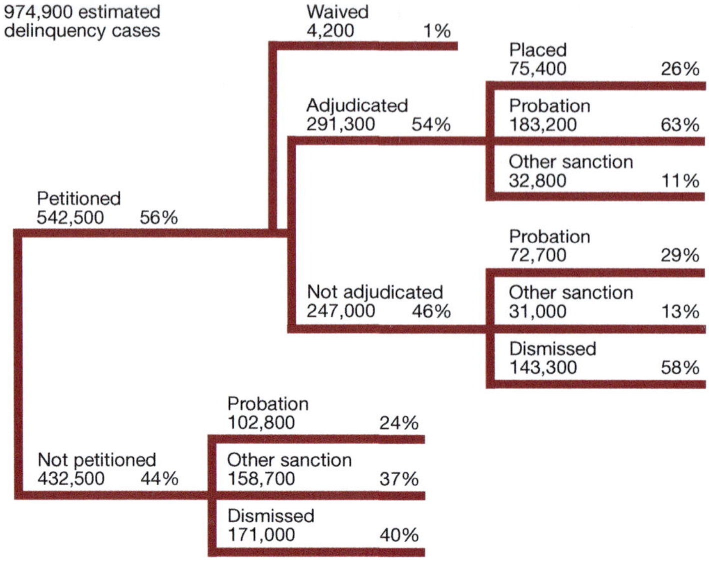

FIGURE 9.2 *Juvenile court processing of delinquency cases, 2014. While a majority of cases (56%) handled by juvenile courts are petitioned, a sizeable proportion (44%) are not petitioned and are either dismissed or provided some form of informal disposition. Of the cases that are petitioned, over half (54%) result in adjudication. Almost two-thirds (63%) of the cases that are adjudicated result in probation as the most severe juvenile court disposition.*

Source: Hockenberry and Puzzanchera (2017:54). Used with permission of the National Center for Juvenile Justice.

handled status offense caseload increased considerably (61%) and then declined 50% through 2014" (Hockenberry and Puzzanchera 2017:68). This decline in the number of petitioned status offense cases occurred for all racial groups. Although males accounted for 58 percent of all petitioned status offense cases in juvenile courts, females made up a substantially larger portion as compared to the delinquency caseload—42 percent. Furthermore, the case rate of petitioned status offense cases increases substantially from age 12 through 16, with the rate at 16 being 7 times greater than at age 12 (Hockenberry and Puzzanchera 2017).

ADJUDICATION HEARINGS

When formal court processing is deemed necessary, cases proceed through a series of hearings, with varying names, that serve particular purposes. Be aware that the names of these hearings and the procedures that they follow vary from state to state. Yet the adjudication processes of most juvenile courts are similar because of similar personnel and due process requirements. "Juvenile court process and practice: Key personnel in the juvenile court process" depicts the work roles in the formal juvenile court processes.

The first adjudication hearing is often referred to as a **probable cause** or **detention hearing**. This hearing makes an initial determination about whether sufficient information and evidence exist to substantiate that a youth was likely involved in activity that violated state criminal or status offense law. Judges also make determinations regarding continued detention in probable cause hearings. An **arraignment hearing** typically follows at a separate time in order to advise the youth of his or her rights and obligations, to read the petition, and to allow the youth to admit or deny the petition. The vast majority of juveniles admit the petition at arraignment (Feld 2014). If the youth denies the petition, an **adjudicatory hearing** follows. This hearing

JUVENILE COURT PROCESS AND PRACTICE: KEY PERSONNEL IN THE JUVENILE COURT PROCESS

- **Juvenile court judges** are the principal players in juvenile courts. Either elected or appointed, depending on the structure of state juvenile courts, juvenile court judges have wide ranging authority and discretion under state statutory law. They preside over all juvenile court proceedings and interpret statutory law, both criminal and procedural, and youth court acts. Juvenile court judges make determinations regarding detention, court procedures, rules of evidence, adjudication, and disposition. In addition, juvenile court judges often supervise juvenile probation departments when probation is a judicial entity.

- **Juvenile prosecutors** are responsible for charging youth with criminal and status offenses and presenting the state's case to the juvenile court. Prosecutors have various titles in different jurisdictions: county attorney, district attorney, state attorney, or United States attorney. Before the due process revolution of juvenile justice (1966–1975), prosecutors normally were not present in juvenile courts because traditional juvenile courts operated under the rehabilitative ideal, using a child welfare approach with informal, family-like procedures, instead of an adversarial process (see Chapter 2). In the last 40 years, prosecutors have taken on a larger role in juvenile court process, especially at intake and during adjudicatory hearings.

- **Defense attorneys** also play a larger role in juvenile court proceedings since the due process revolution in juvenile justice. With juvenile justice proceedings becoming more complex, the right to counsel is essential for youth to have their cases handled with justice and fairness. Knowledge of juvenile court proceedings and trial advocacy, together with an appreciation of adolescent development are necessary skills for effective legal counsel when working with youth accused of delinquent offenses. Nonetheless, recent research has questioned the advantage of defense counsel in juvenile court outcomes, especially at disposition (Peck and Beaudry-Cyr 2016; Feld 2012; Feld and Schaefer 2010; Burruss and Kempf-Leonard 2002).

- **Probation officers** are the eyes, ears, and feet of the juvenile court. Their duties are wide-ranging and carried out with extensive statutory authority and discretion. Duties include intake screening to determine informal or formal case handling, coordinating detention, conducting informal disposition, being present in the courtroom during adjudication and disposition, conducting predisposition investigations and writing predisposition reports, implementing disposition, and most notably, probation supervision.

comes closest to an adversarial trial in adult court, as evidence and witnesses are presented first by the prosecutor and then the defense, following due process of law. The outcome of this fact-finding process is a legal determination by the judge about whether the juvenile committed the offense(s). This is usually referred to as a *finding of fact* or a *finding of delinquency*. If the youth admitted to, or was found to have committed the offense(s), the judge then decides if the youth should be adjudicated a "**delinquent youth**" or adjudicated a "**status offender**." Both terms designate a legal status that results from the juvenile court's determination that the youth violated criminal law (delinquent youth) or status offense law (status offender), and that the youth is in need of juvenile court assistance. Recall from Chapter 2 that most state statutes now use different terms to refer to a status offender, such as "child in need of supervision" (CHINS), "minor in need of supervision" (MINS), "youth in need of intervention" (YINI), or some equivalent term. On the other end of the adjudication continuum is a third legal status, introduced in conjunction with "get tough" policies initiated in the 1980s. Many states statutes were changed to add a third adjudication category of "**serious juvenile offender**," or some equivalent term, to designate youth who commit felony offenses, including crimes against persons, serious property offenses, or offenses involving dangerous drugs. This adjudicatory category allows for more punitive disposition under statutory law.

Procedural due process rights during adjudication

In the ten-year period from 1966 to 1975, the U.S. Supreme Court decided a series of cases that injected due process rights, drawn from the U.S. Constitution, into juvenile justice procedures (Feld 2003, 2014; Sickmund and Puzzanchera 2014; Hemmens, Steiner, and Mueller 2013). For juveniles, these procedural due process rights center on formal adjudication procedures in juvenile courts. It would be worthwhile to review the facts and findings of the five Supreme Court cases that constitute the due process revolution in juvenile justice, summarized in Chapter 2.

Foremost among these Supreme Court cases is *in re Gault* (1967).[1] The Court ruled that in adjudicatory hearings, which may possibly result in commitment to secure institutions, juveniles must be given the "essentials of due process," including timely and specific notice of charges, right to counsel, right to confront and cross examine witnesses, and privilege against self-incrimination (Feld 2014; Hemmens et al. 2013; Feld 2012). These essential due process rights provide the foundation for formal adjudicatory hearings.

While each state operates its own juvenile court system, the procedural rights that were extended through the due process revolution apply to all juvenile courts, thereby providing similarity to adjudication procedures across courts, but clearly not uniformity. We will characterize the adjudication process of juvenile courts by identifying key elements of procedural due process (Feld 2014, 2012).

- **Notice of charges**: As discussed earlier in the chapter, a petition is the charging document that initiates formal handling of cases by juvenile courts. Petitions establish the legal basis of the case and their form and content is specified in statutory law. Petitions must extend due process. This means that they must provide timely written notice (adequate time for preparation) and the notice must be given to parents; petitions must be specific, identifying the statutory law that was allegedly violated; and petitions must be concise and understandable.

- **Hearings and evidence**: Adjudicatory hearings in youth courts involve similar due process right as criminal court trial proceedings, except the right to a jury trial (Feld 2014). In fact, adjudicatory hearings are considered criminal prosecutions in most states, following explicit "rules of evidence," which regulate the presentation and admissibility of evidence and witnesses. Case law and state statutory law requires that juveniles be provided with basic due process of law during adjudicatory hearings, including the right to confront and cross-examine a witness, the right to seek suppression of illegally obtained evidence, and the privilege against self-incrimination.
- **Right to counsel**: The U.S. Supreme Court in *in re Gault* (1967) declared that "the assistance of counsel is . . . essential for the determination of delinquency." The Court also acknowledged that involvement of lawyers in juvenile adjudication would result in a more formal and adversarial process. Even with the right to counsel, the role of attorneys in adjudication hearings is not always well established, and is quite variable across cases within a particular juvenile court and across juvenile courts. Three roles are most prominent for defense attorneys in juvenile court: (1) the *adversarial role*, transplanted from criminal courts, provides a zealous defense during adjudicatory hearings; (2) the *guardian ad litem role*, which seeks the "best interests of the child" by providing adult, legal advocacy; and (3) the *social worker role*, in which the attorney serves as a treatment consultant to the court, seeking appropriate rehabilitation for the youth (Feld 2014).

  In most jurisdictions, juveniles may waive their right to counsel, and judges are not required to appoint counsel. The basic constitutional standard is that the juvenile must make a "knowing, intelligent, and voluntary" waiver (Feld 2014:338).
- **Competency:** "Appellate courts have held that the right to counsel has little meaning if the juvenile is incompetent to stand trial, and that counsel cannot be effective if youths are unable to communicate or to cooperate with their attorneys" (Sanborn 2009:139). The competency requirement necessitates that the juvenile understands the nature of the charges and can assist in the preparation and presentation of a defense, including being capable of testifying at the adjudication hearing.

  Recent research contends that there are significant differences in "adjudicative competence" between juveniles and adults such that young people are less likely to fully understand legal proceedings and to provide relevant information to their lawyers. They are also less likely to make reasoned judgments and decisions about their legal situation (Scott et al. 2015a; Feld 2012; Grisso et al. 2003).

  This question of competency is often considered in terms of juvenile cases transferred to adult criminal courts, but it is equally relevant to the formal procedures of contemporary juvenile courts. In fact, a number of states have solidified the due process importance of juvenile competency considerations through enactment of statutory law protections (Bryant, Matthews, and Wilhelmsen 2015; Sanborn 2009). The chapter reading by Elizabeth Scott and her colleagues (2015b) claims that juveniles are less culpable for their involvement in crime and less competent in juvenile justice proceedings. The implications of this developmental argument for sentencing reform are also discussed in the reading.
- **Admit or deny the petition/guilty pleas**: Admissions in juvenile courts are the equivalent of guilty pleas in criminal courts. However, with the introduction of due process rights in juvenile proceedings, some youth courts no longer use the terms "admit" or "deny the petition." Regardless of the terms that are used for pleas, at arraignment, most youth admit the petition that is filed against them (Feld 2014). Admitting the petition or pleading guilty

constitutes a waiver of trial rights, including the right to a hearing, confrontation and cross-examination, privilege against self-incrimination, and proof beyond a reasonable doubt (Feld 2014). The resulting due process question relates to whether or not the admission or plea is "valid"—entered into "knowingly, intelligently, and voluntarily," and whether the record provides sufficient factual basis (Feld 2014:348; Feld 2012).

Even though most youth in juvenile courts admit the petition or plead guilty, the proportion of these admissions or guilty pleas that result from plea bargaining is unknown (Burrow and Lowery 2015). **Plea bargaining** involves negotiation between the defense attorney and the prosecutor in which the youth agrees to admit (plead guilty) to the petition, in exchange for keeping the case in juvenile court, without waiver to adult criminal court, reducing the charge(s), and/or leniency in disposition/ sentencing. Even though plea bargaining is extremely common in adult criminal courts (up to 95 percent of disposed cases in state courts), little is known about the extent of plea bargaining in juvenile justice or how its use varies across jurisdictions (Burrow and Lowery 2015; Mears 2000). Additionally, plea bargaining policies, procedures, and practices have been studied in only a limited number of jurisdictions. This research suggests that plea bargaining is growing in use and acceptance, but not necessarily with the procedural safeguards of due process that are extended in adult criminal courts (Burrow and Lowery 2015; Mears 2000; Sanborn 1993). Few courts, for example, investigate the voluntariness of juvenile admissions or pleas (Sanborn 1993).

- **Record and appeal**: The *in re Gault* (1967) decision left two constitutional rights unresolved: the right to a transcript of the proceedings and the right to appellate review (Sickmund and Puzzanchera 2014). The confidentiality and informality of the traditional juvenile court meant that these rights were unnecessary when courts operated in the best interests of the child. State statutes now routinely require that a record be made of juvenile court proceedings and that the adjudication process conclude with a written finding of fact regarding the petition. Nonetheless, state laws vary greatly with regard to the extent and timing of the right to appellate review. State statutory laws often restrict appellate review until after the final order of disposition (Feld 2014).
- **Procedural rights of status offenders**: At least initially, the *in re Gault* decision applied only to "loss of liberty" cases in which institutional confinement was a possible disposition after a finding of delinquency or conviction. The question remained, however, whether the essentials of due process introduced by this decision applied to less serious offenses, especially status offenses. Barry Feld (2014:351) observes that "states may provide somewhat different and less extensive procedural rights for status offenders." State statutory and case law vary considerably with regard to the extent to which essential due process rights are extended to status offenders, including the privilege against self-incrimination, the right to counsel, and the criminal law burden of proof—beyond a reasonable doubt.

Adjudication: Extent, trends, and demographics

In 2014, 30 percent of all delinquency cases handled by juvenile courts resulted in delinquency adjudications—a proportion that has changed little since 1997 (Hockenberry and Puzzanchera 2017:44). Figure 9.2 shows that in that same year, 54 percent of petitioned delinquency cases resulted in adjudication and 46 percent were not adjudicated. The number of adjudicated cases grew from 338,138 in 1985 to 627,223 in 1997, and then declined by 54 percent to 291,300

TABLE 9.1 Cases adjudicated delinquent in juvenile court, 2014

Most serious offense	Number of cases adjudicated	Percentage of petitioned cases adjudicated	Percentage of petitioned cases adjudicated								
			Age		Gender		Race				
			≤ 15	≥ 16	Male	Female	White	Black	Hispanic	Am. Indian	Asian
Total delinquency	291,300	54	54	53	55	49	54	50	59	65	55
Person offenses	77,500	51	52	50	53	46	51	49	57	64	57
Property offenses	95,700	54	55	52	55	48	55	50	57	67	54
Drug law violations	33,200	52	55	51	53	51	53	48	55	63	45
Public order offenses	84,900	57	56	58	59	53	58	52	64	63	61

Person offenses: criminal homicide, forcible rape, robbery, aggravated assault, simple assault, other violent sex offenses, other person offenses.
Property offenses: burglary, larceny-theft, motor vehicle theft, arson, vandalism, trespassing, stolen property, other property offenses.
Drug law violations: a broad offense category, including unlawful sale, purchase, cultivation, transportation, or use of controlled or prohibited drug.
Public order offenses: obstruction of justice, disorderly conduct, weapons offenses, liquor law violation, nonviolent sex offenses, other public order offenses.

Source: Hockenberry and Puzzanchera (2017:44, 47).

in 2014. This decline in the number of cases adjudicated since 1997 occurred for all offense categories—person, property, drugs, and public order (Hockenberry and Puzzanchera 2017).

With considerable variation in each offense category, person offense cases were least likely to be adjudicated delinquent (51 percent), while public order offense cases (57 percent) were most likely to be adjudicated delinquent (see **Table 9.1**). Younger juveniles (15 years or younger) were slightly more likely than older juveniles to be adjudicated delinquent. Petitioned delinquency cases involving males were more likely to be adjudicated delinquent than those involving females. Petitioned cases involving black youth were less likely to be adjudicated delinquent than those involving white or Asian youth, while petitioned cases involving Hispanic and American Indian youth were most likely to result in delinquency adjudication (Hockenberry and Puzzanchera 2017:44, 47).

Figure 9.2 also shows that 46 percent of the petitioned delinquency cases were not adjudicated. The largest portion of these cases were dismissed (40 percent). For other non-adjudicated cases, however, juvenile courts may still impose a variety of dispositions, including out-of-home placement, probation, restitution, and community service. The various dispositions of non-adjudicated cases are often based on a **consent decree with petition**—an agreement between the juvenile court judge, parents, youth, and probation officer.

Most petitioned status offense cases do not result in adjudication. **Figure 9.3** shows that in 2014, 42 percent of the petitioned status offense cases were adjudicated, while 58 percent were not adjudicated. From 1995 to 2002 the number of cases in which youths were adjudicated a status offender by juvenile courts increased by 82 percent, and then declined through 2014 by 64 percent, to 42,500 adjudicated status offense cases. This decline in the number of status offender adjudications occurred for all categories of status offenses—runaway, truancy, curfew, ungovernability, and liquor law. Truancy cases (42 percent) constituted the largest portion of adjudicated status offender caseloads of juvenile courts, followed by cases involving

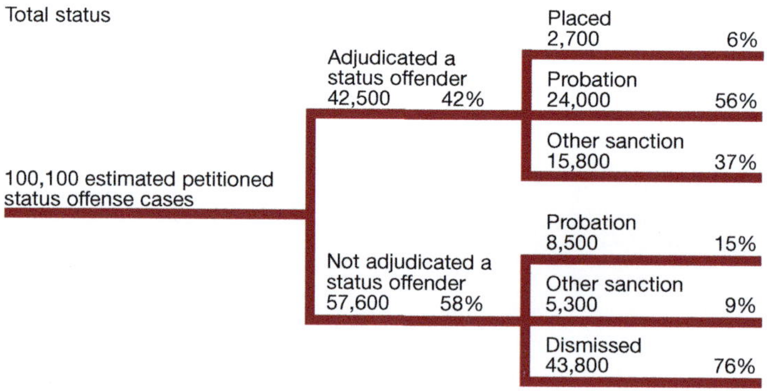

FIGURE 9.3 *Juvenile court processing of petitioned status offense cases, 2014. Juvenile Court Statistics report only petitioned status offense cases, not status offense cases that are dismissed or dealt with informally without petition. Well over half (58%) of the petitioned status offense cases are not adjudicated, and of these cases more than three-fourths (76%) are dismissed. Of the adjudicated status offense cases, over half (56%) result in probation as the most severe disposition.*

Source: Hockenberry and Puzzanchera (2017:88). Used with permission of the National Center for Juvenile Justice.

liquor laws (19 percent), ungovernability (12 percent), curfew (9 percent), runaway (7 percent), and miscellaneous (12 percent). The likelihood of adjudication in status offense cases was greater for males than females, for older status offenders (16 years or older), and for whites, as compared to other racial and ethnic groups (Hockenberry and Puzzanchera 2017:82, 83; 2015:78).

DISPOSITION

Once a youth is adjudicated a delinquent youth or a status offender, the court decides the most appropriate sanction, commonly referred to as **formal disposition**. Disposition is similar to sentencing in adult courts, yet it is distinctive in purpose and process. Traditionally, disposition has been one of the key decision points in which the juvenile court considers "the best interests of the child," seeking an individualized, rehabilitative, and least restrictive resolution to cases that are officially processed. Disposition is imposed at a *dispositional hearing*, which is separated in time and purpose from adjudication hearings (see Figure 9.1 The juvenile court processes of intake, adjudication, and disposition).

Predisposition report

After adjudication but prior to the dispositional hearing, a **predisposition report** is usually ordered by the juvenile court judge. Authorized by court order and statutory law, the report is written by the probation officer to provide an assessment of the youth and his or her background and social environment. Even with recent initiatives for punishment and accountability, the predisposition report attempts to provide assessment information to the judge so that disposition can be individualized and directed at rehabilitation. Since most youth admit the petition, the judge, at disposition, often has limited knowledge of the case. As a result, information provided to the judge through the predisposition report is especially relevant to making disposition individualized and rehabilitative.

Information for the predisposition report is gathered primarily through interviews with the youth and parents, and by checking official records such as state and federal criminal record systems and court records. In addition, the investigating probation officer usually interviews the arresting officer, other family members, and school personnel.

The predisposition report is commonly organized with three major sections: the offense section, a social history, and a summary and recommendation. The offense section covers four main areas: an official version of the offense, usually provided by the police report; commentary regarding the juvenile's version of the offense; prior record, including previous arrests, petitions, adjudications, and dispositions; and a victim impact statement (required by some state statutes). The social history section offers an assessment of the youth and his or her family background, educational experiences and achievements, friends, employment, and neighborhood context. The final section, the summary and recommendation, is the shortest, but perhaps most important section because judges often give it the most attention. Two areas of concise discussion are included in this final section. First, an evaluative summary highlights and summarizes the key findings of the assessment. Second, the probation officer offers a recommendation regarding disposition that is followed by the judge in most cases. In addition to the predisposition report, various supplemental assessments can be ordered by the court, including psychological, educational, chemical dependency, and family assessments.

Dispositional hearing

Juvenile court disposition is distinct from adjudication in philosophy, purpose, and process. The dispositional hearing is not a fact-finding or adversarial process; rather, it maintains an individualized and rehabilitative focus, pursuing the least restrictive option. The proceedings of the dispositional hearing are often not specified in statutory law. Rules of evidence do not strictly apply, nor are due process rights fully extended. For example, in conducting the dispositional hearing, the judge may provide the defense only limited opportunity to cross-examine witnesses and to contest evidence. As the subject areas of the predisposition report suggest, non-legal factors become the center of attention in the dispositional hearing. The youth's attitude, family background, school experiences, and friends all have an important influence on disposition. Disposition attempts to fulfill multiple, seemingly inconsistent goals, including public safety, nurturance, deterrence, accountability, and rehabilitation.

Dispositional options in statutory law

Disposition results in a court order prescribing sanctions; almost always more than one disposition is involved. (See "Case in Point: A Dispositional Order in Juvenile Court" at the beginning of the chapter for an illustration of a disposition order.) For example, probation is commonly included with restitution and community service. Under state statutory law, a full range of dispositions are possible, including:[2]

- Probation
- Foster or group home placement
- Placement in a residential treatment center
- Placement in a secure facility
- Placement at an assessment center
- Further medical or psychological evaluation of the youth, parents, or guardian
- Counseling for the youth, parents, or guardian
- Alcohol or drug treatment
- Commitment to a mental health facility
- Requirement that parents or guardians provide special treatment, care, or services to the youth that the court may designate
- Educational program
- Vocational training
- Mediation
- Teen court
- Drug court or some other specialized, therapeutic court
- Restitution
- Community service
- Home arrest
- Intensive supervision
- Electronic monitoring
- Drug testing
- Confiscation of the youth's driver's license
- Fine

- Payment of court costs
- Payment of victim counseling costs.

A disposition of out-of-home placement usually involves a court order of **commitment**. Commitment is the juvenile court's legal authorization for out-of-home placement of a youth who has been adjudicated delinquent. Legal custody is transferred to "the state"—more precisely to a state agency such as the juvenile court or department of corrections.

Disposition: Extent, trends, and demographics

Probation was the most restrictive disposition given in 63 percent of delinquency cases that were adjudicated in 2014 (183,200 cases; see Figure 9.2). Out-of-home placement ("Placed") was used in 26 percent of adjudicated cases, resulting in residential placement at a long-term secure facility (such as a state training school), boot camp, residential treatment center, or group home. The proportion of adjudicated cases with a disposition of out-of-home placement declined from 1985 to 2004, from 31 percent to 25 percent. Since 2005, the proportion of adjudicated youth court ordered into out-of-home placement has remained stable at about 26 or 27 percent. Over the same time period, the proportion of probation dispositions increased somewhat from 57 percent to 63 percent. Other sanctions, including drug court, non-residential community programs, restitution, and community service, were used in 13 percent of the adjudicated cases in 2014 (Hockenberry and Puzzanchera 2015, 2017; Sickmund and Puzzanchera 2014).

Once adjudicated, juveniles that were younger (15 years or younger), female, white, Hispanic, American Indian, and Asian were more likely than comparative categories to be placed on probation. In contrast, adjudicated cases involving older juveniles (16 years or older), males, blacks, and Hispanics were more likely to result in out-of-home placement (Hockenberry and Puzzanchera 2017).

Figure 9.3 shows that probation is also the most common dispositional order in adjudicated status offense cases. Juvenile court data from 2014 show that probation was the most restrictive disposition in 56 percent of adjudicated status offense cases. The percentage of adjudicated status offense cases resulting in probation was higher for youth who were younger (15 years or younger), female, and black.

Juvenile courts ordered out-of-home placement in 6 percent of all adjudicated status offense cases in 2014 (see Figure 9.3). The offense profile of adjudicated status offense cases resulting in out-of-home placement shows that 22 percent were for ungovernability, 19 percent for truancy, 18 percent for liquor law violations, 2 percent for curfew, and 18 percent for miscellaneous status offenses (including tobacco violations, violations of a court order, or offenses coded "other" by the reporting agency). The percentage of adjudicated status offense cases resulting in out-of-home placement was fairly equal across age and gender, and for white, black and Hispanic youth, with the exception of runaway offenses, for which a higher percentage of white youth were ordered into out-of-home placement (Hockenberry and Puzzanchera 2017).

Changes in philosophy and practice in juvenile disposition

Traditionally, the juvenile court pursued disposition that was individualized, rehabilitative, and the least restrictive option. The transformations in juvenile justice that were discussed in Chapter 2 altered the philosophy and practice of disposition in contemporary juvenile courts.

Three developments in juvenile disposition are especially noteworthy: blended sentences in juvenile courts, the death penalty for juveniles, and sentences of life without parole. A fourth innovation in disposition called therapeutic courts will be described in Chapter 11 under the topic of community-based corrections.

Blended sentencing

With the advent of more punitive measures in juvenile justice, 14 states have adopted "blended sentencing" (Sickmund and Puzzanchera 2014). These statutory laws authorize juvenile court judges to impose adult criminal court sanctions on certain offenders, depending on age, criminal history, and type of offense. The sanctioning powers of juvenile courts in these states have been expanded so that some juvenile offenders may receive the same penalties that adult offenders face, even when those juvenile offenders remain under the jurisdiction of the juvenile court. The most common type of blended sentence involves imposition of both a juvenile and adult sentence, with the adult sentence being suspended on the condition that the youth successfully completes the juvenile disposition. Blended sentencing is discussed more fully in Chapter 8.

Death penalty for juveniles

In *Roper v. Simmons* (2005), the U.S. Supreme Court ruled that it is unconstitutional to impose capital punishment for crimes committed while under the age of 18.[3] The 5–4 decision overturned statutes in 25 states that previously allowed the death penalty for youth under age 18. In this case, a premeditated murder was carried out by Christopher Simmons, age 17, together with a younger accomplice. Simmons confessed to the murder and provided evidence. The jury returned a guilty verdict and recommended the death penalty, even after considering the mitigating factors that Simmons had no criminal history and was under the legal age of majority. The criminal court judge sentenced Simmons to death. The case was appealed to the Supreme Court on grounds that the death penalty for a juvenile is "cruel and unusual punishment," in violation of the Eighth Amendment.

The Court acknowledged that the Eighth Amendment must be interpreted in light of "the evolving standards of decency that mark the progress in a maturing society," to determine which forms of legal punishments are so disproportionate to be considered "cruel and unusual." In the majority opinion, Justice Kennedy noted three general differences between adolescents and adults that make juveniles less responsible, or less culpable, for their behavior, and, as a result, make capital punishment for juveniles legally unjustifiable: (1) juveniles "lack maturity" and have an "underdeveloped sense of responsibility"; (2) "juveniles are more vulnerable or susceptible to negative influences and outside pressures, including peer pressure"; and (3) "the character of a juvenile is not as well formed as that of an adult." Some of the legal arguments associated with the reduced culpability of juveniles are presented in the application box "Juvenile justice law: *Roper v. Simmons* (2005)—majority and dissenting opinions."

Life without parole for juveniles

Following the Roper decision, the Supreme Court in the cases *Graham v. Florida* (2010)[4] and *Miller v. Alabama* (2012)[5] took up the issue of whether a sentence of life without parole is similarly cruel and unusual punishment when applied to juveniles. In the Graham decision, the Supreme Court held that life without the possibility of parole is cruel and unusual punishment for juveniles convicted of a non-homicide offense.

JUVENILE JUSTICE LAW: *ROPER V. SIMMONS* (2005)—BRIEF EXCERPTS FROM THE MAJORITY AND DISSENTING OPINIONS

Justice Kennedy delivered the opinion of the Court. (Notice that in legal writing, references are not cited within parentheses, but follow in the text as a separate sentence.)

> The susceptibility of juveniles to immature and irresponsible behavior means their irresponsible conduct is not as morally reprehensible as that of an adult. *Thompson, supra,* at 835 (plurality opinion). Their own vulnerability and comparative lack of control over their immediate surroundings mean juveniles have a greater claim than adults to be forgiven for failing to escape negative influences in their whole environment. See *Stanford*, 492 U. S., at 395 (Brennan, J., dissenting). The reality that juveniles still struggle to define their identity means it is less supportable to conclude that even a heinous crime committed by a juvenile is evidence of irretrievably depraved character. From a moral standpoint it would be misguided to equate the failings of a minor with those of an adult, for a greater possibility exists that a minor's character deficiencies will be reformed.

An excerpt from Justice O'Connor's dissenting opinion.

> Adolescents *as a class* are undoubtedly less mature, and therefore less culpable for their misconduct, than adults. But the Court has adduced no evidence impeaching the seemingly reasonable conclusion reached by many state legislatures: That at least some 17-year-old murderers are sufficiently mature to deserve the death penalty in an appropriate case. Nor has it been shown that capital sentencing juries are incapable of accurately assessing a youthful defendant's maturity or of giving due weight to the mitigating characteristics associated with youth.

An excerpt from Justice Scalia's dissenting opinion, joined by Chief Justice Roberts and Justice Thomas.

> Murder, however, is more than just risky or antisocial behavior. It is entirely consistent to believe that young people often act impetuously and lack judgment, but, at the same time, to believe that those who commit premeditated murder are—at least sometimes—just as culpable as adults. Christopher Simmons, who was only seven months shy of his 18th birthday when he murdered Shirley Crook, described to his friends *beforehand*—"[i]n chilling, callous terms," as the Court puts it, *ante*, at 1—the murder he planned to commit. He then broke into the home of an innocent woman, bound her with duct tape and electrical wire, and threw her off a bridge alive and conscious. *Ante*, at 2.

Source: *Roper v. Simmons* (2005), Washington, DC: Supreme Court of the United States. Retrieved November 9, 2017 (www.supremecourt.gov/opinions/04pdf/03-633.pdf).

Terrance Graham had been charged and convicted of a probation violation for home invasion robbery, committed at the age of 16. In the Miller decision, the Supreme Court banned mandatory sentences of life without parole for juveniles, even when imposed for youth convicted of homicide. The ruling still allowed state courts to impose life without parole sentences for homicide offenses committed by juveniles, but such sentences could not be mandatory, based on state mandatory sentencing laws. In imposing life without parole sentences, courts must take up individualized consideration of the juvenile and the offense. In this case, Evan Miller, age 14, together with a friend, beat a neighbor with a baseball bat and then set fire to his trailer, resulting in his death. Miller was charged and convicted in adult court of murder in the course of arson, a crime with a mandatory minimum sentence of LWOP in Alabama (Sickmund and Puzzanchera 2014).

The second reading in this chapter by Elizabeth Scott and her colleagues describes the Supreme Court's rationale for these three decisions: *Roper v. Simmons* (2005), *Graham v. Florida* (2010), and *Miller v. Alabama* (2012). "In short, children are different from adults, and these differences have implications for criminal punishment" (Scott et al. 2015b:1).

SUMMARY AND CONCLUSIONS

Formal proceedings in juvenile courts involve two primary components: adjudication and disposition. Adjudication is initiated by a legal document, called a petition, filed by the prosecutor's office or the probation department, which charges the youth with a violation(s) of statutory law. The adjudicatory hearing is a fact-finding process with due process rights, resulting in judicial determinations regarding whether the youth has, in fact, violated criminal law as alleged in the petition and whether the youth should be legally declared a "delinquent youth," a "status offender," or a "serious juvenile offender." In 2014, 54 percent of the petitioned delinquency cases were adjudicated in juvenile courts, as compared to 42 percent of the petitioned status offense cases. While a majority of cases that are not adjudicated are dismissed, juvenile courts may still provide for disposition in these cases, often through a consent decree with petition—an agreement between the juvenile court judge, parents, youth, and probation officer. Depending on state statutory law, juvenile courts may impose various dispositions in cases that are not adjudicated, including probation, treatment, counseling, restitution, community service, and out-of-home placement.

If a youth is adjudicated a delinquent youth or a status offender, the court determines the most appropriate sanction at a dispositional hearing. The dispositional hearing is usually separated in time, purpose, and procedures from adjudication hearings. Disposition maintains an individualized and rehabilitative focus, while pursuing the least restrictive option. A predisposition report, written by a probation officer, informs disposition through assessment of the youth and his or her background and social environment. The predisposition report is commonly organized with three major sections: the offense section, a social history, and a summary and recommendation. A full range of dispositions are normally authorized under state statute, including probation, out-of-home placement, treatment, educational program, counseling, mediation, restitution, community service, fines, drug testing, and electronic monitoring. Disposition may also involve a court order of commitment—a transfer of legal custody to the state. The court order of disposition almost always includes more than one dispositional option; for example, probation is commonly included with restitution and community service. Now would be a good time to review "Case in point: A dispositional order in juvenile court," which opened the chapter!

READING 9.1

"THE RIGHT TO COUNSEL IN JUVENILE COURT: THE CONUNDRUM OF ATTORNEYS AS AN AGGRAVATING FACTOR AT DISPOSITION."

Barry C. Feld and Shelly Schaefer. 2010. *Justice Quarterly* 27:713–741.

Feld and Schaefer provide a thorough discussion of the right to counsel in juvenile court in light of the in re Gault (1967) decision by the U.S. Supreme Court. While juveniles often waive the right to counsel, when counsel is appointed, the involvement of defense counsel in the case proves to be an aggravating factor in sentencing.

Progressive reformers who created the juvenile court used informal procedures to adjudicate delinquents and to impose rehabilitative dispositions in a child's "best interests" (Rothman, 1980; Schlossman, 1977). The Supreme Court in *In re Gault* (1967) granted delinquents procedural safeguards at trial, including the right to counsel, because of the gap between juvenile courts' rehabilitative rhetoric and punitive reality. Gault's increased formality legitimated punishment, contributed to greater severity in juvenile sentencing practice, and made providing adequate safeguards all the more imperative (Feld, 1988a, 2003b). Unfortunately, the presence of counsel consistently appears to be an aggravating factor when judges sentence delinquents. After controlling for legal variables, judges sentence youths who appear with counsel more severely than they do those who appear without an attorney (Burruss & Leonard, 2002; Feld, 1988b; 1991; GAO, 1995). Several explanations may account for this finding: lawyers who appear in juvenile court are incompetent and prejudice their clients' cases; judges pre-determine sentences and appoint counsel when they anticipate out-of-home placements; or judges punish delinquents who exercise procedural rights (Feld, 1989, 1993).

This article assesses the implementation of law reform in Minnesota to improve delivery of legal services in juvenile courts. Section "Right to Counsel in Juvenile Court" examines the procedural assumptions of juvenile courts and the struggle to implement Gault's mandate to provide counsel. It describes the inadequate delivery of legal services and the generally negative impact that lawyers have on clients' case-outcomes. Section "Law Reform to Provide Counsel and Decriminalize Misdemeanors" examines the process of law reform in Minnesota in the mid-1990s. As part of a nationwide trend to "get tough" on youth crime, Minnesota in 1995 adopted substantive juvenile justice reforms—offense-based waiver and blended sentencing laws and expanded use of delinquency convictions to enhance adult criminal sentences (Feld, 1995; Podkopacz & Feld, 2001). To complement these substantive changes, the new law mandated appointment of counsel or stand-by counsel for youths charged with felonies or who faced out-of-home placements, and consultation with a lawyer by youths charged with misdemeanors. The Governor vetoed funds to pay for additional lawyers. Within months after the law took effect and as a cost-saving strategy, the legislature decriminalized many misdemeanors, converted them into status offenses for which judges could not impose out-of-home placements, and eliminated juveniles' right to counsel (Weldon, 1996). Section "Data" describes the data used to conduct this pre- and post-reform legal impact study. Section "Findings and Analyses" compares how juvenile courts in Minnesota processed 30,270 youths in 1994—the year before the statutory changes—with how they processed 39,369 youths in 1999 after they implemented the changes. We analyze the contradictory impact of efforts to increase rates of representation and to foster judicious non-intervention—converting misdemeanors into petty offenses and restricting judges' sentencing authority to deny youth counsel. We assess how these competing reforms affected delivery of legal services and the impact of lawyer on juvenile court sentencing practices. Finally, we consider the broader policy implications of our findings.

Right to counsel in juvenile court

Juvenile courts melded a new vision of childhood with new theories of social control, introduced a judicial-welfare alternative to the criminal justice system, and enabled the state, as *parens patriae*, to monitor ineffective childrearing (Feld, 1999, 2003b). The *parens patriae* doctrine legitimated intervention to supervise children and supported claims that proceedings were civil rather than criminal. Courts' status jurisdiction enabled them to control noncriminal misbehavior such as sexual activity, truancy, or immorality (Platt, 1977; Sutton, 1988). Juvenile courts eschewed criminal procedural safeguards and rejected juries, excluded lawyers, and conducted confidential hearings (Feld, 1999; Rothman, 1980; Tanenhaus, 2004).

The Supreme Court in *In re Gault* (1967) rejected Progressives' rehabilitative rhetoric, critically examined juvenile courts' reality, and found that their procedural deficiencies violated the Constitution. The Court concluded that juvenile courts must provide fundamentally fair procedures including notice of charges, a hearing, assistance of counsel, an opportunity to confront and cross-examine witnesses, and the privilege against self-incrimination (Feld, 1984). Although *Gault* likened the seriousness of a delinquency proceeding to a felony prosecution, the Court relied on the Fourteenth Amendment Due Process Clause rather than the Sixth Amendment which protects adult defendants' right to counsel (*Gideon v. Wainwright* 1961). The Court did not require appointment of counsel, but only directed judges to advise a child and parent of the right to counsel and, if indigent, to have counsel appointed (*In re Gault* 1967).

Presence of counsel in juvenile courts

When the Court decided *Gault*, lawyers seldom appeared in juvenile courts (Barrett, Brown, & Cramer, 1966). Although states amended their juvenile codes to comply with *Gault*, the law-in-action lagged behind the law-on-the-books and most states failed actually to deliver legal services. Evaluations of initial compliance with *Gault* found that most judges did not advise juveniles of their rights and the vast majority did not appoint counsel (Canon & Kolson, 1971; Ferster, Courtless, & Snethen, 1971; Lefstein, Stapleton, & Teitelbaum, 1969; Stapleton & Teitelbaum, 1972). Studies in the 1970s and early 1980s reported that judges failed to appoint counsel for most juveniles (Aday, 1986; Bortner, 1982; Clarke & Koch, 1980; Kempf-Leonard, Pope, & Feyerherm, 1995). Research in Minnesota in the mid-1980s reported that most youths appeared without counsel and that judges removed from their homes and confined many unrepresented youths (Feld, 1989, 1993). A comparative study of rates of representation in six states reported that only three of them appointed counsel for a substantial majority of juveniles (Feld, 1988b). Studies in the 1990s described judges' failure to appoint lawyers for many youths who appeared in court (Burruss & Kempf-Leonard, 2002; GAO, 1995). The General Accounting Office (GAO, 1995) reported that rates of representation varied widely among and within states and that judges tried and sentenced many unrepresented youths. Burruss and Kempf-Leonard (2002) found geographic variation in representation in Missouri and reported that attorneys' presence increased juveniles' likelihood of receiving out-of-home placements.

In the mid-1990s, the American Bar Association (ABA, 1993, 1995) published two reports on juveniles' legal needs, which reported that many youths lacked counsel, and concluded that lawyers who represented delinquents lacked adequate training and often failed to provide competent representation. Since the late-1990s, the ABA and the National Juvenile Defender Center have conducted state-by-state assessments of juveniles' access to counsel in a dozen states and report that many, if not most, youth appear without counsel and that lawyers representing delinquents often provide substandard legal assistance because of structural impediments to effective advocacy (e.g., Brooks & Kamine, 2003; Bookser, 2004; Celeste & Puritz, 2001; Puritz & Brooks, 2002; Puritz, Scali, & Picou, 2002). Moreover, regardless of how inadequately lawyers perform, juvenile courts appear incapable of correcting their own errors (Berkheiser, 2002). Defense attorneys rarely, if ever, appeal adverse decisions and often lack a record with which to challenge an invalid waiver of counsel (Berkheiser, 2002; Bookser, 2004; Crippen, 2000; Harris, 1994; Puritz & Shang, 2000).

Waivers of counsel in juvenile court

There are several reasons that many youths appear in juvenile courts without counsel. Public defender legal services may be inadequate or absent in nonurban areas (ABA, 1995). Judges may give cursory advisories of the right to counsel, imply that a rights colloquy and waiver are just a legal technicality, and readily find waivers of counsel in order to ease courts' administrative burdens (ABA, 1995; Berkheiser, 2002; Bookser, 2004; Cooper, Puritz, & Shang, 1998). In other instances, judges may not appoint counsel if they expect to impose a non-custodial sentence (Burrus & Kempf-Leonard, 2002; Feld, 1984, 1989; Lefstein et al., 1969).

Many juveniles are unrepresented because judges allow and find they waived counsel (ABA, 1995; Berkheiser, 2002; Cooper et al., 1998; Feld, 1989). In most states, judges gauge juveniles' waivers of rights by assessing whether they were "knowing, intelligent, and voluntary" under the "totality of the circumstances" (*Fare v. Michael C.* 1979; *Johnson v. Zerbst* 1938; Berkheiser, 2002). Judges consider factors like age, education, IQ, and prior police contacts, and exercise broad discretion to decide whether a youth understood and waived her rights (Feld, 1984, 1989, 2006). In most states, juveniles may waive counsel without consulting with either a parent or an attorney (Berkheiser, 2002; Feld, 2006). In addition, judges frequently failed to give any counsel advisory, often neglected to create any record of a waiver colloquy, and readily accepted waivers from manifestly incompetent children (Berkheiser, 2002).

Research on juveniles' exercise of *Miranda* rights raises questions about their ability to make knowing, intelligent, and voluntary waivers. Many juveniles do not understand a *Miranda* warning or counsel advisory well enough to make a valid waiver (Grisso, 1980, 1981; Grisso et al., 2003). Although older juveniles understood *Miranda* warnings about as well as adults, substantial numbers of both groups misunderstood some element of the warning. Even youths who understand the abstract words of an advisory of counsel may not appreciate the function or importance of rights (ABA, 1995; Grisso, 1980, 1997; Grisso et al., 2003).

Research on adolescents' adjudicative competence raises further questions about their capacity to exercise rights (Bonnie & Grisso, 2000; Grisso et al., 2003). To be competent to stand trial, a defendant should be able to understand proceedings, make rational decisions, and consult with counsel (*Dusky v. United States* 1960; *Drope v. Missouri* 1975). Analysts report significant age-related differences between adolescents' and young adults' competence, legal understanding, and quality of judgment (Grisso et al., 2003; Redding & Frost, 2001). As a result of reduced adjudicative competence and compromised ability to exercise rights, juveniles do not understand legal proceedings as well as adults and waive counsel at higher rates (Harlow, 2000).

Presence of counsel as an aggravating factor in sentencing

Historically, juvenile court judges discouraged adversarial representation and organizational pressures to maintain stable, cooperative relationships with others in the system impeded effective advocacy (Bortner, 1982; Clarke & Koch, 1980; Feld, 1984; Stapleton & Teitelbaum, 1972). Lawyers who appear with juveniles often put their clients at a disadvantage (Bortner, 1982; Burruss & Kempf-Leonard, 2002; Feld, 1988b, 1989). After controlling for legal variables like present offense, prior record, and pre-trial detention status, judges removed from home and incarcerated delinquents who appeared with counsel more frequently than they did unrepresented youths (Bortner, 1982; Burruss & Kempf-Leonard, 2002; Clarke & Koch, 1980; Duffee & Siegel, 1971; Feld, 1989; Guevara, Herz, & Spohn, 2008; Guevara, Spohn, & Herz, 2004). The presence of counsel *per se* appears to be an aggravating factor when judges sentence juveniles (Bortner, 1982; Burruss & Kempf-Leonard, 2002; Clarke & Koch, 1980; Feld, 1988b, 1989, 1993; GAO, 1995; Koch, 1980).

Several possible reasons may account for why juveniles with lawyers fare worse than those who are unrepresented. First, lawyers who appear in juvenile courts may be incompetent and prejudice their clients' cases (Knitzer & Sobie, 1984; Lefstein et al., 1969; Stapleton & Teitelbaum, 1972). Even in states in which judges routinely appoint counsel, many lawyers provide ineffective representation (Knitzer & Sobie, 1984). Public defender offices may assign their least capable lawyers or send new attorneys to juvenile court to gain trial experience (Flicker, 1983; Handler, 1965). Court-appointed lawyers may place a higher priority on maintaining good relations with the judges who appoint them than vigorously defending their young clients (Feld, 1989; Flicker, 1983). Conditions under which many defense attorneys work constitute a structural impediment to quality representation (ABA, 1995; Cooper et al., 1998; Jones, 2004). Observations and qualitative studies consistently report adverse working conditions—crushing caseloads, penurious compensation, lack of support services, inexperienced attorneys, and inadequate supervision—that detract from effective representation (Brooks & Kamine, 2003; Celeste & Puritz, 2001; Jones, 2004; Puritz & Brooks, 2002; Puritz et al., 2002).

Alternatively, judges may appoint lawyers when they expect to impose more severe sentences and this could account for the relationship (Aday, 1986; Canon & Kolson, 1971). In most states, the same judge presides at a youth's arraignment, detention hearing, adjudication, and disposition, and she may appoint counsel when she anticipates imposing a more severe sentence (Feld, 1984). However, if judges appoint lawyers at youths' arraignments or detention hearings because they expect to incarcerate them later, have they already prejudged the case? If they only appoint lawyers when they anticipate more severe dispositions, then can an attorney still provide an effective defense (Burruss & Kempf-Leonard, 2002; Guevara et al., 2008)?

Finally, judges may sentence represented delinquents more severely than unrepresented ones because a lawyer's presence insulates them from appellate reversal (Duffee & Siegel, 1971). While judges may not punish juveniles just because they have a lawyer, they may sentence youths more leniently who "throw themselves on the mercy of the court" (Burruss & Kempf-Leonard, 2002; Guevara et al., 2004). The sentencing differential associated with counsels' presence mirrors the harsher sentences adults receive who exercise their right to a jury trial rather than plead guilty (Engen & Steen, 2000). Juvenile court judges may punish youths whose lawyers invoke formal procedures, disrupt routine procedures, or question their discretion.

If many effects of representation are negative, then some may question why to require counsel in juvenile court. Since *Gault*, legal changes have transformed the juvenile court from a nominally rehabilitative social welfare agency into a scaled-down, second-class criminal court (Feld, 1988a, 1999, 2003b). When youth confront a legal institution exercising coercive powers, only lawyers can effectively invoke procedural and substantive safeguards to protect against erroneous state intervention. The direct consequence of delinquency convictions and sentences makes procedural justice critical (Feld, 1988a). The use of prior convictions to sentence delinquents more harshly, to waive juveniles to criminal court, and to enhance adult sentences makes providing competent counsel all the more imperative (Feld, 2003a).

Law reform and unintended consequences

In addition to intended results, purposeful actions often produce unintended consequences which may be contrary to the original goal or which may generate an unexpected benefit (Merton, 1936). Instances abound of justice system reforms intended to reduce offender populations which perversely have a contrary, net-widening effect. Net-widening occurs when reformers introduce a new sanction to be used in lieu of another, more severe sanction, and which decision-makers then use on an inappropriate population. Diversion programs intended to channel youths away from juvenile courts instead bring less-seriously delinquent youths into the system (Klein, 1979). Intensive supervision probation programs intended to keep offenders in the community instead result in closer supervision and higher rates of probation revocation for technical violations (Peterisilia & Turner, 1993). Judges apply sentencing reforms to less serious offenders than those envisioned and impose more severe punishment on those whom they previously treated leniently (Morris & Tonry, 1990). The 1995 Minnesota juvenile blended sentencing law produced a net-widening effect. Instead of using blended sentences in lieu of transfer, judges imposed tougher sentences on youths whom they previously treated as ordinary delinquents and through subsequent probation revocations consigned younger, less serious youths to adult prisons (Podkopacz & Feld, 2001).

In this study, we assess the cumulative impact of law reforms. Because judges working in complex organizations have to implement these changes, we examine whether they conformed with or deviated from the legislature's intent to improve delivery of legal services and to reduce incarceration without representation. Because attorneys' presence appears to be an aggravating factor in sentencing delinquents, we examine how mandating appointment of counsel affects juveniles' dispositions. And, as with any law reform, we look for unintended consequences.

Law reform to provide counsel and decriminalize misdemeanors

Although a few states require juveniles to consult with a lawyer (e.g. *D.R. v. Commonwealth* 2001), the majority allow youths to waive counsel unaided (Berkheiser, 2002). Like many states, Minnesota has struggled to provide adequate defense representation for delinquents. Studies in the mid-1980s reported that most youths appeared without counsel, found significant geographic variations in rates of representation, and observed that judges removed from home or confined many unrepresented youths (Feld, 1989, 1991, 1993).

In 1990, the Minnesota Supreme Court appointed the Juvenile Representation Study Committee to examine juveniles' access to counsel and to recommend policy changes. The Study Committee found that most juveniles appeared without counsel and reported geographic disparities in legal access (Juvenile Representation Study Committee, 1991; Feld, 1995).

It recommended mandatory, non-waivable appointment of counsel for juveniles charged with felony or gross misdemeanor offenses and in any proceeding that could lead to out-of-home placements (Juvenile Representation Study Committee, 1991). It recommended that juveniles charged with misdemeanor offenses consult with counsel prior to any waiver. Because counties used different methods to provide legal defense, the Committee could not estimate either current expenditures or predict the costs of implementing its recommendations and the legislature did not enact its proposals (Feld, 1995).

Mandating representation and vetoing funding

In 1992, the Minnesota Supreme Court, Governor, and legislature created the Juvenile Justice Task Force to recommend policies on transfer to criminal court, juvenile court sentencing practices, uses of delinquency convictions, and increased procedural safeguards (Feld, 1995; Juvenile Justice Task Force, 1994). The legislature unanimously enacted changes in waiver criteria and procedures, created a new form of blended sentencing—Extended Jurisdiction Juvenile (EJJ) prosecutions—that combined juvenile and criminal court sentencing options, and expanded use of delinquency convictions to enhance adult criminal sentences (Feld, 1995, 2003a; Podkopacz & Feld, 2002).

The increased punitiveness of waiver and delinquency-sentencing policies prompted the legislature to expand juvenile courts' procedural safeguards. The Task Force confirmed inadequate delivery of legal services and recommended that judges appoint counsel for juveniles facing felony charges or out-of-home placement (Feld, 1995; Juvenile Justice Task Force, 1994). Although youth charged with a misdemeanor could waive counsel, the Task Force recommended that she consult with counsel prior to any waiver. Because the Juvenile Representation Study Committee (1991) could not assess the costs of its proposals, the Task Force calculated the additional costs of a full-representation defender system at about $5.5 million dollars (Feld, 1995).

The 1994 legislature unanimously enacted the Task Force's procedural reform recommendations and provided, in part, that:

> Before a child who is charged by delinquency petition with a misdemeanor offense waives the right to counsel or enters a plea, the child shall consult in person with counsel who shall provide a full and intelligible explanation of the child's rights. The court *shall appoint* counsel, or stand-by counsel if the child waives the right to counsel for a child who is:
>
> (1) charged by delinquency petition with a gross misdemeanor or felony offense; or
> (2) the subject of a delinquency proceeding in which out-of-home placement has been proposed.
>
> (Minn. Stat. § 260.155(2) (West, 1995)) (emphasis supplied)

Rules of procedure made appointment of counsel or stand-by counsel mandatory in cases involving felony or gross misdemeanor charges or out-of-home placement. The law required any youth charged with a misdemeanor to meet with a lawyer prior to any waiver of counsel (Feld, 1995). Even if a child charged with a misdemeanor waived counsel, court rules authorize judges to appoint stand-by counsel to assist a youth (Minn. R. Juv. Proc. 3.02(2)). As another incentive to appoint counsel, court rules prohibited judges from considering prior misdemeanor convictions obtained without counsel in later probation, contempt, or home-removal proceedings (Feld, 1995). The legislature replaced the county-by-county patchwork method of delivering legal defense services with a statewide public defender system to represent youths in delinquency and extended jurisdiction proceedings (Minn. Stat. Ann. § 611.15 (West, 1995)).

The legislature also appropriated funds necessary to implement the new law. The Task Force estimated that a full-representation juvenile defender system would cost an additional $5.5 million dollars. The legislature appropriated $2.65 million for the initial six-month period with annual appropriations thereafter (Feld, 1995). On May 5, 1994, Minnesota Governor Arne Carlson signed the Juvenile Crime Bill and simultaneously *line-item vetoed* the appropriations necessary to implement the changes (Feld, 1995). He mandated appointment of counsel, vetoed the funds to meet that obligation, and imposed financial costs and administrative burdens on public defender whose caseloads increased by 150% or more (Feld, 1995; Weldon, 1996).

Decriminalizing misdemeanors to foster judicious non-intervention

The new law took effect on 1 January 1995, and within months, caseload increases overwhelmed public defenders. The same number of lawyers tried to represent substantially more clients without additional resources (Weldon, 1996). In light of the Governor's veto, legislators sought to reduce public defender caseloads rather than to appropriate more funds (Weldon, 1996). In March, 1995, legislators enacted a creative solution and decriminalized most common misdemeanors, such as shoplifting, vandalism, larceny and the like. The law retained delinquency jurisdiction and out-of-home placement sanctions for some serious misdemeanors, but relabeled most misdemeanors as petty offenses, that is status offenses (Minn. Stat. §260.015 Sub. 21 (b) (West, 1995)). The law also prohibited out-of-home placement sentences of status offenders (Minn. Stat. §260.195(3) (West, 1995)). Judges could impose fines, community service, probation, restitution, or out-patient drug or alcohol treatment, but they could not remove status offenders from their home. By decriminalizing misdemeanors and barring home-removal sanctions, the legislature sought to eliminate status offenders' right to counsel (Weldon, 1996).

Supreme Court decisions bolstered the strategy to decriminalize misdemeanors, to bar out-of-home placement, and thereby to eliminate status offenders' right to counsel. *Gideon v. Wainwright* (1963) applied the Sixth Amendment's guarantee of counsel to state felony proceedings. Although *Gault* relied on the rationale of *Gideon*, the Court based delinquents' right to counsel on the Fourteenth Amendment Due Process Clause, rather than the Sixth Amendment. *Gault* only dealt with procedural rights for delinquents—youths charged with criminal conduct that could result in institutional confinement—and did not decide the rights of status offenders. In *Argersinger v. Hamlin* (1972), the Court held that a state must appoint counsel for an indigent adult defendant charged with *and* imprisoned for a minor offense. *Argersinger* left unclear whether the right to counsel attached because of the penalty authorized or the actual sentence imposed. *Scott v. Illinois* (1979) held that the sentence the judge actually imposed, rather than the one authorized by the statute determined whether the state must appoint counsel. Justice Brennan dissented in *Scott*, but noted that *Scott*'s actual imprisonment rationale still would encourage states to decriminalize offenses to avoid providing counsel.

> It may well be that adoption by this Court of an "authorized imprisonment" standard would lead state and local governments to re-examine their criminal statutes. A state legislature or local government might determine that it no longer desired to authorize incarceration for certain minor offenses in light of the expense of meeting the requirements of the Constitution. In my view this re-examination is long overdue. In any event, the Court's

> "actual imprisonment" standard must inevitably lead the courts to make this re-examination, which plainly should more properly be a legislative responsibility.
>
> (*Scott v. Illinois*, 1979, pp. 388–389)

Because *Scott* prohibited incarceration without representation, judges could deny counsel to adults in misdemeanor proceedings as long as they did not order confinement. Based on *Scott*'s rationale, the Minnesota legislature could bar out-of-home placement of status offenders and thereby withhold the right to counsel (Weldon, 1996).

Although fiscal constraints drove Minnesota's decriminalization strategy, they produced policy innovations long advocated by juvenile justice reformers. Contemporaneously with *Gault*, the President's Commission on Law Enforcement and Administration of Justice (1967a, 1967b) proposed a two-track juvenile justice system in which states formally adjudicated youths charged with serious crimes and handled informally minor and status offenders (President's Commission, 1967b). The Crime Commission (1967b) and other analysts recommended policies of judicious non-intervention, diversion (Lemert, 1971), or radical nonintervention (Schur, 1973) to avoid stigmatizing youths. These recommendations reflected concerns of labeling theorists about the stigmatic consequences of delinquency adjudications and trepidation about the iatrogenic effects of juvenile court intervention in minor cases (Sanborn & Salerno, 2005). By the mid-1970s, these rationales led to reforms like the federal Juvenile Justice and Delinquency Prevention Act to divert and deinstitutionalize status offenders (Feld, 1999).

We examine the impact of these complementary legal changes. How did mandating counsel for all youths charged with felonies and relabeling many misdemeanors as status offenses with limits on dispositions affect juvenile justice administration? If lawyers are an aggravating factor at disposition, then what effect did mandatory representation have on youths' sentences? Did judges comply with restrictions on appointment of counsel for youths charged with status offenses and did they continue to place these youths out-of-home without benefit of counsel? What was the net impact of these changes on overall confinement of juveniles? . . .

Discussion and conclusion

For several decades, Minnesota's juvenile courts have struggled to comply with *Gault*'s mandate that delinquents receive assistance of counsel. The 1995 law and court rules required judges to appoint counsel or stand-by counsel for all youths charged with felonies and who faced removal from home. The Governor vetoed the funds necessary to implement those requirements. As a creative cost-saving strategy, the legislature redefined most misdemeanors as status offenses, barred out-of-home placements, and thereby eliminated juveniles' constitutional right to counsel. The legislature's crass motive simply to save money unintentionally fostered policies of judicious non-intervention and produced a substantial decline in out-of-home placements.

Notwithstanding the law's cost-saving intent and unambiguous language, it did not achieve the legislature's goals. Judges continued to appoint counsel for about one-fifth of the status offenders despite the statutory prohibition. We can only speculate why judges continued to appoint and public defenders continued to accept representation of status offenders. Appointing counsel for even a small proportion of the vastly more numerous status offenders produced a net increase in the number of youths represented. Because the legislature intended to reduce costs by decriminalizing misdemeanors, what impact did providing counsel have on the Public Defenders' budget and quality of representation?

Both in 1994 and 1999, other than an extensive prior record, the presence of counsel is the strongest predictor of the likelihood of an out-of-home placement. Model III indicates that this effect is most pronounced in the more formal, urban courts. Although we could attribute the relationship between counsel and out-of-home placements simply to lawyers' role as an aggravating factor at sentencing, it more plausibly reflects imperfect judicial compliance with *Scott*—no incarceration without representation. Judges know that they should appoint counsel as a prerequisite to any legitimate out-of-home placement. They also know that appointing counsel reduces the likelihood that appellate courts would overturn their placement decision. Because the 1995 law narrowed the range of offenses for which judges could appoint counsel *and* remove youths from home, it strengthened the relationship between these two judicial decisions. Perhaps, judges surmise their likely disposition early in the proceedings and appoint counsel when they anticipate out-of-home placement. They attempt to conform to *Scott* and to predict, albeit imperfectly, when they will impose more severe dispositions and then appoint counsel in such cases. Even if this accounts for the impact of counsel as an aggravating factor at sentencing, it highlights the fundamental dilemma *Scott* poses. How will judges know at arraignment whether they will remove a youth from home following conviction and therefore appoint counsel without simultaneously prejudging the case and prejudicing the proceedings? It is certainly plausible that *ex parte* communications between the county attorney or probation staff prior to arraignment could alert the judge of the need to appoint counsel, but such conversations without defense counsel present undermine the legitimacy of the process.

Despite judges' improved efforts to conform to *Scott*, judges still removed many unrepresented youths from their homes. Notwithstanding the 1995 law's clear language to provide counsel for youths facing out-of-home placement, lawyers did *not* represent about one quarter (26.7%) of the youths whom judges removed from home. Because lawyers appeared more often with juveniles charged with felonies and serious misdemeanors, status offenders remained the largest proportion of youths whom judges removed from home without representation. We need qualitative studies—courtroom observations or analyses of dispositional hearing transcripts—to determine why out-of-home placements of unrepresented youths continue to occur.

Perhaps the most positive finding of this study is the substantial overall decline (34.5%) in out-of-home placements—judicious non-intervention—that accompanied decriminalization of misdemeanors. Some delinquents may require confinement to protect the community and others may benefit from juvenile court intervention, but judges often lack the ability accurately to diagnose and classify for treatment. Many youths will outgrow the mistakes of adolescence if they are shielded from harsh, life altering interventions that easily disrupt their development. The desire to protect young people from the iatrogenic effects of juvenile court sanctions provided the rationale for diversion and de-institutionalization reforms of the 1970s. Justice Brennan's dissent in *Scott* suggested that increasing the costs of representation could encourage states to decriminalize low-level offenses because judges seldom actually incarcerated offenders convicted of those crimes. Minnesota's cost-saving strategy to avoid providing counsel for status offenders offers a test of his hypothesis and a serendipitous unintended consequence.

[References and notes omitted.]

READING 9.2

"JUVENILE SENTENCING IN A DEVELOPMENTAL FRAMEWORK: THE ROLE OF THE COURTS."

Elizabeth Scott, Thomas Grisso, Marsha Levick, and Laurence Steinberg. 2015b. John D. and Catherine T. MacArthur Foundation, Models for Change.

This reading is from the Models for Change initiative of the MacArthur Foundation. Elizabeth Scott and her colleagues identify five mitigating factors for juvenile sentencing hearings that are drawn from recent research findings on adolescent development.

Three United States Supreme Court decisions in the past decade have delineated the constitutional principle that children are developmentally different from adults in ways that matter for the fair punishment of juvenile offenders. The Court has prohibited the death penalty for juveniles and strictly limited the use of life without parole—prohibiting the sentence for non-homicide offenses and, even for homicide, requiring courts to consider mitigating factors.

The Court's developmental framework is grounded in scientific research and such bedrock principles of criminal law as proportionality, mitigation, culpability, and competence. Some jurisdictions have used the framework to adopt further reforms in juvenile justice, including:

- Abolishing altogether juvenile life without parole (JLWOP).
- Revising or prohibiting mandatory minimum sentences and enhanced sentencing such as "three strikes" rules.
- Rejecting lifetime parole and sex offender registries.
- Reforming transfer laws.
- Addressing expungement and the confidentiality of juvenile records.

The Supreme Court reframes juvenile sentencing

Since 2005, the Supreme Court has transformed the constitutional landscape of juvenile justice. In three strongly worded opinions, the Court prohibited the death penalty for juveniles (*Roper v. Simmons*, 2005), barred the sentence of life without parole (LWOP) for juveniles convicted of a non-homicide offense (*Graham v. Florida*, 2010), and banned the use of mandatory LWOP sentences for juveniles, even those convicted of homicide (*Miller v. Alabama*, 2012).

Together, the Court opinions create a special status for juveniles under the Eighth Amendment's prohibition of cruel and unusual punishment. Citing a large and growing body of behavioral and brain research, the Court affirmed that adolescents are less mature than adults in ways that make them less culpable even for the most serious crimes, less competent to participate in criminal proceedings, and more likely to change over time. In short, children are different from adults, and these differences have implications for criminal punishment.

Although the Court's decisions directly address only the most serious crimes, their implications are much broader. As Justice Roberts pointed out in his *Miller* dissent, the Court, in emphasizing that children are different, has announced a general principle of reduced culpability that applies to the criminal conduct of young offenders across the board. The same developmental factors that mitigate culpability for murder or armed robbery also influence adolescents committing less serious crimes.

Key themes of the framework, grounded in law and science

The three Supreme Court opinions have provided a coherent developmental framework for sentencing adolescents, grounded in scientific research and such bedrock principles of criminal law as proportionality and mitigation. Several key themes carry through the three opinions.

Juveniles are less culpable

The legal principle of proportionality holds that punishment should be based not only on the harm caused by the crime, but also on the culpability of the offender. Juvenile offenders must be held accountable for their crimes; adolescent immaturity does not exculpate young offenders. But their developmental immaturity *does* mitigate their culpability, and it should be taken into account in sentencing decisions.

The court noted three ways in which adolescent immaturity mitigates culpability. First, teenagers' decision-making capacity is reduced due to their "inability to assess consequences" and to the "recklessness, impulsivity, and heedless risk-taking" that contribute to an "underdeveloped sense of responsibility" in adolescents. These typical features of adolescents can be traced to the normal processes of brain development: neuroscientists have found that in adolescents, the brain systems involved in self-regulation (for example, impulse control and thinking ahead) are relatively immature, while the systems that respond to emotional and social stimuli, such as immediate rewards, exhibit heightened activity, partly as a consequence of changes in the brain at puberty. Second, the Court noted that legal minors are susceptible to coercion. They are vulnerable to peer pressure and have limited ability to extricate themselves from their homes and other settings that can contribute to their criminal activity. Finally, the Court observed that much juvenile offending is the product of "transient immaturity"; thus, a youth's criminal activity is less likely than an adult's to be "evidence of irretrievable depravity." These differences between juvenile and adult offenders correlate to conventional sources of mitigation in criminal law.

Juvenile offenders are likely to reform

Brain research has shown that adolescence, like infancy and early childhood, is a period of high neuroplasticity—the capacity of the brain to change in response to experience. This capacity makes young offenders good candidates for rehabilitation. Moreover, as noted above, most adolescent offending is the product of a transient phase, and most adolescents will desist from criminal activity as they mature into adulthood. Thus, lengthy incarceration does little to protect the public, despite the considerable expense it creates for taxpayers. The lengthiest sentence, life without parole, also denies young offenders a meaningful opportunity to reform and to demonstrate their growth and maturity—a point the Court reiterated forcefully in both *Graham* and *Miller*.

Juveniles are less competent

The Court emphasized in *Graham* and *Miller* that severe sentences might result from juvenile defendants' relative incapacity to deal effectively with the police, execute plea agreements, or participate competently in their trials. Several scientifically demonstrated developmental factors contribute to this incapacity, including adolescents' tendencies toward dependence and acquiescence, as well as their impulsiveness and short-sightedness in decision-making. In addition, their cognitive and intellectual abilities often are not fully developed, and most lack knowledge about the legal process. Together, these factors can lead to an impulsive confession, the rash rejection of a plea offer, or the inability to assist counsel by challenging witnesses or pointing to relevant exculpatory or mitigating evidence. Severe sentences might also result because immature teenage defendants may create negative impressions in court. In sum, the Court concluded that a juvenile may simply be less able than an adult to navigate a high-stakes encounter with the police and a criminal proceeding in which his entire future is on the line.

Sentencing juveniles after *Miller*

The Supreme Court did not require states to abolish the discretionary sentence of LWOP for juveniles convicted of homicide. But a fair reading of *Miller*—including the Court's forceful conclusion that the sentence of LWOP will be "uncommon" and its emphasis on the risk of an erroneous LWOP sentence—creates a presumption of immaturity. This implies that the state bears the burden of demonstrating that a juvenile is one of the rare youths who deserve this sentence. In jurisdictions that retain JLWOP, sentencing courts must carefully evaluate the mitigating factors that reduce the culpability of juveniles and make young offenders more likely to reform. Although courts may approach this in different ways, the evaluation should include assessment of the five factors specified in *Miller*, all linked to youthful immaturity and the sources of mitigation discussed above:

1 Immaturity, impetuosity, less capacity to consider future consequences, and related characteristics that impair juveniles' ability to make decisions.
2 A family and home environment from which a child cannot extricate himself or herself.
3 The circumstances of the offense, including the role the youth played and the influence of peer pressure.
4 Impaired legal competency that puts juveniles at a disadvantage in dealing with police or participating in legal proceedings.
5 The youth's potential for rehabilitation.

Because these factors are based on developmental constructs, not all experts will have the training and experience to evaluate them. It is important that forensic *child* psychologists or psychiatrists be involved. These experts have the skills, experience, and tools needed to inform courts making sentencing decisions.

Some states have found that even with an assessment of mitigating factors, the risk of error in applying JLWOP is too high, and the sentence is inherently problematic under the Eighth Amendment. In response, they have abolished the sentence altogether. In Massachusetts, for example, the state's highest court concluded that juveniles' reduced culpability makes LWOP a disproportionate sentence for *any* crime. Moreover, that court said, JLWOP is flawed because it denies the young offender the opportunity to reform.

FIVE MITIGATING FACTORS FOR SENTENCING HEARINGS

1. **Decision-making capacity:** immaturity, impetuosity, and related characteristics that impair the ability to make decisions.
2. **Capacity to resist negative influences:** family circumstances and individual capacities that limit the youth's ability to meet his or her own needs.
3. **Context of the offense:** the circumstances of the offense, including peer pressure and the role the youth played.
4. **Legal competency:** impaired competency that puts the youth at a disadvantage in dealing with police or legal proceedings.
5. **Potential for rehabilitation:** the potential for the youth to desist from offending, on his or her own or with interventions.

The developmental framework and other sentencing reforms

The Supreme Court's developmental framework supports broader sentencing reforms affecting juveniles in the adult system. Two areas where courts are playing an important role in reform involve mandatory minimum sentences and enhanced sentencing.

Mandatory minimum sentences

A sentencing structure that subjects juveniles and adults to the same fixed minimum sentence rejects the core principle that children are less culpable than adults and deserve less punishment. Furthermore, lengthy mandatory sentences, which sometimes are the virtual equivalent of LWOP, deny young offenders the meaningful opportunity to reform. A number of courts have rejected lengthy sentences of juveniles on these grounds. For example, after Miller, the Iowa Supreme Court struck down an order by the Governor commuting the sentences of all juveniles serving LWOP to life with parole eligibility after 60 years. The Court observed that subjecting juveniles to such a lengthy fixed sentence was a rejection of the fundamental principles that young offenders were less culpable than adults and that they should be given a meaningful opportunity to demonstrate reform. A year later, the same court found all mandatory minimum adult sentences to be unconstitutional for juveniles.

Enhanced sentencing

"Three strikes" laws, and others that use previous offenses to enhance the severity of sentences for later offenses, have been criticized even for adult offenders. Some courts have found that this objection is amplified when the earlier convictions are juvenile offenses. The likelihood that the youthful offense was the product of immaturity is too compelling to allow it to be the basis for a later harsh sentence.

Lifetime parole and sex offender registries

Because research shows that juvenile offending does not predict adult criminality, some courts have rejected lifetime parole or lifetime registration for juvenile sex offenders.

Further implications of the developmental framework

Lawmakers influenced by the Supreme Court's developmental framework have undertaken additional reforms, two of which are described briefly here.

Transfer laws

Laws that automatically transfer juveniles to criminal courts for specific offenses subvert the lessons of the developmental framework described in *Miller* and *Graham*. Some legislatures have restricted these laws, recognizing that due to their immaturity, most adolescents belong in the juvenile system and that transfer decisions should be made on an individualized basis, taking into consideration the offender's immaturity and potential for rehabilitation.

Expungement and confidentiality

The stigma of a criminal record has long-term consequences and can exclude individuals from educational opportunities, jobs, voting, and public housing. Mitigating these harmful effects is essential if young people are to become productive members of society. The developmental framework supports efforts to maintain the confidentiality of juvenile records, to automatically expunge minor offenses, and to provide a process whereby more serious offenses may be expunged.

This brief is based on the report "The Supreme Court and the Transformation of Juvenile Sentencing," prepared by Elizabeth Scott, Thomas Grisso, Marsha Levick, and Laurence Steinberg, and available at http://modelsforchange.net/transformation. . . .

[Notes omitted.]

CRITICAL-THINKING QUESTIONS

1 In the dispositional order that opened the chapter, how is the suspended commitment related to the conditions of formal probation?
2 Describe the purpose and content of juvenile court petitions.
3 The formal procedures of juvenile courts can be depicted by the due process rights that have been extended to juveniles during adjudication hearings. Describe several of these procedural rights.
4 How are juvenile court adjudication and disposition distinct in purpose and process?
5 Provide an inventory of juvenile court dispositions.
6 What is a court order of commitment?
7 What do Feld and Schaefer (2010) (chapter reading) mean when they say that appointed counsel may be an aggravating factor when judges sentence youths?
8 Based on the chapter reading by Scott and her colleagues (2015b), identify the five mitigating factors for juvenile sentencing hearings that are drawn from recent research findings on adolescent development.

SUGGESTED READING

Burrow, John D. and Patrick G. Lowery. 2015. "A Preliminary Assessment of the Impact of Plea Bargaining Among a Sample of Waiver-Eligible Offenders." *Youth Violence and Juvenile Justice* 13:211–227.

Peck, Jennifer H. and Maude Beaudry-Cyr. 2016. "Does Who Appears Before the Juvenile Court Matter on Adjudication and Disposition Outcomes? The Interaction between Client Race and Lawyer Type." *Journal of Crime and Justice* 39:131–152.

Scott, Elizabeth, Thomas Grisso, Marsha Levick, and Laurence Steinberg. 2015a. "The Supreme Court and the Transformation of Juvenile Sentencing." John D. and Catherine T. MacArthur Foundation, Models for Change. Available online at: www.modelsforchange.net/publications/778.

USEFUL WEBSITES

For further information relevant to this chapter, go to the following websites.

- **National Council of Juvenile and Family Court Judges:** www.ncjfcj.org/
- **The Annie E. Casey Foundation: Juvenile Justice:** www.aecf.org/work/juvenile-justice/
- **Models for Change: Systems Reform in Juvenile Justice, John D. and Catherine T. MacArthur Foundation:** www.modelsforchange.net/index.html

GLOSSARY OF KEY TERMS

Adjudication: The formal proceedings of juvenile courts, involving a series of court hearings that make judicial findings regarding the "facts of the case." The ultimate purpose of adjudication is twofold: (1) to determine whether the youth is responsible for the offense(s) charged in the petition; and (2) to determine whether the youth should be legally declared a "delinquent youth," a "serious juvenile offender," or a "status offender" by the juvenile court.

Adjudicatory hearing: The formal hearing in juvenile courts in which evidence and witnesses are presented, first by the prosecutor and then the defense, following due process of law. The outcome of this fact-finding process is a legal determination by the judge about whether the juvenile committed the offense(s). This is usually referred to as a *finding of fact* or a *finding of delinquency*. If the youth admitted to, or was found to have committed the offense(s), the judge then decides if the youth should be adjudicated a "delinquent youth," a "serious juvenile offender," or a "status offender" (or some equivalent term).

Arraignment hearing: A judicial hearing during the early stages of adjudication. The judge advises the youth of his or her rights and obligations, the petition is read aloud, and the youth is asked whether she or he admit or deny the petition.

Commitment: The juvenile court's legal authorization for out-of-home placement for a youth who has been adjudicated a delinquent youth. Commitment involves a transfer of legal custody to "the state"—some state agency such as the juvenile court or department of corrections.

Consent decree with petition: In cases that are petitioned but not adjudicated, an agreement for disposition made between the juvenile court judge, parents, youth, and probation officer. Such disposition may include out-of-home placement, probation, restitution, and community service.

Delinquent youth: An adjudicatory status used to designate that a youth has violated the criminal law and is in need of the juvenile court's assistance through disposition. (See Chapter 2 for discussion of the legal definition of "delinquent youth.")

Formal disposition: The juvenile court's response to a youth's admission of a petition or the court's finding that a youth committed an offense(s). The court order of formal disposition may require involvement in rehabilitation programs, community service, restitution, formal probation, out-of-home placement, or confinement.

Petition: A legal document filed in juvenile court by the prosecutor that specifies: the jurisdiction of the juvenile court, the charges in statutory and ordinary language, the facts of the offense including time and place of occurrence, and basic identifying information for the youth and his or her parents.

Plea bargaining: Negotiation between the defense attorney and the prosecutor in which the youth agrees to admit the petition or plead guilty in exchange for some concession such as keeping the case in juvenile court (without waiver to adult criminal court), reducing the charge(s), and/or leniency in disposition or sentencing.

Predisposition report: A court-ordered report written by a probation officer that provides information relevant for court disposition in an effort to make disposition individualized and rehabilitative. The predisposition report is commonly organized with three major sections: offense section, a social history, and a summary and recommendation.

Probable cause hearing: Usually the first adjudication hearing, which makes an initial determination about whether sufficient information and evidence exist to substantiate that a youth was likely involved in activity that violated state criminal or status offense law. Judges also make determinations regarding continued detention.

Serious juvenile offender: An adjudicatory status, determined by juvenile court judges in some states, to designate that a youth has committed a felony offense, including crimes against person, serious property offense, or an offense involving dangerous drugs. This adjudicatory status allows for more punitive disposition under statutory law.

Status offender: An adjudicatory status used to designate that a youth has violated status offense law and is in need of the juvenile court's assistance through disposition. State statutes (youth court acts) use various terms instead of status offender, such as "child in need of supervision" (CHINS), "minor in need of supervision" (MINS), or "youth in need of intervention" (YINI). Almost all of these terms for status offender are typically referred to by some peculiar-sounding acronym. (See Chapter 2 for discussion of the legal definition of "status offender.")

NOTES

1 *In re Gault*, 387 U.S. 1, 87 S. Ct. 1428 (1967).

2 See for example: *Montana Code Annotated 2017*, 41-5-1512 and 1513, accessible online (http://leg.mt.gov/bills/mca/title_0410/chapter_0050/part_0150/sections_index.html); *Minnesota Statutes* 2015, section 260B.198, accessible online (www.revisor.mn.gov/statutes/?id=260B.198&year=2015); Wisconsin Statutes 2013-2014, Chapter 938.34, accessible online (https://docs.legis.wisconsin.gov/statutes/statutes/938/VI/34).

3 *Roper v. Simmons*, 543 U.S. 551, 125 S. Ct. 1183 (2005).

4 *Graham v. Florida*, 560 U.S. 48, 130 S. Ct. 2011 (2010).

5 *Miller v. Alabama*, 132 U.S. 2455, 132 S. Ct. 2455 (2012).

REFERENCES

Bryant, Angela, Gregory Matthews, and Blessing Wilhelmsen. 2015. "Assessing the Legitimacy of Competence to Stand Trial in Juvenile Court: The Practice of CST With and Without Statutory Law." *Criminal Justice Policy Review* 26:371–399.

Burrow, John D. and Patrick G. Lowery. 2015. "A Preliminary Assessment of the Impact of Plea Bargaining Among a Sample of Waiver-Eligible Offenders." *Youth Violence and Juvenile Justice* 13:211–227.

Burruss, George. W., Jr. and Kimberly Kempf-Leonard. 2002. The Questionable Advantage of Defense Counsel in Juvenile Court. *Justice Quarterly* 19:37–68.

Feld, Barry C. 2003. "The Politics of Race and Juvenile Justice: The 'Due Process Revolution' and the Conservative Reaction." *Justice Quarterly* 20:765–800.

Feld, Barry C. 2012. "Procedural Rights in Juvenile Courts: Competence and Consequences." Pp. 664–691 in *The Oxford Handbook of Juvenile Crime and Juvenile Justice*, edited by B. C. Feld and D. M. Bishop. New York: Oxford.

Feld, Barry C. 2014. *Juvenile Justice Administration in a Nutshell*. St. Paul, MN: West.

Feld, Barry C. and Shelly Schaefer. 2010. "The Right to Counsel in Juvenile Court: The Conundrum of Attorneys as an Aggravating Factor at Disposition." *Justice Quarterly* 27:713–741.

Grisso, Thomas, Laurence Steinberg, Jennifer Woolard, Elizabeth Cauffman, Elizabeth Scott, Sandra Graham, Fran Lexcen, N. Dickon Reppucci, and Robert Schwartz. 2003. "Juveniles' Competence to Stand Trial: A Comparison of Adolescents' and Adults' Capacities as Trial Defendants." *Law and Human Behavior* 27:333–363.

Hemmens, Craig, Benjamin Steiner, and David Mueller. 2013. *Significant Cases in Juvenile Justice*. 2nd ed. New York: Oxford.

Hockenberry, Sarah, and Puzzanchera, Charles. 2017. *Juvenile Court Statistics 2014*. Pittsburgh, PA: National Center for Juvenile Justice.

Mears, Daniel P. 2000. "Assessing the Effectiveness of Juvenile Justice Reforms: A Closer Look at the Criteria and the Impacts on Diverse Stakeholders." *Law and Policy* 22:175–202.

Peck, Jennifer H. and Maude Beaudry-Cyr. 2016. "Does Who Appears Before the Juvenile Court Matter on Adjudication and Disposition Outcomes? The Interaction between Client Race and Lawyer Type." *Journal of Crime and Justice* 39:131–152.

Sanborn, Jr., Joseph B. 1993. "Philosophical, Legal, and Systemic Aspects of Juvenile Court Plea Bargaining." *Crime & Delinquency* 39:509–527.

Sanborn, Jr., Joseph B. 2009. "Juveniles' Competency to Stand Trial: Wading Through the Rhetoric and the Evidence." *The Journal of Criminal Law and Criminology* 99:135–213.

Scott, Elizabeth, Thomas Grisso, Marsha Levick, and Laurence Steinberg. 2015a. "The Supreme Court and the Transformation of Juvenile Sentencing." John D. and Catherine T. MacArthur Foundation, Models for Change. Retrieved May 16, 2016 (www.modelsforchange.net/publications/778).

Scott, Elizabeth, Thomas Grisso, Marsha Levick, and Laurence Steinberg 2015b. "Juvenile Sentencing in a Developmental Framework: The Role of the Courts." John D. and Catherine T. MacArthur Foundation, Models for Change. Retrieved May 16, 2016 (www.modelsforchange.net/publications/780).

Sickmund, Melissa and Charles Puzzanchera (eds.). 2014. *Juvenile Offenders and Victims: 2014 National Report*. Pittsburgh, PA: National Center for Juvenile Justice.

Chapter 10

JUVENILE PROBATION

CHAPTER TOPICS

- **Key features of juvenile probation**
- **Scope and structure of juvenile probation**
- **Use of probation: Extent, trends, and demographics**
- **Probation conditions**
- **Probation supervision**
- **Revocation**

CHAPTER LEARNING OBJECTIVES

After completing this chapter, students should be able to:

- Describe the key features of juvenile probation.
- Discuss the legal standard that probation conditions be "reasonable and relevant."
- Contrast the various supervision styles of probation officers.
- Explain the key components of evidence-based practice in juvenile probation.
- Define and briefly describe juvenile probation revocation.

CHAPTER CONTENTS

CASE IN POINT

A SUPERVISION AGREEMENT

The Case in Point that opened Chapter 9 presented a hypothetical order of disposition for Kent Clausen, a youth 16 years of age. That dispositional order adjudicated him a "delinquent youth" and issued a suspended execution of "commitment" to the state department of corrections. Instead, Kent was placed on probation with court-ordered conditions. Here we present the associated "supervision agreement," which is a document that sets out the terms of probation supervision. The supervision agreement follows closely from the order of disposition.

STATE OF INDIANA	**IN YOUTH COURT**
5th JUDICIAL DISTRICT	**SUPERVISION AGREEMENT**

IN THE MATTER OF THE WELFARE OF:
KENT CLAUSEN

Pursuant to the provisions of the Youth Court Act of the State of Indiana, this Court has ordered that Kent Clausen be under the supervision of District Court Services. It is this Court's high hope that your association with a probation officer during the period of supervision will be an experience that will help you understand the rules of our community and attain the highest degree of good citizenship.

You will be under the supervision of this Court for an indefinite period, until the Court releases you from this obligation. The Court will review your progress every six (6) months. You should understand that pursuant to law, this Court has jurisdiction over your case until you reach your twenty-first (21st) birthday.

The rules of probation are divided into two groups. The first group are those General Conditions of Supervision that are routinely assigned to anyone who is under the supervision of this Court. The second group are those Special Conditions of Supervision that the Court and your Probation Officer feel are necessary. You are expected to follow both groups of rules.

GROUP I – GENERAL CONDITIONS OF SUPERVISION

1. You will obey all local, state, and federal laws.
2. You are to attend school regularly and follow all rules of the school; and you will maintain passing grades.
3. You will make no change in address, school, or employment without first consulting your probation officer.
4. You will obey parents and let them know where you are going and with whom.
5. You will report promptly to your probation officer as directed.
6. You will not leave the State of Indiana without consulting your probation officer.
7. You will avoid undesirable places and bad companions.
8. You will not be in possession of or consume any alcohol or illicit drugs.

GROUP II – SPECIAL CONDITIONS OF SUPERVISION

1. While under the supervision of this Court, you will be working with Probation Officer Charles Stevens whose office is located in the Morris County Courthouse in the City of Lanchester. He is immediately available to you at all times at the phone number: 219-460-6142.
2. While under the supervision of this Court, you will be expected to live with your parents, Kirk and Karen Clausen at 104 Sunset Drive, Lanchester, Indiana.
3. You will participate in cognitive behavior therapy until you successfully complete treatment, as determined by your counselor.
4. You will submit to random drug testing and UA's upon request of your probation officer. In addition, you will submit to a search of your person or living area at the request of your probation officer.
5. You will pay restitution in the amount to be determined by the Court, to be paid in full by the time you reach 18 years of age.

IN WITNESS THEREOF, I have hereunto set my hand and caused to be affixed the Seal of the Juvenile Court of Morris County at the Courthouse in the city of Lanchester, Indiana, this 2nd day of October 2016.

Mary M. Malloy	*Charles Stevens*
Judge of the Juvenile Court	Probation Officer

I hereby certify that I have read the foregoing agreement and that I understand its contents. I agree that I will make every effort to follow its provisions.

Kent Clausen	*Karen Clausen*
Youth	Parent

Probation is the most frequently imposed disposition in juvenile courts. In 2014, formal probation was used in almost two-thirds of all adjudicated delinquency cases (see Figure 9.2 in Chapter 9). Even in delinquency cases that are dealt with informally by juvenile courts (not petitioned or not adjudicated), at least one-fourth received probation as an informal disposition. Probation is also the most common disposition for petitioned status offense cases in juvenile courts. Over half of all adjudicated status offense cases result in formal probation (see Figure 9.3 in Chapter 9).[1] Thus, probation is the backbone of the juvenile court and juvenile corrections. This chapter examines juvenile probation, first describing its key features, structure, and use, then exploring conditions of probation, supervision, and revocation.

KEY FEATURES OF JUVENILE PROBATION

Juvenile probation is an informal or formal disposition that is based in the community, involving conditions (court-imposed rules) and supervision by a probation officer. Most youth placed on probation also receive other dispositions that complement and enhance the conditions and supervision of probation. For example, in addition to probation, a property offender may be ordered by the court to pay restitution, or a drug offender may be ordered into chemical dependency counseling. These additional dispositions, used in combination with probation, are customarily written into the court order of probation.

Informal probation typically utilizes a court-approved agreement called a *consent adjustment without petition* or a *consent decree without adjudication*; each of these legal terms indicates how far the case has proceeded into the adjudication processes of the juvenile court. Formal probation is grounded in a court order of disposition (see the dispositional order presented at the beginning of Chapter 9). Many juvenile court jurisdictions also use an additional legal document that spells out the terms of supervision. This document, often call a *supervision agreement*, is usually signed by the judge, the probation officer, the parent or guardian, and the youth. The "case in point" that opened this chapter provides an example of a supervision agreement.

Both informal and formal probation allow the youth to remain in the community, albeit under the supervision of a probation officer and with court-imposed conditions. As such, probation is intended to provide disposition that is "the least restrictive alternative," and the conditions that are imposed are intended to be individualized and rehabilitative (Feld 2014; Griffin and Torbet 2002).

SCOPE AND STRUCTURE OF JUVENILE PROBATION

Juvenile probation was the cornerstone of the original juvenile court, established in Chicago through the enactment of the *Illinois Youth Court Act of 1899*. The Act granted probation officers extensive authority and discretion in cases handled by the court. Section 9 of the statute states:

> In the case of a delinquent child the court may continue the hearing from time to time, and may commit the child to the care and guardianship of a probation officer duly appointed by the court, and may allow said child to remain in its own home, subject to the visitation of the probation officer; such child to report to the probation officer as often as may be required and subject to be returned to the court for further proceeding whenever such action may appear to be necessary; or the court may commit the child to the care and

> guardianship of the probation officer, to be placed in a suitable family home, subject to the friendly supervision of such probation officer; or it may authorize the said probation officer to board out the said child in some suitable family home . . . .
>
> (NCJFCJ 1998:5)

Across the United States,

> juvenile probation is the oldest and most widely used vehicle through which a range of court-ordered services is rendered. Probation may be used at the "front end" of the juvenile justice system for first-time, low-risk offenders or at the "back end" as an alternative to institutional confinement for more serious offenders.
>
> (Torbet 1996:1)

The range of court-ordered services include intake screening (described in Chapter 9), investigation and assessment for the predisposition report (also described in Chapter 9), and probation supervision (Shepherd 1996). "Juvenile Justice Process and Practice: The Work of Probation Officers" briefly describes the many duties of juvenile probation officers.

The organization and administration of juvenile probation varies from state to state. Two structural dimensions are most important. First, are probation services a *judicial* or an *executive branch* responsibility? Second, are probation services administered at the *local* or *state* level? Most frequently, probation services are administered by judicial agencies; this is the case in 20 states and the District of Columbia, with about half of these being *state judicial agencies* and half being *local juvenile courts*. In 15 states, probation administration is a combination of

JUVENILE JUSTICE PROCESS AND PRACTICE: THE WORK OF PROBATION OFFICERS

Probation officers perform a number of important tasks in the juvenile justice process:

- **Intake screening and informal disposition**: initial authorization for detention, preliminary inquiry, consent adjustment without petition, petition (providing information), consent decree with petition.
- **Predisposition investigations and reports**: data and information gathering, interviewing, assessment, diagnostic recommendations.
- **Other court reports**: preliminary inquiry, alcohol/drug assessments, progress reports, review reports, revocation reports.
- **Direct services to youth and families**: individual, family, and group counseling.
- **Supervision**: compliance checks, some surveillance, electronic monitoring, formal and informal adjustments, review hearings, revocations.
- **Program coordination**: volunteers, community service, restitution, referral to other programs and services.
- **Revocation**: revocation reports, participates in revocation hearings.

Sources: Griffin and Torbet (2002), Shepherd (1996), Torbet (1996).

structures, usually with probation services administered by the *local juvenile court* in urban counties and by a *State executive system of probation* in smaller counties. In an additional 15 states, probation is administered by an *executive organization*, most commonly a *State executive system of probation* (OJJDP 2013; Griffin and King 2006; Torbet 1996).

THE USE OF PROBATION: EXTENT, TRENDS, AND DEMOGRAPHICS

"Probation was the most restrictive disposition used in 63% (183,200) of the cases adjudicated delinquent in 2014, compared with 60% (336,600) of the adjudicated caseload in 2005" (Hockenberry and Puzzanchera 2017:52). The percentage of adjudicated delinquency cases resulting in probation was relatively stable from 1985 through 1994, increased modestly through 2000, and then remained level through 2014. Of the adjudicated delinquency cases resulting in probation in 2014, 33 percent were property offenses, 28 percent were person offenses, 26 percent were public order offenses, and 13 percent were drug offenses (Hockenberry and Puzzanchera 2017).

Table 10.1 shows the number and profile of adjudicated cases, and the percent resulting in probation, ranging from 55 percent of adjudicated public order offenses to 74 percent of adjudicated drug offenses. The table also reveals that probation is more likely for youth age 15 or younger than for older youth, for females than for males, and for whites, American Indians, and Asians than for blacks and Hispanics. Thus, the percentage of adjudicated delinquency cases resulting in probation varies by type of offense, age, gender, race, and ethnicity.

Probation is also the most common disposition for petitioned status offense cases in juvenile courts. Over half (56 percent) of all adjudicated status offense cases result in formal probation. The percentage of adjudicated cases resulting in probation varied from 60 percent in the mid- to late 1990s to 50 percent in 2005 and 2006, rising to an average of 56 percent through 2014. Of the adjudicated status offense cases resulting in probation in 2014, 45 percent were truancy offenses, 21 percent were liquor law violations, 15 percent were ungovernability, 8 percent were miscellaneous offenses, and 4 percent were curfew violations. Probation is more likely for younger status offenders (age 15 or younger), for females, and black youth. Just as for delinquency cases, the percentage of adjudicated status offense cases resulting in probation varies by type of offense, age, gender, and race (Hockenberry and Puzzanchera 2017).

PROBATION CONDITIONS

Probation conditions are court-imposed rules that offenders must obey in order to live in the community and avoid confinement. In this way, probation involves conditional release into the community. Probation conditions are written into a legal document. In some juvenile court jurisdictions, probation conditions are part of the court order of disposition; other juvenile courts use a standardized supervision agreement.

Probation conditions are of two types: *general conditions* that apply to everyone on probation and *individualized conditions* (sometimes called *special* or *specific conditions*). General conditions involve common rules of probation such as abiding by all state laws, attending school regularly, and obeying parents. Individualized conditions are usually derived from specific needs identified in the predisposition report. Urinalyses, participation in various treatment programs, counseling, and restitution are examples of special conditions. A major reason for the extensive use of probation is that probation conditions serve multiple purposes. They provide public safety through

TABLE 10.1 Adjudicated delinquency cases resulting in probation, 2014

Most serious offense	Number of cases adjudicated	Percentage of petitioned cases adjudicated	Percentage of petitioned cases adjudicated								
			Age		Gender		Race or Ethnicity				
			≤ 15	≥ 16	Male	Female	White	Black	Hispanic	Am. Indian	Asian
Person offenses	77,500	65%	68%	62%	64%	71%	68%	64%	63%	64%	71%
Property offenses	95,700	64	66	61	63	67	65	62	63	67	72
Drug law violations	33,200	74	75	73	74	75	76	69	72	76	NA
Public order offenses	84,900	55	59	53	56	55	55	54	57	61	71
Total delinquency	291,300	63	65	60	62	66	64	61	62	66	72

Person offenses: criminal homicide, forcible rape, robbery, aggravated assault, simple assault, other violent sex offenses, other person offenses.
Property offenses: burglary, larceny-theft, motor vehicle theft, arson, vandalism, trespassing, stolen property, other property offenses.
Drug law violations: a broad offense category, including unlawful sale, purchase, cultivation, transportation, or use of controlled or prohibited drug.
Public order offenses: obstruction of justice, disorderly conduct, weapons offenses, liquor law violations, nonviolent sex offenses, other public order offenses.

Source: Adapted from Hockenberry and Puzzanchera (2017:44, 53, 54, 56, 57).

supervision, they render punishment through restriction of freedom, they deter future crime, and they promote offender accountability and rehabilitation. Thus, probation has adapted to the changing philosophies of the juvenile justice system. "Case in point: A supervision agreement," which opened this chapter, provides an example of a supervision agreement that specifies the terms of supervision, including the conditions that were imposed by the court in the dispositional order.

Juvenile courts have extensive discretion when imposing conditions of probation (Cromwell, del Carmen, and Alarid 2002). Although a wide range of probation conditions have been authorized under appellate court review, the basic standard to emerge is that the conditions be *reasonable and relevant*. Probation conditions must be clear and not excessive (reasonable), and they must be related to the offense, to the prevention of future delinquency, or to public safety (relevant) (Feld 2014). For example, is a probation condition restricting freedom of association constitutional? A Florida appellate court case *In the Interest of D. S. and J. V. Minor Children* (1965) dealt with two juveniles who were found guilty of simple assault and placed on probation.[2] One of the conditions of their probation was that they were not to associate with gang members, under the rationale that this would prevent further delinquency. Their appeal alleged that such restriction of freedom of association was unconstitutional. The appellate court ruled that this condition was both reasonable and relevant (Hemmens, Steiner, and Mueller 2004).

PROBATION SUPERVISION

Probation supervision refers to the monitoring and assistance of probationers by probation officers. The approach to supervision taken by probation officers determines the relative emphasis given to offender rehabilitation or enforcement of probation rules. Styles of supervision have varied over the history of juvenile probation.

Styles of probation supervision

A descriptive typology of probation supervision styles can be constructed from two important dimensions: rehabilitation and control, as shown in **Figure 10.1** (Jordon and Sasfy 1974; see also Ward and Kupchik 2010; Seiter and West 2003; Klockers 1972). *Rehabilitation* refers to the degree to which probation officers emphasize reform and the role they take in bringing about offender change. *Control* refers to the level of monitoring and surveillance by probation officers and how closely they enforce probation conditions. The relative emphasis on these two important aspects of supervision influences probation officers' views and approaches to: (1) probation conditions as a vehicle for change, (2) enforcement of conditions through monitoring and surveillance, and (3) readiness to revoke probation (Czajkoski 1973; Klockers 1972).

The *moral reformer* style of supervision was the original approach used in probation, first practiced by John Augustus, a Boston shoemaker who advanced probation in 1841. Like many others of his day, John Augustus viewed crime and delinquency as a moral problem, requiring moral guidance. Augustus worked closely with the offenders released to him, getting involved in many aspects of their lives—family, work, church, recreation—and providing assistance. He believed that with proper guidance, offenders could be morally reformed. Following this tradition, early juvenile probation officers often used a moral-reformer style of supervision. Active involvement in the daily lives of juvenile offenders was meant to promote rehabilitation and high levels of control.

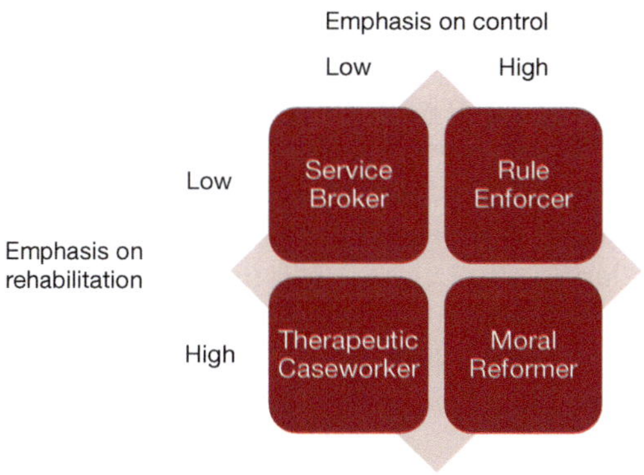

FIGURE 10.1 *A model of probation supervision.*
Source: Adapted from Jordan and Sasfy (1974:29).

The professionalization of the juvenile court that began in the 1920s was associated with the greater use of full-time, highly trained probation officers, rather than volunteers. State statutes began to require probation officers to have a college degree. Consistent with the child-savers' view that the juvenile court should be more of a welfare system than a judicial system, professional probation officers emphasized a *therapeutic casework* supervision style (Feld 1999). Probation officers engaged in case assessment, in which they evaluated the needs of their "clients" and developed rehabilitative goals derived from their assessment. Probation officers also provided direct services—they engaged in therapeutic counseling, including individual, family, and peer counseling.

Beginning in the 1960s, growing consideration was given to the community's role in generating and responding to crime and delinquency. In this context, a community-based approach to probation supervision developed. Rather than having probation officers engage in therapeutic casework, the *service broker* supervision style emphasized the need to use resources in the community, including educational programs, job training, job placement, community mental health, certified counselors, and drug treatment. It was thought that by using community resources, the offender would be better able to be reintegrated back into the community. With this approach to supervision, probation officers became brokers of community services and resources.

The final supervision style to emerge was that of the *rule enforcer.* Associated with the "get tough" approach to crime and delinquency during the 1980s and 1990s, the law-enforcer style of supervision seeks to provide offender accountability and public safety. The get tough approach is accomplished through supervision that emphasizes restriction of freedom, enforcement of probation conditions, monitoring and surveillance, and revocation of probation for rule violation.

Techniques of probation supervision

Regardless of supervision style, probation supervision is accomplished primarily through three basic techniques: (1) interviews with probationers and others, (2) random urinalysis to test for the presence of drugs, and (3) records checks. These supervision techniques are used in office visits, in visits with the youth in his or her daily activities (field visits), and in contacts with people who associate with the youth (collateral contacts). As a result, probation officers conduct interviews in their offices and at probationers' homes, schools, and places of work. Most commonly, interviews are simply informal talks with the offenders and their parents, teachers, counselors, and employers. Depending on supervision style, interviews with probationers may be therapeutic, involving counseling techniques, or they may be directed at information gathering to bring about offender accountability and enforcement of conditions. Urinalysis is most commonly conducted randomly during office visits, but it may also be done during field visits at home, school, or work. Probation officers also routinely check records that are kept by various agencies, including police reports, detention intakes, school attendance records, and grades. Records information like this is normally gathered through collateral contacts with people and agencies that are relevant to the probation case. These collateral contacts supplement the probation officers' knowledge about probationers' daily activities and attitudes.

The first reading for this chapter by Craig Schwalbe and Tina Maschi (2011) examines probation officers' strategies to encourage and enforce compliance with probation conditions. Specifically, the study examines the use of confrontational tactics (coercion) and client-centered approaches across offense characteristics, youth demographics, and psychosocial characteristics of the youth (see also Schwartz et al. 2017; Schwalbe and Maschi 2009).

Intensive probation supervision

Intensive supervision probation (ISP) is a development in probation supervision that attempts to provide public safety and offender accountability through intensive monitoring and supervision of the probationer. As an alternative to secure confinement, ISP is highly structured in terms of conditions and supervision standards. ISP officers have greatly reduced caseloads that allow for much higher levels of supervision. ISP commonly involves the use of electronic monitoring devices (at least in initial phases), a specified number of contacts per week, mandatory school and work checks, random urinalysis, and a required number of community service hours. Although these standards are intended to provide public safety, they are also designed to promote competency development by monitoring performance in school and work.

Effectiveness of community supervision tied to rehabilitative services

The effectiveness of probation supervision is difficult to gauge because of the extensive variability in supervision both within and across court jurisdictions—in styles of supervision, caseload size, level of supervision, and services offered. Evaluation research clearly shows, however, that supervision alone, including intensive supervision, does not work, but must be combined with treatment services to reduce recidivism (Cullen and Jonson 2017; Lipsey et al. 2010; Bonta et al. 2008; Petersillia and Turner 1993; Lipsey 1992). Based on extensive review of evaluation research in juvenile justice, Mark Lipsey and his colleagues (2010:24) found that a therapeutic approach includes a number of categories of evidence-based practices:

- **Counseling**: individual, group, and family counseling, mentoring
- **Skill building**: social, academic, and vocational skills
- **Multiple coordinated services**: case management and service referrals
- **Restorative justice**: restitution, victim-offender mediation
- **Behavioral monitoring**: observation to detect bad behavior, intensive probation or parole supervision.

These findings speak clearly to the need for a range of services, including rehabilitative components, in both regular probation supervision and ISP.

Evaluation research also shows that the most effective rehabilitation uses treatment strategies that are known to produce change in juvenile offenders by promoting mental and behavioral health. Most notably, cognitive behavioral therapy (CBT) is an evidence-based intervention strategy for a variety of behavioral health problems and mental disorders, including substance abuse, conduct disorder, sex offenses, and post-traumatic stress disorder (PTSD). CBT focuses on cognitively restructuring distorted and erroneous cognitions (thoughts, beliefs, and attitudes, sometimes called "thinking errors") and developing new adaptive cognitive skills to regulate thoughts, emotions, and behaviors (Andrews and Bonta 2017; Cullen and Jonson 2017; Van Voorhis and Salisbury 2016).

The use of behavioral health screening and risk/need assessment in probation supervision

Another key element of evidence-based practice in juvenile probation is the use of behavioral health screening and risk/need assessment. After extensive study, the National Center for Mental Health and Juvenile Justice (NCMHJJ) established the need for mental health and substance abuse assessment of youth involved in the juvenile justice system (Skowyra and Cocozza 2007). Behavioral health screening was deemed essential to the task of more accurately identifying mental health and substance abuse needs of court-involved youth. The NCMHJJ also advocated for the use of behavioral health screening and assessment to guide treatment strategies in individual cases. Behavioral health screening and assessment are usually distinguished in terms of time frame and scope. *Screening* is a brief process that can be conducted by laymen or trained clinicians. The purpose of screening is to, as early as possible, identify youth who display fairly immediate behavioral health needs. Mental health assessment is used when screening indicates the need for further evaluation. *Assessment* uses multiple sources of information, but is based most extensively on standardized assessment instruments that are given by trained clinicians.

The NCMHJJ also emphasizes that behavioral health screening and assessment should be performed in conjunction with an assessment of risk for future violence and delinquent offending (Skowyra and Cocozza 2007). Predictions of delinquency have traditionally relied on "subjective assessments, professional judgments, intuition, or 'gut-level feelings'" (Gottfredson and Moriarty 2006:180). Much research shows, however, that predictions of delinquency that rely on human judgments are far less accurate and valid than those grounded on risk assessment instruments that classify youth according to their likelihood of future delinquent offending (Guy et al. 2015; Andrews and Bonta 2017).

The second chapter reading by Guy and her colleagues (2015) describes how behavioral health screening and risk/need assessment are utilized in juvenile probation. This excerpt of a technical report establishes the need for and benefit of behavioral health screening and risk/need assessment. They also describe several screening and assessment instruments and how they can best be used in juvenile probation. To do so, the authors advocate for a therapeutic framework known as "risk-needs-responsivity," commonly referred to as the RNR model. The RNR model utilizes behavioral health screening and risk/need assessment in guiding probation case management (see also Andrews and Bonta 2017; Vincent et al. 2016; Haqanee and Peterson-Badali 2015; Bonta et al. 2011).

House arrest and electronic monitoring

House arrest and electronic monitoring are usually coupled to provide intensive supervision of youth pending court action or as a dispositional condition of probation. *House arrest* requires the youth to stay home except for specific time periods that have been approved for him/her to be away, such as school and work. Compliance is checked through frequent probation officer contracts and an electronic monitoring device. *Electronic monitoring systems* are either active or passive. *Active systems* utilize GPS (Global Positioning Satellite) tracking technology that allows the monitoring agency to create individualized inclusion and exclusions zones, mapping, and daily schedule parameters through which 24-hour tracking is conducted. Probation officers are notified either immediately or according to programmed intervals. *Passive systems* involve an ankle transmitter bracelet and a home monitoring unit, using a land-line or cellular signal. Random phone calls generated by computer must be responded to by the probationer in an established time period.

REVOCATION

Violations of probation conditions may result in a highly discretionary judicial decision called revocation. **Revocation** is the legal termination of probation by the court when the youth commits a new offense or violates the conditions of probation (Feld 2014). Probation conditions are imposed by the courts, and consequently the decision to revoke probation rests with the court that imposed the conditions. It is the probation officer, however, who initiates the revocation process with a revocation report to the court, which must establish probable cause for the *petition to revoke probation*. The probation officer has extensive discretion in deciding whether to deal with the probation violation informally or formally through a revocation hearing. Judges also have considerable discretion in deciding whether to revoke probation. The revocation hearing follows due process of law, with certain rights that have been extended through state statutory law and appellate court review (Feld 2014; Cromwell et al. 2002). Upon the finding that probation conditions have been violated, the judge may continue the youth on probation, perhaps with new conditions, or the judge may revoke the probation and impose a new disposition.

SUMMARY AND CONCLUSIONS

Probation is the most frequently imposed disposition in juvenile courts, for both delinquency cases and petitioned status offense cases. The use of probation varies by type of offense, and by age, gender, and race of the youth. Probation is usually combined with other dispositions, such as restitution or community service, and it involves a set of court-imposed rules, called conditions that must be obeyed in order to live in the community and avoid residential placement. Although a wide range of probation conditions have been authorized under appellate court review, the basic standard to emerge is that conditions must be "reasonable and relevant."

Community supervision is provided by probation officers who vary greatly in their supervision styles, especially in terms of the degree to which they emphasize control and reform. By distinguishing the relative emphasis on control and rehabilitation, four supervision styles are evident: *moral reformer* (high in control, high in rehabilitation); *therapeutic-caseworker* (low in control, high in rehabilitation); *service-broker* (low in control, low in rehabilitation); and *rule enforcer* (high in control, low in rehabilitation).

Evidence-based practice in juvenile probation points to the importance of a therapeutic approach, involving behavioral health screening and risk/need assessment, as well as rehabilitation services. Evaluation research reveals five categories of effective rehabilitative programs: counseling (including mentoring); skill building; multiple coordinated services involving case management and service referrals; restorative justice (including restitution and victim-offender mediation); and behavioral monitoring (Lipsey et al. 2010).

While research shows that probation supervision alone does not work, three supervision practices are popular in many contemporary juvenile court jurisdictions. First, intensive supervision probation (ISP) attempts to provide public safety and offender accountability through intensive monitoring and supervision of the probationer. Second, house arrest confines youth to their home, except for specific time periods that have been approved for them to be away, such as school and work. Compliance is checked through frequent probation office contacts and an electronic monitoring device. Third, electronic monitoring utilizes electronic surveillance devices to monitor the youth's location and schedule of activities.

Revocation is the legal termination of probation by the court when the youth commits a new offense or violates the conditions of probation. The probation officer initiates the revocation process with a revocation report to the court. The revocation report must establish probable cause for the petition to revoke probation, which instigates a revocation hearing. The revocation hearing follows due process of law, with certain rights that have been extended through state statutory law and appellate court review.

READING 10.1

"CONFRONTING DELINQUENCY: PROBATION OFFICERS' USE OF COERCION AND CLIENT-CENTERED TACTICS TO FOSTER YOUTH COMPLIANCE."

Craig S. Schwalbe and Tina Maschi. 2011. *Crime and Delinquency* 57: 801–822.

Schwalbe and Maschi (2011) examine probation officers' strategies to encourage and enforce compliance with probation conditions. Through analysis of a survey of probation officers, the study describes and specifies the use of confrontational tactics (coercion) and client-centered approaches across offense characteristics, youth demographics, and psychosocial characteristics.

For juvenile probation officers, youth compliance with probation requirements is a fundamental concern. Probation is formally defined as a period of suspended sentence when the delinquent juvenile submits to monitoring by a probation officer (PO) and agrees to participate in court-mandated interventions to remediate conditions that contribute to risk of future delinquency (Griffin & Torbet, 2002). When youths violate the terms of their probation, they risk exposure to increased sanctions and deeper penetration into the juvenile justice system. Because more than 60% of youths adjudicated delinquent are ordered to probation supervision (Snyder & Sickmund, 2006), the success of probation, which relies in large part on the cooperation of youths with its conditions, is a large concern for juvenile justice scholars and policy makers. Unfortunately, research with juvenile offenders suggests that many violate the terms of their probation or parole and that from a third to a half will reoffend (Cottle, Lee, & Heilbrun, 2001; Piquero, 2003; Schwalbe, 2007).

Gaps in the literature on compliance promoting practices hamper efforts to develop a knowledge base of effective probation strategies. The best practice literature on probation and evidence from allied human services fields offers advice and guidelines generally falling into two categories: confrontational tactics and client-centered approaches. However, these guidelines have not been experimentally evaluated, leaving POs uninformed about the optimal balance between confrontational tactics and client-centered approaches. Furthermore, efforts to develop training curricula and evidence-based probation approaches are hindered by a lack of knowledge about current practices in the field. This study builds on the extant literature by examining the practices POs use to enforce and encourage compliance among adjudicated youths. It describes the strategies employed by POs with adjudicated youths and tests hypotheses about the influence of youth legal and social factors as well as PO characteristics on these strategies and tactics.

Confrontational tactics in probation

Confrontational tactics deter youthful noncompliance by informing youths' expectations about the certainty and severity of potential consequences for noncompliant behaviors (Griffin & Torbet, 2002; Walsh, 2001). Confrontational tactics can take the form of benign reminders about the consequences of nonconforming behaviors or more assertive or aggressive approaches, such as threatened consequences. These strategies are rooted in a deterrence approach to juvenile justice. Deterrence theory suggests that antisocial behavior originates in a subjective cost-benefit analysis of delinquency and in expectations about the likelihood of detection (Kurlychek, Torbet, & Bozynski, 1999; Matsueda, Kreager, & Huizinga, 2006; Maxwell & Gray, 2000; Ward, Stafford, & Gray, 2006). That is, delinquent behaviors are more likely when youths value the rewards of delinquent behaviors more than their negative consequences and when youths believe that the chances of being caught are low. POs may employ confrontational tactics to influence youths' values, attitudes, and perceptions about perceived rewards and consequences for delinquency and noncompliant behaviors (Griffin & Torbet, 2002; Walsh, 2001).

The effects of deterrence-informed probation strategies on youth outcomes have not been evaluated. Nevertheless, the best practice and training literature suggests that youthful noncompliance should be addressed firmly, directly, and consistently (Griffin & Torbet, 2002). For instance, Walsh (2001) recommended that for many offenders, "any legal violation, no matter how minor, [should] result in official action" (p. 131). Moreover, the Graduated Sanctions approach advanced by the Office of Juvenile Justice and Delinquency Prevention (OJJDP), relying as it does on an escalating sanction severity for chronic and serious offenses, ensconces this approach as the formal policy of many jurisdictions across the United States (Bender, King, & Torbet, 2006; Howell, 1995, 2003; Kurlychek et al., 1999; Maloney, Romig, & Armstrong, 1988; Wiebush, 2002). Maxwell and Gray (2000) provided indirect evidence in support of deterrence-based strategies in a study of adult probationers. Among adults sentenced to an intensive probation program (N = 516), participants who had a higher expectation of punishment for drug or alcohol use had lower rates of program failure than participants with a low expectation of detection and punishment.

Client-centered approaches in probation

Approaches grounded in traditional casework models and emerging research in evidence-based practices present an array of alternatives to deterrence-informed confrontation and coercion

(Pratt, Cullen, Blevins, Daigle, & Madensen, 2006). The essence of these approaches is the development of a strong working relationship or affective bond between the PO and the juvenile that enables the PO to influence youthful compliance through role modeling, persuasion, problem solving, or other interpersonal means. Such approaches have deep roots in the juvenile justice system. In one of the earliest texts about probation, Flexner and Baldwin (1914) described the imperative of winning the confidence of children and their parents. He suggested that "their [probation officers'] real strength lies not in the power which the court has over parents and children, but in the use of the same human qualities which characterize helpful relations between people generally" (p. 138). Later, Young (1937) wrote against "ordering and forbidding" techniques in favor of the casework approach built on careful study of individual cases and close personal relations between POs and probationers. For both writers, personal influence, rather than force or authority, was portrayed as the strongest tool of the probation officer.

Three streams of empirical evidence lend contemporary support for client-centered approaches in probation and inform ongoing developments in the field. The first is the growing evidence in favor of cognitive-behavioral principles in the treatment of delinquent youths (Landenberger & Lipsey, 2005; Lipsey & Wilson, 1998). Cognitive-behavioral interventions emphasize the roles of beliefs, attitudes, social skills, and problem-solving capacity in the development of conditions such as antisocial behavior as well as in their remedy. Prototypical cognitive interventions focus on increasing skills for social engagement and on challenging faulty or unhelpful belief structures (Goldstein, Glick, & Gibbs, 1998). For probation officers, approaches informed by cognitive-behavioral research may include modeling of interpersonal problem-solving skills and the use of behavioral management plans that include incentives and rewards for compliant and cooperative behaviors.

The second stream can be found in the growing interest among justice systems in Motivational Interviewing (Alexander, Van Benschoten, & Walters, 2008; Clark, 2005; Clark, Walters, Gingerich, & Meltzer, 2006). Motivational Interviewing is a brief intervention designed to help people overcome ambivalence and engage in health-promoting behavior change (Miller & Rollnick, 2002). Although it was developed in the field of addictions, it has been tested in numerous settings and is gaining acceptance in justice-related settings as well (Feldstein & Ginsburg, 2006; Miller & Mount, 2001). A defining feature of Motivational Interviewing is its reliance on empathic listening and its nondirective approach, which eschews direct confrontation. Miller and Mount (2001) showed that training for probation officers in Motivational Interviewing can increase the frequency of nondirective counseling strategies such as reflection, reframing, and affirmation. Although we are not aware of any evaluations of Motivational Interviewing by probation officers, there is a growing chorus of interest in this approach, and it is commonly recommended for justice settings of all kinds.

A third stream of evidence is emerging in research with adult probation programs. Skeem and colleagues study predictors and effects of the working alliance in probation and parole among adult offenders who have severe mental health problems (Skeem, Emke-Francis, & Louden, 2006; Skeem, Encandela, & Louden, 2003; Skeem, Louden, Polaschek, & Camp, 2007; Vidal & Skeem, 2007). Their research suggests that structural characteristics of probation programs shape typical probation strategies with this population. For instance, rather than employing negative pressure and coercive approaches common in standard probation, officers in specialized mental health probation programs employ more problem-solving approaches and outreach. Furthermore, their research indicates that strong working alliances in probation, like that across all human service settings in which the alliance has been studied, are associated with more positive outcomes, including greater compliance, fewer violations, and less recidivism.

Predictors of confrontational and client-centered approaches

Whether probation officers employ more confrontational approaches or more client-centered approaches may depend on the intersection of PO traits and characteristics with youth offending histories, youth psychosocial need profiles, and with youth demographic characteristics. As an example, one may expect POs to confront youths who exhibit patterns of more serious or chronic delinquency, whereas POs may employ more client-centered approaches with youths who have greater psychosocial needs such as mental health problems or family discord (Campbell & Schmidt, 2000; Fader, Harris, Jones, & Poulin, 2001; Lyons, Baerger, Quigley, Erlich, & Griffin, 2001; Matarazzo, Carrington, & Hiscott, 2001; Schwalbe, Hatcher, & Maschi, 2009). Evidence from probation officers themselves suggests that they vary in their attitudes toward punishment (Leiber, Schwarze, Mack, & Farnworth, 2002; Lopez & Russell, 2008; Shearer, 2002). One would expect, for instance, that POs who strongly endorse punishment would tend to employ confrontational tactics, negative pressures such as threatened consequences, and swift execution of negative sanctions. Moreover, evidence suggests that latent or preconscious stereotypes about youths of color and about female offenders prime POs toward a more confrontational approach through their effect on attitudes toward punishment (Gaarder, Rodriguez, & Zatz, 2004; Graham & Lowery, 2004).

In an earlier study (Schwalbe & Maschi, in press), we examined predictors of probation approaches, as reported by POs who responded to a Web-based survey ($N = 308$). Results from that study showed that POs tended to employ a balanced approach with youths. That is, they utilized about equal amounts of accountability-based approaches, which included direct measures of confrontational approaches, and rehabilitation-based approaches. The roles of youth age, level of psychosocial needs, and PO attitudes toward treatment and punishment in the overall intensity of PO approaches stood out as predominant findings of that study. Notable youth and PO characteristics that did not predict the intensity of probation approaches included youth race, gender, and offending characteristics.

Current study

The present study examined interpersonal probation strategies, including confrontational approaches and client centered approaches, used by POs to encourage and enforce compliance. These strategies were conceptualized on a continuum of approaches where the continuum mid-point represented a balanced approach and where the continuum endpoints represented either more frequent use of confrontation compared to client-centered approaches on the one end or more frequent use of client-centered approaches compared to confrontation on the other. These analyses were designed to identify youth characteristics and PO characteristics that predicted extreme probation strategies. Findings from this study point to youth-related and PO-related factors that contribute to more or less confrontational and punitive approaches in probation supervision.

Methods

Sample

A Web-administered electronic survey was conducted with the membership of the American Probation and Parole Association (APPA). Actively employed probation officers who supervised juvenile offenders were eligible to participate. Survey respondents were entered into a drawing for one of 10 $20 e-gift certificates to a well-known online retailer. In total, 384 respondents entered the Web-based portal to register for the drawing; 308 respondents completed the survey. Survey respondents were recruited via an announcement in an electronic newsletter that targets probation officers (n = 11, 3% of total), a direct e-mail invitation to the membership list of the organization of probation officers (n = 225, 59% of total), and two follow-up e-mails spaced at approximately 2-week intervals (n = 68 [18%] and n = 80 [21%], respectively). Because the APPA database does not identify members according to the focus of their work in probation (i.e., adult, juvenile) and because the APPA membership includes affiliated organizations in addition to individual members, it is impossible to calculate response rates or to accurately describe the sampling frame of juvenile probation officers.

Measures

The aim of the survey was to elicit probation strategies and practices used by officers with a specific youth during the preceding 3-month period. Respondents randomly selected an index juvenile from their caseloads using procedures adapted from a similar study of child welfare caseworkers (Hansen & Warner, 1994). Respondents were directed to insert their names into an alphabetical list of their juvenile caseloads and to select the next youth on the list who met the following criteria: (a) has been formally adjudicated, (2) has been known to the respondent for at least 3 months, and (c) is under 18 years old. Respondents then completed a survey of youth demographic, offending, and psychosocial characteristics; of probation approaches used in the preceding 3-month period; and questions about attitudes and demographic characteristics of the survey respondent. Measures are described in more detail in the section that follows.

Probation Practices Assessment Survey (PPAS)

The study utilized the PPAS compliance practices subscales (Schwalbe & Maschi, in press). The compliance practices subscales measure the frequency of 15 strategies and approaches employed by POs during the past 3 months to encourage youth compliance. Compliance practice subscales include *confrontation tactics* (4 items, a = .81; e.g., "How often did you threaten consequences like violation of probation or detention placement?"), *counseling tactics* (6 items, a = .75; e.g., "How often did you ask the youth about how his/her current behavior is related to his/her long-term goals?"), and *behavioral tactics* (5 items, a = .80; e.g., "How often did you offer incentives for completing tasks?"). Each item was measured on a 7-point Likert scale ranging from *never* to *every contact.*

Three outcome variables were derived from the PPAS compliance practices subscales. In the first, a continuum of confrontation tactics and counseling tactics was calculated by subtracting the counseling tactics scale score from the confrontation tactics scale score. Values approaching zero indicate that counseling and confrontation were used at about equal levels with the index youth; positive values indicate more frequent use of confrontation, whereas negative values indicate more frequent use of counseling. The second outcome, a continuum of confrontation tactics and behavioral tactics, was calculated in the same manner. Finally, a third continuum was calculated that averaged counseling tactics and behavioral tactics into a single score and subtracted this combined score from the confrontation tactics scale score.

Youth characteristics

Respondents completed 31 questions about youth demographics (i.e., age, gender, and race), offending characteristics (i.e., severity, type, and prior adjudications), and psychosocial characteristics (i.e., school functioning; involvement in specialized mental health, substance abuse, and child welfare service systems; peer relationships; drug and alcohol involvement; and parental criminality). Survey items were adapted from previously validated risk and needs assessment instruments such as the North Carolina Assessment of Risk, the Joint Risk Matrix, and the Youth Level of Service/Case Management Inventory (Hoge & Andrews, 2003; Schwalbe, Fraser, & Day, 2007; Schwalbe, Fraser, Day, & Cooley, 2006). Respondents reported known alcohol use and known illicit drug use on 4-point scales ranging from *does not use* to *uses more than once per month* and whether youths were known to associate with gang members. To each of these items (alcohol use, drug use, and gang association), respondents had the option to respond "information not available." Two measures of school problems were obtained: whether youths were suspended from school or were truant from school during the past 3 months. Five items measuring involvement in specialized health and social services prior to the most recent adjudication were combined into an additive index of *prior social service involvement* (i.e., outpatient mental health treatment, inpatient mental health treatment, outpatient substance abuse treatment, inpatient substance abuse treatment, and child welfare involvement).

Compliance

POs completed a 9-item youth compliance scale. The compliance scale measures the frequency of cooperative youth behaviors on a 7-point Likert scale ranging from *never* to *always*. Four items indicated compliant behaviors (i.e., attended scheduled meetings with the probation officer, attended scheduled meetings with other service providers, was polite toward the probation officer, and was forthcoming and told the truth to the probation officer); four items indicated noncompliant behaviors (i.e., missed appointments with the probation officer, missed appointments with other service providers, lied or misrepresented the truth to the probation officer, and yelled at or swore at the probation officer). Items measuring noncompliant behaviors were reverse-scored so that higher scores represent greater compliance. In addition, a single item measured global compliance (i.e., overall cooperation with the PO). Factor analysis of the specific compliance items (i.e., omitting global compliance) revealed three subscales: *truth telling* (2 items, α =.72), *polite behaviors* (2 items, α = .57), and *attendance* (4 items, α =.77).

Probation officer characteristics and attitudes

Respondents reported on their demographic characteristics (i.e., age, gender, and race), years of experience in juvenile justice settings, and education level. In addition, they completed the 6-item *attitude toward punishment* scale (α = .75; Leiber et al., 2002), two items measuring respondent beliefs about the *helpfulness of probation officers* with youths who have alcohol and mental health problems (α = .66), and two items measuring respondent beliefs about the *effectiveness of mandated treatment* on drug problems and mental health problems (α = .87; Polcin & Greenfield, 2003). . . .

Discussion

Findings from this study showed that confrontational approaches are widespread in standard probation practice. Scores on the PPAS confrontation tactics subscale suggested that POs employ some type of confrontation in about half of their contacts with youths. Equally prevalent were the use of client-centered approaches, however. Thus, the first overriding finding of this study affirmed that confrontational approaches were employed in balance with client-centered approaches. Balanced approaches to probation supervision are consistent with the Balanced and Restorative movement in juvenile justice policy and with graduated sanctions policies (Maloney et al., 1988; Wiebush, 2002). Moreover, research on intensive probation programs with adult offenders suggests that a balanced approach is associated with less violation of probation (VOP) and less recidivism than either a more extreme law enforcement approach (i.e., confrontation) or casework approach (i.e., counseling or behavioral tactics) (Paparozzi & Gendreau, 2005). Thus, probation officers who employ a balanced approach are functioning in step with policy prescriptions and may be aligned with empirical evidence as well.

Although a balanced approach was reported by many respondents, the second overriding finding of our study was that POs employed more extreme approaches contingent on key youth and PO characteristics. For instance, illicit drug use frequency stood out as a prominent predictor of confrontation. In every model, more frequent illicit drug use led to greater use of confrontation compared to alternative interpersonal strategies and tactics. Clearly, the tendency of POs to employ confrontational approaches with respect to youth drug use was out of step with contemporary trends in the field of addictions (Miller & Rollnick, 2002). Research with Motivational Interviewing underscores the benefits of maintaining a nondirective approach to reduce client defensiveness and resistance and to increase client engagement with the treatment process. Results of this study suggested that either POs had not been trained in this approach or that they were unwilling to abandon directive approaches, such as confrontational tactics, altogether. As indicated above, POs clearly embraced both intervention styles. This finding points to the need for research to study how POs package both types of strategies and to evaluate their relative effectiveness for youths with substance use problems in the context of probation.

Three youth-related factors tended to decrease confrontational tactics: youth age, prior service utilization, and youth compliance. The finding that younger youths received more confrontation than older youths was unexpected. This finding may indicate a greater hope or urgency for prevention with younger youths compared to their older peers, thereby justifying more frequent confrontation. On the other hand, POs may have expected more independence from older youths, granting them more latitude to make choices and to face court consequences. The gendered effect of prior social service utilization demonstrated in this study suggested that POs were more prone toward problem-solving approaches for females than for males when prior service use was high. Such a finding is consistent with the chivalry hypothesis in which juvenile justice systems seek to protect female offenders from harsh sanctions (Chesney-Lind & Sheldon, 1998; Leiber & Mack, 2003). In this case, girls with previously identified treatment needs were the beneficiaries of a more gentle and positive approach.

The interaction between gender and race suggested that the chivalry hypothesis was conditional, however. Whereas the chivalry hypothesis was supported for White females who received less confrontation than African American females, POs reported more confrontation with African American females than any other group. The tendency of POs to confront these girls was consistent with the stereotype sex role hypothesis, whereby the juvenile justice system employs coercive and controlling interventions to enforce a middle-class standard of female role behaviors (Chesney-Lind & Sheldon, 1998; Leiber & Mack, 2003). Results of this study suggest that although White girls benefited from officer protection, African Americans encountered more pressure to conform.

Among all youth factors, the most consistent predictor of confrontational approaches was youth compliance. In bivariate analyses, each dimension of youth compliance (i.e., global compliance, attendance, polite behaviors, and truth telling) predicted less confrontation. Thus, it appears that when presented with youthful noncompliance, POs defaulted to more deterrence-oriented and accountability-oriented tactics and strategies. Of note across all of our findings was the prominence of PO perceptions of youth truth telling or honesty. More than any other aspect of youth compliance, results of this study demonstrated that POs valued youth honesty and that probation strategies were conditioned on this perception. Whether POs were accurate in their assessments of youth honesty cannot be ascertained from the available data, nor can we know whether the youths themselves or their parents would agree with PO assessments of honesty. Nevertheless, results of this study point to the wide-ranging influence of PO impressions of youthful honesty and dishonesty in their intervention decisions.

Among PO characteristics, the effect of officer age stands out, about which several interpretations are possible. For instance, that older officers were more likely to employ client-centered approaches relative to confrontational tactics could reflect a cohort effect based on overriding policies toward youth well-being and accountability that have changed during the past quarter century. POs hired earlier entered a justice system that was more strongly oriented toward the well-being of youths relative to the current policy framework that prioritizes accountability and public safety. Alternatively, this finding may also reflect the effects of maturity, in which older officers are less reactive to youthful noncompliance. The former explanation points to the challenge of retooling staff as agency policies change. The latter explanation suggests the need for close supervision of younger, less experienced staff in their use of client-centered approaches and confrontational tactics.

This study had at least four notable limitations related to its measurement and sampling designs. First, it is likely that POs' reports of their tactics and strategies were biased by limitations of recall. Our study design sought to attenuate this limitation by constraining the duration of recall to a period commonly employed for case reassessment (3 months) and by linking PO reports to a specific youth rather than to an average youth or to their whole caseload. In these ways, the survey primed respondents to think in specific rather than general terms. Second, it is not clear that POs' definitions about specific strategies, "confrontation," for instance, would be invariant across other participants or observers. As this study represented the perspectives of POs on their use of interpersonal strategies, it would be instructive to obtain the perspectives of youths, parents, and objective observers as well. Third, as respondents to our study belonged to a professional association of probation officers, they represented a skilled and motivated subset of POs whose experiences and use of probation strategies may or may not represent the typical PO serving in the field. Finally, structural variables, such as local agency policies, philosophies, and procedures, were not included in the survey and were therefore unavailable for this analysis. Alongside youth and PO characteristics, structural factors such as these would be expected to influence probation strategies as well.

Despite these limitations, this study opens new avenues for future research toward an evidence-based approach to juvenile probation. The probation strategies examined here need to be evaluated for their effects on outcomes such as youth and family cooperation, engagement in treatment, VOP, and recidivism. Such an evaluation should strive to identify an optimal balance of confrontational and client-centered approaches. Moreover, such an evaluation should identify styles and approaches to confrontation that are more or less effective with key justice outcomes. Currently, best practices in the field are based on nonempirical literature on practice with involuntary and mandated clients in corrections and social work. By advancing into longitudinal and experimental evaluations, the literature could inform training curricula for probation officers and build a more sturdy evidence base for probation practice. In the long run, this stream of research promises to guide POs toward an optimal balance between confrontational approaches and traditional client-centered strategies that foster youths' prosocial development and successful completion of probation requirements.

[References omitted.]

READING 10.2

"INTRODUCTION" (PP. 8–22) IN *ADVANCING USE OF RISK ASSESSMENT IN JUVENILE PROBATION.*

Laura S. Guy, Gina M. Vincent, Thomas Grisso, and Rachael Perrault. 2015. Washington, DC: National Criminal Justice Reference Service.

This reading is the introduction of a technical report on research sponsored by the U.S. Department of Justice, which studied the impact of implementing risk assessment and behavioral health screening in juvenile probation. These instruments, together with a decision-making model for case planning, were used in three demonstration sites in two states. The introduction to this report provides an overview to the use of assessment in probation, describing the major instruments used for behavioral health screening and risk/need assessment.

Juvenile probation

Probation departments in juvenile justice systems nationwide play many roles to assist the courts and meet the needs of youth about whom the courts must make legal and rehabilitation decisions. Juvenile probation officers (JPOs) are the caseworkers of the juvenile justice system. They assemble initial information about the youth soon after their arrest, often provide that information to the court to determine the need for pretrial detention, and have input into decisions about adjudicating the charges or employing an informal adjustment of the case. If a youth is adjudicated delinquent, JPOs typically provide the court information for the "disposition" phase of the case, based on their interviews and investigation of the youth's background, regarding the youth's needs related to rehabilitation. Finally, JPOs often monitor youth while they are on probation as part of their disposition, including community aftercare if the youth is returning from a period of secure juvenile correctional placement.

The JPO's evaluation of the youth for "post-adjudication" or "disposition" decisions of the court is a central focus of the present study. Many courts rely on JPOs at this point to offer recommendations regarding the placement and programming for the youth that will meet the objectives of the court. Those objectives include provision of treatment and rehabilitation services in the youth's best interest and to reduce the likelihood of future recidivism, and to provide those services in a manner that protects public safety during rehabilitation.

Providing information to the courts to meet these objectives necessarily requires the JPO's inquiry into several key questions. They can be summed up as questions about "risk" and "risk factors" or "needs." What is the risk that this youth will engage in behaviors that may endanger others during the period of rehabilitation? For this specific youth, what is contributing to those risks? And what risk factors, or criminogenic needs, of the youth must be met to reduce that risk?

As we explain in more detail later, in recent years juvenile probation departments have begun to rely on structured tools to assist JPOs in their collection of information about youths to address these placement and rehabilitation questions. The present study focused on the proper implementation of these tools and their effect on JPOs' disposition decisions. The tools they employ typically are screening tools for behavioral health needs, and risk/needs assessment tools.

Behavioral health screening

. . . [R]esearch about the high prevalence of behavioral health problems among juvenile justice-involved youth (e.g., Teplin et al., 2002) began to appear about two decades ago. This resulted in widespread recognition of the need to identify youths' behavioral health problems at every decision point in juvenile justice processing. Subsequently, the term "behavioral health problems" has become more common in this field, referring both to behavioral health problems (such as depression, anxiety, suicide risk, problems involving impulse control) and to substance use problems.

Need for behavioral health identification

As the high prevalence of behavioral health problems became apparent, increasingly juvenile justice programs recognized the importance of identifying them when processing youth for purposes of determining proper dispositions. Treatment was considered important for two broad reasons: to meet the system's "parental" obligation to care for youth in its custody, and to reduce the likelihood of recidivism to the extent that behavioral health disorders (especially substance use) may contribute to further offending (Grisso, 2004).

Arising from that concern was recognition of the need to be able to identify youths' behavioral health problems at various points in juvenile justice processing, such as probation intake, intake to pretrial detention, and admission to juvenile corrections. In most cases it was unrealistic to expect the juvenile justice system to have trained mental health professionals (psychiatrists or psychologists) available to evaluate every youth. This recognition led to the development of a growing number of structured tools that JPOs, detention centers, and juvenile corrections programs could use to signal probation and detention personnel to youths' behavioral health needs (Grisso, Vincent & Seagrave, 2005).

Tools for behavioral health screening

Among the most widely used methods for identifying youths' behavioral health needs in juvenile justice are "screening" tools. Screening for behavioral health problems is a brief, objective method that sorts youth into two categories: those who are *highly unlikely* to have serious behavioral health problems, and those who *might have* such problems. Therefore, screening tools for behavioral health problems are not diagnostic; they do not determine a youth's specific behavioral health needs. They identify whether a youth shows enough evidence of symptoms or distress (e.g., suicidal thoughts) to suggest that the youth is in need of further evaluation by a mental health professional to assess the type and seriousness of a youth's behavioral health needs. The purpose of screening, therefore, is much like "triage." The majority of youth involved in juvenile justice have some type of behavioral health needs, yet not all of them are serious enough to require intervention at the time they are being seen in juvenile justice. Screening identifies those youth who are more likely to have serious behavioral health needs that require immediate attention (Skowyra & Cocozza, 2007).

In recent years a number of screening tools have been developed to assess mental health, substance use, and suicide risk in juvenile justice settings (Grisso et al., 2005). Behavioral health screening methods typically are sufficiently brief and structured to require no mental health training and to be completed in 10–15 minutes, so that they can be used with every youth at any particular decision point in juvenile justice. The most widely used behavioral health screening tool in juvenile justice currently is the Massachusetts Youth Screening Instrument-Second Version (MAYSI-2; Grisso & Barnum, 2000, 2006), now used statewide in juvenile probation, detention and/or corrections programs in over forty states. Described in more detail later, the MAYSI-2 is a self-report instrument on which youth respond to 52 items inquiring about various thoughts and feelings that contribute to six clinical scales (e.g., Depressed-Anxious, Suicidal Ideation, Alcohol/Drug Use). Cut-off scores on the scales, based on national norms for 70,000 juvenile justice youth, are used to signal the need for further assessment. Over 60 studies have examined its reliability, validity and utility (reviewed in Grisso et al., 2011).

The authors have developed and published procedures for implementing MAYSI-2 in JJ programs, including training of staff, putting in place standardized administration procedures, including training, monitoring fidelity of administration, monitoring compliance with protocol, creating data bases, and measuring outcomes (Skowyra & Cocozza, 2007). Regarding use specifically in juvenile probation, our efforts over the past several years have resulted in routine MAYSI-2 screening in all juvenile probation offices in four states. We have accumulated a national database for MAYSI-2 data in probation comprising over 25,000 cases from 141 probation offices in 7 states. Thus we have national normative data to which to compare future probation cases. Our recent research with detention centers, as well as its implementation and outcomes (Williams & Grisso, 2011), has provided evidence that juvenile detention centers' responses to youths' mental health problems are increased when MAYSI-2 is implemented. We anticipate that this will be the case with probation officers as well.

Assessing and managing risk for offending

As noted in our discussion of juvenile probation, JPOs are required to assess the risk that a youth will engage in behaviors that may endanger others during the period of rehabilitation, and to provide the court a picture of what is contributing to that risk so that the system can plan appropriate interventions. For most of the 100 years of the juvenile justice system, this assessment relied simply on the judgment of the JPO. In recent years, however, the practice of using structured and validated tools to assist in that judgment has become more common, for at least two reasons. First, scientific studies clearly show that unstructured judgments of these sorts are no better than chance, whereas use of validated structured methods significantly increase the accuracy and quality of such judgments (e.g., Bonta, Law, and Hanson, 1998; Guy, 2008; Hanson & Morton-Bourgon,

2009). Second, legislative advances have prompted the more routine use of structured and validated tools. For example, in 2002, the Juvenile Justice Delinquency and Prevention Act (JJDPA) urged juvenile justice experts to assist states in ". . . the design and utilization of risk assessment mechanisms to aid juvenile justice personnel in determining appropriate sanctions for delinquent behavior" (JJDPA, 2002, p. 18). The act also stated that delinquency should be addressed by quality prevention programs "designed to reduce risks and develop competencies in at-risk juveniles that will prevent, and reduce the rate of, violent delinquent behavior" (JJDPA, 2002, p. 1). In 2014, this Act came into consideration for reauthorization.

This goal has become more attainable in the past ten years, given the advent of several valid risk assessment tools designed specifically for use with youth in juvenile justice. Thus most state and county juvenile justice agencies have adopted risk assessment tools in the past decade, while a few are currently contemplating adoption (Wachter, 2014). They are being encouraged by a trend in juvenile justice to use data and research to drive decisions for justice-involved youth in a manner that promotes both public safety and youth potential, doing so in a manner that increases fairness through standardized and structured procedures.

New approaches to risk assessment with structured and validated tools are highly compatible with this most recent culture shift in juvenile justice because risk assessment tools, although not infallible, can contribute to public safety and promote youth potential in two ways. First, they offer validated input to inform the decision about whether youth are in need of secure custody or can be better served in the community. Second, modern risk assessment tools improve the ability of systems to help youth become productive members of the community when they leave the juvenile justice system, because many tools evaluate not only the degree of risk, but also the factors that are likely contributing to that risk. Those factors are called "criminogenic needs"— a youth's needs that are catalysts for that youth's delinquency. There is scientific evidence that indicates case planning focused on the key factors leading to offending can improve outcomes, thereby increasing longer-range public safety (e.g., Loung & Wormith, 2011; Vieira, Skilling & Peterson-Badali, 2009). Therefore, risk assessment enhances public safety by informing both placement and programming decisions before the court. Risk assessment also enhances case management practices outside of the court.

Risk assessment tools for juvenile justice

As noted earlier, the field of risk assessment in juvenile justice contexts has been heavily influenced by recent development of structured tools that have the potential to identify juveniles' criminogenic needs that appear to be related to their offending and develop an estimate of risk of re-offending. Analysis of the information obtained through use of the tools is then used to guide intervention to reduce re-offending.

Several risk assessment instruments for youth exist that have good data from multiple studies to support their use. Two of the most widely researched instruments (based on the number of peer-reviewed publications) for assessing future offending among juveniles are the *Youth Level of Service/Case Management Inventory* (YLS/CMI; Hoge & Andrews, 2002) and the *Structured Assessment of Violence Risk in Youth* (SAVRY; Borum, Bartel, & Forth, 2006). Both instruments in essence are checklists of risk factors that have been shown by research and consultation with professionals to be related to reoffending among youth (the SAVRY also contains protective factors). The main difference between the instruments is the way in which the evaluator uses information about the risk factors. With the YLS/CMI, the evaluator sums the number of items that were rated as "yes, present" to compute a total score that corresponds with an estimated level of risk (Low, Medium, High, or Very High). Risk assessment instruments that involve predetermined rules about how to combine such information and leave no room for discretion are referred to as actuarial instruments. Although many people use the YLS/CMI in this way as an actuarial instrument, the manual encourages evaluators to subsequently consider whether any of several additional items related to the youth or his or her family are relevant for the case. After engaging in that step, evaluators then should decide whether the initial risk level associated with the total score should be adjusted upwards or downwards. This is known as an "over-ride" option.

In contrast, evaluators using the SAVRY consider not only whether any of the risk items are present, but also how relevant each item is for the given case. Considering all of this information, as well as any relevant case-specific information, evaluators are encouraged to engage in "case formulation" techniques that involve developing theories about how the particular risk and protective factors work together to drive the youth's risk for delinquency. Typically, evaluators using the SAVRY make a judgment about whether the youth is at relatively low, moderate, or high risk for engaging in violence or general delinquency. The model of decision-making that the SAVRY follows is termed *Structured Professional Judgment* (see Guy, Douglas, & Hart, in press).

Benefits of using risk assessment tools

There are a number of benefits of using validated risk assessment tools compared to unstructured practices in which caseworkers collect whatever data they routinely choose to obtain and make judgments based solely on their individual beliefs about those data. Use of these tools encourages *consistency* and *rational data collection*. Risk assessment tools assure that caseworkers collect a particular set of data on a range of factors and do so for every case. Moreover, use of such a tool assures that data are collected on factors that have known relationships to future re-offending, based on research with those factors. Tools also should increase transparency, in that caseworkers are better able to demonstrate the basis for their placement decisions when explaining their decisions.

Risk assessment tools *lead to more valid placement decisions*. They allow for placement and treatment decisions that are commensurate with a youth's risk level and needs, which in turn have been shown to be related to decreased risk for reoffending.

The use of risk assessment tools has been found to lead to *results that are more appropriate for youth and also reduce the costs of juvenile justice intervention*. For example, in one study, out-of-home placement rates dropped by 50%, use of maximum levels of supervision dropped by almost 30%, and use of community services decreased except for high-risk youths (Vincent, Guy, Gershenson, & McCabe, 2012). These results suggest that unstructured assessment by caseworkers typically overestimates the need for more restrictive placements. Reductions in out-of-home placements (Justice Policy Institute, 2014), and conceivably use of maximum levels of supervision, translate into cost reductions for the juvenile justice system and taxpayers. Further, they do this with *appropriate attention to public safety*, to the extent that higher-risk youth are identified for more restrictive interventions.

The risk-needs-responsivity framework

Following risk assessment, decisions about risk management may be employed within a conceptual framework known as "risk-needs-responsivity" (RNR). The RNR framework includes three primary principles.

First, the *risk principle* suggests that the highest risk offenders should receive the most intensive interventions to reduce their risk of continued offending. Conversely, low risk cases have a much lower chance of reoffending even in the absence of services and therefore should be given minimal attention. There is some evidence that when low risk offenders are placed in intensive interventions with higher risk, more antisocial offenders, this exposure can contribute to low-risk offenders' later delinquency. Theoretically this is due to "deviancy training" or "deviant peer contagion" (Gatti et al. 2009).

Second, the *need* principle suggests that interventions to reduce risk should focus on criminogenic needs of youth: basically, needs that contribute to delinquency and offer a potential explanation for a youth's re-offending. Targeting a youth's specific criminogenic needs for intervention reduces risk for reoffending.

The *specific responsivity* principle suggests that the selection of interventions should consider offenders' specific characteristics that may affect their response to an intervention. For example, some youth may have greater intelligence than others, or may have different behavioral health problems, that influence the likelihood of their positive responsivity.

Most RNR research has been conducted with adult offenders, including large meta-analytic studies (e.g., Andrews & Dowden, 2006); however, research with the youth population is growing. Research supports the notion that matching services with the needs and responsivity factors of individual youth can lead to reductions in recidivism, and that failure to match (providing "one size fits all" plans) may result in higher recidivism (Vieira et al., 2009). Luong and Wormith (2011), for example, reported that recidivism significantly increased as the number of untreated needs increased ($r = .28$). For high-risk offenders, the match between an assessed need and an identified intervention was associated with a 38% reduction in reconviction. Taken as a whole, the evidence for RNR supports the notion that supervision and human service interventions must consider individual differences.

Bridging the research-to-practice gap: The study of implementation processes

Despite positive advances in policy, in our work with states involved in the MacArthur Foundation's *Models for Change* initiative, we have discovered that many juvenile probation offices fit one of the following categories regarding their use of behavioral health screening and/or risk assessment:

- They do not have such tools in place, or
- They have tools in place but not tools that have been validated, or
- They have valid tools in place but they have not developed, or are not maintaining, policies and practices regarding the use of the tools.

The first two of these are failures to use validated tools that are available. The third is the failure to *implement* validated tools in a manner that assures their benefits. If validated risk assessment and behavioral health tools are not applied according to the procedures with which they were validated, the value of their validity as tools is lost.

Implementation has been defined as "active and planned efforts to mainstream an innovation within an organization" (Greenhalgh, Robert, Macfarlane, Bate, & Kyriakidou, 2004, p. 582). It has been described more specifically as the process of putting a procedure into operation, or "the use of strategies to introduce or change. . .interventions within specific settings" (Proctor et al., 2009, p. 26). Implementation of assessment methods and interventions can go astray in many ways and for many reasons. Examples provided in Vincent, Guy and Grisso's (2012) guidelines for implementation of risk assessment procedures include such things as caseworkers' failure to actually use tools even when required by local policy, or improper administration or scoring of tools. Administration of tools may occur in unstandardized ways, such as poor conditions under which data were obtained or improper instructions to youth and parents. Scores may be interpreted in ways that are not consistent with the manualized instructions.

Explanations for successes and failures of implementation typically point to factors operating at multiple systemic levels (Ferlie & Shortell, 2001), including characteristics of the intervention, characteristics of the organization adopting the intervention, and contextual factors (Rabin et al., 2008). Implementation is important to study because the potential impact of an intervention is linked directly to the quality of procedures followed when putting it in place. Adoption of a behavioral health screening tool or a risk assessment tool will not lead to any changes in the way youth are processed if the tool is not implemented with fidelity.

In the absence of sound implementation procedures, use of the tool or intervention is compromised by lack of appropriate training, lack of service options, unclear decision-making procedures, and disappointment that implementation of the tool did not achieve targeted goals (e.g., decreasing numbers of youth in secure placement, ensuring appropriate placement). . . .

Different stakeholders likely will place more or less importance or value on particular implementation-level outcomes. For example, cost may be most important to policy makers and administrators, whereas feasibility may be most important to direct service providers. Little is known about timing in the implementation process in terms of when each construct is relatively more important; this type of knowledge may be important insofar as indicators of implementation success can be identified and addressed early during an implementation if observed to be compromised. Longitudinal studies that measure multiple implementation outcomes before, during, and after implementation therefore would be beneficial.

Research on implementation of behavioral health screening

Some studies have examined whether behavioral health screening changes outcomes. For example, Williams and Grisso (2011) implemented the MAYSI-2 in nine detention centers and found significant increases in mental health referrals during four months following implementation compared to four months prior to implementation. Neither this study, however, nor any others of which we are aware, have systematically varied implementation factors to determine their relative effect on practices or quality of behavioral health screening. Williams and Grisso did find, however, staff who were provided brief training of detention staff on the behavioral health needs of youth prior to implementation showed only minimal signs of increased knowledge about the matter, none of which survived after four months. Gains in referral to mental health services as a result of MAYSI-2 implementation were unrelated to differences between detention centers in the degree to which they retained the above training.

Research on implementation of risk assessment in juvenile justice settings

Several risk assessment studies have demonstrated the importance of proper implementation practices. Some of them have found that risk assessment tools often are not implemented well or systematically. For example, in a study of 12 courts that implemented risk assessment procedures in four states (Shook & Sarri, 2007), researchers found that only half of the court professionals (including probation officers) were using the tools regularly in their decision-making. Researchers in Maryland examined the potential impact of implementing a standardized risk assessment tool on service referrals and out-of-home placement decisions (Young, Moline, Farrell, & Bierie, 2006). They used an extensive implementation process that involved stakeholders at multiple levels, peer training for staff, and data monitoring. They found some shifts in service referrals and placement decisions in line with the assessment, but average adherence to administering the risk assessment tool as the policy required was still only 55%.

Research examining implementation factors with risk assessment tools in juvenile probation (Vincent, Guy, Gershenson, et al., 2012) found that merely teaching probation officers how to reliably complete an evidence-based risk assessment tool did not ensure that they would use the tool in their decisions. The study examined the relation between risk level and out-of-home placement decisions (mainly detention, group homes, and secure correctional facilities) for two time periods: (a) Pre-Implementation—after staff received training on a risk assessment tool but prior to implementation of a clear office policy or training about how to use the tool in decision-making, and (b) Post-Implementation—after office policies and training on use of the tool in decision-making occurred and were applied in practice.

The study discovered that certain aspects of case management, such as the number of service referrals made and out-of-home placement decisions, were not in line with youths' risk level until after a number of the risk assessment implementation steps were complete (e.g., adopting policies, training staff on RNR principles). In fact, prior to completing all implementation steps, probation officers had a tendency to assign more services to lower risk youth and fewer services to higher risk youth. Moreover, consistent with findings from Young et al. (2006) and the research of others (Bonta, Bogue, Crowley, & Mottuk, 2001; Bonta et al., 2011), it was essential for stakeholders (particularly judges) to buy into the process and for sound implementation methods to be used. Otherwise, risk assessment was not incorporated into decision-making or reflected in youths' case outcomes (Vincent, Guy, Gershenson, et al., 2012).

In order to counteract these barriers and achieve good outcomes, it is essential to develop an appropriate assessment system for the justice agency that involves sound training, consideration of staffs' concerns and resistance to change, and appropriate data gathering and monitoring of the system's improvements over time (Bonta et al., 2001; Ferguson, 2002).

What works: Risk assessment implementation guide

In the interest of developing a comprehensive implementation protocol for a risk assessment system, our team created the *Risk Assessment in Juvenile Justice: A Guidebook for Effective Implementation* (Vincent, Guy, & Grisso 2012), which outlines eight steps of implementation. These steps were derived from research and the experiences of many practitioners in the field who assisted with the development of the Guide. The steps range from Step 1: Getting the System Ready for risk tool adoption to Step 8: Promoting Sustainability.

Using most of the steps that are now outlined in the implementation Guide, with funding from the MacArthur foundation, our research team assisted two states (Louisiana and Pennsylvania) in implementing either the SAVRY or the YLS/CMI in their juvenile probation offices. We followed standardized methods for risk assessment tool implementation and training at each office. This was a multi-site, pre-post study with propensity-score matching in six juvenile probation offices and a sample of 2260 youth. The findings indicated good to excellent inter-rater reliability among JPOs using the risk assessment tools in the field (Guy & Vincent, 2011; Vincent, Guy, Fusco, & Gershenson, 2012), significant changes in the practices of JPOs and knowledge of youth developmental issues and actual risk (Vincent, Paiva, Cook, Guy, & Perrault,

2012), significant declines in rates of youth being sent to out-of-home placements in each site that had been placing 30% or more of their youth (Vincent, Guy, Gershenson, et al., 2012; Vincent & Guy, 2012; Vincent, Guy, Cook, Gershenson, & Paiva, 2011), and significant declines in use of maximum levels of supervision in all but one site where supervision data were available (Vincent, Guy, Gershenson, et al., 2012; Vincent & Guy, 2012; Vincent et al., 2011). However, recidivism actually declined in only one site, whereas it stayed constant in all the others.

The training and implementation steps also led to changes in the way the average JPO thought about youth and case planning. Vincent, Paiva, et al. (2012) found a significant reduction in the number of youth JPOs perceived as likely to re-offend after putting risk assessment in place. After taking into account the specific site and several characteristics of the JPOs (such as years of experience working in juvenile justice and authoritarian beliefs), we found that officers changed from perceiving 45 to 50 percent of their youth as likely re-offenders to thinking that only 30 percent were likely to re-offend. A control sample of JPOs in an office that did not implement a risk assessment instrument did not significantly change their estimates of youths' recidivism. Following implementation of risk assessment practices, there also was a significant increase in the number of JPOs who considered evidence-based risk factors when they made their disposition recommendations. After a risk assessment was implemented, according to quantitative and qualitative analyses of interviews with JPOs, they were significantly more likely to consider a youth's dynamic risk factors (criminogenic needs) when recommending dispositions and services in the community. Moreover, supervision levels on probation were assigned according to an individual youth's level of risk, rather than using a "one size fits all" approach. . . .

[References omitted.]

CRITICAL-THINKING QUESTIONS

1. Considering the probation supervision agreement presented at the beginning of the chapter, distinguish between "general conditions" and "special conditions."
2. Discuss how the use of probation varies by type of offense, and by age, gender, and race of youth.
3. What are probation conditions? What does it mean that probation conditions must be "reasonable and relevant"?
4. How do the supervision styles of probation officers vary?
5. Evaluation research shows that probation supervision alone does not work, but must be combined with treatment services to reduce recidivism. Explain.
6. In the first chapter reading, Schwalbe and Maschi (2011) examine probation officers' use of both confrontational tactics and client-centered approaches to encourage and enforce compliance with probation conditions. Describe and distinguish these two approaches to probation supervision.
7. The second reading by Guy and her colleagues (2015) claims that, for most of the 100-year history of juvenile justice, assessment of future offending relied solely on the subjective judgment of juvenile probation officers. How has assessment of future offending changed in recent years?

SUGGESTED READING

Bonta, James, Tanya Rugge, Terri-Lynne Scott, Guy Bourgon, and Annie K. Yessine. 2008. "Exploring the Black Box of Community Supervision." *Journal of Offender Rehabilitation* 47:248–270.

Griffin, Patrick and Patricia Torbet (eds.). 2002. *Desktop Guide to Good Probation Practice.* Pittsburgh, PA: National Center for Juvenile Justice. Available online: www.ncjj.org/Publication/Desktop-Guide-to-Good-Juvenile-Probation-Practice.aspx.

Schwalbe, Craig S. and Tina Maschi. 2009. "Investigating Probation Strategies with Juvenile Offenders: The Influence of Officers' Attitudes and Youth Characteristics." *Law and Human Behavior* 33:357–367.

Vincent, Gina M., Laura S. Guy, Rachael T. Perrault, and Bernice Gershenson. 2016. "Risk Assessment Matters, But Only When Implemented Well: A Multisite Study in Juvenile Probation." *Law and Human Behavior* 40:683–696.

USEFUL WEBSITES

For further information relevant to this chapter, go to the following websites:

- **American Probation and Parole Association**: www.appa-net.org/eweb/StartPage.aspx
- **National Center for Juvenile Justice: search "probation"**: www.ncjj.org/
- **National Council on Crime and Delinquency: "Assessment"**: www.nccdglobal.org/assessment
- **Statistical Briefing Book: "Juveniles on Probation"**: www.ojjdp.gov/ojstatbb/probation/overview.html

GLOSSARY OF KEY TERMS

Intensive supervision probation (ISP): A development in probation supervision that attempts to provide public safety and offender accountability through intensive monitoring and supervision of the probationer.

Juvenile probation: An informal or formal disposition that is based in the community, involving conditions (court-imposed rules) and supervision by a probation officer.

Probation conditions: Court-imposed rules that are a central part of the disposition of probation. Juveniles placed on probation by the court must obey these conditions in order to live in the community and avoid confinement.

Probation supervision: Monitoring and assistance of probationers by probation officers. The approach to supervision taken by probation officers determines the relative emphasis given to offender rehabilitation or enforcement of probation rules.

Revocation: The legal termination of probation by the court when the youth commits a new offense or violates the conditions of probation.

NOTES

1 Hockenberry and Puzzanchera (2017:88) note that 38 percent of the adjudicated status offense cases involved only minimal probation supervision because the court also ordered some form of treatment or counseling program, restitution, and/or community service.

2 *In the Interest of D. S. and J. V., Minor Children*, 652 So.2D 892 (Fla. Appl. 1995).

REFERENCES

Andrews, D. A. and James Bonta. 2017. *The Psychology of Criminal Conduct*. 6th ed. London: Routledge.

Bonta, James, Guy Bourgon, Tanya Rugge, Terri-Lynne Scott, Annie K. Yessine, Leticia Gutierrez, and Jobina Li. 2011. "An Experimental Demonstration of Training Probation Officers in Evidence-Based Community Supervision." *Criminal Justice and Behavior* 38:1127–1148.

Bonta, James, Tanya Rugge, Terri-Lynne Scott, Guy Bourgon, and Annie K. Yessine. 2008. "Exploring the Black Box of Community Supervision." *Journal of Offender Rehabilitation* 47:248–270.

Cromwell, Paul F., Rolando V. del Carmen, and Leanne Fiftal Alarid. 2002. *Community-Based Corrections*. 5th ed. Belmont, CA: Wadsworth.

Cullen, Francis T. and Cheryl Lero Jonson. 2017. *Correctional Theory: Contest and Consequences*. Los Angeles: Sage.

Czajkoski, Eugene H. 1973. "Exposing the Quasi-Judicial Role of Probation Officers." *Federal Probation* 37:9–13.

Feld, Barry C. 1999. *Bad Kids: Race and the Transformation of the Juvenile Court*. New York: Oxford University Press.

Feld, Barry C. 2014. *Juvenile Justice Administration in a Nutshell*. St. Paul, MN: West.

Gottfredson, Stephen D. and Laura J. Moriarty. 2006. "Statistical Risk Assessment: Old Problems and New Applications." *Crime and Delinquency* 52:178–200.

Griffin, Patrick and Melanie King. 2006. "National Overviews." *State Juvenile Justice Profiles*. Pittsburgh, PA: National Center for Juvenile Justice. Retrieved January 24, 2017 (www.ncjj.org/stateprofiles).

Griffin, Patrick and Patricia Torbet (eds.). 2002. *Desktop Guide to Good Probation Practice*. Pittsburgh, PA: National Center for Juvenile Justice. Retrieved September 22, 2016 (www.ncjj.org/Publication/Desktop-Guide-to-Good-Juvenile-Probation-Practice.aspx).

Guy, Laura S., Gina M. Vincent, Thomas Grisso, and Rachael Perrault. 2015. *Advancing Use of Risk Assessment in Juvenile Probation*. National Criminal Justice Reference Service. Retrieved January 11, 2017 (www.ncjrs.gov/pdffiles1/ojjdp/grants/249155.pdf).

Haqanee, Zohrah and Michele Peterson-Badali. 2015. "Making 'What Works' Work: Examining Probation Officers' Experiences Addressing the Criminogenic Needs of Juvenile Offenders." *Journal of Offender Rehabilitation* 54:37–59.

Hemmens, Craig, Benjamin Steiner, and David Mueller. 2004. *Significant Cases in Juvenile Justice*. Los Angeles: Roxbury.

Hockenberry, Sarah, and Puzzanchera, Charles. 2017. *Juvenile Court Statistics 2013*. Pittsburgh, PA: National Center for Juvenile Justice.

Jordan, Frank and Joseph M. Sasfy. 1974. *National Impact Program Evaluation: A Review of Selected Issues and Research Findings Related to Probation and Parole*. Washington, DC: Mitre Corporation.

Klockers, Carl B., Jr. 1972. "A Theory of Probation Supervision." *Journal of Criminal Law, Criminology, and Police Science* 63:550–557.

Lipsey, Mark W. 1992. "Juvenile Delinquency in Treatment: A Meta-Analytic Inquiry into the Variability of Effects." Pp. 83–127 in *Meta-Analysis for Explanation: A Casebook*, edited by T. D. Cook, H. Cooper, D. S. Cordray, H. Hartmann, L. V. Hedges, R. J. Light, T. A. Louis, and F. Mosteller. New York: Russell Sage Foundation.

Lipsey, Mark, James C. Howell, Marion R. Kelly, Gabrielle Chapman, and Darin Carver. 2010. *Improving the Effectiveness of Juvenile Justice Programs: A New Perspective on Evidence-Based Practice*. Washington, DC: Center for Juvenile Justice Reform. Retrieved January 12, 2017 (http://cjjr.georgetown.edu/wp-content/uploads/2014/12/ebppaper.pdf).

National Council of Juvenile and Family Court Judges (NCJFCJ). 1998. *Juvenile and Family Court Journal* 49(4):1–5

Office of Juvenile Justice and Delinquency Prevention (OJJDP). 2013. "Organization and Administration of Delinquency Services." *OJJDP Statistical Briefing Book*. Released on April 05, 2013. Retrieved January 24, 2017 (www.ojjdp.gov/ojstatbb/structure_process/qa04203.asp?qaDate=2013).

Petersillia, Joan and Susan Turner. 1993. "Intensive Probation and Parole." Pp. 281–335 in *Crime and Justice: A Review of Research*, edited by M. Tonry. Chicago: University of Chicago.

Schwalbe, Craig S. and Tina Maschi. 2009. "Investigating Probation Strategies with Juvenile Offenders: The Influence of Officers' Attitudes and Youth Characteristics." *Law and Human Behavior* 33:357–367.

Schwalbe, Craig S. and Tina Maschi. 2011. "Confronting Delinquency: Probations Officers' Use of Coercion and Client-Centered Tactics to Foster Youth Compliance." *Crime and Delinquency* 57:801–822.

Schwartz, Katherine, Andrew O. Alexander, Katherine S. L. Lau, Evan D. Holloway, and Matthew C. Aalsma. 2017. "Motivating Compliance: Juvenile Probation Officer Strategies and Skills." *Journal of Offender Rehabilitation* 56:20–37.

Seiter, Richard P. and Angela D. West. 2003. "Supervision Styles in Probation and Parole: An Analysis of Activities." *Journal of Offender Rehabilitation* 38:57–75.

Shepherd, Robert E., Jr. (editor). 1996. *The ABA Juvenile Justice Standards, Annotated*. Chicago: American Bar Association. Retrieved December 27, 2016 (www.ncjrs.gov/pdffiles1/ojjdp/166773.pdf).

Skowyra, Kathleen R. and Joseph J. Cocozza. 2007. *Blueprint for Change: A Comprehensive Model for the Identification and Treatment of Youth with Mental Health Needs in Contact with Juvenile Justice*. National Center for Mental Health and Juvenile Justice. Delmar, NY: Policy Research Associates.

Torbet, Patricia McFall. 1996. "Juvenile Probation: The Workhorse of the Juvenile Justice System." *Juvenile Justice Bulletin*. Washington, DC: Office of Juvenile Justice and Delinquency Prevention. Retrieved December 6, 2016 (www.ncjrs.gov/pdffiles/workhors.pdf).

Van Voorhis, Patricia and Emily J. Salisbury (eds.). 2016. *Correctional Counseling and Rehabilitation*. 9th edition. London: Routledge.

Vincent, Gina M., Laura S. Guy, Rachael T. Perrault, and Bernice Gershenson. 2016. "Risk Assessment Matters, But Only When Implemented Well: A Multisite Study in Juvenile Probation." *Law and Human Behavior* 40:683–696.

Ward, Geoff and Aaron Kupchik. 2010. "What Drives Juvenile Probation Officers? Relating Organizational Contexts, Status Characteristics, and Personal Convictions to Treatment and Punishment Orientations." *Crime and Delinquency* 56:35–69.

Chapter 11

COMMUNITY-BASED CORRECTIONS AND RESTORATIVE JUSTICE

CHAPTER TOPICS

- **Rise of community-based corrections**
- **Range of community-based programs**
- **Balanced and restorative justice**
- **Specialized courts**

CHAPTER LEARNING OBJECTIVES

After completing this chapter, students should be able to:

- Describe the history of community-based corrections, beginning in the 1960s.
- Discuss the range of community-based programs at various points in the juvenile justice process, including diversion, community treatment, and aftercare.
- Describe various intermediate sanctions, including day reporting centers, house arrest, electronic monitoring, restitution, and community service.
- Describe various types of community-based residential placement.
- Identify the unique characteristics of a balanced and restorative approach to delinquency.
- Contrast the approach and goals of specialized courts, including problem-solving and teen courts, with the approach and goals of traditional juvenile courts.

CHAPTER CONTENTS

CASE IN POINT

A RESTORATIVE APPROACH TO JUVENILE DELINQUENCY

John and Will were teenagers growing up in a small town in Virginia, a town where there were relatively few structured social activities for teenagers, so teenagers sometimes "created their own fun." One Friday night, John and Will were walking down a street where a new home was under construction. It was to be an impressive home, and included several custom windows in its lavish design. Without giving it much thought, John and Will threw rocks at the home, breaking several windows and causing several thousands of dollars in damage.

Neither of the boys had been in trouble with the law before. This was simply a moment of poor judgment that got entirely out of hand. The couple whose new home was damaged did not want to see the boys' lives tarnished by a criminal record for their first offense. They also had insurance to replace the broken windows, so they were not concerned about the monetary cost of the damage. What they wanted was for the boys to take responsibility for their actions and to learn important lessons in the process.

Trying to prevent formal juvenile court processing, the juvenile prosecutor in this small town sat down together with John and Will, the couple whose home was damaged, the boys' parents, and other members of the community to develop a restorative response to the damage the boys caused. The boys admitted to their actions and apologized for their destruction of someone else's property. The group then decided that an appropriate course of action with the boys would include not only informal probation, but also 70 hours of community service, which John and Will would complete by working with Habitat for Humanity to construct homes for low-income families.

The goal was not only to respond to the boys' harmful behavior, but also to teach them a lesson about the value of a home. This restorative approach held John and Will accountable for their actions and gave them an opportunity to "right the wrong" they had committed, but it also actively involved the victims and members of the community in determining a response designed to achieve goals other than simply punishment.

Juvenile court disposition seeks correctional options that are individualized, rehabilitative, and least restrictive. Reflecting the "rehabilitative ideal," juvenile court disposition has traditionally involved a wide range of correctional options, including probation (discussed in Chapter 10), community-based corrections, and residential placement (discussed in Chapter 12). In this chapter, we consider community-based responses to delinquency, including diversion, community treatment, specialized problem-solving courts, residential placement, and after-care programs. We also discuss contemporary restorative justice approaches, which emphasize offender accountability, community safety, and competency development. Finally, we consider the development of specialized problem-solving courts, such as juvenile drug court and mental health courts, which focus on treatment rather than punishment.

RISE OF COMMUNITY-BASED CORRECTIONS

The rise of community-based corrections in the 1960s and 1970s coincided with transformations of the juvenile justice system associated with the enactment of the Juvenile Justice and Delinquency Prevention Act of 1974 (described in Chapter 2). This was no accident. The President's Commission on Law Enforcement and Administration of Justice, established in 1965, recommended that nonviolent offenders be handled in the community rather than the juvenile courts. The logic of this recommendation stems from the second revolution's serious questioning regarding whether the rehabilitative ideal could be accomplished: "the great hopes originally held for the juvenile court have not been fulfilled. It has not succeeded significantly in rehabilitating delinquent youth, in reducing or even stemming the tide of delinquency, or in bringing justice and compassion to the child offender" (President's Commission 1967a:80, 1967c). In addition, the Commission emphasized the importance of dealing with delinquency in the context in which it develops—the local community:

> crime and delinquency are symptoms of failures and disorganization of the community. . . . The task of corrections, therefore, includes building or rebuilding social ties, obtaining employment and education, securing in the larger sense a place for the offender in the routine functioning of society. This requires not only efforts directed toward changing the individual offender, which have been almost the exclusive focus of rehabilitation, but also mobilization and change of the community and its institutions.
>
> (President's Commission 1967b:7)

Instead of rehabilitation, the major goal of community-based corrections is *reintegration*—correctional efforts designed to keep juvenile offenders in the community and to help them participate in community life.

In the late 1960s and 1970s, several states passed legislation, typically called *community corrections acts*, which endorsed the community corrections model by providing funding and other incentives for community-based facilities and services. Beginning in the second half of the 1970s, federal financial support through the Office of Juvenile Justice and Delinquency Prevention (OJJDP) led to the development of community-based programs that utilized community resources. Community-based programs tend to be diversionary, attempting to deal with delinquency in the community rather than in the juvenile justice system. As we have already stressed, diversion occurs throughout the juvenile justice system. With regard to juvenile corrections, diversion refers to the use of community-based programs that provide needed services to delinquent youth in the local community, regardless of the point at which the case is diverted. Community-based programs also try to deinstitutionalize juvenile corrections, keeping delinquent youth in the local community, rather than placing them in correctional institutions.

A wide variety of community-based juvenile correctional programs were developed during this time period. Chief among them were youth service bureaus that provided various services to youth and families, including individual, peer, and family counseling; crisis hotlines; drop-in centers; job placement services; educational tutoring; and recreational programs (President's Commission 1967a:83, 1967c). Foster care programs; community service programs; and various residential programs, including group homes that emphasize treatment and education, drug treatment centers, and halfway houses, were also developed. From their beginning, community-based correctional programs have tried to promote delinquency prevention, diversion, and community reintegration as an alternative to placement in secure, custodial correctional institutions.

RANGE OF COMMUNITY-BASED PROGRAMS

Community-based responses to delinquency include diversion, community treatment, certain types of residential placement, and aftercare.

Diversion

Diversion is the tendency to deal with juvenile matters informally, before petition or adjudication, by referring cases to special programs and agencies inside or outside the juvenile justice system. Police officers sometimes divert cases to special programs within the department or to a variety of community resources such as family counseling and drug treatment. Probation officers, when screening cases that have been referred to the juvenile court, have legal authority to decide whether cases should be dealt with formally or informally. Informal handling may involve a diversionary referral to a community treatment option. Prosecutors can choose not to petition a case and instead to provide for some informal handling of a case, often involving a referral to community resources.

Efforts to accomplish this have included the creation of community agencies and *Youth Service Bureaus* that provide various services to young people, such as counseling, skill development, educational services, vocational and job training, advocacy, and social services. Diversion represents an attempt to respond to the problem behaviors of youth, but without the adverse effects of juvenile court processing (e.g., labeling and stigmatization, an official record).

States have adopted procedures for administering diversion agreements, which typically require an individual to admit his or her involvement in delinquency and to enter voluntarily into a diversion agreement. Such agreements may include informal probation supervision and participation in court-approved programs or in specialized courts, such as drug courts (Feld 2014). "Components of diversion programs include: developing court intake and prosecutorial screening criteria; providing counseling; performing chemical dependency assessments and making referrals to treatment agencies where appropriate; connecting diverted offenders with community resources; and monitoring juveniles' performance and compliance" (Feld 2014:191–192). In some states, diversion programs emphasize restorative justice, which we discuss later in this chapter.

Researchers have found it difficult to evaluate the effectiveness of diversionary efforts, in part because of a lack of consensus about how to define diversion (Mears 2012). Feld (2009, 2014) has also expressed concern about net-widening effects of diversion. *Net-widening* refers to the expansion of social control efforts. Feld argues that diversionary practices might be used to induce youth to participate in programs with the threat of formal processing of cases if the youth do not comply. If the youth who are diverted receive supervision and services, but would otherwise have had their cases dismissed, then diversion actually increases social control of youth in these cases. The section entitled "Expanding ideas: Adolescent Diversion Project" describes a diversion program that has been rated "effective" based on rigorous research.

EXPANDING IDEAS: ADOLESCENT DIVERSION PROJECT

CrimeSolutions.gov is a registry of evidence-based practices that provides information about programs and practices that have been shown, through rigorous research, to be effective or promising for preventing crime and delinquency. One of the community-based programs rated "effective" is the Adolescent Diversion Project (ADP), for juveniles who are 13–15 years old.

Program goals

The ADP is a strengths-based, university-led program that diverts arrested youth from formal processing in the juvenile justice system and provides them with community-based services. Based upon a combination of theoretical perspectives, the goal of the ADP is to prevent future delinquency by strengthening youth's attachment to family and other prosocial individuals, increasing youth's access to resources in the community, and keeping youth from potentially stigmatizing social contexts (such as the juvenile justice system).

The program began in 1976, through a collaboration among Michigan State University, personnel from the Ingham County (MI) Juvenile Court, and members of the community in response to a rise in juvenile crime and the need for cost-saving alternatives to the formal processing of juveniles.

Key personnel

The ADP is run by the Psychology Department at Michigan State University. Undergraduate psychology students . . . are trained for 8 weeks in specific behavioral intervention techniques and advocacy, followed by 18 weeks of intensive supervision while they work with juveniles referred by the Intake Division of the Ingham County Juvenile Court.

Program components

The ADP focuses on creating an alternative to juvenile court processing within a strengths-based, advocacy framework. During the 18-week intervention, the caseworkers (i.e., student volunteers) spend 6–8 hours per week with the juveniles in their home, school, and community. The caseworkers work one-on-one with juveniles in order to provide them with services tailored to their specific needs. Caseworkers focus on improving juveniles' skills in several areas, including family relationships, school issues, employment, and free-time activities. For example, caseworkers teach youth about resources available in the community so that juveniles can access these resources on their own once the program is over.

The first 12 weeks of services are called the active phase, and case workers spend time each week with juveniles while providing direct assistance in behavioral contracting and advocacy efforts. During the last four weeks of services, called the follow-up phase, case workers spend a little less time each week assisting juveniles in those same areas, but their role is that of a consultant, preparing juveniles to use the techniques and strategies they've learned following the end of the program.

Evaluation

Two evaluation studies of this program have found significant differences in rates of official delinquency between juveniles who participated in the ADP and those in the control groups. For example, one study found that "at the 1-year follow-up, diverted youth who received services through ADP had a 22 percent recidivism rate, compared to a 32 percent recidivism rate for diverted youth who received no services and a 34 percent recidivism rate for youth who went through traditional court processing." However, these studies also found no significant differences in *self-reported* delinquency between juveniles who participated in the ADP and those in the control groups.

The ADP is also quite cost effective. The project costs approximately $1,021 per youth for the 18-week intervention, compared to the $13,466 spent by a local juvenile court for the average youth served.

Source: CrimeSolutions.gov (2013).

Community treatment

Community treatment typically involves adjudicated youth. Probation (discussed in Chapter 10) is the most widely used community-based sanction for youth who are adjudicated delinquent. Other community-based sanctions for adjudicated youth include day reporting centers, house arrest and electronic monitoring, restitution, community service, and intensive probation supervision. These sanctions are sometimes referred to as **intermediate sanctions** because, in terms of severity, they exist between the more lenient response of probation and the harsher response of placement in residential facilities. Community-based dispositions for adjudicated youth may also involve treatment options, including counseling, drug treatment, and mental health services.

Day reporting centers assist probation officers with the task of monitoring probationers. Some individuals who are placed on probation are court ordered to report in person to a day reporting center, to participate in designated activities such as drug testing, drug abuse education, job skills training, job placement services, and counseling. Probationers may also be required to call the centers throughout the day, and can expect phone calls from staff at the centers at random times throughout the day and at home following curfew. Day reporting centers are also used to provide community-based services to at-risk youth.

Juveniles placed on probation may also be required, through *house arrest*, to remain in their homes, except at specified times, such as to attend school or work. House arrest may be enforced through *electronic monitoring*, which requires probationers to wear a non-removable monitoring device that signals the probation department if they leave their house. House arrest combined with electronic monitoring provides a cost effective alternative to placement in a detention center.

Restitution requires offenders to accept responsibility for the harm they have caused and to compensate the victim or the community for their actions, either monetarily or by providing services. Monetary restitution involves the offender paying the victim for harm done (e.g., costs associated with property damage or physical injuries). Service restitution involves the offender providing some service to the victim or the community, and is typically completed under the supervision of a probation officer. Juvenile court judges often order monetary restitution as a condition of probation, though the specific amount must be reasonable in terms of the youth's ability to pay it (Feld 2014). Restitution programs attempt to achieve several goals: holding juveniles accountable, providing reparation to victims, and rehabilitating juveniles.

Judges may impose *community service*, such as cleaning up parks or doing maintenance work for public agencies, as a condition of probation. The intent of community service is to encourage juveniles to accept responsibility for their actions, to benefit the community harmed by delinquency, and to provide juveniles with work experience (Feld 2014).

Community-based residential placement

Community-based residential placement for juveniles includes group homes, foster homes, and shelter care. *Group homes* are residential placement settings that attempt to provide individualized treatment, such as individual or group counseling, educational programming, and social and job skills training, either within the facility or in the community. Youth in these types of facilities may be allowed to attend school or work in the community. Most group homes are privately operated and community-based. They are often located in neighborhoods, and they use community resources and services in an attempt to integrate youth into the local community. In 2015, group homes held 9 percent of delinquent offenders and 20 percent of status offenders who were in residential placement (Sickmund et al. 2017).

Foster home placements are often used by juvenile courts when a youth's home life is determined to be harmful or especially chaotic. They are also sometimes used for non-violent delinquents, as an alternative to more restrictive institutional placements such as detention centers, and for transitional placement of delinquents who are returning to the community from institutional placement.

Shelter care placements tend to hold youth for relatively short periods of time. Shelter care is typically used for youth who need temporary emergency placement, have run away from home, have been abused by their parents, or have engaged in minor delinquency. Shelter care may involve counseling and crisis intervention services. In 2015, shelters held 2 percent of delinquent offenders and 9 percent of status offenders who were in residential placement (Sickmund et al. 2017). Chapter 12 discusses the full range of residential placement, including group homes and shelter care.

Aftercare

Aftercare programs provide support, supervision, and services to delinquent youth after residential placement. Aftercare may occasionally involve placement in group homes, foster care, or shelter care. Traditionally, youth released from residential placement are placed on *parole*. Parole involves conditions and supervision, just like probation, but parole follows residential placement. In many states, parole supervision is provided by officers who are both probation and parole officers. We discuss aftercare and reentry services in detail in Chapter 12.

BALANCED AND RESTORATIVE JUSTICE

Contemporary correctional efforts in **balanced and restorative justice** are often community-based because they attempt to actively involve community members and use community resources in delinquency prevention and intervention. Restorative approaches to offending emerged primarily in other parts of the world, most notably Australia and New Zealand. They were introduced in the U.S. as part of a reaction against the punitive, "get-tough" responses to delinquency that began here in the 1980s, such as transfer of serious juvenile offenders to adult criminal courts. The number of restorative justice programs in the U.S. increased significantly during the 1990s (Bazemore 2012). By the late 1990s, 35 states had adopted some form of restorative justice legislation or policy (O'Brien 2000). This approach is typically non-residential.

Howard Zehr (2014), one of the founders of the restorative justice movement, describes the difference between restorative justice and traditional criminal or juvenile justice systems by examining the questions they raise. In traditional justice systems, the questions are: "What laws have been broken? Who did it? What do they deserve?" In a restorative approach to justice, the questions are: "Who has been hurt? What are their needs? Whose obligations are these [needs]?" The box entitled "Juvenile justice policy and practice: Principles of balanced and restorative justice" describes key principles of a restorative approach to delinquency.

The balanced and restorative approach to juvenile justice is directed at three fundamental goals: offender accountability, competency development, and public safety. Unlike more retributive responses to delinquency, which attempt to punish offenders in proportion to the harm they have caused to victims, restorative justice provides an opportunity for offenders to take responsibility for their actions and attempt to repair the damage done, either to the victim or to the community more generally. This *accountability* may happen in the form of restitution or service to the victim, community service, apologies, or behavioral agreements. The goal of *competency development* is based on the idea that, while in the juvenile justice system, youth should be provided with opportunities and skills training that help them become more productive and responsible members of the community. The goal of *public safety* recognizes the need for community protection, but also emphasizes the capacity of the community to manage youths' behavior and the value of keeping juvenile offenders in their communities whenever possible (Bazemore and Washington 1995).

JUVENILE JUSTICE POLICY AND PRACTICE: PRINCIPLES OF BALANCED AND RESTORATIVE JUSTICE

Kay Pranis, an early proponent of restorative justice, identifies 11 key principles of the balanced and restorative justice philosophy:

1 Crime is injury.
2 Crime hurts victims, communities, and juvenile offenders and creates an obligation to make things right.
3 All parties should be a part of the response to the crime, including the victim if he or she wishes, the community, and the juvenile offender.
4 The victim's perspective is central to deciding how to repair the harm caused by the crime.
5 Accountability for the juvenile offender means accepting responsibility and acting to repair the harm done.
6 The community is responsible for the well-being of all its members, including both victims and offenders.
7 All human beings have dignity and worth.
8 Restoration or repairing the harm and rebuilding relationships in the community is the primary goal of juvenile justice.
9 Results are measured by how much repair was done rather than by how much punishment was inflicted.
10 Crime control cannot be achieved without active involvement of the community.
11 The juvenile justice process is respectful of different cultures and backgrounds—whether racial, ethnic, geographic, religious, economic, age, abilities, family status, sexual orientation, or other—and all are given equal protection and due process.

Source: Pranis (1998:5).

In restorative justice, victims, offenders, and communities are all viewed as stakeholders in the process of responding to delinquency. Efforts are made to actively involve all three in the process of determining how best to repair the damage caused by delinquency as early and as fully as possible.

The balanced and restorative approach to juvenile corrections tries to accomplish these three goals through *restorative conferencing*, which includes several strategies to bring together the victim, offender, and other members of the community in a non-adversarial, community-based process (Belbott 2003). Gordon Bazemore and Mark Umbreit (1997) describe four restorative conferencing models:

1 *Victim–offender mediation:* With the assistance of a trained mediator, victims voluntarily meet with offenders in a safe and structured setting. The victim is allowed to tell the offender about the crime's physical, emotional, and/or financial impact and to ask the offender questions about the crime. Together they work out a restitution plan for the offender (Belbott 2003).

2 "*Community reparative boards* are composed of small groups of citizens who have received intensive training and conduct public, face-to-face meetings with offenders who have been ordered by the court to participate. During the meeting, board members discuss with the offender the nature and seriousness of the offense" (Belbott 2003:324). They also develop agreements that sanction offenders, and monitor compliance and submit reports to the court.

3 *Family group conferencing model:* "To initiate a family group conference, a trained facilitator contacts the victim and the offender to explain the process and invite them to participate. The victim and offender are asked to identify key members of their support system who will also be asked to attend. Participation is voluntary. The conference usually begins with the offender describing the incident, after which the other participants describe how the incident has affected their lives. . . . After the discussion, the facilitator asks the victim what he or she wants the outcome of the conference to be" (Belbott 2003:324). The group then collectively seeks to resolve the offense through an agreement that outlines what is expected of the offender.

4 *Circle sentencing* is based on traditional practices of indigenous groups in Canada and the United States. "Circle sentencing includes participation of the victim, offender, both of their families and friends, personnel from the justice agency, police department and relevant social service agencies, and interested community members who together develop a sentencing plan that addresses the concerns of all the parties" (Belbott 2003:325).

Research suggests that restorative approaches are an effective alternative to traditional juvenile court responses to delinquency (Bazemore and Umbreit 1995, 2001). Studies have examined the effects of restorative processes on both recidivism and victim satisfaction. Some have argued, however, that recidivism is not the primary focus of restorative justice, and thus, evaluations should focus on outcomes such as victim satisfaction and reparation of harm to victims and the community.

Research examining victim satisfaction when restorative approaches are used, compared to traditional court processes, consistently shows significantly higher levels of victim satisfaction with restorative approaches (Sherman and Strang 2007; Daly 2005). Studies also show that reparative actions by offenders (e.g., restitution and community service) have positive effects on victim satisfaction (Butts and Snyder 1991; Schneider 1986). These types of reparative actions and restorative processes also contribute to reductions in recidivism among offenders, though the effects are often modest (Sherman et al. 2015; Haynes, Cares, and Ruback 2014; Hipple, Gruenewald, and McGarrell 2014; Bergseth and Bouffard 2013; Jeong, McGarrell, and Hipple 2012; Bonta et al. 2008; Sherman and Strang 2007; see also Weatherburn and Macadam 2013).

The first reading for this chapter, by James Bonta and his colleagues (2008), presents a meta-analysis of research on the effectiveness of restorative justice and its impact on recidivism. It concludes that restorative interventions are associated with relatively small but statistically significant reductions in recidivism, particularly for low-risk offenders.

Despite research suggesting positive effects of restorative approaches, several challenges have prevented wider use of restorative approaches in the U.S. Gordon Bazemore (2012), a major advocate of restorative justice practices, describes these challenges, including an emphasis on more punitive approaches to delinquency and concerns about the informal nature of restorative practices, the absence of mandates or incentives for referral to restorative programs, and widening the net of social control by drawing into the juvenile justice system individuals who otherwise would have been handled outside that system (see also McAlinden 2011). According to Bazemore,

> The problem is that current juvenile justice practitioners (whether in probation, diversion, or residential care) claim to want restorative practices, while in fact marginalizing them. In much of the world, on the other hand, restorative justice is either mandated for many cases, or used in some fashion as a vital non-adversarial, problem-solving, decision-making process ideal for developing diversion, and dispositional and reentry recommendations.
> (Bazemore 2012:713)

Restorative justice has not yet received this degree of systematic use in the U.S.

SPECIALIZED COURTS

Specialized courts include both problem-solving courts and teen courts. The use of **problem-solving courts** for juveniles began in the mid-1990s, following their initial use in the adult criminal justice system in the late 1980s (Butts, Roman, and Lynn-Whaley 2012). These courts are sometimes called treatment courts or therapeutic courts. The purpose of such courts is to offer treatment and rehabilitation rather than simply punishment, and to focus on the offender rather than the offense. Key components of problem-solving courts include offender accountability, competency development, treatment programs, and close supervision and monitoring. The most common types of problem-solving courts for juveniles are drug courts and mental health courts. Teen courts are also now used in almost every state.

Drug courts

Drug courts emerged in 1989 in the adult criminal justice system. In the 1980s and 1990s, drug arrests increased substantially, and drug offenders were overwhelming court systems. Law enforcement agencies and criminal courts saw the need for effective diversion programs and new ways of responding to drug offenders. To meet this need, the federal government provided significant funding to promote and implement drug courts (Butts et al. 2012). Juvenile drug courts began to appear in the mid-1990s, and by 2013, there were 422 juvenile drug courts in use across the U.S. (Latessa and Smith 2015).

Juveniles whose cases are sent to drug courts are given an opportunity to have their charges dismissed or their dispositions modified, if they complete a course of drug treatment under court supervision. Juveniles who do not successfully complete the treatment program must typically serve a sentence as long as, or perhaps longer than they would have otherwise served. Youth with violence in their criminal histories, with co-occurring substance abuse and mental health disorders, or who have failed prior treatment attempts have typically been excluded from drug courts. Most participants in juvenile drug courts are 15 to 17 years old (Butts et al. 2012).

For each juvenile whose case is sent to drug court, case managers develop a comprehensive plan of services, including drug treatment and any other needed services, such as mental health services, educational assistance, and job training. Juveniles must comply with frequent drug tests and attend frequent court hearings to review progress. The approach in these hearings is team-oriented, and typically involves the judge, program staff (including the prosecutor, defense attorney, probation officer, and treatment providers), and members of the juvenile's family.

JUVENILE JUSTICE POLICY AND PRACTICE: CORE ELEMENTS OF JUVENILE DRUG COURTS

In their discussion of the components that juvenile drug courts typically share, Jeffrey Butts and his colleagues describe these five elements:

1. Individualized and less adversarial courtroom procedures allow judges and other drug court staff to collaborate openly in motivating young offenders to desist from drug use and sustain desistance.
2. Treatment plans are consistent with the goals established for each youth during court hearings.
3. A visible and consistent system of sanctions and rewards (both in and out of the courtroom) encourages prosocial behavior while deterring deviant behavior among juvenile clients.
4. An effective system of case management services matches offenders and services to ensure consistency in the application of rewards and sanctions.
5. Courts, and especially judges, draw upon their community standing and their leadership skills to ensure the availability of high-quality treatment and supervision services and to hold the services system accountable for youths, their families, and the community.

Source: Butts, Roman, and Lynn-Whaley (2012:617).

These individuals work together to provide the juvenile with services, as well as sanctions for non-compliance and incentives and rewards for progress through the program. Offenders are typically involved in the drug court process for 12 to 18 months—until they have a lengthy record of clean drug tests and program compliance (Butts et al. 2012). The box entitled "Juvenile justice policy and practice: Core elements of juvenile drug courts" describes five essential elements of juvenile drug court programs.

Research on juvenile drug courts is quite limited and has shown mixed results. Studies using a matched comparison design (which compare juveniles who were assigned to drug court with those who were assigned to standard probation) found that drug court participants were no less likely than juveniles given probation to use drugs following program participation. In fact, the majority of juveniles assigned to drug court were unsuccessful in meeting drug court requirements (Gilmore, Rodriguez, and Webb 2005; Rodriguez and Webb 2004; see also Sullivan et al. 2014). Studies have also shown better outcomes for drug court participants when Multisystemic Therapy (discussed in Chapter 13) is incorporated into drug court programs (Henggeler 2007; Henggeler et al. 2006).

The second reading for this chapter, by Lesli Blair and her colleagues (2015), presents an evaluation of drug court intervention programs, including their processes and outcomes. This evaluation of nine juvenile drug courts in three regions of the U.S. was sponsored by the Office of Juvenile Justice and Delinquency Prevention.

In 2016, the OJJDP released evidence-based, treatment-oriented guidelines for juvenile drug courts. These guidelines are intended to improve the functioning of drug courts by supporting

JUVENILE JUSTICE POLICY AND PRACTICE: EVIDENCE-BASED PRACTICE RECOMMENDATIONS FOR JUVENILE DRUG COURTS

The National Center for Mental Health and Juvenile Justice, in collaboration with the Louisiana Supreme Court Drug Court Office, provides a set of evidence-based practice recommendations for juvenile drug courts. These recommendations highlight key components that are necessary in order to maximize the effectiveness of juvenile drug court programs. They are organized into three areas: screening and assessment, treatment, and outcome monitoring.

Screening and assessment recommendations

1. All screening and assessment tools used within a juvenile drug court should be standardized, scientifically sound, and appropriate for the population served.
2. Clear decision rules and response policies should be in place as a part of any screening protocol.
3. A thorough assessment process should be completed for every youth accepted into the juvenile drug court to validate substance abuse or dependence diagnoses.
4. Any screening and assessment process within juvenile drug courts should be designed to assess and address the presence of co-occurring mental health disorders.
5. Policies should be in place that clearly establish what information will be shared and how it will be communicated.

Treatment recommendations

1. Treatment offered by the juvenile drug court must be comprehensive.
2. Service plans must be well-coordinated and flow smoothly across "levels of care," treatment providers and social service providers.
3. Programs should collaborate in and encourage the adoption of evidence-based practices.
4. Families' needs must be addressed and they must be fully engaged partners.
5. Integrated treatment should be provided to youth with co-occurring disorders.

Outcome monitoring recommendations

1. A sustainable outcome monitoring process should be in place that collects information on key program characteristics and youth outcomes.
2. Information collected through the outcome monitoring process should be stored electronically, so that data analysis and report development can be easily completed.
3. A clear data collection process should be articulated.
4. Data collected as a part of the outcome monitoring process should be reviewed on a regular basis.
5. Information collected should be summarized and disseminated to key stakeholders.
6. Juvenile drug courts should seek out support for conducting a full outcome evaluation.

Source: Hills, Shufelt, and Cocozza (2009:6–7).

judges and other drug court staff through training, technical assistance, and programmatic initiatives (OJJDP 2016). Similarly, in 2009, the National Center for Mental Health and Juvenile Justice presented evidence-based practice recommendations for juvenile drug courts (Hills, Shufelt, and Cocozza 2009). The box entitled "Juvenile justice policy and practice: Evidence-based practice recommendations for juvenile drug courts" presents these recommendations.

Mental health courts

Like drug courts, **mental health courts** first emerged in the adult criminal justice system in the late 1990s to address challenges posed by offenders with mental health problems. The first juvenile mental health court opened in 2001 (Butts et al. 2012). Research clearly shows high rates of mental health disorders among juvenile offenders (Teplin et al. 2002), and it has fueled calls for better intervention strategies for these offenders. For example, research has found that 46 percent of youth referred to a juvenile probation intake department had some form of diagnosable mental health disorder (Wasserman et al. 2005), and 50–75 percent of juveniles placed in secure correctional facilities had diagnosable disorders (Coalition for Juvenile Justice 2000). Juvenile mental health courts were developed to provide a multidisciplinary team approach to address the needs of the significant portion of juvenile offenders who have mental health disorders. In 2007, there were 18 juvenile mental health courts in the U.S., and 20 additional jurisdictions that intended to open juvenile mental health courts (Council of State Governments 2008).

Juvenile mental health courts are designed primarily for non-violent juvenile offenders who have been diagnosed with a serious mental illness. Most courts use mental health screening and assessment tools to identify juveniles who are eligible to participate based on the seriousness of their mental illness and exclude youth with minor disorders (Butts et al. 2012). The primary goal is to connect youth with community-based mental health services, but public safety is also a consideration in determining who is eligible for participation. The emphasis is on reducing the impact of the underlying mental illness, with the assumption being that effective management of symptoms will decrease offenders' involvement in the juvenile justice system (Latessa and Smith 2015). Mental health courts typically operate after adjudication but before disposition (Cocozza and Shufelt 2006). Some courts, however, operate at the pre-adjudication stage. Mental health court participation is voluntary. A concern with juvenile mental health courts, as with drug courts, is the possibility for net-widening.

Juvenile mental health courts are similar to juvenile drug courts in their team-oriented, offender-based approach and close court supervision through regular review hearings. The team typically consists of case managers, mental health providers, probation officers, defense attorney, and prosecutor. Together, they develop individualized treatment plans, monitor juveniles' compliance and progress, and make recommendations to the court. The treatment options may include individual, group, and family therapy, as well as medication management services (Butts et al. 2012). Mechanisms for monitoring compliance may include community supervision, home visits, and electronic monitoring. Successful program completion may result in the juvenile's record being expunged or charges being dropped. The typical length of mental health court involvement ranges from 10 to 18 months (Cocozza and Shufelt 2006).

Research examining the effectiveness of juvenile mental health courts is extremely limited. Given variation in mental health court models used in different jurisdictions, evaluation becomes quite difficult. A recent study found that youth who participated in mental health court had lower recidivism rates than youth who were assigned to other forms of diversion and probation, including intensive supervision probation (Heretick and Russell 2013). Butts and his colleagues (2012:626) summarize the limited research this way: "At best, the research suggests that the model has merit, but the realities of program implementation render client results unpredictable."

Teen courts

Teen courts, also called youth courts or peer courts, are voluntary diversion programs. The idea of teen courts emerged in the 1970s, but it was in the late 1990s and early 2000s that the number of teen courts increased dramatically (Butts et al. 2012). The growth in popularity of teen courts was due in part to the active financial support they received from the OJJDP. In 1993, an estimated 80 teen courts existed in the U.S. (Godwin 2000). By 2006, this number had grown to more than 1,250 teen courts (National Youth Court Center 2006), and in 2007, these courts considered more than 116,000 cases (Schneider 2007).

Teen courts are given authority through an agreement between prosecutors and police to defer formal charges for youth who agree to participate (Butts et al. 2012). The primary sources of referrals to teen courts are police, juvenile courts, and juvenile probation departments. Schools may also make referrals in some jurisdictions. Teen courts are typically used for status offenders and first-time non-serious delinquent offenders. The most common offenses referred to teen courts are shoplifting, disorderly conduct, minor assault, and alcohol possession (Butts and Buck 2000).

In these courts, offenders receive meaningful, though unofficial consequences, administered by people their own age. Youth are responsible for what happens in the courtroom. Prosecutors, defense attorneys, and jury members are all teenagers; in about half of teen courts, the judge is as well. This structure provides an opportunity for offenders to see other teenagers in responsible roles, to see that most young people are law abiding, and to see that it is law-abiding juveniles, not offenders, who are respected (Butts et al. 2012).

Rather than the warning that first-time offenders might receive in the traditional juvenile justice system, offenders in teen courts always receive some type of sanction. These sanctions are often restorative in nature, such as requiring the offender to replace stolen property, repair property damage, or complete community service to repay the broader community harmed by delinquency. Offenders are often required to write letters of apology to their victims or their parents. They may be required to serve later on a teen court jury, or to participate in educational programs, such as drug or alcohol classes or those focused on decision-making skills. These various sanctions attempt to teach juveniles accountability for their actions.

Despite the popularity of teen courts, there are few studies that employ rigorous research designs (e.g., use of a comparison group) to evaluate their effectiveness. Studies that have used rigorous research designs have found mixed results. Some research finds that teen court participants are less likely than those in the comparison group to reoffend (Butts, Buck, and Coggeshall 2002; Hissong 1991). Other studies find no differences between the two groups in the likelihood of reoffending (North Carolina Administrative Office of the Courts 1995; Seyfrit, Reichel, and Stutts 1987) or a higher rate of reoffending among teen court participants (Stickle et al. 2008).

SUMMARY AND CONCLUSIONS

Community-based corrections, which began to be widely used in the 1960s and 1970s, emphasize the community's role in causing and responding to delinquency and utilize community resources. The goal of handling juvenile offenders in the community whenever possible is consistent with the changing view of delinquency that emerged through the enactment of the Juvenile Justice and Delinquency Prevention Act of 1974, especially its emphasis on reintegration.

Community-based responses to delinquency include diversion, community treatment, certain types of residential placement, and aftercare. Diversion is the referral of cases, before petition or adjudication, to programs and agencies inside or outside the juvenile justice system. These programs and agencies may provide services such as counseling, drug treatment, vocational and job training, and educational services, sometimes administered through Youth Service Bureaus.

Community treatment typically involves adjudicated youth who receive intermediate sanctions such as day reporting centers, house arrest and electronic monitoring, restitution, community service, and intensive probation supervision. Community-based treatment options may also include counseling, drug treatment, and mental health services. Community-based residential placements include group homes, foster homes, and shelter care, where juveniles receive individualized treatment and have access to a variety of community resources. Aftercare programs provide support, supervision, and services to delinquent youth after residential placement.

Balanced and restorative approaches to juvenile justice are often community-based, attempting to actively involve community members and use community resources in responding to delinquency. The goals of balanced and restorative justice are offender accountability, competency development, and public safety. Offenders are asked to take responsibility for the harm they have caused, and victims and community members are actively involved in determining the best way for offenders to repair that harm. This process happens through several different restorative conferencing strategies, including victim-offender mediation, community reparative boards, family group conferencing, and circle sentencing.

The use of specialized courts, including problem-solving courts and teen courts, began or expanded in the 1990s. Drug courts and mental health courts are two types of problem-solving courts that exist for juveniles. Both focus on treating the underlying problems that give rise to delinquency, rather than simply punishing individuals for offending. Both types of courts use a team-oriented approach in which case managers, treatment providers, judges, probation officers, and attorneys work together to develop individualized treatment plans and monitor juveniles' compliance and progress. Teen courts are voluntary diversion programs used for status offenders and first-time non-serious delinquent offenders. Teenagers serve as prosecutors, defense attorneys, jury members, and sometimes judges in teen courts, and offer an opportunity for offenders to view other teens in responsible and respected roles.

READING 11.1

"RESTORATIVE JUSTICE AND RECIDIVISM: PROMISES MADE, PROMISES KEPT?"

James Bonta, Rebecca Jesseman, Tanya Rugge, and Robert Cormier. 2008. Pp. 108–120 in *Handbook of Restorative Justice: A Global Perspective*, edited by D. Sullivan and L. Tifft. New York: Routledge.

Bonta and his colleagues (2008) examine research on the effectiveness of restorative justice and its impact on recidivism. Through a meta-analysis, the study empirically analyzes the results of prior research on restorative justice and recidivism and finds that restorative interventions are associated with relatively small but statistically significant reductions in recidivism, particularly for low-risk offenders.

Without a doubt, restorative justice (RJ) has attracted widespread attention and it has challenged our traditional notions of justice and the application of justice. RJ offers an alternative to the traditional adversarial and mainly offender-centered system of justice by assigning a greater role in dealing with crime to victims and community members. Throughout the world many countries are not only experimenting with RJ but also enshrining RJ principles into law and policy. In short, RJ may represent the beginnings of a paradigm shift.

Fundamentally, restorative justice is an approach to justice that focuses on repairing the harm caused by crime while holding the offender responsible for his or her actions. Restorative justice programs, at their best, are designed to render a more satisfying sense of justice by engaging the parties directly affected by a crime – victims, offenders, and community – in a process where collectively they can identify and address their needs in the aftermath of a crime, and seek a resolution that affords reparation, healing, and prevents future harm. Enmeshed in this definition of restorative justice are a number of outcomes that restorative justice program evaluators need to address. These include, but are not limited to, the extent to which harm was repaired, the nature and quality of the engagement, the level of satisfaction of the parties with the process and the outcomes, the extent to which needs were identified and addressed satisfactorily for each of the parties, the impact on the offender and, in this respect, most notably, whether the likelihood of recidivism is reduced.

The last of these intended outcomes, reducing recidivism, is one that restorative justice has in common with two other prominent approaches to addressing criminal behavior, i.e. deterrence, which is based on the premise that punishment can serve to reduce the likelihood that offenders will reoffend, and rehabilitation, which is based on the premise that appropriate treatment of offenders reduces recidivism. The focus of this chapter is an examination of the evidence regarding restorative justice and its impact on recidivism in the context of the more extensive literature on the effects of deterrence and rehabilitation on recidivism.

What do we know about recidivism reduction?

Before reviewing the RJ research specifically as it relates to recidivism, it is helpful to summarize the research on the effects of deterrence and rehabilitation on recidivism. We will deal first with deterrence, as the evidence is relatively straightforward and unequivocal.

There are a number of reasons why societies punish those who transgress laws and norms. First, punishing offenders demonstrates to the public that justice was served. For many, there is something inherently satisfying to have an element of offenders getting their 'just deserts' (von Hirsch 1976). The punishment of offenders also expresses society's disapproval of certain acts, thereby communicating cultural norms and values. Finally, punishment is intended to deter offenders and others from behaving in an antisocial manner. It is to this last reason for having criminal justice sanctions that we turn our attention.

Punishing offenders has become prevalent in many industrialized nations as evidenced by increasingly stringent laws and methods for dealing with offenders. This popularity is no better seen than in the United States. Fueled by 'three strikes (and even two strikes) and you're out' laws, America has the highest incarceration rate in the world, at least among countries that report their prison populations. It houses one-quarter of the world's prison population with nearly two million offenders incarcerated (Walmsley 2002). Add to this more than four million offenders under community supervision and it is little wonder that one of every thirty-two American citizens in 2003 was under some form of correctional control (Glaze and Palla 2004). And these are only the numbers for adults.

Not only have the laws become more stringent, leading to high incarceration rates, so have the conditions of correctional control. In terms of custody, the US has 'no-frill prisons' where even basic amenities such as radio, television and access to daily exercise are removed. Community correctional control is no longer limited to probation; there is now a wide range of intermediate sanctions that are *added* to probation and parole. Probation and parole in many jurisdictions includes electronic monitoring, urinalysis and sometimes even public humiliation. As Erwin (1986) wrote nearly twenty years ago, probation is under pressure to 'turn up the heat' and be as punishing as prison.

The popularity of the get-tough movement is not restricted to the US. Other countries have seen rising prison populations and the imposition of stricter controls over offenders. For example, in the UK the prison population grew 7 percent between 2001 and 2002 (Councell 2003). The apparent insatiable appetite of the public to cause suffering upon offenders appears, however, to be subsiding. Legislators and policy-makers are beginning to realize that getting tough on criminals is extremely expensive. Concerns have been raised that getting tough on offenders comes at the expense of funding social programs such as health, education, and crime prevention (Austin et al. 1999; Greenwood 1998). Moreover, and quite simply, punishment does not appear to deter offenders from further crime.

The evidence for the ineffectiveness of criminal justice sanctions comes from both narrative and meta-analytic reviews of the research findings. A narrative literature review is a conventional approach to summarizing empirical studies on a particular topic. Studies are identified, read, and evaluated based on the reviewer's judgment of the findings. Andrew von Hirsch and his colleagues (von Hirsch et al. 1999) conducted such a review on the effects of punishment on offender recidivism and found limited support for deterrence. The problem with the narrative review is that it is dependent upon the qualitative assessment of findings by the reviewer(s) and final conclusions are limited to a simple 'vote count' (i.e. how many studies favor a certain conclusion and how many do not).

Meta-analysis has come to replace the traditional narrative literature review as the preferred approach to summarizing the findings from studies. The advantages offered by meta-analysis are many. First, this method is more rigorous in its approach to examining studies, as meta-analysis uses a structured and transparent methodology to examine the features of a study that relate to the issue of interest. Next, all study results, whether they are statistically significant or not, are coded. Counting only statistically significant results can be misleading, especially when sample size is small. Lastly, meta-analysis provides a *quantitative* summary of the findings. Assigning a quantitative weight to the findings, or what is commonly referred to as an 'effect size,' allows for an estimate of the magnitude of the findings, its relationship to various characteristics of the study, and by pooling the effect size with other studies it increases the power of the findings beyond that which a single study can provide.

Studies on the same topic often report their results in different ways. The problem is taking the different results and being able to compare them. The solution lies with the meta-analytic technique of statistically transforming the findings from individual studies to a standardized quantitative weight or an effect size. For example, if conducting a meta-analysis on the effects of a certain type of diet on weight loss then there may be a need to transform the weight losses that are reported in various studies as pounds or stones into kilograms. There are a number of effect sizes that can be chosen by the meta-analyst (e.g. Cohen's *d*, odds-ratio). However, in this chapter we describe studies that use either the Pearson correlation coefficient (*r*) or phi. The phi coefficient is the same as the Pearson correlation coefficient when used with dichotomous data.

To date, there have been two meta-analytic reviews that have addressed the question of whether sanctions impact on recidivism. Smith et al. (2002) conducted the first meta-analysis involving over a hundred studies with 442,471 offenders. Smith et al. (2002) found that serving a prison sentence, as compared to a community sentence, was not associated with a reduction in recidivism (phi = 0.07; CI = 0.05–0.09). CI is the confidence interval that gives the range of values that are likely to occur around the mean effect size and is usually set at 95 percent. Thus, the finding of a CI in the range of 0.05 to 0.09 means that there is a 95 percent likelihood that the true population mean will fall within this range. It is important to note that the CI for this particular finding did not include zero, meaning that the result was not due to simple chance. If the confidence interval includes zero then the findings are not statistically significant using the conventional 0.05 probability level. Another advantage of reporting the CI associated with a mean effect size is that if we are examining two or more relationships and the CIs overlap then we cannot be certain that one relationship is greater than the other. Here, the mean phi coefficient was 0.07 and it was positive, indicating that incarceration was associated with an *increase* in recidivism (a negative phi would have indicated a decrease in recidivism).

Smith et al. (2002) also found that the length of time incarcerated was not associated with reductions in recidivism (phi = 0.03, CI = 0.02–0.04). On the contrary, longer periods of incarceration were associated with an increase in recidivism. To simplify the interpretation of phi, the value approximates percentages, and a phi of 0.03 suggests an increase in recidivism in the neighborhood of 3 percent. Their second major set of analyses focused on the effects of intermediate sanctions (e.g. electronic monitoring programs, boot camp, drug testing, etc.). Once again, intermediate sanctions had no impact on recidivism (phi = –0.01, CI = –0.02–0.00).

The second meta-analysis comes from the larger review of the offender rehabilitation literature (Andrews and Bonta 2003). Within the Andrews and Bonta (2003) review there were 101 tests of the impact of sanctions on recidivism. The mean effect size (*r* in this case) was –0.03 with a 95 percent confidence interval of –0.05 to –0.03. Because the coding direction was reversed from that in the Smith et al. (2002) review, the negative sign indicates that sanctions were associated with increases in recidivism. Specifically, it was rehabilitation programs that were associated with decreases in recidivism *(r* = 0.12, CI = 0.09–0.14). Thus, two independent meta-analyses confirmed the earlier findings from the von Hirsch et al. (1999) narrative review of the deterrence literature but this time with quantitative precision. The overall conclusion is that deterrence does not 'work.'

So, if deterrence does not reduce recidivism then what about the delivery of rehabilitation services to offenders? We turn now to the literature on offender rehabilitation and recidivism.

Offender rehabilitation and recidivism

In our discussion of the research on deterrence we noted the meta-analysis reported by Andrews and Bonta (2003). Although they found that deterrence, if anything, had a negative impact, the focus of their meta-analytic review was on the effectiveness of providing human service interventions to offenders. On this latter point, there was a significant relationship between human service delivery and reduced recidivism. Of 273 tests of the impact of human service programs (e.g. family therapy, skill-building, substance abuse interventions, etc.) on recidivism, the average *r* was 0.12 (CI = 0.09–0.14). In other words, for those offenders who receive treatment, the recidivism rate is 12 percent lower than for offenders who do not receive treatment. This reduction in recidivism may not be dramatic but it is certainly more impressive than the findings with deterrence (note that the confidence intervals for deterrence and treatment do not overlap).

The review of offender treatment by Andrews and Bonta (2003) is consistent with the findings from other meta-analytic reviews focusing on different kinds of offenders and social contexts. For example, Lipsey (1989) reviewed the treatment literature for juvenile delinquents and reported an average effect size estimate of 0.10 based on 443 effect sizes. Redondo and his colleagues (Redondo et al. 1999) examined forty-nine European studies and found a mean effect size of 0.15. There have been more than a dozen meta-analytic reviews of the offender rehabilitation literature and their findings are remarkably consistent (McGuire 2001) in showing that treatment 'works.'

Most reviews of the treatment literature make only broad differentiations among the treatment programs. It has been recognized since the 1980s that not all offender treatment programs are equally effective (Andrews 1980; Palmer 1983). However, the principles of differential treatment were not clearly formulated and empirically demonstrated until 1990 (Andrews, Bonta and Hoge 1990; Andrews et al. 1990).

In 1990, Andrews, Bonta and Hoge presented three important principles for effective rehabilitation. They were the principles of Risk, Need, and Responsivity. The Risk principle states that the intensity of human service intervention should be proportional to the offender's risk to re-offend. That is, more intense levels of services should be directed to the higher-risk offender and minimal services directed to the low-risk offender. Many therapists like to treat low-risk clients who are cooperative, verbal, intelligent and motivated, but the research shows that treating low-risk offenders has minimal impact on recidivism *(r* = 0.03, ninety-six tests; Andrews and Bonta 2003). It is the higher-risk offender that shows the most benefit from treatment *(r* = 0.10, 278 tests).

The Need principle makes a distinction between criminogenic and non-criminogenic needs. Criminogenic needs are offender needs that are functionally related to criminal behavior. They are dynamic, changeable risk factors. Some examples are substance abuse, cognitions supportive of crime and social support for crime. Examples of non-criminogenic needs are vague feelings of emotional discomfort, self-esteem and increasing group cohesiveness. In order to reduce recidivism, treatment programs must target criminogenic needs ($r = 0.19$, 169 tests).

An offender may be high risk and with clearly defined criminogenic needs, but treatment may have little impact if it is not delivered in a way that the offender can understand and that motivates him/her. Many offenders have a concrete thinking style, are poorly educated, and have a restless, energetic temperament. Placing them in a treatment program that is dependent on 'talking it out' and discussing abstract ideas is unlikely to help. The Responsivity principle speaks to tailoring the treatment to the learning style of the individual. For most offenders, this means a structured, cognitive–behavioral style of intervention that is rich in concrete exercises and that shapes the desired behavior with the appropriate use of interpersonal rewards and punishments. Behavioral forms of intervention work best with offenders ($r = 0.23$, seventy-seven tests).

In the Andrews et al. study (1990), the presence of these principles was clearly associated with reductions of recidivism. When treatment programs adhered to all three principles (i.e. appropriate treatment) the mean phi coefficient was 0.32 (fifty-four tests). When none of the principles were followed (i.e. inappropriate), treatment actually made things worse with an increase in recidivism ($r = -0.07$, thirty-eight tests).

An updated analysis of the expanded treatment database reinforced the conclusion that rehabilitation programs adhering to the three principles led to reductions in recidivism ($r = 0.26$, sixty tests; Andrews and Bonta 2003). The more recent findings also showed that treatment was more effective when delivered in the community. The mean effect size was 0.35 for appropriate programs delivered in the community and 0.17 for similar programs delivered in prison/residential settings. Moreover, the number of principles that are followed is associated with a step-wise reduction in recidivism. When only one principle was followed the mean r was 0.02 and for two principles, $r = 0.18$.

In summary, there is convincing evidence that treatment programs with certain characteristics can reduce recidivism. Those programs associated with reductions in reoffending are those that target the criminogenic needs of higher-risk offenders using behavioral intervention techniques. This, we do know. Can restorative justice programs have a similar effect and, if so, under what conditions? We turn to these questions next.

A meta-analysis of the impact of restorative justice on recidivism

In order to answer the question of whether or not restorative justice programs can impact offender recidivism, we undertook a meta-analytic review of the pertinent literature. The present review is an update and expansion of the meta-analyses conducted by Bonta and his colleagues (Bonta et al. 2002) and Latimer et al. (2001). These earlier reviews found a small relationship between restorative justice interventions and reductions in recidivism. Bonta et al. (2002) reported an average reduction of recidivism of 3 percent and Latimer et al. (2001) found a 7 percent reduction. Although the two reviews found different effect size estimates, the overlapping confidence intervals from the two studies suggest that the differences are not significant.

The reviews, however, were heavily weighted by studies that included court-imposed restitution and community service agreements. For many (e.g. Bazemore 2000; Zehr 2004), court-ordered reparation does not represent restorative justice because the parties are not engaged in a process that leads to a restorative agreement. With the recent publication of studies that better fit a more refined definition of restorative justice, it is time to re-examine the literature and explore the impacts from programs that more fully involve victims and the community.

As with earlier reviews (Bonta et al. 2002; Latimer et al. 2001), our net was cast widely in selecting studies to include in our meta-analysis. Restorative justice was broadly defined as 'any intervention that attempts to repair the harm caused by the offender to the victim or the community.' Consequently, court-imposed restitution and community service with limited victim involvement remained along with studies of victim offender mediation. Newer interventions such as family group conferencing and community forums were added to the database. We decided to keep court-imposed restoration schemes for two reasons. First, it would allow us to make comparisons of court-ordered reparation programs with non-coercive reparation programs. Second, many of the early studies of court-ordered restitution and community service provided restorative justice rationales involving offender accountability and repairing the harm.

To be included in the review, the study had to meet the following three criteria. First, there had to be a comparison group of some type (comparison groups were coded as to whether they were the result of random assignment, some type of matching, etc.). Second, post-program recidivism data had to be reported in a way that permitted the calculation of an effect size. As all the studies provided results that could be used to construct two-by-two tables (type of treatment and recidivism outcome), the phi coefficient was selected as our effect size measure. Finally, the assessment of recidivism had to be based on a longitudinal research design. Retrospective analysis of criminal histories and cross-sectional comparisons were omitted.

Over fifty variables were coded for each study. The variables could be grouped into three main categories. The first category dealt with evaluation methodology and measured such things as type of research design (e.g. random, quasi-experimental, etc.), the comparability of the control group to the RJ group (e.g. checks for group equivalence conducted) and length of follow-up. The second category assessed participant characteristics (e.g. adult or youth, race, age, etc.). The last category dealt with the characteristics of the program (e.g. was restitution required? was participation mandatory? did the program follow restorative justice principles? etc.). Given the strong evidence concerning the effectiveness of offender rehabilitation programs in reducing recidivism, we also coded for the presence of treatment programming and its appropriateness following the principles of effective rehabilitation.

Our review of the literature uncovered thirty-nine studies that met the criteria for inclusion. Most (72.1 percent) of the programs were from the United States, and approximately half of the programs were situated within a court setting (see **Table 1** for a summary of program characteristics). Given that the studies dated back to 1976 when restorative justice was in its infancy, it is not surprising that 36.1 percent of studies were categorized as having minimal adherence to today's standards of restorative justice. Only 31.1 percent of the studies provided a detailed description of the restorative justice model. Not shown in the table, 52.7 percent of cases involved face-to-face meetings between victims and offenders. The mean attrition rate (i.e. percent who did not complete the program) was 21.5 percent.

Perhaps because of our study selection criteria, we found that most evaluations used acceptable research designs. Random assignment was conducted in 29.5 percent of the studies and another 54.1 percent used quasi-experimental, matched designs, while the remaining studies used control groups selected for their convenience and availability or a pre-post design. Fully 83.3 percent of studies made efforts to verify the equivalence of the experimental and control groups. Most

TABLE 1 Characteristics of restorative justice interventions

Age of program (percent)	
Less than two years	42.6
Two years or more	57.4
Type of setting (percent)	
Court	50.8
Police	16.4
Probation/parole	26.2
Institution/residential	6.6
Program ownership (percent)	
Criminal justice agency	63.9
Private agency	26.2
Public, non-criminal justice agency	9.8
Participation mandatory (percent)	35.0
Treatment provided (percent)	15.0
Adherence to RJ principles (percent)	
Minimal	36.1
Moderate	21.3
High	42.6
Staff trained in RJ (percent)	74.5
Elements of . . .	
Victim offender mediation or reconciliation (percent)	62.3
Restitution	82.0
Community service	82.0
Family group conference	24.6
Community forum	8.2

(84.7 percent) of the control groups were exposed to traditional criminal justice processing. The remaining control groups consisted of either an alternative restorative justice program or a treatment intervention.

As presented in **Table 2**, most of the offenders in the restorative justice programs were low-risk, male, Caucasian youth. Very few programs targeted serious cases such as violent offenders or those who committed crimes against the person. Although not a focus of our review, this highly select group also displayed very high rates of satisfaction with restorative justice. On average, 87.7 percent of offenders expressed satisfaction with their experience. Victims expressed slightly lower rates of satisfaction (81.6 percent).

The thirty-nine studies yielded sixty-seven effect size estimates for recidivism. The number of effect size estimates exceeds the number of studies because a study may report more than one comparison. For example, Umbreit and Coates' (1992) study yielded two effect sizes (one for a victim offender mediation program in Oakland, California, and another for a program in Minneapolis, Minnesota). The most common measure of recidivism was reconviction (50.8 percent) followed by rearrest (44.1 percent). The average follow-up interval was 17.7 months. The average phi coefficient for all programs was 0.07 and the CI did not include zero (**Table 3**).

TABLE 2 Characteristics of the participants

Sample (percent)	
Juvenile	75.0
Adult	25.0
Gender (percent)	
Male	97.7
Female	2.3
Race (percent)	
Caucasian	79.2
Black	6.3
Other	14.5
Mean age (years)	18.7
Prior record (percent)	46.1
Low risk (percent)	72.0
Major offense type (percent)	
Person	14.2
Property	67.3
Vandalism	8.2
Other	10.3

In other words, restorative justice interventions do have an impact on recidivism in the order of a 7 percent reduction. Further inspection of Table 3 finds little variation in the mean effect size across sample (juvenile/adult) and type of RJ intervention (e.g. victim offender mediation, restitution). The overlapping CIs indicate that there are no differences between programs with youthful offenders and adult offenders, nor does one particular RJ intervention perform better than another.

Exploring further what could possibly influence the magnitude of the phi coefficient, we examined the role of the evaluation methodology used in the studies. There were no differences in the mean effect size among the studies that used random assignment, quasi-experimental designs or even studies with poor methodologies (e.g. control with no checks for equivalence). However, the year of publication was related to phi ($r = 0.25$, $p < 0.05$) with studies after 1995 yielding larger effect size estimates than studies prior to 1996 (average phi of 0.12 and 0.04 respectively).

The positive effects found with recent evaluations may be due to the fact that these RJ programs have more developed and conceptually refined models of restorative justice. The restorative justice rationale/model underlying the programs was more clearly formulated in the recent studies. No study after 1995 was coded 'vague or poor' in their description of a restorative justice model. Most of the recent programs (65 percent) were highly structured as evidenced by manuals or formalized routines. In the earlier programs, only 10 percent were coded as highly structured. Furthermore, all the programs after 1995 described staff as being specifically trained in the delivery of restorative justice services. Finally, prior to 1996 only 18.4 percent of the programs were coded as 'high adherence to RJ' whereas the rate jumps to 82.4 percent for programs published in 1996 or later.

TABLE 3 Restorative justice interventions and recidivism (CI)

Type of sample/program	RJn	N	k	phi	CI
All programs	11,701	25,771	67	0.07	0.06–0.08
Juvenile	9,595	21,766	50	0.06	0.05–0.07
Adult	1,858	3,507	16	0.09	0.06–0.12
Victim offender mediation	3,440	6,949	40	0.08	0.06–0.10
Restitution	10,822	23,934	55	0.08	0.07–0.09
Community service	10,495	23,252	57	0.07	0.06–0.08
Family group conference	1,878	3,741	16	0.09	0.06–0.12
Community forum	705	1,435	5	0.11	0.06–0.16

Notes: RJn = rj sample size; N = total sample size including control; k = number of effect sizes; CI = 95 percent confidence interval.

The recent studies could be characterized as not only being more true to restorative justice principles, but also these programs were not simply mere 'add-ons' to criminal justice sanctions. Many of the early RJ programs were closely tied to criminal justice sanctions, usually in the form of restitution and community service. Sometimes offenders met the victim or negotiated through a mediator the terms and conditions for repairing the harm. However, criminal justice officials administered most of the early interventions where the court assigned the amount of restitution or community service with minimal victim involvement. A closer analysis of the data shows that RJ interventions that were contextualized within criminal justice sanctions showed little effect on recidivism (phi = 0.01) whereas programs that were outside of the sanctioning process were more effective in reducing recidivism (phi = 0.10, $t = 2.26$, $df = 49$, $p < 0.05$).

Treatment, restorative justice and recidivism

As reviewed earlier, offender rehabilitation programs can have significant impacts on reducing recidivism. Human service interventions, without differentiation according to risk, need and responsivity, produce a mean effect of 0.12. This effect size is of the same order as that found for RJ programs that operate outside of the criminal sanctioning process (0.10). RJ programs that are court-ordered reparation programs have an average effect size of 0.01, almost identical to that found with criminal justice sanctions. Only eleven interventions had any evidence of treatment provided to offenders. There was no difference in the effect size for those who received treatment (0.09) and those who did not (0.07). The treatments provided were further coded as to their adherence to the principles of effective interventions. Three programs could not be evaluated because of a lack of information and six programs were coded as inappropriate. The six inappropriate programs produced a mean effect size of 0.01. The Bonta et al. (2002) study was the only one that was coded as appropriate and it had a mean effect size of 0.31.

In recent years, justice practices have been extended to offenders who have committed more serious crimes and to higher-risk offenders. We make a distinction between those who have committed serious, violent crimes and those who are at a high risk to re-offend. They are not necessarily the same. An offender with no prior record but who has committed a serious crime can be at low risk to re-offend (Rugge et al. 2005). Five RJ programs, all published after 1997, targeted mostly violent offenders. The mean phi coefficient was 0.15 but the range was high (0.02 to 0.26). Although this result appears promising, more studies are needed.

With respect to offender risk level, thus far our data suggest that RJ interventions have no impact on recidivism for the higher-risk offender (phi = −0.01, n = 17). Surprisingly, RJ programs targeting low-risk offenders showed a greater impact on recidivism (phi = 0.08 for low-risk offenders vs −0.01 for the higher-risk offenders; $t = 2.14$, $df = 54$, $p < 0.05$). This finding raises two questions. Why would restorative justice work better, in terms of recidivism reduction, with lower-risk offenders than with higher-risk offenders and why does it have absolutely no impact on higher-risk offenders?

The effectiveness of RJ programs with low-risk offenders is contrary to the rehabilitation literature where treatment provided to low-risk offenders is largely ineffective. In trying to understand this finding it is helpful to be reminded that low-risk offenders, by definition, have very few criminogenic needs that require attention. Moreover, when considering only the offender, RJ targets increasing acceptance of responsibility for the harm caused, empathy for the victim and stimulating feelings of remorse and shame. None of these factors are established criminogenic needs that are functionally related to criminal behavior (Andrews and Bonta 2003). Yet, we see reductions in re-offending.

There are two possible explanations that account for the reduced recidivism. First, the control groups in the studies were exposed to traditional criminal justice processing. Labeling theorists would argue that official processing might actually increase offending because the offender assumes the criminal label given by the criminal justice system. There is some evidence that interventions with low-risk offenders can sometimes increase recidivism (Andrews et al. 1990; Bonta et al. 2000). In other words, the exposure to criminal justice processing experienced by comparison groups may not be without effect. Some offenders may have worsened, thereby accentuating differences with the restorative justice groups.

A second explanation may relate to the reintegrative shaming model forwarded by Braithwaite (1989, 1999). Reintegrative shaming with its non-stigmatizing approach to labeling (the traditional criminal justice system's approach) may be well suited for the low-risk offender. Low-risk offenders are individuals who still have relatively close ties to the norms and values of society. The harms that they have caused to victims and the communities can be addressed without the heavy-handed approach of criminal justice processing. In a sense, their deviation from the norm is not so great that it cannot be corrected with something as simple as meeting the victim or involving community volunteers in repairing the harm. Rebuilding relationships is not insurmountable for the low-risk offender and can form the basis for 'relational rehabilitation' (Bazemore 1999).

With the higher-risk offender, we have an individual with a variety of criminogenic needs who generally has weak bonds to society. In this case, restorative justice may well be deficient in reducing recidivism. As more and more restorative justice experimentation is extended to higher-risk offenders, the hazard of doing harm becomes a possibility. With the higher-risk offender, appropriate treatment interventions will be needed to reduce recidivism, and yet the evidence thus far suggests that restorative justice practitioners are ill equipped to deal with these offenders. The studies that we reviewed found that when treatment was given, the treatment was likely to be inappropriate. The very first principle for effective treatment intervention requires an assessment of offender risk, and this is almost absent in the literature on restorative justice. Only five studies used an actuarial, evidence-based measure of offender risk. It may not be the role of restorative justice facilitators to deliver treatment programming; yet it would be useful if they would recognize the need for treatment and the type of programming that would assist in reducing offender recidivism, and make the appropriate referrals for treatment.

Summary and implications

Our meta-analytic review of the literature on restorative justice and recidivism provides a number of observations about what we know and what we need to know. We can summarize them as follows:

1. RJ interventions, on average, are associated with reductions in recidivism. The effects are relatively small but they are significant. It is also clear that the more recent studies are producing larger effects.
2. There is evidence to indicate that court-ordered RJ programs have no impact on recidivism. Programs that operate in a non-coercive environment and that attempt to involve victims and community members in a collaborative manner produce the largest effect size estimates.
3. RJ interventions appear more effective with low-risk offenders. This may be because low-risk offenders are diverted from the potential harm caused from traditional criminal justice processing and they are easier to reintegrate into the mainstream culture.
4. For high-risk offenders, restorative justice may be insufficient to decrease recidivism. If restorative justice practitioners continue to deal with the higher-risk offenders, then careful consideration of delivering appropriate treatment programming to these offenders in conjunction with the restorative process will be required.

We saw from our restorative justice meta-analysis that considerable progress has been made, particularly since 1996. We anticipate that as new evaluations of restorative justice and its impact on recidivism are published we will reach a point where we can derive some basic principles of practice for restorative justice that are associated with a reduction in recidivism. The establishment of treatment principles in the offender rehabilitation field has contributed significantly to program development. Similar principles in the area of restorative justice would surely be a welcome addition to basic principles that relate to the underlying philosophy of restorative justice and safeguarding the rights and interests of the parties (see the United Nations Basic Principles on the Use of Restorative Justice Programs in Criminal Matters; United Nations 2002). The goal is to elucidate the elements of restorative justice interventions that will meet a range of objectives, including repairing harm, producing a satisfying sense of justice, meeting the needs of victims, and increasing the likelihood that offenders will adopt law-abiding lives.

[References omitted.]

READING 11.2

"JUVENILE DRUG COURTS: A PROCESS, OUTCOME, AND IMPACT EVALUATION."

Lesli Blair, Carrie Sullivan, Edward Latessa, and Christopher J. Sullivan. 2015. *Juvenile Justice Bulletin.* Washington, DC: Office of Juvenile Justice and Delinquency Prevention.

Lesli Blair and her colleagues (2015) provide an evaluation of drug court intervention programs, including their processes and outcomes. This evaluation of nine juvenile drug courts in three regions of the U.S. was sponsored by the Office of Juvenile Justice and Delinquency Prevention. Because the findings of this evaluation generally do not support juvenile drug courts, the report authors conclude with recommendations for improving juvenile drug courts.

The first juvenile drug court was implemented in 1995 (Sloan and Smykla, 2003); since then, their use has grown considerably. According to the Office of National Drug Control Policy, 447 juvenile drug courts were in operation as of June 30, 2013 (National Institute of Justice, 2014). Despite the rapid growth of juvenile drug courts, studies concerning their effectiveness have yielded inconsistent results. Some studies have failed to find significant differences or have yielded mixed results (Anspach, Ferguson, and Phillips, 2003; Hartmann and Rhineberger, 2003; Koetzle-Shaffer, 2006; O'Connell, Wright, and Clymer, 2003), whereas others have found significant differences in key outcomes, including reduced recidivism rates (Latessa, Shaffer, and Lowenkamp, 2002; Rodriguez and Webb, 2004; Thompson, 2002), for drug court youth and those going through normal juvenile court processing. Recent meta-analyses of drug court studies found that juvenile drug courts have a slight positive effect on some outcomes for juveniles but not as strong an effect as their counterparts in the adult justice system (Drake, 2012; Koetzle-Shaffer, 2006; Latimer, Morton-Bourgon, and Chretien, 2006; Mitchell et al., 2012).

These mixed results, coupled with methodological limitations of juvenile drug court research, have hindered the field in drawing conclusive evidence of the courts' effectiveness. Even when evaluations have found the courts to be effective, researchers frequently have not been able to sufficiently explain which aspects of the courts' programming led to the positive outcomes. Given the existing findings, further research would help to better distinguish between models of successful and unsuccessful juvenile drug courts, resulting in:

- Evidence-based blueprints for guiding the development of new programs.
- A higher quality of programming.
- More efficient methods for finding funding and targeting resources.
- More effective juvenile drug court processes.

The juvenile drug court study

This bulletin summarizes key findings from a multisite study of juvenile drug courts that the Office of Juvenile Justice and Delinquency Prevention funded. The study had two main goals: (1) to update the research regarding the ability of juvenile drug courts to reduce recidivism and (2) to determine whether the selected juvenile drug courts were using evidence-based approaches, the characteristics of which might result in more positive outcomes and serve as models for drug court professionals and policymakers. The researchers conducted both an outcome evaluation and a process evaluation to consider youth outcomes relative to the quality of juvenile drug courts and their programming.

Methods

This section provides a brief overview of the authors' methods. Additional, detailed information about the authors' methods and statistical analysis can be found in the final report: www.ncjrs.gov/pdffiles1/ojjdp/grants/241643.pdf.

Participants and sampling procedures

Nine drug courts, representing different regions and populations nationwide, participated in the study (see table 1). Two courts are located on the west coast, three are in the Pacific Northwest, three are in the Midwest, and one is in the Northeast. The authors chose small, medium, and large localities, each served by three courts, for the study. The courts represented a mix of preadjudication and postadjudication drug court models. Over a 3 1/2 -year recruitment period, the authors asked all of the youth who participated in these juvenile drug courts to take part in the study. The youth and their parents or guardians provided informed consent. The authors matched each youth in drug court with a youth on probation from the same jurisdiction to form the study's drug court and control comparison groups. Youth were matched on gender, race, level of risk, and level of need for substance abuse treatment. Enrollment at each of the sites ranged from 72 to 296 youth, which was split evenly between the drug court group and the comparison group. The authors then compared outcomes for juveniles in drug court with outcomes for youth on traditional probation.

The researchers reviewed each youth's court file to complete the data collection for both groups. They collected data concerning sociodemographics, current offense, criminal history, assessments, education, family, employment, substance abuse, mental health, and other topics (e.g., gang involvement, abuse history) and additional data on drug tests, violations, incentives, treatment referrals, and case closures.

Measures

Data collected during the process evaluation measured the effectiveness of the drug court structure, procedures, and treatment programming. The authors used the Evidence-Based Correctional Program Checklist–Drug Court (CPC–DC) to evaluate the programs. The CPC–DC is a tool that researchers at the University of Cincinnati developed to assess drug court programs; it measures how closely drug and other therapeutic courts adhere to known principles of evidence-based, effective intervention.

The researchers constructed the CPC–DC using previous studies of both adult and juvenile drug courts and items from previously validated process evaluation tools (e.g., Lowenkamp, Holsinger, and Latessa, 2005; Koetzle-Shaffer, 2006; Shaffer et al., 2008). Although the CPC–DC itself was not validated within this study due to limited sample sizes, it highlighted the extent to which the studied juvenile drug courts' practices were in line with the literature on effective juvenile courts and drug courts.

To measure adherence to evidence-based practices, the researchers administered the CPC–DC during a 5-month period between months 13 and 17 of the active recruitment phase.

TABLE 1 Scores on the Correctional Program Checklist – Drug Court

Court	Overall	Development, coordination, staff and support	Quality assurance	Capacity	Assessment practices	Treatment	Content
1	55.8%	66.7%	28.6%	50.0%	88.9%	44.4%	59.3%
2	46.5	66.7	42.9	56.3	55.6	33.3	40.7
3	46.5	77.8	42.9	62.5	44.4	33.3	37.0
4	44.2	77.8	0.0	43.8	33.3	50.0	44.4
5	37.2	55.6	0.0	31.3	44.4	38.9	40.7
6	60.5	77.8	28.6	56.3	88.9	50.0	63.0
7	25.6	22.2	28.6	25.0	22.2	27.8	25.9
8	51.2	55.6	42.9	50.0	66.7	44.4	51.9
9	46.5	44.4	42.9	43.8	55.5	44.4	48.1

Note: The Correctional Program Checklist–Drug Court measures drug courts' adherence to evidence-based practices. Each area and all domains are scored and are rated as highly effective (65–100 percent), effective (55–64 percent), needs improvement (46–54 percent), or ineffective (45 percent or less).

The CPC–DC consists of two instruments: one for the formal drug court (CPC–DC) (see table 1) and another for the major referral agencies providing treatment and services to the drug court clients (CPC–DC: RA). Researchers assessed 35 referral and treatment agencies using the CPC–DC: RA.

The CPC–DC and CPC–DC: RA are divided into two categories: capacity and content. The capacity measures assess whether the drug court and its referral agencies have the foundation to deliver evidence-based interventions and services for offenders and consist of two domains:

1. development, coordination, staff and support, and
2. quality assurance.

The content measures focus on the substantive aspects of the drug court and its referral agencies and also consist of two domains: (1) assessment practices and (2) treatment characteristics. The content measures the extent to which the drug court and its referral agencies adhere to the principles of risk, need, and responsivity (RNR) and treatment.

The drug court tool consists of 41 indicators, and the referral agency tool has 49 indicators. Each category and each domain is scored and is rated as highly effective (65 to 100 percent), effective (55 to 64 percent), needs improvement (46 to 54 percent), or ineffective (45 percent or less). The authors totaled scores in all domains and then calculated the overall assessment score using the same scale. Not all of the domains are given equal weight, and some items do not apply to this study and, thus, were not scored. Data collection is carried out by a minimum of two trained evaluators and comprises the following:

- Conducting structured interviews with program staff, youth, and family members.
- Observing drug court staff meetings, court sessions, and treatment groups and the services provided to them.
- Reviewing related program information—such as participant files, policy and procedure manuals, schedules, and treatment materials.

After the researchers reviewed the data, they scored the program and provided a narrative summary to the program staff.

Findings

As shown in figure 1, youth who attended drug court fared worse than the probation (comparison) group regarding new referrals and adjudications during both the supervision and post-supervision stages. Only three of the nine drug courts showed evidence of lower recidivism rates for drug court youth when compared with probation youth, and only one drug court evidenced significantly lower recidivism rates for drug court youth when compared with probation youth. These findings suggest that, overall, the juvenile drug courts studied did not have a significant impact on outcomes, given their objectives; instead, youth in juvenile drug courts generally had a significantly greater likelihood of recidivism than youth on probation. This was true even when the multivariate analyses controlled for time at risk, risk level, need for substance abuse, and key sociodemographic variables. These findings also held when accounting for site-level effects in multilevel regression models. The researchers also analyzed outcome measures across different characteristics of drug court participants, including risk level, length of supervision period, race/ethnicity, gender, and age. For example, there were statistically significant differences

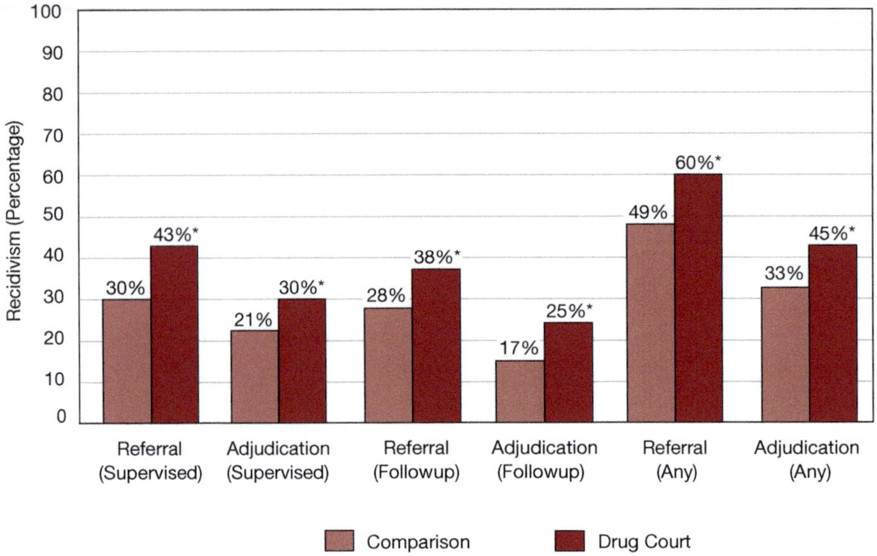

* Percentages are significant at p < .05.

FIGURE 1 *Overall recidivism outcomes: drug court youth versus comparison youth*

between drug court youth and probation youth in the likelihood of a new referral or adjudication for youth who were in the moderate- and high-risk categories (see Figures 2 and 3).

Table 1 and Table 2 report the CPC–DC percentage scores for the drug courts and an average score for their affiliated referral agencies. Past research on the CPC indicates that when agencies

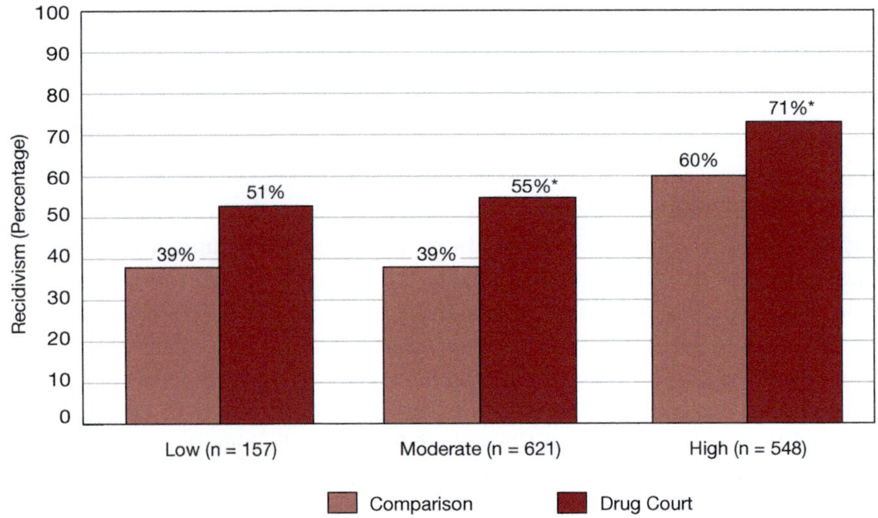

* Percentages are significant at p < .05.

FIGURE 2 *New referral following program entry by risk level: drug court youth versus comparison youth*

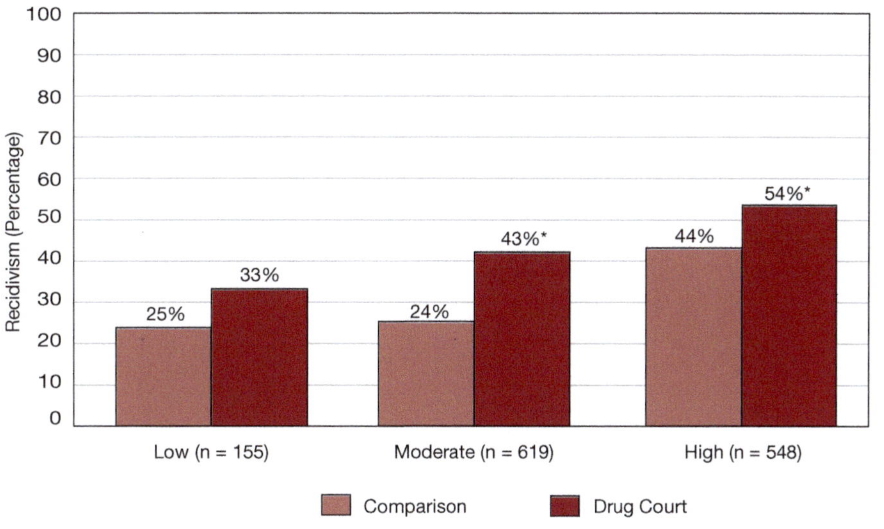

* Percentages are significant at $p < .05$.

FIGURE 3 *Adjudication following program entry by risk level: drug court youth versus comparison youth*

attain a score in the "effective–highly effective" range, recidivism rates decline. Only two of the drug courts scored in the "effective" category, and only one drug court's referral agencies had an average score in the "highly effective" category. These results indicate that the drug courts and referral agencies in general were not adhering to evidence-based practices. However, the one drug court that evidenced significant findings in favor of the drug court group was the drug court whose referral agencies averaged in the "highly effective" category. Otherwise, there was little correlation between the CPC–DC scores and overall outcomes.

The results for the content categories of the CPC–DC and CPC–DC: RA suggest that, overall, the sites were not adhering to the RNR principles in a way that is consistent with evidence-based practices. Many of the juvenile drug courts were not adequately assessing their clients for risk, needs, and barriers to treatment success. Even when conducted, the courts often did not share these assessments with the referral agencies that provided treatment. This is cause for concern because assessment and treatment practices are the foundation for delivering evidence-based practices. Treatment practices were also generally lacking in adherence to evidence-based recommendations. For example, treatment for drug court youth predominantly involved talk therapy and was based on educational precepts (i.e., general counseling techniques). These approaches have proved to be relatively ineffective in changing young offenders' behavior (Lipsey, 2009). Alternatively, the desirability of high-quality treatment services is illustrated by the fact that the one court that achieved significant reductions in recidivism had referral agencies that averaged a "highly effective" overall score on the CPC–DC: RA, which captured the adherence of treatment agencies to evidence-based practices. Quality assurance was also a major area in need of improvement. In fact, all nine drug courts scored in the "ineffective" category in this area, and only half of the referral agencies scored in the "effective" or "highly effective" category.

After the authors completed site visits, they also examined whether the drug courts were adhering to the 16 strategies that the National Drug Court Institute recommends (Bureau of

TABLE 2 Average referral agency scores on the Correctional Program Checklist – Drug Court

Court	Overall	Leadership, staff and support	Quality assurance	Capacity	Assessment practices	Treatment	Content
1 (n = 1)	35.3%	50.0%	50.0%	50.0%	75.0%	20.7%	27.3%
2 (n = 2)	38.6	75.0	0.0	56.3	0.0	32.6	29.4
3 (n = 4)	47.5	75.0	37.5	66.7	12.5	39.9	37.5
4 (n = 5)	65.7	75.7	50.0	71.1	65.0	63.3	63.5
5 (n = 1)	60.8	78.6	75.0	77.8	25.0	55.2	51.5
6 (n = 3)	42.7	64.3	25.0	55.6	58.3	32.0	35.4
7 (n = 9)	48.2	72.0	38.9	63.9	5.6	45.5	40.5
8 (n = 6)	54.1	75.0	37.5	65.8	8.3	53.1	47.7
9 (n = 4)	47.0	69.7	56.3	66.7	25.0	37.7	36.2

Note: The Correctional Program Checklist–Drug Court: Referral Agency instrument measures treatment referral agencies' adherence to evidence-based practices. Each area and all domains are scored and are rated as highly effective (65–100 percent), effective (55–64 percent), needs improvement (46–54 percent), or ineffective (45 percent or less).

Justice Assistance, 2003). Each of the 16 strategies has multiple associated recommendations for implementation, for a grand total of 152 recommendations. However, as this was an ad hoc comparison, the authors found relatively little overlap between the items of the CPC–DC and the 16 strategies and their accompanying recommendations. Only 31 of the 152 recommendations paralleled CPC–DC or CPC–DC: RA indicators. Despite this, the courts routinely implemented only 22 of the 31 matched recommendations, examples of which follow:

- Holding regular meetings to discuss each drug court youth.
- Involving the necessary court and treatment staff in these meetings.
- Providing sufficient case management and supervision.
- Requiring a sufficient frequency of drug tests.
- Rewarding progress in the drug court (youth receiving reinforcement for their positive behavior).

Areas the courts were not meeting the recommendations included:

- Instituting sufficient quality assurance processes (e.g., having a program evaluator or participating in an outcome study).
- Implementing effective treatment practices (e.g., offender reassessment, specific responsivity matching, evidence-based treatment, aftercare).
- Providing adequate staff training.

Recommendations for improving juvenile drug courts

The authors offer the following suggestions, based on the process evaluation findings, for improving juvenile drug courts:

- Staff who work in the drug court or provide treatment should be trained and required to use core correctional practices in their work with youth. These practices include effective reinforcement, effective disapproval, effective use of authority, anticriminal modeling, problem solving, and relationship skills. These staff should also be required to use evidence-based approaches, namely, cognitive-behavioral interventions and structured social learning.
- Drug courts should conduct a standardized risk and needs assessment with every client and share the results with all of their referral agencies. These results should be used to ensure that low-risk youth are not admitted to drug court, that areas of criminogenic need are being targeted, and that a sufficient dosage of treatment is provided.
- Youth should be screened into and out of these programs on the basis of validated substance abuse assessments. The program should accept only youth with a clear need for substance abuse treatment.
- Drug court and treatment staff should use the results of each client's assessments (risk, needs, and responsivity) to create an individualized case plan to avoid a one-size-fits-all approach. Drug court staff and treatment staff should operate from the same set of goals and objectives for each youth.
- In addition to focusing on substance abuse, drug courts should target other central criminogenic factors for change. These include antisocial attitudes, thoughts, values, and beliefs; antisocial peers and a lack of prosocial peers; antisocial personality characteristics;

coping and problem-solving skills; school and work performance; and family risks (e.g., supervision and consistent discipline).

- Drug courts should have established completion standards that are progress based, not time based. Youth should exhibit reductions in substance use and increases in knowledge and skills, which will help them remain substance free and crime free.
- Drug courts should ensure that their internal practices and the practices of their referral agencies adhere to the principles of effective intervention, namely, RNR and fidelity. Supervisors should regularly observe staff delivering case management and treatment services to drug court participants and coach these staff to improve their service delivery, as needed.
- Drug court programs should regularly collect and analyze data on key indicators, such as changes in risk and needs scores, completion rates, recidivism rates, and other areas youth should be improving based on the services delivered (e.g., school attendance and performance, changes in behavior at home).
- Drug court programs should be evaluated using a risk-controlled comparison group to ensure that the program is reducing recidivism when compared with other practices within the same jurisdiction. For example, drug court youth should be compared with similarly situated (in terms of risk/needs) youth on probation or youth placed in other local court programs.

Study limitations

Analyses that combined CPC–DC and CPC–DC: RA scores with recidivism outcomes revealed no clear pattern between the overall CPC–DC or the CPC–DC: RA scores and the main effect-size values for new referrals or adjudications. This may be a result of the small variation in scores on the CPC–DC and CPC–DC: RA across the sites and minor differences in the effectiveness and program fidelity among the nine drug courts. As such, the CPC–DC has not been established as a valid instrument to measure the effectiveness of drug courts. However, the measures of the CPC–DC are based on empirically derived best-practices.

Another limitation to this study is the use of official data as the main outcome measure. Although the authors administered a self-report followup survey, the response rate was too low to add any insight to the findings. As such, they used official referral and adjudication data to measure the success of the drug courts. These data do not capture all offenses that participants may have committed during followup, nor are they able to capture the extent of other outcomes that may have resulted from participation in drug court (e.g., reduction in drug use).

Conclusion

Although numerous studies have examined the effectiveness of juvenile drug courts, this research offers a fairly well-controlled outcome study and a review of key intervention features within these programs. The study's findings do not generally support juvenile drug courts; most sites saw higher rates of recidivism for drug court youth when compared with youth on probation. These findings were also valid across key subgroups when multivariate analyses included important controls. However, the drug courts studied generally did not adhere closely to evidence-based practices, which might explain the findings in part. The process evaluation does offer some suggestions for improvement. Juvenile drug courts could improve by following the recommendations of evidence-based practices, as measured by the CPC–DC.

However, given previous literature and the findings of the current study, there are still unanswered questions about whether, and under which circumstances, juvenile drug courts can be an effective intervention for substance-using youth. It is possible that the drug court model, as currently implemented, may not be an optimal fit for some youth. These juveniles may naturally age out of substance-using behavior with few negative consequences, suggesting that they may not benefit from drug court practices that were designed for serious addicts in the adult justice system. Juveniles are still developing cognitively and socially (see Cauffman and Steinberg, 2012; National Research Council, 2013), so they may not weigh risks and consequences the same way as adult drug court participants. This may contribute to the general success of adult drug courts and the mixed success of juvenile drug courts. The study suggests that researchers, policymakers, and practitioners must pay more attention to questions regarding (1) the target population involved in the juvenile drug court system (Who), (2) the nature of the drug court process in relation to the target population (How), and (3) the quality of the programming that youth receive within the drug court system (What).

[References omitted.]

CRITICAL-THINKING QUESTIONS

1 Consider the case of John and Will that opened this chapter. What is your reaction to the approach used in their case, and what makes this approach "restorative"?
2 What is the role of the community in community-based corrections?
3 What are the unique characteristics of a balanced and restorative approach to delinquency?
4 How do problem-solving courts, such as drug courts and mental health courts, and teen courts differ from traditional juvenile courts?
5 To what extent does research support the use of specialized courts? Does research generally show that these courts are effective at reducing delinquency?
6 The reading by Bonta and his colleagues shows that restorative approaches are associated with reductions in recidivism. How might you explain why this relationship between restorative justice and reduced recidivism exists?
7 Imagine that you are a state legislator who has read the *Juvenile Justice Bulletin* on juvenile drug courts included in this chapter. Would you continue to support the use of this type of specialized court in your state after reading this bulletin? Why or why not?

SUGGESTED READING

Bazemore, Gordon. 2012. "Restoration, Shame, and the Future of Restorative Practice in U.S. Juvenile Justice." Pp. 695–722 in *The Oxford Handbook of Juvenile Crime and Juvenile Justice,* edited by B. C. Feld and D. M. Bishop. New York: Oxford University Press.

Bergseth, Kathleen J. and Jeffrey A. Bouffard. 2013. "Examining the Effectiveness of a Restorative Justice Program for Various Types of Juvenile Offenders." *International Journal of Offender Therapy and Comparative Criminology* 57:1054–1075.

Butts, Jeffrey A., John K. Roman, and Jennifer Lynn-Whaley. 2012. "Varieties of Juvenile Court: Nonspecialized Courts, Teen Courts, Drug Courts, and Mental Health Courts." Pp. 606–635 in *The Oxford Handbook of Juvenile Crime and Juvenile Justice,* edited by B. C. Feld and D. M. Bishop. New York: Oxford University Press.

Jeong, Seokjin, Edmund F. McGarrell, and Natalie Kroovand Hipple. 2012. "Long-Term Impact of Family Group Conferences on Re-Offending: The Indianapolis Restorative Justice Experiment." *Journal of Experimental Criminology* 8:369–385.

Sullivan, Christopher J., Lesli Blair, Edward Latessa, and Carrie Coen Sullivan. 2014. "Juvenile Drug Courts and Recidivism: Results from a Multisite Outcome Study." *Justice Quarterly* 32:291–318.

USEFUL WEBSITES

For further information relevant to this chapter, go to the following websites.

- **OJJDP Guide for Implementing the Balanced and Restorative Justice Model:** www.ojjdp.gov/pubs/implementing/contents.html
- **OJJDP Juvenile Drug Treatment Court Guidelines**: www.ojjdp.gov/pubs/250368.pdf
- **Evidence-Based Practice Recommendations for Juvenile Drug Courts**: www.ncmhjj.com/resources/evidence-based-practice-recommendations-juvenile-drug-courts/
- **National Center for Mental Health and Juvenile Justice (NCMHJJ)**: www.ncmhjj.com/
- **NCMHJJ, Research and Program Brief**: "A Blueprint for Change: Improving the System Response to Youth with Mental Health Needs Involved with the Juvenile Justice System": www.ncmhjj.com/wp-content/uploads/2013/07/2006_A-Blueprint-for-Change.pdf
- **Youth Courts**: An Empirical Update and Analysis of Future Organizational and Research Needs: www.ncjrs.gov/pdffiles1/ojjdp/grants/222592.pdf

GLOSSARY OF KEY TERMS

Aftercare: The assistance, services, and programs that follow residential placement upon a resident's release.

Balanced and restorative justice: An approach to delinquency that attempts to actively involve victims and community members and use community resources in delinquency prevention and intervention. This approach is directed at three goals: offender accountability, competency development, and public safety.

Community treatment: Community-based sanctions and treatments that typically involve adjudicated youth. These include day reporting centers, house arrest, restitution, community service, intensive probation supervision, counseling, drug treatment, and mental health services.

Community-based residential placement: Out-of-home placement of youth in group living facilities such as group homes, foster homes, and shelter care. These facilities may occasionally be used for aftercare.

Diversion: The tendency to deal with juvenile matters informally, without formal processing and adjudication, by referring cases to special programs and agencies inside or outside the juvenile justice system.

Drug courts: Specialized courts that give juveniles an opportunity to have their charges dismissed or their dispositions modified, if they complete a course of drug treatment under court supervision. The therapeutic approach in these courts involves a comprehensive plan of drug treatment services, graduated sanctions, and incentives and rewards for progress.

Intermediate sanctions: Community-based residential placements and sanctions that, in terms of severity, exist between the more lenient response of probation and the harsher response of placement in custodial institutions.

Mental health courts: Specialized courts that are designed primarily for non-violent juvenile offenders who have been diagnosed with a serious mental illness. The therapeutic approach in these courts involves a comprehensive plan of mental health services, graduated sanctions, and incentives and rewards for progress.

Problem-solving courts: Specialized courts designed to offer treatment and rehabilitation rather than simply punishment. The most common types of problem-solving courts for juveniles are drug courts and mental health courts. Sometimes called treatment courts or therapeutic courts.

Teen courts: Specialized courts that are voluntary diversion programs, typically used for status offenders and first-time non-serious delinquent offenders. Offenders receive restorative sanctions, administered by other teenagers. Given authority through an agreement between prosecutors and police to defer formal charges for youth who agree to participate.

REFERENCES

Bazemore, Gordon. 2012. "Restoration, Shame, and the Future of Restorative Practice in U.S. Juvenile Justice." Pp. 695–722 in *The Oxford Handbook of Juvenile Crime and Juvenile Justice*, edited by B. C. Feld and D. M. Bishop. New York: Oxford University Press.

Bazemore, Gordon and Mark Umbreit. 1995. "Rethinking the Sanctioning Function in Juvenile Court: Retributive or Restorative Responses to Youth Crime." *Crime and Delinquency* 41:296–316.

Bazemore, Gordon and Mark Umbreit. 1997. *Balanced and Restorative Justice for Juveniles: A Framework for Juvenile Justice in the 21st Century*. Washington, DC: Office of Juvenile Justice and Delinquency Prevention.

Bazemore, Gordon and Mark Umbreit. 2001. "A Comparison of Four Restorative Conferencing Models." *Juvenile Justice Bulletin*. Washington, DC: Office of Juvenile Justice and Delinquency Prevention.

Bazemore, Gordon and C. Washington. 1995. "Charting the Future of the Juvenile Justice System: Reinventing Mission and Management." *Spectrum: The Journal of State Government* 68:51–66.

Belbott, Barbara A. 2003. "Restorative Justice." Pp. 322–325 in *Encyclopedia of Juvenile Justice*, edited by M. D. McShane and F. P. Williams. Thousand Oaks, CA: Sage.

Bergseth, Kathleen J. and Jeffrey A. Bouffard. 2013. "Examining the Effectiveness of a Restorative Justice Program for Various Types of Juvenile Offenders." *International Journal of Offender Therapy and Comparative Criminology* 57:1054–1075.

Blair, Lesli, Carrie Sullivan, Edward Latessa, and Christopher J. Sullivan. 2015. "Juvenile Drug Courts: A Process, Outcome, and Impact Evaluation." *Juvenile Justice Bulletin*. Washington, DC: Office of Juvenile Justice and Delinquency Prevention.

Bonta, James, Rebecca Jesseman, Tanya Rugge, and Robert Cormier. 2008. "Restorative Justice and Recidivism: Promises Made, Promises Kept?" Pp. 108–120 in *Handbook of Restorative Justice: A Global Perspective*, edited by D. Sullivan and L. Tifft. New York: Routledge.

Butts, Jeffrey A. and Janeen Buck. 2000. "Teen Courts: A Focus on Research." *Juvenile Justice Bulletin*. Washington, DC: Office of Juvenile Justice and Delinquency Prevention.

Butts, Jeffrey A., Janeen Buck, and Mark Coggeshall. 2002. *The Impact of Teen Court on Young Offenders*. Washington, DC: The Urban Institute.

Butts, Jeffrey A., John K. Roman, and Jennifer Lynn-Whaley. 2012. "Varieties of Juvenile Court: Nonspecialized Courts, Teen Courts, Drug Courts, and Mental Health Courts." Pp. 606–635 in *The Oxford Handbook of*

Juvenile Crime and Juvenile Justice, edited by B. C. Feld and D. M. Bishop. New York: Oxford University Press.

Butts, Jeffrey A. and Howard Snyder. 1991. *Restitution and Juvenile Recidivism.* Monograph. Pittsburgh, PA: National Center for Juvenile Justice.

Coalition for Juvenile Justice. 2000. "Handle with Care – Serving the Mental Health Needs of Young Offenders." *2000 Annual Report.* Washington, DC: Coalition for Juvenile Justice.

Cocozza, Joseph J. and Jennie L. Shufelt. 2006. "Juvenile Mental Health Courts: An Emerging Strategy." *Research and Program Brief.* Washington, DC: National Center for Mental Health and Juvenile Justice.

Council of State Governments. 2008. *Mental Health Courts: A Primer for Policymakers and Practitioners.* New York: Council of State Governments Justice Center, Criminal Justice/Mental Health Consensus Project.

CrimeSolutions.gov. 2013. "Program Profile: Adolescent Diversion Project (Michigan State University)." Office of Justice Programs. Retrieved March 6, 2017 (www.crimesolutions.gov/ProgramDetails.aspx?ID=332).

Daly, Kathy. 2005. "A Tale of Two Studies: Restorative Justice from a Victim's Perspective." In *New Directions in Restorative Justice: Issues, Practice, and Evaluation*, edited by E. Elliot and R. M. Gordon. Cullompton, UK: Willan Publishing.

Feld, Barry C. 2009. *Cases and Materials on Juvenile Justice Administration.* 3rd ed. St. Paul, MN: West.

Feld, Barry C. 2014. *Juvenile Justice Administration in a Nutshell.* 3rd ed. St. Paul, MN: West.

Gilmore, Amna Saddik, Nancy Rodriguez, and Vincent J. Webb. 2005. "Substance Abuse and Drug Courts: The Role of Social Bonds in Juvenile Drug Courts." *Youth Violence and Juvenile Justice* 3:287–315.

Godwin, Tracy. 2000. *National Youth Court Guidelines.* Washington, DC: Office of Juvenile Justice and Delinquency Prevention.

Haynes, Stacy Hoskins, Alison C. Cares, and R. Barry Ruback. 2014. "Juvenile Economic Sanctions: An Analysis of Their Imposition, Payment, and Effect on Recidivism." *Criminology and Public Policy* 13:31–60.

Henggeler, Scott W. 2007. "Juvenile Drug Court: Emerging Outcomes and Key Research Issues." *Opinions in Psychiatry* 20:242–246.

Henggeler, Scott W., Colleen A. Halliday-Boykins, Phillippe B. Cunningham, Jeff Randall, Steven B. Shapiro, and Jason E. Chapman. 2006. "Juvenile Drug Court: Enhancing Outcomes by Integrating Evidence-Based Treatments." *Journal of Consulting and Clinical Psychology* 74:42–54.

Heretick, Donna M. L. and Joseph A. Russell. 2013. "The Impact of Juvenile Mental Health Court on Recidivism among Youth." *OJJDP Journal of Juvenile Justice* 3:1–10.

Hills, Holly, Jennie L. Shufelt, and Joseph J. Cocozza. 2009. "Evidence-Based Practice Recommendations for Juvenile Drug Courts." National Center for Mental Health and Juvenile Justice, in collaboration with the Louisiana Supreme Court Drug Court Office; Models for Change. Retrieved January 26, 2017 (www.ncmhjj.com/resources/evidence-based-practice-recommendations-juvenile-drug-courts/).

Hipple, Natalie Kroovand, Jeff Gruenewald, and Edmund F. McGarrell. 2014. "Restorativeness, Procedural Justice, and Defiance as Predictors of Reoffending of Participants in Family Group Conferences." *Crime and Delinquency* 60:1131–1157.

Hissong, Rod. 1991. "Teen Court – Is It an Effective Alternative to Traditional Sanctions?" *Journal for Juvenile Justice and Detention Services* 6:14–23.

Jeong, Seokjin, Edmund F. McGarrell, and Natalie Kroovand Hipple. 2012. "Long-Term Impact of Family Group Conferences on Re-Offending: The Indianapolis Restorative Justice Experiment." *Journal of Experimental Criminology* 8:369–385.

Latessa, Edward J. and Paula Smith. 2015. *Corrections in the Community.* 6th ed. New York: Routledge.

McAlinden, Anne-Marie. 2011. "'Transforming Justice': Challenges for Restorative Justice in an Era of Punishment-Based Corrections." *Contemporary Justice Review* 14:383–406.

Mears, Daniel P. 2012. "The Front End of the Juvenile Court: Intake and Informal Versus Formal Processing." Pp. 573–605 in *The Oxford Handbook of Juvenile Crime and Juvenile Justice*, edited by B. C. Feld and D. M. Bishop. New York: Oxford University Press.

National Youth Court Center. 2006. *National Program Directory and National Resources 2006–2007*. Lexington, KY: National Youth Court Center. Retrieved January 29, 2017 (www.youthcourt.net/content/view/74).

North Carolina Administrative Office of the Courts. 1995. *Report on the Teen Court Programs in North Carolina*. Raleigh, NC: North Carolina Administrative Office of the Courts.

O'Brien, Sandra. 2000. *Restorative Juvenile Justice Policy Development and Implementation Assessment: A National Survey of States*. Ft. Lauderdale, FL: Florida Atlantic University, Balanced and Restorative Justice Project.

Office of Juvenile Justice and Delinquency Prevention (OJJDP). 2016. *Juvenile Drug Treatment Court Guidelines*. Washington, DC: OJJDP.

Pranis, Kay. 1998. *Guide for Implementing the Balanced and Restorative Justice Model*. Washington, DC: OJJDP.

President's Commission on Law Enforcement and Administration of Justice. 1967a. *The Challenge of Crime in a Free Society*. Washington, DC: GPO.

President's Commission on Law Enforcement and Administration of Justice. 1967b. *Task Force Report: Corrections*. Washington, DC: GPO.

President's Commission on Law Enforcement and Administration of Justice. 1967c. *Task Force Report: Juvenile Delinquency and Youth Crime*. Washington, DC: GPO.

Rodriguez, Nancy and Vincent J. Webb. 2004. "Multiple Measures of Juvenile Drug Court Effectiveness: Results from a Quasi-Experimental Design." *Crime and Delinquency* 50:292–314.

Schneider, A. 1986. "Restitution and Recidivism Rates of Juvenile Offenders: Results from Four Experimental Studies." *Criminology* 24:533–552.

Schneider, J. M. 2007. "Youth Courts: An Empirical Update and Analysis of Future Organizational and Research Needs." *Hamilton Fish Institute Reports and Essays Serial*. Washington, DC: Hamilton Fish Institute on School and Community Violence, The George Washington University.

Seyfrit, Carole L., Philip L. Reichel, and Brian L. Stutts. 1987. "Peer Juries as a Juvenile Justice Diversion Technique." *Youth and Society* 18:302–316.

Sherman, Lawrence W. and Heather Strang. 2007. *Restorative Justice: The Evidence*. London, UK: The Smith Institute.

Sherman, Lawrence W., Heather Strang, Evan Mayo-Wilson, Daniel J. Woods, and Barak Ariel. 2015. "Are Restorative Justice Conferences Effective in Reducing Repeat Offending? Findings from a Campbell Systematic Review." *Journal of Quantitative Criminology* 31:1–24.

Sickmund, Melissa, T. J. Sladky, Wei Kang, and Charles Puzzanchera. 2017. "Easy Access to the Census of Juveniles in Residential Placement." Retrieved August 26, 2017 (www.ojjdp.gov/ojstatbb/ezacjrp/).

Stickle, W. P., N. M. Connell, D. M. Wilson, and D. Gottfredson. 2008. "An Experimental Evaluation of Teen Courts." *Journal of Experimental Criminology* 4:137–163.

Sullivan, Christopher J., Lesli Blair, Edward Latessa, and Carrie Coen Sullivan. 2014. "Juvenile Drug Courts and Recidivism: Results from a Multisite Outcome Study." *Justice Quarterly* 32:291–318.

Teplin, Linda A., Karen M. Abram, Gary M. McClelland, Mina K. Dulcan, and Amy A. Mericle. 2002. "Psychiatric Disorders in Youth in Juvenile Detention." *Archives of General Psychiatry* 59:1133–1143.

Wasserman, Gail A., Larkin S. McReynolds, Susan J. Ko, Laura M. Katz, and Jennifer R. Carpenter. 2005. "Gender Differences in Psychiatric Disorders at Juvenile Probation Intake." *American Journal of Public Health* 95:131–137.

Weatherburn, Don and Megan Macadam. 2013. "A Review of Restorative Justice Responses to Offending. *Evidence Base* 1:1–20.

Zehr, Howard. 2014. *The Little Book of Restorative Justice*. New York: Good Books.

Chapter 12

RESIDENTIAL PLACEMENT AND AFTERCARE SERVICES

CHAPTER TOPICS

- **Residential placement**
- **Aftercare and reentry services**

CHAPTER LEARNING OBJECTIVES

After completing this chapter, students should be able to:

- Distinguish the various types of residential placement facilities.
- Characterize youth who are committed to residential placement by juvenile courts.
- Summarize the key findings of evaluation research on effectiveness of residential treatment programs.
- Describe the role and vital importance of aftercare and reentry services in juvenile justice.

CHAPTER CONTENTS

CASE IN POINT

RESIDENTIAL PLACEMENT IN A GROUP HOME

As a high school sophomore, Scott was the Oregon state champion wrestler at 160 pounds. The summer following his state championship, Scott appeared before the Lincoln County Youth Court for aggravated assault and underage drinking. He had been there a number of times before for a variety of delinquent offenses. Because of his continued involvement in serious law violations, Scott was adjudicated a "delinquent youth" and committed to the Oregon Youth Authority for placement at MacLaren Youth Correctional Facility. Execution of this disposition was suspended and he was instead placed at a group home for delinquent boys in a small town some distance from where he lived. Upon successful completion of the community-based group home program, Scott was to be released back to his parents with aftercare services offered through a parole officer.

The suspended sentence was a great relief to Scott because he was apprehensive about being placed in a custodial institution like MacLaren. But he was also apprehensive about a group home in a new town, where he would have to go to a new high school because the group home used public schools and did not offer an in-house or alternative school.

In late summer, Scott entered the group home and enrolled at the local high school. While the school counselor who enrolled him was supportive and encouraging, most teachers were apprehensive about how a delinquent youth from the group home might be disruptive in class, even though they knew the school liaison counselor from the group home would actively monitor classroom behavior, homework, and academic achievement. The group home also had tight security with staff monitoring, strict rules, and a rigorous daily schedule. The group home also employed an evidence-based, cognitive-behavioral treatment program. Nonetheless, students from the small town ostracized youth from the group home, and they rarely sought to get to know them, partly because group home youth rarely stayed more than a single school year and more so because local youth didn't want to associate with "bad kids"—the "group home boys."

But Scott was a state wrestling champion and he had an outgoing personality. Would he be more readily accepted at school? Not at first. Scott had to prove himself to the wrestling team, other students, and teachers, and the proof had to be demonstrated over months. Viewing his stay at the group home as a last chance to turn his life around, Scott put much effort into school and the group home treatment program, and he slowly gained acceptance and experienced success in both contexts. It also helped that Scott won another state wrestling championship, this time for a new high school.

Most state youth court acts declare that juvenile courts should:

> provide for the care, protection, and mental and physical development of children . . ., whenever possible, in a family environment, separating the child from the child's parents only when necessary for the child's welfare or in the interests of public safety. . .
>
> (Ohio Revised Code, Title XXI, Chapter 2151.01).

Accordingly, out-of-home placement for adjudicated youth is a disposition used only after family and community-based programs have been utilized to the fullest extent possible. Nonetheless, in 2014, 1 in every 4 adjudicated delinquency cases (26 percent) resulted in out-of-home placement. Contemporary juvenile corrections incorporates a wide range of residential facilities for out-of-home placement, including community-based shelter care, foster homes and group homes; specialized residential treatment centers such as drug and mental health treatment facilities; rural youth ranches and wilderness camps; and secure institutions such as detention centers, boot camps, state training schools, and juvenile prisons (Hockenberry and Puzzanchera 2017).

This chapter examines **residential placement** for youth who have been adjudicated delinquent and committed for out-of-home placement. As described in Chapter 9, a juvenile court disposition of **commitment** provides legal authorization for out-of-home placement (Feld 2014). Legal custody is transferred to a state agency such as the juvenile court or department of corrections. "Aftercare" and reentry services provided following out-of-placement will also be discussed.

RESIDENTIAL PLACEMENT

Residential placement facilities vary tremendously in terms of administrative control (private or public operation), size, physical setting, level of custody and security, length of placement, and the degree to which they pursue rehabilitation. Two data sources, described in Chapter 4, depict the use of residential placement across the United States. The Census of Juveniles in Residential Placement (CJRP) provides information on all juveniles held in residential facilities on a particular date (a census reference date), including their date of birth, race, gender, placement status, most serious offense charged, court adjudication status, date of admission, and security level. The Juvenile Residential Facility Census (JRFC) gathers data on how facilities operate and the services they provide, including level of security, capacity and crowding, facility ownership and operation, and juvenile injuries and deaths while in custody. In select years, additional information is collected regarding specific services, such as education, substance abuse treatment, and mental and physical health services provided to juveniles in placement (Sickmund and Puzzanchera 2014). A third data source is featured in the first chapter reading by Andrea Sedlak and Karla McPherson (2010): The Survey of Youth in Residential Placement (SYRP).

The CJRP provides brief descriptions of the major types of residential facilities employed in juvenile corrections and asks residential placement facilities to classify themselves. These descriptions depict the range of facilities that provide residential placement for delinquent youth (Sickmund et al. 2017, Glossary).

- **Detention center:** A short-term facility that provides temporary care in a physically restricting environment for juveniles in custody pending court disposition and, often, for juveniles who are adjudicated delinquent and awaiting disposition or placement elsewhere, or are awaiting transfer to another jurisdiction.
- **Shelter:** A short-term facility that provides temporary care similar to that of a detention center, but in a physically unrestricting environment. Includes runaway/homeless shelters and other types of shelters.
- **Reception/diagnostic center:** A short-term facility that screens persons committed by the courts and assigns them to appropriate correctional facilities.
- **Group home:** A long-term facility in which residents are allowed extensive contact with the community, such as attending school or holding a job. Includes halfway houses. . . .
- **Boot camp:** A secure facility that operates like military basic training. There is emphasis on physical activity, drills, and manual labor. Strict rules and drill instructor tactics are designed to break down youth's resistance. Length of stay is generally longer than detention but shorter than most long-term commitments.
- **Ranch/wilderness camp:** A long-term residential facility for persons whose behavior does not necessitate the strict confinement of a long-term secure facility, often allowing them greater contact with the community. Includes ranches, forestry camps, wilderness or marine programs, or farms.
- **Residential treatment center:** A facility that focuses on providing some type of individually planned treatment program for youth (substance abuse, sex offender, mental health, etc.) in conjunction with residential care. Such facilities generally require specific licensing by the state that may require that treatment provided is Medicaid-reimbursable. . . .
- **Long-term secure facility:** A specialized type of facility that provides strict confinement for its residents. Includes training schools, reformatories, and juvenile correctional facilities.

The one-day count of the CJRP in 2015 revealed that there were 31,487 youth committed to residential correctional facilities as a result of being adjudicated delinquent (Sickmund et al. 2017).[1] **Table 12.1** shows that a substantial proportion of these youth—almost 80 percent—were placed in residential facilities for delinquent offenses; 15 percent for technical violations of probation, parole, or court order; and 5 percent for status offenses. Person offenses made up 38 percent of all commitments to residential placement, with another 23 percent due to property

TABLE 12.1 Number and percentage of committed juveniles in residential placement: Offense by type of facility (Census of Juveniles in Residential Placement, 2015)

Offense type	Total count and percentage		Detention center		Shelter		Reception/ diagnostic center		Group home		Boot camp		Ranch or wilderness camp		Residential treatment center		Long-term secure	
	Count	%	Count	%	Count	%	Count	%	Count	%	Count	%	Count	%	Count	%	Count	%
Total committed	**31,487**	**100**	**3,972**	**13**	**519**	**<2**	**564**	**2**	**3,756**	**12**	**244**	**1**	**935**	**3**	**10,439**	**33**	**11,058**	**35**
Delinquent offenses	**24,935**	**79**	**2,506**	**8**	**325**	**1**	**482**	**1**	**2,953**	**9**	**122**	**<1**	**698**	**2**	**7,934**	**25**	**9,915**	**31**
Person offenses	12,015	38	1,000	3	142	<1	237	<1	1,291	4	36	<1	219	1	3,594	11	5,496	17
Property offenses	7,208	23	807	3	109	<1	146	<1	844	3	57	<1	297	1	2,263	7	2,685	9
Drug offenses	1,790	6	272	<1	34	<1	37	<1	275	1	6	<1	47	<1	666	2	453	1
Public order offenses	3,922	12	427	1	40	<1	62	<1	543	1	23	<1	135	<1	1,411	4	1,281	4
Technical violations	**4,839**	**15**	**1,373**	**4**	**40**	**<1**	**46**	**<1**	**457**	**1**	**116**	**<1**	**168**	**<1**	**1,642**	**5**	**997**	**3**
Status offenses	**1,713**	**5**	**93**	**<1**	**154**	**2**	**36**	**<1**	**346**	**1**	**6**	**<1**	**69**	**<1**	**863**	**3**	**146**	**<1**

Source: Sickmund et al. (2017).

offenses. The number of youth committed to residential placement in 2015 (31,487) was less than half the number committed eighteen years earlier, in 1997 (75,406).

Table 12.1 also reveals that residential treatment centers and long-term secure facilities held over two-thirds of the delinquent youth committed to residential placement (33 percent and 35 percent, respectively). In addition, sizeable portions of the committed youth were placed in detention centers (13 percent) and group homes (12 percent). Altogether, over 9 out of 10 of the youth committed to residential placement are in these four types of residential placement: long-term secure facilities, detention centers, residential treatment centers, and group homes. Consequently, our discussion of residential placement will focus on these four major types.

Custodial institutions

Long-term secure facilities and *detention centers* are often referred to as **custodial institutions** because of their emphasis on secure confinement. A secure correctional facility is "designed to physically restrict the movements and activities of juveniles . . . held in lawful custody" (JJDPA 2002:4).

Detention centers are primarily short-term facilities that provide a physically restrictive environment for youth pending juvenile court adjudication, disposition, or placement. Less often, detention may also be used as a disposition or sentence of short-term, secure confinement for youth who have been adjudicated delinquent in juvenile court or convicted in adult court. Chapter 8 described juvenile detention in greater detail, revealing that 40 percent of the youth in detention centers were being held before adjudication, 14 percent were awaiting disposition, 16 percent were awaiting placement, and 22 percent were in detention as a result of a juvenile court commitment or a criminal court conviction, with a sentence of detention. This last group of detained youth is represented in Table 12.1 under the "Detention Center" column, which shows that almost 13 percent of the youth committed to residential placement were placed in detention centers. Thus, a sizeable portion of the youth in residential placement as a result of a juvenile court order of commitment were placed in detention centers, the most restrictive form of secure confinement.

Over one-third (35 percent) of the youth committed to residential placement were placed in long-term secure facilities, most commonly state training schools or juvenile correctional facilities (see Table 12.1). These custodial institutions are usually large, state facilities, providing long-term secure confinement for serious juvenile offenders (Sickmund and Puzzanchera 2014). The number of commitments to long-term secure facilities has declined by 71 percent from 38,238 commitments in 1997 to 11,058 in 2015 (Sickmund et al. 2017). State training schools and juvenile correctional centers vary considerably from campus-like grounds with cottages to large, secure buildings much like adult prisons. Most custodial institutions are large facilities, housing 50 to 150 residents (Sickmund et al. 2017). Like their predecessor, the reform school (see Chapter 2), state training schools are typically divided into smaller housing units called cottages, and they typically operate on a school-day schedule. Juvenile correctional institutions are more prison-like, but still offer a school-based approach.

Although contemporary state training schools and juvenile correctional centers tend to emphasize custody over rehabilitation, they commonly offer programs for competency development, especially education and job training. Additionally, long-term secure facilities typically incorporate behavior modification programs in an effort to promote behavior change and to teach daily living skills. With increasing emphasis on the mental health issues of serious, violent

JUVENILE JUSTICE PROCESS AND PRACTICE: A SECURE MENTAL HEALTH TREATMENT CENTER

Mendota Juvenile Treatment Center (MJTC) is a 29-bed secure facility that provides comprehensive mental health treatment to serious and violent juvenile offenders. The facility is located on the grounds of the Mendota Mental Health Institute, which primarily provides forensic treatment for adult males. Youth are typically transferred to MJTC when they are unresponsive to rehabilitation services provided in traditional custodial institutions such as state training schools or juvenile correctional institutions.

> MJTC seeks to rehabilitate youth by focusing on helping participants understand interpersonal processes, acquire social skills, and improve normative social connections. MJTC is informed by social control theory and the theory of defiance and attempts to improve a participant's hostility toward authority figures and strengthen his connections to normative social behaviors, beliefs, and relationships.
>
> (MMHI 2017)

The treatment program utilizes behavior modification to encourage compliance and positive behavior, and involves academic support, group therapy for anger management, treatment directed at specific issues such as substance abuse or sexual offending, and individual therapy. Treatment may also involve psychotropic medication, which is overseen by a staff psychiatrist.

Sources: MMHI (2017); OJJDP's Model Program Guide (2012).

juvenile offenders, some states have incorporated mental health treatment into long-term secure confinement. For example, the Mendota Juvenile Treatment Center (MJTC) in Wisconsin provides comprehensive mental health treatment in a secure facility to serious, violent juvenile offenders who have been unresponsive to rehabilitation services in traditional custodial institutions. The program is described in "Juvenile court process and practice: A secure mental health treatment center." OJJDP's Model Program Guide classifies MJTC as a "promising" model program.

The second chapter reading by Michelle Inderbitzin (2007) describes a participant observation study of a cottage unit at a state training school for chronic and violent male offenders. The author's ethnographic observations of staff and resident interaction in "Blue Cottage" focuses on how cottage staff balance custody and treatment in this maximum-security institution. Inderbitzin (2007:348) observes that "cottage staff members were put in the difficult position of juggling their roles as corrections officers, counselors, and surrogate parents."

"Get tough" initiatives in juvenile corrections during the 1980s and 1990s led to the development of a third type of custodial institution: *boot camps.* Widely implemented during this period, boot camps provide relatively short-term residential placement in a military-style environment. A regimented schedule stresses discipline, physical training, work, and education. The number of committed youth placed in boot camps has diminished greatly in recent years, from 3,593 in 1997 (5 percent of the youth committed for residential placement) to 244 in 2015 (less than

1 percent of the youth committed for residential placement)—a 93 percent decline. The decline in boot camp commitments is due largely to evaluation research showing that this particular type of residential placement is ineffective at reducing recidivism (Meade and Steiner 2010).

Reception and diagnostic centers constitute a fourth type of custodial institution. These facilities are short-term residential facilities used for screening and assessing youth who have been adjudicated delinquent and committed for residential placement. Screening and assessment are used to guide subsequent residential placement or to determine security classification for placement in a state training school or juvenile correctional facility. When used for security classification, reception centers may be a unit within a long-term secure facility, rather than a separate residential facility.

Residential treatment centers

One-third (33 percent) of the youth committed to residential placement are placed in residential treatment centers (see Table 12.1). *Residential treatment centers* typically provide intensive treatment services for youth with "significant psychiatric, psychological, behavioral, or substance abuse problems who have been unsuccessful in outpatient treatment or have proved too ill or unruly to be housed in foster care, day treatment programs, and other nonsecure environments" (DSG 2011:1). Residential treatment centers are considered less restrictive and more therapeutic than custodial institutions, and they are thought to be less stigmatizing than psychiatric hospitals. These facilities usually provide a combination of substance abuse and mental health treatment, sometimes involving medication management. Despite a common orientation of offering treatment services, residential treatment centers vary extensively in the degree to which family, peer, school, and community resources are utilized. Some programs, for example, emphasize family counseling services in anticipation of restoring the family unit following residential placement. Other residential treatment centers emphasize mobilizing positive peer influences for therapeutic purposes, especially in addressing substance abuse problems.

Group homes

Group homes provide placement for 12 percent of all adjudicated offenders who were committed to residential facilities (see Table 12.1). Most group homes are relatively small (ten or fewer youth) and privately operated. They are community based, located in neighborhoods and utilizing community resources and services, including public schools. Group homes attempt to provide youth with stable, positive group-living situations in order to promote and teach acceptable behavior, social relationship skills, and academic achievement. In general, group homes attempt to promote positive experiences in an effort to instill a sense of success. Traditionally, many group homes operated using the *Teaching-Family Model*, developed by researchers at the University of Kansas in the early 1970s (McElgunn 2012; Fixen et al. 2007). A married couple, referred to as "teaching-parents," direct the treatment program and have broad and extensive responsibilities, including supervising the activities of the youth in school, in the community, in their natural homes, and in the group home; correcting problem behaviors and teaching appropriate behavior; and developing positive relationships with parents, juvenile court personnel, and social service and mental health agencies. They also develop and maintain budgets and policies to operate the home (Fixen et al. 2007).

As distinguished from residential treatment centers, group homes tend to focus more on effective social relationship skills and less on mental health issues. A contemporary example of an evidence-based treatment program used in group homes operated by Methodist Home for Children in North Carolina is the Value-Based Therapeutic Environment (VBTE). Program counselors teach youth that their behavioral choices are related to six values: respect, responsibility, spirituality, compassion, empowerment, and honesty. Applying these values to their own lives, youth gain insight into how their behaviors affect those around them, and they receive consistent feedback from program staff about how to modify these behaviors (Strom et al. 2017). The OJJDP Model Program Guide classifies the VBTE as "promising," as depicted in the "Juvenile justice process and practice" box entitled "OJJDP model program guide—evidence-based residential treatment centers," which appears later in the chapter.

Boarding schools, ranches, and wilderness camps

A wide variety of additional residential facilities provide services to youth who usually have *not* been adjudicated delinquent and committed for placement. These facilities include therapeutic boarding schools, ranches, and camps for "troubled youth," sometimes referred to as "pre-delinquents." The CJRP data presented in Table 12.1 include out-of-home placements in ranches and wilderness camps for youth who have been adjudicated and committed, but these particular residential programs are more commonly oriented to non-delinquent youth or youth that have been diverted from formal juvenile court processing.

Boarding schools, ranches, and *wilderness camps* vary tremendously in size, programming, and the degree to which they emphasize treatment. Some of these facilities are quite large, housing 50 or more youth, usually in smaller units such as a team, cottage, or house where unit staff try to provide a family-like environment. The safety and therapeutic value of these residential programs for troubled youth has been seriously questioned since the 1990s. In 2007, the Government Accounting Office (GAO) published a report on their investigation into allegations of abuse and death of youth enrolled in residential treatment programs between 1990 and 2007 (GAO 2007). The investigation took a case study approach to allegations of abuse and death, primarily at wilderness and boot camp residential programs, and found significant evidence of mismanagement in these particular cases.

The industry of residential programs for troubled youth has been largely unregulated, with accreditation standards and practices emerging at the state, federal, and professional association levels. The largest professional association in this industry is the National Association of Therapeutic Schools and Programs, a non-accrediting, membership association. The Federal Trade Commission (2008) recommends that decisions for residential placement be made with careful consideration of official licensing and accreditation for the facility's programs—educational, mental health, counseling, and rehabilitation.

Characteristics of residential placement facilities

The most recent Juvenile Residential Facility Census (JRFC) was conducted in October 2014. The census provides key characteristics of 1,852 residential facilities across the U.S. that house justice-involved youth. Some of the more distinctive characteristics are as follows (Hockenberry, Wachter, and Sladky 2016).

- **Type of facility**: Of the 1,852 total residential facilities, 776 classified themselves as residential treatment centers, 664 as detention centers, 360 as group homes, 176 as training schools, 143 as shelter facilities, 61 as reception/diagnostic centers, and 31 as ranch/wilderness camps.
- **Public or private operation**: Of the residential facilities, 1,008 (54 percent) are public and 844 (46 percent) are private. Public residential facilities house 71 percent of the justice-involved youth, while private facilities house 29 percent.
- **Size of facilities**: Most residential facilities (56 percent) are small, housing 20 or fewer youth, although more than half of the youth were held in medium-sized facilities, with 21–100 youth. More than half of all group homes and shelter facilities are small, accommodating 10 or fewer youth. Residential treatment centers also tend to be small, but somewhat larger than group homes and shelter facilities. Training schools and reception/diagnostic centers are most commonly of medium size, with 21–100 youth. However, about one-fifth (21 percent) of all training schools are large, housing over 100 youth.
- **Security features**: While security features vary extensively across the various types of residential facilities, almost 90 percent of facilities restrict residents through the use of locked doors, gates, or fences (Sickmund et al. 2017). Security features include locking residents in their sleeping rooms to confine them, secure day rooms, locked internal doors to secure specific areas, locked outside door, external gates in fences or walls that are locked to confine residents, and razor wire on fences or walls. Group homes are the least secure type of residential facility, while training schools, detention centers, and reception/diagnostic centers are the most secure. Fifty percent of training schools, 47 percent of detention centers, and 39 percent of reception/diagnostic centers report the use of external gates in fences or walls with razor wire (Hockenberry et al. 2016)
- **Screening residents for needs**: **Table 12.2** reveals that most residential placement facilities screen residents with regard to educational needs, mental health, substance abuse problems, and suicide risk. Screening of educational needs and suicide risk was particularly common across the different types of residential placement facilities, as was substance abuse screening, but to a lesser degree. However, the depth of evaluation varied considerably across the four areas of need, and across the different types of residential facilities. For example, while almost three-quarters of the residential facilities screened "all youth" for substance abuse problems, the range was from 57 percent at shelters to 86 percent at reception/diagnostic centers. Furthermore, the most common form of evaluation for substance abuse problems was through staff-administered questions, visual observation of the youth, or a self-reported checklist asking about the resident's substance use and abuse. Similarly, while almost 9 out of 10 residential facilities evaluated educational needs, a vast majority of the facilities used previous academic records, rather than more precise educational assessment tools and education specialists. Mental health was the least commonly evaluated need. Less than 60 percent of facilities evaluated all residents for mental health need. However, this form of assessment was most commonly done by an in-house mental health professional (Hockenberry et al. 2016).
- **Educational services**: Table 12.2 also shows that most residential placement facilities provide both middle school (78 percent) and high school (87 percent) educational services. Ranches or wilderness camps and detention centers reported the highest percentage of middle and high school educational services, whereas group homes reported the lowest percentage. Provisions for special education and GED preparation services were also common across residential facilities, with ranches or wilderness camps and residential treatment centers

TABLE 12.2 Screening residents for needs and treatment services offered in residential placement facilities (Juvenile Residential Facility Services Census, 2014)

	Total facilities	Detention center	Shelter	Reception/ diagnostic center	Group home	Ranch or wilderness camp	Residential treatment center	Long-term secure
SCREENING "ALL YOUTH" FOR NEEDS								
Educational	88%	89%	69%	91%	82%	97%	93%	94%
Mental health	58	38	36	67	56	43	76	69
Substance abuse problems	74	71	57	86	71	59	78	76
Suicide risk	89	98	91	96	75	76	89	96
EDUCATIONAL SERVICES								
Provide middle school	78	88	87	80	65	81	85	77
Provide high school	87	91	90	90	79	100	92	87
Special education	77	78	81	82	68	89	89	80
GED preparation	67	66	67	74	65	89	84	71
ONSITE TREATMENT SERVICES								
Mental health	85	86	69	93	80	87	86	89
Substance abuse	69	67	51	79	58	81	73	92
Sex offender	36	24	25	52	28	10	43	62
Violent offender	22	21	17	57	15	23	23	55

Sources: Hockenberry et al. (2016:9); OJJDP (2016).

reporting the highest percentage of these educational services and groups homes reporting the lowest percentage (Hockenberry et al. 2016).

- **Onsite treatment services**: Table 12.2 indicates that, with the exception of shelters, a sizable majority (85 percent) of all residential placement facilities offer onsite mental health treatment services. Substance abuse treatment is also widespread, being offered in 85 percent of all facilities. Sex offender treatment and violent offender treatment are far less common than mental health and substance abuse treatment. In recent years, attention has been directed at the development of effective gender-specific programming. "Expanding Ideas: Gender-Specific Programming" describes these developments.

EXPANDING IDEAS: GENDER-SPECIFIC PROGRAMMING

In 2004, the Office of Juvenile Justice and Delinquency Prevention assembled a panel of scholars and practitioners to study girls' delinquency in order to better understand and respond to girls' involvement in delinquency. The *Girls Study Group* reviewed the research on factors that predict or prevent delinquency. While some of these factors applied equally to both boys and girls, others were particularly influential for girls. The risk factors that were found to affect predominantly girls' delinquency included early puberty, sexual abuse or maltreatment, depression and anxiety, and romantic partners. Factors that were found to protect against girls' delinquent involvement included caring adults, school success and religiosity. A box in Chapter 13, "Expanding ideas: Gender-specific risk and protective factors," expands on these risk and protective factors for girls' delinquency (Zahn et al. 2009).

Furthermore, the profiles of boys and girls involved in juvenile justice systems are different. Compared to boys,

> Girls appear to have greater odds of co-morbid mental health conditions and are particularly associated with major depression, posttraumatic stress disorder, separation anxiety, and disruptive disorders. Girls tend to be younger when detained than boys, have been detained for less-serious crimes or status offenses, and have higher rates of family dysfunction.
>
> (DSG 2010:3, references omitted)

Given these differences, the Girls' Study Group advocated for the development of gender-specific programming in juvenile justice. Several evaluation studies, however, found that gender-specific programming provided little evidence of effectiveness (Zahn et al. 2009; Chesney-Lind, Morash, and Stevens 2008). In response to this inability to identify effective gender-specific programs, Matthews and Hubbard (2009) provide five strategies that could be used to develop effective programs for girls: (1) using comprehensive and individualized assessment; (2) building helping, therapeutic relationships; (3) using a gender-responsive, cognitive-behavioral approach; (4) promoting healthy interpersonal connections, and (5) recognizing within-girl differences that can differentiate smaller groups of girls for which particular programs may be effective (see also DSG 2010:5).

Characteristics of youth committed to residential placement

Across different types of offenses, males (86 percent), and black (41 percent) and Hispanic (21 percent) youth make up a disproportionate percentage of youth committed to residential placement (Sickmund et al. 2017). More specifically, **Table 12.3** shows that 16–17-year-old youth make up over half (54 percent) of the youth committed to residential placement, and this holds true for all offense categories. While males constitute the vast majority of youth in residential placement for delinquent offenses (88 percent), females constitute a larger percentage of youth in residential placement for status offenses (37 percent). Minority youth account for two-thirds (68 percent) of youth committed to residential placement, with black youth representing the largest share of juvenile offenders in placement (41 percent) (Hockenberry 2016:12). Racial disparity in residential placement is also evident in the disproportionate percentages of black youth committed for person offenses (43 percent) and property offenses (44 percent) and Hispanic youth committed for drug offenses (25 percent). White youth constitute almost half (48 percent) of all residential placements for status offenses.

Outcomes of residential placement and evidence-based practice

Research evaluating the effectiveness of residential placement began in the early 1970s when psychologists developed and evaluated the *Teaching-Family Model*, used widely in group homes that were becoming increasingly popular at that time (McElgunn 2012; Fixen et al. 2007). While this research provided valuable information on program implementation and effectiveness, the research designs used for evaluation do not meet present-day criteria for establishing evidence-based practice, nor is there reason to believe that the findings are generalizable to other types of residential placement (Farmer et al. 2016).

The contemporary emphasis on evidence-based practice in juvenile corrections and particularly in residential placement began with the work of Mark Lipsey in the early 1990s. He used a statistical method call "meta-analysis," which provides a "systematic synthesis of quantitative research results" (Lipsey, Wilson, and Cothern 2000:1). In an influential OJJDP bulletin, Lipsey and his colleagues (2000:1) addressed two fundamental questions: "Can intervention programs reduce recidivism rates among serious delinquents?" and "If so, what types of programs are most effective?" Two types of treatment programs were shown to be most effective: interpersonal skills programs, involving training in social skills and anger control, and teaching family homes based in the community. Positive but less consistent results were found for multiple service programs and community residential programs (primarily outside of the juvenile justice system). A number of treatment programs were found to be ineffective, including milieu therapy (in which the residential environment is structured to support treatment goals) drug abstinence programs, wilderness/challenge programs, and employment programs.

As described more fully in Chapters 2 and 13, delinquency prevention and intervention efforts are increasingly driven by evaluation research that seeks to establish whether particular strategies, methods, and programs effectively reduce the likelihood of delinquent offending. Various program registries of evidence-based practice have been developed, including the OJJDP Model Program Guide. The evidence-based residential treatment programs identified as "very effective" and "promising" by this particular registry are briefly described in the box entitled "Juvenile justice process and practice: OJJDP Model Program Guide—evidence-based residential treatment centers.

TABLE 12.3 Age, sex, and race/ethnicity of youth committed to residential placement (Census of Juveniles in Residential Placement, 2015)

	Total count	Age				Sex		Race or ethnicity					
		< 13	14–15	16–17	18–20	Male	Female	White	Black	Hispanic	American Indian	Asian	Other
Committed	**31,487**	**3%**	**23%**	**54%**	**20%**	**86%**	**14%**	**33%**	**41%**	**21%**	**2%**	**<1%**	**3%**
Delinquent offenses	**24,935**	**3**	**22**	**54**	**21**	**88**	**12**	**32**	**42**	**21**	**2**	**<1**	**3**
Person offenses	12,015	3	22	50	24	87	13	31	43	21	2	<1	3
Property offenses	7,208	3	24	56	17	89	11	30	44	20	2	<1	3
Drug offenses	1,790	2	17	64	18	84	16	45	25	25	2	<1	2
Public order offenses	3,922	4	24	51	20	92	8	34	40	21	2	<1	2
Technical violations	**4,839**	**3**	**22**	**57**	**18**	**81**	**19**	**32**	**38**	**13**	**2**	**<1**	**2**
Status offenses	**1,713**	**7**	**31**	**54**	**7**	**63**	**37**	**48**	**32**	**21**	**3**	**<1**	**4**

Source: Sickmund et al. (2017).

JUVENILE JUSTICE PROCESS AND PRACTICE: OJJDP MODEL PROGRAM GUIDE—EVIDENCE-BASED RESIDENTIAL TREATMENT CENTERS

Multidimensional treatment foster care—adolescents	**very effective**	A behavioral treatment alternative to residential placement for adolescents who have problems with chronic antisocial behavior, emotional disturbance, and delinquency. This program is rated Effective. It was associated with a significant drop in official criminal referral rates, involvement in criminal activities, and days spent in lock up among MTFC-A boys. Similarly, the program was associated with a significant reduction in delinquency and days spent in lock up among MTFC-A girls.
Methodist home for children's value-based therapeutic environment (VBTE) model	**promising**	A nonpunitive treatment model that concentrates on teaching juvenile justice–involved youth about prosocial behaviors as alternatives to antisocial behaviors. The program is rated Promising. It had significant effects on new charges and convictions for person offenses, but it did not significantly affect charges and convictions for property, drug, and public order offenses. Youths who received the treatment did spend significantly fewer total days incarcerated compared with control youths.
Residential student assistance program (RSAP)	**promising**	A substance abuse intervention program developed for high-risk adolescents living in residential facilities. The program is rated Promising. Intervention youth were significantly less likely to use alcohol and marijuana, and reported less other drug use compared to the comparison group.

Source: OJJDP Model Program Guide. Retrieved December 12, 2017 (www.ojjdp.gov/mpg/Program). Programs by topic: "Detention, Confinement, and Supervision," and "Residential Treatment Centers."

Recent evaluation research examines key dimensions of "quality of care" and their effects on "outcomes" of residential placement. Farmer and her colleagues (2017) identify four fundamental aspects of quality of care: safety, treatment, staffing, and setting. *Safety* consists of rules, structures, and discipline that are fair and not excessive; *treatment* involves a deliberate therapeutic approach that promotes positive growth and development, and enhanced psychological and social functioning; *staffing* has to do with training, supervision, turnover, continuity, and youth/staff ratios; and *setting* relates to facility cleanliness, size, and family-like atmosphere. These key program characteristics influence treatment outcomes, including decreased psychological pathology and depression, and enhanced prosocial behavior and family functioning (Boel-Studt and Tobia 2016; Bettmann and Jasperson 2009). Their research findings reveal that several program processes are associated with better outcomes of residential care: behavior modification programs that are positively focused; youths' perceptions of staff fairness and helpfulness; age/interest-appropriate activities; staff preservice training; and prohibition of physical restraint (Farmer et al. 2017; see also James, Thompson, and Ringle 2017).

AFTERCARE AND REENTRY SERVICES

Each year approximately 100,000 youth are released from out-of-home placements and are confronted with the challenge of reintegration back into the communities where they live (Barton 2006; Altschuler and Armstrong 2001). **Aftercare** programs provide reintegrative services that prepare and monitor out-of-home placed youth for reintegration back into their communities (DSG 2010; Altschuler and Armstrong 2001). The contemporary term for aftercare services is *reentry*. Traditionally, youth released from residential placement are placed on **parole**. Parole involves conditions and supervision, just like probation. Although similar, probation and parole are distinguished in relation to residential placement: probation is used before placement and parole afterwards. In many states, parole supervision is provided by officers who are both probation and parole officers.

The use of the term "aftercare" is a bit misleading because the process does not simply begin after youth are released from residential placement (DSG 2010). Ideally, the aftercare process begins shortly after adjudication and continues throughout the time that youth are in residential placement. Aftercare programs then provide services and supervision to youth as they transition back into the community (Ballentine, Morris, and Farmer 2012; Geis 2003).

Recent estimates show that as many as 75 percent of youth released from residential placement will require another out-of-home placement within a year (Tyler et al. 2017; Narendorf and McMillen 2010). Youth leaving residential placement often have a variety of co-occurring needs, including academic problems, criminal behavior, drug and alcohol dependency, mental health issues, and medical needs (Tyler et al. 2016). The importance of linked systems of care for providing effective treatment to court-involved youth with multiple service needs is discussed more fully in Chapter 14.

Important elements of aftercare

Recent research has identified the important elements of aftercare services for youth departing residential placement (Tyler et al. 2017; Tyler et al. 2016; Tyler et al. 2014). Findings from surveys administered to social service practitioners show a high level of support for the importance of aftercare. Ninety-two percent of social service practitioners gave aftercare the highest importance rating. Findings suggest that family, safety, mental health, and substance abuse supports are the most important elements of aftercare that should accompany parent training and academic support. Specific services identified include intervention for self-harm and suicidal thoughts, access to mental health services, coping with trauma, and managing medication for behavior/mental health.

These findings are consistent with prior research supporting the importance of aftercare action plans to help youth who begin to struggle during the process of reintegration back into the community (Trout and Epstein 2010). They also connect to findings from prior studies about the importance of providing continuity and consistency for youth and families at admission, during care, and after discharge from residential placement (Tyler et al. 2014). The need for aftercare programs to address mental health and substance abuse issues is also consistently cited in the prior literature (Trout et al. 2014a; Trout et al. 2014b). In his review of aftercare services, Steve Geis (2003) identifies a series of evidence-based aftercare intervention strategies, including targeting specific dynamic and criminogenic risk factors; implementing a plan that is strictly adhered to by trained personnel; requiring staff and offenders to make frequent contact; using cognitive and behavioral treatments; and targeting offenders with the highest risk of recidivism.

Financial constraints are uniformly listed as the greatest barrier to providing aftercare services. The financial costs associated with providing care to youth after release from residential placement are often too great for families to cover without financial assistance. An examination of ways in which public funding sources for assisting families of youth after reentry into the community is a critical element of a successful aftercare process. Not only do these services provide needed care for youth, they also provide connections to resources, service providers, and other families in the local community (Tyler et al. 2016; Tyler et al. 2014).

Model aftercare programs

One of the most widely implemented contemporary aftercare programs is the *intensive aftercare program* (IAP) (Altschuler, Armstrong, and MacKenzie 1999; Altschuler and Armstrong 1994, 1996). The IAP model is designed to reduce recidivism among high-risk parolees by combining intensive supervision with treatment, as a bridge between residential placement and reentry into the community. Five principles guide the structured reentry process:

1. Prepare youth for progressively increased responsibility and freedom in the community.
2. Facilitate youth–community interaction and involvement.
3. Work with the offender and targeted community support systems (e.g., schools, family) on qualities needed for constructive interaction and for the youth's successful community adjustment.
4. Develop new resources and supports where needed.
5. Monitor and test the youth and the community on their ability to deal with each other productively.

(Wiebush, McNulty, and Le 2000:2, enumerated)

IAP focuses on developing individualized parole reentry plans through careful case selection, assessment, and classification. In essence, it is a balanced and restorative approach to aftercare in that it provides intensive supervision and treatment services, balanced incentives, and graduated consequences (see Chapter 11 for further information on restorative justice). While the IAP incorporates many aftercare elements that are considered "best practices" by aftercare specialists, evaluation research has shown that the aftercare program did not significantly reduce recidivism and therefore cannot be considered a "best practice" (Wiebush et al. 2005).

A recent aftercare program that incorporates the use of mobile text technology to monitor youth with substance abuse issues upon reentry is the Educating and Supporting Inquisitive Youth in Recovery (ESCYIR) program. ESCYIR is a 12-week aftercare intervention program in Los Angeles County, California. Participants in the program receive daily text messages to their mobile phones that include personalized monitoring questions, health advice, and other relapse-related information to assist with successful reentry into the community.

Two evaluations of the initial ESCYIR program have been conducted since the program piloted in 2012. In the first evaluation, researchers compared the number of relapses after the completion of treatment for youth who were randomly assigned to participate in the ESCYIR program and for a control group of youth who received traditional aftercare services. Findings show that youth who received text messages in the ESCYIR program had significantly fewer relapses, used fewer types of substances, and took part in more 12-step meetings and other extracurricular activities than youth in the control group (Gonzales et al. 2014).

The second study was a continuation of the evaluation by Gonzales and her colleagues (2014). Data gathered 6 months and 9 months after completion of treatment showed that youth in the ESCYIR had significantly fewer relapses for the primary drug for which they were receiving treatment, were more likely to engage self-help resources, and were more confident about not relapsing than peers in the control group (Gonzales et al. 2016). The findings suggest that ESCYIR is a promising program for reducing substance abuse relapse and subsequent return to treatment. It is a low cost and convenient program incorporating an effective and widely accessible text-based format for service delivery. The OJJDP Model Programs Guide website listed below provides additional information on evidence-based aftercare programs.

Evaluation of aftercare program effectiveness

Two recent meta-analysis studies (described in Chapter 13) have examined the effectiveness of aftercare programs on juvenile recidivism. The evidence in these investigations is drawn from comprehensive searches of research databases, bibliographies of previous meta-analyses, and prior literature reviews. Government documents and reports were also included in the investigations. The studies incorporated in these meta-analyses include both male and female youth from a variety of socioeconomic and ethnic backgrounds.

Both meta-analyses incorporate findings from studies published between 1990 and 2009. The findings show mixed results. In the first meta-analysis, James and her colleagues (2013) reviewed 22 studies that included individuals who ranged in age from 10 to 25 years. The researchers found a small, but significant impact of aftercare on recidivism. In the most recent meta-analysis, Weaver and Campbell (2015) reviewed a total of 30 studies. They also found evidence of an association between receiving aftercare services and reduced recidivism. The impact, however, was not statistically significant.

Even with these two meta-analyses, rigorous examinations of aftercare interventions are limited. Results from more rigorous investigations are needed to make evidence-based decisions about whether or not access to aftercare services systematically impacts recidivism and returns to juvenile justice systems (Tyler et al. 2017).

SUMMARY AND CONCLUSIONS

The latest publication of Juvenile *Court Statistics* reports that 1 in every 4 adjudicated delinquency cases (26 percent) results in out-of-home placement (Hockenberry and Puzzanchera 2017). As a result, contemporary juvenile corrections relies on a wide range of residential facilities for out-of-home placement, including community-based shelter care, foster homes and group homes; specialized residential treatment centers such as drug and mental health treatment facilities; rural youth ranches and wilderness camps; and secure institutions such as detention centers, boot camps, state training schools, and juvenile prisons. In particular, residential treatment centers and long-term secure facilities hold over two-thirds of the delinquent youth committed to residential placement. A substantial portion (80 percent) of the adjudicated youth committed to residential correctional facilities were involved in delinquent offenses, as compared to placement due to technical violations of probation, parole, or a court order (14 percent), or status offenses (5 percent). Delinquent offenders committed to residential placement are disproportionately male and minority youth (Sickmund et al. 2017).

Evaluation research shows that two types of residential treatment are most effective at reducing recidivism: interpersonal skills programs (involving training in social skills and anger control) and teaching family homes (community-based, family-style group homes). Strong but less consistent results were evident for multiple service programs and community residential programs (Lipsey et al. 2000). In addition, several program elements are associated with better outcomes of residential care: positively focused behavior modification practices; youths' perceptions of staff fairness and helpfulness; age- and interest-appropriate activities; preservice staff training; and prohibition of physical restraint (Farmer et al. 2017).

Aftercare and reentry services are essential for successful reintegration of youth after residential placement. Comprehensive aftercare plans begin shortly after adjudication and continue throughout the time that youth are in residential placement. Aftercare programs then provide services and supervision to youth as they transition back into the community. Research shows that successful aftercare services address ongoing mental health and substance abuse issues and provide support to youth and families (Tyler et al. 2017).

READING 12.1

"CONDITIONS OF CONFINEMENT: FINDINGS FROM THE SURVEY OF YOUTH IN RESIDENTIAL PLACEMENT."

Andrea J. Sedlak and Karla S. McPherson. 2010. Washington, DC: Office of Juvenile Justice and Delinquency Prevention.

The Survey of Youth in Residential Placement (SYRP) is the third component in the Office of Juvenile Justice and Delinquency Prevention's set of surveys providing updated statistics on youth in custody in the juvenile justice system. It joins the Census of Juveniles in Residential Placement and the Juvenile Residential Facility Census, which are biennial mail surveys of residential facility administrators conducted in alternating years. SYRP is a unique addition, gathering information directly from youth through anonymous interviews. This bulletin series reports on the first national SYRP, covering its development and design and providing detailed information on the youth's characteristics, backgrounds, and expectations; the conditions of their confinement; their needs and the services they received; and their experiences of victimization in placement.

This bulletin presents findings from the Survey of Youth in Residential Placement about the conditions of confinement for youth in a range of different facilities and programs. Results focus on the structural and operational characteristics of these environments and indicate how youth offenders are distributed across various programs and facilities of different size and complexity.

SYRP research provides answers to a number of questions about the characteristics and experiences of youth in custody, including:

- How are youth grouped in living units and programs?
- Which youth are placed together?
- What activities are available in each facility?
- How accessible are social, emotional, and legal supports?
- What is the quality of the youth-staff relationships?
- How clear are the facility's rules? How clear is the facility's commitment to justice and due process?
- What methods of control and discipline do staff use?

SYRP's findings are based on interviews with a nationally representative sample of 7,073 youth in custody during spring 2003, using audio computer-assisted self interview methodology. Results examined youth offenders' self-reports about conditions in their facility and living unit and in their placement program (i.e., detention, corrections, camp, community-based, or residential treatment). Facility administrators provided additional information by verifying or updating their answers on the most recent Juvenile Residential Facility Census (JRFC) survey, by completing the Census of Juveniles in Residential Placement (CJRP) survey (to give administrative data on the sampled youth), and by providing information about facility structure and operations. Using these data, SYRP describes the custody environment at three different levels: the facility's organization and security, the program characteristics, and the specific conditions in a youth's living unit. . . .

Facility and program characteristics

Facilities that hold juvenile offenders vary widely in size, organizational complexity, and layout. Many are single-function facilities, providing only one type of placement program (e.g., a boot camp or a detention center), while others are more complex. The more complex facilities offer various programs in separate groups of living units. These facilities can occupy multiple buildings on a single campus or have housing units at multiple locations. Facilities and their programs also differ in size, security, the types of offenders they hold, and the average length of stay for their residents. Most youth (93 percent) live in facilities that provide a single primary program. The remaining 7 percent of youth are in operationally complex facilities that provide different programs for different groups of residents. The majority (58 percent) of youth in custody are in facilities that house 100 or fewer youth, and most youth (65 percent) are in public facilities. . . .

SYRP classifies residential programs into five general categories by grouping together living units that have the same primary function. . . . Most youth are in either corrections programs (32 percent) or detention programs (26 percent). The remainder of youth are in community-based programs (18 percent), residential treatment programs (14 percent), or camp programs (10 percent). Overall, 26 percent of youth in residential placement are in programs that have one or more specialized subunits. Specialized subunits include reception/diagnostic units, targeted treatment units (e.g., for sex offenders, violent offenders, drug treatment), and variations of the primary program (e.g., a camp program that includes both a boot camp and a forestry camp, or a community-based program that incorporates a shelter, group homes, and independent living subunits). Most youth in camps (59 percent) reside in a program with specialized subunits. . . .

Security

Facilities are typically classified as "staff secure" or "secure" according to whether locks confine youth in their living units during the day. More than one-third (35 percent) of youth are placed in programs that do not use locks, but almost half (46 percent) are confined by three or more locks during the day. Youth in detention are held most securely, with 83 percent confined by three or more locks during the day. Locks secure youth in buildings (64 percent), in areas within buildings (e.g., corridors, wings, floors) (58 percent), and within external fences or walls (59 percent). Detention and corrections programs use locks for most residents. In addition, 53 percent of youth offenders live in facilities that lock residents into their sleeping rooms under certain conditions.

Types of offenders in different programs

Youth placed in custody have committed a variety of offenses. Including current offenses and past convictions, SYRP shows that all types of offenders are comparably represented in each kind of program.

Some significant, small differences occur across programs. Youth with the most serious career offenses (i.e., murder, rape, or kidnapping) are most prevalent (14 percent or more) in corrections, residential treatment, and community-based programs. Camp programs have the highest percentage of property offenders (30 percent), and detention and camp programs have the highest percentage of drug and public order offenders (11 percent). Female offenders constitute 15 percent of the total youth offender population and are most prevalent in detention (19 percent) and residential treatment programs (29 percent).

Youth placement with other youth

SYRP examined how youth are grouped together in programs and living units and revealed certain imbalances. Placing youth who are different ages or who have dissimilar personal histories or offense records together in programs and living units may not provide these youth with optimal environments for growth and change.

Age

Age differences mark important differences in youth's maturity and experience. These disparities are magnified during childhood and adolescence. Most experts agree that housing young juvenile offenders with older youth is a practice that should be avoided. Separation of adults and juveniles in custody is also one of the core requirements of the Juvenile Justice and Delinquency Prevention (JJDP) Act.

SYRP does not include juveniles who are held in adult prisons and jails, but the findings do reveal considerable age mix in juvenile facilities as well as substantial mixing of juveniles with young adults. Mixing juveniles with young adults poses challenges for implementing developmentally appropriate programming and for safety (Committee on Adolescence, 2001; Steinberg, Chung, and Little, 2004). One-fifth of offenders in juvenile facilities are in living units with others who are 3 or more years older than they are. Moreover, 43 percent of juveniles in placement are housed in living units with young adults. Such units with older offenders tend to have more serious offenders. Juveniles (younger than 18 years old) who are in units with young adults are more than twice as likely as juveniles not living in units with young adults (42 percent versus 20 percent) to be living with youth whose most serious career offense is murder.

Sex

Thirty-six percent of youth in custody live in facilities that house both males and females. Similarly, 35 percent of programs are coed. However, coed placement in living units is uncommon (6 percent). Coed placement predominates in detention programs—86 percent of youth are in a coed program and 17 percent are in a coed living unit.

Race/ethnic group

The core requirements of the JJDP Act mandate that states must work to improve their response to disproportionate minority contact. Despite the requirement, SYRP findings on differences in custody rates (Sedlak and Bruce, forthcoming) reconfirm the numerous earlier studies that have demonstrated that minority youth are still disproportionately represented in the placement population (Hsia, Bridges, and McHale, 2004; Pope, Lovell, and Hsia, 2002).

In addition, SYRP reveals that different races and ethnicities tend to be held in different types of programs—more Black/ African American youth in placement are in corrections programs compared with other races/ethnicities (42 percent versus 31 percent or less of other races/ ethnicities), more Hispanic youth in placement are in camp programs (17 percent versus 7 percent), and more White youth are in residential treatment programs (20 percent versus 9 percent). These findings confirm that the patterns previously observed only in local samples (Cohen, 1991; Drakeford and Garfinkel, 2000; Kaplan and Busner, 1992; Richissin, 1999) also hold at the national level for the total population of youth in custody. SYRP data can provide a resource for examining factors that might explain the observed distributions, such as youth's backgrounds, offense histories, and service needs.

Placement with other victims

Results indicate that youth with experiences of physical or sexual abuse tend to be clustered together in the same living units. These patterns could stem from deliberate programming decisions, whereby youth with similar abuse histories are housed together for specialized treatment. Clustering of abuse victims is particularly strong for females. This may reflect the joint influence of two dynamics: females have fewer placement alternatives and they are more likely to have experienced prior physical or sexual abuse.

One-fourth (25 percent) of youth in custody report past experiences (prior to placement) of frequent or injurious physical abuse and nearly one-eighth (12 percent) acknowledge prior sexual abuse. Among youth with physical abuse histories, 77 percent of males and 95 percent of females are in living units where more than 20 percent of residents claim they were physically abused. A similar pattern is evident for prior sexual abuse: victims of both sexes are more likely to be living with higher percentages of other victims (52 percent of male victims and 84 percent of female victims).

Coplacement of offender types

SYRP shows that most youth (63 percent) live in units where the majority of other residents are person offenders. Nearly one-fifth of the less serious career offenders (status offenders, technical parole violators, and youth who report no offense) are placed in living units with youth who have killed someone, and about one-fourth reside with felony sex offenders. . . . Extensive mixing of youth who have dramatically different offense histories raises concern about the safety of the less serious offenders. From another perspective, placing youth together who have committed the same specific kind of offense (e.g., robbery, felony sex, felony drug) can have a reinforcing effect, increasing the probability that a juvenile will recidivate on the shared crime (Bayer, Pintoff, and Pozen, 2004).

These facts may seem somewhat surprising in light of the assumption that more serious offenders are remanded to the more secure placement contexts. However, the career offense categories in this survey depend on self-reports of both prior convictions and current offenses. Current placements will substantially depend on current offenses and assessed risks (Austin, Johnson, and Weitzer, 2005) as well as youth's needs and the types of placements available at the time.

Unlike serious career offenders for robbery or drug offenders, sex offenders are more typically separated. SYRP indicates that youth who are in custody for a current rape offense are in living units where the majority of residents have rape offense histories (55 percent on average), whereas youth who are in custody for current offenses other than rape are in units where just 6 percent of residents (on average) are felony sex offenders. This type of clustering is dictated to a considerable extent by treatment programs geared toward specific types of offenders. In fact, nearly three-fourths (74 percent) of youth in custody for a current rape offense are in specialized living units for sex offenders.

Placement with nonoffenders

Some facilities house youth who are in custody because the juvenile court wants to protect them (i.e., they have been neglected or abused), they do not have a parent or guardian, or their families have voluntarily placed them in a private facility for specific services, such as mental health or substance abuse treatment. SYRP surveys only offender youth, but administrative data on their facilities also indicate whether they are housed with nonoffender youth. Twelve percent of youth in residential placement reside in facilities that also house nonoffenders. Ten percent participate in programs with nonoffenders, and 8 percent reside in primary living units with nonoffenders.

Physical and program environment

The physical features of a facility and the programs it provides define day-to-day reality for youth in custody. SYRP asks youth about their sleeping arrangements, the reasons for any difficulty sleeping, the cleanliness of the environment, the quality of the food and of the recreation and educational programs, and the amount of time they spend watching television.

Sleeping arrangements

Slightly more than one-third (36 percent) of youth in custody sleep in a private room, so most youth share their room with one or more other residents. About 17 percent stay in a room with 10 or more other residents. Sleeping arrangements vary with security level—more youth who are locked in during the day have private sleeping rooms (42 percent) compared with youth who are not locked in during the day (23 percent). Sleeping arrangements also vary with type of program. For instance, 60 percent of youth in detention programs have single rooms, whereas 55 percent of youth in camp programs share their rooms with 10 or more other youth.

Difficulty sleeping

Important changes in sleep patterns occur during adolescence, shifting to later circadian cycles (Carskadon, Vieri, and Acebo, 1993). At the same time, traditional schedules (e.g., the early start of the school day) do not accommodate these new daily cycles, so most teens suffer from chronic sleep deprivation (Carpenter, 2001; Carskadon et al., 1998; Carskadon, 2005). Adolescents' sleep problems have been the focus of increased attention in recent years, with some policymakers recommending that schools shift their start times. Researchers have explored the implications of juveniles' sleep deprivation, documenting its association with poorer grades (National Sleep Foundation, 2006), depression (Graham, 2000), behavior problems (Stein et al., 2001), and increased suicide risk (Liu, 2004).

SYRP finds that youth in custody report more sleep problems compared with high school-aged youth in the general population. About one-third (34 percent) of youth in custody say they "often" or "always" have a problem falling asleep at night, whereas only 11 percent of 9th to 12th graders in the general population say they have difficulty falling asleep "every night" or "almost every night." Just 28 percent of youth in custody say they have "no problem" falling asleep, compared with almost half (48 percent) of 9th to 12th graders who "rarely" or "never" have that problem (National Sleep Foundation, 2006). Females tend to have more trouble falling asleep then males. More females report that they have trouble sleeping "often" (23 percent vs. 16 percent) or "always" (20 percent vs. 16 percent), whereas more males say they have no problem falling asleep (30 percent vs. 18 percent).

Youth's view of facilities and amenities

SYRP asks youth to describe their facility by choosing characteristics from a list of positive and negative qualities. More than half of youth in custody have polarized views on these items. One-fourth of youth (25 percent) select no positive feature to describe their facility, while just slightly more (29 percent) identify no negative feature. . . .

Television

Youth also indicated that they watched an average of 2.9 hours of television on a typical weekday. These numbers are comparable to those in the general American population, where youth watch an average of 2.5 hours of television a day (Woodard and Gridina, 2000). Youth in community-based programs spend the most time watching television (averaging 3.5 hours per day). The number of hours youth say they watch television is unrelated to whether they think their facility has a good recreation program.

Safety

Several questions focus on issues related to youth's safety in their facilities, including whether they know what to do in case of fire or how to get help if they are threatened, whether they ever left their facility without permission, and whether they are afraid of being attacked while living there.

Most youth in custody (78 percent) say they know what to do in case of fire in their facility. Only 5 percent report having left their facility without permission. More than one-third of youth (38 percent) say they fear attack by someone, which includes 25 percent who fear attack by another resident, 22 percent who are afraid that a staff member will physically attack them, and just 15 percent who fear attack by someone coming into the facility from the outside. Ninety percent of youth report that they know how to find help if they are threatened or assaulted. . . .

More females than males say they fear being attacked (44 percent versus 36 percent). More girls express fear of attack from another resident and from someone outside the facility.

Access to support

SYRP asks youth about their access to different types of support, including their families, emotional support from facility staff, and legal representation.

Family contact

The vast majority of youth in custody (92 percent) said that since arriving at their facility, they had some contact with their families, either through phone calls or visits. Nearly 9 in 10 youth talked with their family on the telephone, and more than two-thirds had an in-person visit.

The percentage of youth in contact with family varies by program type. While most youth have spoken on the telephone with their families, fewer youth in detention (80 percent) and camps (74 percent) have done so compared with those in other programs (93 percent). Fewer youth in corrections (61 percent) and camp programs (63 percent) report in-person visits with their families. Fewer youth in camps (80 percent) have any family contact compared with youth in other programs (camps are commonly in remote locations). Frequency of family contact also depends on the program. Youth in corrections and camp programs are nearly twice as likely to have a low rate of family contact. Thirty-nine percent of corrections and camp youth have family contact less than once a week, compared with 20 percent of youth in other programs.

One-third (33 percent) of youth who have no in-person visits indicate that this is due to time constraints (facility visiting hours are inconvenient) or distance (their family lives too far away). One-fifth of those who have no phone calls or no visits say that their families have resource constraints (e.g., a phone call would be long distance, a visit would cost too much, or the family does not have transportation). About one in seven (14 percent) youth without contact claim that the lack of contact exists because their facility does not allow it. Relatively few youth without contact say it is because they do not want to talk or visit with their family (7 percent) or because their family does not want to talk or visit with them (6 percent).

The majority of all youth in custody (59 percent) say that it would take their families 1 hour or longer to travel to visit them. For more than one-fourth of youth (28 percent), their families would have to travel 3 hours or longer to see them.

Emotional support from facility staff

Eighty-four percent of youth in custody know how to find a staff member to talk to if they are upset. Youth in residential treatment programs are most likely to know how to find this support (93 percent) and those in camps are least likely (77 percent).

Legal counsel

Improving access to legal counsel has been a policy concern (Hsia and Beyer, 2000; Puritz and Scali, 1998), but SYRP shows that youth's access to legal support is infrequent. Only a minority of youth in custody report that they have a lawyer (42 percent), have requested contact with a lawyer (20 percent), or requested and received access to a lawyer (13 percent).

Youth in detention facilities are most likely to have a lawyer (50 percent) and to request contact (28 percent). More females (49 percent) have lawyers than males (41 percent).

Facility climate

SYRP asks questions about relationships between youth and facility staff, gang memberships, and whether youth were offered contraband.

Youth–staff relations

Youth distrust of facility staff and conflict with them can undermine program efforts to alter delinquent career paths and elevate discipline, control, and safety issues. Overall, youth in custody are lukewarm in their ratings of staff. Based on consensus within living units, 43 percent of youth are living in units with relatively poor youth-staff relations. Youth in unlocked units are more than twice as likely to live in units with good youth-staff relations (26 percent versus 12 percent). Those in locked units are almost twice as likely to live where youth-staff relations are poor (53 percent versus 28 percent).

In selecting specific characteristics to describe staff, about one-half of youth (49 percent) feel staff are friendly and 47 percent describe staff as helpful. More than one-third say that staff genuinely seem to care about them (38 percent), are fun to be with (38 percent), and act as good role models (34 percent). In contrast, 40 percent of youth say staff are hard to get along with, 38 percent say staff are disrespectful, and 29 percent describe staff as mean. Youth in community-based and residential treatment programs have the most positive perceptions of staff.

Gangs

The presence of gangs in a facility can exacerbate conflicts and disruptions and complicate facility operations. Nearly one-third of the custody population professes some gang affiliation—a level of gang involvement consistent with rates among high-risk youth (Thornberry, 1998). A majority of youth in custody (60 percent) report that there are gangs in their facilities.

On average, youth in residential placement are in living units where 19 percent of residents are members of gangs in the facility. Most youth (64 percent) are living in units where one-fifth or fewer of the residents are gang members, less than one-third (30 percent) are in living units where between one-fifth and one-half of youth are gang members, and 6 percent are living in units with a majority of gang members.

The presence of gangs can affect the custody environment for all youth present. SYRP reveals that the presence of gangs in a facility is significantly related to the percentage of youth who say they have been offered contraband (24 percent versus 8 percent) and to the percentage of youth who are in living units characterized by poor youth-staff relations (51 percent versus 30 percent). Certain problematic conditions tend to cluster in custody environments. When problems escalate, facilities sometimes engage in last-resort control methods. For instance, when there are gangs in a facility, significantly more youth are in living units where one or more residents say that staff sprayed them with pepper spray (38 percent versus 18 percent).

Contraband

One indicator of disregard for rules involves whether youth can easily obtain prohibited items such as alcohol, drugs, and weapons. Sixteen percent of youth in custody say they have been offered such contraband since they arrived at their facility. Youth most frequently report they have been offered marijuana (12 percent) and other illegal drugs (10 percent). Primarily, youth say other residents offered the contraband (12 percent), rarely implicating staff (6 percent) or someone outside the facility (4 percent).

More residents in community-based programs report offers of contraband (26 percent). These offers are often likely to come from other residents (16 percent) or from outside the facility (13 percent). Additionally, males report being offered contraband twice as often as females (18 percent versus 9 percent).

Rules and justice

SYRP asks youth whether they understand the rules at their facility, know how to file a complaint, receive fair and reasonable treatment, have been placed in solitary confinement, or have experienced other methods of control.

Clarity and consistency of rules

Youth should be given copies of the facility's rules and should learn and follow them. Seventy-five percent of youth say they received a copy of the facility's rules when they arrived, and 90 percent believe they understand the rules. The majority of youth (68 percent) feel that facility rules are applied equally to all residents.

Access to a grievance process

Youth who wish to file a grievance about staff should have access to an adequate grievance process that is readily available, easy to use, and impartial (Roush, 1996). However, the findings reveal that one-third of youth in custody (33 percent) have some type of problem with the grievance process; either they do not know how to file a complaint (19 percent) or are concerned about retribution if they do so (20 percent).

Fair and reasonable treatment

Best practice fosters juvenile accountability through principles of balanced and restorative justice (Beyer, 2003), but many youth in custody do not perceive fairness or justice in their facility environments. One-half of youth in custody report that staff apply punishment without cause, and more than one-third claim that staff use unnecessary force. About one-third (34 percent) think that staff treat residents fairly, and less than one-third (30 percent) say punishments are fair. These views are strongly correlated with whether youth live in units that are locked during the daytime. Youth in locked units have more negative views of fair and reasonable treatment in all categories compared with youth in units that are staff secure in the daytime.

Discipline

Common disciplinary measures in a facility involve group punishment, which 49 percent of youth have experienced, and removing special privileges (such as television), which 43 percent have experienced. Twenty-six percent of youth in custody have been confined to their rooms, 24 percent were placed in solitary confinement, 23 percent were given extra chores or work, and 20 percent were moved to another location in the facility. . . .

Solitary confinement

Maintaining discipline and control is critical but challenging, considering that the large majority of youth in custody have previous involvement with the juvenile justice system and most (57 percent) have a history of person offenses (Sedlak and Bruce, forthcoming). Nevertheless, some may find SYRP findings on the prevalence of solitary confinement both surprising and problematic.

More than one-third of youth in custody (35 percent) report being isolated—locked up alone or confined to their room with no contact with other residents. The vast majority of youth who were isolated (87 percent) say this was for longer than 2 hours and more than one-half (55 percent) say it was for longer than 24 hours. Best practice guidelines recommend that solitary confinement exceed 24 hours only if the facility director explicitly approves and that youth who are held in solitary confinement for longer than 2 hours see a counselor (Roush, 1996). SYRP has no information on procedures for approving lengthy times in solitary confinement, but the interview does ask youth whether they talked to a counselor about their feelings or emotions. The majority (52 percent) of those isolated longer than 2 hours indicate that they have not talked to a counselor since coming to the facility.

Control and use of restraints

Best practice dictates that restraints should be used only for youth who are out of control (Roush, 1996). More than one-fourth of youth in custody (28 percent) say that facility staff used some method of physical restraint on them—whether handcuffs, wristlets, a security belt, chains, or a restraint chair. Although the questions mean to ask youth about their experiences at the facility, some youth may report being handcuffed or otherwise restrained during transportation to or from the facility, which would be common for youth in more secure placement environments. This possibility should qualify interpretations of their reports regarding these restraints.

However, this qualification would not apply to youth's answers about experiences with a restraint chair or pepper spray. The Office of Juvenile Justice and Delinquency Prevention's Performance-Based Standards program dictates using a restraint chair or pepper spray only as a last resort following appropriate protocol (Council of Juvenile Correctional Administrators, 2007). SYRP indicates that these practices, although infrequent, are used—4 percent of youth say that facility staff placed them into a restraint chair and 7 percent report that staff used pepper spray on them.

Apart from these personal experiences, however, SYRP reveals that these practices indirectly affect a much larger segment of youth in custody. Thirty percent of youth in custody live in units where one or more residents experienced the use of pepper spray and more than one in five youth in custody (21 percent) are in living units where staff used pepper spray on more than 10 percent of residents. Twenty-nine percent of youth live with one or more residents who received time in a restraint chair, and 16 percent are in units where more than 10 percent of residents report that staff placed them into a restraint chair.

Conclusion

Although youth's self-reports have limitations, the findings reported here convey internally consistent patterns. Moreover, they portray confinement conditions and raise concerns that have been longstanding issues in juvenile justice (Guarino-Ghezzi and Loughran, 2006), indicating areas where future policies and practices can measurably improve the custody environments. The findings in this bulletin highlight several areas where confinement conditions do not meet best practice guidelines and where improvement efforts could begin, including the following:

- **Prioritize developmentally appropriate programming and document its implementation and success.** SYRP revealed a considerable age mix within living units. One in five young offenders are housed in living units with offenders who are 3 or more years older than they are, and more than two in five juveniles are housed with young adults who are 18 years or older. These arrangements present barriers to creating developmentally appropriate programming and undermine youth safety. Moreover, no systematic information exists regarding facilities' efforts to implement programs, interventions, or activities designed for specific age ranges or on the success of facilities' efforts.
- **Explore factors that might explain disproportionate confinement of minorities.** SYRP confirms that minority youth continue to be disproportionately represented in the population of youth in custody. The study also reveals that, even within the placement population, different races and ethnicities tend to be assigned to different types of programs. Exploring the information that SYRP collects on youth's backgrounds, offense histories, and service needs may help explain these different placement rates and patterns.
- **Improve understanding of the risks and benefits of mixing different types of offenders versus grouping youth with similar offense histories.** SYRP indicates that a number of less serious offender youth are housed in living units with some of the most serious offenders. It also shows that youth who are grouped together in living units often share common backgrounds, such as membership in a gang or a history of physical or sexual abuse (possibly because the facility contains a specialized treatment program).

  Mixing youth with different offense histories and backgrounds raises safety concerns, but grouping youth who have committed similar offenses may enhance deviancy training (i.e., bonding with other group members around deviance and reinforcing the delinquent behavior). Although studies have demonstrated the negative effects of aggregating offenders, they have also shown that these negative effects do not occur in all circumstances or for all youth (Dodge, Dishion, and Lansford, 2006). Further research should specifically identify how and when deviance training occurs. Such research can help guide recommendations for grouping offender youth to minimize safety issues and avoid deviance training.
- **Ensure that youth know the facility fire safety procedures.** Best practice guidelines dictate that facilities post a clear evacuation plan and hold regular, documented fire drills (Roush,

1996). SYRP results show that more than one in five youth in custody (22 percent) do not know what to do if there is a fire in their facility.

- **Select placement locations that facilitate family contact.** Although family interventions can be more effective with delinquent youth than individual treatment (Perkins-Dock, 2001; Quinn, 2004; Quinn and VanDyke, 2004), involving families is often difficult while the youth is incarcerated. SYRP shows that most youth have contact with their families but indicates that more than one-fourth of youth are placed a considerable distance from their families—requiring the family to travel 3 hours or longer to visit the youth. When assigning youth to placements, the court should consider how the facility's location could affect their family's involvement in an intervention program.
- **Increase access to legal counsel, particularly before adjudication.** The *Juvenile Justice Standards* (Institute for Judicial Administration–American Bar Association, 1980), developed as a result of the 1974 Juvenile Justice and Delinquency Prevention Act (P.L. 93–415), require legal representation for juveniles from the outset of the court process. However, SYRP indicates that less than one-half of all youth in custody (42 percent) have a lawyer and just one-half (50 percent) of those held in detention facilities have a lawyer.
- **Improve the quality of youth-staff relations, require fair treatment, and establish an effective grievance process.** Positive relationships with older, prosocial role models can counteract the negative effects of placing delinquent youth with other youth offenders (Dodge, Dishion, and Lansford, 2006). Unfortunately, poor relations with staff characterize life in custody for more than two in five youth (43 percent). A majority of youth in custody say punishments are unfair, while more than one-third feel that staff use unnecessary force. Similarly, one-third of youth have difficulties with their facility's grievance process—either they do not know how to file a complaint or they fear retribution if they do so. Standards for staff conduct should require that staff treat youth fairly and issue fair and reasonable punishments commensurate with the infraction. The facility should maintain a grievance process that is clear and universally understood and that includes protections for youth who submit complaints.
- **Implement best practice guidelines in the use of solitary confinement and of last-resort control methods of pepper spray and restraint chairs.** SYRP indicates that, contrary to best practice guidelines (Roush, 1996), the majority of youth who were isolated longer than 2 hours did not see a counselor. When youth are held in solitary confinement for longer than 24 hours, facility staff should document the specific circumstances and verify that the facility director explicitly approved the period of confinement in that particular case. Staff should also establish timely records detailing the situations where staff use pepper spray or a restraint chair, verifying that the events warranted these measures and that staff followed appropriate protocol.

[References and notes omitted.]

The Survey of Youth in Residential Placement (SYRP) webpage provides much additional information on research design and methods, as well as a series of bulletins and full reports: https://syrp.org/default.asp.

READING 12.2

"A LOOK FROM THE INSIDE: BALANCING CUSTODY AND TREATMENT IN A JUVENILE MAXIMUM-SECURITY FACILITY."

Michelle Inderbitzin. 2007. *International Journal of Offender Therapy and Comparative Criminology* 51:348–362.

Michelle Inderbitzin describes her participant observation study of a cottage unit at a state training school for chronic and violent male offenders. The author's ethnographic observations of staff and resident interaction in "Blue Cottage" focuses on how cottage staff balance custody and treatment in this maximum-security state training school.

. . . Today, as juvenile justice agencies prioritize public safety and the accountability of adolescent offenders, many state training schools function essentially as juvenile prisons (Bortner & Williams, 1997), and staff members must learn how to balance their duties as both correctional officers and counselors to young offenders. Although training schools share many characteristics of adult prisons, there are also key differences. In general, juvenile facilities offer more focus on rehabilitation, a kinder tone, and a more supportive environment (Hubner, 2005; O'Neil, 1988). Many young offenders are able to build meaningful relationships with members of the cottage staff; they come to rely on them in their daily interactions, and they turn to them for practical advice.

The staff members in this study work in a living unit of one state's end-of-the-line training school for adolescent males. In this role, they are charged with attempting to change some of the most violent and criminal youth in the state into more-conforming adults and more-responsible citizens. They are given few tools to enable this transformation, just a maximum-security setting, an innocuous mission statement, and their own good intentions. Failure rates are high, expectations are low, and they come to work each shift prepared to mete out punishment, counseling, and advice to the boys in their care, serving as multifaceted guardians to young men who have had few conforming role models in their lives. While the war on crime continues outside the institution's locked buildings and razor-wire fences, staff members wage their own daily battles within the confines of the cottage, trying to control, change, and save one young man at a time.

Members of the cottage staff are the pivotal figures (Bortner & Williams, 1997; Feld, 1977) in the institution's handling of juvenile offenders. Unlike earlier times when training schools employed "cottage parents" and separate professional counselors and social workers (Polsky, 1962/1987), the nature of the job now requires the staff to simultaneously take on many roles—counselor, corrections officer, coach, and surrogate parent. This is particularly challenging because the position of the cottage staff dictates oscillation between custody and treatment goals, creating conflict and ambiguous role definitions for individuals trying to balance both (Carroll, 1974). This was similar to what Singer (1996) found in his research in a juvenile institution:

> An explicit goal of the facility that might not be documented easily is that of maintaining the institution's custodial orientation. Security is an important concern and at times conflicts with the institution's treatment-oriented mandate. . . . The task of administrators and staff simultaneously to treat and to punish juvenile offenders is an extremely difficult one.
>
> (pp. 177, 184)

. . .

Method

. . . The data for this ethnographic study were gathered through participant observation in the state's end-of-the-line training school during a period of approximately 15 months. This training school housed chronic and violent male offenders ranging in age from 15 to 20. They were adjudicated delinquent for offenses including drug dealing, multiple property crimes, serious violent and/or sexual assaults, armed robbery, and homicide. Most of them had done time in other juvenile institutions, and this was often their last stop before facing adult consequences for their crimes. As such, it seemed to be an important piece of the juvenile justice experience. If they were going to become conforming citizens, this would be a final opportunity before the contaminating exposure of adult prisons.

Although able to spend time with administrators and security staff and visit other living units, the author took a cue from earlier studies in which the cottage is viewed as central to the institutional experience (Bortner & Williams, 1997; Feld, 1977; O'Neil, 1988; Polsky, 1962/1987) and made the "Blue" cottage the particular focus of this study. The Blue cottage held between 18 and 26 violent offenders; on a typical day, there would be 20 boys in Blue and 2 to 3 staff members working per shift. During the time in the field, both the boys in the cottage and the staff members were observed, as the author listened to them, asked questions, and paid attention to the interactions that took place within and between the two groups.

Over the course of the study, the average visit was once a week, usually for 7 or 8 hours at a time. Visits were generally centered around weekends or evenings when the boys would be back from school or their jobs around the campus and would be spending time in the cottage. On different occasions, the author attended staff meetings, dinners, recreation, and even the high school graduation of 2 of the boys in the cottage. Most frequently, however, time was spent simply hanging out in the cottage, watching, listening, and interacting with the residents and staff. Initially, as Polsky (1962/1987) had found several decades earlier, "The explanation of the observer's role was not credible to them. . . . No one really understood the role of a sociologist" (p. 120). In fact, nearly everyone at the institution assumed the author was trying to get a job as a staff member. With no other terminology available to them, employees often referred to the author as an intern. To combat this, it was expressed as clearly as possible that the purpose was research, and the author initially made an effort to stay at a distance from the staff.

Over time, the author carved out a unique spot in the cottage and was able to move among groups, the residents, and the staff and have candid dialogue with all. In ongoing conversations, staff members told about the boys who passed through Blue, their backgrounds, and their issues, and they provided insights into their own lives and goals. In listening carefully to them, it was possible to conduct the kind of study "which seeks to discover hypotheses as well as to test them" (Becker, 1970, p. 26). Staff members shared what they felt was most important and most challenging about their jobs. They explicitly and implicitly discussed the problems inherent in juvenile institutions where workers are expected to be both keepers and counselors. They shared stories of their successes, their disappointments, and their frustration.

Extensive field notes were taken, detailing observations, experiences, and impressions after each period in the cottage. As opposed to surveys and interviews, which offer a perspective at one point in time, fieldwork offered the opportunity for many interactions with the same staff members and residents. Because of this, it was possible to follow up on issues they raised, to watch as changes were implemented, and to get perspectives and opinions over time. Analytic induction was then used to contextualize their experiences as they fit into the larger issues of crime, punishment, and the treatment of juvenile offenders. . . .

Pathways into the Blue cottage

At any given time, approximately 8 staff members were assigned to the Blue cottage; 2 or 3 staff members worked a typical shift. There was a short chain of command in each cottage. The program manager was in charge of the cottage and generally worked the day shift on Mondays to Fridays; his assistant, the cottage supervisor, generally worked evenings and weekends and handled many of the day-to-day details of life in the living unit. Of the staff members assigned to the cottage, the majority were male. One or two female staff members were assigned to the cottage during this study, but it was a very male-dominated setting, and the females often worked graveyard shifts when the residents were locked down for the night or during the day when most of the boys were away from the cottage. One female staff member went on maternity leave at the beginning of this study and never returned to Blue. Many shifts were staffed exclusively by males; by contrast, there was never a shift staffed solely with females.

Staff members ranged in age from their late 20s to their late 50s. Although located in a rural area with a predominately White population, the Blue cottage did have 4 African American males working in it at different points in the research, making it the most racially diverse living unit in the institution. Although gender, race, and age undoubtedly had an impact on the relationships between staff members and residents, they never seemed to be a primary issue. The boys tended to respond more to the individual's attitude and treatment of them rather than to physical characteristics. Staff members took on different roles in the cottage, some acting as big brothers, coaches, and friends, whereas others acted as surrogate parents or grandparents. In all cases, the staff members had the power to punish and reward the adolescent inmates for their behavior and their attitudes (Kivett & Warren, 2002). . . .

Characteristics of the Blue cottage

Working at the Blue cottage presented special challenges. Although the institution's lock-up unit (IMU—the Intensive Management Unit) housed the boys with the most serious behavior problems, it generally had them only temporarily. The IMU operated with the residents locked in their rooms for the vast majority of the time. The staff and the inmates communicated through intercoms in the cells, and the staff controlled the floor (unlocking doors one at a time to let boys go to the bathroom or get a pencil or an aspirin) from a glass-enclosed booth. There were several locked doors between the staff and the residents. Staff members had very little physical contact with the residents, and the boys were never free to interact with each other. The Blue cottage, by contrast, housed the institution's problem children who were allowed to be in a less restrictive atmosphere. Although there were locked rooms within the locked cottage, the Blue staff and residents had a great deal of interaction and movement within the cottage. With such relative freedom, there was greater potential for assaults where both staff and residents could be injured.

The Blue cottage had the reputation for housing the worst offenders at the toughest juvenile institution in the state. To some extent, members of the Blue staff members blamed the administration for making them into the hardest cottage by sending them the meanest, most volatile, and most difficult offenders. At the beginning of this study, Blue was a cottage for violent offenders, and virtually all of the young men who were assigned to Blue were minority boys who claimed affiliation with various gangs. Blue was also sometimes assigned boys who had intimidated and/or assaulted staff members at other institutions; it was, in effect, a dumping ground for the school's—and indeed the state's—intractable children.

Across the campus, the Blue cottage seemed to be viewed as more lax than the other cottages, the staff thought to be less stringent in enforcing the rules and instilling discipline. It elicited many comments when other employees heard that a researcher was spending time in the Blue cottage, including the observation that Blue was an "interesting choice" and that one would see just about anything one wanted to see in Blue. Even some members of the Blue staff, well aware of the cottage's unsavory reputation, were initially concerned about being transferred to work in it, but most enjoyed the cottage once they were assigned to it and had settled into the routine. In a private conversation, Kyle, the Blue supervisor, explained that Blue was often sent some of the institution's "problem staff" in addition to the problem children, but he said that he and the program manager made an extra effort to work with those employees, and they usually improved and worked out fine.

Roles and responsibilities of the cottage staff

Ultimately, the cottage staff did much of the work of the institution; their job covered a wide range of duties, responsibilities, and risks. Working in a maximum-security facility, the staff members were first and foremost in charge of custody. It was their job to keep control of their young inmates; they were in charge of the safety of the boys in the cottage, the safety of their fellow staff members, and the safety of the community. In addition to custody issues, cottage staff members were in charge of the treatment and rehabilitation of their residents. As Singer (1996) explains, balancing custody and treatment presents many challenges: "The task of administrators and staff simultaneously to treat and punish juvenile offenders is an extremely difficult one . . . there is a bottom line concern with maintaining discipline, order, and security" (p. 184).

In their treatment role, each member of the cottage staff served as a counselor for a caseload of boys, monitoring the boys' progress and helping them to plan for their futures. As part of their responsibilities, cottage staff members also ran all of the programming and treatment groups that took place in the cottage. Finally, staff members spent time and effort trying to deal with potential problems informally, working to prevent fights, negotiating with the boys and offering them choices whenever possible, and developing cooperative relationships with inmate leaders (Bartollas, Miller, & Dinitz, 1976; Feld, 1977; Inderbitzin, 2005; Polsky, 1962/1987).

The history of violence and victimization in training schools has been well documented (Bartollas et al., 1976; Feld, 1977; Wooden, 2000). It particularly makes sense that a cottage of violent offenders would be a place where trouble might erupt. In trying to control their volatile population, part of the Blue staff's responsibility was to constantly watch for grudges and flaring tempers to try to prevent injuries from occurring as a result of fights between the residents. The staff did not carry weapons of any sort, just two-way radios and one pair of handcuffs for the cottage. When they needed backup to deal with the residents, they radioed security, and security staff members rushed over to provide the extra manpower. But the Blue cottage staff did their best to watch over and control their residents without resorting to calling security. They understood that they needed to maintain order, but they also knew that they could not always use official or formal means (Feld, 1977; Sykes, 1958). Because incidents that required outside help were relatively rare and generally quite serious in nature, Kyle said that when security did get a call from the Blue cottage, they "came running," expecting the worst.

In the daily life of the cottage, at least one staff member was "on the floor at all times," and he or she kept careful watch over the residents in the common areas of the cottage. The staff kept track of how many of the boys were in the communal shower and bathroom at any given time; they also kept a close eye on the laundry room, which was one of the closed spaces in which the residents could temporarily get out of sight to settle a score. The staff at the Blue cottage attempted to prevent fights rather than react to them, trying to de-escalate potential problems before they blew up into a full-fledged assault (Kivett & Warren, 2002). To do so, staff members would frequently call individual boys into the office to talk with them before they could get themselves into trouble. Some of the boys were known to be "loose cannons" likely to explode at any time. Yet even under the careful watch of the staff, the residents found ways to fight each other; if the staff became aware of a fight in progress, they would generally jump in to break it up, risking injury to themselves.

As one example, during this research, 5 members of one gang assaulted another resident in Blue. They were all in one room fighting, and at least one of the boys had a weapon—a broken piece of a fan with a long piece of wire sticking out of it. Brandon, a physically strong staff member, rushed into the fracas to break it up, and he pulled 2 of the boys into headlocks, one in each arm. While in that position, one of the boys managed to bite him. In the end, the 5 residents who were determined to have initiated the assault were sent to the IMU and the rest of the cottage was put on lockdown—with all of the boys locked in their rooms—until things settled down. Kyle explained later that the graveyard worker who was also on duty was "not much of a presence," so Brandon was basically on his own in breaking up the fight.

In attempting to keep the cottage as safe as possible, some staff members took a proactive role in removing potential weapons and contraband from the residents' possession. Luke claimed that he knew all of the hiding spots in the residents' rooms. He would occasionally go through the rooms when the boys were out of the cottage and find all sorts of forbidden items: tobacco, pornography, drags, shanks (sharp objects used for stabbing), razor blades, tattoo machines, and items stolen from other areas in the institution. Luke said that when he found contraband, he would quietly remove it from the rooms. It was a less confrontational method of dealing with the contraband, and "no one had to lose face." He explained that he would not discipline the residents for the contraband "unless they were stupid enough to ask what happened to their stuff." In that case, he said, he would give them disciplinary checks, not for the contraband, but for "being idiots." If the contraband were just in the room, he said, it could belong to either roommate, but if one were dumb enough to claim it, he deserved the "idiot check." Luke said that he felt like he was helping to make the cottage a safer place to live and work by quietly removing the weapons and contraband.

After any incident in the cottage, such as an assault or a theft, the staff would have to hold an investigation and fill out the institution's paperwork. Investigations often consisted of calling the residents into the office one by one to question them. The "inmate code" would hold in most cases as the residents did not want to be known as snitches, and they refused to rat on each other, saying, "I didn't see nothing, *you know.*"

In one such incident, an assault took place while the boys were at recreation at the institution's gym. Ron, who was the nearest staff witness, was forced to work late to write the report detailing the incident.

In the meantime, the boy who committed the assault was sent directly to the IMU, and the Blue cottage was locked down while other Blue staff members conducted an investigation. Although most were unwilling to share any information, residents were individually called out to be asked if they saw anything, and one eventually "spilled his guts," giving his interpretation of who started the fight and what it was over. Kyle explained that investigating an incident was like solving a puzzle: You had to figure out which part of each person's story was true and then put all of the pieces together.

When kids were sent to the IMU, the Blue staff's job was not yet done. Any time a resident was going to spend some time at IMU, his counselor had to go through his room and pack away all of his clothes and personal possessions because he would only be allowed to wear state-issued coveralls in the IMU. The counselors carefully documented each item in an effort to prevent later claims of stolen or missing property. Some also used the opportunity to sift through the boys' possessions and confiscate their pornography and other forbidden items.

Supervising the residents encompassed other challenges as well. Structural constraints, such as being overcrowded and understaffed, made the job all the more difficult for the cottage staff. Although the cottage had 16 rooms, the population sometimes climbed as high as 26 residents. With so many young men in a confined space, the staff grew somewhat resigned to fights, with several commenting, "What do they expect when they send us so many kids?" The more residents in the cottage, the harder it was to maintain control.

Using similar logic, the fewer staff members who were there to provide supervision, the harder it was to keep control. On some nights, the Blue cottage only had 2 staff members working, whereas on other nights there would be as many as 4. Luke talked about how grateful he was when the cottage was allocated another full-time staff member because, with the addition, he said that there should always be at least 3 staff working. He said that on the nights when there were only 2 staff members working, the job became really stressful because anything could happen. With more staff members on a shift, it took off some of the pressure.

Besides providing supervision, the cottage staff's main role was to try to provide counseling and mentoring to their residents. Staff members, in their roles as counselors, generally had 4 or 5 boys on their caseloads whom they were supposed to meet with individually once a week and coordinate their paperwork and their rehabilitation programming. Using language handed down from the early days of reform schools and cottage parents (Platt, 1977; Polsky, 1962/1987), they often referred to the boys on their caseload as their sons, saying things such as "That's my son" or telling others that "Your son needs you." Along with meeting with the boys on their caseloads individually, staff members were also expected to run treatment groups within the cottage once a week, with subjects ranging from life skills to anger management to cultural diversity.

Treatment groups were intended to be relatively small for the residents to fully participate and get individual attention, but they ranged in size from 5 or 6 boys all the way up to 12 or 13. Because all of the residents had to take part in treatment groups to facilitate their rehabilitation, the staff had to figure out what to do with boys who had just entered the cottage and joined in during the middle of a group's curriculum. In a Blue staff meeting, one of the counselors expressed his frustration that boys kept being added to his group when they were sent to Blue, and he asked his coworkers how they managed to catch the new kids up to speed. Luke told him that he just marked down what week the new boys entered his group and that he planned to have them stay through the end of the sessions, attending the next version of the group when it started over until they had eventually covered all of the material. Although far from ideal, it was the best solution Luke could come up with to balance his responsibilities and fulfil his treatment duties.

During this study, the institution changed its treatment program from focusing on the residents' risk factors to focusing on teaching the boys new "competencies." As such, the goals and the plans for the treatment groups had to be revised. Staff members from across the campus were selected to organize the new competency groups and to put together notebooks, complete with lesson plans for each week, for each of the cottages. The "life skills" notebook was full of random pages pulled from the Internet and from other workbooks. Luke, who was in charge of the life skills group for the Blue cottage, learned that the residents had already completed some of the same assignments and workbooks in the institution's school. It was pointless for them to be doing the exact same work twice, he said, but he only found out about the repetitive assignments when the boys told him that they had already done the lesson that he had assigned.

Even more telling about the quality of the care that went into planning the group, half of the notebooks' pages were so badly photocopied that it was literally impossible to read large segments of them, rendering them all but worthless. Similar to earlier findings in juvenile correctional facilities, there was little evidence of any particular treatment model in operation, and Blue staff members clearly felt a lack of institutional support in developing treatment goals and practice (Kelly, 1992, p. 126).

In actually leading the life skills group, Luke tried to make it as practical as possible for the young men. For example, in one of his sessions, he talked to them about sex and responsibility and birth control. He made every effort to give them practical advice and answers. He explained later that one boy showed his inexperience and youth in the group by asking if a girl could get pregnant if she "gave him head" and then swallowed. The older and more experienced residents laughed at him, but Luke cut them off, saying that if the boy really did not know, it was a good question. In trying to act as a positive male role model, Luke made it clear that he was willing to answer all of their sincere questions honestly.

Discussion and conclusions

This study has offered a look inside one state's maximum-security juvenile correctional facility, with particular focus on the often conflicting roles and responsibilities of cottage staff members. Although others have documented the gap between juvenile justice rhetoric and the reality of daily life in institutions (Feld, 1999; Kelly, 1992), it seems that even the rhetoric has changed as there is currently more focus on the young offenders' accountability and punishment rather than on rehabilitation. Within the training school in this study, custody was a key concern, but individual staff members also attempted to model good behavior and to resocialize the young men in their care into more thoughtful, less violent adults.

Feld (1999) has suggested that "juvenile institutions constitute particular hybrids that combine elements of both mental health and *parens patriae* ideology with the ordinary criminal justice system. But, if 'treatment' differs from 'punishment,' then juvenile corrections must do something more than simply confine criminals" (p. 275). What treatment that did take place in the maximum-security training school in this study, and the effort put into it, was left largely to the discretion of the cottage staff members.

Because they work in a job defined by contradictory goals, cottage staff members perform a balancing act as they go about their daily responsibilities, taking on many different roles (Carroll, 1974; Hemnens & Stohr, 2000) and wearing many hats. Staff members set the tone of the cottage and influence virtually every aspect of the residents' lives; in real ways, they define the institutional experience of the young offenders assigned to their care (O'Neil, 1988).

In attempting to apply Feld's (1977) correctional typology to the Blue cottage, it became clear that at least some members of the staff would characterize Blue as treatment oriented, with much of their attention directed toward trying to help rehabilitate their residents. More objectively, the Blue cottage best fit Feld's individual custody model, where staff members see themselves "serving a dual function" of detaining dangerous young people but also attempting to provide them with personal discipline and skills that would give them a better chance to succeed on their return to the community (Feld, 1977, p. 53).

Although custody was arguably the primary goal of the staff members, as Singer (1996) found in his study, "it would be too easy to dismiss the treatment-oriented mission ... the staff that worked in the institution was largely motivated to provide for the best interests of its resident population" (p. 183). Members of the Blue cottage staff clearly spent more time thinking about their treatment groups and strategies for helping the boys on their caseloads than they did thinking about custody issues, which became largely automatic for them after working in the institution for a period.

In dealing with the stress arising from the dual responsibilities of treatment and custody, staff members would have undoubtedly benefited from supportive psychological counseling, but none was provided by or available in the institution. Without such support, staff members adopted their best common-sense approach in dealing with their everyday duties in the cottage and tried to encourage and look out for each other whenever possible.

One of the key differences between the Blue cottage and the cottages that Feld (1977) describes is that in Feld's study, staff members were allowed to form their own cottage teams, so "there was substantial interpersonal and ideological compatibility within units" (p. 302). In the institution in this study, staff members were assigned to the Blue cottage, and some were clearly treatment-oriented people workers, others were more custody-oriented rule enforcers (Farkas, 2000), and others fell somewhere in between.

In general, the Blue cottage seemed to be more treatment oriented than most of the cottages in the institution. In visits to other cottages, the staff members seemed less flexible, and more emphasis seemed to be placed on obedience and conformity. The leaders of the Blue cottage staff—the program manager and the cottage supervisor—were treatment oriented, and their perspectives influenced the tone of the cottage. But it was sometimes an uneasy compromise, and much of the friction that did arise stemmed from these competing ideologies. Just as individual staff members had to learn to balance their roles and responsibilities, the cottage too hung in the balance between treatment and custody.

While balancing all of the responsibilities inherent in their pivotal role in a juvenile correctional facility, individual staff members made a valiant attempt to establish meaningful relationships with the boys in their care, hoping to influence them to choose a more positive, conforming path. Although they had little training and few resources, they attempted, in their own words, to send their "sons" back into the community "less violent and more educated," more mature, and better able to make considered decisions. In doing so, they embraced the message articulated by Ayers (1997) in his study of children in juvenile court: "You can change your life. With considerable effort, that message might come to inform all our work with children, even children in crisis, even tough kids in terrible places. You can change your life" (p. 200).

[References omitted.]

CRITICAL-THINKING QUESTIONS

1 What were some of the challenges faced by Scott in his out-of-home placement at a group home, as described in the "Case in point" at the beginning of the chapter?
2 Describe how residential placement facilities vary in terms of operational control, size, physical setting, level of custody and security, length of placement, and degree of emphasis on rehabilitation.
3 Provide a brief characterization of delinquent youth who are committed to residential placement.
4 Summarize the key findings of evaluation research on effectiveness of residential treatment programs.
5 What are aftercare services and why are they important for successful transition from residential placement to reentry within the community?
6 Describe the physical and program environment of residential facilities discussed in the reading by Sedlak and McPherson (2010).
7 As depicted in the reading by Inderbitzin (2007), identify and briefly describe the dual roles of staff members in the Blue Cottage at the state training school she studied.

SUGGESTED READING

Bettmann, Joanna E. and Rachael A. Jasperson. 2009. "Adolescents in Residential and Inpatient Treatment: A Review of the Outcome Literature." *Child and Youth Care Forum* 38:161–183.

Hockenberry, Sarah. 2016. "Juveniles in Residential Placement, 2013." National Report Series Bulletin. Washington DC: Office of Juvenile Justice and Delinquency Prevention.

Hockenberry, Sarah, Andrew Wachter, and Anthony Sladky. 2016. "Juvenile Residential Facility Census, 2014." National Report Series Bulletin. Washington DC: Office of Juvenile Justice and Delinquency Prevention.

Mendel, Richard A. 2010. "The Missouri Model: Reinventing the Practice of Rehabilitating Youthful Offenders: Summary Report." Baltimore, Maryland: The Annie E. Casey Foundation. Retrieved December 12, 2017 (http://missouriapproach.org/publications/2010/12/8/annie-e-casey-foundation-report.html).

USEFUL WEBSITES

For further information relevant to this chapter, go to the following websites.

- **Center for Technology and Behavioral Health**: www.c4tbh.org/program-review/educating-supporting-inquisitive-youth-in-recovery-esqyir/
- **Easy Access to the Census of Juveniles in Residential Placement**: www.ojjdp.gov/ojstatbb/ezacjrp/
- **The Missouri Approach**: A Revolutionary Approach to Juvenile Justice Reform: http://missouriapproach.org/
- **OJJDP's Model Program Guide**: www.ojjdp.gov/mpg/Topic. Link to "Residential Treatment Centers," "Secure Confinement," and "Reentry/Aftercare."

GLOSSARY OF KEY TERMS

Aftercare: Reentry and reintegrative services that prepare and monitor out-of-home placed youth for reintegration back into their communities.

Commitment: The juvenile court's legal authorization for out-of-home placement for a youth who has been adjudicated a delinquent youth. Commitment involves a transfer of legal custody to a state agency such as the juvenile court or department of corrections.

Custodial institutions: Closed and secure residential facilities for delinquent youth, providing long-term custody.

Parole: The conditions and supervision provided after release from residential placement, intended to smooth the transition back into the community.

Residential placement: Court-authorized or court-ordered out-of-home placement of a youth in a group living facility.

NOTE

1 In 2015, 48,043 youth were placed in residential facilities; one-third (15,816) were "detained" and two-thirds (331,487) were "committed" (Sickmund et al. 2017). Our discussion focuses on youth committed to residential placement as a result of juvenile court adjudication. Traditionally, detained youth are said to be "held" in custody, while committed youth are said to be "placed" in a residential facility.

REFERENCES

Altschuler, David M. and Troy L. Armstrong. 1994. "Intensive Aftercare for High Risk Juveniles: A Community Care Model—Summary." Washington, DC: Office of Juvenile Justice and Delinquency Prevention.

Altschuler, David M. and Troy L. Armstrong. 1996. "Aftercare Not Afterthought: Testing the IAP Model." *Juvenile Justice* 3:15–22.

Altschuler, David M. and Troy L. Armstrong. 2001. "Reintegrating High-Risk Juvenile Offenders into Communities: Experiences and Prospects." *Corrections Management Quarterly* 5:79–95.

Altschuler, David M., Troy L. Armstrong, and Doris Layton MacKenzie. 1999. "Reintegration, Supervised Release and Intensive Aftercare." *Juvenile Justice Bulletin*. Washington, DC: Office of Juvenile Justice and Delinquency Prevention.

Ballentine, Kess L., Ashley N. Morris, and Elizabeth M. Z. Farmer. 2012. "Following Youth after Out-of-Home Placement: Navigating a Data Collection Obstacle Course." *Residential Treatment for Children and Youth* 29:32–47.

Barton, William H. 2006. "Incorporating the Strengths Perspective into Intensive Juvenile Aftercare." *Western Criminology Review* 7:48–61.

Bettmann, Joanna E. and Rachael A. Jasperson. 2009. "Adolescents in Residential and Inpatient Treatment: A Review of the Outcome Literature." *Child and Youth Care Forum* 38:161–183.

Boel-Studt, Shamra M. and Lauren Tobia. 2016. "A Review of Trends, Research, and Recommendations for Strengthening the Evidence-Base and Quality of Residential Group Care." *Residential Treatment for Children and Youth* 33:13–35.

Chesney-Lind, Meda, Merry Morash, and Tia Stevens. 2008. "Girls' Troubles, Girls' Delinquency, and Gender Responsive Programming: A Review." *The Australian and New Zealand Journal of Criminology* 41:162–189.

Development Services Group, Inc. (DSG). 2010. "Gender-Specific Programming." Literature Review. Washington, DC: Office of Juvenile Justice and Delinquency Prevention. Retrieved November 4, 2017 (www.ojjdp.gov/mpg/litreviews/Gender-Specific_Programming.pdf).

Development Services Group, Inc. (DSG). 2011. "Residential Treatment Centers." Literature Review. Washington, DC: Office of Juvenile Justice and Delinquency Prevention. Retrieved April 27, 2017 (www.ojjdp.gov/mpg/litreviews/Residential_Treatment_Centers.pdf).

Farmer, Elizabeth M. Z., Maureen L. Murray, Kess Ballentine, Mary Elizabeth Rauktis, and Barbara J. Burns. 2017. "Would We Know It If We Saw It? Assessing Quality of Care in Group Homes for Youth." *Journal of Emotional and Behavioral Disorders* 25:28–36.

Farmer, Elizabeth M. Z., H. Ryan Wagner, Barbara J. Burns, and Maureen Murray. 2016. "Who Goes Where? Exploring Factors Related to Placement among Group Homes." *Journal of Emotional and Behavioral Disorders* 24:54–63.

Federal Trade Commission. 2008. "Residential Treatment Programs for Teens." Retrieved June 13, 2017 (www.consumer.ftc.gov/articles/0185-residential-treatment-programs-teens).

Fixen, Dean L., Karen A. Blasé, Gary D. Timbers, and Montrose M. Wolf. 2007. "In Search of Program Implementation: 792 Replications of the Teaching-Family Model." *The Behavior Analyst Today* 8:96–110.

Feld, Barry C. 2014. *Juvenile Justice Administration in a Nutshell*. St. Paul, MN: West.

Geis, Steve V. 2003. "Aftercare Services." Juvenile Justice Bulletin. Washington, DC: Office of Juvenile Justice and Delinquency Prevention.

Gonzales, Rachel, Mayra Hernandez, Debra A. Murphy, and Alfonso Ang. 2016. "Youth Recovery Outcomes at 6 and 9 Months Following Participation in a Mobile Texting Recovery Support Aftercare Pilot Program." *American Journal of Addictions* 25:62–68.

Gonzales, Rachel, Alfonso Ang, Debra A. Murphy, Deborah C. Silk, and M. Douglas Anglin. 2014. "Substance Abuse Recovery Outcomes among a Cohort of Youth Participating in a Mobile-Based Texting Aftercare Pilot Program." *Journal of Substance Abuse Treatment* 47:20–26.

Government Accounting Officer (GAO). 2007. "Residential Treatment Programs: Concerns Regarding Abuse and Death in Certain Programs for Troubled Youth." Washington, DC: GAO. Retrieved June 13, 2017 (www.gao.gov/new.items/d08146t.pdf).

Hockenberry, Sarah. 2016. "Juveniles in Residential Placement, 2013." National Report Series Bulletin. Washington, DC: Office of Juvenile Justice and Delinquency Prevention.

Hockenberry, Sarah and Charles Puzzanchera. 2017. *Juvenile Court Statistics 2014*. Pittsburgh, PA: National Center for Juvenile Justice.

Hockenberry, Sarah, Andrew Wachter, and Anthony Sladky. 2016. "Juvenile Residential Facility Census, 2014." National Report Series Bulletin. Washington, DC: Office of Juvenile Justice and Delinquency Prevention.

Inderbitzin, Michelle. 2007. "A Look from the Inside: Balancing Custody and Treatment in a Juvenile Maximum-Security Facility." *International Journal of Offender Therapy and Comparative Criminology* 51:348–362.

James, Chrissy, Geert Jan M. Stams, Jessica J. Asscher, Anne Katrien De Roo, and Peter H. van der Laan. 2013. "Aftercare Programs for Reducing Recidivism Among Juvenile and Young Adult Offenders: A Meta-Analytic Review." *Clinical Psychology Review* 33:263–274.

James, Sigrid, Ronald W. Thompson, and Jay L. Ringle. 2017. "The Implementation of Evidence-Based Practices in Residential Care: Outcomes, Processes, and Barriers." *Journal of Emotional and Behavioral Disorders* 25:4–18.

Juvenile Justice and Delinquency Prevention Act of 2002 (JJDPA 2002). Retrieved June 7, 2017 (www.ojjdp.gov/about/jjdpa2002titlev.pdf).

Lipsey, Mark W., David B. Wilson, and Lynn Cothern. 2000. "Effective Intervention for Serious Juvenile Offenders." *Juvenile Justice Bulletin*. Washington, DC: Office of Juvenile Justice and Delinquency Prevention.

Matthews, Betsy and Dana Jones Hubbard. 2009. "Moving Ahead: Five Essential Elements for Working Effectively with Girls." *Journal of Criminal Justice* 36:494–502.

McElgunn, Peggy. 2012. "Teaching-Family Model: Insuring Quality Practice." *Reclaiming Children and Youth* 21:40–42.

Meade, Benjamin and Benjamin Steiner. 2010. "The Total Effects of Boot Camps That House Juveniles: A Systematic Review of the Evidence." *Journal of Criminal Justice* 38:841–853.

Mendota Mental Health Institute (MMHI). 2017. "MMHI – Mendota Juvenile Treatment Center." Madison, WI: MMHI. Retrieved May 6, 2017 (www.dhs.wisconsin.gov/mendota/programs/juv-treatment.htm).

Narendorf, Sarah C. and J. Curtis McMillen. 2010. "Substance Use and Substance Use Disorders as Foster Youth Transition to Adulthood." *Children and Youth Services Review* 32:113–119.

Office of Juvenile Justice and Delinquency Prevention (OJJDP). 2016. *Statistical Briefing Book*. Washington, DC: Office of Juvenile Justice and Delinquency Prevention. Retrieved July 3, 2017 (www.ojjdp.gov/ojstatbb/corrections/qa08502.asp?qaDate=2014).

OJJDP's Model Program Guide. 2012. "Program Profile: Mendota Juvenile Treatment Center." Washington, DC: Office of Juvenile Justice and Delinquency Prevention. Retrieved June 6, 2017 (www.crimesolutions.gov/ProgramDetails.aspx?ID=274).

Ohio Revised Code, Title XXI Courts—Probate—Juvenile, Chapter 2151: Juvenile Court. Retrieved April 25, 2017 (http://codes.ohio.gov/orc/2151).

Sedlak, Andrea J. and Karla S. McPherson. 2010. "Conditions of Confinement: Findings from the Survey of Youth in Residential Placement." Washington, DC: Office of Juvenile Justice and Delinquency Prevention.

Sickmund, Melissa and Charles Puzzanchera (eds.). 2014. *Juvenile Offenders and Victims: 2014 National Report*. Pittsburgh, PA: National Center for Juvenile Justice.

Sickmund, Melissa, T. J. Sladky, Wei Kang, and Charles Puzzanchera. 2017. "Easy Access to the Census of Juveniles in Residential Placement." Retrieved August 26, 2017 (www.ojjdp.gov/ojstatbb/ezacjrp/).

Strom, Kevin J., Joshua A. Hendrix, Debbie Dawes, and Stephanie Hawkins Anderson. 2017. "An Outcome Evaluation of the Methodist Home for Children's Value-Based Therapeutic Environment Model." *Journal of Experimental Criminology* 13:101–124.

Trout, Alexandra L. and Michael H. Epstein. 2010. "Developing Aftercare, Phase I: Consumer Feedback." *Children and Youth Services Review* 32:445–451.

Trout, Alexandra. L., Steven Hoffman, Michael H. Epstein, and Ronald W. Thompson. 2014a. "Family, Teacher and Parent Perceptions of Youth Needs and Preparedness for Transition upon Youth Discharge from Residential Care." *Journal of Social Work* 14:594–604.

Trout, Alexandra. L., Steven Hoffman, Jacqueline Huscroft-D'Angelo, Michael J. Epstein, Kristin Duppong Hurley, and Amy L. Stevens. 2014b. "Youth and Parent Perceptions of Aftercare Supports at Discharge from Residential Care." *Child and Family Social Work* 19:304–311.

Tyler, Patrick M., Ronald W. Thompson, Alexandra L. Trout, Matthew C. Lambert, and Lori L. Synhorst. 2016. "Availability of Aftercare for Youth Departing Group Homes." *Residential Treatment for Children and Youth* 33:270–285.

Tyler, Patrick M., Alexandra L. Trout, Michael H. Epstein, and Ronald Thompson. 2017. "Provider Perspectives on Aftercare Services for Youth in Residential Care." *Journal of Child and Family Studies* 26:1603–1613.

Tyler, Patrick M., Alexandra L. Trout, Michael H. Epstein, and Ronald Thompson. 2014. "Provider Perspectives on Aftercare Services for Youth in Residential Care." *Residential Treatment for Children and Youth* 31:219–229.

Weaver, Robert D. and Derek Campbell. 2015. "Fresh Start: A Meta-Analysis of Aftercare Programs for Juvenile Offenders." *Research on Social Work Practice* 25:201–212.

Wiebush, Richard G., Betsie McNulty, and Thao Le. 2000. "Implementation of the Intensive Community-Based Aftercare Program." Juvenile Justice Bulletin. Washington, DC: OJJDP.

Wiebush, Richard G., Dennis Wagner, Betsie McNulty, Yanqing Wang, and Thao N. Le. 2005. *Implementation and Outcome Evaluation of the Intensive Aftercare Program: Final Report*. National Council on Crime and Delinquency. Washington, DC: Office of Juvenile Justice and Delinquency Prevention.

Zahn, Margaret A., Jacob C. Day, Sharon F. Mihalic, and Lisa Tichavsky. 2009. "Determining What Works for Girls in the Juvenile Justice System." *Crime and Delinquency* 55:266–293.

PART IV

Partnerships in juvenile justice

Chapter 13

DELINQUENCY PREVENTION

CHAPTER TOPICS

- **Risk-focused delinquency prevention**
- **Evidence-based practice in delinquency prevention**
- **Implementation fidelity**
- **Model programs in delinquency prevention**

CHAPTER LEARNING OBJECTIVES

After completing this chapter, students should be able to:

- Describe the risk-focused prevention perspective.
- Explain the innovation of evidence-based practice in delinquency prevention.
- Identify the key elements of program implementation fidelity.
- Provide an overview of several delinquency prevention programs that have been evaluated as "model programs."

CHAPTER CONTENTS

CASE IN POINT

BREAKING THE LURE OF THE STREETS THROUGH DELINQUENCY PREVENTION

Melissa was a 13-year-old girl who persistently ran away from home. Home was a small rural town in Oregon. Her destination was always the streets of Portland. Melissa's parents had given up hope for a "normal teenage daughter," and their relationship with her was cold and brittle. In fact, they did not always call in a runaway report to the police when she left home. But her probation officer (PO) was determined in her efforts to break Melissa's persistent pattern of running away. In addition to running away, Melissa also displayed an array of other status offenses, including curfew violations, truancy, and underage drinking. Based on this pattern of behavior, the Youth Court adjudicated Melissa a "youth in need of intervention"—the legal determination of a status offender—and through the informal intervention of the PO, the Youth Court tried to reform her behavior.

On one of Melissa's runs—one that lasted three weeks—a "street crime officer" with the Portland Police Department took her into custody for prostitution. Apparently Melissa had connected with a pimp and he alone received the profit from her trade. Melissa was transported to Juvenile Hall (the city detention center) and her PO was called to transport her back to her home jurisdiction for juvenile court processing. Given Melissa's unstable behavior, the Juvenile Court decided to place her in the protective custody of a short-term, semi-secure proctor home, used in lieu of secure confinement in a detention center (in this small rural town, the local jail). During this time, the PO advocated for Melissa with the Youth Court, seeking to involve the family in an intensive form of family therapy, called Multisystemic Therapy (MST). The PO was able to convince the Juvenile Court to use MST as a pre-petition diversion program: if the family successfully completed the program, the charges would not be petitioned for formal juvenile court processing, thereby providing incentive for program participation.

While the program will be described more fully later in this chapter, MST works with chronic juvenile offenders who have a long history of arrests. Highly trained MST therapists work intensely with delinquent youth and their families—they are on call 24-7. MST therapy seeks to improve parenting skills, especially family management and parent-child interaction, enhance school involvement and performance, and build job skills. The therapist and parents also introduced the youth to pro-social activities as an alternative to antisocial activities.

Over the course of several months of therapy, Melissa's parents made considerable progress in parenting skills, and they reestablished a relationship with their daughter. In so doing, they reclaimed hope for her and they became invested in her. Melissa's behavior stabilized and she began to develop a stronger relationship with her parents. How might this outcome be different had formal adjudication and commitment to some type of juvenile custodial institution occurred instead of this more preventive intervention?

Although juvenile justice systems are the primary mechanism by which communities respond to delinquent acts, delinquency prevention programs represent a proactive approach to juvenile crime, attempting to prevent it before it occurs. In the late 1960s, the President's Commission on Law Enforcement and the Administration of Justice issued a series of important reports. One of them, the *Task Force Report on Juvenile Delinquency and Youth Crime*, concluded:

> In the last analysis, the most promising and so the most important method of dealing with crime is by preventing it—by ameliorating the conditions of life that drive people to commit crime and that undermine the restraining rules and institutions erected by society against antisocial conduct.
>
> (President's Commission on Law Enforcement and Administration of Justice 1967:4)

Delinquency prevention became a national priority through the Juvenile Justice and Delinquency Prevention (JJDP) Act of 1974. The JJDP Act also created the Office of Juvenile Justice and Delinquency Prevention (OJJDP), whose charge was, and still is, to assist states and local communities in developing policies, practices, and programs directed at delinquency prevention. The resulting prevention perspective stands in sharp contrast to formal processes of juvenile justice.

This chapter describes contemporary delinquency prevention. The field has been transformed in recent years with the advent and expansion of evidence-based practice. We first depict the risk-focused prevention perspective, which is based on the empirical identification of risk factors that predict delinquent behavior. We then describe evidence-based practice in delinquency prevention, followed by the associated consideration of what makes for successful implementation of prevention programs—this is referred to as "implementation fidelity." Lastly, we present three model programs that illustrate evidence-based practice in delinquency prevention. The notion of "best practices" is extremely popular today, but true best practices are substantiated by evaluation research that gauges effectiveness, as provided in evidence-based practice.

RISK-FOCUSED DELINQUENCY PREVENTION

The word *adolescence* is derived from the Latin verb *adolēscere*, meaning "to grow up" or "come to maturity."[1] Adolescence is a distinct and transitory period of development between childhood and adulthood "characterized by increased experimentation and risk taking, a tendency to discount long-term consequences, and heightened sensitivity to peers and other social influences" (National Research Council 2013:1). In combination, these three cognitive patterns bring about an adolescent preference for behaviors that are exciting, peer-oriented, and provide immediate rewards.

Adolescent experimentation and risk taking include behaviors such as alcohol and drug use, disruption and underachievement in school, reckless driving, precocious sexual activity, and juvenile delinquency. Psychologists contend that these **risk-taking behaviors** sometimes serve an "adaptive function," allowing youth to try out different behaviors, negotiate peer pressure, explore self-identity, and acquire adult skills (National Research Council 2013; Collins and Steinberg 2006; Gardner and Steinberg 2005). At the same time, risk-taking behaviors may pose a significant harm to the youth and others, and may compromise healthy psychosocial development (Steinberg and Morris 2001; Jessor 1992; Dryfoos 1990).

Several aspects of risk-taking behavior are especially consequential for developmental outcomes. First, youth involved in one form of risk-taking behavior are likely to be involved in others, multiplying their impact (Welsh et al. 2013; Thornberry, Huizinga, and Loeber 2004; Huizinga et al. 2000; Elliott, Huizinga, and Menard 1989). Second, risk-taking behaviors most often occur in the context of peers, and are exacerbated by peer influence (Gardner and Steinberg 2005). Third, it is evident from research findings that youth who display risk-taking behaviors early in life are more likely to develop persistent and serious patterns of risk-taking behaviors (Broidy et al. 2003; Loeber, Farrington, and Petechuk 2003). As a result, delinquency prevention programs seek to reduce the occurrence of risk-taking behaviors during the adolescent years because they compromise successful adolescent development.

For most youth, however, experimentation and risk-taking behaviors do not extend beyond adolescence, as psychosocial maturity is achieved. In fact, only a small percentage of youth who engage in risk-taking behaviors persist into adulthood (Steinberg, Cauffman, and Monahan 2015; National Research Council 2013; Moffitt 1993). Contemporary theory and research reveal that psychosocial maturation during the adolescent and young adult years involves the development of three key social and psychological capabilities:

1 **Temperance**. The ability to control impulses, including aggressive impulses.
2 **Perspective**. The ability to consider other points of view, including those that take into account longer-term consequences or that take the vantage point of others.
3 **Responsibility**. The ability to take personal responsibility for one's behavior and resist the coercive influences of others (Steinberg et al. 2015:3 [enumerated]; see also Monahan et al. 2009; Steinberg and Cauffman 1996).[2]

These key elements of psychosocial maturity are established primarily through three conditions that are critically important to healthy adolescent development (National Research Council 2013; Steinberg, Chung, and Little 2004). First, the presence of a parent or parent figure who is involved with, and invested in, the adolescent. The parent–child relationship is characterized by warmth, firmness and support. Second, peer group association that both values and models prosocial behavior, especially academic success (Brown et al. 2008). Third, parents, schools, and work provide opportunities for youth to develop critical thinking and decision-making skills, facilitating decisions that are both autonomous and responsible.

Risk factors

Research has consistently identified a number of risk factors that increase the likelihood of risk-taking behaviors and, ultimately, negative developmental outcomes (Green et al. 2008). A **risk factor** is any individual trait, social influence, or environmental condition that leads to greater likelihood of risk-taking behaviors and ultimately negative developmental outcomes during the adolescent years (Hoge, Vincent, and Guy 2013). Exposure to multiple risk factors significantly increases the risk of future problem behaviors (Green et al. 2008). The OJJDP Study Group on Serious and Violent Juvenile Offenders and the Study Group on Very Young Offenders reviewed this literature and concluded that a limited number of risk factors are commonly identified through research (Loeber et al. 2003; Wasserman et al. 2003; Hawkins et al. 2000; see also Tanner-Smith, Wilson, and Lipsey 2013; Hawkins et al. 2009; Green et al. 2008). These risk factors are listed in "Expanding ideas: Risk factors predictive of juvenile delinquency." These risk factors are grouped into five categories or "domains": individual, family, peer group, school, and neighborhood and community factors. Contemporary approaches to delinquency prevention argue that these risk factors must be first identified through research and then addressed through evidence-based practice (Bulman 2014; Welsh et al. 2013; Farrington and Welsh 2007; Wassermann et al. 2003).

Two types of risk factors can be distinguished: static and dynamic (Hoge et al. 2013; Vincent, Guy, and Grisso 2012; Andrews and Bonta 2010). **Static risk factors** are background characteristics of the youth that cannot be changed through prevention programs, including the early age of onset of risk-taking behaviors, history of aggressive behavior and violence, and parental criminality. **Dynamic risk factors** are characteristics of the youth and his/her environment that can be changed through intervention, such as antisocial attitudes and values, association with delinquent peers, dysfunctional family relationships, and antisocial personality traits (impulsiveness, risk-taking, and low self-control). Delinquency prevention programs focus on the latter because of their potential for change.

Protective factors and resiliency

Not all youth exposed to risk factors become delinquent. In fact, some flourish despite these detriments and adversities (Bartol and Bartol 2009; Hawkins et al. 2009; Werner 2005). Understanding such **resiliency** provides a unique angle from which to approach delinquency prevention: to build strengths and skills that allow youth to resist the pressures and temptations for delinquency. *Strength-based* approaches to prevention seek to promote protective factors that have been found in research to prevent involvement in delinquency. **Protective factors** are those individual traits and social circumstances that allow youth to adapt positively to adverse environments. After reviewing the research literature on resiliency, Curt Bartol and Anne Bartol (2009:97) identify nine key competencies that are strongly substantiated as protective factors (see also Vincent et al. 2012; Hawkins et al. 2009; Farrington and Welsh 2007).

EXPANDING IDEAS: RISK FACTORS PREDICTIVE OF JUVENILE DELINQUENCY

Individual factors

- verbal deficits (affecting listening, reading, problem solving, speech, writing, and memory)
- inattentiveness, impulsiveness, hyperactivity
- difficult temperament
- negative emotionality (disagreeable, oppositional, defiant, rebellious)
- weak constraint, limited behavioral inhibition, low self-control
- low intelligence and academic failure
- risk-taking/sensation seeking
- early onset of problem behaviors
- aggression
- social withdrawal
- attitudes favorable to risk-taking behaviors

Family factors

- poor family management and direct controls (monitoring and supervision, standards for behavior, recognizing and responding to problem behaviors)
- lax, harsh, and inconsistent discipline
- child maltreatment (especially neglect)
- low levels of parental involvement
- weak family attachment and indirect controls
- parental attitude favorable to deviance
- parental criminality, substance abuse, psychopathology
- family and marital conflict
- family disruption, including divorce and separation
- residential mobility

School and academic factors

- early and persistent classroom disruption and antisocial behaviors
- poor academic performance
- weak social bonds to school
- limited academic aspirations
- truancy and dropping out
- frequent school transition
- school with high rate of delinquency
- low academic quality of school
- low parent and community involvement in school

Peer-related factors

- association with delinquent peers
- peer rejection
- delinquent attitudes and behaviors are modeled, imitated, and reinforced in a delinquent peer group
- delinquent values and attitudes
- learned techniques for committing crimes
- gang membership

Neighborhood and community factors

- concentrated disadvantage (concentrated poverty, social isolation, joblessness)
- social disorganization (poverty, cultural heterogeneity, and residential mobility)
- ineffective social control (collective efficacy)
- delinquent and criminal subculture (tradition of crime, socialization, availability of drugs and access to weapons)

Sources: Drawn primarily from Hawkins et al. (2000). See also Tanner-Smith et al. (2013); Hawkins et al. (2009); Green et al. (2008); Farrington and Welsh (2007); Loeber et al. (2003); Wasserman et al. (2003).

1 Connections to competent, emotionally warm, caring adults
2 Social experiences with supportive, prosocial peers
3 Language skills and cognitive ability
4 Self-regulation skills
5 Interpersonal skills
6 Attention and focus skills
7 Positive attitude and emotions
8 Positive views of self and abilities
9 Intrinsic motivation to be effective

"Expanding ideas: Gender-specific risk and protective factors" identifies risk and protective factors that are unique to girls, drawn from analysis conducted by OJJDP's Girls Study Group.

EXPANDING IDEAS: GENDER-SPECIFIC RISK AND PROTECTIVE FACTORS

The Office of Juvenile Justice and Delinquency Prevention (OJJDP) convened the Girls Study Group in order to examine girls' delinquency. Part of their study involved a review of research on factors that lead to delinquent behavior or prevent it from occurring. One of the resulting technical reports, "Charting the Way to Delinquency Prevention in Girls" provides the following summary of risk and protective factors that are unique to girls (Zahn et al. 2008:4–5).

Risk factors

- **Early puberty**. Early puberty increases girls' risk for delinquency, particularly if they come from disadvantaged neighborhoods and have dysfunctional families. This disparity between biological and social maturity can lead to increased conflict with parents or negative associations with older boys or men.
- **Sexual abuse or maltreatment**. Compared to boys, girls experience more sexual victimization overall, including sexual assaults, rapes, and sexual harassment. However, all types of maltreatment (sexual, physical, and neglect) can increase the risk of delinquency for both sexes.
- **Depression and anxiety**. Depression and anxiety disorders have been associated with delinquency. Girls receive these diagnoses more frequently than boys.
- **Romantic partners**. When a youth's boyfriend or girlfriend commits a crime, he or she may also engage in delinquent behavior. For less serious crimes, girls are influenced more by their boyfriends than boys by their girlfriends. For serious crimes, they are equally affected. . . .

Protective factors

- **Caring adult.** Girls who had a caring adult in their lives during adolescence were less likely to commit status or property offenses, sell drugs, join gangs, or commit simple or aggravated assault during adolescence. They also were less likely to commit simple assault as young adults. . . .

- **School success.** Girls who experienced success in school during adolescence committed fewer status and property offenses and were less likely to join gangs in adolescence. School success helped protect them from involvement in simple and aggravated assault in adolescence and young adulthood. However, these girls were more likely to commit property offenses in young adulthood.
- **Religiosity.** Girls who placed a high importance on religion during adolescence were less likely to sell drugs in early adolescence.

Source: Risk and protective factors, and their descriptions are taken from Zahn et al. (2008:4–5).

Risk-focused delinquency prevention is based on the simple proposition that to prevent risk-taking behaviors from occurring, we need to identify the factors that lead to such behaviors and then find ways to reduce them (Lehman, Hawkins, and Catalano 1994:94; see also Welsh et al. 2013; Farrington and Welsh 2007). The task of identifying and reducing risk factors and enhancing protective factors, however, is not simple or easy. Only in the last 25 years have researchers been able to clearly identify "both the risk factors that produce delinquency and the interventions that consistently reduce the likelihood that it will occur" (Greenwood 2008:186; see also Welsh et al. 2013; Greenwood 2006; Farrington and Welsh 2007; Thornberry et al. 2004; Burns et al. 2003).

EVIDENCE-BASED PRACTICE IN DELINQUENCY PREVENTION

Contemporary delinquency prevention efforts are increasingly driven by evaluation research that seeks to establish whether particular strategies, methods, and programs effectively reduce the likelihood of delinquent offending. Greenwood and Welsh (2012:495) summarize this approach: "**Evidence-based practice** involves the use of scientific principles to assess the available evidence on program effectiveness and to develop principles for best practice in any particular field." As discussed in Chapter 2, evidence-based practice is one of the most significant movements in contemporary juvenile justice reform (McKee and Rapp 2014; Greenwood and Welsh 2012; Lipsey and Howell 2012).

While the rigor of evaluation research varies, five standards are key (Mihalic and Elliott 2015:127–128; see also Blueprints 2017; Dodge and Mandel 2012; Greenwood and Welsh 2012; Byrne and Lurigio 2009; Greenwood 2006, 2008; Welsh and Farrington 2007). These include:

1 **Intervention specificity**: The program clearly identifies a specific behavioral outcome that is sought, the mechanisms by which the outcome is achieved, and the target population for the intervention.
2 **Evaluation quality**: The effectiveness of the program must be established using a strong research design, including random assignment of subjects and experimental or quasi-experimental design.
3 **Intervention impact**: Evidence from scientifically-sound evaluation research shows "significant positive change in intended outcomes that can be attributed to the program" (Mihalic and Elliott 2015:128).

4 **Dissemination readiness**: "The program is available for dissemination and has the necessary organizational capability, manuals, training, technical assistance and other support required for implementation with fidelity in communities and public service systems" (Mihalic and Elliott 2015:128). Cost–benefit analysis is also available.
5 **Sustained outcomes**: The intervention program has lasting positive effects for a minimum of 12 months.

Using these standards, the Center for the Study and Prevention of Violence at the University of Colorado developed a registry of prevention and intervention programs that have been found to effectively promote positive youth development (Mihalic and Elliott 2015). This **program registry of evidence-based practice** is called *Blueprints for Healthy Youth Development*, or *Blueprints* for short. Blueprints currently identifies nine "Model Programs" and nine "Promising Programs" in terms of effective "program outcomes" for "delinquency and criminal behavior" (Blueprints 2017). A number of these Model Programs will be described more fully in the following section. Two other program registries of evidence-based practice have been developed and are widely used in the field of juvenile justice: OJJDP's *Model Programs Guide,* created by the Office of Justice programs, and the *National Registry of Evidence-Based Programs and Practices*, sponsored by the Substance Abuse and Mental Health Services Administration (SAMHSA). "Expanding ideas: Program registries of evidence-based practice" provides links to the websites of these registries.

The model programs approach to evidence-based practice seeks to identify particular programs of proven effectiveness, and then guide implementation for successful results. The model programs that have been identified are sometimes referred to as "brand name" programs because they

EXPANDING IDEAS: PROGRAM REGISTRIES OF EVIDENCE-BASED PRACTICE

Three program registries for evidence-based practice are widely used for delinquency prevention and intervention. The websites for each of these registries identify and describe model programs that have been found to be effective through evaluation research. A word of caution: these registries use different criteria for assessing program effectiveness and different terminology to classify the degree of effectiveness (Mihalic and Elliott 2015:126).

- **Blueprints for Healthy Youth Development**, Center for the Study and Prevention of Violence at the University of Colorado Boulder: www.blueprintsprograms.com/
- **Model Programs Guide,** Office of Juvenile Justice and Delinquency Prevention: www.ojjdp.gov/mpg/. The Model Programs Guide is integrated with **CrimeSolutions.gov:** www.crimesolutions.gov/ (under "Topic," use "Juveniles" and then "Delinquency Prevention"). OJJDP also provides an implementation guide for Model Programs Guide users, called **iGuides,** which identifies ten steps to plan for successful implementation of prevention programs: www.ojjdp.gov/mpg-iguides/.
- **National Registry of Evidence-based Programs and Practices,** Substance Abuse and Mental Health Services Administration: www.samhsa.gov/nrepp

are often "developed by a single investigator or team over a number of years and proven through careful replications, supported by millions of dollars in federal grants" (Greenwood 2008:192). Well-known evidence-based programs include Functional Family Therapy, Multisystemic Therapy, Multidimensional Treatment Foster Care, and Nurse-Family Partnership (Greenwood and Welsh 2012).

In contrast to this model programs approach, evidence-based practice can also be "generic" when research is used to uncover strategies and methods, rather than particular programs, which are effective at reducing future offending (Greenwood and Welsh 2012; Lipsey and Howell 2012; Lipsey et al. 2010). This approach to evidence-based practice is usually accomplished through a statistical technique called **meta-analysis**, which estimates the effects of intervention methods and strategies found across evaluation studies. The most prominent criminologist in this effort is Mark Lipsey who, in 1992, conducted the first meta-analysis focusing on juvenile justice. Lipsey found that effective strategies shared a number of common features, including targeting high-risk offenders who, even though they have high re-offense rates, have the most room for improvement (Lipsey et al. 2010:23). Effective intervention methods are therapeutic, rather than controlling, and they are based on a number of key features:

- **Skill building**: cognitive-behavioral techniques, social skills, academic and vocational skills;
- **Counseling**: individual, group, and family counseling, mentoring;
- **Multiple coordinated services**: case management and service referrals;
- **Restorative justice**: restitution, victim-offender mediation;
- **Behavioral monitoring**: observation to detect bad behavior, intensive probation or parole supervision (Lipsey et al. 2010:23–25; Lipsey 2009; Lipsey and Cullen 2007).

Lipsey and his colleagues (2010) also offer a practical guide for local communities to progressively evaluate and refine prevention and intervention programs according to the methods that have been found to be effective in meta-analysis research. The *Standardized Program Evaluation Protocol* (SPEP) is an evaluation tool that assigns points (maximum overall score is 100 points) to delinquency prevention and intervention programs according to how closely their characteristics match those associated with programs found to be effective in meta-analysis (Lipsey et al. 2010:29). Higher scores indicate greater correspondence, and each of the characteristics used in the tool can be assessed in order to refine the program for greater effectiveness, based on what has been shown to work in similar programs.

Evidence-based practice has increasingly embraced two additional dimensions of effectiveness: risk/need assessment and cost-benefit analysis. **Risk/need assessment** instruments use items that measure key factors that have been found to statistically predict the likelihood of future delinquency—the "risk" element of these assessment tools. Common risk factors in risk/need assessment instruments include prior delinquent offending, substance abuse, family problems, peer delinquency, and school-related problems (Schwalbe 2008). These risk factors also recognize "criminogenic needs"—the "need" element of these assessment tools—when the predictors that are identified can be changed through intervention. Earlier in the chapter we referred to these predictors that can be changed as "dynamic risk factors." Examples of dynamic risk factors include antisocial attitudes and values, association with delinquent peers, dysfunctional family relationships, and antisocial personality traits (impulsiveness, risk-taking, and low self-control) (Vincent et al. 2012; Andrews and Bonta 2010). In contrast, "static risk factors" also predict the likelihood of future delinquency, but cannot be changed through intervention. Examples of static risk factors include the early age of onset of problem behaviors, history of aggressive behavior and violence, and parental criminality.

Risk/need assessment instruments have evolved with use and evaluation, providing better predictive validity and reliability, and becoming more theoretically informed and more relevant and applicable to prevention and intervention efforts (Hoge et al. 2013; Vincent et al. 2012; Andrews and Bonta 2010; Andrews, Bonta, and Wormith 2006). As such, risk/need assessment instruments have taken on the dual task of predicting future delinquency (risk assessment) and informing intervention ("criminogenic need" assessment).

Cost–benefit analysis of delinquency prevention and intervention programs seeks to "comprehensively identify and measure the benefits and costs of a program," including those that occur during and after participation in the program (National Research Council 2013:167; see also Dodge and Mandel 2012). Cost–benefit analysis "may be viewed as a way to calculate society's return from investing in an intervention" (National Research Council 2013:167; see also Rocque et al. 2014; Dodge and Mandel 2012; Cohen and Piquero 2009; Farrington and Welsh 2007). The Washington State Institute for Public Policy is unquestionably the pace-setter in cost–benefit analysis, conducting evaluation research of programs in order to inform funding decisions by the Washington State Legislature.

Whether one chooses to intervene with juvenile offenders when they are institutionalized, in group or foster homes, or on probation, states and localities can adopt programs that produce remarkably large economic returns. The same is true for programs that seek to divert juveniles before they are convicted of further crimes. Indeed, some programs deliver $10 or more of benefits for each $1 of cost (National Research Council 2013:168; based on Washington State Institute for Public Policy 2011 and Drake, Aos, and Miller 2009).

As the effectiveness of delinquency prevention and intervention programs receives increasing attention, so, too, does the drive to implement model programs in the most effective manner. As a result, identifying and implementing evidence-based practices has become a priority for both governmental and private agencies (Rocque et al. 2014; Dodge and Mandel 2012; Greenwood and Welsh 2012; Lipsey and Howell 2012; Lipsey et al. 2010; Greenwood 2006, 2008; Mihalic et al. 2004a).

IMPLEMENTATION FIDELITY

Although some scholars have offered lists of common features shared by effective programs, such generalizations fail to appreciate what makes different prevention programs effective (Lerner and Galambos 1998; Dryfoos 1990). The wide array of risk and protective factors makes it almost impossible to address them all, and different programs target different problem behaviors and contexts (Mihalic and Elliott 2015). For example, some prevention programs that focus on bullying in schools have been found to be effective because they target a particular risk factor—early aggressiveness—which predicts later violence. The effectiveness of bullying prevention is likely to be determined by program characteristics that are quite different from other forms of delinquency prevention, even those that are applied in school contexts.

Beyond program features, effective delinquency prevention depends on implementation **fidelity**—"the degree to which a program's core services, components, and procedures are implemented as originally designed" (CrimeSolutions.gov 2016). Even programs that have been evaluated as effective through research must be implemented fully to produce the desired effects.

The Blueprints project conducted an evaluation of implementation quality, looking at aspects of program implementation rather than program features (Mihalic et al. 2004b). Nine model programs at 147 sites were part of the study. Questionnaires were administered at each site every four months, over a two-year period. The study revealed six key elements of program implementation (Mihalic et al. 2004b:3–9; see also Elliott and Mihalic 2004):

1 **Effective organization.** Successful programs depend on strong administrative support for the implementing staff; agency stability; a shared vision of program goals; and inter-agency links, especially with other programs involved in clients' treatment plans.
2 **Qualified staff.** Program success is fostered by staff who support the program and who are motivated to implement the program day in and day out. Program staff must also be skilled, experienced, and have the necessary credentials to carry out the program. They must also be given the time necessary to implement the program, especially a new program. Paid staff has been found to be more effective than volunteers.
3 **Program champion(s).** Every successful program needs a person who champions the program—who motivates, innovates, guides, and fosters program delivery.
4 **Program integration.** Success is most likely when a program is integrated into a larger organizational structure, in which the prevention program supports and augments the host agency's goals and objectives. Bullying prevention, for example, is most effectively implemented within a school context in which student safety and security are taught as part of the academic curriculum.
5 **Training and technical assistance.** A strong training program followed with technical assistance cultivates employee confidence and ability and allows for more effective program implementation.
6 **Implementation fidelity.** Sometimes referred to as *integrity*, fidelity has to do with the degree to which the program is actually delivered as it was designed. Successful programs tend to be those that closely follow the goals and methods of the program's design.

Similarly, OJJDP has recently developed a web-based guide for program implementation, called *Model Programs iGuides* (short for implementation guides). Designed to be used before identifying and implementing an evidence-based program, iGuides provides information on the key steps and common problems of implementing a model program. "Expanding ideas: Program registries of evidence-based practice" provides a link to the iGuides website.

MODEL PROGRAMS IN DELINQUENCY PREVENTION

Delinquency prevention programs can be classified into three main approaches: (1) universal prevention; (2) selective prevention; and (3) indicated prevention (Farrington and Welsh 2007). **Universal prevention** programs (or primary prevention) target the general population of youth and include campaigns to prevent smoking and drug use, to promote problem-solving and dispute resolution skills through classroom education, and to provide classes on parenting skills to all parents.[3] **Selective prevention** programs (or secondary prevention) target youth or groups of youth who are "at risk" due to multiple risk factors in their lives. **Indicated prevention** programs (or tertiary prevention) target identified juvenile offenders in order to prevent or eliminate a serious pattern of delinquent offending. As mentioned earlier in this chapter, one of the fundamental principles of evidence-based practice is that intervention is more effective with high-risk offenders who, even though they have high re-offense rates, have the most room for improvement (Lipsey et al. 2010:23). As a result, indicated prevention programs have received greater public policy attention in recent years than in the past (Dodge and Mandel 2012; Greenwood and Welsh 2012; Lipsey and Howell 2012).

The best way to gain insight into delinquency prevention programs is through case examples. Here we offer three descriptions of prevention programs that have been evaluated as "Model Programs" through Blueprints for Healthy Youth Development: Life-Skills Training, Nurse-Family Partnership, and Multisystemic Therapy. "Expanding ideas: Examples of Blueprints' model programs for prevention and intervention" provides brief program descriptions of three additional model programs designed to prevent delinquent behavior. Moreover, you may wish to explore other model prevention programs that have been evaluated as effective by the three main model program registries, identified in "Expanding ideas: Program registries of evidence-based practice."

Life skills training: Drug use prevention curriculum

Life Skills Training (LST) is a universal prevention program that provides a three-year drug use prevention curriculum to sixth or seventh graders, with booster sessions during the following two years. The curriculum is "designed to prevent or reduce gateway drug use (tobacco, alcohol, and marijuana) by providing social resistance skills training to help students identify pressures to use drugs and resist drug offers" (Mihalic et al. 2004a:47). LST is implemented primarily in school classrooms by teachers using direct instruction, discussion, and positive reinforcement. The first year involves 15 lessons, and the booster sessions include 10 lessons in year two and 5 lessons in year three. Lessons have three basic skill-training components: (1) Personal Self-Management Skills teaches students to examine self-image and how it influences behavior, and to develop skills in goal setting, problem solving, decision making, and stress management; (2) Social Skills teaches students communication skills, including assertiveness and making and refusing requests; and (3) Resistance Skills teaches students to recognize common misconceptions about drugs and violence, and through coaching and practice, students learn resistance and refusal skills in dealing with peers and media pressure to use drugs (Blueprints 2017).

In numerous evaluations, LST has been found to reduce alcohol, tobacco, and marijuana use by 50–75 percent for students completing the curriculum, compared to control group students. Reductions in smoking and use of inhalants, narcotics, and hallucinogens were demonstrated through the 12th grade. The effectiveness of LST on violence and delinquency has also been established. "Studies testing LST have not only demonstrated short-term effects, but also provide evidence of its long-term effectiveness, with several studies providing 5–6 year follow-up data, and one study providing 10-year follow-up data" (Blueprints 2017; see also Mihalic et al. 2004a).

Nurse–family partnership: Prenatal and infancy home visits by nurses

Nurse–family partnership is a selective prevention program designed for low-income, first-time single mothers. The nurse visitation program targets three risk factors associated with the development of early antisocial behavior in children: adverse maternal health-related behaviors during pregnancy, child abuse and neglect, and troubled maternal life course. Nurse visitation programs are selective prevention programs because they target a particular at-risk group.

Public health nurses with small caseloads make prenatal and infancy home visits every one to two weeks and continue home visitation until the child is two years old. Nurses provide support and instruction on prenatal health, infancy caregiving, personal health, child development, parenting, pursuing education, and career development. Extensive evaluation shows that the program reduced rates of child abuse and neglect by helping mothers learn effective parenting skills and personal controls. Mothers receiving nurse home visits had fewer months on welfare, fewer behavioral problems, and lower arrest and conviction rates than mothers who did not participate in the program. Adolescents whose mothers participated in the nurse visitation program were less likely to run away, be arrested, or be convicted of a crime. Compared to the children of nonparticipants, these adolescents smoked fewer cigarettes, consumed less alcohol, and had fewer behavioral problems related to alcohol and drug use. By the time a child reached age 15, cost savings were estimated at four times the original investment, as a result of reductions in crime, welfare and health care costs, and taxes paid by working parents (Blueprints 2017; Mihalic et al. 2004a; Olds, Hill, and Rumsey 1998).

Multisystemic therapy: Intensive treatment for chronic juvenile offenders

Multisystemic Therapy (MST) is an indicated prevention program that targets chronic juvenile offenders, providing intensive family- and community-based treatment. Highly trained therapists with small caseloads and 24-7 availability provide direct therapeutic services to youth and their families, addressing "the known causes of delinquency on an individualized, yet comprehensive basis." MST seeks to generate positive change in the youth's "natural settings—home, school, and neighborhood—in ways that promote prosocial behavior while decreasing antisocial behavior." Within the youth's natural setting, MST seeks to "empower parents with the skills and resources needed to independently address the inevitable difficulties that arise in raising teenagers, and to empower youth to cope with the family, peer, school, and neighborhood problems they encounter" (Blueprints 2017).

At the family level, MST seeks to foster effective parenting. This includes helping parents to remove obstacles that get in the way of effective parenting, such as parental substance abuse, lack of social support, and martial conflict. MST also promotes parenting skills, including monitoring and supervision of the youth, and effective discipline techniques, communication, and problem solving. At the peer level, MST intervention discourages interaction with delinquent and drug-using friends, while encouraging interaction with prosocial peers. At the school level, intervention encourages opening lines of communication between parents and teachers, and parental monitoring of the youth's school performance. At the individual level, cognitive behavioral therapy is used to enhance social skills and to encourage the youth to respond assertively to negative peer pressure (Blueprints 2017).

MST is supported by numerous evaluations that consistently demonstrate positive outcomes for serious juvenile offenders, including violent offenders, substance abusing offenders, and juvenile sex offenders. MST has been shown to impact serious delinquency behavior, drug use, arrests, incarceration, family relations, peer relations, and psychiatric problems (Blueprints 2017).

As these delinquency prevention programs illustrate, prevention programs operate at various levels—individual, family, school, and community—and they are based in varying service sectors—mental health, public health, education, child welfare, and juvenile justice. Regardless of where they occur, prevention programs seek to keep youth out of the juvenile justice system and they attempt to integrate youth into the family, school, and community (Farrington and Welsh 2007).

EXPANDING IDEAS: EXAMPLES OF BLUEPRINTS' MODEL PROGRAMS FOR PREVENTION AND INTERVENTION

Functional Family Therapy (FFT)

- **Target behaviors**: Delinquency and Criminal Behavior; Illicit Drug Use
- **Brief description**: A short-term family therapy intervention and juvenile diversion program helping at-risk children and delinquent youth to overcome adolescent behavior problems, conduct disorder, substance abuse and delinquency. Therapists work with families to assess family behaviors that maintain delinquent behavior, modify dysfunctional family communication, train family members to negotiate effectively, set clear rules about privileges and responsibilities, and generalize changes to community contexts and relationships.

GenerationPMTO

- **Target behaviors**: Antisocial-Aggressive Behavior; Anxiety; Conduct Problems; Delinquency and Criminal Behavior; Externalizing; Illicit Drug Use; Internalizing; Mental Health—Other
- **Brief description**: A group- or individual-based parent training program that teaches effective family management strategies and parenting skills, including skill encouragement, setting limits/positive discipline, monitoring, problem solving, and positive involvement, in order to reduce antisocial and behavior problems in children.

Positive Action

- **Target behaviors**: Academic Performance; Alcohol; Anxiety; Bullying; Delinquency and Criminal Behavior; Depression; Emotional Regulation; Illicit Drug Use; Positive Social/Prosocial Behavior; Sexual Risk Behaviors; Tobacco; Truancy—School Attendance; Violence
- **Brief description**: A school-based social emotional learning program for students in elementary and middle schools to increase positive behavior, reduce negative behavior, and improve social and emotional learning and school climate. The classroom-based curriculum teaches understanding and management of self and how to interact with others through positive behavior, with school climate programs used to reinforce the classroom concepts school-wide.

Source: Blueprints (2017). Program search using the "Delinquency and Criminal Behavior" filter. Target behaviors ("program outcomes") and brief descriptions are derived from this source.

SUMMARY AND CONCLUSIONS

Delinquency prevention programs represent a proactive approach to juvenile crime, attempting to prevent it before it occurs. The various approaches to delinquency prevention seek to reduce the occurrence of adolescent risk-taking behaviors, such as alcohol and drug use, disruption and underachievement in school, reckless driving, precocious sexual activity, and juvenile delinquent, because they compromise successful adolescent development. For most youth, however, risk-taking behaviors do not extend beyond adolescence, as psychosocial maturity is achieved. Psychosocial maturation during the adolescent and young adult years involves development of three key social and psychological capabilities: temperance, perspective, and responsibility (Steinberg et al. 2015).

Contemporary approaches to delinquency prevention argue that these risk factors must first be identified through research and then addressed through a broad range of prevention programs at the individual, family, school, and community levels. Delinquency prevention programs can be classified as *universal*, targeting the general population of youth, *selective*, targeting individual youth or groups of youth who are "at risk" due to multiple risk factors in their lives, and *indicated*, targeting juvenile offenders in order to prevent or eliminate a serious pattern of delinquent offending. We also considered several delinquency prevention programs that have been evaluated as successful and identified as "model programs."

Delinquency prevention efforts are increasingly driven by evaluation research that tries to establish whether particular strategies, methods, and programs effectively reduce the likelihood of delinquent offending, an approach called evidence-based practice. Several model program guides are available that identify delinquency prevention and intervention programs of demonstrated effectiveness. Another form of evaluation research called meta-analysis estimates the effectiveness of particular intervention strategies and methods across a number of evaluation studies. Evidence-based practice also involves risk/need assessment, to identify the criminogenic needs of youth and to determine their likelihood of reoffending, and cost–benefit analysis, to comprehensively measure the financial impact of programs.

READING 13.1

"CHANGING LIVES: PREVENTION AND INTERVENTION TO REDUCE SERIOUS OFFENDING."

Phil Bulman. 2014. Washington, DC: Office of Juvenile Justice and Delinquency Prevention.

This "Justice Research" report from the Office of Juvenile Justice and Delinquency Prevention summarizes a technical report from a panel of experts assembled by OJJDP, called the Study Group on Transitions from Juvenile Delinquency to Adult Crime. This brief report summarizes "Bulletin 6: Changing Lives: Prevention and Intervention to Reduce Serious Offending" by Brandon C. Welsh and his colleagues (Welsh et al. *2013).*

Decades of study have revealed much about risk factors for delinquency and crime. Individual characteristics and various factors can increase the probability of offending and may also predict substance abuse, teenage pregnancy, dropping out of school and other problems during adolescence and early adulthood. Because risk factors can predict future criminal behavior, prevention and intervention programs focus on mitigating them in a young person's life. In addition, longitudinal studies have identified protective factors that inhibit criminal behavior. Programs that strengthen these protective factors can reduce the risk of delinquency. Most prevention and intervention programs that address risk factors have not been adequately evaluated, but high-quality studies are emerging. Randomized controlled trials and other rigorous studies have shown that many of these programs have positive effects on offending in addition to other outcomes.

This bulletin focuses on the highest quality evaluation studies and research reviews. Grouped by program focus—family, school, peers and community, individual, employment—the bulletin assesses early childhood, juvenile, and early adulthood programs that have demonstrated measurable impacts on offending in early adulthood or up to age 29.

Family-based programs

Family-based programs target risk factors such as poor child rearing. Psychologists deliver some programs; public health professionals deliver others. This section discusses programs for young children and for adjudicated delinquents.

Young children

Only a few programs that focus on early childhood have demonstrated that they have an impact on reducing offending in early adulthood. One was a parent training program that yielded positive results for young children but showed no impact for participants when they were between ages 16 and 21.

The best-known home visiting program, and the only one with a direct measure of delinquency, is the Nurse–Family Partnership initially carried out in Elmira, NY. Four hundred first-time mothers were randomly assigned to receive home visits from nurses during pregnancy or during the child's first two years or to a control group that received no visits. Nurses visited mothers in the experimental groups every two weeks, advising them on prenatal and postnatal care, infant development, the importance of nutrition, and avoiding smoking and drinking during pregnancy.

Results showed that postnatal visits—particularly to poor, unmarried teenage mothers—were associated with a significant decrease in reported abuse and neglect during the child's first two years. In a 15-year follow-up, significantly fewer experimental group mothers were identified as committing child abuse and neglect. By age 15, children of the higher risk mothers in the experimental group had significantly fewer arrests than controls. By age 19, girls in the experimental group had significantly fewer arrests, and girls of the higher risk mothers had significantly fewer children of their own and less Medicaid use. However, few effects were observed for boys.

Adjudicated delinquents

Multisystemic therapy

This therapy, designed for serious juvenile offenders, may include individual, family, peer, school and community interventions, including parent training and other skill-building sessions. It is often referred to as family-based treatment. Three evaluations of randomized experiments have measured the impact of multisystemic therapy on offending in early adulthood (the experimental groups received multisystemic therapy).

- **Substance-abusing offenders:** 118 substance-abusing juvenile offenders received either multisystemic therapy or the usual community services. The mean age at treatment was 15.7 and at follow-up was 19.6. The experimental group had significantly lower yearly conviction rates than did the controls for violent crimes but not for property crimes. Effects on long-term drug use were mixed, with higher rates of marijuana abstinence for the experimental group but no effect on cocaine use.
- **Violent offenders:** 176 serious and violent juvenile offenders received either multisystemic therapy or individual therapy. The mean age at treatment was 13.7 and at follow-up was 28.8. The experimental group had significantly lower recidivism rates than did the controls (50 percent versus 81 percent), including lower rates of rearrest for violent offenses (14 percent versus 30 percent). Experimental participants also had 54 percent fewer arrests and 57 percent fewer days of confinement in adult detention facilities.
- **Sex offenders:** 48 high-risk juvenile sex offenders received either multisystemic therapy or the usual community services. The mean age at treatment was 14 and at follow-up was 22.9. The experimental group reported lower recidivism rates than did the controls for sexual (8 percent versus 46 percent) and nonsexual (29 percent versus 58 percent) crimes. Experimental participants also had 70 percent fewer arrests for all crimes and spent 80 percent fewer days in detention facilities.

Functional family therapy

This approach modifies patterns of family interaction through modeling and reinforcement to encourage clear communication and minimize conflict. A long-term follow-up of a randomized experiment involving 54 juvenile offenders compared family therapy with probation services. The mean age at treatment was 15.4 for the experimental group and 15.3 for the control group. Most were between ages 20 and 22 at follow-up. Family therapy participants reported a lower rate of rearrest compared with their control counterparts.

Multidimensional treatment foster care

This approach includes both individual therapeutic care for adolescents in foster care and training in parent management skills. A short-term follow-up of a randomized experiment involving 81 serious and chronic female juvenile offenders compared multidimensional treatment with group care. The age at treatment was between 13 and 17 and at follow-up was between 15 and 19. Multidimensional care was more effective than group care as measured by days in locked settings, number of criminal referrals and self-reported delinquency.

A two-year follow-up of a randomized experiment involving 79 adolescent males compared multidimensional treatment to group home care. The age at treatment was between 12 and 17 and at follow-up was between 16 and 19. Multidimensional treatment was significantly more effective than group home care as measured by referrals for violent offending and self-reports of violent behavior. Only 5 percent of participants in the multidimensional program had two or more criminal referrals for violent offenses compared with 24 percent of the group home adolescents.

School-based prevention programs

Only three school-based prevention programs have demonstrated that they have an impact on reducing offending in early adulthood: the Seattle Social Development Project, the Montreal Longitudinal-Experimental Study and the Good Behavior Game.

Seattle Social Development Project

This project combines parent training, teacher training and skills training for children. About 500 first-graders were randomly assigned to experimental or control classes in the original study. Parents and teachers in the experimental classes received child management instruction designed to increase children's attachment to parents and their bonding to school. They also learned how to teach children positive ways to solve problems.

A follow-up at age 18 found that the group that participated in the full program through grade six reported significantly less violence, less alcohol abuse and fewer sexual partners than the group that participated in grades five and six only or the control group. In the latest follow-up, the group that participated in grades one through six reported significantly better educational and economic attainment and mental and sexual health by age 27, but no effects were found for substance abuse or criminal activity at ages 24 or 27.

Montreal Longitudinal-Experimental Study

This study combined skills training, parent training and teacher support. About 250 disruptive 6-year-olds from low socioeconomic neighborhoods were assigned randomly to two groups, experimental and control. The experimental group learned how to improve social skills and self-control. Coaching, peer modeling, role playing and reinforcement strategies were used in small group sessions at school. Parents were trained in parent management, family crisis management and techniques for nonpunitive and consistent discipline.

By age 12, three years after the end of treatment, the boys in the experimental group committed significantly less burglary and theft and were significantly less likely to get drunk or get into fights than the boys in the control group. The experimental boys also had significantly higher school achievement. At every age from 10 to 15, the experimental boys had significantly lower self-reported delinquency scores than the control boys. The differences in delinquency between the two groups increased as the follow-up progressed. However, the experimental boys were only slightly less likely to have a juvenile court record up to age 15 (7 percent compared with 9 percent). The experimental boys were also less likely to be gang members or to get drunk or take drugs but were not significantly less likely than the controls to have intercourse by age 15.

The latest follow-up was a criminal record check at age 24. Those in the experimental group were less likely to have a record than their control counterparts (22 percent compared with 33 percent).

Good Behavior Game

The Good Behavior Game encourages children to learn how to regulate their own and their classmates' behavior. In an experimental study in 19 urban elementary schools in Baltimore, first-grade students were randomly assigned to groups that had equal numbers of disruptive children. The two-year program began with tangible rewards, such as stickers, for entire groups that exhibited good behavior. Eventually, they moved to less tangible rewards such as longer recess times.

After one year, teachers and peers rated the experimental students as less aggressive and shy than control students. The most positive effects were for students rated most aggressive at baseline. Among boys with the highest baseline aggression ratings, the positive effects endured through sixth grade.

Between ages 19 and 21, male participants in the highest risk group engaged in significantly less violent and criminal behavior than their control counterparts (34 percent compared with 50 percent). They also had significantly lower rates of drug dependence.

Peer- and community-focused programs

Peer-focused programs to prevent offending concentrate on reducing the influence of delinquent friends and increasing the influence of healthier friends. There are no outstanding examples of effective intervention programs for delinquency and later offending based on peer risk factors.

Children at Risk

The most important prevention program whose success seems to be based mainly on reducing peer risk factors is the Children at Risk program, which targeted high-risk adolescents with an average age of 12 who lived in poor neighborhoods of five American cities. Participants were identified in schools and randomly assigned to experimental or control groups. Initial reports were disappointing, but a one-year follow-up showed that, according to self-reports, experimental participants were less likely to have committed violent crimes or sold drugs.

Mentoring programs

Community-based prevention covers a wide array of programs such as after-school programs, mentoring, youth groups and resident groups. Although evidence is insufficient to support claims that after-school programs are effective, mentoring programs have been shown to produce a significant 10-percent reduction in offending on average. Mentoring is more effective when the average duration of each contact between mentor and mentee is greater and when mentoring is combined with other interventions. However, no studies have included follow-ups in the early adult years.

Communities That Care

Communities That Care and other comprehensive community initiatives work to bring together key people to target a range of risk factors. Findings from a randomized controlled trial involving 4,400 students in 24 American communities found that the program significantly reduced the initiation of delinquent behavior and both alcohol and cigarette use between grades five and eight. However, there are no follow-ups into early adulthood.

Individual-level programs

These programs target individual-level risk factors for offending in early childhood, adolescence and early adulthood. They may focus on intellectual stimulation for preschool children, social skills training that targets traits such as impulsivity and low empathy in childhood, or treatment of substance abuse and improving mental health in young adults. Several preschool programs have demonstrated that they have an impact on reducing offending in early adulthood.

Perry Preschool project

The Perry Preschool project included 123 children in Ypsilanti, Mich., who were divided into experimental and control groups. Children in the experimental group attended a daily preschool program, backed up by weekly home visits, when they were ages 3 and 4. The goal was to provide intellectual stimulation that would increase their thinking and reasoning abilities and lead to later school achievement.

The program had long-term benefits. At age 19, subjects in the experimental group were more likely to be employed, to have graduated from high school and to have received college or vocational training and were less likely to be arrested. By age 27, the experimental group had only half as many arrests as the controls, an average of 2.3 compared with 4.6. They were more likely to have graduated from high school, had significantly higher earnings and were more likely to be homeowners. Among female participants in the experimental group, more were married, and fewer of their children were born out of wedlock.

The most recent follow-up, which included 91 percent of the original sample at age 40, found important differences between the experimental and control groups. Participants in the experimental group had significantly fewer lifetime arrests for violent crimes (32 percent compared with 48 percent), property crimes (36 percent compared with 58 percent) and drug crimes (14 percent compared with 34 percent) and were significantly less likely to have been arrested five or more times (36 percent compared with 55 percent). In addition, they had significantly higher levels of schooling (77 percent graduated from high school compared with 60 percent), better employment records and higher incomes.

Child–Parent Center program

The Child–Parent Center program gave disadvantaged children ages 3 and 4 an active learning preschool program and family support. Educational enrichment continued into elementary school up to age 9. The program operated in 24 centers in impoverished Chicago neighborhoods. An evaluation found that, compared with the control group, those in the program group were significantly less likely to be arrested for any offense (17 percent compared with 25 percent). They also had lower rates of multiple offenses and violent offenses at age 18 and a significantly higher rate of high school completion (50 percent compared with 39 percent). At age 24, participants in the experimental group had significantly lower rates of felony arrests (17 percent compared with 21 percent) and lower rates of incarceration (21 percent compared with 26 percent).

Carolina Abecedarian Project

The Carolina Abecedarian Project targeted 111 low-income children, 98 percent of whom were African American, deemed to come from multirisk families. The experimental group received full-time preschool care in addition to social services; the control group received only social services. At age 21, fewer of those in the experimental group reported misdemeanor or felony arrests or incarceration. Also, significantly fewer were marijuana users or had become teenage parents, and significantly more had attended college or university.

Employment-based training programs

These programs for adolescents and young adults focus on increasing employment rates among people at risk of serious offending.

Intensive residential training programs

Job Corps is the only residential program that has demonstrated desirable effects on offending in early adulthood. It also has positive effects on subsequent earnings.

Job Corps improves the employability of at-risk young people (ages 16–24) by offering vocational training, education and health care. It serves about 60,000 people annually. A three-year follow-up of a randomized experiment that included 15,400 people found that Job Corps produced statistically significant reductions in criminal activity, improved educational attainment and greater earnings. The arrest rate among participants was 29 percent compared with 33 percent for control counterparts. Tax data analysis showed that earnings gains continued for the oldest participants eight years after completing the program.

Ex-offender job training for older males

These programs may be useful for those who are old enough to be "aging out" of crime. Few evaluations of programs that serve this population exist. Two programs from the 1970s that reduced offending in early adulthood were the Supported Work program and the Baltimore Life Experiment. One analysis found that the Supported Work program was highly effective at reducing offending and improving employment for ex-offenders older than age 26, but not for younger participants.

Transition to adulthood

Few studies have examined the impact of interventions on criminal behavior outcomes during the transition from late adolescence to early adulthood. Most focus exclusively on juvenile or adult populations, but results are largely consistent. Four interventions with ample studies show effectiveness:

1 **Cognitive behavioral therapy** produces on average a 22-percent reduction in offending rates. Most studies focus on either juveniles or adults. There is no reason to expect that this approach would be any less effective among offenders in the transitional age group.
2 **Educational, vocational and employment programs** show mixed results. Some find a modest 10-percent decrease in offending, others find the mean effect to be about 20 percent, and still others have found no effect on reoffending rates.
3 **Substance abuse treatment** is commonly provided to offenders, and treatment programs produce a range of positive effects, from about 4- to 20-percent reductions in reoffending rates.
4 **Treatment for sex offenders** varies, and analyses of effectiveness have all looked broadly at this category of program rather than at specific interventions. Reductions in general reoffending rates (not limited to sex crimes) range from 24 to 36 percent.

Costs and benefits

The financial benefits of programs often outweigh their costs, as they both reduce offending in the young adult years and save money in the long run. According to research conducted by the Washington State Institute for Public Policy (WSIPP), this was true of multidimensional treatment foster care ($8 saved per $1 expended), functional family therapy ($10 saved per $1 expended), multisystemic therapy ($3 saved per $1 expended), vocational education in prison ($12 saved per $1 expended), cognitive-behavioral therapy in prison ($22 saved per $1 expended), drug treatment in prison ($6 saved per $1 expended), and employment training in the community ($12 saved per $1 expended). . . .

Program effectiveness

NIJ's CrimeSolutions.gov uses proven research to determine what works in criminal justice, juvenile justice and crime victim services. CrimeSolutions.gov rates some of the programs discussed in this summary as being effective or promising in reducing serious crime rates among young people . . . .

Evidence ratings from CrimeSolutions.gov

Title	Evidence Rating
Effective	
Multisystemic Therapy	✓+ ✓+ ✓+
Functional Family Therapy	✓+ ✓+ ✓+
Multidimensional Treatment Foster Care	✓+ ✓+ ✓+
Nurse–Family Partnership	✓+ ✓+ ✓+
Good Behavior Game	✓+ ✓+ ✓+
Perry Preschool Project	✓+
Promising	
Communities That Care	✓ ✓ ✓
Montreal Longitudinal-Experimental Study	✓
Child–Parent Center	✓
Job Corps programs	✓

Note: A rating with one icon denotes programs evaluated in one study or meta-analysis. A rating with multiple icons denotes programs evaluated across multiple studies.

READING 13.2

"EVIDENCE-BASED PROGRAMS REGISTRY: BLUEPRINTS FOR HEALTHY YOUTH DEVELOPMENT."

Sharon F. Mihalic and Delbert S. Elliott. 2015. *Evaluation and Program Planning* 48:124–131.

It is nice to get the "inside story" on policies and programs. This article describes the origin, development, and operation of the Blueprints for Healthy Youth Development registry of evidence-based prevention and intervention programs, as offered by the designers of the registry, Delbert Elliott and Sharon Mihalic.

Introduction

Prior to 1990, the general consensus in the research community about the effectiveness of prevention programs was that "nothing worked," or to be more precise, nothing had been demonstrated in evaluations of programs and practices to be effective in preventing delinquency, antisocial behavior or dysfunctional, health compromising behavior (Martinson 1974; Romig, 1999; Sechrest, White, and Brown 1979). However, over the last two decades, there have been major advances in both evaluation research and program design and development. This work has provided a rich body of evidence demonstrating that some programs and practices are effective, both for preventing the onset of problem behaviors and for successfully intervening with those caught up in these types of behavior (Greenwood 2006; Institute of Medicine 2008; Sherman et al. 2002). Moreover, these programs often have positive effects on other important outcomes such as mental health, academic achievement, parenting practices and family well-being, and employment. This change in findings about the effectiveness of prevention programs and practices is the result of both major improvements in the quality of evaluation research and improved program design and implementation.

We now have a better understanding of what does and does not work, and this has led to a new interest in identifying and implementing programs that have been demonstrated by rigorous evaluations to be effective. This current drive for proven, evidence-based programs has also been fueled by huge financial deficits at both the federal and state levels, leading to serious consideration of the high costs of violence, crime, drug abuse, school dropout and other problem behaviors and the efficiencies associated with investments in more cost-effective, proven programs and practices. In 2002, the White House encouraged all federal agencies to support evidence-based programs and to discontinue programs without evidence of effectiveness (Office of Management Budget 2001; 2002), and it is now common practice that federal and state funding for prevention programs be restricted to evidence-based programs and practices.

This paper seeks to better inform policymakers, practitioners and citizens about the importance and advantages of using evidence-based programs to improve the life course of children, taking a closer look at the Blueprints for Healthy Youth Development registry as one source of important information on this topic.

Defining evidence-based programs

An evidence-based program is a set of coordinated services/activities that demonstrate effectiveness [on some desired outcome] based on research (Children's Services Council n.d.). Most researchers agree that the evidence of program effectiveness should minimally come from quasi-experimental or experimental evaluation. Randomized experiments are the "gold standard" for determining the effectiveness of a program (Campbell and Boruch 1975; Shadish, Cook, and Leviton 1991). Some argue that a higher standard should be placed on programs that will be taken to scale, such as requiring randomized controlled trials (Coalition for Evidence-Based Policy 2014; Elliott 2013) or evidence of sustained effects and replication (Elliott and Mihalic 2004).

A number of agencies and groups have developed standards for assessing the research for the effectiveness of programs in order to designate them as evidence-based. However, the standards adopted by each agency differ, with some applying a more rigorous standard than others. For example, some agencies that rate programs will only accept a randomized controlled trial as sufficient evidence (http://evidencebasedprograms.org), while some will accept both randomized controlled trials and closely matched quasi-experimental designs (http://blueprints programs.com). The higher standards, such as randomization, replication, and sustainability, will result in fewer programs, but it is critical that there be a high degree of confidence in the effectiveness of a program before endorsing and taking a program to scale.

The problem is that a lower standard comes with a greater risk of failure when programs are subsequently implemented on a wide scale. For example, evaluations conducted with RCTs have, in a number of instances, invalidated earlier findings from studies with quasi-experimental comparison group designs. Examples include hormone replacement therapy which was once a recommended treatment for postmenopausal women, based upon comparison group studies, until two large-scale randomized controlled studies showed that it increased the risk of coronary heart disease, stroke, and breast cancer; dietary fiber to prevent colon cancer was shown to have no effect; and an oxygen-rich environment for premature infants was shown to increase blindness (Baron 2007).

A number of "design replication" studies have been carried out to examine whether and under what circumstances comparison-group studies can replicate the results of randomized controlled trials. These studies test comparison-group methods against randomized methods by first comparing the outcomes of the program group to a randomly assigned control group, and next comparing the same program participants with a comparison group selected through methods other than randomization. Twelve of these studies have been summarized by Cook, Shadish, and Wong (2008). Their review suggests that comparison group studies without close matching often produce inaccurate estimates of an intervention's effects. This is true even when statistical techniques are used to adjust for observed differences between the two groups. Often studies match only on demographic variables, and these studies consistently fail to reproduce the results of experiments. Comparison group designs are more likely to produce valid results when there is careful matching of the treatment and comparison groups at pretest, especially on the pretest measures of the outcome and geographic location.

The evidence used to inform policy decisions must be scientifically valid. Randomized controlled trials are first and foremost in generating this evidence, followed closely by matched comparison designs. Non-equivalent comparison group designs or methods that fail to use a control group do not provide an acceptable standard of evidence, as they often produce erroneous results. Other factors in design and implementation of an evaluation must also be considered to ensure that the evaluation is producing valid results. These include, but are not limited to: adequate sample size, baseline equivalence, low attrition, lack of differential attrition, valid outcome measures, appropriate unit of analysis, intent to treat analysis, and appropriate statistical techniques. The Society for Prevention Research has adopted a similar set of standards that must be met if a program or policy is to be called tested and effective (Society for Prevention Research n.d.).

The quality of evidence is not the only consideration in defining an evidence-based program. If these programs are to be replicated, there must be specificity in the program description that clearly shows how its theoretically grounded components produce the intended impact. It is, therefore, important to identify the outcomes the program is designed to change and the specific risk, protective, and promotive factors that will mediate that change. It is also important to designate the targeted population, which should not be based upon assumption, but upon evidence of the program's success with that population. Theoretically driven programs also involve detailed instructions on how to deliver the intervention, duration of the intervention, and amount of training required. Failure to implement the program within the specified guidelines often results in smaller or null effects (Mihalic 2004). While some may question the importance of using theoretically driven programs, recent studies indicate that interventions which make extensive use of theory tend to have larger effects on behavior than interventions that make less or no use of theory (Taylor, Conner, and Lawton 2012; Webb et al. 2010).

Widespread dissemination of programs with evidence of effectiveness from poorly designed studies, as well as implementation of programs with poor fidelity, is a waste of limited funds and undermines the public confidence in prevention science when the outcomes that were promised are not achieved.

Why has policy changed over the last decade to support evidence-based programs?

Budget shortfalls at national and local levels have created a need for greater efficiency and accountability in systems working with children and youth. Despite tremendous outlays of money each year for support services to families and youth, research is not being used with sufficient frequency, intensity and quality to impact human services and has not provided the full potential benefits to consumers and communities (Baron 2012; Sawhill and Baron 2010). Baron (2012) uses as an example Department of Education data showing that "reading and math achievement of 17-year-olds—the end product of our K-12 educational system—has not improved over 40 years, despite a 90 percent rise in public spending per student (adjusted for inflation)." In the same report, he also states that "in education, although the college graduation rate has risen, the high school graduation rate peaked around 81 percent in the early 1970s. Since then, it has been stuck between 75 and 80 percent."

However, there are examples showing that when evidence-based programs are integrated into these systems, taxpayers enjoy cost savings and youth benefit from better outcomes. In 2004, the Florida Legislature voted to initiate the Department of Juvenile Justice's Redirection project to address the growing number of juvenile offenders who were being committed to residential facilities for non-legal violations of probation. The Redirection project diverted, or redirected, these youth from residential placement to evidence-based, community-based treatments, relying on three programs (Functional Family Therapy, Multi-systemic Therapy, and Brief Strategic Family Therapy). During the eight-year period through 2012, Redirection saved the Juvenile Justice System $183 million. Additionally, Redirection youth, compared to matched youth in residential commitment with the same risk profiles, had 19 percent fewer subsequent adjudications and 31 percent fewer subsequent placements. These reductions came with an average cost saving of $22,000 per youth served in Redirection. The program has been consistently shown to enhance public safety and save taxpayer dollars (Redirection 2012).

Pennsylvania also invested in evidence-based programs, especially Blueprints programs, with costs and benefits assessed for seven of those programs (Big Brothers Big Sisters, LifeSkills Training, Multidimensional Treatment Foster Care, Multisystemic Therapy, Functional Family Therapy, Nurse Family Partnership, and Strengthening Families). Using a conservative and widely accepted methodology developed by the Washington State Institute for Public Policy (WSIPP, 2013) and applied to data on the effectiveness of the programs in Pennsylvania, these programs achieved a return on investment of $317 million in reduced corrections costs, welfare and social services burden, drug and mental health treatment, and increased employment and tax revenue. That figure translates into a return between $1 and $25 per dollar invested (Jones et al. 2008).

After decades of reacting to problems with short-term, ineffective, or unevaluated approaches, and in some instances even believing in the pessimistic perspective that nothing works (Martinson 1974; Regnery 1985; Sechrest et al. 1979), we as a society have become more proactive in addressing the behavioral problems of youth and now pursue programs that have proven to demonstrate positive outcomes. Successes such as those mentioned above fuel the momentum. This has come as the science of prevention has evolved, and we have learned much about the factors leading to youth violence and poor developmental outcomes. Programs have been developed based upon research identifying specific risk and protective factors, and knowledge about how to successfully mitigate these factors, resulting in successful outcomes. Also, evaluation and statistical methods have evolved, bringing greater assurance of the effectiveness of programs. Such assurance has helped federal and local agencies, as well as private foundations, to be more proactive in promoting and/or requiring the use of evidence-based programs.

Creation of evidence-based registries

With an increased focus on what works, several federal and private registries have been created to help people sift through the findings and claims regarding evidence-based programs. These registries, while helpful, also create confusion among users because they vary widely in their focus and criteria for assessing effectiveness. Some registries were created to examine programs with specific outcomes. For instance, Blueprints, until recently, only examined outcomes of violence, delinquency, and substance use. Thus, a user looking for a program to address depression would previously not have found any listed. The terminology used to classify programs also varies, with some calling programs that meet the highest level of evidence "Model" and some labeling these programs as "Effective" or "Exemplary." The criteria used to assess program effectiveness also vary from registry to registry. For instance, while one registry may call a program "Model," another might list the same program as "Promising" or perhaps not list it at all because it does not meet the evidentiary standard. Registries also differ in whether or not they share information on programs reviewed but not meeting criteria.

Confusion around these differences often results in users assuming that if a program appears on a list that it has the same level of evidence as any other program on the list. For instance, a survey of state education agency directors that administered the Safe and Drug Free Schools and Communities Act in 2004–2005 found that all states rely on federal lists to determine whether programs are evidence-based; however, they were willing to recommend any program that appeared on the lists, even if the evidence was weak (Hallfors, Pankratz, and Hartman 2007).

Some help in understanding the evidence and ratings underlying these lists can be found on the Blueprints website which includes a "Matrix of Federal and Privately Rated Programs" that have been assessed by various registries (http://blueprintsprograms.com/resources/matrix.pdf). This matrix shows how a program has been rated across 5 agencies, including Blueprints, Coalition for Evidence-Based Policy, CrimeSolutions.gov, OJJDP Model Programs Guide, and SAMHSA-NREPP. Programs with consistently high ratings across several of the agencies should be ones that are given priority when searching for evidence-based programs to adopt. Users can also easily determine the top tier programs, regardless of the labeling used by each agency. The criteria used by each agency for assessing effectiveness are also provided.

Advantages of evidence-based programs

Assurance that the program works

There are numerous advantages in using evidence-based programs, but the biggest may be the assurance that the program works—the higher the scientific standard, the greater the assurance. Many people cling to the adage, "it's better to do something than nothing." Unfortunately, some things that are implemented with the best of intentions do harm to youth. Lipsey (1992) reported that approximately one-third (29%) of controlled evaluations of juvenile programs found negative effects. For instance, Scared Straight programs, which are currently being glamorized by a popular television network, have shown that the experimental groups reoffended between 1% and 30% more than the control groups (significance not provided) in seven of nine randomized studies reported on in a systematic review by Petrosino, Turpin-Petrosino, and Finckenauer (2000). The other two studies did not report group failure rates, and only one study reported positive effects (on new court intakes). Despite the best of intentions, this program led to more crime, showing that programs can not only fail, but may even do more harm than good.

Another example of a harmful program is the 21st Century Community Learning Centers, an afterschool program authorized by Congress in 1994. Nearly all centers offer recreational opportunities ranging from unstructured free time to organized sports. Programs also offer enrichment activities such as dance, drama, and music, as well as workshops on developmental topics such as building leadership skills and resolving conflicts with peers. The national evaluation found higher rates of negative behaviors (suspensions, disciplinary actions, calls to parents about bad behavior) in the treatment group, along with no differences in academic performance and mixed findings on developmental outcomes. The only positive outcome was that program youth felt safer than control youth (James-Burdumy, Dynarski, and Deke 2007, 2008). This program grew quickly with an appropriation of $40 million in fiscal year 1998 to $1.49 billion in fiscal year 2014 (http://www.afterschoolalliance.org/policy21stcclc.cfm), despite evaluation evidence of its harmful effects. Investments in such ineffective and sometimes harmful programs are a waste of scarce violence prevention dollars and undermine public confidence in prevention science when the intended results are not achieved.

Cost–benefit data available

A second advantage is that cost–benefit data are often available for evidence-based programs, usually showing that the monetary benefits of implementing the program outweigh the costs. These data have been reported for various evidence-based programs by the Washington State Institute for Public Policy (WSIPP 2013). For example WSIPP reports $25.61 in monetary benefits per $1 spent in implementing the LifeSkills Training program. Similarly, research at Pennsylvania State University reports $25.72 in benefits from LifeSkills Training per $1 spent, with an estimated $16,160,000 in potential economic benefit statewide (Jones et al. 2008). WSIPP estimates that the implementation of a modest or aggressive portfolio of evidence-based programs in the State of Washington between 2008 and 2030 could save the taxpayers from $1.9 to $2.6 billion, respectively (Aos, Miller, and Drake 2006). In the current decade of cost containment, showing that programs can actually generate savings is an important decision-making tool when deciding which investments in programs should be made.

Packaged/manualized materials available

Evidence-based programs offer packaged/manualized materials that explain what should be delivered to whom, when, where and how. The materials usually include protocols or checklists for monitoring implementation fidelity. In many of the evidence-based programs, quality assurance procedures are integral to the program and serve to improve the quality of implementation and the likelihood of results. Training and technical assistance are also available and are typically mandatory. An evidence-based program with packaged materials is usually much more time and cost-efficient than developing one's own program. Also program development should always be followed by evaluation, and this can be an extremely costly endeavor. An evidence-based program does not require evaluation in every new site during the adoption and early implementation stage, as its effectiveness has already been established. It is more important to monitor implementation fidelity to ensure that the program is being implemented as intended in order to ensure the best results. After the program has been established at a site, some form of evaluation may be warranted to ensure the program is having its intended effect at the site. It should be noted, however, that a program evaluation establishes effectiveness with a specific targeted population. A new evaluation is required when a program is implemented outside the population for which evidence exists.

Current use of evidence-based programs

The advantages of evidence-based programs in resolving the youth development issues faced by our nation seem unquestionable. Yet, the adoption of these programs has lagged behind the growth in the number of programs being made available. In mental health, the time lag between development of an evidence-based practice and its integration into routine practice is estimated to be 20 years (Hoagwood 2003–2004; Institute of Medicine Committee on Quality of Healthcare in America 2001). The implementation of evidence-based programs in school settings has grown over the years since national surveys first assessed their use, from 34.4% in 1999 to 42.6% in 2005 to 46.9% in 2008 (Ringwalt et al. 2011; Ringwalt et al. 2009). Respondents in these surveys were also asked to identify which curriculum they used the most since most school districts use multiple curricula. Although nearly half the school districts used an evidence-based program in 2008, only 26% of schools used the evidence-based program most frequently. Other studies have shown a similar pattern, reporting that a majority of schools use evidence-based prevention curricula, but they are rarely the most commonly used curricula (Pankratz and Hallfors 2004). Additionally, Hallfors and Godette (2002) found that only 19% were implementing evidence-based curricula with fidelity. The use of evidence-based programs in other domains is even lower. Kumpfer and Alvarado (2003) estimate that in 2003 only 10% of family programs were evidence-based. Much more needs to be done to inform funders and practitioners of the benefits of evidence-based programs, the availability of programs that meet specific needs, the outcomes that can be achieved, and cost benefits that result. This has been the mission of Blueprints for Healthy Youth Development since 1996.

Blueprints for Healthy Youth Development

Background

Blueprints for Healthy Youth Development, formerly known as Blueprints for Violence Prevention, was one of the early leaders in the movement to identify evidence-based programs, promoting and using a rigorous standard. Blueprints, hosted at the University of Colorado Boulder—Center for the Study and Prevention of Violence, began in 1996 with several small grants and received major funding from the Office of Juvenile Justice and Delinquency Prevention beginning in 1997. The original focus was on the prevention of youth violence, delinquency, and substance use. In the latter half of 2010, with funding from the Annie E. Casey Foundation, the focus expanded to include youth programs to improve emotional and physical health and well-being, positive relationships, and academic success. The outcomes of interest involve more than preventing harmful behavior—they also involve positive behaviors and healthy development.

Blueprints identifies and recommends programs for children, youth and families that have undergone rigorous evaluations which have demonstrated strong evidence of effectiveness. Blueprints provides one of the highest standards in the field for quality programming.

Blueprints standard

The Blueprints' standards for recommending a program are among the most rigorous in the field. Many of the program registries ask for nominations and only review those studies submitted by the program developers. Thus, studies with null results may be omitted from the review process. Although Blueprints does review nominated programs, Blueprints additionally performs an exhaustive search of the literature on a monthly basis to find programs related to the outcomes of interest (delinquency, substance use, emotional and physical well-being, academic success, and positive relationships). A Blueprints program review typically considers all evaluations of a program. A comprehensive write-up of every program identified is completed. Each program write-up includes a description of the program, target audience, risk and protective factors, evaluation methodology, outcomes, generalizability, and limitations of each evaluation conducted for that program. A program then undergoes an internal review administered by Blueprints staff to determine if it might meet Blueprints criteria. Programs that pass this initial screening will undergo a second review conducted externally by the Blueprints Advisory Board of experts.

Blueprints considers four criteria for certifying a program:

- Evaluation quality: Studies must be of sufficient methodological quality to confidently attribute results to the program.

- Intervention impact: The preponderance of evidence from the high quality evaluations indicates significant positive change in intended outcomes that can be attributed to the program, and there is no evidence of harmful effects.
- Intervention specificity: The program description clearly identifies the outcome the program is designed to change, the specific risk and/or protective factors targeted to produce this change in outcome, the population for which it is intended, and how the components of the intervention work to produce this change.
- Dissemination readiness: The program is currently available for dissemination and has the necessary organizational capability, manuals, training, technical assistance and other support required for implementation with fidelity in communities and public service systems. Cost information and monitoring tools must also be available.

Blueprints programs must meet all four criteria. Programs are rated as either "Promising" or "Model." Promising programs meet the minimum standard of effectiveness, requiring a minimum of (a) one high quality randomized controlled trial or (b) two high quality quasi-experimental evaluations. Model programs meet a higher standard and provide greater confidence in the program's capacity to change behavior and developmental outcomes. Model programs require replication with a minimum of (a) two high quality randomized controlled trials or (b) one high quality randomized controlled trial plus one high quality quasi-experimental evaluation. There is also a requirement for sustained positive intervention impact for a minimum of 12 months after the program intervention ends.

To date, of more than 1300 programs assessed, 54 programs have qualified for Blueprints certification. While many programs with randomized or quasi-experimental designs have been evaluated, they often fail to meet the evaluation quality standard. . . . Some of the more common problems that prevent certification of a program include: (a) the failure to demonstrate baseline equivalence, (b) failure to determine if attrition differs by study condition, (c) randomizing subjects at one level (such as school) and conducting the analysis at a different level (such as individual), and (d) failure to follow and analyze all subjects as assigned to their original condition (intent to treat).

Blueprints website

Blueprints has developed a new website (http://blueprintsprograms.com) that highlights the model and promising programs in five outcome domains: problem behavior, emotional regulation, academic success, physical health and well-being, and positive relationships. Easy-to-use program searches allow users to match programs to identified needs. Searches can be run using criteria such as risk and protective factors, program outcomes achieved, type of program, or targeted population (i.e., age, gender, race/ ethnicity), as well as several other factors. Each program listed on the website contains information on:

- description of the intervention,
- program goals,
- risk and protective factors,
- logic model (if available),
- outcomes achieved,
- training and technical assistance,

- contact information,
- program costs,
- funding strategies,
- cost–benefit information (if analyzed by Washington State Institute for Public Policy),
- full write-ups describing all evaluations of a program, including methodology, outcomes, and limitations.

The website includes links to needs assessment surveys for those who want to match a program to the needs identified in their schools or communities. The Blueprints website provides a brief description of the standards that various federal and private agencies use to rate programs, as well as a matrix of programs with the rating given by each of those agencies, allowing a comparison of ratings across agencies (http://blueprintsprograms.com/resources).

The information provided on the Blueprints website, as well as a national/international Blueprints Conference (http://blueprintsconference.com) held every two years, has led to greater awareness and use of evidence-based programs. The Blueprints website has served as a resource for governmental agencies, schools, foundations, and community human service organizations trying to make informed decisions about their investments in youth programs.

Lessons learned

Throughout the 17 plus years of the Blueprints project, the most important lesson that we have learned, and have struggled to impart, is that the standard for recognizing an evidence-based program must be high in order to maintain the public's confidence. In the earliest years of the project, Blueprints identified a model program, Quantum Opportunities, based upon a multi-site evaluation (Hahn 1994, 1995). This evaluation examined outcomes in each of the national sites participating in the study, and the demonstration appeared successful. Later, a large multi-site replication by the Department of Labor found only a few, largely inconsistent effects (Rodriguez-Planas 2012), and some of the primary behavioral outcomes were negative at one of the replicating sites (unpublished report). This program had to be removed from the Blueprints list.

This happened again with another program, CASASTART, a comprehensive case management strategy for preventing drug use and delinquency for small groups of high-risk adolescents, ages 11–13, living in highly distressed neighborhoods. Although this program was only on the Blueprints list as promising, based upon one successful large-scale randomized trial conducted by the Urban Institute (Harrell et al. 1997; Harrell, Cavanagh, and Sridharan 1998), a later evaluation conducted by the Blueprints team found no effects, and some iatrogenic effects for girls (Mihalic et al. 2011). This program was subsequently retracted by the program developers. However, many agencies were already using the program and were left with decisions of whether to continue or abandon the program. Some were in the midst of grants, while others were in the process of renewing grants that would support implementation. While most agencies ultimately decided to continue the use of the program, believing that they were having success with their youth, there was confusion as to how to handle the unexpected news.

These examples reinforce the reasoning for maintaining a high standard. We cannot afford to take programs to scale prior to rigorous testing. When a program has not been adequately tested and later evidence suggests that the program should be removed from a list, this shakes the confidence of the public. In the examples above, the original trials were conducted in a rigorous manner with random assignment, and later studies failed to replicate. This reinforces the need for replication as a part of the standard. There is always a chance of instances such as these happening, but to accept programs with an even lower standard than Blueprints could multiply such problems. The only way to avoid these costly and confusing problems is to endorse standards of the highest quality, especially when taking programs to scale.

Blueprints maintains a rigorous standard; however, we suggest that as time goes by even our standard could be strengthened, especially by requiring independent replication. Currently, Blueprints model programs require replication; however, those studies are typically done by the program developers. There is accumulating evidence that programs evaluated by the program developers report effect sizes considerably larger than trials conducted by independent researchers (Eisner 2009). This can be attributed to specific biases that can be inadvertently built into an evaluation at various steps in the process. Additionally, program developers evaluating their own programs provide a range of technical assistance resources that are often not available in real-world applications. At the current time, adoption of that standard would limit the number of model programs to less than a handful. We are hopeful that over time, researchers and funders will see the value of independent replication and more independent studies will be conducted.

Conclusion

Human services systems spend millions of dollars each year to address the problems that prevent youth from attaining developmental milestones and reaching their full potential. Unfortunately, even with the best of intentions, much of this work has not demonstrated the intended benefits, and some of the work done in public service agencies is conducted with little attention to behavioral outcomes. This has been changing, especially over the last decade, with an increased emphasis on accountability and promotion of evidence-based programs. However, public service systems and schools do not always know which programs would be best in meeting their needs. Often choices are made because of "hearsay" testimonial or other reasons not based on evidence. These systems need assistance in choosing programs that are effective and that represent a good match to the needs, programming, and staffing of the system.

Blueprints for Healthy Youth Development helps to meet those needs. Blueprints maintains a registry of programs that meet the highest standards of quality, and each program has been deemed ready for dissemination. The rigor underlying evaluations of Blueprints programs can assure users that they can make a real difference in preventing antisocial behavior and promoting positive behavior, academic success, emotional well-being, physical health and positive relationships.

The Blueprints website (http://blueprintsprograms.com) provides useful information on every model and promising program. There are easy-to-use program searches that help users find a program that matches their selection criteria. Users can search for a program by the outcomes they are interested in impacting, by a specific type of program, by risk and protective factors, and by the intended target of intervention (such as age, gender, race/ethnicity). Program information includes descriptions of the intervention, targeted audience, risk and protective factors, contacts, training and technical assistance, program costs, funding strategies, and cost–benefit data. There are also full descriptions of all studies conducted of a program, with information on methodology, outcomes, and limitations. The information is comprehensive, some of which cannot be found on other registries.

Blueprints will continue to promote the use of evidence-based programs and the use of high standards to identify those programs. Blueprints conducts a conference every two years with this as a major goal. Blueprints remains a leader in setting the standards for identifying evidence-based programs and for promoting the use of these programs nationally and internationally.

[References omitted.]

CRITICAL-THINKING QUESTIONS

1 How might the outcome of Melissa's case, presented at the beginning of the chapter, have been different if formal adjudication and commitment to some type of juvenile residential placement occurred instead of the more preventive intervention that was used?
2 What does the term *adolescents at risk* mean and how is it related to delinquency prevention efforts?
3 Explain the statement: Risk-focused prevention is based upon the simple premise that to prevent a risk-taking behavior from occurring, we need to identify the factors that increase the risk of that behavior and then find ways to reduce the risk.
4 Briefly characterize the evidence-based practice approach to delinquency prevention.
5 What are some of the dangers of ignoring evidence-based delinquency prevention practices?
6 The prevention and intervention programs described in the reading by Bulman (2014) are grouped according to "program focus." Identify the six focus areas and provide an example of each.
7 Using the reading by Mihalic and Elliott (2015), briefly explain how the Blueprints model program registry evaluates evidence, data, and research methods to determine which programs meet their high standard of proven efficacy.

SUGGESTED READING

Dodge, Kenneth A. and Adam D. Mandel. 2012. "Building Evidence for Evidence-Based Policy Making." *Criminology & Public Policy* 11:525–534.

Elliott, Delbert S. and Sharon Mihalic 2004. "Issues in Disseminating and Replicating Effective Prevention Programs." *Prevention Science* 5:47–53.

Greenwood, Peter W. and Brandon C. Welsh. 2012. "Promoting Evidence-Based Practice in Delinquency Prevention at the State Level: Principles, Progress, and Policy Directions." *Criminology & Public Policy* 11:493–513.

Lipsey, Mark W. and James C. Howell. 2012. "A Broader View of Evidence-Based Programs Reveals More Options for State Juvenile Justice Systems." *Criminology & Public Policy* 11:515–523.

McKee, Esther Chao and Lisa Rapp. 2014. "The Current Status of Evidence-Based Practice in Juvenile Justice." *Journal of Evidence-Based Social Work* 11:308–314.

USEFUL WEBSITES

For further information relevant to this chapter, go to the following websites.

- **Blueprints for Healthy Youth Development**, Center for the Study and Prevention of Violence at the University of Colorado Boulder: www.blueprintsprograms.com
- **Model Programs Guide**, Office of Juvenile Justice and Delinquency Prevention: www.ojjdp.gov/mpg
- **Model Programs iGuides**, Office of Juvenile Justice and Delinquency Prevention: www.ojjdp.gov/mpg-iguides/iguide-categories.html
- **National Registry of Evidence-based Programs and Practices**, Substance Abuse and Mental Health Services Administration: www.samhsa.gov/nrepp

GLOSSARY OF KEY TERMS

Cost–benefit analysis: In evaluating delinquency intervention programs, cost–benefit analysis seeks to "comprehensively identify and measure the benefits and costs of a program," including those that occur during and after participation in the program (National Research Council 2013:167).

Dynamic risk factors: Characteristics of the youth and his/her environment that can be changed through intervention, such as antisocial attitudes and values, association with delinquent peers, dysfunctional family relationships, and antisocial personality traits (impulsiveness, risk-taking, and low self-control).

Evidence-based practice: "Involves the use of scientific principles to assess the available evidence on program effectiveness and to develop principles for best practice in any particular field" (Greenwood and Welsh 2012:495).

Fidelity: "The degree to which a program's core services, components, and procedures are implemented as originally designed" (CrimeSolutions.gov 2016).

Indicated prevention (or tertiary prevention): Targets identified juvenile offenders in order to prevent or eliminate a serious pattern of delinquent offending.

Meta-analysis: A statistical technique that estimates the effects found across evaluation studies of intervention methods and strategies.

Protective factors: Individual traits, abilities, and social circumstances that allow youth to adapt positively to adverse environments.

Program registry of evidence-based practice: A systematic guide to model programs for delinquency prevention and intervention. The model programs that are identified and described have been found to be effective through evaluation research.

Resiliency: Achieving healthy psychosocial development and positive functioning despite stress, hardship, and adversity (risk factors).

Risk-taking behaviors: Exciting, pleasure-seeking acts such as alcohol and drug use, disruptive acts and underachievement in school, reckless driving, precocious sexual activity, and juvenile delinquency. Risk-taking behaviors may be harmful for the youth and others and they may compromise psychosocial maturation in the adolescent and young adult years.

Risk factor: Any individual trait, social influence, or environmental condition that leads to greater likelihood of risk-taking behaviors and ultimately negative developmental outcomes during the adolescent years.

Risk/need assessment: Standardized assessment instruments to identify the likelihood or "risk" of future offending or reoffending, and the "criminogenic needs" of the youth—those factors that lead to delinquency and can be changed.

Selective prevention (or secondary prevention): Prevention programs target youth or groups of youths who are "at-risk" due to multiple risk factors in their lives.

Static risk factors: Background characteristics of the youth that cannot be changed through prevention programs, including the age of onset of problem behaviors, history of aggressive behavior and violence, and parental criminality.

Universal prevention (or primary prevention): Prevention programs that target the general population of youth and include campaigns to prevent smoking and drug use, to promote problem-solving and dispute resolution skill through classroom education, and classes on parenting skills offered to all parents.

NOTES

1 *Latdict: Latin Dictionary and Grammar Resources* (www.latin-dictionary.net/search/latin/adolescere), accessed January 26, 2016. See also *Oxford English Dictionary* (http://dictionary.oed.com), accessed January 26, 2016.

2 Another approach to adolescent development focuses on positive youth development. Lerner and his colleagues emphasize the "Five C's" of positive youth development: confidence, competence, character, caring, and connection (Arbeit et al. 2014).

3 Farrington and Welsh (2007:94) point out that there are very few truly "universal" programs, provided to all youth and families because prevention programs are a limited resource that usually must be targeted to those in greatest need. Thus, universal programs are often applied selectively.

REFERENCES

Andrews, D. A. and James Bonta. 2010. *The Psychology of Criminal Conduct.* 5th ed. Cincinnati, OH: Anderson.

Andrews, D. A., James Bonta, and J. Stephen Wormith. 2006. "The Recent Past and Near Future of Risk and/or Need Assessment." *Crime and Delinquency* 52:7–27.

Arbeit, Miriam R., Sara K. Johnson, Robey B. Champine, Kathleen N. Greenman, Jacqueline V. Lerner, Richard M. Lerner. 2014. "Profiles of Problematic Behaviors across Adolescence: Covariations with Indicators of Positive Youth Development." *Journal of Youth and Adolescence* 43:971–990.

Bartol, Curt R. and Anne M. Bartol. 2009. *Juvenile Delinquency and Antisocial Behavior: A Developmental Perspective.* 3rd ed. Upper Saddle River, NJ: Pearson Prentice Hall.

Blueprints for Healthy Youth Development (Blueprints). 2017. Center for the Study and Prevention of Violence at the Institute of Behavioral Science, University of Colorado Boulder. Retrieved October 26, 2017 (www.blueprintsprograms.com).

Broidy, Lisa M., Daniel S. Nagin, Richard E. Tremblay, John E. Bates, Bobby Brame, Kenneth A. Dodge, David Fergusson, John L. Horwood, Rolf Loeber, Robert Laird, Donald R. Lynam, Terrie E. Moffitt, Gregory S. Pettit, and Frank Vitaro. 2003. "Developmental Trajectories of Childhood Disruptive Behaviors and Adolescent Delinquency: A Six-Site, Cross-National Study." *Developmental Psychology* 39:222–245.

Brown, B. Bradford, Jeremy P. Bakken, Suzanne W. Ameringer and Shelly D. Mahon. 2008. "A Comprehensive Conceptualization of the Peer Influence Process in Adolescence." Pp. 17–44 in *Understanding Peer Influence in Children and Adolescents*, ed. M. J. Prinstein and K. A. Dodge. New York: Guilford Press.

Bulman, Phil. 2014. "Changing Lives: Prevention and Intervention to Reduce Serious Offending." Washington, DC: Office of Juvenile Justice and Delinquency Prevention.

Burns, Barbara J., James C. Howell, Janet K. Wiig, Leena K. Augimeri, Brendan C. Welsh, Rolf Loeber, and David Petechuk. 2003. "Treatment, Services, and Intervention Programs for Child Delinquency." Washington, DC: Office of Juvenile Justice and Delinquency Prevention.

Byrne, James M. and Arthur J. Lurigio. 2009. "Separating Science from Nonsense: Evidence-Based Research, Policy, and Practice in Criminal and Juvenile Justice Settings." *Victims and Offenders* 4:303–310.

Cohen, Mark A. and Alex R. Piquero. 2009. "New Evidence on the Monetary Value of Saving a High-Risk Youth." *Journal of Quantitative Criminology* 42:89–109.

Collins, W. Andrew and Steinberg, Laurence. 2006. "Adolescent Development in Interpersonal Context." Pp. 1003–1077 in *Handbook of Child Psychology: Vol. 3, Social, Emotional, and Personality Development*, 6th ed., edited by N. Eisenberg, W. Damon, and R. M. Lerner. Hoboken, NJ: John Wiley & Sons.

CrimeSolutions.gov. 2016. "Glossary." National Institute of Justice. Retrieved February 3, 2016 (www.crimesolutions.gov/Glossary.aspx).

Dodge, Kenneth A. and Adam D. Mandel. 2012. "Building Evidence for Evidence-Based Policy Making." *Criminology and Public Policy* 11:525–534.

Drake, Elizabeth K., Steve Aos, and Marna G. Miller. 2009. "Evidence-Based Public Policy Options to Reduce Crime and Criminal Justice Costs: Implications for Washington State." *Victims & Offenders* 4:170–196.

Dryfoos, Joy G. 1990. *Adolescents at Risk: Prevalence and Prevention*. New York: Oxford.

Elliott, Delbert S., David Huizinga, and Scott Menard. 1989. *Multiple Problem Youth: Delinquency, Substance Use, and Mental Health Problems*. New York: Springer-Verlag.

Elliott, Delbert S. and Sharon Mihalic. 2004. "Issues in Disseminating and Replicating Effective Prevention Programs." *Prevention Science* 5:47–53.

Farrington, David P. and Brandon C. Welsh. 2007. *Saving Children from a Life of Crime*. New York: Oxford.

Gardner, Margo and Laurence Steinberg. 2005. "Peer Influence on Risk Taking, Risk Preference, and Risky Decision Making in Adolescence and Adulthood: An Experimental Study. *Developmental Psychology* 41:625–635.

Green, Amy E., Ellis L. Gesten, Mark A. Greenwald, and Octavio Salcedo. 2008. "Predicting Delinquency in Adolescence and Young Adulthood: A Longitudinal Analysis of Early Risk Factors." *Youth Violence and Juvenile Justice* 6:323–342.

Greenwood, Peter. 2006. *Changing Lives: Delinquency Prevention as Crime Control*. Chicago: University of Chicago.

Greenwood, Peter. 2008. "Prevention and Intervention Programs for Juvenile Offenders." *The Future of Children* 18:185–210. Retrieved February 7, 2015 (www.princeton.edu/futureofchildren/publications/docs/18_02_09.pdf).

Greenwood, Peter W. and Brandon C. Welsh. 2012. "Promoting Evidence-Based Practice in Delinquency Prevention at the State Level: Principles, Progress, and Policy Directions." *Criminology & Public Policy* 11:493–513.

Hawkins, J. David, Todd I. Herrenkohl, David P. Farrington, Devon Brewer, Richard F. Catalano, Tracy W. Harachi, and Lynn Cothern. 2000. "Predictors of Youth Violence." Washington, DC: Office of Juvenile Justice and Delinquency Prevention.

Hawkins, Stephanie R., Phillip W. Graham, Jason Williams, and Margaret A. Zahn. 2009. "Resilient Girls—Factors that Protect Against Delinquency." Girls Study Group: Understanding and Responding to Girls' Delinquency. Washington, DC: Office of Juvenile Justice and Delinquency Prevention.

Hoge, Robert D., Gina Vincent, and Laura S. Guy. 2013. "Bulletin 4: Prediction and Risk/Needs Assessment" (NCJ 242934). Study Group on the Transitions between Juvenile Delinquency and Adult Crime. Washington, DC: National Criminal Justice Reference Service. Retrieved October 6, 2014 (https://ncjrs.gov/pdffiles1/nij/grants/242934.pdf).

Huizinga, David A., Rolf Loeber, Terence P. Thornberry, and Lynn Cothern. 2000. "Co-Occurrence of Delinquency and Other Problem Behaviors." *Juvenile Justice Bulletin*. Washington, DC: Office of Juvenile Justice and Delinquency Prevention.

Jessor, Richard. 1992. "Risk Behavior in Adolescence: A Psychosocial Framework for Understanding and Action." *Developmental Review* 12:374–390.

Lehman, Joseph D., J. David Hawkins, and Richard F. Catalano. 1994. *Corrections Today* (August):92–100.

Lerner, Richard M. and Nancy L. Galambos. 1998. "Adolescent Development: Challenges and Opportunities for Research, Programs, and Policies." *Annual Review of Psychology* 49:413–446.

Lipsey, Mark W. 1992. "Juvenile Delinquency in Treatment: A Meta-Analytic Inquiry into the Variability of Effects." Pp. 83–127 in *Meta-Analysis for Explanation: A Casebook*, edited by T. D. Cook, H. Cooper, D. S. Cordray, H. Hartmann, L. V. Hedges, R. J. Light, T. A. Louis, and F. Mosteller. New York: Russell Sage Foundation.

Lipsey, Mark W. 2009. "The Primary Factors that Characterize Effective Interventions with Juvenile Offenders: A Meta-Analytic Overview." *Victims & Offenders* 4:124–147.

Lipsey, Mark W. and Francis T. Cullen. 2007. "The Effectiveness of Correctional Rehabilitation: A Review of Systematic Reviews." *Annual Review of Law and Social Science* 3:297–320.

Lipsey, Mark W. and James C. Howell. 2012. "A Broader View of Evidence-Based Programs Reveals More Options for State Juvenile Justice Systems." *Criminology & Public Policy*, 11:515–523.

Lipsey, Mark, James C. Howell, Marion R. Kelly, Gabrielle Chapman, and Darin Carver. 2010. *Improving the Effectiveness of Juvenile Justice Programs: A New Perspective on Evidence-Based Practice.* Washington, DC: Center for Juvenile Justice Reform. Retrieved October 31, 2017 (http://cjjr.georgetown.edu/wp-content/uploads/2015/03/ImprovingEffectiveness_December2010.pdf).

Loeber, Rolf, David Farrington, and David Petechuk. 2003. "Child Delinquency: Early Intervention and Prevention." Washington, DC: Office of Juvenile Justice and Delinquency Prevention.

McKee, Esther Chao and Lisa Rapp. 2014. "The Current Status of Evidence-Based Practice in Juvenile Justice." *Journal of Evidence-Based Social Work* 11:308–314.

Mihalic, Sharon F. and Delbert S. Elliott. 2015. "Evidence-Based Programs Registry: Blueprints for Healthy Youth Development." *Evaluation and Program Planning* 48:124–131.

Mihalic, Sharon, Abigail Fagan, Katherine Irwin, Diane Ballard, and Delbert Elliott. 2004a. "Blueprints for Violence Prevention." Washington, DC: Office of Juvenile Justice and Delinquency Prevention.

Mihalic, Sharon, Katherine Irwin, Abigail Fagan, Diane Ballard, and Delbert Elliott. 2004b. "Successful Program Implementation: Lessons from Blueprints." Washington, DC: Office of Juvenile Justice and Delinquency Prevention.

Moffitt, Terrie E. 1993. "Adolescence-Limited and Life-Course-Persistent Antisocial Behavior: A Developmental Taxonomy." *Psychological Review* 100:674–701.

Monahan, Kathryn C., Laurence Steinberg, Elizabeth Cauffman, and Edward P. Mulvey. 2009. "Trajectories of Antisocial Behavior and Psychosocial Maturity from Adolescence to Young Adulthood." *Developmental Psychology* 45:1654–1668.

National Research Council. 2013. *Reforming Juvenile Justice: A Developmental Approach*, edited by Richard J. Bonnie, Robert L. Johnson, Betty M. Chemers, and Julie A. Schuck (Committee on Assessing Juvenile Justice Reform). Committee on Law and Justice, Division of Behavioral and Social Sciences and Education. Washington, DC: The National Academies Press.

Olds, David, Peggy Hill, and Elissa Rumsey. 1998. "Prenatal and Early Childhood Nurse Home Visitation." Washington, DC: Office of Juvenile Justice and Delinquency Prevention.

President's Commission on Law Enforcement and Administration of Justice. 1967. *Task Force Report: Juvenile Delinquency and Youth Crime.* Washington, DC: GPO.

Rocque, Michael, Brandon C. Welsh, Peter W. Greenwood, and Erica King. 2014. "Implementing and Sustaining Evidence-Based Practice in Juvenile Justice: A Case Study of a Rural State." *International Journal of Offender Therapy and Comparative Criminology* 58:1033–1057.

Schwalbe, Craig S. 2008. "A Meta-Analysis of Juvenile Justice Risk Assessment Instruments: Predictive Validity by Gender." *Criminal Justice and Behavior* 35:1367–1381.

Steinberg, Laurence and Elizabeth Cauffman. 1996. "Maturity of Judgment in Adolescence: Psychosocial Factors in Adolescent Decision Making." *Law and Human Behavior* 20:249–272.

Steinberg, Laurence, Elizabeth Cauffman, and Kathryn C. Monahan. 2015. "Psychosocial Maturity and Desistance from Crime in a Sample of Serious Juvenile Offenders." Washington, DC: Office of Juvenile Justice and Delinquency Prevention.

Steinberg, Laurence, He Len Chung, and Michelle Little. 2004. "Reentry of Young Offenders from the Justice System: A Developmental Perspective." *Youth Violence and Juvenile Justice* 2:21–38.

Steinberg, Laurence and Amanda Sheffield Morris. 2001. "Adolescent Development." *Annual Review of Psychology* 52:83–110.

Tanner-Smith, Emily E., Sandra Jo Wilson, and Mark W. Lipsey. 2013. "Risk Factors and Crime." Pp. 89–111 in *The Oxford Handbook of Criminological Theory*, edited by F. T. Cullen and P. Wilcox. New York: Oxford.

Thornberry, Terence P., David Huizinga, and Rolf Loeber. 2004. "The Causes and Correlates Studies: Findings and Policy Implications." *Juvenile Justice* 9:3–19.

Vincent, Gina M., Laura S. Guy, and Thomas Grisso. 2012. "Risk Assessment in Juvenile Justice: A Guidebook for Implementation." Models for Change: System Reform in Juvenile Justice. MacArthur Foundation. Retrieved April 25, 2014 (www.modelsforchange.net/publications/346).

Washington State Institute for Public Policy. 2011. "Return on Investment: Evidence-Based Options to Improve Statewide Outcomes." Olympia, WA: Washington State Institute for Public Policy. Retrieved September 30, 2014 (www.wsipp.wa.gov/rptfiles/11-07-1201.pdf).

Wasserman, Gail A., Kate Keenan, Richard E. Tremblay, John D. Cole, Todd I. Herrenkohl, Rolf Loeber, and David Petechuk. 2003. "Risk and Protective Factors of Child Delinquency." Washington, DC: Office of Juvenile Justice and Delinquency Prevention.

Welsh, Brandon C. and David P. Farrington. 2007. "Scientific Support for Early Prevention of Delinquency and Later Offending." *Victims and Offenders* 2:125–140.

Welsh, Brandon C., Mark W. Lipsey, Frederick P., Rivara, J. David Hawkins, Steve Aos, Meghan E. Peel, David Petechuk. 2013. "Bulletin 6: Changing Lives: Prevention and Intervention to Reduce Serious Offending" (NCJ 242936). Study Group on the Transitions between Juvenile Delinquency and Adult Crime. Washington, DC: National Criminal Justice Reference Service. Retrieved January 13, 2015 (https://ncjrs.gov/pdffiles1/nij/grants/242936.pdf).

Werner, Emmy E. 2005. "What Can We Learn About Resilience From Large-Scale Longitudinal Studies?" Pp. 91–105 in *Handbook of Resilience in Children*, edited by S. Goldstein and R. B. Brooks. New York: Kluwer Academic/Plenum Publishers.

Zahn, Margaret A., Stephanie R. Hawkins, Janet Chiancone, and Ariel Whitworth. 2008. "Charting the Way to Delinquency Prevention for Girls." Girls Study Group: Understanding and Responding to Girls' Delinquency. Washington, DC: Office of Juvenile Justice and Delinquency Prevention.

Chapter 14

LINKING SYSTEMS OF CARE

CHAPTER TOPICS

- **A system of care approach**
- **Major systems of care for court-involved youth**
- **Linking systems of care for children and youth**

CHAPTER LEARNING OBJECTIVES

After completing this chapter, students should be able to:

- Describe the system of care philosophy.
- Define youth maltreatment and the impact it has on the service needs of youth in the juvenile justice system.
- Identify the major systems of care that provide services for youth in juvenile justice systems.
- Explain the importance of identifying prior victimization and trauma exposure in the linking systems of care for children and youth approach.

CHAPTER CONTENTS

CASE IN POINT

MARCIE, A MULTISYSTEM YOUTH

Marcie's first involvement with the juvenile court occurred when she was 13 years old. School officials found her smoking marijuana with two other students in the alley next to the junior high school. Disciplinary records show that she regularly cut classes, often skipping school altogether, and twice had been involved in physical altercations with other students. Examination of her social and family history reveals a much broader scope of treatment needs prior to official contact with the juvenile justice system.

At the age of four, Marcie was abandoned by an alcoholic mother who was fleeing an abusive relationship with Marcie's biological father. At that time, she entered the foster care system. Prior to her fifth birthday, she began receiving medical care for stomach pains. The doctor diagnosed her with stomach ulcers, thought to be the result of stress and worry. When Marcie started kindergarten, these physical problems worsened and she often missed school due to chronic stomach pain. Marcie struggled with school; in particular, she had difficulty learning to read. Diagnosed with dyslexia and attention-deficit/hyperactivity disorder prior to the second grade, she was on an individualized learning plan and was reading below a fifth-grade level at the time of her arrest for possession of marijuana.

Marcie's story is not unique. Despite declines in the number of juveniles entering justice systems across the United States, treatment needs for court-involved youth have become more apparent (Hockenberry and Puzzanchera 2017; Herz et al. 2012; Abram et al. 2004). As we have seen in previous chapters, juvenile courts have traditionally assumed responsibility for coordinating services for youth, sometimes through diversion and community-based programs, and other times through direct services provided by court personnel, particularly probation officers. Court personnel, however, are beginning to realize that a variety of services fall outside the expertise of juvenile courts, especially specialized services such as educational support, medical care, mental health care, and substance abuse treatment. In this chapter, we focus on the development of a linked system of care for children and youth approach. The discussion begins with an overview of the system of care philosophy. We then discuss the major systems outside the juvenile justice system where court-involved youth receive care. The chapter concludes with a brief discussion of wraparound services in the juvenile justice system and introduces a recent program launched by the Office for Victims of Crime that advances a linking system of care approach.

A SYSTEM OF CARE APPROACH

From its inception, the juvenile justice system promoted both a rehabilitate and preventative approach. This approach is consistent with mandates to manage juvenile offenses in a largely community-based approach that emphasizes the needs of juveniles as a guiding principle over the need to punish them. In Chapter 2, on the Origins and Transformation of Juvenile Justice, we discussed how the rehabilitative ideal of the juvenile court came under attack beginning with the "due process revolution" in the mid-1960s.

By the 1980s the "get tough" approach, along with increases in both the number and severity of juvenile offenses, prompted several initiatives for punishment and accountability. Funds for publicly available services for juveniles began to shrink. Across the United States, juvenile justice systems began addressing treatment needs previously provided through public services within the community.

Outside of the juvenile justice systems, other major systems providing services to juveniles (e.g., child welfare, education, healthcare, mental health, and substance abuse treatment) were adapting specialized approaches. In many instances, information gathered within each of these systems was not easily accessible across systems by other service providers. This so-called "silo effect" resulted in the development of care plans for juveniles that were specific to needs within a single system, despite the growing body of evidence about service needs across multiple systems.

Origins of the system of care philosophy

The system of care movement traces its origin back to the 1960s. We begin our discussion 20 years later, with work in the mental health system, focusing on severely emotionally disturbed youth (Stroul and Friedman 1986). This work, grounded in a multi-system approach, recognizes that emotionally disturbed youth and their families require coordinated services beyond the mental health system. The system of care approach builds on the 1984 initiation of the Child and Adolescent Service System Program and is the first approach of its kind that systematically addresses children's mental health (Hodges, Ferreira, and Israel 2012).

In their original statement, Stroul and Friedman (1986:3) define a **system of care** as "a comprehensive spectrum of mental health and other necessary services which are organized into a coordinated network to meet the changing needs of children and their families." Stroul and Friedman (1986:17) outline the principles that guide the system of care philosophy, including three systems of care core values:

1. **Family driven and youth guided**, with strengths and needs of the family determining the types and mix of services and supports provided.
2. **Community based**, with the locus of services as well as system management resting within a supportive, adaptive infrastructure of structure, processes, and relationships at the community level.
3. **Culturally and linguistically competent**, with agencies, programs, and services that reflect the cultural, racial, ethnic, and linguistic differences of the populations they serve to facilitate access to and utilization of appropriate services and supports and to eliminate disparities in care.

The system of care approach seeks to improve collaboration and coordination between service providers across systems where youth and their families receive care. The intent of the approach is to work at the local services level to expand access to available services and improve connections between providers across the systems where essential services are located. Mental health services are a key piece of the system of care framework that also includes juvenile justice services and each of the major systems of care discussed later in this chapter.

Closely aligned with the work of Stroul and Friedman is an approach that emerged during the 1980s in a number of juvenile justice systems: "wraparound services" for court-involved youth. **Wraparound services** recognize the importance of multi-system treatment and the need to address barriers and challenges for providing comprehensive health and human services to youth and their families (Wilson 2008). For court-involved youth, wraparound services are services such as mental health and physical health services that are "wrapped around" the juvenile court services that are provided to address delinquent behavior. Wraparound services maintain some or all of the following objectives (Rossman 2001:2–3):

- Identifying gaps in service delivery and assigning organizational responsibility for implementing needed services.
- Reducing barriers to obtaining services (e.g., streamlining application procedures, reducing geographical distance between provider and client, decreasing unacceptably long waiting periods before treatment commences).
- Conserving institutional resources by sharing some efforts across systems or by reducing unnecessary duplication of efforts.

The role of youth maltreatment in the system of care

A recent report published by the Children's Bureau of the United States Department of Health and Human Services shows that in 2014, child protective service agencies across the U.S. received 3.6 million referrals involving more than 6 million children and youth (Child Welfare Information Gateway 2016). As many instances of maltreatment do not come to the attention of child protective services or other service agencies that work with youth, the actual numbers are undoubtedly much larger.

Youth maltreatment occurs when a parent or caregiver is responsible for or allows abuse or neglect of a youth. Youth maltreatment includes physical, sexual, and emotional abuse, as well as physical, emotional, and educational neglect. Youth maltreatment consists of both actual physical or emotional harm and placing youth in danger of physical or emotional harm. The box entitled "Juvenile justice process and practice: Dimensions of youth maltreatment" presents six of the most common types of youth maltreatment.

JUVENILE JUSTICE PROCESS AND PRACTICE: DIMENSIONS OF YOUTH MALTREATMENT

The National Incidence Study of Child Abuse and Neglect originated from requirements in the 1974 Child Abuse and Training Act. Administered four times since 1976, most recently in 2005 and 2006, the National Incidence Study of Child Abuse and Neglect collects data on common forms of maltreatment, including:

Physical abuse. Acts that cause or could have caused physical injury. This includes excessive corporal punishment.

Sexual abuse. Sexual activity either with or without force. This includes contacts for sexual purposes, prostitution, pornography, and other sexually exploitative acts.

Emotional abuse. Verbal threats and emotional assaults. This includes terrorizing a child, administering unprescribed and potentially harmful substances, and willful cruelty or exploitation not covered by other types of maltreatment.

Physical neglect. Disregard of physical needs and physical safety. This includes acts of abandonment, illegal transfers of custody, expulsion from the home, failure to seek remedial health care or delay in seeking care, and also includes inadequate supervision, food, hygiene, clothing, or shelter.

Emotional neglect. Lack of attention to emotional and developmental needs, and emotional well-being. This includes inadequate nurturance or affection, permitting maladaptive behavior, and exposure to domestic violence or other maladaptive behaviors or environments.

Educational neglect. Failure to provide for educational needs. This includes permitting chronic truancy, failure to enroll, or other inattention to educational needs.

Source: Sedlak et al. (2010).

The connection between youth maltreatment and the likelihood of multiple system treatment needs is well documented (Haight et al. 2016; Herz, Ryan, and Bilchik 2010; Wolpaw and Ford 2004). Youth who have experienced maltreatment are more likely to experience academic problems, elevated rates of trauma exposure, mental health problems, post-traumatic stress disorder, and substance abuse. **Trauma** includes physical and emotional responses to events that threaten the life or emotional integrity of a youth or someone critically important to him or her. These findings suggest the need for approaches that advocate for coordination and co-operation of youth service providers across multiple systems where youth receive care.

Delinquency, juvenile justice, and the system of care approach

Multiple terms describe youth who are involved in both the child welfare and juvenile justice systems. These include **dual-status youth**, a youth who is involved in both the child welfare system and the juvenile justice system, though not necessarily at the same time. The most general and most commonly used term to describe youth with treatment needs in the juvenile justice and at least one other system is "crossover youth." A **crossover youth** is any youth who has experienced maltreatment and engages in delinquency (Baglivio et al. 2016; Herz et al. 2012; Herz et al. 2010). The box entitled "Juvenile justice process and practice: Definitions for juveniles receiving services across multiple systems" presents the definitions that are used to identify youth receiving services in more than one system.

A recent study found that 92 percent of crossover youth were first involved in the child welfare system and then become known to the juvenile justice system (Huang, Ryan, and Herz 2012). Research findings show that maltreated youth are at a 47 percent greater risk of becoming involved in delinquency than youth who do not experience maltreatment (Ryan and Testa 2005). The dual involvement of youth in the child welfare and juvenile justice systems often compounds vulnerable youth risk for problematic developmental outcomes such as mental health issues, educational problems, and vocational difficulties (Haight et al. 2016; Thomas 2015).

JUVENILE JUSTICE PROCESS AND PRACTICE: DEFINITIONS FOR JUVENILES RECEIVING SERVICES ACROSS MULTIPLE SYSTEMS

Multiple terms describe juveniles who receive services in more than one system of care. The common use of multiple terms often used interchangeably, impacts practice, policy, and the data gathered to describe trends and patterns. Herz, Ryan, and Bilchik (2010) identify and provide definitions of three terms that distinguish juveniles by the amount of juvenile justice system involvement they experience.

1 **Crossover youth** is any youth who has experienced maltreatment and engaged in delinquency regardless of system involvement. Crossover youth, in other words, experience maltreatment and delinquency, but they may or may not formally enter the child welfare and/or juvenile justice systems.

2 **Dually-involved youth** is a subgroup of crossover youths who are concurrently known to both the child welfare and juvenile justice systems at some level. Their contact may be preventative (i.e., having a voluntary case in child welfare and/or receiving informal diversion in juvenile justice), formal (i.e., having substantiated allegations for abuse and/or neglect or being adjudicated delinquent in the delinquency court), or a combination of both.

3 **Dually-adjudicated youth** is a subgroup of dually involved youths that includes youths who entered both systems, were formally processed by both systems, and are under the formal care and control of both systems.

The Center for Juvenile Justice Reform at Georgetown University has developed an evidence-based approach for dealing with youth involved in both the child welfare and juvenile justice systems, called the "Crossover Youth Practice Model." The model explains why maltreated youth are more likely to be involved in delinquency and offers evidence-based intervention methods that address the needs of crossover youth. The three-phase model seeks to minimize the involvement of maltreated youth in the juvenile justice system through improved communication and coordination between service providers in the child welfare and juvenile justice systems, earlier and more individualized intervention, and increased family engagement (Haight et al. 2016). In collaboration with partners from the Casey Family Programs, the Crossover Youth Practice Model is in operation or in the process of implementation in 96 counties across 21 states (Center for Juvenile Justice Reform 2015).

MAJOR SYSTEMS OF CARE FOR COURT-INVOLVED YOUTH

The impact of maltreatment and the trauma associated with it appears in a number of public service systems outside of child welfare and juvenile justice systems (Burns et al. 2003). Here we discuss five of the most common external systems where youth who are involved in the juvenile justice system also receive services in other systems: child welfare, education, mental health, medical care, and substance abuse treatment.

Child welfare system

As described above, youth known in both the juvenile justice and child welfare systems are the most common form of crossover youth. This is particularly true for **deep-end youth**—those youth adjudicated delinquent and subsequently placed in a residential facility. Recent studies present varying estimates of the number of crossover youth receiving services in both systems, depending on how broadly dual-system involvement is defined. Estimates of youth involved in the child welfare system who are also known in the juvenile justice system range from more than one-third to nearly 50 percent (Lee and Villagrana 2015; Herz et al. 2010; Thomas 2015). Fieldwork conducted in local jurisdictions across the United States shows even higher levels of crossover youth, with approximately two-thirds of the juvenile justice populations across the jurisdictions examined having some level of contact with the child welfare system (Herz et al. 2012).

Crossover youth involved in the juvenile justice system and child welfare system represent a complex and particularly vulnerable population. They are subject to both the child welfare system that monitors abuse and neglect, and the juvenile justice system that responds to delinquent acts. As a group, crossover youth generally do not receive the comprehensive services needed to address their histories of abuse, neglect and/or trauma, and they frequently move from one system to another because of the lack of coordination across systems. As a result, youth are sometimes asked to repeat explanations of traumatic experiences previously shared in earlier interactions with service providers in other systems.

Involvement in both juvenile justice and child welfare systems has multiple consequences, including elevated levels of recidivism, and more frequent and prolonged contacts with the juvenile justice system. In addition, crossover youth experience more frequent placement changes, substantially higher placement costs, extensive behavioral health problems, poor educational outcomes, and higher overall system costs (Thomas 2015).

Education

Schools are perhaps the primary location where the risk factors associated with the early onset of delinquent behavior are observed. In addition, school settings are often the social context in which disruptive behavior first becomes evident in the form of bullying, physical aggressiveness, and difficult temperament. In a North Carolina study, between 70 and 80 percent of the children who received services for mental health problems were seen by providers in the education sector, usually guidance counselors and school psychologists (Grisso 2008).

Furthermore, research consistently shows that court-involved youth are likely to experience problems in school. Findings show that academic attainment is a protective factor against involvement in delinquency, but academic failure is a risk factor for delinquency. Academic problems often result in the inability to develop positive relationships with peers, leading to increases in school dropout levels and greater likelihood of involvement in delinquency (Farn and Adams 2016; Lee and Villagrana 2015; Leone and Weinberg 2012).

Access to sufficient academic services is particularly important for youth in residential placement. On an average day, more than 48,000 juveniles reside in residential placement facilities across the United States (OJJDP 2017). Findings from the Survey of Youth in Residential Placement show that less than half of the youth spent at least six hours in school and only half reported that the facility they were residing in had a "good" educational program (Sedlak and McPherson 2010).

Mental health system

Seventy percent of all youth in the juvenile justice system have a diagnosable mental health disorder (Skowyra and Cocozza 2007). This is more than three times higher than the percentage among youth in the general population (20 percent). As many as 30 percent of court-involved youth report suffering from a serious behavioral disorder (Underwood and Washington 2016; Espinosa, Sorenson, and Lopez 2013; Skowyra and Cocozza 2007).

Research strongly and consistently indicates that conduct disorders, attention-deficit hyperactivity disorder, and their co-occurrence increase the likelihood of delinquent behavior (Grisso 2008). Mental health experts contend that effective intervention requires integrated, community-based intervention that provides services across mental health, education, child protective, and juvenile justice agencies (Schubert and Mulvey 2014; Grisso 2008).

The absence of available community-based mental health services across the country has resulted in the misuse and overuse of the juvenile justice system to address mental health issues. Many youth whose primary service needs are for mental health issues, not for serious delinquent behavior, end up in the juvenile justice system; however, juvenile justice personnel typically lack training and expertise in treating mental health problems (Herz et al. 2012; Underwood and Washington 2016).

Medical care system

Compared to youth in the general population, court-involved youth are more likely to report chronic medical issues, such as hypertension, asthma, arthritis, dental concerns, and joint or back/neck pain (Clark and Gehshan 2007). These medical needs place additional strain on the limited resources available to provide care for court-involved youth and extend the scope of care that juvenile justice staff provide to youth. Research findings show that more than two-thirds of youth in residential placement have some type of health care need. The most commonly reported health care needs relate to dental, vision, or hearing issues. Health care needs associated with illness experienced during placement are also common (Sedlak and McPherson 2010).

For many court-involved youth, the health care received during involvement in the juvenile justice system will be the only professional care they receive to address physical health problems. Problems associated with providing health care to court-involved youth are particularly challenging during the transition from residential placement back into the community. Research findings indicate that treatment gaps for physical health needs are particularly problematic for youth who are returning to poor neighborhoods where fewer health care services are available (Clark and Gehshan 2006).

Substance abuse treatment

Research conducted by the National Center on Addiction and Substance Abuse at Columbia University (2004) shows that substance abuse among court-involved youth is prevalent. As many as 80 percent of youth in the juvenile justice system are under the influence of alcohol or drugs at the time of the delinquent offense, are arrested for an alcohol or drug offense, test positive for alcohol or drugs, admit having substance use and addiction problems, or some combination of these. The percentage of youth in the juvenile justice system with a documented substance abuse disorder (46 percent) is nearly six times higher than for youth in the general population (8 percent) (Substance Abuse and Health Administration 2015).

These patterns are consistent with those reported by Sedlak and McPherson (2010), based on the Survey of Youth in Residential Placement. More than half of the respondent's report that they were drunk or high on drugs several times a week or more during the months before residential placement. Over two-thirds report problems related to substance use, such as getting into trouble while they were high, not meeting their responsibilities, or having a blackout experience.

Effective substance abuse treatment requires clinical intervention and a rigorous therapy schedule. Because of existing challenges, many youth who could benefit from substance abuse treatment do not receive it. As many as one-third of all residential placement facilities do not systematically screen admitted youth for substance use issues. Only half of juveniles in residential placement are in facilities that use standardized assessment tools to identify substance use problems (Sedlak and McPherson 2010). This is consequential, as youth who receive treatment for substance abuse disorders and addiction are less likely to commit a drug-related offense in the year after admission to treatment (Grella et al. 2001).

LINKING SYSTEMS OF CARE FOR CHILDREN AND YOUTH

Up to this point in the chapter, we have discussed the system of care approach that was among the first and most successful efforts to connect youth with services across multiple systems. In this section, we begin using the term "linking systems of care." One of the important takeaways from the evidence showing crossover by court-involved youth into systems of care outside of the juvenile justice system is the multiple contexts where treatment needs of youth can initially be revealed. This creates a need not only to provide access to care across systems, but also to work to connect these systems together. The innovation to provide services across systems is referred to as **linking systems of care**.

A focus on evidence-based practice connects many of the models built on the system of care philosophy. **Evidence-based practice** involves the use of data gathered through research and evaluation as the basis for decision-making. It advances the view that data reduce subjectivity, thus providing a more objective approach for decision-making, policy development, and the establishment of what has been called "best practices."

As mentioned in earlier chapters that discuss evidence-based practice (see Chapters 2, 10, and 13), early identification of service needs for youth is a key aspect of comprehensive care. The use of screening to identify needs and assessment to inform the best course of action to address identified needs is a key component of evidence-based practice. **Screening instruments** are simple to use and ideally require only a few minutes to administer. These tools are common in both clinical and non-clinical settings as a means of identifying referral need for more in-depth assessment. **Assessment instruments** are more extensive. Their purpose is to classify problem behaviors and provide evidence for effective treatment. Most assessment tools require clinical training to administer them and require significantly more time to complete than simple screening tools.

Assessment instruments to uncover trauma exposure are a strategic part of the Linking Systems of Care for Youth and Children approach presented below. The box entitled "Expanding ideas: Trauma assessment instruments" presents information about four commonly used trauma assessment instruments.

A recent innovation that builds on the importance of evidence-based practice and early identification of treatment needs from the system of care philosophy is the Linking Systems of Care for Youth and Children program. This program is part of the "Vision 21" initiative sponsored by the Office for Victims of Crime at the National Institute of Justice, which seeks to transform

EXPANDING IDEAS: TRAUMA ASSESSMENT INSTRUMENTS

A number of instruments are currently available to uncover trauma exposure. Some of these tools are specific to uncovering trauma exposure in small children. Others have been modified or developed specifically to uncover trauma exposure among adolescents. Below are links to websites that describe four of these instruments and contain additional links to research about them.

- **Adverse Childhood Experiences,** Centers for Disease Control and Prevention: www.cdc.gov/violenceprevention/acestudy/index.html
- **Child and Adolescent Needs and Strengths,** National Child Traumatic Stress Network: www.nctsnet.org/nctsn_assets/pdfs/measure/CANS-MH.pdf
- **Juvenile Victimization Questionnaire,** Crimes Against Children Research Center: www.unh.edu/ccrc/jvq/index_new.html
- **UCLA PTSD Reaction Index for DSM-5,** National Center for Posttraumatic Stress Disorder, U.S. Department of Veterans Affairs: www.ptsd.va.gov/professional/assessment/child/ucla_child_reaction_dsm-5.asp

the delivery of crime victim services and ensure that service providers are equipped to meet the needs of crime victims in the twenty-first century. The Linking Systems of Care for Youth and Children program incorporates the emphasis on coordination and collaboration of service delivery at the local level, with input from children, youth, and their families. Linking Systems of Care incorporated the core concepts in Stroul and Friedman's original system of care approach. The program also includes at its foundation the importance of identifying gaps and barriers for treatment and the need to reduce duplication of efforts from earlier system of care and wraparound services models.

The Linking Systems of Care for Youth and Children program emphasizes the need to identify exposure to violence, crime, and abuse, and address the trauma associated with these experiences. The program promotes the development of prevention and intervention strategies aimed at reducing violence and victimization among youth. It recognizes that youth who experience violence, abuse, and associated trauma may initially require attention within one of the systems of care, followed by coordinated efforts across systems to identify prior victimization and trauma among youth.

The title of the approach "linking systems of care" is revealing. It emphasizes the importance of connecting youth with services across multiple systems, the trademark of the system of care approach developed by Stroul and Friedman, and the wraparound services discussed earlier in the chapter. The linking systems of care approach adds to this an emphasis on connecting services and service providers across systems so that more comprehensive screening and assessment for prior victimization and trauma exposure can take place. Providing comprehensive, coordinated care and treatment for youths who experience prior victimization and trauma is also a focus of the linking systems of care approach.

Exposure to violence, crime, and abuse

Exposure to violence, crime, and abuse is a focal point of the linking system of care approach because of extensive research findings showing association with numerous negative outcomes for youth, including physical and mental health issues and increased levels of delinquency (Finkelhor, Omrond, and Turner 2007). The National Survey of Children's Exposure to Violence is the most comprehensive source of information to gauge the prevalence of exposure to violence. Data from the survey measure exposure to violence, including conventional crimes such as robbery and theft, various forms of parental maltreatment, peer and sibling victimization, sexual victimization, school violence, bullying, and cyber violence. The findings from the most recent survey in 2011 show that 60 percent of the sample reported experiencing violence in their home, school, or community (Finkelhor et al. 2015).

Research findings show that youth exposed to violence, crime, and abuse are likely to report multiple types of experiences. **Poly-victimization** occurs when youth report that they have experienced multiple forms of victimization. Youth who experience poly-victimization are at increased risk of subsequent victimization and psychological trauma (Finkelhor et al. 2015; Finkelhor et al. 2009). In a study of court-involved youth, researchers found that girls report higher levels of poly-victimization than males (Ford et al. 2013). These experiences create treatment needs for both boys and girls that are often unmet unless there is effective collaboration and coordination between staff in the juvenile justice system and service providers in other systems.

Trauma-informed care

Psychological trauma and post-traumatic stress disorder are prevalent among youth in the juvenile justice system (Dierkhising et al. 2013; Ford et al. 2013; Smith and Saldana 2013). Court-involved youth report very high levels of trauma exposure, with 70 to 90 percent reporting a history of at least one potentially traumatic experience (Sedlak and McPherson 2010; Abram et al. 2004). This level is greater than the 20 percent of youth in the general population who report exposure to a traumatic event. Youth in the juvenile justice system report exposure to multiple types of trauma. The range of possible traumas include various forms of violence exposure and abuse, serious injury, the loss or separation of a loved one due to an unexpected death or parental incarceration, and living through a natural disaster (Dierkhising et al. 2013).

The ability to identify trauma due to exposure to violence, crime, and neglect within the Linking Systems of Care for Youth and Children program reflects a larger movement in recent years within the juvenile justice system to become trauma informed. Efforts to increase awareness of trauma and its consequences among youth, and staff who provide services to them are a priority in best practices approaches. The National Child Traumatic Stress Network is a leader in promoting trauma-informed care and the development of trauma awareness training, including a specific module for the juvenile justice system. The box entitled "Juvenile justice process and practice: Essential elements of a trauma-informed juvenile justice system" presents these elements.

The Vision 21 Linking Systems of Care for Youth and Children demonstration project began in January 2015. The project, sponsored by the Office of Victims of Crime, is built upon three broad objectives to: 1) promote healing for victims of crime; 2) coordinate prevention and intervention services for youth and families experiencing trauma; and 3) build capacity within communities to meet the needs of youth exposed to violence. Participants in the project work collaboratively to accomplish these objectives. The project is state specific and reflects a shift away from national level program development to state specific model development. The Office of Victims of Crime is guiding states to develop the general framework of the approach. Individual States will adopt and develop this framework to address the specific needs of youth and their families.

As the project moves forward, potential barriers may affect full implementation of the program. Practitioners have concerns about the use of trauma and prior victimization screening tools and the amount of pressure on existing resources that needs identified using these tools will generate. Some fear that the amount of need uncovered will be beyond the capacities of existing community services. Privacy issues are another significant barrier. Information sharing across systems must take place in order to minimize the need for youth and their families to retell their stories and to promote coordinated and collaborative care. Currently, legal and policy obstacles complicate or prevent the sharing among agencies of information about youth receiving care in more than one system.

SUMMARY AND CONCLUSIONS

Providing for the treatment needs of youth in the juvenile justice system has become an increasingly complex goal. Despite declines in the number of youth entering the juvenile justice system across the United States, the variety of treatment needs of court-involved youth continue to be a policy and practice concern. In many instances, youth treatment needs require specialized care that is beyond the scope of practitioners in the juvenile justice system, due to lack of

JUVENILE JUSTICE PROCESS AND PRACTICE: ESSENTIAL ELEMENTS OF A TRAUMA-INFORMED JUVENILE JUSTICE SYSTEM

In their work to increase trauma-informed care, the National Child Traumatic Stress Network identified eight essential elements of a trauma-informed juvenile justice system. These include:

1. **Trauma-informed policies and procedures**
   Trauma-informed policies and procedures make juvenile justice organizations safer and more effective by ensuring the physical and psychological safety of all youth, family members, and staff and promoting their recovery from the adverse effects of trauma.
2. **Identification/screening of youth who have been traumatized**
   Carefully timed traumatic stress screening is the standard of care for youth in the juvenile justice system.
3. **Clinical assessment/intervention for trauma-impaired youth**
   Trauma-specific clinical assessment and treatment and trauma-informed prevention and behavioral health services are the standard of care for all youth identified as impaired by posttraumatic stress reactions in the screening process.
4. **Trauma-informed programming and staff education**
   Trauma-informed education, resources, and programs are the standard of care across all stages of the juvenile justice system.
5. **Prevention and management of secondary trauma stress**
   Juvenile justice administrators and staff at all levels recognize and respond to the adverse effects of secondary traumatic stress in the workplace in order to support workforce safety, effectiveness, and resilience.
6. **Trauma-informed partnering with youth and families**
   Trauma-informed juvenile justice systems ensure that youth and families engage as partners in all juvenile justice programming and therapeutic services.
7. **Trauma-informed cross system collaboration**
   Cross system collaboration enables the provision of continuous integrated services to justice-involved youth who are experiencing posttraumatic stress problems.
8. **Trauma-informed approaches to address disparities and diversities**
   Trauma-informed juvenile justice systems ensure that their practices and policies do address the diverse and unique needs of all groups of youth and do not result in disparities related to race, ethnicity, gender, gender-identity, sexual orientation, age, intellectual and developmental level, or socioeconomic background.

Source: National Child Trauma Stress Network (n.d.).

training and expertise. The variety of youth treatment needs and the disappearance of local community-based resources that have historically been available to meet those needs places additional time and resource strain on juvenile justice systems.

The system of care approach provides decades of research findings and evidence-based practice establishing the need for comprehensive care for court-involved youth and their families. This focus is present in the wraparound services approach that emerged in juvenile justice systems in the 1980s. The need to identify service needs for youth and children in a way that minimizes service gaps and eliminates the need for them to repeat traumatic life experiences is an important consideration for improving current practice. Recent advancements in the linking systems of care approach add awareness of the numerous places where treatment needs for youths may initially be uncovered. In this chapter, we emphasized schools as an important context where treatment needs are often first observed.

The system of care approach and the programs based on this philosophy seek to connect services across the various systems that provide care and treatment to youth. The research presented in this chapter provides evidence of treatment needs across multiple systems for court-involved juveniles. Coordination and collaboration among the various service delivery systems present a contemporary challenge that is key to effectively managing the resources available to juvenile justice systems.

READING 14.1

"TRAUMA HISTORIES AMONG JUSTICE-INVOLVED YOUTH: FINDINGS FROM THE NATIONAL CHILD TRAUMATIC STRESS NETWORK."

Carly B. Dierkhising, Susan J. Ko, Briana Woods-Jaeger, Ernestine C. Briggs, Robert Lee, and Robert S. Pynoos. 2013. *European Journal of Psychotraumatology* 4:1–12.

Dierkhising and her colleagues present data from the National Child Traumatic Stress Network Core Data Set. Findings based on self-reports from 658 adolescents with recent involvement in the juvenile justice system show early onset of trauma exposure and co-occurring trauma are common.

Youth involved in the juvenile justice system report higher rates of trauma exposure, post-traumatic stress disorder (PTSD), and other mental health problems (e.g., depression, anxiety) compared to the general population (Schufelt and Cocozza, 2006; Wolpaw and Ford, 2004; Wood, Foy, Layne, Pynoos, and James, 2002). Justice-involved youth also tend to experience multiple types of trauma, or polyvictimization, before they reach the juvenile justice system (Abram et al., 2004). Yet, less is known about the details of their trauma histories such as prevalence rates of a broad range of trauma types, rates of co-occurring trauma across childhood, and the age of onset of trauma exposure.

Trauma exposure and PTSD among justice-involved youth

The relation between trauma exposure and juvenile justice involvement has been consistently documented (Chamberlain and Moore, 2002; Ford, Chapman, Hawke, and Alpert, 2007; Kerig and Becker, 2010; Widom and Maxfield, 1996). Youth who report child maltreatment both through official case records or self-reports, are found to be at higher risk for delinquent or criminal involvement in both adolescence and adulthood (Smith and Thornberry, 1995; Widom and Maxfield, 1996). In addition, more severe forms of maltreatment (i.e., chronic or frequent maltreatment) have been found to be associated with more severe and chronic delinquent behavior and the relation between child maltreatment and justice involvement holds across gender and ethnicity (Smith and Thornberry, 1995; Widom and Maxfield, 1996). Other forms of trauma exposure, beyond child maltreatment, have also been linked to delinquency and justice involvement, such as community violence, domestic violence, and traumatic loss (Foy, Ritchie, and Conway, 2012; Kerig, Ward, Vanderzee, and Moeddel, 2009; Wood et al., 2002).

Prevalence rates of trauma exposure among youth involved in the juvenile justice system highlight this robust relation. One study found 92 percent of justice-involved youth reported exposure to at least one type of trauma, and that exposure to multiple traumas was the norm (Abram et al., 2004). Females tend to report higher rates of interpersonal victimization, particularly sexual assault, while males report higher rates of witnessing violence (Cauffman, Feldman, Waterman, and Steiner, 1998; Ford et al., 2007; Foy et al., 2012). For instance, 29 percent of incarcerated females compared to 3 percent of their incarcerated male counterparts reported being raped or molested (Wood et al., 2002), and 48 percent of incarcerated males compared to 17 percent of incarcerated females reported witnessing some type of violent act (Cauffman et al., 1998).

In light of the high rates of trauma exposure among justice-involved youth, many prevalence studies have focused specifically on the development of PTSD among this population. Rates of PTSD tend to vary between 3 and 50 percent among incarcerated youth (Ford et al., 2007) with a 30 percent prevalence rate on average. For example, a study comparing 96 females and 93 males incarcerated in the California Youth Authority found that nearly half of the females (49 percent) met the criteria for PTSD compared to about one-third (32 percent) of males (Cauffman et al., 1998). Another study of randomly selected youth (N =898) in a pre-trial detention center in Cook County, Illinois found about 11 percent of males and 15 percent of females met the criteria for PTSD (Abram et al., 2004). The discrepancies among prevalence rates are attributed to regional differences among study participants, the use of varying assessment instruments, and the time at which the assessment occurs during juvenile justice processing (Wolpaw and Ford, 2004).

While trauma exposure and PTSD are common among justice-involved youth, it is not yet clear what the mechanisms of influence are between trauma and delinquency (Ardino, 2012; Kerig, 2012a). The few studies that have begun to illuminate this process focus on emotional and cognitive processes as mediating mechanisms (Allwood, Baetz, DeMarco, and Bell, 2012; Allwood and Bell, 2008; Kerig and Becker, 2010). For instance, post-traumatic stress symptoms and cognitions supportive of violence have been found to mediate the relation between violence exposure (i.e., family and community violence exposure) and self-reported delinquency among a community sample of adolescents (Allwood and Bell, 2008). Post-traumatic stress symptoms have also been found to mediate the relation between violence exposure and additional mental health problems among an incarcerated sample of adolescents (Kerig and Becker, 2012). Importantly, gender differences are consistently found when delineating the relation between trauma and delinquency indicating varying trajectories from trauma to delinquency for males and females (Kerig and Becker, 2012).

An understudied aspect in the developmental trajectory of trauma and delinquency is the age of onset of trauma in this population. This is surprising given the extensive literature on the age of onset of delinquent behavior; one of the most robust predictors of chronic and persistent delinquency (Natsuaki, Ge, and Wenk, 2008; Sampson and Laub, 1993). This literature indicates that the experience of risk factors (e.g., parenting problems, conduct problems, academic failure, peer rejection) early in life is associated with more chronic delinquency and that children who begin their delinquent careers in childhood, rather than later in adolescence, become the most consistent and chronic offenders (Moffitt, 1993; Patterson, DeBaryshe, and Ramsey, 1989). Given the importance of timing in the development of delinquent behaviors, it follows that timing of trauma may also be related to adverse outcomes. The timing of a traumatic experience is also important given that youth who experience trauma early in life are more likely to experience other types of trauma later in life (Finkelhor, Ormrod, and Turner, 2007) and the experience of multiple trauma types is associated with increased post-traumatic stress reactions, difficulties in emotion regulation, and internalizing problems (Finkelhor, Turner, Hamby, and Ormrod, 2011). However, these associations have not been explored among justice-involved samples. Expanding our knowledge regarding the age of onset of trauma exposure can enhance our understanding of the developmental implications of trauma exposure and justice involvement.

Mental health and associated risk factors among justice-involved youth

Justice-involved youth often experience additional adversity and mental health problems, beyond trauma exposure and PTSD, either preceding or concurrent with justice involvement. In a nationally representative study, approximately 70 percent of justice-involved youth met criteria for at least one mental health disorder, and among those youth 79 percent met criteria for two or more diagnoses (Schufelt and Cocozza, 2006). The most common disorders include disruptive disorders, substance use disorders, anxiety disorders, and mood disorders. PTSD and other mental health problems tend to co-occur among highly traumatized samples as well. For instance, in the National Survey of Adolescents, Ford and colleagues (2010) found that adolescents exposed to multiple trauma types compared to non-exposed adolescents had double the risk for major depressive disorder, triple the risk for PTSD, and 5–8 times the risk for comorbid disorders (Ford, Elhai, Connor, and Frueh, 2010).

Substance-use problems, academic problems, and concurrent child welfare involvement are also common among justice-involved youth. For instance, 1.9 million of the 2.4 million youth arrested in 2000 reported a substance-abuse problem, were arrested for a drug-related offense, and/or were under the influence at the time of their arrest (National Center on Addiction and Substance Abuse, 2004). Poor academic performance is associated with increased delinquent involvement (Maguin and Loeber, 1996), and many youth drop out of school after release from a juvenile justice facility (Buffington, Dierkhising, and Marsh, 2010). Additionally, up to 42 percent of youth in the juvenile justice system are crossover youth, youth who report involvement in both the juvenile justice and child welfare systems, with females representing a higher proportion of crossover youth (Herz and Ryan, 2008; Herz, Ryan, and Bilchik, 2010). While these risk factors are thought to contribute to and/ or co-occur with justice involvement, they are often associated with PTSD and trauma exposure also. However, less is known about the associations among these risk factors in justice-involved samples. A better understanding of these associations can improve intervention and prevention efforts for youth.

The current study

This study describes detailed trauma histories, mental health problems, and associated risk factors (i.e., academic problems, substance/alcohol use, and concurrent child welfare involvement) among adolescents with recent involvement in the juvenile justice system. Justice-involved youth include 658 adolescents (aged 13–18 years) from the National Child Traumatic Stress Network Core Data Set (NCTSN-CDS) who report recent involvement in the juvenile justice system as indexed by being detained or under community supervision by the juvenile court. Four primary questions guide this descriptive study: (1) What are the prevalence rates of trauma types, mental health problems, and associated risk factors (i.e., academic problems, substance/alcohol use, and concurrent child welfare involvement) among justice-involved youth?; (2) Are there gender differences in trauma types, mental health problems, and associated risk factors?; (3) At what age are youth first experiencing trauma and does trauma co-occur (i.e., multiple trauma types occurring within a single year)?; and (4) How is age of onset of trauma associated with mental health problems and related risk factors among males and females?

Method

Participants

The National Child Traumatic Stress Network (NCTSN) is a federally funded initiative that seeks to raise the standard of care and increase access to services for traumatized children and their families. As part of this initiative, the Core Data Set (CDS) was established to standardize assessment protocols across all funded NCTSN clinical sites. These sites included a range of community-based mental health clinics, child welfare settings, juvenile justice programs, hospitals, schools, and residential treatment centers. Data were collected between 2004 and 2010, from 56 sites located across the country and includes baseline assessments and follow-up treatment information and outcomes. All participants (N =14,088 children and adolescents from birth to 21 years) were referred for trauma-focused treatment and assessed on various clinical measures, such as mental health problems, functional impairment, treatment types, and service system utilization. Extensive training on assessment administration and data entry was provided to all participating sites. A clinical service provider working with the referred youth and their parents/caregivers completed all assessment instruments. Only baseline assessments were used for this study.

The justice-involved subgroup (n =658) includes adolescents aged 13–18 years who indicated recent involvement with the juvenile justice system as defined by either: (1) being in a detention center, training school, jail, or prison (14.6 percent); (2) having seen a probation officer or court counselor (57.9 percent); or (3) both (27.5 percent) within the past 30 days. The sample is racially and ethnically diverse with 40.1 percent identifying as White, 21.6 percent identifying as Black, 31.4 percent identifying as Hispanic, and 6.9 percent identifying as Other. The sample is composed of more females (54 percent) than males (46 percent) and the average age is 15.7 years (SD = 1.3). The majority of the sample lives at home with their parents (53.6 percent), with 23.9 percent in either a correctional facility or residential treatment center, 8.4 percent with other family members, 6.9 percent in foster care, and 7.2 percent in another living situation (i.e., homeless, independent, or other). Approximately two-thirds (67.5 percent) of the sample reported eligibility for public insurance.

Instruments

Trauma exposure

The trauma history profile (THP) is a comprehensive assessment of an individual's trauma history including type of trauma and when it occurred in the life span. The THP includes information regarding age of onset and whether more than one trauma type co-occurred in the same year. The THP is derived from the trauma history component of the UCLA PTSD-Reaction Index (PTSD-RI: Steinberg, Brymer, Decker, and Pynoos, 2004) and expanded to include 19 trauma types. The provider at intake or early in the course of service delivery completed it. Trauma history information is obtained retrospectively from multiple informants, including the adolescent, parents/caregivers, and/or other relatives. Definitions for many of the trauma types were adapted from the National Child Abuse and Neglect Data System (NCANDS) Glossary, a national database of child abuse and neglect reports.

Post-traumatic stress reactions

The UCLA PTSD-RI was used to capture the frequency of post-traumatic stress symptoms over the past month, with response options ranging from 0 (none of the time) to 4 (most of the time). Scoring algorithms permit tabulation of a PTSD-RI total score, as well as Criterion B, C, and D symptom subscale scores. For this study, a total PTSD score is a summed continuous variable created from the symptom items that correspond to diagnostic criteria as defined by the Diagnostic and Statistical Manual for Mental Health Disorders (DSM-IV-TR: American Psychiatric Association [APA], 2000). A clinical cut-off of 38 is then used to categorize those in the clinical range (i.e., most likely to meet criteria for PTSD) as described by Steinberg and colleagues (2004). Clinically significant symptom cluster scores (i.e., Criterion B-D) are derived from whether or not a specific number of symptoms were present in each cluster based on the DSM-IV-TR criteria. For Criterion B, the DSM-IV-TR requires the presence of at least one symptom in the past month, for Criterion C at least three symptoms, and for Criterion D at least two symptoms. A symptom is considered "present" when the respondent indicates the symptom occurred much of the time (2–3 times a week in the past month) or most of the time (almost every day in the past month). Psychometric properties are fairly robust with good to excellent internal reliability across age, racial/ ethnic groups, and gender (Steinberg et al., 2004, 2013).

Internalizing and externalizing problems

The Child Behavior Checklist (CBCL; Achenbach and Rescorla, 2001) was used to assess internalizing and externalizing symptoms. The CBCL is completed by a parent or caregiver who knows the child well. This widely used measure consists of 118 items scored on a 3-point scale ranging from 0 (not true) to 2 (often true) and yields scores on two broad band scales of internalizing and externalizing, as well as scores on DSM-IV-oriented scales, and empirically based syndrome scales that reflect emotional and behavioral problems and symptoms. The measure has been found to have sound psychometric properties with respect to reliability and validity, across racially and ethnically diverse samples.

Associated risk factors

To assess for academic problems, and substance/alcohol use, clinicians used a 3-point scale ranging from 0 (not a problem), 1 (somewhat a problem), and 2 (very much a problem) to rate the degree of impairment in youth within the last 30 days. Responses indicating "somewhat a problem" and "very much a problem" were collapsed to create a dichotomous variable. Child welfare involvement was determined when youth indicated that they received services within the last 30 days from the child welfare system (yes/no). For this study, items assessing involvement in foster care, Department of Social Services (DSS), and child welfare were collapsed to create a child welfare involvement variable. . . .

Discussion

Overview of findings

This study describes the trauma histories, mental health problems, and associated risk factors among adolescents with recent involvement in the juvenile justice system. Mental health problems were prevalent with nearly one-quarter (23.6 percent) of youth meeting criteria for PTSD. Furthermore, over half of the sample indicated post-traumatic stress symptoms in the clinical range on at least one symptom cluster. Youth overwhelmingly presented with academic problems, substance/alcohol use, and concurrent child welfare involvement. Findings also reveal that youth with recent involvement in the justice system tended to be exposed to trauma beginning early in life and continued to experience multiple types of trauma. Additionally, early age of onset of trauma was associated with exposure to multiple types of trauma for both males and females, while early age of onset was differentially associated with mental health problems among males and females.

Practice implications

Findings from this study have implications for both practitioners and policymakers. At the practice level, it is clear that screening for trauma exposure, PTSD, and internalizing problems is needed among justice-involved youth. The juvenile justice system is in a unique position to address the multiple problems that impact the lives of justice-involved youth as it has contact with, and often oversight of, this vulnerable population. Beyond screening, clinical assessments are imperative to clearly identify clinical disorders and related functional impairments that guide treatment planning. In light of scarce resources, screening and assessment tools can, and should, be used to direct resources to those most in need.

While PTSD is prevalent among the sample, it was also found that many youth who do not meet criteria for a diagnosis of PTSD are still experiencing clinically significant post-traumatic stress symptoms within individual symptom clusters. For practitioners working with this population, utilizing a conservative cut-off score or methodology when screening for PTSD may more accurately identify youth experiencing clinically significant post-traumatic stress reactions. With this screening method, a follow-up clinical assessment could then be used to evaluate how symptoms may be adversely impacting youth's functioning.

An essential aspect of an effective screening and assessment process is the availability of evidence-based practices for justice-involved youth experiencing trauma reactions. Fortunately, there is an emerging literature on promising practices and evidence-based treatments for justice populations (Kerig, 2012b). Trauma Affect Regulation: Guide for Education and Therapy (TARGET; Ford and Russo, 2006) has been found to reduce disciplinary incidents and punitive sanctions (Ford and Hawke, 2012) and, when compared to treatment as usual, a reduction in mental health problems among incarcerated youth (Marrow, Knudsen, Olafson, and Bucher, 2012). Other interventions have built upon existing evidence-based treatments by adding a trauma-informed approach (Kerig and Alexander, 2012; Smith, Chamberlain, and Deblinger, 2012). For example, an innovative pilot study of an intervention which integrated components of Trauma Focused-Cognitive Behavioral Therapy (TF-CBT; Cohen, Mannarino, and Deblinger, 2006) with Multidimensional Treatment Foster Care (MTFC; Chamberlain, 2003) found a reduction in trauma-related symptoms and delinquency compared to treatment as usual (Smith et al., 2012). Continued intervention studies are needed to further support and disseminate trauma-focused treatment for justice-involved youth.

In light of the prevalence of trauma and post-traumatic stress, staff who have direct and consistent contact with justice-involved youth, such as probation officers and detention staff, should be trained to understand trauma and post-traumatic reactions so they are best equipped to recognize potential emotional distress and post-traumatic stress reactions (Griffin, Germain, and Wilkerson, 2012; Marrow et al., 2012). While these staff members are not expected to conduct a clinical assessment (nor are they qualified to), knowledge of trauma and post-traumatic stress can facilitate a better understanding and anticipation of the problems that may arise for justice-involved youth. In addition, trauma-informed training can help staff members who are not clinically trained to make appropriate referrals to mental health practitioners when needed, as they may have the most frequent and direct contact with youth. Indeed, recent research has shown that implementation of a trauma-informed approach using both trauma training for direct care staff and a trauma-focused intervention was effective in reducing psychological distress among youth and improving management of youth problem behaviors (e.g., reductions in seclusions and restraints) when compared to treatment as usual (Marrow et al., 2012).

Policy implications

It is important for policymakers to acknowledge that justice-involved youth have strikingly high rates of trauma exposure and that this trauma typically begins early in life, is often in multiple contexts (e.g., home, community, school), and persists over time. In light of these findings, prevention and intervention policies should target young children exposed to violence in order to reduce the likelihood of re-victimization and mental health problems, as well as prevent future justice involvement. For youth who do come to the attention of the juvenile court, it is imperative that the system is prepared to meet the needs of chronically traumatized youth with significant mental health problems. Policies that support a trauma-informed juvenile justice system should emphasize trauma screening and assessment, evidence-based trauma treatment, cross-system engagement, and promote resilience and engagement among youth and families (Griffin et al., 2012; Ko and Sprague, 2007).

Attention should also be paid to youth who are not diverted at the point of contact with the juvenile court, resulting in incarceration in a detention or residential treatment facility. These youth are, perhaps, most vulnerable as all other prior interventions have not been successful and they are more likely to recidivate as a juvenile or as an adult, and have poor long-term economic, academic, and mental health outcomes (Justice Policy Institute, 2009; Widom and Maxfield, 1996). Incarceration can be traumatic for youth and abusive practices that are common among large-scale detention facilities may continue to expose youth to trauma and abuse (Mendel, 2011). Policies that promote safety and treatment in these facilities are needed in order to protect and rehabilitate youth in the deepest parts of the juvenile justice system.

These findings also highlight important gender differences among justice-involved youth. We found early age of onset of trauma exposure was significantly correlated with increased post-traumatic stress reactions among females but not males. Additionally, females reported significantly higher rates of post-traumatic stress reactions compared to males. These findings indicate a need for a gender responsive approach. Acknowledging and addressing the distinct needs of males and females is an integral part of juvenile justice reform efforts, while additional research and funding mechanisms to enhance gender responsiveness are needed (Office of Juvenile Justice and Delinquency Prevention [OJJDP], 1998; Watson and Edelman, 2012).

Limitations and strengths

The current study's findings must be considered in light of its limitations. Importantly, the sample consists of clinically referred adolescents from non-randomly selected treatment sites, which limits generalizability. Nevertheless, it is one of the few studies of justice-involved youth that includes a multi-state sample with consistent use of selected measures across states. Justice-involved youth were aggregated to include both detained youth and youth in the community under supervision by the juvenile court which can obscure potential between-group differences. Yet, even using this broader definition of justice-involved youth we found comparable rates of mental health problems and trauma exposure to previous studies. This provides support for enhancing services for youth with varied levels of involvement in the justice system. Youth in the CDS were clinically referred for trauma treatment, meaning their inclusion in the CDS is predicated on trauma exposure, which contributes to potential over-estimation of prevalence rates of trauma exposure. However, it also allowed for the inclusion of a broader range of trauma types and more detailed trauma histories.

Despite these limitations, these findings expand the literature by utilizing a comprehensive trauma history assessment, including a broad range of traumas and age at time of exposure, among a large, multi-state sample. This methodology provides a deeper understanding of justice-involved youth's trauma histories and later mental health problems, which have essential practice and policy implications. Future research should continue to explore developmental pathways from trauma exposure to justice involvement by focusing on the implications of timing of trauma exposure and cumulative exposure across development in order to identify key points for intervention.

[References omitted.]

READING 14.2

"CHILDREN'S EXPOSURE TO VIOLENCE, CRIME, AND ABUSE: AN UPDATE."

David Finkelhor, Heather Turner, Anne Shattuck, Sherry Hamby, and Kristen Kracke. 2015. *Juvenile Justice Bulletin.* Washington, DC: Office of Juvenile Justice and Delinquency Prevention.

Finkelhor and his colleagues (2015) present the results from the second administration of the National Survey of Children's Exposure to Violence, a self-report survey gauging past-year and lifetime exposure to violence, crime, and abuse. Findings show that many children are exposed to multiple potentially trauma inducing events.

This bulletin discusses the second National Survey of Children's Exposure to Violence (NatSCEV II), which was conducted in 2011 as a follow-up to the original NatSCEV I survey. The U.S. Department of Justice (DOJ) and the Centers for Disease Control and Prevention (CDC) sponsored both surveys. The Crimes against Children Research Center of the University of New Hampshire conducted the NatSCEV I survey between January and May 2008. NatSCEV I represented the first comprehensive national survey of children's past-year and lifetime exposure to violence, crime, and abuse in the home, school, and community across children and youth from ages 1 month to 17 years.

As in the first NatSCEV survey, NatSCEV II researchers interviewed a nationally representative sample of children and their caregivers regarding the children's exposure to violence, crime, and abuse across several major categories: conventional crime, child maltreatment, victimization by peers and siblings, sexual victimization, witnessing and indirect victimization (including exposure to community violence, family violence, and school violence and threats), and Internet victimization. (For more detailed information on the types of violence that children were questioned about in NatSCEV I, see Finkelhor, Turner, Ormrod, Hamby, and Kracke, 2009). In addition to the types of exposure to violence, crime, and abuse covered in the original survey, NatSCEV II asked participants about several new types of exposure in the categories of conventional crime, child maltreatment, peer and sibling victimization, and Internet victimization.

In general, NatSCEV II confirms the earlier survey's findings regarding the extent of children's past-year and lifetime exposure to violence, crime, and abuse, with few significant changes in reported exposures between the two surveys. In the NatSCEV II sample, approximately three in five children (57.7 percent) experienced at least one exposure to five aggregate types of violence in the past year (physical assault, sexual victimization, maltreatment, property victimization, and witnessing violence). Among the individual categories of exposure, declines somewhat outnumbered increases; however, NatSCEV II recorded significant changes from 2008 (all declines) in exposure to only 6 of 54 types of exposure to violence covered in the survey: property victimization and robbery (past year), being flashed by a peer (past year and lifetime), statutory sex offenses (past year and lifetime), school bomb threats (past year and lifetime), and assault by juvenile siblings (lifetime).

NatSCEV II recorded high levels of past-year exposure to various individual categories of direct victimization. In 2011, approximately 2 in 5 children and youth surveyed (41.2 percent) were victims of at least one assault in the past year, and approximately 1 in 10 (10.1 percent) were injured in an assault. Approximately 1 in 20 children and youth (5.6 percent) were sexually victimized in the past year. Approximately one in four children and youth (24.1 percent) were victims of property crimes (including robbery, vandalism, and theft) in the past year. The reported rate of child maltreatment (including physical, sexual, and emotional abuse; neglect; and custodial interference or family abduction) in the past year was 13.8 percent.

Approximately 1 in 4 study participants witnessed a violent act in the past year (22.4 percent), and approximately 1 in 12 witnessed family violence in the past year (8.2 percent). Approximately 1 in 30 children and youth (3.7 percent) experienced bomb or attack threats against their schools. The rate of indirect exposure to household theft was 7.9 percent in the past year.

Multiple exposures to violence among children and youth continued to be a concern, with nearly one-half (48.4 percent) of NatSCEV II participants reporting more than one type of direct or witnessed victimization in the past year—nearly 1 in 6 (15.1 percent) reported 6 or more types of direct or witnessed victimization and 1 in 20 (4.9 percent) reported 10 or more types of direct or witnessed victimization over the same period.

In 2011, reported rates of lifetime exposure to violence continued to be high, especially for the oldest youth (ages 14–17), showing how exposure to violence accumulates as a child grows. For example, approximately 7 in 10 of these youth (69.7 percent) had been assaulted during their lifetimes, and a similar proportion (71.5 percent) witnessed violence during their lifetimes. In addition, more than half of these youth (56.6 percent) were victims of property crimes during their lifetimes. Lifetime exposure to major categories of violence for all youth surveyed in 2011 ranged from approximately 1 in 10 (9.5 percent) for sexual victimization to more than half (54.5 percent) for any assault. During their lifetimes, one in four (25.6 percent) were victims of maltreatment, two in five (40.2 percent) were victims of property crimes, and two in five (39.2 percent) witnessed violence.

Background

Childhood exposure to violence, crime, and abuse can lead to serious consequences for the health and well-being of those exposed, both during childhood and throughout adulthood (Shonkoff, Boyce, and McEwen, 2009; Fang et al., 2012). Child maltreatment, peer victimization, and exposure to family and community violence have all been shown to be connected to developmental difficulties, problem behavior, and physical and mental health effects extending throughout the lifespan (Danese et al., 2009; Sachs-Ericsson et al., 2005; Widom, DuMont, and Czaja, 2007; Bensley, Van Eenwyk, and Wynkoop Simmons, 2003). Children exposed to violence, crime, and abuse are more likely to abuse drugs and alcohol; suffer from depression, anxiety, and posttraumatic stress disorder; fail or have difficulties in school; and become delinquent and engage in criminal behavior. (For a more detailed discussion of the problem of child victimization, see Finkelhor, Turner, Ormrod, Hamby, and Kracke, 2009, and the sources cited therein.) Measuring child victimization accurately and comprehensively is crucial to reducing child victimization because those assessments help child welfare professionals identify and provide services to child victims of violence and their families and provide programs to educate children, their families, and those who work with children at risk for violence (including educators, social workers, medical professionals, and juvenile justice professionals). Unfortunately, earlier studies that measured children's exposure to violence often were limited in the age ranges and types of exposure to violence studied as well as where the exposure to violence took place (i.e., they were limited to violent incidents in the home, the school, or the community instead of studying incidents in all of these locations) (Shonkoff, Boyce, and McEwen, 2009; Finkelhor, 2008; Nansel et al., 2003). Most of these studies tended to concentrate on specific forms of violence, such as child maltreatment, domestic violence, bullying, or community violence. This meant that data could not be combined to provide an accurate assessment of the total level of violence, crime, and abuse in a child's environment. These studies also tended to look at specific characteristics of violent events (e.g., location, victim, or perpetrator) rather than viewing them from the perspective of the totality of the child's experience. As a result, controversies persist about the most common forms of victimization, the age of greatest exposure to various types of victimization, and trends across time as children grow (Almeida et al., 2008; Mulford and Giordano, 2008; Pepler et al., 2008). In addition, few earlier studies analyzed the effect of polyvictimization—the cumulative effect over time of repeated exposures to multiple forms of violence, including a greater risk of exposure to other forms of violence and accumulation of multiple adversities and trauma symptoms (Dong et al., 2004; Finkelhor, Ormrod, and Turner, 2007).

To support a more regular and systematic nationwide assessment of children's exposure to violence, crime, and abuse, DOJ supported the collection of critical nationwide data to assess the full range and scope of children's exposure to violence (both direct and indirect) in the home, school, and community. CDC joined with DOJ to support the collection of data on variables for safe, stable, and nurturing relationships as protective factors for vulnerable youth. NatSCEV I, conducted in 2008, was the first such assessment (Finkelhor, Turner, Ormrod, and Hamby, 2009); the bulletin presenting survey findings was published in 2009 (Finkelhor, Turner, Ormrod, Hamby, and Kracke, 2009). NatSCEVI represented the first nationwide attempt to measure children's past-year and lifetime exposure to violence across a number of categories, from relatively minor and common forms of violence (such as siblings hitting one another) to more serious forms of violence (such as sexual victimization, including attempted and completed rape and statutory sex offenses, assaults with a weapon, and assaults that resulted in injury). It also represented the first comprehensive attempt to capture the full range of childhood exposure to violence, crime, and abuse in the home, school, and community in a single survey, collecting data on 48 types of exposure across 7 domains: conventional crime, child maltreatment, peer and sibling victimization, sexual victimization, witnessing and indirect victimization, school violence and threats, and Internet violence and victimization (Finkelhor, Turner, Ormrod, Hamby, and Kracke, 2009). It further represented the first attempt to systematically measure witnessing violence and indirect violence in the home, school, and community, including children's witnessing of intimate partner violence and other violence within the family, and witnessing and other exposure to shootings, assaults, and murder in the community. The NatSCEV I survey was the most detailed survey to that date and the first national survey to examine children's witnessing and exposure to intimate partner violence and other family violence (Hamby et al. 2011). The rates of exposure to intimate partner violence and other family violence were considerably higher than in previous surveys that captured more limited data on these exposures. NatSCEV II confirms these magnitudes, indicating that exposure to violence within the family remains a matter of grave concern for those who work with our nation's youth.

The second survey in this assessment, NatSCEV II (conducted in 2011), gathered information about the past-year and lifetime exposure to violence among a new group of 4,503 children ages 1 month to 17 years. The updated survey asked participants about children's exposure to the same general categories of violence, crime, and abuse as in NatSCEV I. To monitor this nationwide problem over time, NatSCEV II generally replicated the first survey in terms of sample size, sampling procedures, and the questions asked of participants, although it asked some new questions that went into greater depth about exposure to assaults by adults, child maltreatment and neglect, peer and sibling victimization, and cell phone harassment. Beyond the measures of violence exposure, the survey also has information about mental health status, delinquency, family environment, and other childhood adversities.

The addition of questions about cell phone harassment helps to increase understanding of whether the greater use of electronic communication media by youth increases or moderates violence between peers. As youth socialize and communicate electronically, they may be spending less time in face-to-face contact situations where assaults and physical violence can occur (Common Sense Media, 2012; Vahlberg, 2010). They may also be doing more of their risk taking and independence testing online, which may provide some safeguards against immediate physical exposure to violence. The engrossing quality of the Internet may also have undercut some of the boredom and alienation among youth that has in the past been associated with delinquency and criminal pursuits (Common Sense Media, 2012; Rideout, Foehr, and Roberts, 2010). At the same time, when children and youth get into threatening situations, cell phone technology now affords them a way of summoning help or recording misbehavior, which may act as a deterrent (Crime in America.net, 2011; Klick, MacDonald, and Stratmann, 2012).

The new questions in NatSCEV II regarding child maltreatment, neglect, or abandonment solicited additional details about conditions in the child's household related to that maltreatment and neglect and gathered information about possible unsanitary, unsafe, or threatening conditions that the child might be subjected to that would require immediate intervention. Similarly, the additional questions about peer and sibling victimization solicited additional information about the types of relational aggression that a child or youth might be subjected to from classmates or acquaintances, including ostracism and the spreading of hurtful lies and rumors, and made it clear that those behaviors are components of relational aggression. In addition, the new questions about assaults by adults captured general information relating to assaults by adults against children that NatSCEV I did not capture, allowing more exact measurement of all forms of violence by adults against children.

Major findings from the NatSCEV II survey

Like NatSCEV I, NatSCEV II estimates both past-year and lifetime exposure to violence across a number of categories, including physical assault, bullying, sexual victimization, child maltreatment and neglect, property victimization, and witnessed and indirect victimization. . . . Some of the more notable findings are outlined below (see Finkelhor et al., 2013, for more details).

The NatSCEV II survey confirmed NatSCEV I's finding that children's exposure to violence is common; nearly 60 percent of the sample (57.7 percent) had been exposed to violence in the past year, and more than 1 in 10 reported 5 or more exposures. This exposure occurs across all age ranges of childhood and for both genders.

Assaults and bullying

Two in five children (41.2 percent) were physically assaulted during the past year, and 1 in 10 (10.1 percent) was injured. Siblings and nonsibling peers were both common perpetrators, and assaults from both groups were most common during middle childhood. Assaults by siblings were most common among 6- to 9-year-olds, with 28.0 percent being victims in the past year, and assaults by nonsibling peers were most common among 10- to 13-year-olds, with 23.5 percent being victims in the past year. However, both sibling and nonsibling peer assaults were common throughout childhood and adolescence: Among 2- to 5-year-olds, 26.3 percent were assaulted by siblings and 16.4 percent were assaulted by nonsibling peers in the past year; among 14- to 17-year-olds, 13.6 percent were assaulted by siblings and 18.4 percent were assaulted by nonsibling peers in the past year. NatSCEV II was the first survey to report in general on assaults on children by adults; these were less common than assaults by peers and siblings, with a past-year rate of 5.0 percent and a lifetime rate of 10.2 percent for all children and youth. Both past-year and lifetime rates of assault by adults were similar for boys and girls; past-year rates of assault by adults were highest for 14- to 17-year-olds, but the difference across the age range from 6 to 17 years was not significant.

Some specific types of assaults occurred to smaller groups of youth in the previous year: dating violence to 3.2 percent of youth who were age 12 or older, bias attacks to 1.8 percent, gang or group assault to 1.7 percent, and attempted or completed kidnapping to 0.6 percent. Boys experienced more assaults overall (45.2 percent vs. 37.1 percent for girls) and had particularly disproportionate levels of assault with injury (13.0 percent vs. 7.1 percent), gang/group assault (2.5 percent vs. 0.9 percent), and nonsexual assault to the genitals (9.3 percent vs. 1.0 percent). Girls were targets of more dating violence (4.7 percent vs. 1.9 percent). Assault with injury, dating violence, and nonsexual assault to the genitals were higher among the oldest youth.

Bullying-type victimizations were also common, with 13.7 percent of children and youth being physically intimidated within the past year and 36.5 percent being victims of relational aggression within the past year. (The terms "physical intimidation" and "relational aggression" were used instead of the more common terms of physical and emotional bullying, which in their technical definition require a "power imbalance" in the relationship between victim and perpetrator.) Past-year rates of exposure to relational aggression and Internet/cell phone harassment were higher for girls (NatSCEV II, unlike the first survey, asked specifically about cell phone harassment). Past-year rates of physical intimidation for boys and girls were comparable but did differ by age, with the highest rate experienced by children younger than 10. Among other victimization types occurring in the past year, relational aggression was highest for 6- to 9-year-olds, and Internet/cell phone harassment was highest for 14- to 17-year-olds.

The overall estimate for assault in 2011 was down 2.2 percentage points compared to 2008, and most specific forms of assault also showed declines. However, except for the decline in lifetime exposure to sibling assault, none of the changes in victimization in the past year, and none of the changes in assault from 2008 to 2011 were statistically significant.

Sexual victimization

Nearly 6 percent (5.6 percent) of the total sample experienced a sexual assault victimization in the past year. (Sexual assault includes attempted and completed rape and contact sex offenses by adults and peers but excludes sexual harassment.) Girls ages 14–17 represented the highest risk group, with 22.8 percent experiencing a sexual victimization and 10.7 percent experiencing a sexual assault in the past year. Among this group, 8.1 percent reported an attempted or completed rape, 13.6 percent were sexually harassed, and 12.9 percent were exposed to an unwanted Internet sexual solicitation in the past year.

NatSCEV II shows lifetime estimates for sexual victimization for 14- to 17-year-olds by gender: during their lifetimes, 17.4 percent of the older girls and 4.2 percent of the older boys said they had experienced a sexual assault. Completed rape occurred for 3.6 percent of girls and 0.4 percent of boys. Sexual assault by a known adult occurred for 5.9 percent of girls and 0.3 percent of boys. Sexual assault by an unknown adult occurred for 3.8 percent of girls and 0.1 percent of boys. One category of sexual victimization, peer flashing, saw a significant decline from 2008 in both past-year and lifetime rates.

Child maltreatment and neglect

Child maltreatment includes physical abuse, emotional abuse, neglect, sexual abuse by a known adult, and custodial interference or family abduction (defined as one parent taking, keeping, or hiding a child to prevent the child from being with the other parent; Finkelhor, Turner, Ormrod, and Hamby, 2009). Altogether, 13.8 percent of the sample experienced such maltreatment in the past year, and 25.6 percent experienced it during their lifetimes. The lifetime rate of child maltreatment for the oldest subgroup, 14- to 17-year-olds, was 41.2 percent. Emotional abuse by a caregiver was the most frequent; the past-year rate was 8.0 percent for the total sample and the lifetime rate was 25.7 percent for 14- to 17-year-olds. The rate for physical abuse by a caregiver was 3.7 percent for the full sample in the past year and 18.2 percent for 14- to 17-year-olds in their lifetimes. The rate for neglect was 6.5 percent for the full sample in the past year and 22.3 percent for 14- to 17-year-olds in their lifetimes. Gender differences were evident for physical abuse only, with boys experiencing somewhat higher rates in the past year (4.5 percent vs. 2.9 percent for girls). Rates of both physical and emotional abuse were significantly higher for older children. There were no significant changes in the rate of child maltreatment from 2008 to 2011.

Property victimization

Property victimization, consisting of robbery, vandalism, and theft by nonsiblings, occurred to 24.1 percent of children and youth during the past year. Vandalism was more common for boys (8.7 percent vs. 4.8 percent for girls), and theft was more common among older youth. Property victimization as a whole and robbery specifically declined significantly from 2008.

Witnessing and indirect victimization

Almost a quarter of the sample (22.4 percent) had witnessed violence in the past year, either in the family or in the community. In addition, 8.2 percent had witnessed a family assault, and 6.1 percent had witnessed a parent assault another parent (or parental partner) in the past year. Over their lifetimes, more than one in five children surveyed (20.8 percent) witnessed a family assault, and more than one in six (17.3 percent) witnessed one parent assault another parent or a parental partner. Among the oldest youth (ages 14–17), the lifetime rate of witnessing any family assault was 34.5 percent, and 28.3 percent of these youth had witnessed one parent assaulting another. There were few significant gender or age differences in the witnessing of family assaults.

In the case of witnessing a community assault, the rate for all children and youth was 16.9 percent in the past year and 58.9 percent over the lifetime of the oldest youth. The rate for lifetime exposure to shootings (including hearing gunshots as well as seeing someone shot) was 16.8 percent for the oldest group of youth (ages 14–17), but the rate for exposure to warfare was only 2.0 percent. Among all children and youth, 7.9 percent had been exposed to household theft in the past year and 3.7 percent had been exposed to a bomb threat or other attack threat in their school in the past year. Past-year and lifetime exposure to school bomb and attack threats significantly declined since 2008.

Multiple exposures

Altogether, 57.7 percent of the children had experienced at least one of five aggregate types of direct or witnessed victimization in the year prior to this survey (physical assault, sexual victimization, maltreatment, property victimization, or witnessing family/community violence). Exposures to multiple types of violence were also common. Among all children and youth surveyed, nearly half (48.4 percent) had experienced more than one specific victimization type involving direct or witnessed victimization (out of 50 possible types), nearly 1 in 6 (15.1 percent) experienced 6 or more types, and nearly 1 in 20 (4.9 percent) had been exposed to 10 or more different forms of victimization. . . .

Victimization and delinquency

Among children age 6 and older, violent delinquency dropped by 30 percent from 2008 to 2011, and property delinquency decreased by 40 percent. In 2011, 16.5 percent of the youth engaged in an act of violent delinquency, and 12.1 percent engaged in an act of property delinquency. (For a comprehensive discussion of the relationship between victimization and delinquency, with reference to the NatSCEV I findings, see Cuevas et al., 2013.)

Comparison of selected NatSCEV I and NatSCEV II survey results

The rates reported here for 2011 have been compared to rates from the 2008 NatSCEV I survey, which was also based on a nationally representative sample of children and youth ages 1 month to 17 years (Finkelhor, Turner, Ormrod, and Hamby, 2009; Finkelhor, Turner, Ormrod, Hamby, and Kracke, 2009).

Comparing the exposure rates between the two surveys suggests a mixture of stability and change. The percentage experiencing any of the five direct and witnessed aggregate types of exposure to violence, crime, and abuse (assaults and bullying, sexual victimization, child maltreatment, property victimization, and witnessing and indirect victimization) in the past year fell by 2.3 percentage points, but that change was not significant. Declines outnumbered increases somewhat among the specific types of exposures, but there were only 6 types out of 54 whose changes were significant for either the past year or lifetime. Assault by juvenile siblings (lifetime) declined, being flashed by a peer and statutory sex offenses (past year and lifetime) declined, property victimization (past year) and robbery (past year) declined, and school bomb threats (past year and lifetime) declined.

These trends are consistent with other evidence: the National Crime Victimization Survey showed post-2008 declines in violent crime and property crime exposure among youth (Finkelhor, 2013; Robers et al., 2012; White and Lauritsen, 2012) and, according to Federal Bureau of Investigation statistics, the overall trend in crime as tracked by reports to the police was down 4, 6, and 5 percent, respectively, for each successive year from 2008 to 2011 (Federal Bureau of Investigation, 2010, 2011, 2012, 2013). Rates for substantiated child maltreatment fell during the period 2008 to 2011, including declines in sexual abuse within the family (Finkelhor, Jones, and Shattuck, 2013), and police reports of crime and homicide dropped. . . .

[References omitted.]

CRITICAL-THINKING QUESTIONS

1. How does the information about Marcie in the "Case in point" at the beginning of the chapter support the importance of a system of care approach?
2. Why is coordination and collaboration among systems of care important for responding to youth crime and delinquency?
3. What are the implications of increased dependence on juvenile justice systems to provide mental health and physical health care for court-involved youth?
4. Why is it important for the system of care approach to be community-based?

5 Why is it important for juvenile justice systems to be trauma informed?
6 In the first chapter reading, Dierkhising and her colleagues (2013) argue for the need to understand the implications of trauma exposure and mental health issues. Why is this important in terms of both practice and policy in juvenile justice systems?
7 The second reading by Finkelhor and his colleagues (2015) addresses the importance of understanding exposure to violence. How is exposure to violence connected with delinquency and other negative outcomes for youth?

SUGGESTED READING

Farn, Amber and Jill Adams. 2016. *Education and Interagency Collaboration: A Lifeline for Justice-Involved Youth.* Washington, DC: Center for Juvenile Justice Reform, Georgetown University McCourt School of Public Policy.
Herz, Denise, Phillip Lee, Lorrie Lutz, Macon Stewart, and John Tuell. 2012. *Addressing the Needs of Multi-System Youth: Strengthening the Connection between Child Welfare and Juvenile Justice.* Washington, DC: Center for Juvenile Justice Reform, Georgetown University McCourt School of Public Policy.
Lee, Sei-Young and Margarita Villagrana. 2015. "Differences in Risk and Protective Factors between Crossover and Non-Crossover Youth in Juvenile Justice." *Children and Youth Services Review* 58:18–27.
Thomas, Douglass (eds.). 2015. *When Systems Collaborate: How Three Jurisdictions Improved Their Handling of Dual-Status Cases.* Pittsburg, PA: National Center for Juvenile Justice.

USEFUL WEBSITES

For further information relevant to this chapter, go to the following websites.

- **Center for Juvenile Justice Reform**: Working Across Systems of Care, Georgetown University: cjjr.georgetown.edu/about-us/
- **Models for Change, MacArthur Foundation**: www.modelsforchange.net/index.html
- **National Center for Mental Health and Juvenile Justice**: www.ncmhjj.com/
- **National Child Traumatic Stress Network**: nctsnet.org/
- **Office for Victims of Crime Vision 21**: www.ovc.ncjrs.gov/vision21

GLOSSARY OF KEY TERMS

Assessment instruments: Clinical tools used to classify problem behaviors and provide evidence for effective treatment.

Crossover youth: A youth who is involved with the juvenile justice system and at least one additional system of care.

Deep-end youth: A youth who has been adjudicated delinquent and placed in a residential facility.

Dual-status youth: A youth who is involved in both the child welfare system and the juvenile justice system, though not necessarily at the same time.

Evidence-based practice: The use of data gathered through research and evaluation as the basis for decision-making about policy and best practices.

Linking systems of care: An extension of the system of care approach that advocates for the need to focus on the multiple contexts where youth who have been exposed to violence, crime, and abuse receive care.

Poly-victimization: Exposure to multiple victimizations from various types of violence and abuse.

Screening instruments: Brief tools used in both clinical and non-clinical settings to identify referral need for more in-depth assessment.

System of care: A comprehensive spectrum of mental health and other necessary services which are organized into a coordinated network to meet the changing needs of children and their families.

Trauma: Physical and emotional response to events that threaten the life or emotional integrity of a youth or someone critically important to him or her.

Wraparound services: A youth services approach focusing on the importance of multi-system treatment and the need to address barriers and challenges for providing comprehensive health and human services to youth and their families.

Youth maltreatment: Occurs when a parent or caregiver is responsible for or allows abuse or neglect of a youth. It includes physical, sexual, and emotional abuse, as well as physical, emotional, and educational neglect.

REFERENCES

Abram, Karen M., Linda A. Teplin, Devon R. Charles, Sandra L. Longworth, Gary M. McClelland, and Mina K. Dulcan. 2004. "Posttraumatic Stress Disorder and Trauma in Youth in Juvenile Detention." *Archives of General Psychiatry* 61:403–410.

Baglivio, Michael T., Kevin T. Wolff, Alex R. Piquero, Shay Bilchik, Katherine Jackowski, Mark A. Greenwald, and Nathan Epps. 2016. "Maltreatment, Child Welfare, and Recidivism in a Sample of Deep-End Crossover Youth." *Journal of Youth and Adolescence* 45:625–654.

Burns, Barbara J., James C. Howell, Janet K. Wiig, Leena K. Augimeri, Brendan C. Welsh, Rolf Loeber, and David Petechuk. 2003. "Treatment, Services, and Intervention Programs for Child Delinquency." Washington, DC: Office of Juvenile Justice and Delinquency Prevention.

Center for Juvenile Justice Reform. 2015. *The Crossover Youth Practice Model: An Abbreviated Guide*. Washington, DC: Georgetown University McCourt School of Public Policy.

Child Welfare Information Gateway. 2016. *Child Maltreatment 2014: Summary of Key Findings*. Washington, DC: U.S. Department of Health and Human Services, Children's Bureau.

Clark, Karen and Shelly Gehshan. 2007. *Meeting the Health Needs of Youth Involved in the Juvenile Justice System*. Washington, DC: Joint Center for Political and Economic Studies.

Dierkhising, Carly B., Susan J. Ko, Briana Woods-Jaeger, Ernestine C. Briggs, Robert Lee, and Robert S. Pynoos. 2013. "Trauma Histories among Justice-Involved Youth: Findings from the National Child Traumatic Stress Network." *European Journal of Psychotraumatology* 4:1–12.

Espinosa, Erin M., Jon R. Sorenson, and Molly A. Lopez. 2013. "Youth Pathways to Placement: The Influence of Gender, Mental Health Needs and Trauma on Confinement in the Juvenile Justice System." *Journal of Youth and Adolescence* 42:1824–1836.

Farn, Amber and Jill Adams. 2016. *Education and Interagency Collaboration: A Lifeline for Justice-Involved Youth*. Washington, DC: Center for Juvenile Justice Reform, Georgetown University McCourt School of Public Policy.

Finkelhor, David, Richard K. Ormrod, and Heather A. Turner. 2009. "Lifetime Assessment of Poly-Victimization in a National Sample of Children and Youth." *Child Abuse and Neglect* 33:403–411.

Finkelhor, David, Heather Turner, Anne Shattuck, Sherry Hamby, and Kristen Kracke. 2015. "Children's Exposure to Violence, Crime, and Abuse: An Update." *Juvenile Justice Bulletin*. Washington, DC: Office of Juvenile Justice and Delinquency Prevention.

Ford, Julian D., Damion J. Grasso, Josephine Hawke, and John F. Chapman. 2013. "Poly-Victimization among Juvenile Justice-Involved Youth." *Child Abuse and Neglect* 37:788–800.

Grella, Christine E., Yih-Ing Hser, Vandana Joshi, and Jennifer Rounds-Bryant. 2001. "Drug Treatment Outcomes for Adolescents with Comorbid Mental and Substance Abuse Disorders." *Journal of Nervous and Mental Distress* 189:384–392.

Grisso, Thomas. 2008. "Adolescent Offenders with Mental Health Disorders." *The Future of Children* 18:143–164.

Haight, Wendy, Laurel Bidwell, Won Seok Choi, and Minhae Cho. 2016. "An Evaluation of the Crossover Youth Practice Model (CYPM): Recidivism Outcomes for Maltreated Youth Involved in the Juvenile Justice System." *Children and Youth Services Review* 65:78–85.

Herz, Denise, Phillip Lee, Lorrie Lutz, Macon Stewart, and John Tuell. 2012. *Addressing the Needs of Multi-System Youth: Strengthening the Connection between Child Welfare and Juvenile Justice*. Washington, DC: Center for Juvenile Justice Reform, Georgetown University McCourt School of Public Policy.

Herz, Denise C., Joseph P. Ryan, and Shay Bilchik. 2010. "Challenges Facing Crossover Youth: An Examination of Juvenile-Justice Decision Making and Recidivism." *Family Court Review* 48:305–321.

Hockenberry, Sarah and Charles Puzzanchera. 2017. *Juvenile Court Statistics 2014*. Pittsburgh, PA: National Center for Juvenile Justice.

Hodges, Sharon, Kathleen Ferreira, and Nathaniel Israel. 2012. "'If We're Going to Change Things, It Has to Be Systemic': Systems Change in Children's Mental Health." *American Journal of Community Psychology* 49:526–537.

Huang, Hui, Jospeh P. Ryan, and Denise Herz. 2012. "The Journey of Dually-Involved Youth: The Description and Prediction of Re-Reporting and Recidivism." *Children and Youth Services Review* 34:254–260.

Lee, Sei-Young and Margarita Villagrana. 2015. "Differences in Risk and Protective Factors between Crossover and Non-Crossover Youth in Juvenile Justice." *Children and Youth Services Review* 58:18–27.

Leone, Peter and Lois Weinberg. 2012. *Addressing the Unmet Educational Needs of Children and Youth in the Juvenile Justice and Child Welfare Systems*. Washington, DC: Center for Juvenile Justice Reform, Georgetown University McCourt School of Public Policy.

National Center on Addiction and Substance Abuse. 2004. *Criminal Neglect: Substance Abuse, Juvenile Justice and the Children Left Behind*. New York, NY: Columbia University.

National Child Trauma Stress Network (n.d.). *Essential Elements of a Trauma-Informed Juvenile Justice System*. Retrieved April 4, 2017 (www.nctsn.org/sites/default/files/assets/pdfs/jj_ee_final.pdf).

Office of Juvenile Justice and Delinquency Prevention (OJJDP). 2017. *OJJDP Statistical Briefing Book*. Washington, DC: OJJDP. Retrieved December 12, 2017 (www.ojjdp.gov/ojstatbb/corrections/qa08201.asp?qaDate=2015).

Rossman, Shelli. 2001. *From Prison to Home: The Effect of Incarceration and Reentry on Children, Families, and Communities*. Washington, DC: The Urban Institute.

Ryan, Joseph P. and Mark F. Testa. 2005. "Child Maltreatment and Juvenile Delinquency: Investigating the Role of Placement and Placement Instability." *Children and Youth Services Review* 27:227–249.

Schubert, Carol A. and Edward P. Mulvey. 2014. "Behavioral Health Problems, Treatment, and Outcomes in Serious Youthful Offenders." *Juvenile Justice Bulletin*. Washington, DC: Office of Juvenile Justice and Delinquency Prevention.

Sedlak, Andrea J. and Karla S. McPherson. 2010. "Youth's Needs and Services: Findings from the Survey of Youth in Residential Placement." *Juvenile Justice Bulletin*. Washington, DC: Office of Juvenile Justice and Delinquency Prevention.

Skowyra, Kathleen R. and Joseph J. Cocozza, 2007. *Blueprint for Change: A Comprehensive Model for the Identification and Treatment of Youth with Mental Health Needs in Contact with the Juvenile Justice System*. Delmar, NY: The National Center for Mental Health and Juvenile Justice.

Smith, Dana K. and Lisa Saldana. 2013. "Trauma, Delinquency, and Substance Use: Co-Occurring Problems for Adolescent Girls in the Juvenile Justice System." *Journal of Child and Adolescent Substance Abuse* 22: 450–465.

Stroul, Beth A. and Robert M. Friedman. 1986. *A System of Care for Children and Adolescents with Severe Emotional Disturbances.* Revised ed. Washington DC: Georgetown University Center for Child Development, National Technical Assistance Center for Children's Mental Health.

Substance Abuse and Health Administration. 2015. *Screening and Assessment of Co-Occurring Disorders in the Justice System.* HHS Publication No. (SMA)-15-4930. Rockville, MD.

Thomas, Douglass (eds.). 2015. *When Systems Collaborate: How Three Jurisdictions Improved Their Handling of Dual-Status Cases.* Pittsburg, PA: National Center for Juvenile Justice.

Underwood, Lee A. and Aryssa Washington. 2016. "Mental Illness and Juvenile Offenders." *International Journal of Environmental Research and Public Health* 13:228–242.

Wilson, Kate J. 2008. *Literature Review: Wraparound Services for Juvenile and Adult Offender Populations.* Davis, CA: Center for Public Policy Research, University of California, Davis.

Wolpaw, Jennifer W. and Julian D. Ford. 2004. *Assessing Exposure to Psychological Trauma and Post-Traumatic Stress in the Juvenile Justice Population.* Los Angeles, CA: National Child Traumatic Stress Network.

INDEX

Note: Page numbers in **bold** type refer to **tables**. Page numbers in *italic* type refer to *figures*. Page numbers followed by 'n' refer to notes

For Product Safety Concerns and Information please contact our EU representative GPSR@taylorandfrancis.com Taylor & Francis Verlag GmbH, Kaufingerstraße 24, 80331 München, Germany